Software Engineering

THIRD EDITION

INTERNATIONAL COMPUTER SCIENCE SERIES

Consulting editors   **A D McGettrick**   University of Strathclyde

J van Leeuwen   University of Utrecht

SELECTED TITLES IN THE SERIES

The UNIX System   *S R Bourne*

Software Specification Techniques   *N Gehani and A D McGettrick* (Eds)

The Craft of Software Engineering   *A Macro and J Buxton*

UNIX System Programming   *K F Haviland and B Salama*

PROLOG Programming for Artificial Intelligence   *I Bratko*

Cost Estimation for Software Development   *B Londeix*

Parallel Programming   *R H Perrott*

The Specification of Computer Programs   *W M Turski and T S E Maibaum*

Software Development with Ada   *I Sommerville and R Morrison*

Syntax Analysis and Software Tools   *K J Gough*

Concurrent Programming   *N Gehani and A D McGettrick* (Eds)

Functional Programming   *A J Field and P G Harrison*

Local Area Network Architectures   *D Hutchison*

Comparative Programming Languages   *L B Wilson and R G Clark*

Distributed Systems: Concepts and Design   *G F Coulouris and J Dollimore*

Software Prototyping, Formal Methods and VDM   *S Hekmatpour and D Ince*

C Programming in a UNIX Environment   *J Kay and R Kummerfeld*

High-Level Languages and their Compilers   *D Watson*

Elements of Functional Programming   *C Reade*

Software Development with Modula-2   *D Budgen*

Program Derivation   *R G Dromey*

Programming in Ada (3rd Edn)   *J G P Barnes*

UNIX™ is a trademark of AT & T

THIRD EDITION

Software Engineering

Ian Sommerville

University of Lancaster

Addison-Wesley Publishing Company

Wokingham, England · Reading, Massachusetts · Menlo Park, California
New York · Don Mills, Ontario · Amsterdam · Bonn
Sydney · Singapore · Tokyo · Madrid · San Juan

© 1989 Addison-Wesley Publishers Ltd.
© 1989 Addison-Wesley Publishing Company, Inc.

The programs in this book have been included for their instructional value. They
have been tested with care but are not guaranteed for any particular purpose.
The publisher does not offer any warranties or representations, nor does it
accept any liabilities with respect to the programs.

Many of the designations used by manufacturers and sellers to distinguish their
products are claimed as trademarks. Addison-Wesley has made every attempt to
supply trademark information about manufacturers and their products
mentioned in this book.

Cover designed by Crayon Design of Henley-on-Thames and printed by The
    Riverside Printing Co. (Reading) Ltd. The cover illustration is *Tours: Sunset*
    by J.M.W. Turner, from The Turner Collection, Tate Gallery, London, and
    is reproduced with permission.
Typeset by Quorum Technical Services Ltd, Cheltenham.
Printed and bound in Great Britain by The Bath Press, Avon.

First edition published 1982. Reprinted 1983 and 1984.
Second edition published 1984. Reprinted 1985, 1986, 1987 and 1988.
Third edition printed 1989. Reprinted 1989 and 1990 (twice).

British Library Cataloguing in Publication Data
Sommerville, Ian, *1951–*
    Software engineering. – 3rd ed.
    1. Computer systems. Software
    I. Title
    005.3

    ISBN 0–201–17568–1

Library of Congress Cataloging in Publication Data
Sommerville, Ian.
    Software engineering / Ian Sommerville. — 3rd ed.
        p. cm. — (International computer science series)
    Bibliography: p.
    Includes index.
    ISBN 0–201–17568–1 :
    1. Software engineering. I. Title. II. Series.
QA76.758.S65   1989
005.1—dc19   88–31867
                                    CIP

Preface

Software engineering is critical for the economic well-being of both developed and undeveloped nations. The explosion of computer applications which followed the availability of low-cost computer hardware has meant that the current demand for software exceeds our ability to supply that software and the gap between supply and demand is increasing. We must apply effective software engineering techniques if we are to have any chance of reducing the imbalance.

Like other engineering disciplines software engineering is derivative. It makes use of more fundamental work in computer science, mathematics, psychology and management studies. The aim of the software engineer is to apply knowledge in the most effective way to produce high-quality software systems. The source of that knowledge is irrelevant if it is useful for systems production.

In some cases, our understanding of particular tools and techniques may be incomplete and the techniques may not be built on any formal theory. This does not compromise their utility. After all, our 19th century forebears performed remarkable feats of engineering with little theory by using state-of-the-art knowledge in an effective way. It is the role of computer scientists to seek out the theoretical basis for software engineering; it is the role of software engineers to build useful software systems irrespective of whether or not a sound theoretical basis has been discovered.

This is not to say that engineers should not be aware of computer science theory nor that the theory is of no utility. Indeed, some theoretical work has developed to such an extent that it can now be applied in practical systems construction. Formal systems specifications for large systems have been produced; cognitive scientists have provided a model of human–computer interaction which can be used in user interface design; reliability metrics are useful in assessing systems reliability. Software engineers should monitor developments in computer science and apply these when appropriate to do so.

As in previous editions, the intention of this book is to introduce the reader to state-of-the-art software engineering techniques which are now of practical utility and which can be applied immediately in practical software projects. I do not believe that there is any single solution to the problem of software engineering so I do not preach the benefits of any particular methods, formal or otherwise, to the exclusion of other approaches. Much current research will have no direct long-term applicability so the emphasis is on established techniques rather than on research developments.

Of course, software engineering is a now such a wide-ranging discipline that it would be quite possible to write another book with the material which has been left out of this one. Some topics, such as parallel programming, are not discussed in detail because they are well documented and, in undergraduate courses, are often discussed under other headings such as operating systems design. Other topics, such as software safety, have simply been excluded for lack of space.

Readership

The book is aimed at students in undergraduate and graduate courses and at software engineers in commerce and industry. It may be used in software engineering courses or in courses such as advanced programming and software design to help place these topics in context. Practitioners may find the book useful as general reading and to help update their knowledge on particular topics such as formal specification, object-oriented design or tools and environments. Wherever practicable, examples have been given a practical bias to reflect the type of applications that software engineers must develop.

Very few assumptions have been made about the background of readers of the book. I have assumed a basic familiarity with programming and modern computer systems and some examples rely on knowledge of basic data structures such as stacks, lists and queues. The chapters on formal specification assume knowledge of very elementary set theory. Apart from that, no other mathematical background is required.

Ada is used as the example language but the examples are self-contained and an appendix has been provided giving an overview of the language. Knowledge of Ada is *not* a prerequisite and the examples should be easily understandable by readers with a knowledge of Pascal, C, Modula-2 or other similar high-level programming language.

Changes from earlier editions

This book has now reached its third edition and it is almost 10 years since work on the first edition began. Technology has changed remarkably in that time and it has been necessary to change the book to reflect these technology changes. Changes have also been introduced because of new experience and knowledge of my own and because of suggestions made by readers of earlier editions.

The most obvious change to a reader familiar with previous editions is a structural one. Rather than have a number of fairly long chapters, this edition is now partitioned into two introductory chapters and five major parts with a number of shorter chapters making up each part. However, the ordering of material is similar to that of previous editions in that the early part of the book is concerned with specification and design, the middle of the book with implementation and testing, and the final chapters with software management.

To reflect changes in the subject, there is more material on the early phases of the software life-cycle. The chapters on requirements cover more ground than before, greater emphasis is placed on formal specification, and more material on object-oriented design and on design validation has been included. The chapter on user interface design has been updated. There is less material on programming as the standards have risen enormously in this area since the first edition of the book. A section on software reuse has now been included and CASE tools and software engineering environments are covered in more detail.

The chapters covering testing have been revised and expanded. Static verification techniques are covered in more depth. Part 5, which covers software management, has been expanded to include more management topics. It includes revised versions of previous chapters on cost estimation, maintenance and documentation. It also contains new chapters discussing project planning, configuration management and quality assurance.

Using the book as a course text

A good deal of attention has been paid to making the text usable across a range of software engineering courses. The structure has been redesigned and the material expanded to offer a more flexible, modular coverage. The instructor can devise a variety of different course structures by picking different chapters from the book. At Lancaster, for example, the book is used in four separate courses; an introduction to software engineering; software design; software specification and, with supplementary material, in a course on advanced software engineering.

Each chapter now includes a key point summary, suggested further reading, local references and a list of exercises. The number of diagrams, tables and illustrations has been increased dramatically.

The use of the book as a course text and some suggestions for complementary practical work are discussed in Appendix B (Instructor's Notes).

Supplement

An *Instructor's Guide* is available from the publisher, containing:

- A list of key points to emphasize for each chapter
- Selected solutions to the exercises
- Transparency masters of the program listings and diagrams used in the book

Acknowledgements

Many friends and colleagues have provided invaluable help and advice in the preparation of all of the editions of this text. Members of the Software Engineering Research Groups at the University of Strathclyde and at the University of Lancaster provided a stimulating environment and a source for many of the ideas discussed here.

Particular mention must be made of Ray Welland and Stephen Beer who were the principal architects of the design editing system used as a source of examples in this book. Pete Reid provided material and stimulating discussions on user interface design. John Mariani ably assisted with the work of the Lancaster group.

Thanks are due to all who provided comments on earlier editions of the book and to the reviewers of earlier drafts of this edition. They were Andrew McGettrick of the University of Strathclyde, Ray Welland of the University of Glasgow, David Lee of Marconi Software Systems, Burt Leavenworth of Drexel University, James D. Palmer of George Mason University and others who prefer to remain anonymous. Their comments and suggestions are appreciated.

Finally, my wife Anne and daughters Alison and Jane patiently put up with several months of fatherless evenings while this book was being written. Thank you, Anne, Ali and Jay, for your support.

Ian Sommerville,
Lancaster, June 1988.

Contents

Figure acknowledgements

Figure 2.3 is taken from Ben Shneiderman's *Designing the User Interface*, © 1987, Addison-Wesley Publishing Co., Inc., Reading Mass., Figure 2.1, page 43. Reprinted with permission.

Tables 26.1 to 26.4 are taken from Barry W. Boehm's *Software Engineering Economics*, © 1981, pages 118 and 130. Reprinted with permission of Prentice-Hall, Inc., Englewood Cliffs, NJ.

Chapter 1

Introduction

Objectives

The objectives of this chapter are to define what is meant
by software engineering, to discuss the distinguishing
characteristics of well engineered software and to introduce
the notion of the software process which is the activity of
software production. The notion of software process
models is introduced and two models, the waterfall model
and exploratory programming, are discussed in detail.
Software modifiability and reliability are the most
important attributes of well engineered software and
sections on software evolution and on reliability justify this
choice.

Contents

As the cost of computer hardware decreases, computer systems are being incorporated in more and more products. Millions of personal computer systems are now in use. Some advanced computer applications, such as expert systems, have become economically viable as hardware to support their heavy computation demands can be built at moderate cost. The end result of this proliferation of computer systems into all aspects of life and business is that personal, corporate, national and international economies are increasingly dependent on computers and their software systems. As software costs are the major component of system costs, it is probably not an exaggeration to suggest that the future prosperity of an industrialized economy depends on effective software engineering.

The real costs of software development are immense. Although precise, up-to-date figures are very difficult to establish, it has been suggested (Boehm, 1987) that in 1985 worldwide software costs were in excess of $140 billion. Costs are growing at a rate of 12% per year so if this trend continues, by 1995, worldwide annual software costs will exceed $435 billion (Figure 1.1). Even small improvements in software productivity can therefore result in a significant reduction in absolute costs.

The problems encountered in building large software systems are not simply scaled-up versions of the problems of writing small computer programs. An analogy may be drawn with a road bridge over a river estuary and a footbridge over a stream. Although both are members of the class 'bridges' and hence have some common properties, a civil engineer would never consider designing an estuarial bridge simply by enlarging a footbridge design.

The complexity of small programs (or bridges) is such that the system may be easily understood by one person and all details of the design and construction held in that person's head. Specifications may be informal and the effect of changes immediately obvious. On the other hand, large systems are so complex that it is impossible for individuals to hold and maintain details of each aspect of the project in their minds. Formal techniques of specification and design are necessary; each stage of

Figure 1.1
Predicted annual
software costs.

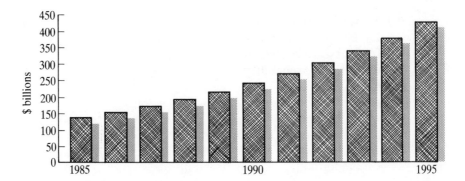

the project must be properly documented and careful management is essential.

Software engineering is defined differently by different people. However, the common factors in these definitions are that software engineering is concerned with software systems which are built by teams rather than individual programmers, uses engineering principles in the development of these systems, and is made up of both technical and non-technical aspects. As well as a thorough knowledge of computing techniques, the software engineer, like any other engineer, must be able to communicate, both orally and in writing. Software engineers should appreciate the problems that system users have in interacting with software whose workings they may not understand. They should understand the project management problems associated with software production.

Furthermore, the term 'software' does not simply encompass the computer programs associated with some application or product. As well as programs, software includes all documentation which is necessary to install, use, develop and maintain these programs. For large systems, the task of constructing such documentation is comparable in magnitude with the task of program development.

The term 'software engineering' was first introduced in the late 1960s at a conference held to discuss what was then called the 'software crisis'. This software crisis resulted directly from the introduction of third generation computer hardware. These machines were orders of magnitude more powerful than second generation machines and their power made hitherto unrealizable applications a feasible proposition. The implementation of these applications required large software systems to be built.

Initial experience in building large software systems showed that existing methods of software development were inadequate. Techniques applicable to small systems could not be scaled up. A number of major projects were late (sometimes years late), cost much more than originally predicted, were unreliable, difficult to maintain and performed poorly. Software development was in a crisis situation. Hardware costs were tumbling while software costs were rising rapidly. There was an urgent need for new techniques and methods which allowed the complexity inherent in large software systems to be controlled.

Now, 20 years later, the 'software crisis' is still with us. Although there have been real improvements in our approach to software engineering, in the tools used for system development and in the education of development staff, the demand for software has increased at a faster rate than improvements in the productivity of software engineers. Furthermore, the advent of microcomputer systems has meant that many more people are now involved in software development and, sadly, some of them are repeating the mistakes made by software engineers in the 1970s.

There is still a need for better tools, techniques and methods and, perhaps most importantly, better education and training. Until now, software engineering has been largely labour-intensive with relatively low capital expenditure per software engineer. As new software development environments come into use, this situation will change and software engineering will become more capital-intensive. Staff will have to be more highly trained and offer greater skills if the most effective use is to be made of expensive environmental support.

1.1   Well engineered software

An obvious question which comes to mind in discussions of software engineering is what distinguishes a well engineered software system from a badly engineered system? A glib answer to this is that if the system does what the user wants, it is well engineered. However, a more general assessment of system quality requires the identification of common attributes which we would expect to find in all well engineered software.

Like all other types of engineering, software engineering is not just about producing products but means producing products in the most cost-effective way. Given unlimited resources, the majority of software problems can probably be solved but the challenge for the software engineer is to produce high-quality software with a finite amount of resources and to a predicted schedule.

Thus, we cannot ignore cost considerations when attempting to define well engineered software. Indeed, one of the attributes of well engineered software, namely maintainability, is a direct result of the fact that the majority of the costs of a software product are incurred after that software has been put into use. Ignoring functionality, there are four attributes which any well engineered software system should possess.

(1)   *The software should be maintainable*   As long-lifetime software is subject to regular change, it is important that the software is written and documented in such a way that changes can be made without undue costs.

(2)   *The software should be reliable*   As discussed in Section 1.3, an appropriate level of reliability is essential if a software system is to be of any use.

(3)   *The software should be efficient*   This does not necessarily mean that the last ounce of performance is squeezed out of the hardware on which the software runs. Indeed, attempting to maximize efficiency can make the software much more difficult to change. Rather, it means that a software system should not make wasteful use of system resources such as memory and processor cycles.

(4)   *The software should offer an appropriate user interface*   It is now
      clear that much software is not used to its full potential simply
      because the interface which it offers makes it difficult to use. The
      user interface design should take into account the capabilities and
      background of the intended system users and should be tailored
      accordingly.

The problem which must be faced by software engineers is attaining the
optimum level for each of these attributes given that some are exclusive
(for example, providing a better user interface may reduce system efficiency) and that all are subject to the law of diminishing returns. This means
that the relationship between cost and improvements in each of these
attributes is not a linear one and small improvements in any of the
attributes can be expensive. Figure 1.2 shows how costs rise as efficiency
improvements are required. Although little space is devoted to discussions
of efficiency in this book, there are some classes of system, like avionic
systems, where efficiency is a prime consideration and it may be necessary
to optimize efficiency at the expense of the other system attributes. The
reason for this is that the software may have to run on a computer where
weight and size considerations restrict the power of the hardware which
can be used and the software may have to run in a relatively small memory
with little or no backing store.

       In such situations, the trade-offs which are required to improve
system efficiency should be made explicit at an early stage in the
development. It should not be left to the individual software engineer to
make decisions on whether maintainability or efficiency should be
optimized. Such decisions must be set out in the contract for the system
and the cost consequences of maximizing efficiency should be explicitly
described to the customer for the software product.

       This book concentrates on techniques which maximize reliability
and maintainability. User interface design is a topic in its own right and
really requires a text to itself (Shneiderman, 1986), but some particularly
relevant aspects of this topic are discussed in Chapter 13.

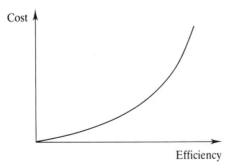

Figure 1.2
Costs versus efficiency.

1.2   The software process

The identification of the 'software crisis' in the late 1960s and the notion that software development is an engineering discipline led to the view that the process of software development is akin to the process which has evolved in other engineering disciplines. Thus, a model of the software development process which was derived from other engineering activities was suggested (Royce, 1970). This was enthusiastically accepted by software project management as it offered a means of making the development process more visible. This model subsequently became known as the 'waterfall model' as the identified activities were structured as shown in Figure 1.3.

This development model was accepted and put into use but it soon became clear that the model was only appropriate for some classes of software system. Although management found the model useful for planning and estimation, the realities of software development did not accord with the activities identified in the model. The software process, those activities involved in software development and maintenance, was actually a more complex and variable process than could be described using a single simple model.

Detailed software process models are still the subject of research but it is now clear that a number of different general models or paradigms of software development can be identified. The original waterfall model is, in fact, one of these general models rather than a detailed process model. Some of these development paradigms are:

(1)   *The waterfall approach*   This views the software process as being made up of a number of stages such as requirements specification, software design, implementation, testing and so on. After each stage is defined it is 'signed off' and development proceeds to the following stage. This approach is widely used and is discussed in more detail later.

(2)   *Exploratory programming*   This approach involves developing a working system, as quickly as possible, and then modifying that system until it performs in an adequate way. This approach is usually used in AI systems development where users cannot formulate a detailed requirements specification and where the notion of system correctness is difficult to gauge. Adequacy rather than correctness is the aim of the system designers.

(3)   *Prototyping*   This approach is similar to exploratory programming in that the first phase of development involves developing a program for user experiment. However, the principal function of the development is to establish the system requirements. This is followed by a re-implementation of the software to produce a production-quality system.

(4) *Formal transformations* This approach involves developing a formal specification of the software system and transforming this specification, using correctness-preserving transformations, to a program.

(5) *System assembly from reusable components* This technique assumes that systems are mostly made up of components which already exist and the system development process becomes one of assembly rather than creation.

The first three of these approaches – namely the waterfall approach, exploratory programming and prototyping – are all used for practical systems development. Some experimental systems have been built using correctness-preserving transformations. The approach based on reusable components has not been tested in practice although it appears to offer advantages for both costs and system reliability. Software reuse is discussed, in general terms, in Chapter 17. Prototyping is discussed in Chapter 6 and formal development in Chapter 7. Further description here concentrates on the conventional 'waterfall' approach and on exploratory programming.

1.2.1 The 'waterfall' model of the life-cycle

The initial model of the software life-cycle was probably first described by Royce (1970) and since then there have been numerous refinements to and variations of the life-cycle model. All of these can be encompassed in the 'waterfall' model (Figure 1.3) whose stages are as follows:

(1) *Requirements analysis and definition* The system's services, constraints and goals are established by consultation with system users. Once these have been agreed, they must be defined in a manner which is understandable by both users and development staff.

(2) *System and software design* Using the requirements definition as a base, the requirements are partitioned to either hardware or software systems. This process is termed systems design. Software design is the process of representing the functions of each software system in a manner which may readily be transformed to one or more computer programs.

(3) *Implementation and unit testing* During this stage, the software design is realized as a set of programs or program units which are written in some executable programming language. Unit testing involves verifying that each unit meets its specification.

(4) *System testing* The individual program units or programs are integrated and tested as a complete system to ensure that the software requirements have been met. After testing, the software system is delivered to the customer.

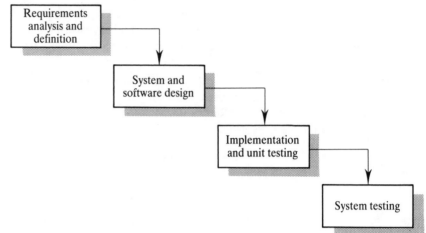

Figure 1.3
The waterfall model of
software development.

(5) *Operation and maintenance* Normally (although not necessarily) this is the longest life-cycle phase. The system is installed and put into practical use. Maintenance involves correcting errors which were not discovered in earlier stages of the life-cycle, improving the implementation of system units and enhancing the system's services as new requirements are perceived.

It is not useful, at this stage, to identify sub-phases within each phase of the waterfall model of the software life-cycle. There is no general agreement on what these sub-phases are and individual projects are normally partitioned in different ways. For management purposes one, more detailed, view of the software life-cycle is suggested in Chapter 25.

It is useful for management purposes to consider the phases of the software life-cycle to be distinct but, in practice, the development stages overlap and feed information to each other. While a design is being developed, problems with requirements are identified; while a program is being coded, design problems are found; and so on. The final life-cycle phase (maintenance) has been omitted from Figure 1.3 and is discussed later. The software process is not a simple linear model but involves a sequence of iterations of the development activities (Figure 1.4).

Unfortunately, with a model which includes frequent iterations it is difficult to identify definite management checkpoints to be used for planning and estimation. Therefore, after some small number of iterations, the tendency is to freeze parts of the development, such as the specification, and to continue with the later development stages. Problems are either left for later resolution, ignored or programmed around. This premature freezing may lead to systems which do not do what the user

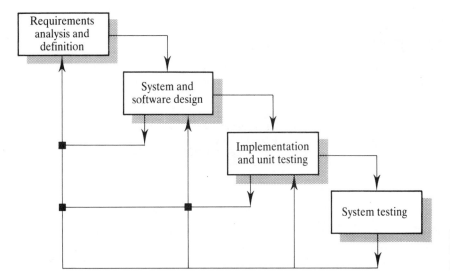

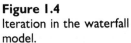

Figure 1.4
Iteration in the waterfall model.

wants and which are badly structured as design problems are circumvented by tricky coding.

The testing phase of the software process, where the complete software system is integrated and exercised, represents the ultimate validation stage in the development cycle. At this stage, the system developer must convince the system buyer that his requirements are met by the system. However, the activities of verification and validation (V & V) pervade the earlier life-cycle stages. It is during these V & V activities that information which is to be fed back to earlier life-cycle phases is normally identified.

Although verification and validation may appear to be synonymous, this is not in fact the case. Perhaps the most succinct expression of the difference between verification and validation is given by Boehm (1981):

Verification : 'Are we building the product right?'
Validation : 'Are we building the right product?'

In short, verification checks if the product which is under construction meets the requirements definition. Validation checks if the product's functions are what the customer really wants.

During the final life-cycle phase, information is fed back to all previous development phases (Figure 1.5). This final phase is an operational phase where the software is put into use. During this use, errors and omissions in the original software requirements are discovered, program and design errors come to light and the need for new software functionality is identified. This means that software modifications are

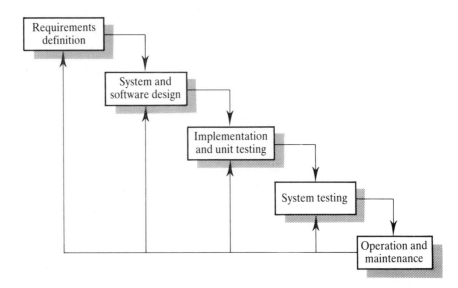

Figure 1.5
The software life-cycle.

necessary and this modification activity is usually called 'software maintenance'.

Maintenance is not simply an error-correction activity but may involve changes in requirements, design and implementation, or it may highlight the need for further system testing. Unfortunately, this is often not properly recognized and software maintenance is simply seen as a single activity carried out after the software product has been delivered. In fact, what really happens is that the development process (or part of it) is repeated many times during the maintenance phase as modifications are incorporated in the software.

One of the aims of software engineering is to reduce overall software costs and it is important to understand how costs are distributed across the software process. Unfortunately, for anything apart from the conventional waterfall model, development costs are not broken down and, even for systems developed using a conventional approach, costs vary dramatically depending on the application, the development organization and the development methods. Furthermore, such cost information is sometimes commercially sensitive so, even when it is collected, only a few organizations will publish software costs. It is thus very difficult to get an overall picture of development costs throughout the software industry.

This makes the task of estimating costs across the software process very difficult. However, some figures given by Boehm (1975) for different types of software system give an approximate indication of cost distribution during software development. These figures are illustrated in Table 1.1. Boehm (1981) has also suggested somewhat different figures where the implementation costs are much higher and design costs much lower. These, however, appear to be based on a life-cycle model with an emphasis which

System type	Phase costs (%)		
	Requirements/design	Implementation	Testing
Command and control systems	46	20	34
Spaceborne systems	34	20	46
Operating systems	33	17	50
Scientific systems	44	26	30
Business systems	44	28	28

Table 1.1
The costs of software development activities.

is different from that of the conventional model. In this alternative model, detailed design is considered to be part of the implementation phase whereas in the model costings in Table 1.1 detailed design is part of the overall software design process.

The above figures show that the software development costs are greatest at the beginning and at the end of the development cycle. This suggests that a reduction in overall software development costs is best accomplished by more effective requirements assessment, design and life-cycle verification and validation.

The need to improve requirements specification and design and to make verification and validation a whole life-cycle activity has promoted other approaches to software development where emphasis is placed on requirements (prototyping model) and validation (formal transformation model). The class of systems which are usually developed using exploratory programming are not covered by the above figures and detailed development costs for these systems are presently unobtainable.

What is not shown in Table 1.1 is the costs of the final life-cycle phase – operation and maintenance. Again there is immense variation in costs from system to system. However, for most large, long-lived, software systems maintenance costs normally exceed development costs by factors which range from two to four, and high maintenance costs appear to be independent of the approach used for software development. Indeed, Boehm (1975) quotes a pathological case where the development cost of an avionics system was $30 per instruction but the maintenance cost was $4000 per instruction. This illustrates how efficiency requirements can lead to very high total life-cycle costs. The general problems of software maintenance are discussed in Chapter 27.

The waterfall model of the life-cycle has been rightly criticized (McCracken and Jackson, 1982; Gladden, 1982) as unrepresentative of the activities which really go on during the software process. Part of the problem with the model is that it does not recognize the role of iteration in the software process, and another failing is that it implies that specifications should be frozen at an early stage in the development process. This leads to software systems whose functionality does not match that which is really required by users. Both the exploratory programming approach and the prototyping approach attempt to resolve these difficulties.

1.2.2 Exploratory programming

Exploratory programming is based on the idea of developing an initial implementation, exposing this to user comment and refining this through many stages until an adequate system has been developed (Figure 1.6).

Exploratory programming appears to be most appropriate for systems where it is very difficult or impossible to establish a detailed system specification. Some might argue that all systems fall into this class but exploratory programming has actually been mostly used for the development of AI systems which attempt to emulate some human capabilities. As we don't understand how humans carry out tasks, setting out a detailed specification for software to imitate humans is impossible. The key to success in this approach is to use techniques which allow for very rapid system iterations so that suggested changes may be incorporated and demonstrated as quickly as possible. This implies the use of a very high-level programming language such as LISP or PROLOG for software development, use of powerful, dedicated hardware systems, and integrated software tools to support the system developer.

One of the important differences between exploratory programming and a specification-based approach to development is in verification and validation. Verification is only meaningful when a program is compared to

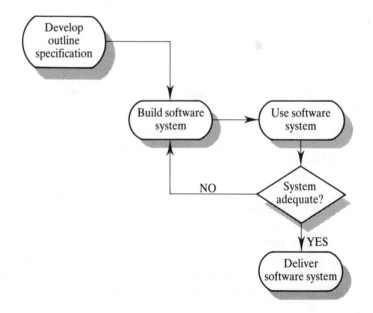

Figure 1.6
Exploratory programming.

its specification. If no specification exists, verification is a nonsense. The notion of a 'correct' program is not a meaningful one and the validation process for programs developed in this way is intended to demonstrate the adequacy of the program rather than its conformance to a specification.

Adequacy, of course, is not a measurable characteristic and only subjective judgements of a program's adequacy can be made. However, this does not invalidate its usefulness – after all, human performance cannot be guaranteed to be correct but we are satisfied if that performance is clearly adequate for the task in hand. As programs are required to emulate human capabilities, the notion of correctness becomes an increasingly limited one and we must design systems so that they do not include unwarranted assumptions about program behaviour.

At the time of writing, the use of an exploratory programming approach has mostly been confined to the development of artificial intelligence systems and it has been little used in the development of large, long-lifetime systems. There are two main reasons for this:

(1)   Existing software management structures are set up to deal with a software process model which results in regular deliverables and where progress may be readily measured. In exploratory programming, it is not cost-effective to produce a great deal of system documentation as the system is subject to such regular change. In order for this model to be used for large systems development, new management techniques will have to be established to control the development process.

(2)   Exploratory programming tends to result in systems whose structure is not well-defined. The reason for this is that continual change corrupts the initial software structure. This means that maintenance of such systems is likely to be difficult and costly particularly when, as is usual with large systems, the system maintainers are not the original developers.

Another potential problem with this approach is that, until now, most users of this approach have been highly qualified and skilled. In large systems development, there is usually a range of skills offered by the development team. It is not clear how less skilled engineers could be used effectively for this mode of development.

These difficulties do not mean that the exploratory programming approach should be rejected. There is no question that there are some classes of system which cannot be developed by setting out specifications then constructing a system according to these specifications. Exploratory programming is the only reasonable development technique in such cases. One possible approach might be to develop a prototype using exploratory programming and use this as a basis for a system rewritten in a more structured way. However, it may well be the case that system maintenance also needs an exploratory approach and it is not clear how this might be supported.

1.3   Software evolution

Large software systems are not static objects. They exist in an environment which is subject to constant change and which may not be completely understood by the implementors of the software. As the environment changes or becomes more fully understood, the software system must either adapt to these changes or become progressively less useful until, ultimately, it must be discarded. This process of change has been termed software evolution and is discussed in an important paper by Lehman (1980) and in greater depth by Lehman and Belady (1985).

Software maintenance is the process of correcting errors in the system and modifying the system to reflect environmental changes. For large systems, this maintenance is accomplished in a series of system 'releases'. Each release is a new version of the system with known errors corrected and incorporating new or updated system facilities.

If the system is implemented in a number of installations it is unlikely that all installations will include all changes in each system release. Furthermore, each installation may make local modifications, tuning the system to the particular environment in which it operates. As a result of these factors, it is inevitable that the versions of the system at each installation drift further and further apart and that general maintenance, applicable to all installations, becomes more difficult. At the moment, we do not have the configuration management techniques to handle this situation when the systems have drifted significantly apart and it seems that only knowledge-based tools will be able to assist with this task.

Lehman suggests that the evolution of a software system is subject to a number of 'laws'. He has derived these laws from experimental observations of a number of systems such as large operating systems. He suggests that there are five laws of program evolution:

(1)   *Continuing change* A program that is used in a real-world environment necessarily must change or become less and less useful in that environment.

(2)   *Increasing complexity* As an evolving program changes, its structure becomes more complex unless active efforts are made to avoid this phenomenon.

(3) *Program evolution* Program evolution is a self-regulating process and measurement of system attributes such as size, time between releases, number of reported errors, etc., reveals statistically significant trends and invariances.

(4) *Conservation of organizational stability* Over the lifetime of a program, the rate of development of that program is approximately constant and independent of the resources devoted to system development.

(5) *Conservation of familiarity* Over the lifetime of a system, the incremental system change in each release is approximately constant.

Lehman's laws (perhaps hypotheses would be a better term) are not universally accepted in the same way as physical laws but they do appear to have some validity for many types of software system. He has used them with some success in the management of new releases of a large operating system. Software evolution is particularly relevant for software maintenance and Lehman's laws are discussed in more detail in Chapter 27.

The reasoning which underlies the first of Lehman's laws is that, when a software system (particularly a large software system) is built to model some environment and is then introduced into that environment, the original environment is modified by the presence of the software system. Therefore, users modify their behaviour as they become familiar with the software system and redefine what they expect of it. The system must then be modified and reintroduced into the environment after which the process starts anew.

The second law reflects the fact that the original program structure was set up to implement a set of initial requirements. As these requirements change incrementally, the original structure is corrupted. To reduce structural complexity thus requires the entire system to be wholly or partially restructured to reflect the requirements at a single point in time.

The third, fourth and fifth laws are not based on software characteristics but are based on the inherent inertia of the human organizations involved in the software development process. Lehman suggests that organizations strive for stability and attempt to avoid sudden or drastic change. Thus, as more resources are added to a software project, the incremental effect of adding new resources becomes less and less until the addition of extra resources has no effect whatsoever. The project at this stage has reached resource saturation.

Whilst the first two of Lehman's laws do appear to be valid, it may be the case that in small, less formal, more responsive organizations Lehman's latter three laws are not valid. The organizational effects on the software may not be universal across organizations.

Given that Lehman's laws are valid, what are the implications for software life-cycle management? Firstly, software maintenance costs are not necessarily a result of errors or omissions and cannot ever be eliminated. What we must do is to adopt techniques which allow changes to be readily incorporated and which retard the deterioration of the system structure. Maintenance must be planned in advance and not simply added as an afterthought. Rapid prototyping may result in a system which is initially more satisfactory but will not dramatically reduce maintenance costs. It should be viewed as a technique for improving quality rather than reducing cost.

Secondly, management should not plan to make very large changes to software systems in a single increment. Rather, changes should be introduced in small increments which implies, perhaps, more frequent system releases. Adding functionality should not be attempted at the same time as curing problems, and some system releases should be dedicated to fault elimination with no attempt being made to introduce new features.

Finally, the laws imply that the most cost-effective way to develop software is to use as few people as possible in each project group as the more people working on a project, the less productive is each individual project member. Most practising software engineers will be aware of this from experience yet there is always a tendency when a software project timetable slips to ignore this and to try to recover by adding staff.

Of course, there are some very large projects which cannot be tackled by a single small project team. In these circumstances, a small team should be responsible for overall system design and should separate the system into a number of independent subsystems which can be developed by small teams and maintained separately. New system releases should concentrate on improving a small number of subsystems and should not attempt to introduce new versions of all subsystems at the same time.

1.4 Software reliability

As computer applications become more diverse and pervade almost every area of everyday life, it is becoming more and more apparent that the most important dynamic characteristic of computer software is that it should be reliable. Reliability takes precedence over efficiency for the following reasons:

(1) Equipment is becoming steadily cheaper and faster. There is less need to maximize equipment usage in preference to human convenience. Paradoxically, however, faster equipment leads to

increasing expectations on the part of the user so efficiency considerations cannot be completely ignored.

(2)   Unreliable software is liable to be avoided by users and, irrespective of how efficient it is, it will soon become worthless. Indeed, if a company attains a reputation for unreliability because of a single unreliable product, this is likely to affect the sales of all of that company's products.

(3)   For some applications, such as a reactor control system or an aircraft navigation system, the cost of system failure is very much greater than the cost of the system itself. There are more and more safety-critical systems coming into use where the human costs of a catastrophic system failure are unacceptable.

(4)   An efficient system can be tuned with considerable success because most execution time is spent in fairly small sections of a program. An unreliable system is much more difficult to improve as unreliability tends to be distributed throughout the entire system.

(5)   Inefficiency is predictable. Programs take a long time to execute. Unreliability is much worse. Software which is unreliable can have hidden errors which can violate system and user data without warning and the results of an error might not be discovered until much later. For example, a fault in a design program used to design aircraft might not be discovered until a number of planes had crashed.

(6)   Unreliable systems can result in information being lost. Data is very expensive and may be worth much more than the computer system on which it is processed. Hence much effort and money is expended in duplicating valuable data.

Informally, the reliability of a software system is a measure of how well it provides the services expected of it by its users. Of course, users do not consider all services to be of equal importance and a system might be viewed as unreliable if it ever failed to provide some critical service. For example, say a system was used to control braking on an aircraft but failed to work under a single set of very rare conditions. Should these conditions arise and the aircraft crash that software might be regarded as unreliable.

On the other hand, say the same software provided some visual indication of its actions to the pilot of the aircraft. Assume this failed once per month without the main system function being affected. It is unlikely, in spite of more frequent failure, that the software would be rated as unreliable. It is possible to provide software reliability metrics such as 'mean time between failures' and 'rate of fault occurrence' (see Chapter 30) but these do not take into account the differing, subjective nature of software faults. It is not clear how useful they are in reliability assessment.

What is most important is perceived reliability – how reliable the system appears to be to users.

The reliability of any system (not merely software systems) is dependent on the correctness of the system design, the correctness of the mapping of the system design to implementation, and the reliability of the components making up the system. For example, the reliability of a motor car depends on the car design, on how well the car is put together, and on how long the components making up the car take to fail. In general, after initial teething troubles, the reliability of most systems is governed by how long it takes the system components to wear out. As the majority of systems have some moving parts, wear is inevitable and it is impossible for these systems to be 100% reliable.

Software systems are unique in this respect. They contain no moving parts and their reliability depends completely on design and implementation correctness. Hardware reliability can be achieved by duplication of components with a new component automatically switching in if component failure is detected. This approach cannot be taken by software systems. If a procedure gives the wrong answer there is no point in trying to execute another identical copy of the same procedure. However, Randell (1975) suggests that greater software reliability might be attained by executing another functionally equivalent but non-identical copy of the procedure. Discussion of this topic is outside the scope of this book.

The key to software reliability lies in the system specification. It is often the case that reliability requirements are expressed in a very informal, qualitative way and it is then extremely difficult to assess whether or not these requirements have been attained. Furthermore, most software specifications are incomplete in that they do not describe what should happen when every possible error condition arises. Rather, they leave decisions like this to the intuition and experience of the system designer. A lack of perceived reliability may not be due to system faults but may be a result of misunderstandings between the specifier and the designer.

This is all very well if a classical approach to software development is adopted. If exploratory programming is used, a system specification at a level which would be useful to assess reliability does not exist. In such circumstances, no trustworthy estimate can be made of system reliability. Conventional verification techniques are of no use in such circumstances and only user reports of perceived reliability can provide feedback to system developers of the system reliability. For this reason, the use of exploratory programming in safety-critical applications is not recommended.

To be realistic, software engineers often have to work with imperfect specifications and cannot evade responsibility for producing reliable systems. Thus, they should work according to 'fail-safe' criteria. As well as meeting the agreed specifications, a program should never produce 'incorrect' output irrespective of the input (no output is better than incorrect output), should never allow itself to be corrupted, should take meaningful and useful actions in unexpected situations and should only fail completely when further progress is impossible. Failure should not affect other components of the system.

It might be imagined that the use of formal methods for system development will necessarily lead to more reliable systems. There is no doubt that a formal system specification is less likely to contain anomalies which must be resolved by the system designer. However, there is no guarantee that such a specification defines a system which meets the user's needs and hence provides a high level of perceived reliability. Indeed, it may be the case that the opaqueness of formal notations makes it more difficult for users to establish whether or not a system is what is required. Paradoxically, it may be less likely that perceived reliability criteria will be met.

Clearly a reliable system must conform to its specification and, if a formal specification has been produced, the system may be proved to meet that specification. The existence of such a proof must increase confidence in the system's correctness (although proofs can contain errors) and hence should lead to greater system reliability. However, it would be most unwise to assume that a system which has been proved to be correct will necessarily be reliable. Proving a program correct depends on making assumptions about that program's environment and, if the major cause of unreliability is environmental rather than inherent in the program, the perceived reliability of the system may not be improved. The role of program proving in the verification and validation process is discussed in Chapter 22.

To achieve high reliability inevitably involves a good deal of extra, often redundant, code built into the system to perform the necessary checking. This reduces the program execution speed and increases the amount of store required by the program. It can dramatically increase development costs. Figure 1.7 shows the relationship between costs and incremental improvements in reliability.

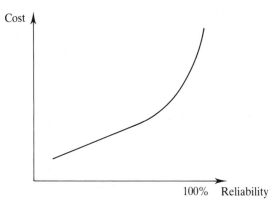

Figure 1.7
Costs versus reliability.

Product reliability is very difficult to quantify and, if arbitrary metrics are used, it is difficult and expensive to check if the system meets the required standards. Because of this, some organizations place constraints on the process of software development on the assumption that adherence to process standards (such as testing standards) will lead to systems whose reliability is acceptable. While there is sense in this, a danger is that adherence to standards becomes more important than software costs or functionality. Furthermore, there is no definitive evidence concerning the relationship between product and process reliability – conforming to a process may do no good at all as far as reliability is concerned.

As well as being reliable at any one point in time, programming systems ought to be reliable over their lifetimes. Because the environments in which these systems operate do change, mechanisms must be built into the software so that it may evolve and continue to offer the same levels of perceived reliability. The topic of software reliability is covered in more detail in Chapter 30.

KEY POINTS

- Software engineering involves technical and non-technical issues. As well as knowledge of specification, design and implementation techniques, software engineers must have some knowledge of human factors and software management.

- Well engineered software is software which provides the services required by its users and which is maintainable, reliable, efficient and provides an appropriate user interface.

- The waterfall model of software development suffers from inadequacies but will continue to be widely used because it simplifies the management of the software process.

- Exploratory programming is not suited to the development of large, long-lifetime software systems.

- Software systems always have to be maintained if they are to remain useful thoughout their life. This need for maintenance arises because the software must fit in with a constantly changing environment.

- The most important dynamic characteristic of a software system is reliability. The reason for this is that the costs of system failure often exceed the costs of developing the software system in the first place.

Further reading

Software Engineering Economics.   In spite of the title, this book is a wide-ranging look at many aspects of software engineering by one of the best respected authorities in this field. Early chapters discuss the software life-cycle and life-cycle costs. (B.W. Boehm. 1981. Prentice-Hall.)

The Cost of Large Software Systems.   This is a relatively old collection of papers and it is surprising and somewhat depressing that so little has changed since this book was published. Papers in this volume by Boehm, Schwartz and Wolverton are of particular interest. (E. Horowitz, (ed.). 1975. Addison-Wesley.)

Programs, Life Cycles and the Laws of Software Evolution.   This paper summarizes several years of work and thought on software evolution. It does take a bit of work to understand it properly but this is worthwhile as the author provides useful insights into software system characteristics. (M.M. Lehman. Proceedings IEEE, **68** (9), 1980. 1060–76.)

Proceedings of an International Workshop on the Software Process.   This is a collection of papers on various aspects of the software process. Whilst some of them are very discursive, there is much of value in this collection. (ACM Software Engineering Notes, **11** (4), 1986.)

References

Boehm, B.W. (1975), 'The high cost of software', in *Practical Strategies for Developing Large Software Systems*, Horowitz, E. (ed.), Reading, Mass.: Addison-Wesley.

Boehm, B.W. (1981), *Software Engineering Economics*, Englewood Cliffs, NJ: Prentice-Hall.

Boehm, B.W. (1987), 'Improving software productivity', *IEEE Computer*, **20** (9), 43–58.

Gladden, G.R. (1982), 'Stop the life cycle – I want to get off', *ACM Software Engineering Notes*, **7** (2), 35–9.

Lehman, M.M. (1980), 'Programs, life cycles and the laws of software evolution', *Proc. IEEE*, **15** (3), 225–52.

Lehman, M.M. and Belady, L. (1985), *Program Evolution. Processes of Software Change*, London: Academic Press.

McCracken, D.D. and Jackson, M.A. (1982), 'Life cycle concept considered harmful', *ACM Software Engineering Notes*, **7** (2), 28–32.

Randell, B. (1975), 'System structure for software fault tolerance', *IEEE Trans. Software Engineering*, **SE-1** (2), 46–58.

Royce, W.W. (1970), 'Managing the development of large software systems', *Proc. WESTCON, Ca.,* USA.

Shneiderman, B. (1986), *Designing the User Interface*, Reading, Mass.: Addison-Wesley.

EXERCISES

1.1 In this chapter, well engineered software was defined as possessing four attributes. List these attributes and suggest four further attributes which such software might possess. Under what circumstances might these be more important than those suggested here?

1.2 Suggest reasons why the waterfall model of the software process is not a true reflection of the activities involved in software development.

1.3 What is the distinction between verification and validation? Illustrate your answer with examples of each of these activities.

1.4 Explain why programs developed using an exploratory programming approach are likely to be difficult to maintain. If you are familiar with LISP, PROLOG or some other exploratory programming language, examine such programs and estimate how hard these would be to change.

1.5 List Lehman's laws and explain how these relate to the software development process.

1.6 Suggest six reasons why software reliability is important. Using an example, explain the difficulties of describing what software reliability means.

1.7 Why is it inappropriate to use reliability metrics which were developed for hardware systems in estimating software systems reliability? Illustrate your answer with an example.

Chapter 2

Human Factors in Software Engineering

Objectives

Human factors are often ignored by software engineers but knowledge of this topic can provide insights into a number of areas of software engineering. The objectives of this chapter are to describe those human factors which are relevant to the software engineering process. These include the way in which we process information, individual and group characteristics, and ergonomics. The chapter starts with a discussion of human diversity and how there seems to be no single ideal programming personality. This is followed by a description of a memory model and cognitive processing. The practical implications of that model are discussed. Group working is then covered and the role of individual personalities, group leadership, group loyalties and group communication is covered. Finally, the importance of ergonomics in workplace design and in the provision of support for software engineering is described.

Contents

In a technical text, it is perhaps unusual to find a chapter on human factors. Its inclusion reflects the author's long-standing conviction that an understanding of the humans who are involved in software engineering as system users, specifiers, designers, programmers and managers helps with the technical processes of systems design and management.

This conviction has been reinforced by the fact that much greater attention is now being paid to human aspects of computer systems, particularly by those involved in user interface design. As discussed in Chapter 13, user interface design must take into account the capabilities and limitations of computer users and a number of studies are now underway which should provide valuable knowledge in this area.

The particular study of human factors and computer systems is a new area of research and, although some seminal works were produced some years ago (Weinberg, 1971; Shneiderman, 1980), there is not a significant body of literature devoted to this topic. Thus, it is necessary to draw on other psychological research and conjecture how this affects software engineering. However, we must be aware that such conjectures are sometimes invalid as the domain in which the original studies were carried out may not be comparable to the software engineering domain.

In spite of the immaturity of this field and the uncertainty over some of the extrapolations from other psychological research, a study of human factors is important and relevant for the following reasons.

(1)   Effective software management is important if large programming projects are to be completed on time, to specification and within budget. To be effective, the software manager must understand his or her staff as individuals and understand how these individuals interact with each other. A better understanding of the psychology of programming helps the manager to understand the human limits involved and to tailor software projects so that programming staff are not set unrealizable objectives.

(2)   Computer systems are used by people and, if the limitations and abilities of these people are not taken into account when designing the system, it will not be used in the best possible way by these humans.

(3)   Programmer productivity is the critical cost factor in software engineering. An understanding of human factors can help identify possible ways of increasing productivity at relatively low cost.

Human factors research is sometimes criticized by pragmatic technicians as common sense and, indeed, some of the conclusions which are drawn in psychological studies simply seem to confirm everyday experience. However, what these technicians sometimes forget is that common sense is actually the result of a great deal of experience and acquired wisdom and that it is worthwhile confirming this experience experimentally and trying to establish some model to explain it.

2.1   Human diversity

Software development is an individual, creative task. It is comparable with composing music, designing buildings and writing books. Although a software engineer may work as part of a team, the team is only necessary because the required software system is so large that it cannot be produced by one person in a reasonable amount of time. Within the team, the work is partitioned and individuals work on their own, creating part of the system.

The individuals involved in software engineering reflect the diversity found in human society. Although predominantly a male profession, there are probably more women employed in software engineering than in any other engineering discipline. Software engineering is a worldwide activity and people of all races are employed as software engineers. Although programming was once seen as an introspective discipline, its expansion has meant that software engineers now exhibit a diverse range of personalities. There seems to be no such thing as a software engineering 'type'.

Psychologists have identified a number of so-called 'personality traits' such as assertive/humble, trusting/suspicious, etc., and have developed tests which allow personality classification according to these traits. An individual personality may be considered to be a combination of all of these traits but is certainly not fixed. Personalities can change depending on individual circumstances, environments, and the personalities of co-workers.

Because personality is a dynamic rather than a static attribute, any attempt to select software engineers on the basis of personality traits is unlikely to be successful. However, using a personality test devised for job aptitude, Perry and Cannon (1966) produced a programmer profile by testing existing programmers. The motivation behind this work was to identify suitable potential programmers. If new recruits are tested and their profiles match with the personality profile of experienced programmers, this may imply that they would make suitable programmers.

Even if the dynamic nature of personality is ignored, Weinberg (1971) points out that it does not follow that personality profile matching will identify good programmers. Different personalities may be suited to different aspects of programming such as systems design, testing, etc. Should the tests attempt to identify a programming personality or should they be more precise and identify program design personalities, program testing personalities, and so on?

Another deficiency of this approach is that the 'ideal' personality profile was obtained by testing programmers already in the profession but without reference to their ability. There is no guarantee that the sample of the programming profession chosen is representative of competent programmers. Finally, an intelligent programmer filling in personality tests might cheat. Instead of presenting their true personality to the tester, they might present the personality which they think the tester wants.

This is a natural human reaction to any kind of assessment and no more culpable than individuals trying to present a favourable picture of themselves at a job interview. Indeed, it can be argued that the ability to recognize and deliver what is required by a user is an attribute which is very desirable in potential software engineers!

There is no evidence to suggest that programming ability is related to any particular personality traits. Weinberg confirms that it is probably impossible to identify programming personalities but suggests that the absence of particular characteristics may mean that individuals are not well suited to software engineering.

One example of such a trait is the ability to withstand a certain amount of stress. The nature of software projects (indeed, any engineering projects) is such that the schedule for the project is imposed on the programmer. Work must be completed by a particular date. As that date approaches, the stress imposed on the software engineer becomes greater. As stress is imposed, performance starts to suffer which causes further delays resulting in more stress and the cycle continues to some sort of unsatisfactory conclusion.

Another personality trait of which a lack might be an impediment to software engineers is adaptive ability. The rate of change of both hardware and software technology is extremely rapid and engineers must be able to adapt to these changes. Without adaptive ability, individuals tend to continue with obsolete practices to the detriment of overall performance. This problem is particularly acute if it is combined with a promotion strategy which results in these individuals becoming managers. They stifle innovation and cause frustration among other technical staff resulting in high staff turnover, low morale and general dissatisfaction.

2.2   Knowledge processing

The activity of software development is a cognitive skill and, like all such skills, is subject to the limitations of people's brains. Of course, there is a great diversity in individual abilities reflecting differences in intelligence, education and experience, but all of us seem to be subject to some basic constraints on our thinking. These result from the way in which information is stored and modelled in our brains so it is worthwhile to examine our knowledge processing model and to try to identify the effects this might have on software development.

2.2.1 Memory organization

As software systems are abstract rather than concrete entities, their development is reliant on the ability of developers to remember their characteristics during the development process. It is, of course, possible to examine a source code listing but the developer must be able to understand and remember the relationship between that listing and the dynamic behaviour of the program and to apply this stored knowledge in developing further program parts.

The retention of information in the memory depends on the memory structure. This seems to be hierarchical with three distinct, connected areas (Figure 2.1):

- A limited capacity short-term memory with very fast access. Input from the senses is received here for initial processing. This memory may be compared to the registers in a computer in that it is simply used in information processing and not for information storage.

- A working memory area which has a larger capacity and a longer access time than short-term memory. This memory area is also used in information processing but can retain more information for longer periods than short-term memory. Again it is not used for information retention over a long period of time. By analogy with the computer, this is like the main store on a system where information is maintained for the duration of a computation.

- Long-term memory which has a very large capacity, relatively slow access time and unreliable retrieval mechanisms (we forget things!). Long-term memory is used for the 'permanent' storage of

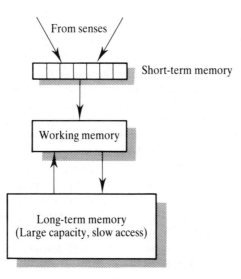

Figure 2.1
Memory organization.

information and information is transferred to and from working memory for processing. To continue the analogy, long-term memory is like disk memory on a computer.

When problems are posed, information about these problems is received in short-term memory and is integrated with existing, relevant information from long-term memory in the working memory area. The result of this integration forms the basis for the problem solution and may be stored in long-term memory for future use. Of course, the solution may be incorrect which involves future revision of the long-term memory. The storage structure there seems to be such that the old, incorrect information is not discarded but is retained to help us avoid repeating the same mistakes.

The limited size of short-term memory places a severe constraint on our cognitive processes. In a classic experiment, Miller (1957) found that the short-term memory can store about seven quanta of information. A quantum of information is not a fixed number of bits – it may be a telephone number, the function of a procedure or a street name. Miller also describes the process of 'chunking' where information quanta are collected together into chunks. These chunks can themselves be collected into larger chunks, etc. This chunking process appears to be the basis of our ability to form abstractions.

If the problem being solved involves the input of more items of information than may be retained in short-term memory, there has to be some kind of information processing and transfer during the input process. This can result in information being lost and errors arising because the information processing cannot keep up with the memory input.

This seems to be a particular problem when the application domain is a new one. For example, if we are presented with pictures of common animals, these can be processed very quickly because they have been known since childhood. On the other hand, if we are presented with descriptions of new software components, it takes much longer to work out what these mean.

Shneiderman (1980) conjectures that the information chunking process is used in understanding programs. The program reader abstracts the information in the program into chunks and these chunks are built into an internal semantic structure representing the program. Programs are not understood on a statement-by-statement basis unless, of course, a statement represents a logical chunk.

Figure 2.2 shows how a simple bubblesort program might be 'chunked' by a reader. Once the internal semantic structure representing the program has been established, this knowledge is transferred to long-term memory and is not readily forgotten. It can usually be realized in different notations without much difficulty.

For example, consider the well known binary search algorithm where an ordered collection of items is searched for a particular item.

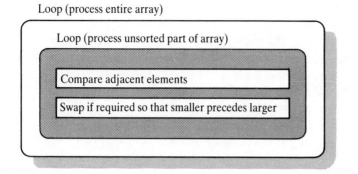

Figure 2.2
Bubblesort chunking.

This involves examining the mid-point of the collection and using our knowledge of the ordering relationship to determine whether or not the key item is in the upper or the lower part of the collection. It is quite obvious that this information is not retained in the form of a program description because, if nothing else, an English language description of the algorithmic model can be produced. A programmer who knows and understands this algorithm can produce a version in Pascal, Ada or another programming language.

The model of how we understand programs in combination with the memory structure knowledge may be used to explain a number of aspects of programming practice. For example, it explains why a structured program should be easier to understand; why programmer ability is language independent; and what is the best way to learn a new programming language. We return to these after the next section where human knowledge modelling is considered in more detail.

2.2.2 Knowledge modelling

Information enters short-term memory and is processed before being stored in long-term memory. In general, we do not store raw information but information abstractions which we call 'knowledge'. Although the distinction between information and knowledge is not a rigid one, a possible view is that neural information processing involves the integration of raw information and existing information to create knowledge.

The knowledge acquired during software development and stored in long-term memory appears to fall into two separate classes:

(1)   *Semantic knowledge*   This is the knowledge of concepts such as the operation of an assignment statement, the notion of a linked list and how a hash search technique operates. This knowledge is acquired through experience and learning and is retained in a representation-

independent fashion. The manner in which the concept was presented to the programmer does not appear to affect the way in which this knowledge is stored.

(2) *Syntactic knowledge* This is the knowledge of details of a representation such as how to write a procedure declaration in Pascal, what standard functions are available in a programming language, whether an assignment is written using an '=' or a ':=' sign, etc. This knowledge is retained in a form which is much closer to raw information and is detailed and arbitrary.

This knowledge organization is illustrated in Figure 2.3, taken from Shneiderman's book on user interface design.

Semantic knowledge is acquired by experience and through active learning where new information is consciously integrated with existing semantic structures. Syntactic knowledge, on the other hand, seems to be acquired by memorization, and new syntactic knowledge is not necessarily integrated with existing knowledge. In fact, new syntactic knowledge may interfere with existing knowledge, as it can only be arbitrarily added to that knowledge rather than integrated with it.

The different acquisition modes for syntactic and semantic knowledge explain the typical situation which arises when an experienced programmer learns a new programming language. Normally, the experienced programmer has no difficulty with the language concepts such as assignments, loops, conditional statements, etc. These are embodied as semantic knowledge and are well understood.

However, the language syntax tends to get mixed up with the syntax of familiar languages. For example, a FORTRAN programmer learning Pascal might write the assignment operator as '=' rather than ':=', a Pascal programmer might write 'type x =...' rather than 'type x is ...' when learning Ada, and so on.

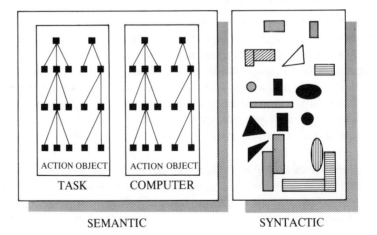

Figure 2.3
Syntactic and semantic knowledge.

The novice programmer has two problems when learning to program. Not only must beginners master the semantic concepts implied in the computational model, they must also master an arbitrary and sometimes obscure syntax. It is difficult for them to distinguish between syntactic and semantic problems and to perform knowledge integration to create the appropriate semantic concepts.

Furthermore, because instructors have successfully understood and processed the semantic information, they sometimes find difficulty in expressing the semantic concepts in terms which are readily understood by novice programmers. The model explains why, for many people, learning to program is a skill which seems to arrive all at once after a period of difficulties. This point is when the semantic and syntactic concepts have been separated and the semantic concepts understood.

The semantic knowledge appears to be stored in two distinct classes, namely knowledge of computing concepts such as the notion of a writable store and knowledge of task concepts such as binary search or radar tracking (Soloway *et al.*, 1982; Card *et al.*, 1983). An orthogonal organization is into high-level concepts, such as the notion of a store, and into detailed, low-level concepts such as the notion that the words in a store are made individually addressable but the bits (usually) are not.

Problem solving involves integration of task and computer concepts. Those involved in software development may not be expert in both of these. Organizational factors such as the need to complete a solution within budget must also be considered as part of the problem-solving process. Thus, a user may be expert in the task concepts, a software designer an expert in the computer concepts, and a manager an expert in the organization factors. Software engineering involves an integration of all of this expertise.

2.2.3 Practical implications

It is all very well to have models of cognitive processes, but the pragmatic software engineer is really interested in how these processes affect software management, design and development. Clearly, user interface design is one area where it is essential to take human knowledge processing capability into account and this is discussed in Chapter 13. Here, we concentrate on the implications of the knowledge processing model in the software development process.

The idea of structured programming – programming using only conditionals and while loops – received a great deal of publicity in the 1970s . It is now recognized that this is by far the best general approach to take to program development because it makes programs easier to understand.

This is explained by the human cognitive model. Recall that short-term memory capacity is limited, information is encoded in chunks and that semantic and syntactic knowledge is stored. If a program can be read top-to-bottom, the abstractions involved in forming chunks can be made sequentially, without reference to other parts of the program. The short-term memory can be devoted to a single section of code. It is not necessary to maintain information about several sections connected by arbitrary goto statements.

For the same reasons, if a programmer actively endeavours to program without the use of goto statements, he or she is less likely to make programming errors. Short-term memory can be devoted to information relevant to the program section being coded. There is no need to retrieve information from working memory about other parts of the program which interfere with that section.

The process of devising and writing a program is, basically, a problem-solving situation. The problem must first be understood, a general solution strategy worked out and, finally, this strategy must be translated into specific actions. The first stage involves the problem statement entering working memory from short-term memory. It is integrated with existing knowledge from long-term memory and analysed. The second stage uses this analysis to work out an overall solution. Finally, some method, such as the top-down development process, described in Chapter 12, is used to develop the general solution and construct a program.

The development of the solution (the program) involves building an internal semantic model of the problem and a corresponding model of the solution. Once this model is built, it may be represented in any appropriate syntactic notation. An experienced programmer who understands a number of programming languages will have approximately the same degree of difficulty in representing that solution, irrespective of which language is actually used.

Programming ability seems to be an ability to take existing computer and task knowledge in combination with new task information and integrate this to create new knowledge. Thus, the problem-solving process is language independent and virtuosity with particular languages is no guarantee of programming skills. Language skills are necessary and take time to develop (particularly for complex languages like Ada) but managers should be wary of hiring staff simply on the basis of previous language experience. It is probably the case that application experience is more important if staff are required to solve a particular problem as this experience means that task concepts are likely to have been absorbed.

However, the representation is more likely to be free of errors if the syntactic facilities of the notation match the lowest level semantic structures which are formulated. Although these may vary from individual to individual, programming teaching now emphasizes assignments, conditional statements, while loops, type declarations, etc., as the lowest level concepts. A programming language should represent these abstractions directly.

Programs written in languages like Pascal should contain fewer errors than those written in FORTRAN or assembly code because low-level semantic concepts can be encoded directly as language statements. Consequently, if the final representation is to be in Pascal, the internal semantics need not be developed to such a level of detail as would be required if the program is represented in FORTRAN.

Because programming ability is language independent and programming language knowledge is held in a representation-independent way, it is relatively easy for programmers who are familiar with one programming language to learn a new language of the same type. All that must be learnt is a new syntax – the concepts are already understood.

This is only true, however, if the semantic concepts underlying both of these languages are the same. For example, a FORTRAN programmer should have little difficulty learning Pascal as both languages are based on the model of a sequential Von Neumann computer. On the other hand, the same programmer could have difficulty learning PROLOG (Clocksin and Mellish, 1982) as its underlying model is quite different.

Beginners may find learning such a language easier than experienced programmers as they would not attempt to fit the language into an existing, understood model. Rather than trying to identify familiar semantic concepts such as assignment statements, loops and conditionals (which don't exist in PROLOG), novices are not constrained by fixed ideas when presented with a programming language.

When organizing programmer education, it should be borne in mind that experienced programmers and inexperienced programmers have quite different requirements. Experienced programmers require to know the syntax of a language whereas inexperienced programmers need to be taught the concepts – how an assignment statement works, the notion of a procedure and so on. For such novice programmers, language-directed editing systems are immensely valuable as they handle a lot of the syntactic detail for the programmer, leaving him or her to concentrate on the semantic concepts of the language. For experienced programmers, who may have evolved a programming style where syntactic program correctness is not always maintained, such editing systems may get in the way.

A language like Ada presents a particular problem. It is based on a Von Neumann model but contains constructs such as packages, tasks and exceptions which may not be familiar to the FORTRAN or Pascal programmer. Thus, these individuals might learn to write simple Ada programs fairly quickly but will need to spend considerably more time in learning the new features of the language. Indeed, such training will make up a major part of the costs of moving to Ada as a standard language for embedded systems development.

2.3 Group working

The popular image of a programmer is of a lone individual working far into the night peering into a terminal or poring over reams of paper covered with arcane symbols. Alternatively the image might be of a technology-mad teenager who is somehow different from his peers and who is most interested in hacking into other computers. Indeed, programmers tend to think of themselves as loners. Cougar and Zawacki (1978) found that data processing professional staff felt that they had a negligible need to work with other individuals.

Although many programming staff work on their own, the majority of software engineers work in teams which vary in size from two to several hundred people. In a study undertaken by IBM (McCue, 1978), the proportion of time spent in various activities was as shown in Figure 2.4. It was found that 50% of a typical programmer's time is spent interacting with other team members, 30% working alone and 20% in activities such as travel and training, which were not directly productive. Thus, while the public and the self-image may be an individual one, the reality is that software engineering is a team activity.

The interaction between team members plays an important role in the overall performance of the group. A well led group whose members recognize each other's abilities and deficiencies and are mutually supportive is likely to perform far better than a group which has been put together by management *dictat* and whose members have little in common in either goals or personalities.

An understanding of group dynamics helps both software managers and those involved in group working. Managers are faced with the difficult tasks of forming groups and, must try to ensure that the groups are balanced in terms of personalities as well as individual technical skills. Software engineers working in groups can achieve better results and more

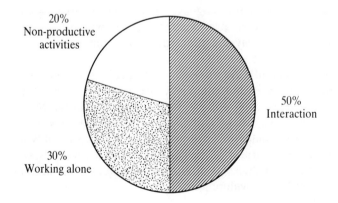

Figure 2.4
Distribution of a software engineer's time.

harmonious working conditions if they understand how the group members interact and how the group, as a separate entity, takes its place within an organization.

2.3.1　Personalities in groups

The formation of a software engineering group brings together individuals, each with their own distinct personality. These personalities sometimes work extremely well together and sometimes clash so dramatically that little or no productive work is carried out. This section attempts to describe why personality clashes sometimes occur and why some groups work together very successfully.

Very roughly, individuals in a work situation can be classified into three types:

(1)　*Task-oriented*　This type of individual is motivated by the work itself. In software engineering, they are technicians who are motivated by the intellectual challenge of software development.

(2)　*Self-oriented*　This type of individual is motivated by a desire for personal success. They are interested in software development as a means of achieving their own goals. Attaining these goals often means that they will move away from technical software development into management as soon as they possibly can.

(3)　*Interaction-oriented*　This type of individual is motivated by the presence and actions of co-workers. Until recently, it was probably the case that few individuals of this type were involved in software development because of the apparent lack of human interaction involved in the process. However, as software engineering becomes more user-centred, it is likely that more interaction-oriented individuals will be drawn into software projects.

Obviously these classes are not rigid and each individual's motivation is made up of elements of each class. Normally, however, one type of motivation is dominant at any one time. However, recall that personalities are not static and that individuals can change. For example, technicians who feel they are not being properly rewarded can become self-oriented and put personal interests before technical concerns.

In an experiment by Bass and Dunteman (1963), task-oriented persons described themselves as being self-sufficient, resourceful, aloof, introverted, aggressive, competitive and independent. Interaction-oriented individuals considered themselves to be unaggressive, with low needs for autonomy and achievement, considerate and helpful. They preferred to work in a group rather than alone. Self-oriented individuals described themselves as disagreeable, dogmatic, aggressive, competitive, introverted and jealous. They preferred to work alone. In the same experiment, it was found that men tended to be task oriented whereas women were more likely to be interaction oriented. Whether this latter observation is a result of natural tendencies or of role stereotyping is not clear.

When individuals worked in groups which were composed entirely of members belonging to the same personality class, only that group made up of interaction-oriented persons was successful. Task-oriented and self-oriented group members felt negatively about their groups. There was, perhaps, an oversupply of leaders. The difficulties encountered when individuals of the same personality class worked together suggest that the most successful groups are made up of individuals from each class with the group leader task-oriented.

Observation suggests that the majority of those involved in computer programming work are task-oriented individuals, motivated primarily by their work. This implies that programming groups are likely to be made up of individuals each of whom will have their own idea on how the same project should be undertaken. This is borne out by frequently reported problems of interface standards being ignored, systems being redesigned as they are coded, unnecessary system embellishments, etc.

The implication of this for software management is that careful attention must be paid to group composition. Selecting individuals who complement each other in terms of personality may produce a better working group than a group selected simply on the basis of programming ability. If a selection on the basis of complementary personalities is impossible (a likely situation bearing in mind that most programmers are task-oriented), the tendency of each group member to go his or her own way implies that strict managerial control may be necessary to ensure that individual goals do not transcend the overall goal of the group.

This control may be more readily achieved if all the members of a project group are given the opportunity to take an active part in each stage of the project. Individual initiative is most likely when one group member is instructed to carry out a task without being aware of the part that task plays in the project as a whole. For example, say a program design is presented to an individual for coding. That individual may see how the design can be improved but, without understanding how that design was arrived at, these improvements could have implications on other parts of the system. If the programmer is involved in the design right from the start, the individual is more likely to identify with that design and to strive to maintain rather than to modify it.

It is an observable fact that the structure of a software system tends to reflect the structure of the group producing that system. For example, if a three-person group is working on a compiler, the result is likely to be a three pass system, with each pass written by one member of the group. On the other hand, if the group structure is hierarchical, with a dominant leader and subordinates, the resulting system is likely to be hierarchical with the leader coding the main program which calls components coded by his or her subordinates.

This phenomenon appears to be inevitable, and attempts to coerce a group into adopting an unnatural system structure are unlikely to succeed. To minimize these clashes between system structure and group structure, the entire group should be involved at the system design stage. An appropriate system structure can then be agreed by group members. Thus, individual group members can see how their work fits into the overall objective of the group. Having been involved in the decision how best to achieve their objective they are less likely to strive for personal rather than group goals.

Clearly, the involvement of all group members at each stage of the project is impossible if the group is large. This implies that, for psychological reasons alone, large groups are less likely to be successful than small groups. This is borne out by a number of experiences of project failure and cost overrun where large programming groups were used and the failure was attributed to the lack of effective group communications.

When a large system requires a large amount of effort, the organization which is most psychologically sound is to partition that system into independent subsystems which are each designed and developed by separate small programming groups.

2.3.2 Egoless programming

The notion of egoless programming was introduced by Weinberg (1971) in his book *The Psychology of Computer Programming*. Egoless programming is a style of project group working which considers programs to be the common property and responsibility of the entire programming group irrespective of which individual group member was responsible for their production. The notion is not confined to programs and it may be generalized to include all software including specifications, designs and user documentation.

Weinberg suggests that this is a good way of working because it makes program production a group rather than an individual effort. His argument is based on the notion that an individual identifies a program as 'his' or 'hers' so is loath to accept that the program may contain errors. This idea is based on the theory of cognitive dissonance, put forward by Festinger (1957).

This theory argues that individuals who hold a set of beliefs or have made a particular decision avoid anything which contradicts those beliefs or that decision. For example, supporters of a political party will normally only attend political speeches made by a member of the same party, in spite of the fact that the material presented in the speech is probably familiar. Buyers of a particular make of computer tend to read articles which praise that computer and to avoid reading material which suggests that other machines are superior.

On the same basis, programmers who consider themselves personally responsible for a program tend to defend that program against criticism, even if it has obvious shortcomings. The programmer's ego is tied up with the program itself. If, however, programmers do not consider their work to be a personal possession but instead common group property, they are more likely to offer their programs for inspection by other group members, to accept criticisms of them, and to work with the group to improve the programs.

The most important distinguishing feature of egoless programming is that it considers programming errors to be normal and expected. No individual blame is associated with these errors. It is not a method of programmer assessment or program quality control. Rather, it is a collective programming effort, undertaken on an informal basis, where the individual who actually coded the program has the same responsibility as all others in the group.

Design and document reviews and code inspections are a derivative of the notion of egoless programming. However, they differ from egoless programming in that they tend to be formally organized as part of the validation process and in that reviews are drawn from outside the development group. Although individual criticism is avoided in the review process, reviews do not really contribute to the group development of software.

As well as improving the quality of programs, documents and designs, the practice of egoless programming also improves intra-group communications. It effectively draws the members of a programming group together and encourages uninhibited communications without regard to status, experience, or sex. Individual members cannot go off and 'do their own thing' but must actively cooperate with other group members throughout the course of the project.

However, there are dangers (discussed below) in groups becoming too tightly knit and introspective. Although egoless programming is to be encouraged, it is best used in combination with more formal inspections and reviews so that the group goals do not diverge from the goals of the organization which includes that group.

2.3.3   Group leadership

The group leader plays a vital role in group functioning and his or her performance may govern the success or otherwise of a software project. While most programming groups have a titular leader or project manager appointed by higher management, that individual may not be the real leader of the group as far as the technical work of the project is concerned.

Some other more technically capable individual may adopt this role with the titular leader being responsible for administrative tasks. This is not necessarily a bad organization. Technical competence and administrative competence are not necessarily synonymous and the roles of technical leader and administrative leader may be complementary.

The actual leader in a software development group is that group member who has most influence on other group members. This influence can be a result of technical abilities, individual status or because of a dominant personality. The leadership may change at different stages of a project. Because of expertise or experience at a particular stage, the best qualified group member may command respect and take over leadership for that stage of the project.

For this reason, and because of the similar motivations of each member of the group, the traditional role of a leader responsible for directing, disciplining and rewarding in an autocratic fashion is not one which is likely to be successful with software engineers. In fact, a classic experiment by Lewin *et al.* (1939) suggests that the traditional leader's role as an autocrat is only suited to situations, such as arise in military engagements, where very rapid decision making is essential.

Their study showed that, when a democratic style of leadership is adopted, group productivity is higher and individual members work better without supervision and are more satisfied with their work. This confirms the intuitive notion that participation of group members at all stages of a project is likely to result in members adopting group goals and cooperating rather than competing.

The leader of a programming group will, in most cases, emerge as the individual who is most technically competent at each stage of the project. If this is not recognized by higher management and an unwanted leader is imposed on the group, this is likely to introduce tensions into the group. The members will certainly not respect the leader and may reject group loyalty in favour of individual goals. This is a particular problem in a fast-changing field such as software engineering where new members may be more up-to-date and better educated than experienced group leaders.

The implication of this is that competent individuals should not be promoted out of programming. It is necessary to provide an alternative career structure for technically able individuals so that they may be properly rewarded yet remain involved in programming. Such a structure has been created by IBM and other organizations in chief programmer teams, described in Chapter 24.

2.3.4 Group loyalties

Being a member of a well led group tends to induce individual loyalty to that group. Each group member identifies with group goals and with other group members. He or she attempts to protect the group, as an entity, from outside interference. Group loyalty implies that there is a coherence in decision making and universal acceptance of decisions once they have been made.

In general, this is a good thing. Group loyalty means that individuals think of the group as more important than the individual members. If a strong group feeling exists, membership changes can be accommodated. The group can adapt to changed circumstances, such as a drastic change in software requirements, by providing mutual support and help.

There are, nevertheless, two important disadvantages of group loyalty which are particularly obvious when the group is cohesive and tightly knit. The disadvantages are the resistance of group members to a change in leadership and a loss of overall critical faculties because group loyalty overrides all other considerations.

If the leader of a tightly knit group has to be replaced and the new leader is not already a group member, the group members may band together against the new leader irrespective of that leader's ability. The new leader will not have the same feelings of group loyalty as the rest of the group and may attempt to change the overall goals of the group. These changes are likely to be met with resistance from existing group members with a consequent decrease in overall productivity. The only practical way of avoiding this situation is, whenever possible, to appoint a new leader from within the group itself.

Another consequence of group loyalty has been termed 'groupthink' by Janis (1972). Groupthink is the state where the critical faculties of the group members are eroded by group loyalties. Consideration of alternatives is replaced by loyalty to group norms and decisions. The consequence of this is that any proposal favoured by the majority of the group tends to be adopted without proper consideration of alternative proposals. Janis suggests that groupthink is most prevalent under conditions of stress. For a software development group, this may be as deadlines and delivery dates approach when it is particularly important to make reasoned decisions.

Software management should make active efforts to avoid groupthink. This may involve formal sessions where group members are encouraged to criticize decisions, and the introduction of outside experts who can offer comments on the group's decisions. It should be policy for some individual outside the group to be involved in reviews of group members' work even when other group members might be better suited technically as reviewers.

Personnel policies can also be used to avoid groupthink. Some individuals are naturally argumentative, questioning, and disrespectful of the status quo. Such people are positive assets in spite of the fact that they may appear to be troublesome. They act as a devil's advocate, constantly questioning group decisions, thus forcing other group members to think about and evaluate their activities.

2.3.5 Group interaction

When involved with a group, members must clearly devote some of their time to communications with other group members. Some of these communications are essential in that they may form part of the activity of egoless programming; they may be collective design meetings or they may be progress reporting sessions. All too often, however, the communication takes place because of an organizational meeting culture, or is necessary because of poor group organization or inadequate documentation practices.

It is desirable to minimize unproductive group communication and to make the best possible use of time for essential interaction. As well as being time consuming, communications among group members and across groups also have to be managed. The more separate communications a group member is involved in, the more difficult these communications are to manage. Consequently, when large numbers of interpersonal communications become the norm, errors are more likely to occur.

Effective communication among the members of a software development group is essential if that group is to work efficiently. The factors which affect the effectiveness of intra-group communications are:

- The size of the group.
- The structure of the group.
- The status and personalities of group members.
- The physical work environment of the group.

The number of potential communication links between members of an n-member group is $n(n-1)$. As the size of a programming group increases, the number of potential communication links between individual members increases as the square of the group size. If there are two members A and B, there are two links AB and BA. If there are three members A, B and C, there are six links. Even in relatively small groups there are a large number of potential communication channels.

Communications between two group members are two-way communication links rather than a single communication. The reason for this is that the status of individuals within a group affects their communications so that a junior programmer (say) would talk to a manager in a different way from the way in which the manager talks to the programmer.

The effectiveness of group communications is influenced by the status, personalities and sexes of group members. Communications between group members of higher and lower status tend to be dominated by higher to lower communications. Lower-status members may be inhibited in opening communications because of their position. This effect of status on communications can be minimized by active efforts of the higher-status individual to encourage uninhibited communication by lower-status members. However, it is almost impossible to eliminate in hierarchical organizations where the progress of a junior member of staff is dependent on reports by more experienced colleagues.

The effectiveness of group communication and hence group efficiency can be influenced by personality clashes between group members. These personality clashes may be due to all members being task-oriented (too many leaders) as discussed previously, or may be the result of personal likes, dislikes and prejudices. Such clashes are difficult for management to resolve – people cannot be coerced into liking each other. If group effectiveness is hampered by personality clashes, the best solution is to reorganize the programming group, transferring some members elsewhere.

The sexual composition of groups also affects intra-group communication. A study by Marshall and Heslin (1976) has shown that both men and women prefer to work in mixed sex groups. The importance of interaction-oriented individuals has already been discussed and, as women tend to be more interaction-oriented than men, the reason for effective performance may be that the female group members act as interaction controllers within the group.

However, with mixed-sex groups there may be problems with role stereotyping. While some men may be content to see a woman adopt the role of interaction specialist, they may be less happy with the idea of a woman adopting an aggressive leadership role. It is important that senior management recognize these potential difficulties and provide support for women who may be placed in such an awkward situation. The problem is, fundamentally, a cultural one and can only be resolved by a long-term change in attitudes towards the role of the sexes in the workplace.

Clearly, some group communications are essential so the aim of the group should be to make these communications as effective as possible. In some ways, the best way to do this is to organize these communications informally rather than formally. Instead of scheduling regular, formal meetings, informal get-togethers over coffee or while travelling can sometimes result in more effective information exchange.

More formal group communications can be structured as either a star or a network (Figure 2.5). In the star organization, the group is structured so that all communications pass through some central coordinator. Therefore, if A wishes to describe some work to other project members in a project where C is the team leader, A would write a descriptive document and pass this to C. C then decides who needs to know about the contents of the document and passes it on to the appropriate group members.

In the network organization, documents produced by group members are circulated to all other group members. It is therefore clearly important that group size is small so that an unreasonable reading load is not placed on group members.

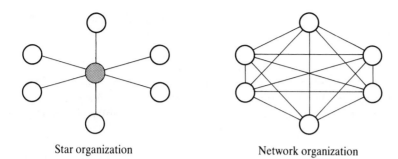

Star organization   Network organization

Figure 2.5
Group communication
patterns.

Research by Leavitt (1951) and Shaw (1964, 1971) suggests that the second alternative is the more effective. In their experiments, the group members preferred to work in loosely structured groups. They also implied that the problem-solving performance of loosely structured groups is superior to that of groups which have a centralized structure. On the other hand, groups where the communication passed through a centralized coordinator seem to be superior for relatively simple tasks such as the collection and dissemination of information.

Further evidence of the superiority of small, loosely structured groups has been provided by Porter and Lawler (1965). They found that the size of an organization correlates negatively with job satisfaction and productivity. It correlates positively with absenteeism and staff turnover. Although their work related to fairly large organizations, their results may also apply to software development groups.

2.4 Ergonomics

The workplace has unquantifiable but extremely important effects on the performance of those working in that environment. Psychological experiments have shown that individual behaviour is affected by room size, furniture, equipment, temperature, humidity, brightness and quality of light, noise and the degree of privacy available. Group behaviour is affected by factors such as architectural organization and telecommunication facilities.

As well as individual productivity, the workplace also affects the general satisfaction of staff. If people are unhappy about their working conditions, staff turnover may be higher so that more costs must be expended on recruitment and training. Software projects may be delayed because of lack of qualified staff.

There has been relatively little attention paid to tailoring the design of buildings specifically for software development. Most software engineering work takes place in environments designed for other functions, principally business offices. Software development staff often work in large open-plan office areas and only senior management have individual offices.

However, studies sponsored by IBM (McCue, 1978) have shown that the open-plan architecture favoured by many organizations was neither liked by software development staff nor helpful as far as productivity was concerned. The most important environmental factors identified in that design study were:

(1) *Privacy* Each programmer requires an area where he or she can concentrate and work without interruption.

(2) *Outside awareness* People prefer to work in natural light and with a view of the outside environment.

(3) *Personalization* Individuals adopt different working practices and have different opinions on decor. The ability to rearrange the workplace to suit working practices and to personalize that environment is important.

Obviously, it is not always possible to custom design buildings specifically for programming. Nevertheless, software management should recognize the importance of the working environment to the individual and provide a pleasant and congenial working environment.

One important implication of McCue's study is that the common practice of grouping programmers together in open-plan offices is not likely to be the most productive organization. Not only are individuals denied privacy and a quiet working environment, they are also limited in the degree to which they can personalize their own workspace.

McCue discovered that providing individual offices for software engineering staff made a significant difference to productivity and conjectured that this was due to the lower level of disruption than that found in open-plan organizations. His conclusions have been adopted by other organizations (Boehm, 1984) who have confirmed this conclusion.

As well as individual effectiveness, group effectiveness and communications are also affected by the physical environment. Development groups require areas where all members of the group can get together as a group and discuss their project, both formally and informally. Meeting rooms must be able to accommodate the whole group in privacy – it is unreasonable to expect group meetings to take place in the corner of some larger office.

Individual privacy requirements and group communication requirements seem to be exclusive objectives but the resolution of this problem, described by McCue, is to group individual offices round larger central rooms which can be used for group meetings and discussions (Figure 2.6).

Although individual offices make for better productivity, they have the disadvantage that it is more difficult for informal communications

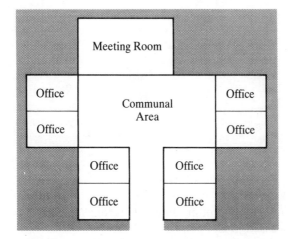

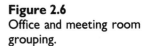
Figure 2.6
Office and meeting room
grouping.

between members of the same or different programming groups to take place. Individuals tend to 'disappear' into their offices and may not communicate much with their co-workers. This is a particular problem for those people who are not gregarious by nature and who are shy about seeking out other people to talk to.

Weinberg suggests that this type of communication is extremely important as it allows problems to be solved and information to be disseminated in an informal but effective way. He cites an anecdotal example of how the removal of a coffee machine to stop programmers 'wasting time' chatting to each other resulted in a dramatic increase in the demand for formal programming assistance. It is important to recognize the value of this informal communication and make implicit provision for it by providing coffee rooms and other informal meeting places as well as formal conference rooms.

2.4.1   Equipment provision

Software engineering became particularly important when hardware costs started to fall rapidly, and this fall in costs has continued and accelerated. There is no evidence that a plateau has been reached, and costs are likely to fall further over the next few years.

The capital costs of computing equipment are now so much less than the human costs involved in software engineering that it is economic nonsense not to provide each software engineer with a significant amount of personal computer power. Existing evidence suggests that individual productivity is increased significantly in situations where software engineers have direct access to a large amount of computer power.

Given that systems are developed for a wide range of different machines, the most effective support system appears to be a network of host computers used for software development which are used to develop

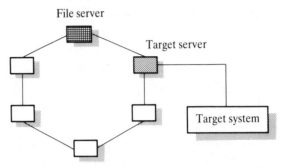

Figure 2.7
Host computer network.

systems for different target machines (Figure 2.7). The software for such a system is discussed in Chapters 18 and 19.

Providing personal computer workstations networked together for equipment support has the following advantages:

- The work of individuals is largely unaffected by the work of others. In timesharing systems, programs such as compilers which have large processing requirements can slow down the system for all other users. With personal systems, users control their own machine.

- Effective networking utilities can be provided to enhance formal and informal group communications. These include electronic notice-boards, computer conferencing systems such as those described by Hiltz and Turoff (1979), and electronic mail systems.

As well as local network access, organizations which have a number of geographically separated sites may find it useful to connect all of these sites via a company-wide area network or may subscribe to public data networking systems.

Effective electronic communication facilities, in conjunction with telephone and facsimile systems, can reduce the number of face-to-face meetings which are required. Electronic mail allows the rapid interchange of documents so that a document may be circulated, commented on, revised and recirculated all in one day. This author's experience has been that electronic discussions tend to be much more focussed than face-to-face meetings, perhaps because there is less scope for digression. However, they do lack immediacy and, obviously, there is no non-verbal communication as occurs in meetings.

An example of a successful project carried out, almost entirely, using telecommunications was the design of the programming language Euclid (Lampson *et al.*, 1977). In future, as telecommunication facilities improve, it is likely that much more use will be made of electronic mail and teleconferencing and major projects will be completed by disparate groups who only meet face-to-face once or twice a year.

KEY POINTS

- It is important that software engineers have some understanding of human factors because the ultimate judge of the usefulness of their software are *human* users. If the software does not take their capabilities and limitations into account it will be found wanting.

- Human memory organization is structured into fast, short-term memory, working memory and long-term memory. Mistakes are minimized when transfers between these memory areas are minimized.

- Knowledge falls into two classes, namely arbitrary syntactic knowledge and deeper semantic knowledge. Semantic knowledge is held in some internal way rather than in a language-oriented way.

- In group working, it is common for leaders who are technically competent to emerge. The titular group leader may simply be responsible for administrative activities.

- Personalities working in groups fall into three classes, namely task-oriented, self-oriented and interaction-oriented.

- Democratic groups tend to be more successful than autocratic groups.

- Group interaction should be structured so that the number of group communication links is minimized.

- The workplace has important but unquantifiable effects on software productivity.

Further reading

The Psychology of Computer Programming. This is a very readable book which uses mainly anecdotal evidence to suggest how programming groups and individual programmers should be managed. It ought to be compulsory reading for every software manager. (G.M. Weinberg. 1971, Van Nostrand Reinhold.)

Software Psychology This is a more academic approach to software psychology which describes various experiments undertaken in this research area. The topics covered are wide ranging from the modelling of conception to how indentation affects program understanding. (B. Shneiderman.1980. Winthrop Publishers.)

Computer Programming and the Human Thought Process. Using a model of thought processes, the author discusses topics such as software tools, top-down design and structured programming. His brain/computer analogy is interesting. (W.J. Tracz. *Software Practice and Experience*, **9** (2), 1979.)

IBM's Santa Teresa Laboratory – Architectural Design for Program Development. This paper describes the original thoughts on workspace design for productivity. More and more organizations are now accepting the importance of architectural design and are adopting these ideas. (G.M. McCue, *IBM Systems*, J., **17** (10), 4–25.)

References

Bass, B.M. and Dunteman, G. (1963), 'Behaviour in groups as a function of self, interaction and task orientation', *J. Abnorm. Soc. Psychol.*, **66** (4), 19–28.

Boehm, B.W. (1984), 'A software development environment for improving productivity', *IEEE Computer*, **17** (6), 30–44.

Card, S., Moran, T.P. and Newell, A. (1983), *The Psychology of Human–Computer Interaction*, Hilldale, NJ: Lawrence Erlbaum Associates.

Clocksin, W. and Mellish, C. (1982), *Programming in PROLOG*, Heidelberg: Springer-Verlag.

Cougar, J.D. and Zawacki, R.A. (1978), 'What motivates DP professionals', *Datamation*, **24** (9).

Festinger, L.A. (1957), *A Theory of Cognitive Dissonance*, Evanston, Ill.: Row Peterson.

Hiltz, S.R. and Turoff, M. (1979), *The Network Nation*, Reading, Mass.: Addison-Wesley.

Janis, I.L. (1972), *Victims of Groupthink. A Psychological Study of Foreign Policy Decisions and Fiascos*, Boston: Houghton Mifflin.

Lampson, B.W., Horning, J.J., London, R.L., Mitchell, J.G. and Popek, G.L. (1977), 'Report on the programming language Euclid', *ACM Sigplan Notices*, **12** (2), 1–79.

Leavitt, H.J. (1951), 'Some effects of certain communication patterns on group performance', *J. Abnorm. Soc. Psychol.*, **54** (1), 38–50.

Lewin, K., Lippit, R. and White, R.K. (1939), 'Patterns of aggressive behaviour in experimentally created social climates', *J. Soc. Psychol.*, **10**, 271–99.

Marshall, J.E. and Heslin, R. (1976), 'Boys and girls together. Sexual composition and the effect of density on group size and cohesiveness', *J. Personality Soc. Psychol.*, **36**.

McCue, G.M. (1978), 'IBMs Santa Teresa Laboratory – Architectural design for program development', *IBM Systems J.*, **17** (1), 4–25.

Miller, G.A. (1957), 'The magical number 7 plus or minus two: some limits on our capacity for processing information', *Psychol. Rev.*, **63**, 81–97.

Perry, D.K. and Cannon, W.M. (1966), 'A vocational interest scale for programmers', *Proc. 4th Annual Computer Personnel Conf.*, ACM, New York.

Porter, L.W. and Lawler, E.E. (1965), 'Properties of organisation structure in relation to job attitudes and behaviour', *Psychol. Bull.*, **64**, 23–51.

Shaw, M.E. (1964), 'Communication networks', in *Advances in Experimental Social Psychology*, New York: Academic Press.

Shaw, M.E. (1971), *Group Dynamics. The Psychology of Small Group Behaviour.* McGraw-Hill, New York.

Shneiderman, B. (1980), *Software Psychology*, Cambridge, Mass.: Winthrop Publishers Inc.

Soloway, E., Ehrlich, K., Bonar, J. and Greenspan, J. (1982),'What do novices know about programming', In *Directions in Human–Computer Interaction*, Badre, A. and Shneiderman, B. (eds), Norwood, NJ: Ablex Publishing Co.

Weinberg, G.M. (1971), *The Psychology of Computer Programming*, New York: Van Nostrand Reinhold.

EXERCISES

2.1 Consider a number of your fellow software engineers. List the types of different personalities which they appear to exhibit.

2.2 Explain why our immediate recall seems to be limited to about seven items.

2.3 Describe human memory organization and explain how this explains why structured programming is effective.

2.4 What is the difference between syntactic and semantic knowledge? From your own experience, write down a number of instances of each of these types of knowledge.

2.5 What are the different types of orientation which can be observed in group working?

2.6 Why is egoless programming an effective technique?

2.7   Explain what you understand by 'groupthink', describe the dangers of this phenomenon and explain how it can be avoided.

2.8   What are the factors affecting group communication? Give four ways in which group communication can be maximized.

2.9   Why are open-plan and communal offices less suitable for software development than individual offices?

2.10 Suggest five ways in which a computer conferencing system can be used in the support of software development.

Part 1

Software Specification

Contents

Chapter 3

Software Specification

Objectives

This chapter serves as an introduction to this part of the book which is concerned with both formal and informal specification techniques and their use in the software process. The place of specification in the software process and the difficulties of producing complete and consistent specifications are covered in the first part of the chapter. Particular attention is paid to identifying the role of formal and informal notations in this process. The structure of a requirements document is described and the importance of planning for requirements evolution discussed.

Contents

The problems which software engineers are called upon to solve are often immensely complex. Understanding the nature of the problem can be very difficult, particularly if the system is new and no non-automated system exists to serve as a model for the software. Establishing the services the system should provide and the constraints under which it must operate is called *requirements analysis*. Once this analysis has been carried out, the requirements must be documented and this activity is called *specification*. We have seen from Chapter 1 that specification is the first activity in the software process.

It is important to make a distinction between user needs and user requirements. An organization may decide that it needs a software system to support its accounting. However, it is unrealistic to present this simple need to a software engineer and expect an acceptable and usable software system to be developed. Rather, information about the problem to be solved must be collected and analysed and a comprehensive problem definition produced. From this definition, a software solution can be designed and implemented.

The principal difficulty which arises in establishing large software system requirements is that the problems being tackled are usually 'wicked' problems. Rittel and Webber (1973) define a wicked problem as a problem for which there is no definitive formulation. For example, an extreme example of a wicked problem is the problem of planning for the next San Francisco earthquake! Any formulation (the requirements) of the problem is bound to be inadequate and, for software systems, the system development is partly concerned with discovering the problem as well as the solution.

There are several reasons why it is impossible to be definitive about a problem specification:

(1) Large software systems are usually required to improve upon the status quo where either no system or an inadequate system is in place. Although difficulties with the current system may be known, it is very hard to anticipate what effects the 'improved' system is likely to have on an organization.

(2) It is usually the case that large systems have a diverse user community and that each user has different, sometimes conflicting, requirements and priorities. The final system requirements are inevitably a compromise.

(3) The procurers of a system (those who pay for it) and the users of a system are rarely the same people. System procurers impose requirements because of organizational and budgetary constraints and these are likely to conflict with perceived user requirements.

There is also a distinction between system goals and system requirements. In essence, a requirement is something that can be tested whereas a goal is a more general characteristic which the system should exhibit. For example, a goal might be that the system should be 'user friendly'. This is not testable as 'friendliness' is a very subjective attribute. An associated requirement might be that all user command selection should take place using command menus.

This distinction exemplifies the terminological problems which are encountered when discussing the requirements definition phase of the software life-cycle. Depending on particular organizations, the so-called requirements specification can be anything from a broad outline statement in natural language of what services the system should provide to a mathematically formal system specification. The line between requirements and design specification is a tenuous one and sometimes the terms are used interchangeably.

Problems arise because of the need to document a system so that it can be understood by potential users and, at the same time, produce a system specification (often called the functional specification) which can act as a basis for a contract between a user and a software supplier. Generally, users prefer a higher level of abstract description than can be provided in a specification which is sufficiently detailed to act as a contract. Furthermore, it is probably impossible to construct a detailed specification without some design activity so further blurring the distinction between requirements and design specification.

It is therefore important that specifications are produced at a number of different levels of abstraction with careful correlations made between these levels. These levels are intended for different classes of reader who must all make decisions about the system procurement and implementation. For the purposes of the chapters in this part of the book, the distinctions between these levels of specification will be made as follows:

- *A requirements definition* is a statement in a natural language of what user services the system is expected to provide. This should be expressed in such a way that it is understandable by non-specialist staff. It should be written so that it is understandable to both client and contractor management and potential system users.

- *A requirements specification* is a statement in a more formal notation which sets out the system services in more detail. This document (sometimes called a functional specification) should be precise so that it may act as contract between the system procurer and software developer. This document must be couched in such terms that it is understandable to technical staff from both procurers and developers, and it is reasonable to assume some understanding of the software engineering process on the part of the procurer. Formal specification techniques may be appropriate for expressing such a specification but this will depend on the background and abilities of the system procurer.

- *A software specification* (design specification) is an abstract description of the software design which is intended to serve as a basis for the design and implementation of the software. There should be a clear relationship between this document and the requirements specification, but the important distinction is that the readers of this are principally software designers rather than users or management. Thus, the use of formal specification techniques is appropriate in such a document. These techniques are introduced in Chapters 7, 8 and 9.

Sometimes, even the formulation of outline requirements for a project is impossible as the application domain is so poorly understood. In such cases, it is unrealistic to expect a definitive requirements definition before system development begins and a process model based on system prototyping is more appropriate than the classical waterfall model. A process model based on prototyping for requirements derivation is discussed in Chapter 6.

The derivation of software requirements is not always considered the province of the software engineer. The systems analyst is sometimes considered responsible for this task, particularly where existing manual systems are to be automated. On the other hand, the definition of requirements for embedded systems and advanced systems is normally taken as a software engineering problem.

In fact, the roles of the systems analyst and the software engineer are complementary. The systems analyst should take responsibility for collecting data on the existing system and for performing a critical analysis of that data to factor out relevant information. He or she should consult with the software engineer so that each understands the required system and should formulate a set of software requirements.

If a process model is used which does not involve system prototyping, the derivation of a requirements specification involves a number of steps.

(1) *Feasibility study* An overall estimate is made of whether the identified user needs are satisfiable using current software and hardware technologies, whether or not the proposed system will be cost-effective from a business point of view, and whether or not it might be developed given existing budgetary constraints. The techniques involved in carrying out such a study are outside the scope of this text and the reader is referred to a systems analysis text (Millington, 1981; Davis, 1983) for further discussion of this phase.

(2) *Requirements definition* A system model is formulated and this is used as the basis for an abstract description of the system requirements. As discussed above, this is primarily a user document which is intended to act as a basis for a more detailed requirements specification document.

(3)   *Requirements specification*   A detailed and precise description of the system requirements is set out to act as a basis for a contract between client and software developer. The creation of this document might be carried out in parallel with some high-level design (indeed, this is often essential) and the design and requirements activities influence each other as they develop. During the creation of this document, errors in the requirements definition are inevitably discovered and it must be modified accordingly.

The sequence of activities and activity iterations are shown in Figure 3.1. In this diagram, activities are shown as round-edged rectangles and deliverables in square boxes.

To illustrate aspects of requirements definition and specification, we use an editing system which manipulates graphical representations of software designs. This system is a real system which is part of the ECLIPSE software engineering environment (Alderson *et al.*, 1985) for which I was responsible for part of the editing system design.

The editor is a design editor rather than a diagram editor. As well as drawing commands, it incorporates procedures to check that the design being documented conforms to the rules of whatever method is being followed. The generated design is stored in a database and may be processed by other tools such as skeleton code generators.

The editing system is not method-specific. The notation and rules of any method where a design is a directed graph may be input and a version of the editor instantiated to support that particular approach. It is intended

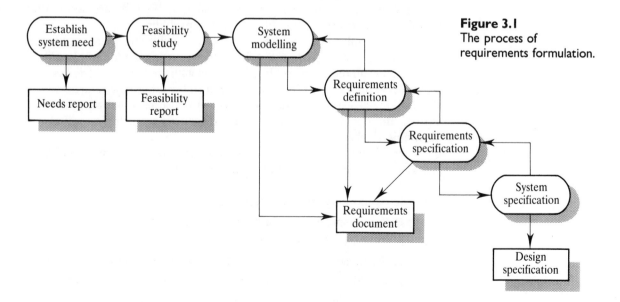

Figure 3.1
The process of
requirements formulation.

to be used as part of a suite of CASE tools (a designer's workbench) which assist the software engineer with design activities.

To provide a linking theme in this book, we draw on this editing system as a source of examples in several different chapters in this part and elsewhere.

3.1 The software requirements document

The software requirements document is a critical document produced during the software life-cycle as it may serve as the basis of a contract between the system procurer and the system contractor. Again, terminology in this area often confuses rather than enlightens as the requirements definition is sometimes seen as a basis for bidding for a system contract and the requirements specification (or functional specification) is the basis for the contract. In essence, the distinction between these is arbitrary and it is important that the combined definition/specification is structured in such a way that it may be readily understood and analysed as a whole.

The software requirements document is not a design document. It should set out what the system should do without specifying how it should be done. The requirements should be stated in such a way that the design may be validated. If the services, constraints and properties specified in the software requirements document are satisfied by the software design then that design is an acceptable solution to the problem.

In principle, the requirements set out in such a document ought to be complete and consistent. Everything the system should do should be specified and no requirement should conflict with any other. In practice, this is extremely difficult to achieve, particularly if the requirements are stated as natural language text. It must be accepted that errors and omissions will exist in the document and it must be structured in such a way that it is amenable to change.

Heninger (1980) claims that there are six requirements which a software requirements document should satisfy:

(1) It should only specify external system behaviour.

(2) It should specify constraints on the implementation.

(3) It should be easy to change.

(4) It should serve as a reference tool for system maintainers.

(5) It should record forethought about the life-cycle of the system.

(6) It should characterize acceptable responses to undesired events.

The software requirements document is a reference tool. It should record forethought about the system life-cycle because it will be used by maintenance programmers to find out what the system is supposed to do. Information in the software requirements document must be precise and easily found. The document should have a detailed table of contents, one or more indexes, a glossary of terms used and a definition of the changes anticipated when the requirements were originally formulated.

We have suggested that there is a logical separation between requirements definition, an abstract statement of requirements understandable by system users and requirements specification, a more detailed description, perhaps expressed in a specialized notation, which serves as a basis for a system contract (see Chapter 5). The requirements document is a combination of these. In practice, the definition and specification may sometimes be presented separately and sometimes as a single consolidated document.

From the point of view of the users, presentation as two separate documents is probably best as this allows users who do not need to know system details to ignore them. From the point of view of system developers and those concerned with requirements validation, presentation as a single consolidated document is best as there is no separation between abstract requirements definition and detailed specification.

If we assume that two separate documents are produced, the requirements definition might have the following structure:

- *Introduction* This should describe the need for the system and should place the system in context, briefly describing its functions and presenting a rationale for the software system. It should describe how the system fits into the overall business or strategic objectives of the organization commissioning the software.

- *The system model* This section should set out the system model showing the relationships between the system components and the system and its environment. It is probably most appropriate to make use of graphical descriptions of the model in this section.

- *Functional requirements* The functional requirements of the system, that is, the services provided for the user, should be described in this section. In a requirements definition, these will normally be described using natural language. Cross-references to a more detailed specification may be included.

- *Hardware* If the system is to be implemented on special hardware, this hardware and its interfaces should be described. If off-the-shelf hardware is to be used, the minimal and optimal configurations on which the system may execute should be set out here.

- *Database requirements* The logical organization of the data used by the system and its interrelationships should be described here.

- *Non-functional requirements* The non-functional requirements of the system, that is, the constraints under which the software must operate, should be expressed and related to the functional requirements.

- *Maintenance information* This section should describe the fundamental assumptions on which the system is based and describe anticipated changes due to hardware evolution, changing user needs, etc.

- *Glossary* This should define the technical terms used in the document. This is principally intended to help non-technical users understand the software requirements document. However, it is also useful for development staff as it establishes a precise definition of terms used in the document. In formulating the glossary, the writer should not make assumptions about the experience or background of the reader.

- *Index* It may be desirable to provide more than one kind of index to the document. As well as a normal alphabetic index, it may be useful to produce an index per chapter, an index of functions and so on.

The requirements specification can assume the existence of a requirements definition and should concentrate on detailed system specifications. Its organization should follow that of the software system being described and extensive use of cross-referencing to the requirements definition is essential.

A consolidated document should follow the structure of a requirements definition but the sections describing functional, non-functional and database requirements should be expanded to include the detailed requirements specification.

The task of developing a software requirements document should not be underestimated. Bell *et al.* (1977) report that the requirements document for a ballistic missile defence system contained over 8000 distinct requirements and support paragraphs and was made up of 2500 pages of text. This is perhaps larger than most systems but it illustrates that a great deal of resources have to be dedicated to the production of a requirements document and that this represents a significant life-cycle cost.

3.2 Requirements evolution

The task of developing software requirements focuses attention on software capabilities, business objectives and other business systems. Naturally, as the requirements definition is developed, a better understanding of users' needs is achieved. This feeds back and causes the perceived requirements to be changed (Figure 3.2). Furthermore, the time required to analyse

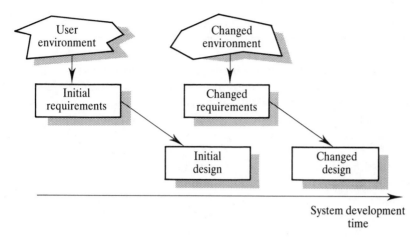

Figure 3.2
Requirements evolution during system development.

requirements and to develop a large system may be several years and it must be expected that requirements changes will be identified in that time. It is therefore important that the inevitability of change is recognized and anticipated when producing a requirements document.

The software requirements document should be organized in such a way that changes can be accommodated without extensive rewriting. If this is not done, changes in the requirements may be incorporated in the system without recording these changes in the definition. This can result in the program and its documentation becoming out of step (Figure 3.3). This situation usually causes problems for the maintenance programmer.

As with programs, changeability in documents is achieved by minimizing external references and making the document sections as modular as possible. Problems are, of course, exacerbated because paper-based documents are used as the means of communication between client and contractor. A requirements document is presented as a book and may not be available in machine-readable form to the system contractor. Thus, changes must be accommodated using the unwieldy system of change

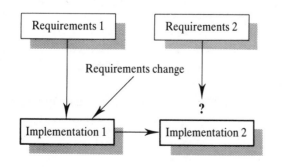

Figure 3.3
Requirements document inconsistency.

control forms and occasional document updates. It is only immediately after the delivery of a document that all of the requirements are summarized in one place.

The answer to this problem is more extensive use of electronic documentation and documentation tools which allow multiple document views and automatic consolidation of change requests and original requirements. However, the diversity of different word and text processing systems make document exchange very difficult and the problem will only be solved when a standard document architecture is established.

Although both functional and non-functional requirements are liable to change, non-functional requirements are particularly affected by changes in hardware technology. As the development time for a large system may be several years, it is likely that the hardware available at the conclusion of the project will be more powerful than that available when the project was conceived. Furthermore, the hardware will evolve throughout the lifetime of the developed software and the non-functional requirements will be modified while the software is in use.

Hardware changes which may occur while the software is being developed can be anticipated. Hardware-dependent non-functional requirements can be specified which assume hardware capability will be available on project completion although that may not be the case when the project commences. No such anticipation can be made for changes during the project's lifetime and the specifier of requirements should avoid, as far as possible, detailed hardware dependencies.

KEY POINTS

- It is very difficult to formulate a definitive specification for large software systems. Thus, it should be assumed that initial system requirements will be both incomplete and inconsistent.

- A requirements definition, a requirements specification and a software specification are all ways of describing specifications at different levels of detail and for different types of reader.

- The requirements document often serves as the basis of a contract between the system procurer and the system contractor.

- Requirements inevitably change. The requirements document should be designed so that it may be easily modified.

Further reading

There are relatively few publications which are exclusively concerned with requirements specification in general. Probably the best overview is in the special issue of *IEEE Computer* listed below.

IEEE Computer, **18** (4), April 1985. This is a journal special issue containing nine papers on requirements engineering. In general it is quite good but is rather parochial inasmuch as it ignores all European work in this area. Important notations for requirements definition such as CORE and JSD were developed outside of North America.

References

Alderson, A., Falla, M. and Bott, M.F. (1985), 'An overview of the ECLIPSE project', in *Integrated Project Support Environments*,. McDermid, J. (ed.), Stevenage: Peter Peregrinus.

Bell, T.E., Bixler, D.C. and Dyer, M.E. (1977), 'An extendable approach to computer aided software requirements engineering', *IEEE Trans. Software Eng.*, **SE-3** (1), 49–60.

Davis, W.S. (1983), *Systems Analysis and Design*, Reading, Mass.: Addison-Wesley.

Heninger, K.L. (1980), 'Specifying software requirements for complex systems. New techniques and their applications', *IEEE Trans. Software Eng.*, **SE-6** (1), 2–13.

Millington, D. (1981), *Systems Analysis and Design for Computer Applications*, Chichester: Ellis Horwood.

Rittel, H. and Webber, M. (1973), 'Dilemmas in a general theory of planning', *Policy Sciences*, **4**, 155–69.

EXERCISES

3.1 Suggest four other wicked problems in addition to the problem of planning for the next San Francisco earthquake.

3.2 Explain why it is useful to draw a distinction between a requirements definition and a requirements specification.

3.3 What are the steps involved in deriving a requirements specification?

3.4 What are the requirements that a requirements document should satisfy?

3.5 You have been given the task of producing guidelines for creating a requirements document which can be readily modified. Write a report setting out standards for the organization of a requirements document which will ensure its maintainability.

Chapter 4

System Modelling

Objectives

The first stage in establishing a system specification is to formulate a model of the 'real-world' entities which are to be represented in the system. In this chapter, the importance of placing the system in context is described and viewpoint analysis is introduced. Model description using graphical notations is covered including finite-state machine modelling of real-time systems. Finally, data modelling using relation models is discussed and illustrated by examples from a design editing system introduced in Chapter 3.

Contents

Once an initial analysis of the user's needs has been carried out, the next step, which is the first stage in requirements definition, is to produce a conceptual model of the software system. This conceptual model is a very high-level view of the system in which the major user services are identified and their relationships documented. This model is a valuable communication tool between system procurers, users and software developers.

For trivial systems this model may exist only in the mind of the engineer responsible for establishing the requirements. He or she understands the systems and knows which functions must be provided as well as the constraints on the operation of these functions. For any non-trivial system, however, a mental model is inadequate. Because the system being modelled is inherently complex, mental models tend to be incomplete and contain ambiguities and conflicts. It is necessary to establish an explicit, precisely defined system model at an early stage and to use this model to understand the system.

There are two distinct approaches which can be used for systems modelling. A functional approach models the system as a set of interacting functions and is typified by the data-flow approach described by DeMarco (1978). Here, the system is considered to be a set of functional transforms with data flowing from one to another. An alternative approach, typified by RML (Borgida *et al.*, 1985), models the system as a set of interacting objects where the operations allowed on each object are encapsulated with the object itself.

Both of these approaches are useful and both reflect human ways of system modelling. However, the proponents of these approaches tend to suggest that their approach should be adopted and others excluded. This is nonsense. Humans are very flexible and, when observing systems, regularly switch from an object-oriented to a functional approach and back again. There is no reason why an artificial distinction between function and entity should be drawn, and the most effective approach to system modelling uses the complementary strengths of each viewpoint.

4.1　System contexts

Requirements misunderstandings are common because the system procurer, different users and the software developer adopt different views of the role of the system in its environment. For this reason, an important part of the system modelling process is to establish a system context where the relationships between the system being specified and other human and computer systems are documented.

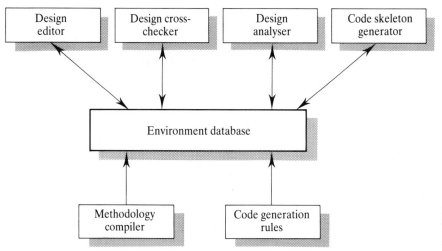

Figure 4.1
The designer's
workbench.

It has been suggested (Borgida *et al.*, 1985) that the majority of effort in deriving system requirements is spent in finding out and documenting knowledge about the environment in which the system is to operate. To express this knowledge, they have devised an object-oriented language (called RML) and we look at the use of this approach when requirements specification is considered. For requirements definition, a more abstract view is necessary than that provided by a specific notation.

Simple block diagrams, supplemented by descriptions of the system entities, are an appropriate starting point for describing system contexts. For example, Figure 4.1 shows the context in which the design editing system operates.

As well as using descriptive names for entities on such diagrams, it is usually valuable to provide a more detailed description of what these entities are expected to do (Table 4.1). This need not describe the entities in full but may refer to other parts of the requirements definition to complete the description.

Figure 4.1 presents a contextual description which shows the existence of other systems but provides no information about the relationships between these systems and how they might be used in the creation of a design. There are various different types of relationship which may be modelled but data-flow relationships (DeMarco, 1978), which show how data is processed by different parts of the system, are particularly useful. Figure 4.2 is a data-flow diagram for the designer's workbench. Notice that logical rather than physical data flow is shown here and the diagram illustrates how the output from one tool is processed by other tools. Figure 4.1 shows that, in fact, all data flow between tools is via the system database.

Table 4.1
Design entity descriptions.

Name	Description
Design editor	An editing system which allows design diagrams to be created, modified, stored in and retreived from the environment database
Methodology compiler	A translation system which takes a formal description of a design method and translates it into tables to drive the design editor.
Code generation rules	A set of rules which set out how code may be generated to represent entities in a particular method. These rules drive the code skeleton generator.

4.2   Viewpoint analysis

When formulating a system model, an engineer must realize that the sources of information about that system (customers, users, or whatever) do not normally think about or describe the system in a top-down manner. Furthermore, for any large system the notion of a single 'top' is illusory and at every decomposition step there are different ways of looking at the system. All of these have a contribution to make to system understanding.

The notion of viewpoint analysis recognizes this and suggests that a system should be described from a number of different viewpoints. Loosely, a viewpoint is any angle from which a system might be considered, so possible viewpoints might be human users, sensors associated with the system, or other computer systems connected to the system being analysed.

As a very simple example of this, consider the automated teller machines which are now common outside banks. These contain an embedded software system to drive the machine hardware and to communicate with the bank's central database. The system accepts customer requests and produces cash, account information, database updates, etc. There are three major, obvious viewpoints from which this system might be considered.

- The customer using the facilities of the machine.
- The auto-teller hardware providing input to and displaying outputs from the system.
- The bank database system on which customer accounts are maintained.

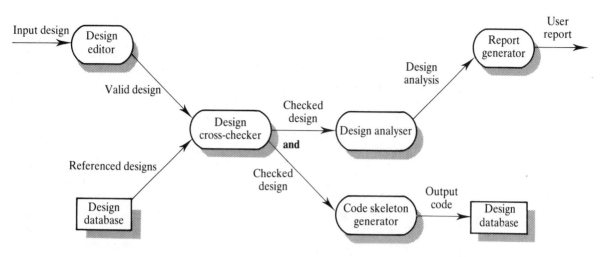

Figure 4.2
Data flow in the
designer's workbench.

Of course, within each viewpoint there may be sub-viewpoints. For example, it is now common for banks to share terminal facilities but only to offer the full functionality of the system to the bank's own customers. Other users are offered more limited facilities. Thus, sub-viewpoints of the customer viewpoint are:

- The bank's own customers.
- Customers of other banks who are using the machine.

For large systems, there may be many more viewpoints and, in principle, all should be considered during requirements analysis. These different viewpoints are likely to place conflicting requirements on a system and it is important to distinguish between direct viewpoints where the requirements must be taken into account and indirect viewpoints whose requirements may be less important. Indirect viewpoints of the auto-teller system might be that of remote diagnostic software used to detect machine faults and that of the service engineer who is responsible for repairing the system hardware.

When performing a viewpoint analysis, three rules should be borne in mind:

(1)   Each viewpoint should be responsible for some information processing.
(2)   Viewpoints should not overlap. That is, functions should not span viewpoints and each function should be performed in a single viewpoint.
(3)   The source or destination of all system information must be an identified viewpoint.

The CORE (Controlled Requirements Expression) method (Mullery, 1979; Looney, 1985) includes viewpoint analysis as an explicit step in the requirements derivation. These viewpoints are set out in a viewpoint structure diagram which is a hierarchical system structure chart showing viewpoints and sub-viewpoints. An example of such a diagram for a bank auto-teller system is shown in Figure 4.3.

The CORE method of requirements analysis and specification has not been widely publicized but is being used more and more in the UK and in Europe. It is used throughout this chapter to illustrate system modelling.

At the time of writing, CORE is being evaluated for use by a number of US defense software contractors. A full description of the method is outside the scope of this chapter but it is appropriate to discuss some of the concepts embedded in CORE in a general discussion of system modelling. Other system modelling techniques such as SADT (Schoman and Ross, 1977) and SREM (Alford, 1977) are discussed in Chapter 5.

4.3   Model Description

A large part of any requirements definition is made up of contextual descriptions simply because this is a description of its interface to the outside world. Much of the work involved in building the system is involved in interfacing to the system's environment. However, it is also important to provide a more detailed system model which outlines the user services which that system is expected to provide. This model description must include details of:

- the system inputs,
- the system outputs,
- the system data processing,
- control in the system.

There are a number of notations which may be used to describe such a model. De Marco (1978) suggests that a data-flow model is appropriate and easily understood by users and such models are discussed as a design aid in Chapter 12. These diagrams are equally useful in systems modelling as they are readily understood by system procurers and users.

CORE uses tabular collection of information about data flows and action diagrams (sometimes called thread diagrams) to describe the processing associated with each viewpoint. Action diagrams are like data-flow diagrams but have additional control information appended to them.

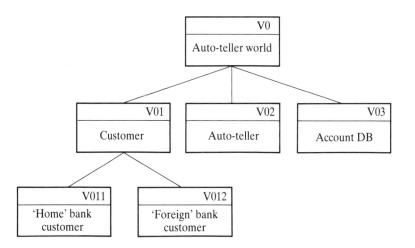

Figure 4.3
A CORE viewpoint
diagram for an auto-teller
system.

Tabular collection diagrams are a useful notational tool as they collect together all of the input, processing and output information for each viewpoint. As viewpoints must be the sources and destinations of inputs and outputs, the tabular collection across viewpoints must be consistent. Any inconsistencies imply an error or omission in the analysis. These are easily detected because of the tabular form. Parts of the collection diagrams for the teller machine and the customer viewpoint are shown in Figures 4.4 and 4.5.

A tabular collection diagram shows where an input comes from (its source), the input itself, the processing as seen by that viewpoint, the outputs and the destinations of these outputs. Thus, Figure 4.4 shows that, from the customer's viewpoint, the teller machine produces a message asking for the card to be input; the customer responds by inputting the card. The action output is the card which is passed to the teller machine. Similarly, the machine requests a PIN; the customer action is to type his or

Figure 4.4
Tabular collection diagram
– customer viewpoint.

CUSTOMER viewpoint (V01)

Source	Input	Action	Output	Destination
Teller m/c (V02)	Card input request	Input card	Card	Teller m/c (V02)
Teller m/c (V02)	PIN input request	Type PIN	Customer PIN	Teller m/c (V02)
Teller m/c (V02)	Collect cash message	Collect cash	Cash	Customer (V01)
			Collection confirm	Teller m/c (V02)

TELLER MACHINE viewpoint (V02)

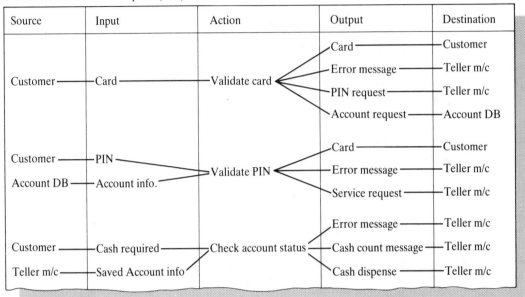

Figure 4.5
Tabular collection diagram – teller machine viewpoint.

her number; the output is the typed number which is sent to the teller machine.

In tabular collections all of the possible inputs and outputs for an action are specified. Thus, if an invalid card is input, the action **Validate card** can produce an error message display and the card returned to the customer. If the card is valid, a request for the customer's PIN is generated as is a request for account information from the account database. For simplicity, the case where a stolen card is retained by the machine has not been included here.

Action diagrams are used to specify processing actions associated with entities in a tabular collection diagram. An action diagram should be generated for every action identified which is a software system action. For customer actions such as **Input card** it is obviously not necessary to generate an action diagram.

The action diagram for **Validate card** is shown in Figure 4.6. The ordering of boxes from left to right is significant and implies time sequentiality. Thus, getting account information from the card takes place before account type checking. Where boxes are aligned, this indicates actions which may be (but need not be) carried out in parallel. Boxes annotated with a circle (as in Figure 4.7) mean a selection from a number of possibilities; boxes annotated with a star (not shown) mean an iteration.

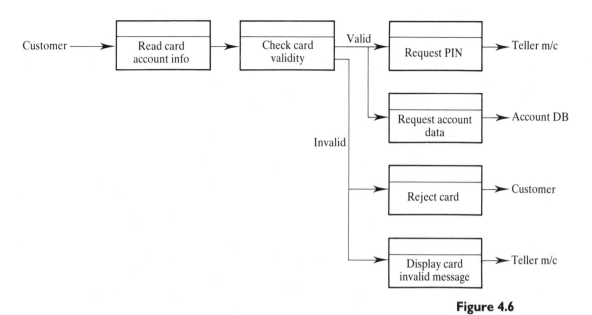

Figure 4.6
Action diagram for card validation.

In general, action diagrams for a single action are (and should be) relatively simple but they don't provide a description of the ordering and interleaving of the actions from the different viewpoints. Therefore, after individual action diagrams have been produced, the next step is to produce combined action diagrams showing how actions are related. In general, there will be a number of these combined action diagrams produced reflecting different system transactions. Figure 4.7 shows a combined action diagram for cash withdrawal.

System modelling based on data flows has been widely used and is easily understood by both users and system developers. Fundamentally, it describes the system as a set of functions. Jackson (1983) suggests, however, that a functional approach may make future modifications difficult. Jackson's suggested technique (JSD) is somewhere between object-oriented design and a functional approach. There are three phases involved which take the analyst from initial model formulation through to a final implementation.

(1) *The modelling phase* The 'real-world' entities which the system is modelling and the actions on these entities are identified. Actions which affect each entity are ordered in time and documented diagrammatically.

(2) *The networking phase* A simulation of the 'real-world' is specified where each entity is represented as a sequential process. System functions are specified in terms of the model.

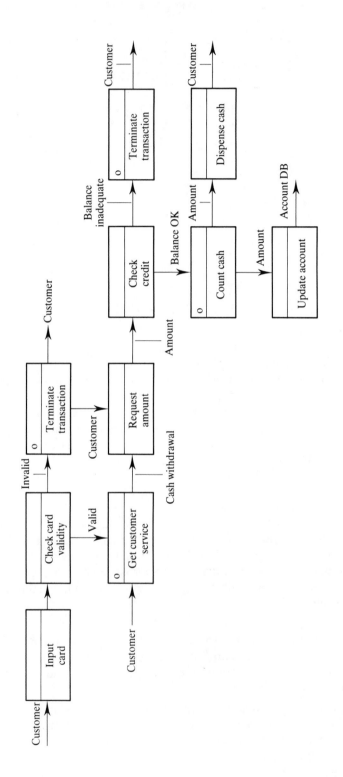

Figure 4.7   Combined action diagram for cash withdrawal.

(3)   *The implementation phase*   The scheduling of processes and timing
        considerations are specified and the model is transformed into an
        implementation.

Notice that JSD has changed from that originally described in Jackson's
book where the method was made up of six steps.

The key to success with Jackson's method is successful identification
of relevant entities. Jackson suggests an approach like that used by Booch
(1987) in deriving an object-oriented design. This involves an informal
analysis of a natural language problem description but this is not a
particularly satisfactory way of tackling the problem. Some users of JSD
have suggested to this author that the initial entity formulation is difficult
and that they prefer an approach to modelling which is based on data
flow.

To some extent, the particular method used for system modelling is
not particularly important. What is important is that some systematic
technique is used for this activity and a model produced which reflects the
system as understood by its users. A model which is complete and
consistent can act as a sound basis for more detailed requirements
definition and specification.

4.4   Real-time systems modelling

The above techniques of system modelling are applicable to the definition
of real-time systems but it is sometimes necessary to supplement such
descriptions with a view of the system which shows how particular input
events result in particular outputs and changes to the state of the system.

Salter (1976) has used finite state machines for system modelling and
considers a general system model to be a function of three elements –
control, function, and data. Intuitively, functions are the information
transformers in the system, data are the inputs and outputs of functions
and control is the mechanism that activates functions in the desired
sequence. The notion of states and state transformations also underlies the
conceptual modelling systems described by Yeh and Zave (1980) and
Heninger (1980).

A finite state machine (FSM) approach is often appropriate for the
modelling of real-time systems where a particular input causes a thread of
actions to be initiated. Figure 4.8 is an FSM model of a simple microwave
oven equipped with buttons to set the power and the timer and to start the
system. The names chosen in the diagram are descriptive but it is necessary
to provide more detail (Table 4.2).

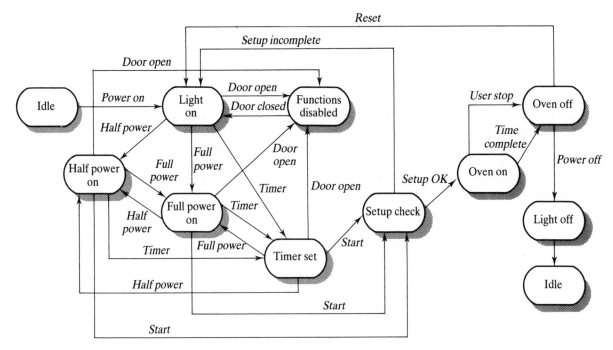

Figure 4.8
System model of a micro-wave oven.

The problem with an FSM approach is that the number of possible states increases very rapidly. This is obvious from Figure 4.8 which is a relatively complex diagram describing a simple system. It is therefore

Table 4.2
Microwave oven state description.

State	Description
Half power on	The power output is set to half power when the half power button is pressed.
Light on	The indicator light is switched on showing that the oven is active.
Functions disabled	Function settings are disabled when the oven door is open. Included for safety reasons.
Setup check	Checks that a valid set of parameters has been set by the user.
Timer set	The timer is set to the user provided value.

necessary to adapt the approach for larger systems so that it is possible to draw and understand the system model. This is often accomplished by drawing individual thread diagrams which show how a sequence of actions 'thread' their way through the system.

Unfortunately, there are no standard abstraction techniques for FSM models so a variety of different approaches to this model abstraction have been adopted. Figure 4.9 shows part of the microwave oven system where only a single message thread has been documented. A thread diagram should be produced for every identifed combination of messages.

It is usually easier for users to understand a requirements document when the system model is presented using a number of different notations and approaches and from a number of different viewpoints. A state machine model is one possible route but system modelling using the system data flows, the threads of control and the life histories of the system data entities may also be valuable.

4.5   Data modelling

Many large software systems require a large database of information. The system takes information from and adds information to this database as it executes. In some cases, this database exists independently of the software system; in others it is created for the system being developed. Part of the systems modelling activity is to define the logical form of this database.

It is sometimes the case that the database is only used by the system which is being developed but it is more common for the information in the database to be shared among a number of programs. Thus, the data model for a system must describe both input and output information. Input

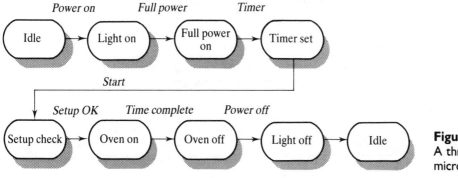

Figure 4.9
A thread diagram for a microwave oven.

information is information which is produced by other systems for processing by the system being developed; output information is information which is intended for subsequent processing.

The data model should only describe information which is shared. There is no need to set out a model for information which is local to the system under development as this is a design consideration. Of course, it is sometimes very difficult to predict which information generated by the system will be required by other tools in future and the data model developed during requirements definition will evolve as the system is maintained.

A useful way of defining the logical form of a database is to use a relational model of data as described by Codd (1970) and by Date (1983). Using the relational model, the logical data structure is specified as a set of tables, with some tables having common keys. This model allows the relationships between data items to be defined without considering the physical database organization.

As an example of a how a relational schema may be used to define a data model, consider the design editing system. This system requires imported data which defines the design method and symbols which are used in a particular editor instantiation. It exports a description of the design semantics for processing by other checking tools.

Space does not allow for a full description of the editor data model and we shall only consider part of the data model here. The editing system includes a program which is used to define the symbols associated with a particular method type. These symbols are put together out of primitives such as Box, Line, Circle, etc., and may be set to be fixed size or of variable size (stretchy). Two relations are required to define the structure of the symbol plus a further relation for each primitive used. The two structure relations and the relation describing the Box primitive are shown in Figure 4.10.

Symbol_information

Type_name	Primitive_set#	Stretchy

Primitive_set

Primitive_set#	Primitive_type	Primitive_id

Box

Primitive_id	Top_coord	Length	Height

Figure 4.10
Relations defining symbol structure.

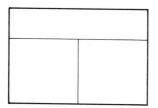

Figure 4.11
An activity symbol.

The symbol information relation shows that each symbol representing a type may be modelled as a type name, a reference to a set of primitives making up the symbol and a flag indicating whether or not the symbol is stretchy. The primitive set relation is made up of a set identifier (as referenced in symbol information) a primitive type and a primitive identifier. Where symbols are made up of several primitives, the primitive set identifier is repeated for each primitive symbol used. The Box relation simply states that boxes are represented by a coordinate defining the top left corner (with reference to some virtual origin), a length and a height.

As an example of the values of these relations for a particular symbol, consider Figure 4.11. Assume the symbol in Figure 4.11 represents a method type called 'Activity'. The relations are shown in Figure 4.12.

Symbol_information

Type name	Primitive set#	Stretchy
Activity	Activity1	No

Primitive_set

Primitive_set#	Primitive_type	Primitive_id
Activity1	Box	Box1
Activity1	Line	Line1
Activity1	Line	Line2

Box

Primitive_id	Top_coord	Length	Height
Box1	(0,0)	3	2

Figure 4.12
Example values for symbol structure relations.

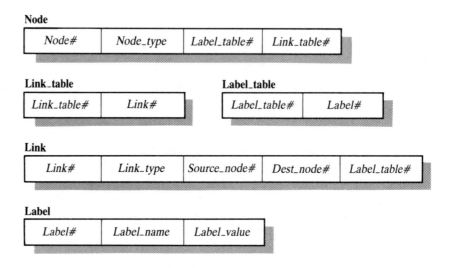

Figure 4.13
Editor output relations.

The design editor is based on the assumption that a design may be represented as a directed graph. The design consists of a set of nodes of different types connected by links which represent the relationships between design nodes. There is a screen representation of this graph which is a design diagram and a separate, distinct database representation. The editing system performs a mapping from the database representation to the screen representation every time it draws a diagram.

The output information produced by the editor should include a logical representation of this graph but not details of its physical screen representation. Thus, post-processing tools are interested in what entities exist, their logical attributes (such as their name) and their connections. These tools are not interested in information such as the entity coordinates or symbol representations.

A slightly simplified form of some of the relations used to define the output from the editing system is as shown in Figure 4.13. To illustrate the values these relations might take, consider a simple design (Figure 4.14) consisting of two named activities connected by a link of type Data_flow. Figure 4.15 shows the relation values.

Although a relational definition of the data does not compromise data independence, it does contain implications of how the data is to be structured in a database. It implies which elements are to be represented as

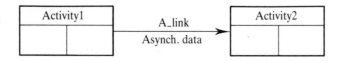

Figure 4.14
Two named activities.

Node

Node#	Node_type	Label_table#	Link_table#
Node1	Activity	LabTab1	LinkTab1
Node2	Activity	LabTab2	LinkTab2

Link_table

Link_table#	Link#
LinkTab1	Link1
LinkTab2	Link1

Label_table

Label_table#	Label#
LabTab1	Label1
LabTab2	Label2
LabTab3	Label3
LabTab3	Label4

Link

Link#	Link_type	Source_node#	Dest. node#	Label_table#
Link1	Data_flow	Node1	Node2	LabTab3

Label

Label#	Label_name	Label_value
Label1	Node_name	Activity1
Label2	Node_name	Activity2
Label3	Link_name	A_link
Label4	Annotation	Asynch. data

Figure 4.15
Example values for editor
output relations.

pointers between entities (those that refer to other relations) and which are
entity attributes. For example, it implies that Node_type is an attribute of
each node which is accessed via some node identifier. It also implies that
the labels and the links associated with nodes are stored separately rather
than as part of the node description.

An alternative technique of data definition, described by Chen
(1976), uses a modified relational model where each relation is a binary
relation. Instead of an entity having attribute values grouped together in a
single relation, these values are all set out in separate simple relations.

Table 4.3
Part of the data dictionary
for the design editor data
model.

Item name	Item type	Logical representation	Used in
Item_name	Field	String	Data_dictionary
Primitive_set#	Field	Numeric	Symbol_information
Symbol_information	Relation		Design_editor_model
Top_coord	Field	[Numeric]2	Box
Type_name	Field	String	Symbol_information

Thus, the Node_table relation above might be described as follows:

Node# '*Has type*' Node_type
Node# '*Has_labels*' Label_table#
Node# '*Has_links*' Link_table#

The advantages of using a binary relational approach to data modelling are that this is a more abstract approach than the relational approach. It is easier to develop a binary relational model in an incremental way. Adding a new type of relation in a binary model rarely involves changes to existing relations whereas changing or augmenting a relational description can involve significant reorganization.

The disadvantage of a binary relational approach is that the description is less intuitive and may be more difficult for the reader to understand. This is particularly likely where readers are client or management staff with little technical database experience, and it seems that a relational view is more acceptable to such readers. Of course, a compromise approach may be adopted where a binary approach is used for development of the model which is then transformed into a relational view for presentation when that development is complete.

During the creation of a data model for a large system, a significant number of named entities will be identified. In addition, names will be allocated to entities created by the system so the end result is a very large number of names which have to be managed and which may have to be unique. Maintaining uniqueness is particularly difficult when a number of people are involved in model development, and requires automated assistance.

A tool which can be used for name management is a data dictionary. A data dictionary is, simplistically, a list of names used by the system arranged alphabetically. As well as the name, there is normally a description of the named entity and, if the name represents a composite object,

Item name	Description
Item_name	The name of known data items. Used as a key to data dictionary entries.
Primitive_set#	An identifier for a set of primitive shapes defining a method symbol.
Symbol_information	A relation holding a description of a method symbol.
Top_coord	The coordinate defining the position of the top left-hand corner of a box.
Type_name	The name of a basic method type.

Table 4.4
Data dictionary descriptions.

there may be a description of the composition. Data dictionaries are valuable in all stages of the software process from initial modelling through to system maintenance.

The key aspect of a data dictionary is that all system names whether they be names of entities, types, relations, attributes or whatever should be entered in the dictionary. Support software should be available to create, maintain and interrogate the dictionary. This software might be integrated with other tools so that dictionary creation is partially automated.

Of course, the data dictionary can itself be considered as a relation with the data name used as the key. Part of the data dictionary for the design editing system's data model is shown in Tables 4.3 and 4.4. Item descriptions have been separated here from other information to simplify the illustrations. In practice, all would be encompassed in a single relation.

KEY POINTS

- A system model presents a description of the real-world entities which are to be represented in the software system.

- Part of the system model should include a context showing how the system relates to other systems.

- Systems rarely have a single 'top' and the model should be created by considering a number of different viewpoints.

- An approach based on data flow is appropriate for modelling the system inputs, processes and outputs.

- Real-time systems can be modelled using finite-state machine diagrams.

- It is important to model the data which is imported to the system by other applications and the data which the system exports. An appropriate model to use here is the relational model.

Further reading

Structured Analysis and System Specification. An excellent book covering data flow modelling. Also useful for background reading in software design. (T. DeMarco. 1978. Yourdon Press.)

CORE – A Debrief Report. The CORE method is poorly documented but has been successful on a number of projects and has been adopted as a standard by a number of large European aerospace companies. This report is far from ideal but is about the best material on CORE which is publicly available. (M. Looney. 1985. NCC Publications, Manchester)

References

Alford, M.W. (1977), 'A requirements engineering methodology for real time processing requirements'. *IEEE Trans. Software Eng.*, **SE-3** (1), 60–9.

Booch, G. (1987), *Software Engineering with Ada*, 2nd edn, Menlo Park, Calif.: Benjamin/Cummings.

Borgida, A., Greenspan, S. and Mylopoulos, J. (1985), 'Knowledge representation as a basis for requirements specification', *IEEE Computer*, **18** (4), 82–101.

Chen, P. (1976), 'The entity relationship model – towards a unified view of data', *ACM Trans. Database Systems*, **1** (1), 9–36.

Codd, E.F. (1970), 'A relational model of data for large shared data banks', *Comm. ACM*, **13**, 377–387.

Date, C.J. (1983), *An Introduction to Database Systems*, Reading, Mass.: Addison-Wesley.

DeMarco, T. (1978), *Structured Analysis and System Specification*, New York: Yourdon Press.

Heninger, K.L. (1980), 'Specifying software requirements for complex systems. New techniques and their applications', *IEEE Trans. Software Eng.*, **SE-6** (1), 2–13.

Jackson, M.A. (1983), *System Development*, London: Prentice-Hall.

Looney, M. (1985), *CORE – A Debrief Report*, Manchester: NCC Publications.

Mullery, G. (1979), ' CORE – A method for controlled requirements specification', *Proc. 4th Int. Conf. on Software Eng.*, Munich.

Salter, K.G. (1976), 'A methodology for decomposing system requirements into data into data processing requirements', *Proc. 2nd Int. Conf. on Software Engineering*, San Francisco.

Schoman, K. and Ross, D.T. (1977), 'Structured analysis for requirements definition', *IEEE Trans. Software Eng.*, **SE-3** (1), 6–15.

Yeh, R.T. and Zave, P. (1980), 'Specifying software requirements', *Proc. IEEE*, **68** (9), 1077–85.

EXERCISES

4.1 What do you understand by the term 'viewpoint analysis'?

4.2 Modify the viewpoint structure diagram shown in Figure 4.3 to include the viewpoint of a bank employee who is responsible for ensuring that the auto-teller machine is stocked with banknotes.

4.3 Construct an action diagram for a bank teller machine which includes a facility allowing a customer to transfer cash from one account to another.

4.4 Many cars now come equipped with anti-lock braking systems. These include sensors to detect wheel lock and controls to activate the car brakes. Produce a system model of an anti-lock braking system. If you are not familiar with the details of such a system, postulate a reasonable model of how it might work.

4.5 A drinks vending machine can dispense coffee with and without milk and sugar. The user deposits a coin and makes a selection by pressing a button on the machine. This causes a cup with powdered coffee to be output. The user places this cup under a tap, presses another button and hot water is dispensed. Draw a finite-state machine model of this system.

4.6 Draw a thread diagram for the action 'dispense coffee with milk' in the above system.

4.7 Draw a finite-state machine model of a heating system controller. Assume that the user can set the temperature required and can also switch the heating system off and on from the controller.

4.8 Explain how the relational model can be used in system data modelling.

4.9 A system is to be procured which holds details of newspaper deliveries in a small town. As well as recording which households take which newspaper, this system also includes billing details and details of customer holidays when newspapers are not delivered. For each delivery person, the system prints a daily list of which newspapers and magazines are to be delivered to which households. Using a relational approach, describe a possible data model for such a system.

4.10 Convert the data model of Exercise 4.9 to a binary relational model. Discuss any difficulties which you encountered in making this conversion.

Chapter 5

Requirements Definition and Specification

Objective

The objective of this chapter is to discuss the problems of requirements definition and specification and to suggest techniques for expressing software requirements in a manner that is understandable to both system developers and system procurers. The importance of separating functional and non-functional requirements is emphasized. A distinction is drawn between requirements definition which is a natural language description of the software requirements and requirements specification which is seen as a more formal requirements description. An Ada-based notation is suggested as an appropriate way of expressing a requirements specification. The problems of expressing non-functional requirements and requirements testability are discussed.

Contents

A software requirements definition is an abstract description of the services which the system is expected to provide and the constraints under which the system must operate. It is read in conjunction with the system model descriptions and provides more detailed information about the system. It should be written in such a way that it is understandable without knowledge of specialized notations.

Commonly, the requirements definition is bundled with a more detailed specification into a single document but it is very important to realize that two distinct activities are involved in creating this document. The first stage involves describing system concepts and the rationale behind decisions made in the system model whereas the later stage is a more detailed activity, involving the precise description of the services that the system must provide. In this book, this first stage is referred to as *requirements definition* and the second stage as *requirements specification*. However, there is no standardized terminology in this area.

Requirements fall into two categories:

- *Functional system requirements*   These are system services which are expected by the user of the system. In general, the user is uninterested in how these services are implemented so the software engineer should avoid introducing implementation concepts in describing these requirements.

- *Non-functional requirements*   These set out the constraints under which the system must operate and the standards which must be met by the delivered system. For example, a non-functional constraint might be a requirement that all information input should be expressible using the ASCII character set. A standard which must be met might be a requirement for the maximum system response time for any user command to be less than 2 seconds.

In principle, the functional requirements of a system should be both complete and consistent. Completeness means that all services required by the user should be specified and consistency means that no one requirement should contradict any other. In practice, for large, complex systems, it is practically impossible to achieve requirements consistency and completeness in the initial version of the software requirements document. As problems are discovered during reviews or in later life-cycle phases, the software requirements document must be corrected.

It is normal practice to express the requirements definition using a mixture of natural language, tables and diagrams. It is essential that the requirements definition should be understandable by senior user personnel who may have no knowledge of specialized notations. Irrespective of developments in specification techniques, it will always be the case that the first stage of requirements expression will be a natural language definition.

4.A.5 The database shall support the generation and control of configuration objects; that is, objects which are themselves groupings of other objects in the database. The configuration control facilities shall allow access to the objects in a version group by the use of an incomplete name.

Figure 5.1
Stoneman requirement
4.A.5.

However, there are good and bad natural language definitions and, unfortunately, it is often the case that the use of language in requirements definitions leaves a great deal to be desired. There is sometimes a confusion between expressing concepts and expressing details so that the description contains an unhappy mixture of information presented at different levels of detail.

It is not the intention here to single out any specific document for criticism. Indeed few requirements documents are in the public domain so it is difficult to find documents of this type which may be freely quoted. However, one document which is available is the Stoneman document (Buxton, 1980) which sets out requirements for an Ada programming support environment (APSE). In general, this is not a badly written document but it does contain some examples of the differing levels of detail which can be found in such documents.

For example, requirement 4.A.5 from the Stoneman document is shown in Figure 5.1. Here we have an example of mixing conceptual and detailed information. This requirement expresses the concept that there should be configuration control facilities provided as an inherent part of the APSE. However, it also includes the detail that those facilities should allow access to the objects in a version group by use of an incomplete name. Clearly this latter detail would have been better left to a section where the configuration control requirements were specified more fully.

There are two major problems which sometimes arise when natural language is used for requirements definition.

(1)   Functional requirements, non-functional requirements, system goals and, sometimes, design information are not clearly distinguished.

(2)   Each paragraph may encompass several individual requirements in a single statement. This is a particular problem where the levels of abstraction of each of the intermixed requirements are different.

Some of the problems of requirements definition are illustrated by examples from the requirements definition for the design editing system whose conceptual model was introduced in Chapter 4. This document was a combined requirements definition and requirements specification which was expressed entirely in natural language. Combing requirements definition and

Figure 5.2
A requirements definition
for an editor grid facility.

> To assist in the positioning of entities on a diagram, the user may turn on a grid in either centimetres or inches, via an option on the control panel. Initially, the grid is off. The grid may be turned on and off at any time during an editing session and can be toggled between inches and centimetres at any time. A grid option will be provided on the reduce-to-fit view but the number of grid lines shown will be reduced to avoid filling the diagram with grid lines.

specification, however, tends to lead to a confusion between concepts and details. This is evident from the example given.

The user of the design editor may specify that a grid should be displayed so that diagram entities may be accurately positioned (Figure 5.2). The first sentence in this requirement actually provides three items of information. Firstly, it tells us that the editing system should provide a grid and presents a rationale for this. Secondly, it gives us detailed information about the grid units (centimetres or inches) and thirdly, it tells how that grid is to be activated by the user. Thus we have a conceptual functional requirement, a non-functional requirement setting out an expected standard and a non-functional requirement constraining the way in which the grid may be activated.

The requirement also gives some but not all initialization information. It specifies that the grid is initially off but does not specify its units when turned on. It provides some detailed information such as the fact that the user may toggle between units and not other information such as the spacing between grid lines.

A natural language requirements definition should be complemented by a requirements specification in a structured language. This specification should have associated natural language comments for the nonexpert who is interested in system details. The definition should concentrate on concepts and refer the reader to the specification for more detailed information. For example, Figure 5.3 might be a simple conceptual grid definition.

This definition concentrates on describing the facility required (the grid) and justifying why it is required. This rationale is critical if a requirements document is to be properly understood and is to be an effective system description for software developers. Without a rationale, some facilities appear arbitrary and the developer may not understand their importance. Notice also the reference to the system specification document where grid details are provided.

It is easy to criticize a requirements definition but much more difficult to write such a document. The writer has a mental model of what is required and has formed a variety of informal relationships within that model. The natural tendency is to express these relationships as they are discovered so that information is not accidentally omitted.

2.6 The grid

2.6.1 The editor shall provide a grid facility where a matrix of horizontal and vertical lines provides a background to the editor window. This grid shall be a passive rather than an active grid. This means that alignment is entirely the responsibility of the user and the system should not attempt to align diagram entities with grid lines.

Rationale:

   A grid helps the user to create a tidy diagram with well spaced entities. Although an active grid can be useful, the user is the best person to decide where entities should be positioned.

2.6.2 When used in 'reduce-to-fit' mode, the spacing of the grid lines shall be adjusted so that the logical grid line spacing is increased.

Rationale:

   If the logical line spacing is not increased, the background will become very cluttered with grid lines.

Specification: ECLIPSE/WORKSTATION_TOOLS/DE/FS. Section 2.6

Figure 5.3
An improved definition for an editor grid facility.

A requirements definition is a difficult document to write and the first version is inevitably unstructured. However, project management should accept the overhead of reorganizing and restructuring the document so that a more readable and usable definition is provided.

   It is not really possible to give a recipe for writing a readable document although the guidelines given in Chapter 29 are applicable. Perhaps the most useful approach is to invent a standard format and to ensure that all requirements definitions adhere to that format. Descriptive paragraphs might be followed by a rationale and a reference to a more detailed specification as shown in Figure 5.3. Use should be made of text highlighting facilities such as emboldening and italicization to add structure to the text, and of graphics to structure the document.

   A further example of this format, taken from the design editor, is shown in Figure 5.4.

5.1 Requirements specification

A notation based on natural language, supplemented by diagrams and tables, is most appropriate for expressing a requirements definition because this must be understood by client and (perhaps) contractor staff who have not been trained in the use of specialized notations. However,

3.5.1 Adding nodes to a design

3.5.1.1 To add a node, the user selects the appropriate node type from the entity type menu. He or she then moves the mouse so that the cursor is placed within the drawing area. On entering the drawing area, the cursor shape should change.

Rationale:

The editor must know the node type so that it can draw the correct shape and invoke appropriate checks for that node. The cursor shape change indicates that the editor is in 'node drawing mode'.

3.5.1.2 The user moves the cursor to the approximate node position and any mouse button is pressed. This should cause the node symbol, in a standard size set up by the symbol definer, to appear surrounding the cursor. It may then be dragged by moving the mouse, with the button depressed, to its required position. Releasing the mouse button fixes the node position and highlights the node.

Rationale:

The user is the best person to decide where to position a node on the diagram. This approach gives the user direct control.

3.5.1.3 If the entity type is such that its symbol may be varied in size, the fact that the symbol size is variable should be indicated as part of the node highlighting.

Specification: ECLIPSE/WORKSTATION_TOOLS/DE/FS. Section 3.5.1

Figure 5.4
The requirements definition for node creation.

as the basis of a system contract, a specification which is written in natural language leaves a great deal to be desired. The reasons for this are:

(1)   Natural language understanding depends on the shared linguistic experience of those responsible for reading and writing the requirements definition. The writer of a definition assumes that the terms which are used in that specification mean the same to the reader as to the writer. This is a dangerous assumption because of the inherent ambiguity of natural language and because a standard computing terminology has not yet been established.

(2)   Unstructured paragraphs of natural language are unable to express the functional architecture of the system in a clear and concise way. Schoman and Ross (1977) define the functional architecture of a system to be a description of the activities performed by the system and the interacting entities within the system. Essentially, it is a formalization of the conceptual model built by the system specifier. As this model is based on abstractions, the notation provided for specifying the model should be capable of expressing these abstractions in an unambiguous manner.

(3)   A natural language requirements specification is over-flexible in that it allows related requirements to be expressed in completely

different ways. This means that the reader of the definition is left with the task of identifying and partitioning related requirements with the consequent likelihood of error and misunderstanding.

(4) Requirements are not partitioned effectively. As a result, the effect of changes can only be determined by examining every requirement rather than a group of related requirements.

It is sometimes suggested that formal specification languages should be used to express system requirements and, indeed, this approach should lead to an unambiguous requirements specification. Such an unambiguous specification is ideal as the basis of a contract as it leaves no room for argument between client and contractor about system functionality. Unfortunately, the current state of user experience (and, realistically, the experience of many software engineers) is such that they would not understand a specification written in a formal specification language and would be unwilling to accept it as a contract basis.

As formal methods become more widely known and adopted, this situation may change but it will probably be many years before formal requirements specifications become the norm. Meanwhile, some compromise notation may be used for requirements specification which adds more structure to the definition than that possible using natural language text.

Notations which have been developed to define requirements all rely on natural language as an expressive base. Instead of using it in an unstructured way, however, they impose some structure on the definition, limit the natural language expressions which may be used and, in some of these languages, enhance the natural language definition by use of graphics.

Languages which have been designed to express software requirements include PSL/PSA (Teichrow and Hershey, 1977), SADT (Schoman and Ross, 1977) and RSL (Bell *et al.*, 1977). Although each language is intended as a general-purpose notation for specifying requirements, these languages were originally designed with different types of application in mind. RSL is designed for specifying time-critical real-time systems, PSL/PSA for information processing systems, and SADT for management information systems. RSL and PSL/PSA are designed to be used in conjunction with software tools which produce reports directly from formally stated requirements. By contrast, an SADT definition is intended to act as finished documentation so there is no need for an associated report generator.

SADT is the proprietary name of a notation developed by Ross (1977) based on a technique called Structured Analysis. Structured Analysis is not intended solely for specifying requirements but is designed as a technique for partitioning, structuring and expressing ideas, irrespective of the language in which these ideas are stated. Structured Analysis relies heavily on graphics to indicate structure and relationships, making use of about 40 distinct graphics symbols. Ross considers a description expressed in this way to bear the same relationship to the implemented system as a blueprint does to the engineering system which it describes.

Although Structured Analysis diagrams use special symbols, Ross maintains that they are easy to read and clear, even to the non-specialist. They are a tool for facilitating human communication but it is difficult to collect the ideas expressed in these diagrams and to check their consistency and completeness with software tools. This is not the case with PSL/PSA and RSL which have been specifically designed for machine processing.

RSL was designed as part of a software requirements engineering methodology (SREM) which was developed to specify the requirements for large defence systems (Bell *et al.*, 1977; Alford, 1977, 1985). SREM is based on a finite state machine model and statements in RSL are processed and collected into a database called the Abstract System Semantic Model (ASSM). To avoid over-complexity, the state machine model is structured into a number of levels of abstraction. A set of automated tools processes the information in the ASSM to generate simulators, produce reports and check the consistency and completeness of the requirements.

An alternative to the use of a requirements statement language to structure and restrict natural language is to use standard forms to achieve the same purpose. A project which used this approach is described by Heninger (1980). Special-purpose forms were designed to describe the input, output and functions of an aircraft software system. The system requirements were specified by filling in these forms. Although the system described by Heninger is a manual one, standardization of the forms would allow machine processing of the requirements to be carried out.

5.1.1 Requirements specification using an Ada-based notation

One of the difficulties of introducing any specialized notation is the high training and start-up costs. These can be reduced when the notation is a derivative of a high-level language such as Ada because more teaching material is available and because those involved in the project may have previous language experience. This approach has been described by Mander (1981) and Hill (1983).

Pure Ada is probably too restrictive to be suitable on its own as a language for requirements definition. However, by relaxing some of the rules of the language and establishing new rules specifying what information must be provided, an Ada-based notation is suitable for requirements definition.

Mander compares requirements definition in Ada to definition in notations such as SADT and PSL/PSA. He concludes that Ada is as expressive as these languages as long as extensive use is made of comments to provide additional information to the reader. A similar approach is described by Luckham and Von Henke (1985) who describe a formal specification language based on Ada. In this language, extra information is provided as formal comments. These are introduced by a special comment symbol so that they may be identified for machine processing.

It is not usually acceptable to specify requirements using Ada on its own as this forces too much implementation detail to be included in the requirements specification. Thus, the language must be extended and used in such a way that its abstraction facilities are utilized and its imperative programming statements avoided. The extensions to the language may be a sublanguage to allow requirements to be specified in a formal way or may take the form of formatted comments and standard style guidelines. Although informal, this latter approach makes the detection of problems during requirements review easier because omissions and inconsistencies are more obvious.

Ada is deficient for requirements specification because it does not provide primitives for set manipulation. When specifying requirements over a collection of entities, the specifier should not be forced into making a decision about how this collection should be represented. Rather, he or she should be allowed simply to consider these collections as sets and should be able to use set operations on them.

Of course, it is possible to model sets in Ada by defining a set abstract data type as a package but this imposes a rather artificial syntax on the set operations. Thus, in the examples below, we use an extended form of Ada where a set is a fundamental type like an array and where set operations are supported. We assume that readers are familiar with this notion and will easily understand these extensions. Ada features and language extensions are described by means of comments when they are used in examples.

An argument against using a programming language like Ada as a basis for describing specifications is that it forces the reader to view the specifications in an operational way. That is, the specification is presented as a set of operations on a system model and is hence less abstract than a purely descriptive approach. This argument is correct. However, this author believes that this can be considered as a strength rather than a limitation of this style of requirements specification.

Humans understand abstractions by building models which may be purely paper models or may have some other representation. Chemists represent molecules by combinations of coloured balls and wires, architects draw up plans of buildings and so on. These models may have equivalent abstract representations but from the point of view of understanding a system, they are very valuable.

From a user's point of view, specifying the requirements as operations on a system model can make those requirements much easier to understand. The dangers, of course, are that, firstly, the model will be constrained by the modelling language and not representative of the application domain and, secondly, the model will be seen as a design model rather than a model to help the user understand the system. Both of these problems can be avoided given sufficiently powerful language abstraction facilities which allow the model representation to be ignored.

When developing a system model to describe requirements, a set of conventions should be established which specifies the way in which the language should be used. For example, if an Ada-based language is used, the exception mechanism may be used to specify all system error handling. Furthermore, a description should be associated with any detailed model specification and this should be expressed using some standard commenting convention.

To show how an Ada-based notation may be used to describe a software system model, some of the facilities of the design editing system introduced earlier in this chapter are described here. The facilities offered by Ada are such that it lends itself to adopting an approach to specification which combines functional and object-oriented viewpoints. This reflects the fact that humans are not constrained to a single approach when describing a system and normally use both functional and object-oriented viewpoints.

Example 5.1
The design editor functions.

```
-- An Ada package specification is a means of gathering together
-- a number of declarations and associating a name with that
-- collection. In the example below, the declarations are
-- procedure declarations although any other valid Ada declarations
-- can also be included. The procedures are the editor operations
-- which provide user services. The package name (Design_editor)
-- encapsulates all of these.

package Design_editor is
    procedure Place_design_entity ;
    procedure Move_design_entity ;
    procedure Delete_design_entity ;
    procedure Annotate_entity_with_text ;
    procedure Resize_node ;
    procedure Annotate_diagram_with_text ;
    procedure Link_design_entity_with_database ;
    procedure Toggle_background_grid ;
    procedure Check_design_correctness ;
    procedure Save_design_to_database ;
    procedure Input_design_from_database ;
    procedure Set_preferences ;
end Design_editor ;
```

At the highest level, the design editor might be viewed as a collection of functions which operate on a design. All that we are doing is writing down descriptive names for the functions which we expect the design editing system to provide. Clearly, this list does not have to be written in Ada but the advantage of using the language is that a processing tool can check the specification to ensure that all facilities which are stated in the overall function list have actually been defined.

The design editor is specified here as a set of functions as this is a natural high-level view of such a system. Examination of this list suggests that the functions fall into three classes:

(1)   Functions which operate on design entities (Move, Delete, Add, Resize, Annotate, Link).

(2)   Functions which operate on a complete design (Check, Save, Input).

(3)   Functions which are concerned with the graphical design display (Annotate, Toggle grid, Set preferences).

This suggests that an object-oriented approach to requirements specification is appropriate because there are a limited number of object classes with functions operating on each. An object-oriented approach sets out the system types and the operations allowed on these types. From a specification point of view, it means that the specification is organized around these types rather than around system functions.

The simple analysis above suggests that there should be three object classes, namely design entities, the design itself and the design display. The design is viewed as a directed graph where the nodes and links may be labelled. Thus, the basic objects on which the design editor operates are nodes, links and labels. Some entities are dependent entities. For example, links are associated with nodes and if a node is deleted it makes no sense for the links to remain on the diagram.

More analysis reveals that nodes and links are fundamentally different types and that the operations on them are different. For example, the operation to create a link should specify the nodes which that link connects, whereas a node may be placed arbitrarily on the diagram. Node creation should involve the user indicating a diagram position where the node symbol is to appear. Node deletion should also imply deletion of attached links as dangling links are semantically meaningless. Link deletion, on the other hand, is a meaningful operation.

Designs are normally constructed on a number of levels where a single node at one level can be 'exploded' to reveal its structure. It therefore makes sense to link a node with the database where a node represents an abstraction of another design component. It makes no sense to link a link with the database.

Example 5.2
The functions associated
with nodes.

```
-- The package Node sets out all of the allowed operations on entities
-- of type Node. These are referenced Node.Delete, Node.Move, etc.
package Node is
    procedure Move ;
    procedure Delete ;
    procedure Add_to_design ;
    procedure Annotate_with_label ;
    procedure Resize ;
    procedure Link_with_database ;
end Node ;
```

Therefore, instead of design entity class, the object classes which might be considered are nodes and links. Thus, for a class Node, the Ada package specification in Example 5.2 identifies the user-level functions which operate on nodes. This is not a design specification so Ada's facilities to define private types and to specify their representation should not be used as they might confuse rather than inform readers of the specification. It is also important only to specify functions which may be user-initiated and not to try to anticipate what other functions may be needed in the system design.

Let us now look at one of these functions, namely the function which adds a new node to the design. Recall that the definition of this stated that the user selected a node type to be added then chose where it should be placed on the diagram. A possible specification for the definition (Figure 5.4) is shown in Example 5.3. This specification provides more information than the requirements definition. It states that, after a node type has been selected from the node type menu, the user must move the cursor to within the drawing area. It also states that the add operation should indicate stretchy symbols by adding stretch blobs to the node and if it is not stretchy it should be highlighted in some other way. The actual node stretching operation is the responsibility of some other procedure.

This procedure specification does not require the use of any extensions to Ada but the operation to move a node, shown in Example 5.4, requires that the labels and links associated with a node should be considered as a set. Its specification is as shown in Example 5.4. Of course, this description could be considered as a high-level design specification rather than a requirements specification in that it describes how a particular design model is transformed by a move operation. There is no clear distinction between a model-based requirements specification and a design but it is important to emphasize that the requirements model and the design model might be quite different. In fact, the move operation in the implemented design editor accords with this specification but its design is completely different from that set out above.

```
-- The procedure Add_to_design describes the actions
-- which should take place when a new node is added
-- to the design.
procedure Add_to_design is
begin
    -- Select the type of node to be placed on the design
    -- A menu of known node types is available and the
    -- selection is made from this
    Node_type := Select_node_type (Node_type_menu) ;
    -- The cursor should now be moved to the drawing area
    loop
        Cursor_position := Track_cursor ;
        exit when Inside_drawing_area (Cursor_position) ;
    end loop ;
    -- when the cursor is in the drawing area, change its shape
    -- to a circle
    Change_cursor_shape (Circle) ;
    -- find the position where the node is to be inserted. This is
    -- indicated by pressing the mouse button
    loop
        Position := Track_cursor ;
        exit when Mouse_button_pressed ;
    end loop ;
    -- draw the shape to be inserted
    Draw_shape (Node_type, Position) ;
    -- the user may drag the shape to another position. Its
    -- final position is when the mouse button is released
    loop
        Position := Track_cursor ;
        Draw_outline (Position) ;
        Draw_shape (Node_type, Position) ;
        exit when Mouse_button_released ;
    end loop ;
    -- Once a node has been placed on a diagram, enter its
    -- details in the design database
    Add_new_node_to_design_database (Node_type, Position) ;
    -- if the symbol size can be changed, indicate this
    -- by drawing stretch blobs on the symbol otherwise
    -- highlight it in some way.
    if Node_symbol_is_stretchy (Node_type) then
        Draw_stretch_blobs (Node_type, Position) ;
    else
        Highlight_node (Node_type, Position) ;
    end if ;
end Add_to_design ;
```

Example 5.3
Ada specification of Add_
to_design.

Example 5.4
The specification of
Move_node.

```
procedure Move_node (Node: NODE_TYPE) is
begin
    -- A node has been selected and highlighted in a previous
    -- operation
    -- this is passed as a parameter to the move operation
    Node_info := Get_from_design_database (Node) ;
    -- To adjust the position, the user simply drags the node using
    -- mouse. The mouse button is pressed during this operation.
    -- Releasing the button, completes the move
    loop
        Node_info.Position := Track_cursor ;
        exit when Mouse_button_released ;
    end loop ;
    -- the for_all construct is not standard Ada. It allows looping to
    -- be expressed without specifying the type of the collection
    -- over which the loop acts. The statement below specifies
    -- that the loop should be executed for all of the links
    -- associated with the selected node. When a node is
    -- moved, links should also be moved.
    for_all Link in Node_info.Links loop
        Link_info := Get_from_design_database (Link) ;
        Position := Get_end_point (Link_info, Node) ;
        Position := Compute_new_end_point (Position,
                               Node_info.Position) ;
        Put_end_point (Position, Node) ;
    end loop ;
    -- Execute the loop for all labels associated with the selected
    -- node. The loop specifies that labels should be moved with
    -- the node.
    for_all Label in Node_info.Labels loop
        Label_info := Get_from_design_database (Label) ;
        Label_info.Position := Add_coord (Label_info.Position,
                               Node_info.Position) ;
    end loop ;
end Move_node ;
```

It is not suggested that Ada is an ideal notation for requirements specification but when it is necessary to supplement a diagram and natural language based requirements definition with more details and when the client and contractor both have Ada experience, it may well be the most cost-effective notation to use. However, its use must be carefully controlled so that the overall system design is not unduly influenced by the requirements specification language.

5.2 Non-functional requirements definition

A non-functional system requirement is some restriction or constraint placed on the system service. One way of looking at non-functional requirements is as a definition of system properties and constraints under which the system must operate. Examples of system properties are its reliability, its response time and its store occupancy. Examples of constraints are the capabilities of the I/O devices attached to the system and the data representations used by other systems with which the required system must communicate. A property checklist is shown in Table 5.1.

Non-functional requirements are such that they tend to conflict and interact with other system functional requirements. For example, it may be a requirement that the maximum store occupied by a system should be 256K because the entire system has to be fitted into read-only memory and installed on a spacecraft. A further requirement might be that the system should be written in Ada but it may be the case that an Ada program providing the required functionality cannot be compiled into less than 256K. Some trade-off must be made either by using some other language, reducing the functionality or by increasing the ROM storage available.

It is normal practice to express non-functional requirements in natural language. This may be as part of a natural language requirements definition or may be in a special section of a requirements definition in a structured language. Figure 5.5 is an example of a non-functional requirement taken from the Stoneman document describing requirements for an Ada support environment. This requirement restricts the freedom

Property	Metric
Speed	Processed transactions/second
	User/event response time
	Screen refresh time
Size	kbytes
	Number of RAM chips
Ease of use	Training time
	Number of help frames
Reliability	Mean time to failure
	Probability of unavailability
	Rate of failure occurrence
	Availability
Robustness	Time to restart after failure
	Percentage of events causing failure
	Probability of data corruption on fail
Portability	Percentage of target-dependent states
	Number of target systems

Table 5.1
Property checklist.

Figure 5.5
Stoneman requirement
4.C.8.

> 4.C.8   It shall be possible for all necessary communication between the APSE and the user to be expressed in the standard Ada character set.

of an APSE designer in his or her choice of symbols which might be used to activate APSE services. It says nothing about the functionality of the APSE and clearly identifies a system constraint rather than a function.

The above requirement is a testable requirement and it is important that the writer of non-functional requirements bears the need for testing in mind when requirements are written. For example, a common system requirement is that the system should be easy to use (Figure 5.6). Leaving aside the fact that there might be two requirements expressed in Figure 5.6 (easy to use and tolerant of error), there is no way in which this requirement can actually be tested. The notions of ease of use and error minimization are subjective and requirements statements of this type are the cause of a great deal of customer dissatisfaction in delivered software systems.

A better expression of this requirement might state it in terms of the time required to learn to make use of the system and the number of errors expected over a given time period (Figure 5.7). This is clearly an imperfect statement of requirement in that ease of use and short training time are not necessarily related. However, it can be tested and this means that it is superior to woolly platitudinous statements about ease of use, user friend-liness or whatever, which tend to pervade requirements definitions.

When expressing non-functional requirements, it is particularly important to state the level of reliability required of the system. In many requirement documents, reliability is implicit, leaving opportunities for dispute between client and contractor over whether or not the system is adequately reliable. By expressing an explicit reliability requirement, the client is forced to consider what real reliability the system should exhibit. The quantification of reliability is discussed in Chapter 30 and one of the reliability metrics described there should be used in expressing reliability requirements.

The major problem in analysing non-functional requirements is that there is a need to separate functional and non-functional requirements yet, at the same time, individual non-functional requirements may relate to one or more functional requirements. If the non-functional requirements are stated separately from the functional requirements, it is sometimes difficult to see the correspondence between them. If stated with the functional

Figure 5.6
An untestable non-
functional requirement.

> The system should be easy to use by experienced controllers and should be organized in such a way that user errors are minimized.

> Experienced controllers should be able to use all of the system functions after a total of two hours training. After this training, the average number of errors made by experienced users should not exceed two per day.

Figure 5.7
A testable non-functional requirement.

requirements, it may be difficult to separate functional and non-functional considerations.

Of course, this fundamental problem is due to the sequential nature of paper-based documentation and can only really be solved when we use electronic document systems supporting multiple document views. Meanwhile, the best we can do is to provide a tabular summary of system properties, non-functional requirements and the particular requirements definition to which these relate.

5.2.1 Information representation

Because of the variety and the complexity of non-functional requirements, it is unlikely that natural language will ever be replaced by formal notations for non-functional requirements definition. However, some types of non-functional requirement which are concerned with the representation of information may be expressed in an Ada-like notation which includes extended facilities for representation specification. Ada already has a for-use clause which allows some representations to be defined.

Say an existing system is made up of a number of processes running on independent processors and the system required is to be integrated with this. Clearly, the existing system has already established representation standards and the new system must conform to these. For example, processes might communicate their state by exchanging messages with other processes. The following definition states the messages which might be expected by the required system.

```
type STATE is (Halted, Waiting, Ready, Running);
for STATE use (Halted => 1, Waiting => 4, Ready => 16,
                Running => 256);
```

This declares that Halted is represented by 1, Waiting by 4, Ready by 16, and Running by 256.

Similarly, say messages are to be sent over some communications line. Clearly, it is desirable to minimize the number of bytes of information transferred and also to conform with any information coding standards. The message might have the following logical structure.

```
type MESSAGE is record
    Sender : SYSTEM_ID;
    Receiver : SYSTEM_ID;
```

```
        Dispatch_time : DATE;
        Length: MESSAGE_LENGTH ;
        Terminator: CHARACTER ;
        Message : TEXT;
    end record;
```

The types used in this record declaration might have the following structure:

```
type SYSTEM_ID is range 20_000..30_000 ;
type YEAR_TYPE is range 1980..2080 ;
type DATE is record
    Seconds: NATURAL ;
    Year: YEAR_TYPE ;
end record ;
type MESSAGE_LENGTH is range 0..10_000 ;
type TEXT is array (MESSAGE_LENGTH) of CHARACTER ;
```

Ada's facilities to specify information representation allow the sizes of type representations to be set out. This is accomplished by using the SIZE attribute and specifying the number of bytes that entities of that type take up.

```
for SYSTEM_ID'SIZE use 2*BYTE ;
for YEAR_TYPE'SIZE use 2*BYTE ;
for MESSAGE_LENGTH'SIZE use 2*BYTE ;
```

Ada also allows the relative location of entities in a record to be set out. If this is not done explicitly, the compiler may rearrange the fields of a record as these are referenced by name rather than position. The record representation specifies that the sender and receiver identifiers are packed into the first word, the date takes up two words, the length and the message terminator are packed into the third word, and the message follows. The first part of the clause indicates that the record should begin on a word boundary. It is assumed that the system is developed on a machine with 32-bit words.

```
for MESSAGE use
    record at mod 8 ;
    -- Sender in first 16 bits
    Sender at 0*WORD range 0..15 ;
    -- Receiver in bits 16–31
    Receiver at 0*WORD range 16..31 ;
    Date at 1*WORD range 0..63 ;
    -- Length starts at the fourth word and takes 16 bits
    Length at 3*WORD range 0..15 ;
    Terminator at 3*WORD range 16..23 ;
    Message at 4*WORD range 0..31 ;
end record ;
```

It may be assumed that the message sent is up to Length characters long and is terminated by the specified termination character.

It must be admitted that Ada's representation specifications are not ideally suited to specifying non-functional requirements even when the area of representation is being addressed. The reason for this is that they are too machine-specific and are dependent on machine word size. However, the ability to perform some automatic checking on the representation is a valuable one and it may be appropriate to use representation clauses rather than natural language in a requirements specification.

KEY POINTS

- There is a distinction between requirements definition and requirements specification. A requirements definition is intended to describe the system to prospective procurers and users; a requirements specification is intended to serve as the basis of a contract between system procurer and system developer.

- Requirements definitions should be presented in a structured way and should exclude unnecessary detail. Graphical high-lighting is suggested as a presentation technique.

- Requirements definitions must be expressed in natural language because potential readers will probably have no knowledge of specialized notations. Natural language is, however, less appropriate for expressing a requirements specification.

- A notation based on Ada can be used for requirements specification by presenting a system model which is described using this Ada-based notation. This is illustrated by example here.

- Non-functional requirements tend to be so varied and complex that natural language must be used for their expression.

- Requirements should be expressed in such a way that they are testable.

Further reading

As discussed in Chapter 3, there is relatively little published work in this area. The special issue of *IEEE Computer* recommended there is also most appropriate as further reading for this chapter.

References

Alford, M.W. (1977), 'A requirements engineering methodology for real time processing requirements', *IEEE Trans. Software Eng*, **SE-3** (1), 60–9.

Alford, M.W. (1985), 'SREM at the age of eight: the distributed computing design system', *IEEE Computer*, **18** (4), 36–46.

Bell, T.E., Bixler, D.C. and Dyer, M.E. (1977), 'An extendable approach to computer aided software requirements engineering', *IEEE Trans. Software Eng,* **SE-3** (1), 49–60.

Buxton, J. (1980), *Requirements for Ada Programming Support Environments: Stoneman*, US Department of Defense, Washington DC.

Heninger, K.L. (1980), 'Specifying software requirements for complex systems. New techniques and their applications'. *IEEE Trans. Software Eng,* **SE-6** (1), 2–13.

Hill, A. (1983), 'Towards an Ada-based specification and design language', *ADA UK News*, **4** (4), 16–34.

Luckham, D. and Von Henke, F.W. (1985), 'An overview of Anna, a specification language for Ada', *IEEE Software*, **2** (2), 9–23.

Mander, K.C. (1981), 'An Ada view of specification and design', *Tech. Rep. 44*, Department of Computer Science, University of York, York, UK.

Ross, D.T. (1977), 'Structured Analysis (SA). A language for communicating ideas', *IEEE Trans. Software Eng,* **SE-3** (1), 16–34.

Schoman, K. and Ross, D.T. (1977), 'Structured analysis for requirements definition', *IEEE Trans. Software Eng,* **SE-3** (1), 6–15.

Teichrow, D. and Hershey, E.A. (1977), 'PSL/PSA: a computer aided technique for structured documentation and analysis of information processing systems', *IEEE Trans. Software Eng*, **SE-3** (1), 41–8.

EXERCISES

5.1 The method of graphical highlighting of requirements is probably only feasible when a document processing system including integrated text and graphics is available. Given that only a text-based system, with multiple fonts and styles, is available, draw up a set of guidelines for presenting requirements definitions in a readable and structured way.

5.2 If you have access to the Stoneman requirements document (or some comparable requirements definition), present a critique of the requirements as expressed in that document.

5.3 Explain why natural language is inappropriate for setting out a requirements specification.

5.4 Discover ambiguities or omissions in the following statement of requirements for part of a ticket issuing system.

This system is intended to automate the sale of rail tickets. Users select their destination, and input a credit card and a personal identification number. The rail ticket is issued and their credit card account charged with its cost.

When the user presses the start button, a menu display of potential destinations is activated along with a message to the user to select a destination. Once a destination has been selected, the user is requested to input his or her credit card, its validity is checked and the user is then requested to input a personal identifier.

5.5 Produce a requirements specification of the above system using an Ada-based notation. You may make any reasonable assumptions about the system. Pay particular attention to specifying user errors.

5.6 Write a set of non-functional requirements for the ticket issuing system of Exercise 5.4 setting out its expected reliability and its response time.

5.7 Using an Ada-based notation, write a requirements specification for the newspaper delivery system described in the exercises in Chapter 4. Include both functional and non-functional requirements. Pay particular attention to the fact that people like to have their newspapers delivered whether or not the computer system is operational.

5.8 Write a more detailed specification for the editor grid facility set out in Figure 5.3.

5.9 Discuss the use of Ada representation clauses in the presentation of non-functional requirements.

5.10 Suggest how the Ada representation clause mechanism might be extended so that it may be used to describe a greater number of non-functional requirements.

5.11 Suggest how an Ada-based notation for requirements specification might be integrated with a graphical modelling notation such as CORE or SADT.

Chapter 6

Requirements Validation and Prototyping

Objectives

During the formulation of a set of requirements, it is important to check the validity of these requirements. This means that the developer should check that the requirements are consistent and that they meet the user's expectations. This chapter discusses the importance of validating software requirements although it emphasizes the fact that requirements necessarily change over a system's lifetime and that there cannot ever be a set of completely 'correct' requirements. Prototyping, the production of a system very quickly, is suggested as a means of requirements validation and a process model based on prototyping is introduced. Various approaches to the development of rapid system prototypes are described.

Contents

Once a set of system requirements has been established, these requirements must be validated to demonstrate that, as far as possible, they reflect an accurate picture of the system desired by the client. If this validation is inadequate, errors in the requirements definition will be propagated to the system design and implementation. Expensive system modifications may be required to correct these errors.

The cost of errors in stating requirements may be very high, particularly if these errors are not discovered until the system is implemented. Boehm (1974) reports that in some large systems up to 95% of the code had to be rewritten to satisfy changed user requirements and also that 12% of the errors discovered in a software system over a three year period were due to errors in the original system requirements. The majority of program maintenance is not actually correction of erroneous code but code modification to support changes to or errors in the original system requirements.

Furthermore, the cost of making a system change resulting from a requirements change is likely to be much greater than repairing design or coding errors. A requirements change implies that the design and implementation must also be changed and the system testing and validation process repeated. This is more expensive than a program bug fix, for example, which involves only changing and retesting part of the code.

Recall, however, the discussion in Chapter 1 on software evolution. Irrespective of how much effort is put into requirements validation, there is no way in which subsequent changes to the requirements can be avoided.

There are four separate steps involved in validating requirements. These are:

(1) The needs of the user should be shown to be valid. A user may think that a system is needed to perform certain functions but further thought and analysis may identify additional or different functions which are required. Of course, there are problems due to the fact that systems have many diverse users and any set of requirements is inevitably a compromise across the user community.

(2) The requirements should be shown to be consistent. Any one requirement should not conflict with any other.

(3) The requirements should be shown to be complete. The definition should include all functions and constraints intended by the system user.

(4) The requirements should be shown to be realistic. There is no point in specifying requirements which are unrealizable using existing hardware and software technology. It may be acceptable to anticipate some hardware developments but developments in software technology are much less predictable.

Demonstrating that a set of requirements meets a user's needs is extremely difficult if an abstract approach is adopted. By reading a definition and specification, users must picture the system in operation and imagine how that system would fit into their work. It is extremely difficult for skilled computer professionals to perform this type of abstract analysis; it is almost impossible for system users. As a result, many systems are delivered which do not meet the user's needs and which are simply discarded after delivery.

Validation should not be seen as a process to be carried out after the requirements document has been completed. Regular requirements reviews involving both users and software engineers are essential while the requirements definition is being formulated. During these reviews, the development team should 'walk' the client through the system requirements explaining the implications of each requirement. Conflicts and contradictions should be pointed out. It is then up to the users and system procurer to modify their requirements to resolve these problems and contradictions.

To counter the problems of user requirements validation, an approach based on prototype development may be adopted. This involves developing a version of the system at an early stage of the requirements definition process, handing this to the user for experiment and modifying the prototype as the requirements are identified. Prototyping is discussed in the following section.

A requirements review is a manual process which involves multiple readers from both client and contractor staff checking the requirements document for anomalies and omissions. The review process may be managed in the same way as design reviews (see Chapter 14) or may be organized on a larger scale with many participants involved in checking different parts of the document.

Requirements reviews are generally successful in detecting many errors in the requirements definition and they are really the only approach which can check the completeness of requirements. However, the consistency of the requirements is best checked using some automated tool and this is only possible when the requirements are expressed in a formal language (Figure 6.1).

Expressing the requirements in an Ada-like notation allows interface inconsistencies to be detected and these are often the most crucial in any large system. If this is supplemented by a precise description of the system expressed using a logic-based notation, behavioural inconsistencies can also be identified using checking tools.

The realism of requirements can be demonstrated, in some cases, by constructing a system simulator. The technique of system simulation is particularly useful to demonstrate that non-functional requirements can be met. One of the tools used in conjunction with the requirements statement language RSL is a simulator generator. This tool analyses an RSL

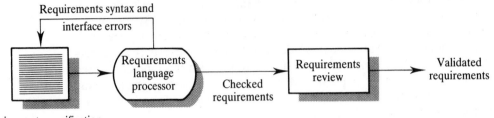

Requirements syntax and interface errors

Requirements language processor

Checked requirements

Requirements review

Validated requirements

Requirements specification in machine-processable language

Figure 6.1
Automated checking of the requirements specification.

definition and automatically generates a system simulator in Pascal. Procedures which simulate each functional definition are provided by the specifier as part of the requirements definition.

The problems of simulation, however, are highlighted by Davis and Vick (1977). They point out that, for complex systems, it can be as expensive and as time consuming to develop the system simulator as it is to develop the system itself. Furthermore, it may be difficult to change the simulator so that changes in the requirements may be impossible to assess by simulation. As a result, simulation has not been extensively used in validating the requirements of large systems although Davis and Vick state that it can result in a significant reduction in requirements errors.

6.1   The prototyping process

The fundamental problem which faces the user who is involved in defining a new software system is that it is difficult to assess how the existence of that system will affect his or her work. For new systems, particularly if these are large and complex, it is probably impossible to make this assessment before the system is built and put into use.

This has led to suggestions, discussed in Chapter 1, that an exploratory approach to systems development should be adopted. This implies presenting the user with a system knowing it to be incomplete and then modifying and augmenting that system as the user's real requirements become apparent.

Alternatively, a deliberate decision might be made to build a 'throw-away' prototype. This is a widely used approach to hardware development where a prototype is built to identify initial problems and, after experimentation, an improved specification is formulated. The prototype is then discarded and a production-quality system built.

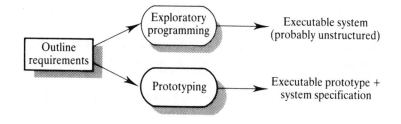

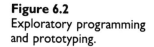

Figure 6.2
Exploratory programming
and prototyping.

The distinction between these two approaches is that exploratory programming starts out with a vague understanding of the system requirements and augments the system as new requirements are discovered. There is no such thing as a system specification and, indeed, systems developed by this approach may be unspecifiable. By contrast, the prototyping approach is intended to discover the system specification so that the output of the prototype development phase is that specification (Figure 6.2).

A software process model based on an initial prototyping stage is illustrated in Figure 6.3. This approach extends the requirements analysis process with the intention of reducing overall life-cycle costs.

The benefits of using a prototype system during the requirements analysis and definition phase of the software life-cycle are:

(1) Misunderstandings between software developers and users may be identified as the system functions are demonstrated.

(2) Missing user services may be detected.

(3) Difficult-to-use or confusing user services may be identified and refined.

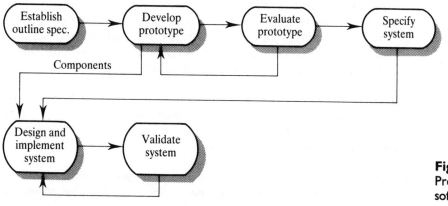

Figure 6.3
Prototyping in the
software process.

(4)   Software development staff may find incomplete and/or inconsistent requirements as the prototype is developed.

(5)   A working, albeit limited, system is available very quickly to demonstrate the feasibility and usefulness of the application to management.

(6)   The prototype serves as a basis for writing the specification for a production quality system.

The process model in Figure 6.3 is based on the assumption that the prototype is developed from some outline system specification, delivered for experiment and modified until the client is satisfied with its functionality. At this stage, a more conventional software process model is entered, a specification is derived from the prototype and the system is re-implemented in a final production version.

Rather than derive a specification from the prototype, it is sometimes suggested that the system specification is the prototype implementation itself. The instruction to the software contractor should simply be 'write a system like this one'. This is a dangerous approach.

(1)   Important system features may have been deliberately left out of the prototype to simplify rapid implementation. In fact, it may not be possible to prototype some of the most important parts of the system such as safety-critical features.

(2)   An implementation is hardly an adequate basis for a contract between client and contractor and certainly has no legal standing.

(3)   Non-functional requirements such as those concerning reliability, robustness and safety cannot be adequately expressed in a prototype implementation.

(4)   The user may not use the prototype in the same way as an operational system. This may be due to unfamiliarity with the system or may be because of some inherent characteristic of the prototype. For example, if the prototype is slow, users may adjust their way of working and, by avoiding some system features, adapt to slow response times. When provided with better response, they may use the system in a completely different way and utilize functions which have not been evaluated.

Complete prototype re-implementation is recommended for long-lifetime systems although, obviously, it may be possible to use components from the prototype in the production-quality system. Re-implementation is recommended for the following reasons:

(1)   Important system characteristics such as performance, security, robustness and reliability may have been ignored during prototype

development so that a rapid implementation could be developed. The nature of the prototype may be such that these cannot be added on to it.

(2)   During the prototype development, the prototype will have been changed to reflect user needs and it is likely that these changes will have been made in an uncontrolled way. This means that only the prototype code exists as a design specification and this is an inadequate basis for long-term maintenance.

(3)   The changes made during prototype development will probably have degraded the system structure so that subsequent changes because of maintenance requirements become more and more difficult to make.

An alternative process model which attempts to combine the advantages of exploratory programming with the control required for large-scale development has been reported by Mills *et al.* (1980). This has been termed evolutionary development (Figure 6.4) and involves developing the requirements and delivering the system in an incremental fashion. Thus, as a part of the system is delivered, the user may experiment with it and provide feedback to later parts of the system. This seems to be a very sensible approach but may only be suited to some classes of client and contractor because of the contractual problems which may arise.

The principal argument against prototyping is that the cost of prototype development represents an unacceptably large fraction of

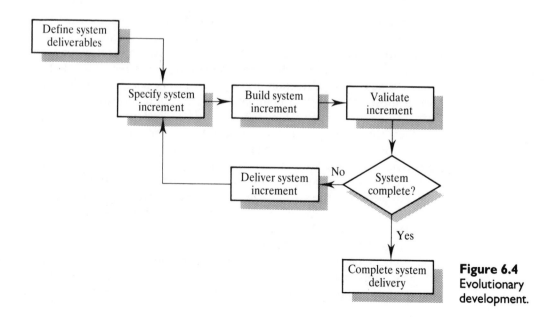

Figure 6.4
Evolutionary
development.

overall system costs. It may be more economic to modify a finished system to meet unperceived needs than to provide an opportunity for the user to understand and refine his needs before the final system is built. By contrast, the cost of a prototype for a mechanical or electronic system which is to be mass produced represents a very small increment in the final unit cost of the system. The cost of system modification after release, which might involve recalling all products, is very large indeed.

6.2 Prototyping techniques

Software prototyping is expensive if the prototype is implemented using the same tools and to the same standards as the final system. However, if a prototype is intended to demonstrate the functional rather than the non-functional aspects of a system, it can be developed at a cost which is significantly lower than that of the final system. There are a number of ways of reducing the development time of a system prototype:

(1)   Use a very high-level language for prototype implementation.
(2)   Relax non-functional requirements such as speed and space requirements.
(3)   Ignore considerations of error action.
(4)   Reduce reliability and program quality standards.

It was once thought that a prototype should have a simpler user interface than a production system. It is now clear that the user interface to a system is one part of the system which can be vastly improved by prototyping, and compromising on user interface implementation is not recommended.

Because error detection and error recovery comprise such a large part of most systems, their elimination drastically reduces the size of the system to be prototyped. Hence the prototype development time is much less than the final system development time. This time can be further reduced by lowering standards of reliability and program quality. As the prototype is thrown away after the final requirements have been established, there is no need for production software standards to be adopted.

By reducing the system size and standards, prototype software can be constructed in any programming language but prototype development time can be reduced by using a very high-level programming language. Very high-level dynamic languages are not normally used for large system development because they need a large run-time support system. This run-time support increases the storage needs and reduces the execution speeds of programs written in the language. As performance requirements

Language	Type	Application domain
Smalltalk	Object-oriented	User interfaces
PROLOG	Logic	Symbolic processing
LISP	Functional	Symbolic processing
SETL	Set-based	Symbolic processing
APL	Mathematical	Scientific systems
4GLs	Database	Business DP
RAPID/USE	Graphical	Business DP
Gist/REFINE	Wide spectrum	Symbolic processing

Table 6.1
Prototyping languages.

can sometimes be ignored in prototype development, however, this is not necessarily a disadvantage.

A number of different high-level languages have been used for prototyping. Table 6.1 summarizes prototype programming languages and suggests the most appropriate application domain where these languages can be applied. However, the domains suggested are not exclusive and the languages may be used for prototyping other classes of application system.

Gomaa (1983) has reported the successful use of APL as a prototyping language. He describes the advantages which accrued from developing a prototype for a process management and information system. He estimates that prototype development costs were less than 10% of the total system costs. In the development of the production system, no requirements definition problems were encountered, the project was completed on time and the system was well received by users.

Another useful prototyping tool is the shell programming language available under UNIX (Bourne, 1978). The UNIX shell is a command language which includes looping and decision constructs. It provides facilities for combining commands which operate on files and strings. In the author's experience, a prototype for an information retrieval system was built, using the UNIX shell, in a day. By contrast, the final system took several weeks to design and implement in Pascal.

The reason why the UNIX shell is an effective prototyping tool is that it provides a means of connecting existing programs together into different useful configurations. This is a very sensible approach but prototyping using the shell is limited because the granularity of the software components which may be connected together is relatively coarse. This means that the function of the individual components is often too general purpose to combine effectively with other components. There appears to be scope for further development of prototyping using existing components with more precise functions than the programs available under UNIX.

However, the UNIX shell only allows the use of simple character stream interfaces and an increasingly important application of prototyping is in user interface prototyping. It is now clear that the usability of an interface is dependent upon its 'look and feel'. These attributes cannot be designed in an abstract way and can only be determined by experiment. Thus prototyping is essential when designing user interfaces.

One of the most powerful prototyping systems for user interfaces (and for other functions) is the Smalltalk system (Goldberg and Robson, 1983). Smalltalk is an object-oriented programming language which is tightly integrated with its environment which is a WIMP interface as described in Chapter 13. Most system interaction is via menus where selections are made by pointing with the mouse. Smalltalk is an excellent prototyping language for two reasons:

(1)   The object-oriented nature of the language means that systems are resilient to change. Thus, rapid modifications of a Smalltalk system are possible without unforeseen effects on the rest of the system. Indeed, Smalltalk is really only suitable for this style of development and is not well suited to a single, monolithic development approach.

(2)   The Smalltalk system and environment is an inherent part of the language and all of the objects defined there are available to the Smalltalk programmer. Thus, a large number of reusable components are available which may be incorporated in the prototype under development.

An alternative to using a very high-level language for prototype development or configuring existing components into a prototype is to use languages and environments which are specifically designed for prototype construction. Examples of such systems are RAPID (Wasserman *et al.*, 1986) and Gist (Balzer *et al.*, 1982, Balzer, 1985).

RAPID is built around a relational database, an implementation language called PLAIN which is designed for building interactive information systems, and a transition diagram interpreter for prototyping user dialogues. It incorporates comparable facilities to those included in CASE workbenches (see Chapter 18) but includes superior facilities for user interface prototyping.

Gist is a non-deterministic language in which the user writes a formal, executable, specification of the system to be prototyped. This specification is refined by the user with automated assistance to produce an executable system prototype. Gist is what is called a wide-spectrum language inasmuch as it incorporates concepts from logic programming, functional programming and imperative programming languages. A LISP implementation of the system is generated by the Gist processor.

As well as a very high-level language, these systems provide a large number of useful software components which can be 'glued' together in a number of prototype configurations. Early experience with both RAPID and the industrialized development of Gist (called REFINE) for rapid prototyping has been encouraging. REFINE is now undergoing commercial evaluation and is described by Smith *et al.* (1985).

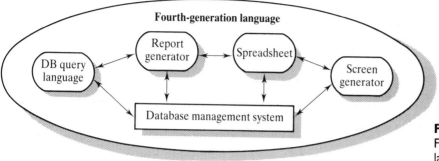

Figure 6.5
Fourth-generation
languages.

For some classes of application, particularly those in commercial data processing, a prototyping approach may supplant the conventional development model as so-called fourth-generation languages (4GLs) are used for systems development. There are now an immense variety of such languages and it is quite clear that their use speeds up the production of some types of system.

Their success is based on the fact that there is a great deal of commonality across data processing applications and many applications are report generation activities using information in a company database. Thus a typical 4GL is based around a database facility and provides a database query language, a report generation package and a package to assist with screen layout design (Figure 6.5). Some spreadsheet-type facilities may also be included. In essence, a 4GL relies on software reuse where routines to access a database and produce reports are provided and the programmer need only describe how these routines are to be controlled.

The argument put forward by the vendors of these products is that system maintenance is much simpler because application development time is very rapid. Systems are typically very much smaller than the equivalent COBOL programs. Rather than be concerned about structuring the system for maintenance, requirements changes are best accommodated by a complete system rewrite.

Using 4GLs for data processing systems development is cost-effective in some cases, particularly for relatively small systems. However, the situation at the moment resembles the Tower of Babel with no standardization or uniformity across languages and a potential cost time-bomb as the requirement to maintain all the different 4GLs is demanded by users. Proponents of these languages seem to be unaware of the problems in the real-time systems community of language proliferation which led to the development of Ada as a standard language for defence systems development.

Although they clearly reduce systems development costs, the effect of 4GLs on overall life-cycle costs for large DP systems is not yet clear. They are obviously to be recommended for prototyping but the lack of standardization may result in long-term maintenance problems.

KEY POINTS

- Typically, requirements errors are more expensive to correct after system delivery than design or implementation errors. Thus, requirements validation is a very important part of the requirements analysis and specification phase.

- Reviews involving both client and contractor are a useful approach to validation.

- Prototyping is a very valuable technique for helping to establish system requirements.

- For some applications or application fragments such as the user interface (see Chapter 13), it is essential to use prototyping to derive the requirements as an abstract analysis is unlikely to yield an acceptable result.

- The use of very high-level languages like Smalltalk or PROLOG is recommended for prototyping

- Fourth-generation languages are effective for prototyping data processing systems. The danger of using these as production rather than prototype systems is that long-term support for some 4GLs is uncertain.

- It is recommended that the prototype should be considered as a 'throw-away' system and should not be used as a basis for further system development.

Further reading

ACM Software Eng Notes **7** (5), 1986. The proceedings of a conference on prototyping. Many papers of interest.

IEEE Trans. Software Eng., **SE-12** (2), 1986. Although this is a special issue on software design methods, the journal also contains four papers on prototyping and program-generation environments.

References

Balzer, R.M., Goldman, N.M. and Wile, D.S. (1982), 'Operational specification as the basis for rapid prototyping', *ACM Software Eng. Notes,* **7** (5), 3–16.

Balzer, R. (1985), 'A 15 year perspective on automatic programming', *IEEE Trans. Software Eng.,* **SE-11** (11), 1257–67.

Boehm, B.W. (1974), 'Some steps towards formal and automated aids to software requirements analysis and design', *IFIP 74,* Amsterdam: North-Holland.

Bourne, S.R. (1978), 'The UNIX shell', *Bell Systems Tech. J.,* **57** (6), 1971–90.

Davis, C.G. and Vick, C.R. (1977), 'The software development system', *IEEE Trans. Software Eng.,* **SE-3** (1), 69–84.

Goldberg, A. and Robson, D. (1983), *Smalltalk–80. The Language and its Implementation,* Reading, Mass.: Addison-Wesley

Gomaa, H. (1983), 'The impact of rapid prototyping on specifying user requirements', *ACM Software Eng. Notes,* **8** (2), 17–28.

Mills, H.D., O'Neill, D., Linger, R.C., Dyer, M., and Quinnan, R.E. (1980), 'The management of software engineering', *IBM Systems. J.,* **24** (2), 414–77.

Smith, D.R., Kotik, G.B. and Westfold, S.J. (1985), 'Research on Knowledge-based software environments at Kestrel Institute', *IEEE Trans. Software Eng.,* **SE-11** (11), 1278–95.

Wasserman, A.I., Pircher, P.A., Shewmake, D.T., and Kersten, M.L. (1986), 'Developing interactive information systems with the user software engineering methodology', *IEEE Trans. Software Eng.,* **SE-12** (2), 326-45.

EXERCISES

6.1 Who should be involved in a requirements review? Suggest how such a review should be conducted.

6.2 Discuss the role of simulation in the requirements validation process.

6.3 Comment on the suitability of the UNIX shell as a prototyping language. Which features of UNIX make it particularly useful in this respect?

6.4 Explain why, for large systems development, it is recommended that prototypes should be 'throw-away' prototypes.

6.5 What features of languages like Smalltalk and LISP contribute to their support of rapid prototyping?

6.6 If you have access to a very high-level language, develop a prototype for the newspaper delivery system introduced in the Exercises in Chapter 4. Use your experience with the prototype to formulate a more definitive set of requirements for such a system.

6.7 If you have experience with Smalltalk or a tool to support user interface prototyping, develop a prototype interface for the automatic ticketing system introduced in Exercise 5.4.

6.8 There are particular difficulties in prototyping real-time embedded computer systems. Suggest what these might be.

Chapter 7

Formal Specification

Objective

The objective of this chapter and the two following
chapters is to introduce formal specification techniques, to
remove some of the mystique surrounding the subject and
to convince software engineers that these are worthy of
further consideration. This chapter sets out the case for
formal specifications and discusses their advantages and
disadvantages. It then introduces the notion of a predicate
and shows how a simple function can be specified by
means of pre- and post-conditions. As an illustration, a
search routine is specified.

Contents

In Chapter 3, the notion of a software specification which was distinct from the requirements definition and requirements specification was introduced. In the same way as the software design process involves a series of transformations which add detail to the design, the process of specification should also be undertaken in a number of stages. This process is illustrated in Figure 7.1 which also shows the involvement of the client and software contractor at each of these stages.

It may seem unusual that a design activity precedes detailed specification in Figure 7.1. Architectural design is the activity of partitioning the requirements to software subsystems and is an essential prerequisite for specification. Without this partitioning, there are no logical elements to specify! Although it might be argued that the modularization of a specification and a design might be different, such an approach is likely to lead to the introduction of errors as a translation is made from the specification to the design.

The involvement of the client decreases and the involvement of the contractor increases as the specification is developed. In the early stages of the process, it is essential that the specification is 'client-oriented'. That is, it should be couched in a way which is understandable to the client and should make as few assumptions as possible about the software design. However, the final stage of the process, which is the construction of a complete, consistent and precise specification, is principally intended for the software contractor and acts as a basis for the software design.

Indeed, the boundary between specification and design is not clear cut and the development of a precise specification might be seen as part of the design process. Although such an activity has probably been practised by good software designers ever since programming began, it is only relatively recently that the development of such detailed and precise specifications has been recognized as a generally useful software process activity.

Of course, the specification stages shown in Figure 7.1 are not independent nor are they necessarily carried out in sequence. A feedback loop exists, as shown in Figure 7.2, where errors, omissions and inconsistencies discovered at one stage of the specification feed back to earlier specification stages.

As a specification is refined, the engineer's understanding of that specification increases. Errors and omissions are detected and these are fed back to allow earlier specifications to be modified. Indeed, error detection is the most potent argument for developing a detailed, precise specification as requirements errors which remain undetected until later stages of the software process are usually expensive to correct.

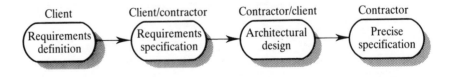

Figure 7.1
Specification stages.

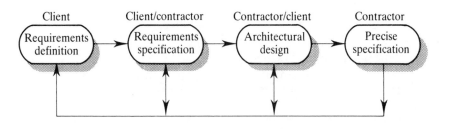

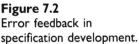

Figure 7.2
Error feedback in
specification development.

The reader will have noticed that the ultimate stage in the specification process shown in Figure 7.1 is referenced as 'Precise specification' and not 'Formal software specification'. This labelling was deliberate as the critical activity is to analyse and document the specification in detail. The principal benefits accrue from detailed analysis rather than particular notations. However, formal techniques are the most effective in assisting with this detailed analysis. Developments over the last decade have meant that formal specification techniques can now be used in the specification of many classes of software system.

7.1   Benefits of formal specification

A formal software specification is a specification expressed in a language whose vocabulary, syntax and semantics are formally defined. The need for a formal semantic definition means that the specification languages cannot be based on natural languages but must be based on mathematics. The advantages of using such a formal language for precise specifications are as follows:

(1)   The development of a formal specification provides insights into and understanding of the software requirements and the software design.

(2)   Given a formal system specification and a complete formal programming language definition, it may be possible to prove that a program conforms to its specification. Thus, the absence of certain classes of system error may be demonstrated. Formal verification is discussed in Chapter 22.

(3)   Formal specifications may be automatically processed. Software tools can be built to assist with their development, understanding and debugging.

(4)   Depending on the formal specification language used, it may be possible to animate a formal system specification to provide a prototype system.

(5)   Formal software specifications are mathematical entities and may be studied and analysed using mathematical methods.

(6)   Formal specifications may be used as a guide to the tester of a component in identifying appropriate test cases. The use of formal specifications in this way is discussed by Hayes (1986).

Research into formal specification techniques was initiated because of interest in formal program verification. However, it is now clear that formal specifications are of value in their own right and that it may be worthwhile to develop a formal specification even when there there are no plans to formally verify the developed system. The other advantages of formal specification are sufficient to justify its use in the software process.

Formal specification techniques are not widely used in industrial software development. Indeed, the specification process model in Figure 7.1 is an idealized one and many if not most organizations commence the design process after the construction of the detailed requirements or functional specification. Formal specification is not widely used because:

(1)   Software management is inherently conservative and is unwilling to adopt new techniques whose payoff is not obvious. It is hard to demonstrate that the relatively high cost of developing a formal system specification will reduce overall software development costs. This author knows of no empirical evidence which suggests that the use of formal methods leads to a significant reduction in life-cycle costs, and conservatism in adopting such methods is understandable.

(2)   Most software engineers have not been trained in the techniques required to develop formal software specifications. Developing specifications requires a familiarity with discrete mathematics and logic. Inexperience of these techniques makes specification development appear difficult.

(3)   System procurers are unlikely to be familiar with formal specification techniques and may be unwilling to fund development activities which they cannot readily influence.

(4)   Some classes of software system are genuinely very difficult to specify using existing specification techniques. In particular, current techniques are not adequate for the specification of the interactive components of user interfaces, and some classes of parallel processing system, such as interrupt-driven systems, are difficult to specify.

(5)   There is widespread ignorance of current specification techniques and their applicability. It is no longer the case that only trivial systems may be specified in a formal way. For example, Earl *et al.* (1986) report on the formal specification of a software engineering environment and Morgan and Sufrin (1984) report on the specification of the UNIX filestore.

(6) Most of the effort in specification research has been concerned with the development of notations and techniques. Relatively little effort has been devoted to tool support yet such support is essential if large-scale specifications are to be developed.

(7) Some members of the computer science community who are active in the development of formal methods misunderstand practical software engineering and suggest that software engineering can be equated with the adoption of formal methods of software development. Understandably, such nonsense makes pragmatic software engineers very wary of their proposed solutions.

The disadvantages of formal specification have militated against their widespread use but many of these disadvantages can be overcome. In the lifetime of this book, we are likely to see the increased use of formal specification as an accepted part of the software process. Tool support for specification development will be an increasingly common feature of software engineering environments.

In Chapter 1, the notion of a software process based on formal transformations was introduced. A formal system specification is a prerequisite for this and the process involves the transformation of that specification through a series of correctness-preserving steps to a finished program (Figure 7.3). Each transformation is sufficiently close to the previous description that the effort of verifying the transformation is not excessive so it can be guaranteed (ignoring verification errors) that the ultimate developed program is a true implementation of the specification.

The advantage of the transformational approach compared to formally verifying that a program meets its specification is that the distance between each transformation is less than the distance between a specification and a program. Program proofs are very long and impractical for

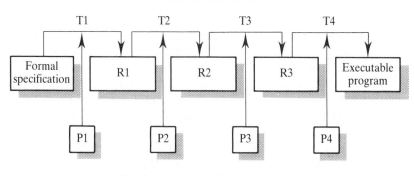

Formal transformations

Proofs of transformation correctness

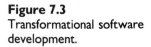

Figure 7.3
Transformational software development.

large-scale systems but a transformational approach made up of a sequence of smaller steps may be more effective. However, the process is not an easy one. Choosing which transformation to apply is a skilled task and proving the correspondence of transformations is difficult.

Few (if any) large-scale systems have been developed using the transformational model of the software process but it is likely that recent developments in formal methods (such as the specification language Z, described in Chapter 9) will make this process a more practical one. Although it is unlikely that a purely transformational approach will ever be adopted for very large systems development, the incorporation of this model into other process models is likely to lead to overall process improvements.

Specification techniques which can be used for non-trivial systems are algebraic specification and model-based specification. These are the subjects of Chapters 8 and 9 respectively. However, before going on to consider these techniques, it is instructive to consider the development of a simple example which will introduce the reader to the notions of formality in specifications.

Paradoxically, perhaps, the approach which is adopted to the discussion of formal specifications is an *informal* one and is not mathematically rigorous. This is partly for space reasons – a rigorous description of formal specification techniques requires a book to itself. Of equal importance, however, is the author's experience that readers without a mathematical background are alienated by formality and tend to reject such material as beyond their abilities. In fact, the practical advantages which result from using formal specification can be achieved without an extensive understanding of the underlying mathematics. An informal approach can illustrate the techniques to readers who are not mathematicians.

An informal approach has been chosen because the intention of these chapters is to convince the reader of the value of formal specifications and to provide some insights into how specifications are developed. We rely on the intuition and intelligence of the reader to understand the notations used and to compensate for the defects and omissions in the formality of the specifications.

One of the reasons why some software engineers have been reluctant to make use of formal specification techniques is unfamiliarity with the notations used to express the specifications. Some notations such as VDM (Jones, 1980) involve the use of a number of specialized symbols which have been invented by the author of the notation and which must be memorized before using VDM specifications. This approach leads to precision but involves a significant learning effort before reading or writing specifications.

By contrast, Larch (Guttag *et al.*, 1985) incorporates a mnemonic notation rather than specialized symbols. This is less alien to many software engineers, particularly if they are not used to learning new mathematical notations. It has the further advantage that it may be typed using a standard keyboard.

In this chapter, and in the following chapter, a mnemonic notation is used because no particular notation developed elsewhere in the example specifications is used. The reader's intuition is relied on to understand the notations used. However, the excellent device used in the Z specification language (Hayes, 1987) of using graphics to structure specifications is adopted. This vastly improves the readability of a specification and has the additional advantage of encouraging the specifier to develop the specification in an incremental way. Examples of this structuring are shown in the following section.

In Chapter 9, however, the specification language Z is used as a basis for describing model-based specifications. Because this is an established language, its mathematical notation is used.

It is only possible in a few short chapters to discuss the specifications of small systems and, inevitably, these concern more detailed components than those discussed in previous chapters. It is possible to use formal specifications for larger systems but the key to success in this is to break the system into fine-grain components.

7.2   Developing a simple formal specification

Perhaps the simplest form of formal specification is axiomatic specification where a system is represented as a set of functions (which are stateless) and each function is specified using pre- and post-conditions. In practice, this is usually possible only with small systems or with system components. Large systems almost always have some state and this technique is not appropriate in such circumstances.

Pre- and post-conditions are predicates over the inputs and outputs of a function. A predicate is simply a boolean expression which is *true* or *false* and whose variables are the parameters of the function being specified.

As well as operators such as =, >=, <=, not, and, or, etc., predicates may also include quantifiers which allow the predicate to be applied to all members of a collection (**for_all**) and to a particular member of a collection (**exists**). These are the universal and existential quantifiers ($\forall$ and $\exists$) used in set theory. The operator **in** is used to select the range over which the quantifier applies. It is analogous to the operator $\in$ used in set theory but applies to arrays as well as sets.

> 1. $A > B$ and $C > D$
>
> 2. exists i, j, k in M..N: $i^2 = j^2 + k^2$
>
> 3. for_all i in 1..10, exists j in 1..10: Squares $(i) = j^2$

Figure 7.4
Predicate examples.

Examples of predicates are shown in Figure 7.4. The first predicate, '$A > B$ **and** $C > D$', states that the value of variable A is greater than the value of B and the value of variable C is greater than that of D. If this is the case when the variables are evaluated, the predicate is true; otherwise it is false.

The predicate '**exists** i, j, k **in** M..N: $i^2 = j^2 + k^2$' illustrates the use of the **exists** quantifier. Given that i, j, and k are integers, it is true if there are values of i, j and k between M and N such that $i^2 = j^2 + k^2$. Thus, if M is 1 and N is 5, the predicate is true as $3^2+4^2=5^2$. If M is 6 and N is 10, the predicate is false as there are no values between 6 and 10 which satisfy this condition.

The predicate '**for_all** i **in** 1..10, **exists** j **in** 1..10: Squares $(i) = j^2$' illustrates the use of the universal quantifier **for_all**. This predicate concerns the values of an array called Squares. It is true if the first ten values in the array are the squares of the integers between 1 and 10.

The development of an axiomatic specification of a function involves a number of stages:

(1) Establish the range of the input parameters over which the function is intended to behave correctly. Specify the input parameter constraints as a predicate.

(2) Specify a predicate defining a condition which must hold on the output of the function if it behaves correctly.

(3) Establish what changes (if any) are made to the function's input parameters and specify these. Of course, a pure mathematical function shouldn't change its inputs but programming languages usually allow function inputs to be modified by passing them by reference.

(4) Combine these into pre- and post-conditions for the function.

As an example, consider a function Search which accepts an array of integers and some integer key as its parameters. The function returns the array index of the member of the array whose value is equal to that of the key. The original input array is unchanged. Assume that the function is defined as follows:

```
function Search ( X: in INTEGER_ARRAY; Key: INTEGER )
            return INTEGER ;
```

The post-condition must refer to the value returned by the function but in this declaration this is anonymous. For convenience, the convention that the name of the function refers to the value returned by the function in predicates is used.

(1)   In order for the function to return a correct output, it must be true that one of the array elements matches the key. The pre-condition therefore states that there must exist some element (called i here) whose value matches an element in the array. Assume that the attributes FIRST and LAST (predefined in Ada) refer to the lower and upper bounds of the array.

exists i **in** (X'FIRST..X'LAST): X (i) = Key

(2)   The function is intended to return the value of the index of the element equal to the key. This can be simply expressed as a predicate using the function name to refer to the returned value. The notation X" refers to the value of the array X after the function has been evaluated.

X" (Search (X, Key)) = Key

(3)   It is not enough simply to specify that a particular value of the array matches the key if that can be achieved by modifying the input array. The specifier must also state that the input is unchanged by the function. Of course, in many programming languages (like Ada or Pascal) this is achieved by passing the function parameters by value rather than by reference.

X = X"

Thus, pre- and post-conditions for the function Search can be written as shown in Figure 7.5.

Now consider a situation where the input array is ordered. This is potentially valuable information to the designer of the algorithm as it allows an efficient binary search algorithm to be used. The ordering of the

```
function Search (X: INTEGER_ARRAY ; Key: INTEGER)
        return INTEGER;

Pre: exists i in X'FIRST..X'LAST: X li) = Key

Post: X" (Search (X, Key)) = Key and
        X = X"
```

Figure 7.5
Specification of the function Search.

> function Search (X: INTEGER_ARRAY ; Key: INTEGER)
>   return INTEGER;
>
> Pre: exists i in X'FIRST..X'LAST: X (i) = Key and
>   for_all i, j in X'FIRST..X'LAST: i < j $\Rightarrow$ X (i) $\leq$ X (j)
>
> Post: X" (Search (X, Key)) = Key and X = X"

Figure 7.6
Specification of Search
with ordered input array.

input can be expressed stating that each array element is either less than or equal to its successor:

for_all i, j **in** X'FIRST..X'LAST: i $\leq$ j $\Rightarrow$ X (i) $\leq$ X (j)

The clause states that for all values which may be referenced in the array, if the index of one value is less than the index of another, this implies that the value of the first is less than the value of the second. The specification of the function now includes an additional clause in the pre-condition (Figure 7.6).

This specification is moderately readable but imagine if a function took a number of arrays as input parameters and it was necessary to write similar predicates applying to each of them. The condition would rapidly increase in size and decline in readability. To counteract this, predicates can be named and parameterized. For example, a predicate called Ordered might be defined as follows:

Ordered (X: INTEGER_ARRAY) =
    for_all i, j **in** X'FIRST..X'LAST: i $\leq$ j $\Rightarrow$ X (i) $\leq$ X (j)

Large specifications are hard to understand so it is important that a specification language contains structuring facilities which allows specifications to be developed incrementally. One of the difficulties with currently used specification languages is their lack of facilities for structuring a specification and this is a problem which must be tackled to make these languages usable in practical software development.

The pre-condition states the condition which must hold if the post-condition is to be valid, but a specification should also set out the behaviour of a component if it is presented with unexpected input. In the above example, how should the function Search behave if there are no array elements that match the input key?

One possible approach to error specification is to have a number of pre/post-condition pairs depending on the number of possible erroneous input ranges. In the case of Search, if the pre-condition is not satisfied, an error predicate can be included. This sets out the post-condition which

```
function Search (X: INTEGER_ARRAY ; Key: INTEGER)
                 return INTEGER;

Pre: exists i in X'FIRST..X'LAST: X (i) = Key

Post: X" (Search (X, Key)) = Key and X = X"

Error: Search (X, Key) = X'LAST + 1
```

Figure 7.7
Specification of Search
with error predicate.

holds in the event of the pre-condition being false. Thus, the revised specification of Search which takes input errors into account is defined in Figure 7.7. Here we see that the error is indicated by returning an integer value which is greater than the value of the upper bound of the array. Thus, the user of search can test the value returned to see if the operation has been successful.

This form of error indication is possible in some cases but is not generally satisfactory. The problem is that the type signature of Search is such that it *must* evaluate to an integer. In fact, it should really evaluate to a tuple where one value is an integer setting out the key matching the index and the error is an error state indicator which is set true if the pre-condition is satisfied. Following chapters return to the problem of specification of error states and show an alternative way of handling error conditions.

This simple problem has been considered at length to illustrate the steps involved in creating a formal specification. These are a consideration of the conditions under which the software component behaves as anticipated, erroneous input conditions, the outputs of a component when presented with erroneous input, the input transformations and the effect on the input parameters of a component. These must be considered in any specification scheme.

KEY POINTS

- Formal system specification is complementary to informal specification techniques.

- Formal specifications are often more concise than equivalent informal specifications.

- Formal specifications are precise and unambiguous. They remove areas of doubt in a specification.

- The principal value of using formal specification techniques in the software process is that it forces an analysis of the system requirements at an early stage. Correcting errors at this stage is cheaper than modifying a delivered system.

- The adoption of formal specification techniques requires some training costs but they can be applied in the development of non-trivial systems.

Further reading

The Specification of Complex Systems. This is an excellent introduction to formal specification techniques by some of the pioneers of the industrial application of formal specification techniques. As well as being relevant reading for this chapter, it is also very useful reading for the remaining chapters on algebraic and model-based specification techniques. (B. Cohen, W.T. Harwood and M.I. Jackson, 1986, Addison-Wesley.)

References

Earl, A.N., Whittington, R.P., Hitchcock, P. and Hall, A. (1986), 'Specifying a semantic model for use in an integrated project support environment', In *Software Engineering Environments*, Sommerville, I. (ed.), London: Peter Peregrinus.

Hayes, I.J. (1986), 'Specification directed module testing', *IEEE Trans. Software Eng.*, **SE-12** (1), 124–33.

Guttag, J.V., Horning, J.J. and Wing, J.M. (1985), 'The Larch family of specification languages', *IEEE Software*, **2** (5), 24–36.

Hayes, I. (ed.) (1987), *Specification Case Studies*, London: Prentice-Hall.

Jones, C.B. (1980), *Software Development – A Rigorous Approach*, London: Prentice-Hall.

Morgan, C. and Sufrin, B. (1984), 'Specification of the UNIX filing system', *IEEE Trans. Software Eng.*, **SE-10** (2), 128–42.

EXERCISES

7.1 You have been given the task of 'selling' formal specification techniques to a software development organization. Outline how you would go about explaining the advantages of formal specifications and countering the problems which might be suggested.

7.2 Write predicates to express the following English language statements.

- There exists an array of 100 sensors and associated control valves. Sensors can take the values high and low and the control valves can be in state open or closed. If a sensor reading is high, the state of the control valve is closed.

- In an array of integers, there is at least one value in that array which is negative.

- In a collection of natural numbers, the lowest number is 20 and the largest number is greater than 250.

- Given a collection of processes which have an integer attribute called DELAY and which may be in states running, waiting or stopped, there is no process which is waiting and whose value of DELAY exceeds 2.

7.3 Write pre- and post-conditions for a function which finds the minimum value in an array of integers.

7.4 Write pre- and post-conditions to define a function called Run_process which acts on a process of the form discussed in Example 7.2. Run_process takes a process identifier as an example and, if the process is waiting, changes its state to running and modifies the DELAY attribute accordingly.

7.5 Write pre- and post-conditions for a function which sorts an array. You may assume the existence of a predicate called PERM which takes two arrays as its parameters and returns true if one is a permutation of the other.

7.6 Write pre- and post-conditions for a function which creates an array where the value of an element whose index is i is i^2.

Chapter 8

Algebraic Specification

Objective

The objective of this chapter is to introduce a specification technique where the actions on an object are specified in terms of their relationships. This is particularly appropriate when used in conjunction with an object-oriented approach to design as it allows the object classes to be formally specified. The introduction to the chapter describes the technique of algebraic specification and it is illustrated by a comprehensive example showing its application to the specification of abstract data types. As a practical illustration of its utility, part of the specification of the design editing system introduced in earlier chapters is also included.

Contents

Algebraic specification is a technique whereby an object is specified in terms of the relationships between the operations that act on that object. It was first brought to prominence by Guttag (1977) in the specification of abstract data types but, since then, the technique has been extended into a general-purpose approach to system specification.

The technique is easiest to understand when the objects specified correspond to abstract data types in some programming language and we shall concentrate on this form of specification here. For an example of a broader system specification using this approach, readers are referred to Cohen *et al.* (1986) who specify a document retrieval system.

There are various notations for algebraic specification which have been developed such as OBJ (Futatsugi *et al.*, 1985) and Larch (Guttag *et al.*, 1985). These are comprehensive notations and space does not permit a description of them here. Rather, a simple notation is used which structures the specification using graphical highlighting (Figure 8.1).

A specification is presented in four parts: an introduction part where the sort of the entity being specified is introduced and the names of any other specifications which are required are set out; an informal description of the sort and its operations; a signature part where the names of the operations on that object and the sorts of their parameters are defined; and an axioms part where the relationships between the sort operations are defined. The name part of a specification can include a generic parameter which is the name of a generic sort. This is explained in Section 8.1.

Loosely, a sort is equivalent to a type in Pascal or Ada. In fact, they are not strictly identical as a sort is the name of a set of objects whereas types in Pascal or Ada are rather different. However, sorts are represented as types in the implementation of a specification and it is often convenient to consider them the same thing.

The introduction part of a specification also includes an **imports** part which names the other specifications which are required in a specification. Importing these specifications makes the defined sorts and their operations available. In general, these operations are simply referenced directly. Names of operations used in imported specifications may be the same as names defined in a specification in which case the name of the imported specification is used to make clear which operation is used.

For example, say a specification called ZONE (Figure 8.12) defines an operation called Create and imports a specification called COORD (Figure 8.2) where an operation with the same name is defined. Within Zone, the name Create refers to the name of the operation which creates an entity of sort Zone. To refer to the operation that creates entities of sort Coord, a dot notation is used as in Ada packages. Thus COORD.Create refers to the operation Create defined in the specification COORD.

The description part of a specification supplements the formal text with an informal description and the signature part sets out the names of the operations which are defined over the sort, the number and sorts of their

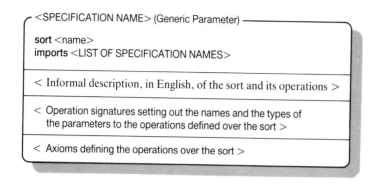

Figure 8.1
The format of an algebraic specification.

parameters and the sort of the result of evaluating the operation. The axioms part defines the operations in terms of their relationships with each other.

Generally, operations fall into two classes:

- *Constructor operations*   Operations that create or modify entities of the sort which is defined in the specification. Typically, these are given names such as Create, Update, Add, etc.

- *Inspection operations*   Operations that evaluate attributes of the sort which is defined in the specification. Typically, these are given names which correspond to attribute names or names such as Eval, Get, etc.

A good rule of thumb which can be used to construct an algebraic specification is to establish the constructor operations and write down an axiom for each inspection operation over each constructor. This suggests that if there are m constructor operations and n inspection operations there should be $m*n$ axioms defined. However, it is sometimes possible to reduce this number of axioms which are required by defining constructors in terms of more primitive constructor operations. This is discussed later in the chapter.

An example of a simple algebraic specification is shown in Figure 8.2 where a sort called Coord is defined. Such a sort might be required in a graphics package. The only operations are to create a coordinate, test coordinates for equality and access the X and Y components.

The specification of Coord imports specifications called BOOLEAN and INTEGER. Assume these define sorts called Boolean and Integer which have their normal intuitive meaning and operations. Notice that in the specification of the Eq operation the operator '=' is overloaded. It is used to separate the left and right sides of the equation and is also used on the right side to compare integers for equality. In principle, this latter use should have been referenced as INTEGER.= but this is so cumbersome that it reduces the readability of the specification. We rely on readers' common sense to understand the meaning of '=' in such situations.

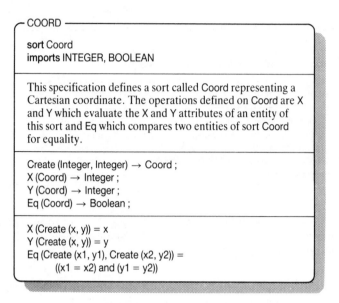

Figure 8.2
The specification of
Coord.

It is usually possible to implement algebraic specifications as an Ada package defining an abstract data type. Example 8.1 shows the package specification (in the Ada sense) for COORD, defined in Figure 8.2. Notice that the type within the package is simply named T. This is meaningful when used in conjunction with the package name as it is referenced as Coord.T.

Example 8.1
An Ada package
specification of Coord.

```
package Coord is
    type T is private ;
    function Create (X, Y: INTEGER) return T ;
    function X (C: T) return INTEGER ;
    function Y (C: T ) return INTEGER ;
    function Eq (C1, C2: T) return BOOLEAN ;
private
    type T is record
        X_pos: INTEGER ;
        Y_pos: INTEGER ;
    end record ;
end Coord ;
```

8.1 The specification of abstract data types

When using algebraic specification, normal practice is to define libraries of specifications of simple sorts such as arrays, lists, queues, etc., and use these as the basis for constructing more complex specifications. Because these simple sorts are probably familiar to readers of this book, discussing their specifications is a good way of illustrating algebraic specification in general. Although it is not always straightforward to use this technique in practical systems (discussed later in this chapter), the basic techniques used for specifying more complex sorts are those illustrated in this section.

We start with a specification of an array, a generic abstract data type which is provided in almost all programming languages. It is considered an abstract data type (although it is not defined as such in Pascal, Ada or most other languages) because it has a restricted set of allowed operations. It is a generic type because the elements of an array can usually be of any other type and, in Pascal or Ada, the array type is instantiated to a more specialized type where the array element type is specified.

The specification of a generic array with operations to create the array, discover the lower and upper bounds, find the value of an array element and assign a value to an array element is set out in Figure 8.3. The specification is parameterized (in Ada terms, it defines a generic) in that it defines arrays of any type Elem. This parameterization facility is important because it is unacceptable to have to specify every single array with different sorts of elements. However, following the notation used in Cohen *et al.* (1986), the generic parameter is of type Elem meaning, in essence, any element type. This is set out initially in the introductory part of the specification, following the name of the specification.

Introducing a generic name means that the specifier can make no assumptions about the operations which are defined on that generic type. Sometimes, however, it is necessary to use operations defined over the generic type in the specification. In this case, the operations required in the specification must also be set out in the introductory part. In Figure 8.3, it is required that an operation called Undefined which evaluates to Elem is provided for the generic type. This is a constant operation (always returns the same value) and it is used to represent the notion that an entity of type Elem has not been given a defined value. Of course, the instantiation of the generic type will have other defined operations, but these are not of interest here.

In the definition of Array, the constructor operations are Create which brings an array into existence and Assign which assigns a value to an array element. The access operations are First and Last which return the lower and upper array bounds and Eval which is used to determine the value of a particular array element.

```
┌─ ARRAY (Elem: [Undefined → Elem]) ──────────────────────┐
│                                                          │
│  sort Array                                              │
│  imports INTEGER                                         │
│                                                          │
├──────────────────────────────────────────────────────────┤
│  This specification defines arrays as collections of     │
│  elements of generic type Elem. Arrays have a lower and  │
│  upper bound (discovered by the operations First and     │
│  Last) and individual elements are accessed via their    │
│  numeric index.                                          │
│      The operation Create takes the array bounds as      │
│  parameters and initializes the values of the array to   │
│  Undefined. The operation Assign creates a new array     │
│  where a particular element has been assigned a value    │
│  and the operation Eval reveals the value of a specific  │
│  element.                                                │
├──────────────────────────────────────────────────────────┤
│  Create (Integer, Integer) → Array                       │
│  Assign (Array, Integer, Elem) → Array                   │
│  First (Array) → Integer                                 │
│  Last (Array) → Integer                                  │
│  Eval (Array, Integer) → Elem                            │
├──────────────────────────────────────────────────────────┤
│  First (Create (x, y)) = x                               │
│  First (Assign (a, n, v)) = First (a)                    │
│  Last (Create (x, y)) = y                                │
│  Last (Assign (a, n, v)) = Last (a)                      │
│  Eval (Create (x, y), n) = Undefined                     │
│  Eval (Assign (a, n, v), m) = if m = n then v else Eval (a, m) │
└──────────────────────────────────────────────────────────┘
```

Figure 8.3
The specification of sort Array.

Given three access operations and two constructor operations, six equations are used to define the abstract array. The specification here is simplified in that it makes no allowance for an access to an array element whose index is outside the array bounds. This can be seen in the Eval operation, which does not check if the element to be accessed falls within the bounds of the array.

The specifications show that the First and Last operations return the bounds of the array as set out in the Create operation, that assigning a value does not change the array size and that the value of an array element is whatever value has been previously assigned to that element. If no value has been assigned, the operation evaluates to Undefined. Thus Create initializes all elements of the array to the value Undefined.

A further example of the algebraic specification technique is shown in Figure 8.4, where a simple list is specified. Lists are commonly used in implementing other data structures and, as we shall see later, the specification set out in Figure 8.4 can be used in the creation of new specifications.

```
┌─ LIST(Elem: [Undefined → Elem]) ─────────────────────────┐
│                                                           │
│  sort List                                                │
│  imports INTEGER                                          │
│ ┌───────────────────────────────────────────────────────┐│
│ │ This specification defines a list where elements are   ││
│ │ added at one end and are removed from the other end.   ││
│ │    The defined operations are: Create, which brings a  ││
│ │ list (initially with no members) into existence; Cons, ││
│ │ which creates a new list with an additional member     ││
│ │ added to the end; Length, which evaluates the list     ││
│ │ size; Head, which evaluates the front element of the   ││
│ │ list; and Tail, which evaluates to a new list with the ││
│ │ head element removed.                                  ││
│ ├───────────────────────────────────────────────────────┤│
│ │ Create → List                                          ││
│ │ Cons (List, Elem) → List                               ││
│ │ Tail (List) → List                                     ││
│ │ Head (List) → Elem                                     ││
│ │ Length (List) → Integer                                ││
│ ├───────────────────────────────────────────────────────┤│
│ │ Head (Create) = Undefined --Error to evaluate an       ││
│ │                             empty list                 ││
│ │ Head (Cons (L, v)) = if L = Create then v else Head (L)││
│ │ Length (Create) = 0                                    ││
│ │ Length (Cons (L, v)) = Length (L) + 1                  ││
│ │ Tail (Create) = Create                                 ││
│ │ Tail (Cons (L, v)) = if L = Create then Create else    ││
│ │                      Cons (Tail (L), v)                ││
│ └───────────────────────────────────────────────────────┘│
└───────────────────────────────────────────────────────────┘
```

Figure 8.4
The specification of sort List.

The constructor operations are Create, Cons and Tail. The access operations are Head and Length. However, it is possible to specify the Tail operation in terms of the other constructor operations, so it is unnecessary to define axioms over the Tail operation for the Head and Length operations.

Notice that attempting to evaluate the head of an empty list results in an Undefined value being returned. The combination of the specifications of Head and Tail show that head evaluates the front of the list and Tail evaluates to the input list with its head removed. Note that the specification of Head states that the head of a list created using Cons is either the value added to the list (if the initial list is empty) or the same as the head of the initial list parameter to Cons. Thus, adding an element to a list does not affect its head unless the list is empty.

The definition of the Tail operation is a recursive one and this is a very common technique used in constructing algebraic specifications. It may not be intuitively obvious that this specifies that the value resulting from the Tail operation is the list which results from taking the input list and removing its head. However, an example may clarify the operation specification.

Say we have a list [5, 7] where 5 is the front of the list and 7 the end of the list. The operation Cons ([5, 7], 9) should return a list [5, 7, 9] and a Tail operation applied to this should return the list [7, 9]. Consider now the sequence of equations that results from replacing the parameters in the above specification with these values.

```
Tail ([5, 7, 9]) =
 Tail (Cons ( [5, 7], 9)) =
  Cons (Tail ([5, 7]), 9) =
   Cons (Tail (Cons ([5], 7)), 9) =
    Cons (Cons (Tail ([5]), 7), 9) =
     Cons (Cons (Tail (Cons ([], 5)), 7), 9) =
      Cons (Cons ([Create], 7), 9) =
       Cons ([7], 9) =
        [7, 9]
```

The systematic rewriting of the axiom for Tail illustrates that it does indeed produce the anticipated result. Readers are invited to verify the axiom for Head using a similar approach.

It is convenient to handle errors in a specification by introducing distinguished undefined values but it is not always easy to implement such values. In fact, few programming languages support the notion of such distinguished values and an alternative approach must be adopted by the implementor.

One such alternative is to implement the operations on an abstract type as procedures and to return an error indicator with each procedure. If the operation succeeds, this indicator is set to Success, otherwise it is set to Failure. The calling procedure may then test the value of the error indicator to discover whether or not the operation has been successful.

This is illustrated in the Ada package specification defining a list below. Notice that this is a generic package so that the elements of the list may be of any type, reflecting the genericity of the specification. Again, the type is simply named T but, when combined with the package name, the readable name List.T results.

```
generic
    -- A private generic type means assignment and equality must be
    -- defined on that type
    type Elem is private ;
package List is
    type T is private ;
    procedure Head (L: T ; V: out Elem ;
                    Err: out ERROR_INDICATOR);
    -- Length can't fail so no need for error indicator
    function Length (L: T) return NATURAL ;
    procedure Tail (L: T ; Err: out ERROR_INDICATOR ) ;
    -- Cons can't fail so no need for error indicator
    function Cons (L: T ; V: Elem ) return T ;
private
```

```
      - - An Ada access type corresponds to a Pascal pointer
      - - The entity referenced by the pointer is defined in the package
      - - body
      - - In this case, it would be a record with one field pointing to the next
      - - list element
      type List_elem ;
      type T is access List_elem ;
   end List ;
```

One of the difficulties in the practical application of formal specification is ensuring the correspondence between the specification and its implementation. The concrete syntax of the programming language and the specification language may be different and it may be necessary to use techniques such as that used in the List implementation to support undefined values. Some mechanism which helps map the specification into an implementation and which will allow readers to see the relationships between the specification and its implementation is required.

There have been two different mechanisms used to assist with relating a specification and its implementation. The first of these is to extend the programming language with specification primitives. This is typified by Anna (Luckham and Von Henke, 1985), which allows Ada programs to be annotated with specifications. An alternative approach is taken in the Larch specification language (Guttag *et al.*, 1985), where a specification is made up of a language-independent and a language-dependent part with a different language-dependent part for each implementation language. As this chapter is more concerned with abstract specifications, this problem is not discussed further here.

I have already alluded to the importance of constructing specifications incrementally and the algebraic approach may be used in this manner. Figure 8.6 illustrates the definition of a sort New_List which is an enriched version of the sort List defined in Figure 8.4. Enrichment is a mechanism that allows specifications to be structured and built out of existing specifications. The sort New_List inherits the operations and axioms defined on List so that these also apply to that sort. In essence, they could be included in the specification NEW_LIST with the name List replaced by New_List. Thus, the operations defined over New_List are set out in Figure 8.5.

```
Create → New_List
Cons (New_List, Elem) → New_List
Head (New_List) → Elem
Tail (New_List) → New_List
Add (New_List, Elem) → New_List
Member (New_List, Elem) → Boolean
Length (New_List) → Integer
```

Figure 8.5
The operations on sort New_List.

```
┌─NEW_LIST (Elem: [Undefined → Elem; .==. → Boolean])──────────
│
│   sort New_List enrich List
│   imports INTEGER, BOOLEAN
│   ─────────────────────────────────────────────────────────
│   This specification defines a list which inherits the operations and
│   properties of the simpler specifications of List and which adds new
│   operations to these.
│       The new operations are Add which adds an element to the
│   front of the list (cf Cons, which adds to the end) and Member
│   which, given a value, tests if the list contains an element matching
│   that value.
│   ─────────────────────────────────────────────────────────
│   Add (New_List, Elem) → New_List
│   Member (New_List, Elem) → Boolean
│   ─────────────────────────────────────────────────────────
│   Member (Create, v) = FALSE
│   Member (Add (L, v), v1) = ((v == v1) or Member (L, v1))
│   Member (Cons (L, v), v1) = ((v == v1) or Member (L, v1))
│   Head (Add (L, v)) = v
│   Tail (Add (L, v)) = L
│   Length (Add (L, v)) = Length (L) + 1
│   Add (Create, v) = Cons (Create, v)
└──────────────────────────────────────────────────────────────
```

Figure 8.6
The specification of an
enhanced List.

Enrichment simply involves inheriting the properties of a sort and is not the same as inheriting a specification with its generic part, its imports part, etc. However, the name of the generic is inherited and it is a requirement that a generic parameter in an enriched specification must include at least the same operations as were previously required. The generic part must be repeated in the specification and, in this case, has been extended over that set out in the specification of List. The parameterization of NEW_LIST includes the equality operation '=='. The notation .==. (Elem, Elem) means that '==' is an infix operator with operands of type Elem. It evaluates to true if its operands are equal, where the precise notion of equality depends on the sort of the entities to which the operator is applied.

The operations added in the specification of New_List are an Add operation which adds an element to the front of the list and a Member operation which tests if a given value is contained in the list. To complete the specification the access operations Head, Tail and Member must be defined over the new constructor (Add) and Member must be specified over previously defined constructor operations.

This process of enrichment can be continued. Say it is intended to specify an ordered list where the values in the list are held in descending order. Thus, the operation to insert a value into the list may place that value at the beginning, in the middle or at the end of the list. Assume also that an operation Remove is required which takes an element from the ordered list, maintaining the ordering. The operations on this sort are set out in Figure 8.7.

```
Create → Ordered_List
Insert (Ordered_List, Elem) → Ordered_List
Remove (Ordered_List, Elem) → Ordered_List
Head (Ordered_List) → Elem
Tail (Ordered_List) → Ordered_List
Member (Ordered_List, Elem) → Boolean
Length (Ordered_List) → Integer
```

Figure 8.7
The operations on sort Ordered_List.

The operations shown in Figure 8.7 do not include the constructor operations Add and Cons which were defined over the sort New_List. The reason for this is that, if these operations were included, it could not be guaranteed that the ordering of the list would always be maintained. The enrichment clause in Figure 8.8 therefore incorporates an **excluding** part which sets out the operations that are not inherited by Ordered_List.

Figure 8.8 shows a specification for the sort Ordered_List. Notice that the generic parameter Elem must have an operation .>. (greater than) which allow comparisons to be made. The 'greater than' operator compares two elements and evaluates to true if its left-hand operand is greater than its right-hand operand. The precise meaning of 'greater than' depends on the actual parameter sort. For example, for integers, the operator

```
ORD_LIST ( Elem: [Undefined → Elem; .==. → Boolean;
                               .>. → Boolean ] )

sort Ordered_List enrich New_List excluding (Cons, Add)
imports INTEGER, BOOLEAN

This specification defines a list in which the members are arranged
in descending order. It is an enrichment of sort New_List which
means that it inherits its operations but the Cons and Add operations
must be hidden to make sure that ordering is not compromised.
They are replaced by a constructor operation called Insert which
inserts a member into the correct position in the ordering.
   A new operation, Remove, which removes a list member
matching the given parameter, is defined.

Insert (Ordered_List, Elem) → Ordered_List
Remove (Ordered_List, Elem) → Ordered_List

Head (Insert (Create, v)) = v
Tail (Insert (Create, v)) = Create
Head (Insert (L, v)) = if v > Head (L) then v else Head (L)
Tail (Insert (L, v)) = if v > Head (L) then L else Insert (Tail (L), v)
Member (Insert (L, v), v1) = (v == v1) or Member (L, v1)
Length (Insert (L, v)) = Length (L) + 1
Remove (Create, v) = Create
Remove (Insert (L, v), v1) = if v == v1 then L else
                               Insert (Remove (L, v1), v)
```

Figure 8.8
The specification of an ordered list.

Create → Queue
Cons (Queue, Elem) → Queue
Head (Queue) → Elem
Tail (Queue) → Queue
Length (Queue) → Integer
Get (Queue) → (Elem, Queue)

Figure 8.9
The operations on sort
Queue.

should have its usual meaning but, for other sorts, ordering may be arbitrary.

The definitions of the Head and Tail operations show the list is ordered. Only if a value inserted in the list is greater than the head of the list is that value the result of the head operation. Similarly, if the value inserted is greater than the list head, the Tail operation returns the original list without the inserted value. Insertion in the correct place is guaranteed because inserting an element into an empty list makes a new singleton list. The Remove operation is defined in terms of the Create and Insert constructor operations. It specifies that only a value which is equal to a value previously inserted into the list may be removed.

In the above examples of specifications, the operations on a sort have been shown as functions which evaluate to a single value. In many cases, this is a reasonable model of the system which is being specified. However, there are some classes of operation which, when implemented, involve modifying more than one entity. For example, the familiar stack pop operation returns a value from a stack and also removes the top element from the stack.

It is, of course, possible to model such operations using multiple simpler operations, but a more natural approach is to define operations that return a tuple rather than a single value. Thus, the stack pop operation might have the signature:

Pop (Stack) → (Elem, Stack)

Rather than returning a single value, the function has multiple output values. This is illustrated in a specification of a queue which can be specified as an enrichment of sort List with an added operation called Get which evaluates to a pair consisting of the first item on the queue and the queue minus its head. The operations on sort Queue are shown in Figure 8.9 and the queue specification in Figure 8.10.

QUEUE (Elem: [Undefined → Elem])

sort Queue **enrich** List
imports INTEGER

This specification defines a queue which is a first-in, first-out data structure. It can therefore be specified as a List where the cons operation adds a member to the end of the queue.

    However, an operation called Get is required which evaluates the head of the queue and, at the same time, creates a new queue consisting of the tail of the input queue. Thus, the output from this function is specified as a tuple.

Get (Queue) → (Elem, Queue)

Get (Create) = (Undefined, Create)
Get (Cons (Q, v)) = (Head (Q), Tail (Cons (Q, v)))

Figure 8.10
The specification of a queue.

8.2   Design editor specification

In previous chapters a design editing system has been used as a source of examples. The interface between this editor and the underlying data store was designed as a set of abstract data types and these were algebraically specified. This interface, called the abstract data interface (ADI), represents a portability interface for the editor (Figure 8.11). To move the editor to another system, it must be re-implemented on that system.

    The ADI is made up of a number of abstract types such as Node, representing a node on a design, Link, representing a link, and Label, representing an annotation to the design. Nodes and Labels are deemed to

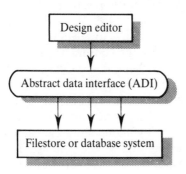

Figure 8.11
The design editor architecture.

exist within rectangular areas on the design diagram called zones, where a zone has a position, length and height. Part of this was discussed as the logical data model in Chapter 4.

The editor user can point at an entity on the design diagram using the mouse, click the mouse button, and hence select the entity. Once an entity has been selected, a range of operations such as Translate, Resize, TextEdit on the entity is allowed. Selection is detected by taking the coordinate of the mouse click and finding the zone that contains this coordinate. Thus, the operations on zones must include a way of checking that a coordinate lies within a zone. The Translate operation is supported directly with a zone operation, as is the Resize operation. Other operations such as TextEdit are not supported directly through the ADI.

The algebraic specification of a zone is shown in Figure 8.12. Note that an Undefined operation is provided (evaluating to a zone at the origin with zero length and height) and the Contains operations tells us that the zone position is the position of its top left corner. We also define an ordering operation '>'. Arbitrarily, zone Z1 is deemed to be '>' zone Z2 if the X-coordinate of Z1 is greater than the X-coordinate of Z2. If the X-coordinates of zones are the same, the zone with the shortest height is deemed to be the greater of the two zones. This operator is included in the specification of zone because we wish to specify the collection of zones as an ordered list (Figure 8.14).

In the editing system, actions are object-oriented. An object on the display is selected by pointing at it with the mouse and clicking on that object. This causes it to be highlighted and subsequent operations act on the selected object. In the system implementation, the effect of select is to return a pointer to a zone in a list of zones and this is passed to subsequent operations.

Pointers are not available in the formal specification but the intent of a specification is to model a system and not to provide an alternative implementation. Thus, the operation of selection is modelled by identifying the zone containing a specified coordinate (the position where the mouse is clicked).

However, it is not acceptable simply to find any zone in the collection that contains the mouse position. The reason for this is obvious from Figure 8.13, which shows several overlapping zones. The intended effect of the selection operation is to select the innermost zone rather than an arbitrary zone containing the coordinate. This can be accomplished by ordering the zones in the collection according to the X-coordinate of their position and searching the zone list for a selection in such a way that the zone with the greatest X-coordinate that contains the mouse coordinate is discovered before other zones which might also contain that coordinate. This can be accomplished by maintaining the list in descending order and searching for the zone from the head of the list. The first zone found that contains the coordinate is the most deeply nested zone.

ZONE

sort Zone
imports COORD

A zone represents a rectangular area on a picture which has a position (defined as the position of its top left corner), a height and a length. The operations on entities of this sort are Position, Length and Height which evaluate the zone position, length and height respectively and Translate, Resize and Contains operations.

The Translate operation adjusts the position of a zone by moving it to the coordinate specified and the Resize operation defines a new zone with the same position but different dimensions. The height and length are unchanged. The Contains operation is used to test if an entity of type Zone encloses the specified coordinate and the equality operation (==) to test if zones are equal. The greater than operation (>) is arbitrary in that the zone with the greater X-coordinate is deemed to be the greatest. However, this definition is helpful when finding a zone in a collection.

Create (Coord, Integer, Integer) → Zone
Position (Zone) → Coord
Length (Zone) → Integer
Height (Zone) → Integer
Translate (Zone, Coord) → Zone
Resize (Zone, Integer, Integer) → Zone
Contains (Zone, Coord) → BOOLEAN
.==. (Zone, Zone) → BOOLEAN
.>. (Zone, Zone) → BOOLEAN
Undefined → Zone

Position (Create (C, l, h)) = C
Length (Create (C, l, h)) = l
Height (Create (C, l, h)) = h
Translate (Create (C, l, h), C1) = Create (C1, l, h)
Contains (Create (C, l, h), C1) = X (C1) $\geq$ X (C) and X (C1) $\leq$ X (C) + l
                    and Y (C1) $\leq$ Y (C) and Y (C1) $\geq$ Y (C) − h
.==. (Create (C, l, h), Create (C1, l1, h1)) =
          COORD.Eq (C, C1) and l = l1 and h = h1
.>. (Create (C, l, h), Create (C1, l1, h1)) = (X (C) > X (C1)) or
                    (X (C) = X (C1) and h < h1)
Undefined = Create (COORD.Create (0, 0), 0, 0)

Figure 8.12
The specification of sort Zone.

Figure 8.14 shows the specification of Zone_List as an enrichment of Ordered_List with a Select operation which examines the list starting with the head of the list. Because of the way in which the operation '>' on zones is defined, the zone with the greatest X-coordinate (the most deeply nested) will be discovered first. If zones have a common position but a different size, the zone with the least height will be discovered first.

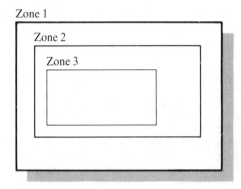

Figure 8.13
Nested zones.

Figure 8.14 also illustrates how a generic specification (Ordered_List) is instantiated to be a list of a specific type. The operator ':=' expresses the binding of the generic parameter Elem (in ORDERED_LIST) to the specific parameter Zone in the specification ZONE_LIST.

Algebraic specification was found to be a useful practical technique in the development of the design editing system although no attempt was made to verify the implementation against the specification. Its principal value was in clarifying the design of the system data interface ensuring that this was orthogonal and consistent.

Algebraic specification was appropriate in this application because the editor interface was structured as a number of abstract types where the state was concealed. As discussed in the following chapter, there are other situations where exposing state information simplifies the specification, making it more concise than a corresponding algebraic specification. Algebraic specification is not always the best technique but, it is a simple intuitive technique for specifying data abstractions.

```
┌─ ZONE_LIST (Elem := Zone) ──────────────────────────────
│
│ sort Zone_List enrich Ordered_List
│ imports Zone
├──────────────────────────────────────────────────────────
│ This specification defines a structure which holds a list of zones. It
│ is defined as an enrichment of Ordered_List but has a specific
│ operation called Select which, given a coordinate, finds the first
│ zone in the list which contains that coordinate.
├──────────────────────────────────────────────────────────
│ Select (Zone_List, Coord) → Zone
├──────────────────────────────────────────────────────────
│ Select (Create, C) = Undefined
│ Select (Insert (ZL, Z), C) = if ZONE.Contains (Head (Insert (ZL, Z)), C)
│                      then Head (Insert (ZL, Z)) else
│                            Select (Tail (Insert (ZL, Z)), C)
└──────────────────────────────────────────────────────────
```

Figure 8.14
The specification of a
Zone_List.

KEY POINTS

- Algebraic specification involves setting out the operations on an object and specifying them in terms of their relationships.

- An algebraic specification consists of two formal parts: a signature part where the operations and their parameters are set out, and an axioms part where the relationships between these operations are defined. If the specification is built using other specifications these should be indicated, and it is good practice to supplement the formal description with an informal explanation of the operations.

- Enrichment of a sort (type) is the name given to creating a new sort by inheriting the operations and axioms of an existing sort and adding new operations and axioms to it.

- Errors in operations can be specified by adding special operations called something like Undefined. These are constant operations which evaluate to the appropriate sort. In the implementation of a specification, the error can be indicated by a function returning an error flag.

- Algebraic specification is probably easiest to scale up when an object-oriented approach is taken to large systems design.

Further reading

The Specification of Complex Systems.   This excellent introductory text contains a good chapter discussing algebraic specification. A simple electronic mail system is used as an example and it is compared to the same system described using a model-based approach. (B. Cohen, W.T. Harwood and M.I. Jackson, 1986, Addison-Wesley.)

'The design of data type specifications'.   A good introduction to the specification of abstract data types. Other papers of interest are also included in the book containing this paper. (J.V. Guttag, E. Horowitz and D.R. Musser, in *Current Trends in Programming Methodology*, Vol. 4, ed. R.T. Yeh, 1978, Prentice-Hall.)

References

Cohen, B., Harwood, W.T. and Jackson, M.I. (1986), *The Specification of Complex Systems*, Wokingham: Addison-Wesley.

Futatsugi, K., Goguen, J.A., Jouannaud, J.P. and Meseguer, J. (1985), 'Principles of OBJ2', *Proc. 12th ACM Symp. on Principles of Programming Languages*, New Orleans, 52–66.

Guttag, J. (1977), 'Abstract data types and the development of data structures', *Comm. ACM,* **20** (6), 396–405.

Guttag, J.V., Horning, J.J. and Wing, J.M. (1985), 'The Larch family of specification languages', *IEEE Software*, **2** (5), 24–36.

Luckham, D. and Von Henke, F.W. (1985), 'An overview of Anna, a specification language for Ada', *IEEE Software*, **2** (2), 9–23.

EXERCISES

8.1 Explain how the technique of algebraic specification can be applied to the specification of abstract data types.

8.2 An abstract data type, Stack has the following operations:

- New: Bring a stack into existence
- Push: Add an element to the top of the stack
- Top: Evaluate the element on top of the stack
- Retract: Remove the top element from the stack and return the modified stack
- Is_empty: True if there are no elements on the stack

Write an algebraic specification of Stack. Make any reasonable assumptions you like about the semantics of the stack operations.

8.3 Modify the example presented in Figure 8.3 (array specification) by adding a new operation called ArrayUpdate which assigns all the values of one array to another array given that the arrays have the same number of elements.

8.4 An abstract data type called String has a signature defined as follows:

```
New → String
Cat (String, String) → String
Length (String) → Integer
Substr (String, Integer, Integer) → String
```

Using your intuitive model of character strings, explain in English what these operations are likely to do. Write the axioms that formally define your informal English specification.

8.5 Using the equation rewriting approach as used in Example 8.4, verify that the operation Insert ([10, 7, 4], 8) on ordered lists (Figure 8.8) causes the list [10, 8, 7, 4] to be built. (Hint: Show that the head of the list is 10 and the tail is [8, 7, 4].)

8.6 Using the same technique with values of your choice, demonstrate the Remove operation in the same specification (Figure 8.8).

8.7 Write a formal algebraic specification of a sort Symbol_table whose operations are informally defined as follows:

- Create: Bring a symbol table into existence.
- Enter: Enters a symbol and its type into the table.
  The operation fails if the name is in the table.
- Lookup: Returns the type associated with a name in the table.
  The operation fails if the name is not in the table.
- Delete: Removes a name, type pair from the table, given a name as a parameter. The operation fails if the name is not in the table.
- Replace: Replaces the type associated with a given name with the type specified as a parameter. The operation fails if the name is not in the table.

8.8 Discuss how your specification would have to be modified if a block-structured symbol table was required. A block-structured symbol table is one used in compiling a language with block structure like Pascal where declarations in an inner block override the outer block declarations if the same name is used.

8.9 Write a formal algebraic specification of the block-structured symbol table.

8.10 Using an example of your choice, demonstrate that the Lookup operation in the block-structured symbol table finds the name in the innermost block in a situation where duplicate names have been entered in the table.

8.11 Write a formal algebraic specification of a binary tree with the following informally defined operations:

- Create: Brings a binary tree into existence
- Is_empty: True if the tree is empty

- Left: Evaluates to the left subtree of the tree
- Data: Evaluates to the data held in a tree node
- Right: Evaluates the right subtree of the tree
- Contains: True if the tree contains a value matching its parameter
- Enter: Adds an element to the tree in order so that all of the elements in the left subtree of a tree have data values less than the root value and vice versa for the right subtree.

(Hint: Define a simpler constructor operation called Add which simply puts an entry into the tree and define Enter in terms of this constructor.)

If you are not familiar with binary trees, it is suggested that you consult a book on simple data structures before tackling this example.

8.12 For all of the abstract data types you have specified, write Ada package specifications defining a package to implement the abstract type. Pay particular attention to error handling.

Chapter 9

Model-Based Specification

Objectives

Algebraic specification fits well with information hiding but can impose an artificial approach for some classes of system. Model-based specification is a complementary technique where the system is modelled using mathematical entities, such as sets, whose properties are well understood. This technique is illustrated using simple examples in this chapter. The specification language used, called Z, has recognized the importance of both presentation and specification reuse. Z allows specifications to be highlighted graphically and integrated with other specifications. This chapter discusses Z schemas and how functions and sequences can be used in modelling systems. The language and specification technique is illustrated using examples.

Contents

Model-based specification is a technique that relies on formulating a model of the system using well understood mathematical entities such as sets and functions. System operations are specified by defining how they affect the overall system model. By contrast with the algebraic approach, the state of the system is exposed and a richer variety of mathematical operations is available.

Using a model-based technique, state changes are straightforward to define, all of the specification for each operation is grouped and, typically, model-based specifications are more concise than corresponding algebraic specifications.

Probably the best known model-based specification technique is VDM (Jones, 1980, 1986). However, in this text, model-based specification is illustrated using a notation called Z (pronounced Zed not Zee) which is a specification language first suggested by Abrial (1980) and later developed at the University of Oxford (Hayes, 1987). Z is based on typed set theory because sets are mathematical entities whose semantics are formally defined.

Z has been chosen as a basis for discussing model-based specification here because its authors have paid particular attention to the presentational aspects of the specification. Formal specifications can be difficult and tedious to read – especially when they are presented as large mathematical formulae – and this, understandably, has inhibited many software engineers from investigating the potential of formal specifications. This has been recognized by the designers of Z and Z specifications are normally presented in small, easy-to-read chunks which are distinguished from associated commentary using graphical highlighting.

In an introductory chapter like this one, it is only possible to give an overview of how model-based specifications can be developed. One of the difficulties in presenting such an overview is the large amount of notation, and a complete description of Z notation would be almost as long as this chapter. Notation is therefore introduced as it is used and a large part of the specification language is not covered. The reader must turn to Hayes (1987) for a fuller description of Z and its uses.

In this chapter, symbolic notation rather than a mnemonic alternative is used because this is the normal way of presenting model-based specifications. Unfortunately, Z relies on a rather unusual character set and this makes typing a specification difficult on simple text preparation systems. Although this problem can be resolved using special-purpose editors, it is an unnecessary hindrance to the more widespread adoption of formal specification techniques.

9.1   Z schemas

A specification in Z is presented as a collection of schemas where a schema introduces some specification entities and sets out relationships between these entities. The developers of Z emphasize that, to be most effective, formal specification must be supplemented by a good deal of supporting, informal description, and the schema presentation has been designed so that it stands out from surrounding text (Figure 9.1).

Figure 9.1 is a specification of a container which can be filled with 'things'. Such a specification might be used in modelling a factory automation system where containers of parts are automatically filled by a computerized system.

The top line of the schema introduces the schema name and the part between this and the dividing line is called the *signature*. The signature sets out the names and types of the entities introduced in the schema. Figure 9.1 introduces two entities namely contents and capacity which are modelled as natural numbers. A natural number is an integer which is greater than or equal to zero.

The schema *predicate* (the bottom part of the specification) sets out the relationships between the entities in the signature by defining a predicate over the signature entities which must always hold. In this case, the predicate states the obvious fact that the contents cannot exceed the capacity of the container.

This specification says nothing about the size of the container or what the container is intended to hold. It merely states that it can't hold a negative number of things and that its contents are discrete. Thus, if the container was used for holding liquids, its contents could probably only be known imprecisely. In general, existing formal specification techniques are not well-suited for describing systems which rely on real, imprecise numbers, and this is an area which requires development before they can be applied in some classes of application system.

The specification in Figure 9.1 can be viewed as a building block which can be used in further specifications and we shall see shortly how this is used. Figure 9.2 shows a specification of a further building block, namely

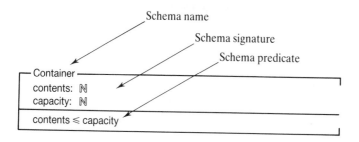

Figure 9.1
A Z schema.

```
┌─Indicator ─────────────────────────────────────────────┐
│ light: {off, on}
│ reading: ℕ
│ danger: ℕ
├─────────────────────────────────────────────────────────
│ light = on  ⟺  reading ⩽ danger
└─────────────────────────────────────────────────────────┘
```

Figure 9.2
The specification of an
indicator.

an indicator which might be associated with a container to provide information about its contents.

The signature in Figure 9.2 introduces three entities, namely light which is modelled by the values off and on, reading which is modelled as a natural number, and danger which is also modelled as a natural number. The intention is that the light and the reading might have some physical manifestation in the real system which provides an operator with information about the system. If the reading reaches some dangerous value, the light should be switched on.

Again, an indicator as specified here is a very general-purpose entity and no attempt will be made, at this stage, to specify what the danger level should be. Thus, the predicate part simply states that if the reading is less than or equal to the danger value, the value of light should be on. The symbol ⟺ means logically equivalent so that a low reading is logically equivalent to the light being on.

Given the specification of an indicator and a container, they can be combined (Figure 9.3) to define a hopper which is a type of container. We wish to define a hopper which has a capacity of 5000 'things' and whose light comes on when it is less than 10% full. Notice that again we need not specify what is held in the hopper.

The effect of combining specifications is to make a new specification which inherits the signatures and the predicates of the included specifications. Thus, hopper inherits the signatures of Container and Indicator and their predicates. These are combined with any new signatures and predicates which are introduced in the specification. In Figure 9.3, three new predicates are introduced.

These predicates are written on separate lines and an implicit 'and' separates the predicates. Thus reading equals contents and capacity equals

```
┌─Hopper ─────────────────────────────────────────────────┐
│ Container
│ Indicator
├─────────────────────────────────────────────────────────
│ reading = contents
│ capacity = 5000
│ danger = 50
└─────────────────────────────────────────────────────────┘
```

Figure 9.3
The specification of a
hopper.

```
┌─Hopper ─────────────────────────────────────────────────┐
│  contents: ℕ                                             │
│  capacity: ℕ                                             │
│  reading:  ℕ                                             │
│  danger:   ℕ                                             │
│  light: {off, on}                                        │
│ ─────────────────────────────────────────────────────── │
│  contents ≤ capacity                                     │
│  light = on⟺reading ≤ danger                             │
│  reading = contents                                      │
│  capacity = 5000                                         │
│  danger = 50                                             │
└──────────────────────────────────────────────────────────┘
```

Figure 9.4
The expanded
specification of a hopper.

5000 and danger equals 50 and the inherited predicates must hold. It is permitted to write these on the same line in which case the 'and' symbol (∧) must separate them.

Figure 9.4 shows the expanded specification of Hopper where the signatures and the predicates of Container and Indicator have been explicitly merged.

Operations can be specified using schemas in a similar way. Figure 9.5 shows the specification of an operation to fill a hopper. The fill operation adds a specified number of entities to the hopper. For the moment, we will ignore the problem of trying to add too much to the container.

Two new notions are introduced in Figure 9.5, namely:

- delta schemas and
- inputs.

In the schema named FillHopper, the name amount is suffixed by a ? character which means that it should be taken as an input to the operation. The ? is part of the name and, by convention, names whose final character is a ? are always taken to indicate inputs. As we shall see in later specifications, names which terminate with a ! symbol are operation outputs.

The predicate for FillHopper specifies that the contents after completion of the operation (referenced as contents') should equal the sum of the contents before the operation and the amount added to the hopper. In

```
┌─FillHopper ─────────────────────────────────┐
│  Δ Hopper                                    │
│  amount?: ℕ                                  │
│ ──────────────────────────────────────────── │
│  contents' = contents + amount?              │
└───────────────────────────────────────────────┘
```

Figure 9.5
The specification of the
hopper filling operation.

```
┌─ Δ Hopper ─────────────────────────────────────────────────┐
│                                                             │
│  Hopper                                                     │
│  Hopper'                                                    │
│                                                             │
└─────────────────────────────────────────────────────────────┘
```

Figure 9.6
A delta schema.

addition, the previous predicates which applied to Hopper still apply before and after the operation. By convention, the values of an entity after an operation are referenced by decorating the name of that entity with a prime mark ('). Normally, these decorated names are introduced by using a delta schema (Figure 9.6). This schema includes both the schema called Hopper and a 'decorated' Hopper schema where the names introduced in Hopper are decorated with a quote mark. Thus, the names contents', capacity', light', danger' and reading' are introduced. The predicates which apply in Hopper also apply in Hopper' and, when the delta schema is used in other schemas, they are also inherited.

The convention in writing Z specifications is to use delta schemas without definition and, when they are encountered by the reader, they indicate that the effect of the operation is likely to change one or more values. Some operations do not result in a change of value but still find it useful to reference the values before and after the operation. These cases can be catered for by incorporating a schema as defined in Figure 9.7.

Figure 9.7 (a Xi schema where Xi is the name of its initial letter) shows a schema which includes the delta schema and a predicate which states explicitly that the values are unchanged. Notice that this predicate includes an explicit 'and' operation between its components.

In the description of FillHopper given in Figure 9.5, we ignored the possibility of adding an amount to the hopper which would cause it to overflow. Of course, the constraints associated with Hopper exclude the possibility of overflow but give no clue to what should happen if an attempt is made to add too much to the hopper.

In practice, of course, a specification should take this into account and should define what should happen in the event of an overflow situation occurring. Figure 9.8 shows the specification of an operation called SafeFillHopper which includes a predicate stating that the amount added should be such that the capacity of the hopper should not be exceeded.

To supplement the specification in Figure 9.8, we must also include a specification of what happens if an attempt is made to add too much to the hopper. Let us assume that the effect of trying to overfill a hopper is to abort

```
┌─ Ξ Hopper ─────────────────────────────────────────────────┐
│                                                             │
│  Δ Hopper                                                   │
│                                                             │
├─────────────────────────────────────────────────────────────┤
│                                                             │
│  capacity = capacity'  ∧   contents = content'  ∧           │
│  reading = reading'  ∧    light = light'  ∧    danger = danger' │
│                                                             │
└─────────────────────────────────────────────────────────────┘
```

Figure 9.7
An unchanged schema.

```
┌─SafeFillHopper ──────────────────────────────────────┐
│                                                       │
│  Δ Hopper                                             │
│  amount?: ℕ                                           │
│ ──────────────────────────────────────────────────── │
│  contents + amount? ≤ capacity                        │
│  contents′ = contents + amount?                       │
│                                                       │
└───────────────────────────────────────────────────┘
```

Figure 9.8
The specification of
hopper fill operation
avoiding overflow.

the fill operation (nothing is added to the hopper) and to print a warning
message on an operator's console. This specification is shown in Figure 9.9.
Figure 9.9 introduces a name r! which refers to an output value. As indicated
above, the convention for referencing output values is to suffix them with an
exclamation mark (!). The name r! is declared to be a sequence of characters
(to hold a message) and, as before, amount? is a natural number.

```
┌─OverFillHopper ──────────────────────────────────────┐
│                                                       │
│  Δ Hopper                                             │
│  amount?: ℕ                                           │
│  r!: seq CHAR                                         │
│ ──────────────────────────────────────────────────── │
│  capacity < contents + amount?                        │
│  contents = contents′                                 │
│  r! = "Hopper overflow"                               │
│                                                       │
└───────────────────────────────────────────────────┘
```

Figure 9.9
The specification of
hopper overfilling.

The predicate associated with OverFillHopper states that it holds
when the capacity of the hopper is less than the current contents plus the
amount to be added. It also states that the contents are unchanged and that
the value r! is 'hopper overflow'. Of course, we could have incorporated an
'unchanged' schema rather than a delta schema here but this is simply a
question of style.

To complete the specification of hopper filling, SafeFillHopper and
OverFillHopper must be combined. This is shown in Figure 9.10 where the
schemas are combined using a disjunction (or) operator. The effect of this
operator is to merge the signatures of the schemas SafeFillHopper and
OverFillHopper and to combine the predicates, separating them with an 'or'
operator (Figure 9.11).

Schemas in Z are a powerful concept and other operators exist to
manipulate schemas. For example, parts of schemas can be hidden so that

```
┌─FillHopperOp ────────────────────────────────────────┐
│                                                       │
│  SafeFillHopper  ∨  OverFillHopper                    │
│                                                       │
└───────────────────────────────────────────────────┘
```

Figure 9.10
The specification of
hopper filling with error
check.

```
┌─FillHopperOp────────────────────────────────────────────────┐
│                                                              │
│  Δ Hopper                                                    │
│  amount?: ℕ                                                  │
│  r!: seq CHAR                                                │
│                                                              │
├──────────────────────────────────────────────────────────── │
│  (contents + amount? ≤ capacity                              │
│  contents' = contents + amount?)                             │
│  ∨                                                           │
│  (capacity < contents + amount?                              │
│  contents = contents'                                        │
│  r! = "Hopper overflow")                                     │
└──────────────────────────────────────────────────────────── ┘
```

Figure 9.11
Expanded specification of
FillHopperOp.

some information hiding can be practised. The reader will already have inferred that schemas can be used as type names and they can be used to identify sets. An alternative more concise form of schemas is also allowed where schemas are written linearly without graphical highlighting. These are not discussed here but they are covered in Hayes (1987).

9.2 Specification using functions

One of the most commonly used techniques in model-based specification is to use functions or mappings in writing specifications. In programming languages, a function is an abstraction over an expression. When provided with an input, it computes an output value based on the value of the input. It is possible to think of Z functions or mappings in a comparable way but they are really a set of pairs where each pair shows how an output relates to an input. A *partial function* is a function where not all possible inputs have a defined output. For example, the function SmallSquare below shows the values of the squares of the numbers from 1 to 7.

$$\text{SmallSquare} = \{1 \mapsto 1, 2 \mapsto 4, 3 \mapsto 9, 4 \mapsto 16, 5 \mapsto 25,$$
$$6 \mapsto 36, 7 \mapsto 49\}$$

Here we see that 1 is mapped onto 1, 2 to 4, 3 to 9 and so on. Hence, the term *mapping* is sometimes used. In an implementation, of course, an algorithm is used to compute the result from the input but the effect is identical to a mapping specification.

The *domain* of a function (written dom f in Z, where f is the function name) is the set of inputs over which the function has a defined result. The range of a function (written rng f in Z) is the set of results which the function can produce. A function is a *partial function* if its input is a member of some set T but its domain (those inputs which produce a result) is a subset of T.

```
┌─ DataDictionaryEntry ────────────────────────────────────────┐
│                                                              │
│  type: {process, data_flow, data_store, user_input, user_output} │
│  description: seq CHAR                                       │
│ ────────────────────────────────────────────────────────── │
│  #description ≤ 2000                                         │
└──────────────────────────────────────────────────────────────┘
```

Figure 9.12
The format of a data
dictionary entry.

If an input i is in the domain of some function f (i ∈ dom f), the associated result may be specified as f (i), that is, f (i) ∈ rng f. For example, in the function SmallSquare defined above, SmallSquare (2) = 4, SmallSquare (5) = 25 and so on. The domain and range of square are as follows:

dom SmallSquare = {1, 2, 3, 4, 5, 6, 7}
rng SmallSquare = {1, 4, 9, 16, 25, 36, 49}

Functions can be used to model data structures. For example, in Chapter 4 we introduced the notion of a data dictionary which, for each system name, held its type and a description of that type. Data dictionaries can be useful throughout the system development process but, for simplicity here, let us assume that the types in the data dictionary are those used in data-flow diagrams. The type and associated description associated with a data dictionary entry are shown in Figure 9.12. The type is constrained to be either a process, a data flow, a data store, a user input or a user output. The description is a sequence of characters and there is an arbitrary restriction here, expressed as a predicate, that this description should be less than 2000 characters in length. The operator #, applied to sequences or sets, given the number of members in the sequence or set.

This schema can be incorporated in a schema describing a data dictionary (Figure 9.13). The schema DataDictionary defines ddict to be a partial function (indicated by the tagged arrow) from NAME to DataDictionaryEntry. Given a name, the associated type and description can be discovered. Notice how the enclosure of the schema name in curly brackets defines a set.

A set called NAME has also been introduced, but not defined. The conventions of Z allow a set to be introduced without definition. This is indicated by writing its name in upper-case characters. Names, whose

```
┌─ DataDictionary ────────────────────────────────┐
│                                                  │
│  DataDictionaryEntry                             │
│  ddict: NAME ↦ {DataDictionaryEntry}             │
│                                                  │
└──────────────────────────────────────────────────┘
```

Figure 9.13
A data dictionary specified
as a mapping.

```
┌─MakeNewEntry────────────────────────────────────────────────┐
│ Δ DataDictionary                                             │
│ name?: NAME                                                  │
│ entry?: DataDictionaryEntry                                  │
├──────────────────────────────────────────────────────────────┤
│ name? ∉ dom ddict                                            │
│ ddict' = ddict ∪ {name? ↦ entry?}                            │
└──────────────────────────────────────────────────────────────┘
```

Figure 9.14
Adding an entry to the
data dictionary.

precise specification is not important at this stage, can be used without cluttering the specification with extraneous information.

Now consider the definition of operations on the data dictionary. Say we wish to define the following operations:

(1)   AddDictionary Entry This operation takes a name and a data dictionary entry as parameters. If the name is not in the data dictionary it is added to the dictionary. If the name is in the dictionary and the type in the dictionary and the type in the parameter match, the new entry is added to the data dictionary replacing the previous entry.

(2)   GetDescription Given a name, this operation evaluates the description associated with that name.

(3)   DeleteEntry Given a name, the entry associated with that name is deleted from the data dictionary.

For brevity, we do not include the specification of errors such as trying to remove a name which does not exist in the dictionary, trying to add a name with a non-matching type and so on. In a complete specification these would be included using a technique as shown in Examples 9.8 to 9.10.

The specification of AddDictionaryEntry encompasses two possibilities which are described in separate schemas (Figures 9.14 and 9.15). The signature of the schema named MakeNewEntry shows that the inputs are a name and an associated entry. A delta schema, showing that the dictionary may be modified by the operation, is also included. The predicate part states that if the input name is not a member of the domain of ddict then the name and entry should be considered as a set and the union of this set and ddict should be taken to give the value of ddict after the operation. Set union is a valid operation because a partial function is a set of pairs.

```
┌─ReplaceEntry────────────────────────────────────────────────┐
│ Δ DataDictionary                                             │
│ name?: NAME                                                  │
│ entry?: DataDictionaryEntry                                  │
├──────────────────────────────────────────────────────────────┤
│ name? ∈ dom ddict ∧ ddict (name?).type = entry?.type         │
│ ddict' = ddict ⊕ {name? ↦ entry?}                            │
└──────────────────────────────────────────────────────────────┘
```

Figure 9.15
Replacing a data
dictionary entry.

Figure 9.15 is similar and shows the specification of the operation where the name is already in the data dictionary. The predicate part states that if the name is in the domain of the function and the type associated with entry? and the type in the dictionary referenced by the name are the same, then the function overriding operator ($\oplus$) is used to replace the existing entry with the new entry. The dot notation A.B is used to reference parts of a type. Thus entry?.type refers to the type part of the entry associated with the name.

The function overriding operator is, perhaps, best illustrated with a simpler example. Say we have a function which maps names to telephone numbers.

$$phone = \{Ian \mapsto 3390, Ray \mapsto 3392, Steve \mapsto 3427\}$$

The domain of phone is {Ian, Ray, Steve} and the range is {3390, 3392, 3427}. Now assume we have another function newphone defined as follows.

$$newphone = \{Steve \mapsto 3386, Ron \mapsto 3427\}$$

The operation phone $\oplus$ newphone results in the following function:

$$phone \oplus newphone = \{Ian \mapsto 3390, Ray \mapsto 3392, Steve \mapsto 3386, Ron \mapsto 3427\}$$

Notice that a new mapping for Ron has been added and that the existing mapping for Steve has been modified. The function overriding operator acts like a set union operator if the name is not in the set. If the name is in the set, the name and its associated value are replaced.

The complete add operation is specified by a disjunction of the schemas named MakeNewEntry and ReplaceEntry (Figure 9.16).

The operation which retrieves the description associated with a name is a simple one. Its specification is shown in Figure 9.17. In the schema GetDescription, we see the use of the Xi (unchanged) schema which indicates that the operation does not change the value of the data dictionary. The predicate part specifies that if the name is in the dictionary, the description associated with that name is evaluated. Notice how the name ddict is used in the same way as a function name in a programming language, with the name acting as a parameter. It must be emphasized, however, that no computation is implied.

```
┌─AddDictionaryEntry ──────────────────────┐
│                                           │
│  MakeNewEntry ∨                           │
│  Replace Entry                            │
│                                           │
└───────────────────────────────────────────┘
```

Figure 9.16
Adding an entry to the data dictionary.

```
┌─GetDescription ──────────────────────────────────────────────┐
│                                                                │
│ Ξ DataDictionary                                               │
│ name?: NAME                                                    │
│ desc!: seq CHAR                                                │
├────────────────────────────────────────────────────────────── │
│ name? ∈ dom ddict                                              │
│ desc! = ddict (name?). description                             │
└────────────────────────────────────────────────────────────── ┘
```

Figure 9.17
Accessing a data
dictionary entry.

The operation to remove an item from the data dictionary makes use of a special operator acting on functions. This is called the domain subtraction operator which is written ◁. Using the above example of telephone numbers, if Ian is to be removed from the domain of phone, this would be written

{Ian} ◁ phone

The resulting function is:

{Ray ↦ 3392, Steve ↦ 3427}

The specification of the remove operation for the data dictionary is shown in Figure 9.18.

```
┌─DeleteEntry ─────────────────────────────────────────────────┐
│                                                                │
│ Δ DataDictionary                                               │
│ name?: NAME                                                    │
├────────────────────────────────────────────────────────────── │
│ name? ∈ dom ddict                                              │
│ ddict' = {name?} ◁ ddict                                       │
└────────────────────────────────────────────────────────────── ┘
```

Figure 9.18
Deleting a data dictionary
entry.

The domain subtraction operator removes a member from the domain of a function. The predicate in Figure 9.18 states firstly that a name must be in the data dictionary before it can be removed. After the application of the domain subtraction operator the name of the identifier to be removed is not a member of the domain of the function. Its related value in the range of the function is thus inaccessible and has been effectively removed.

9.3   Specification using sequences

The above example of a data dictionary specification modelled the data dictionary as a set with no implied ordering on the entries in the dictionary. It is more normal, perhaps, to think of a dictionary as ordered. We have already seen the sequence construct in Z when discussing output messages and this construct can be used in the specification of an ordered dictionary.

Informally, a sequence is a collection where the elements are referenced by their position in the collection. Thus if a sequence is named S, S (1) references the first element in the sequence, S (5) references the fifth element and so on. More formally, a sequence of X is a mapping where the positive integers have associated values in X and the domain of the mapping includes all integers from 1 to n. n is the length of the sequence (Figure 9.19).

```
┌─ SEQUENCE ────────────────────────────────────────────┐
│                                                        │
│  s:  ℕ⁺ ↦ ELEM                                         │
│                                                        │
├────────────────────────────────────────────────────────┤
│  ∃ n:  ℕ⁺ · dom s = 1..n                               │
└────────────────────────────────────────────────────────┘
```

Figure 9.19
Sequence definition.

To define the data dictionary as a sequence, a slightly different data dictionary entry is specified where the name is included as part of the entry (Figure 9.20). Again notice how the existing specification has been reused in creating the entry with the new format.

We can now specify a data dictionary where the entries are held in ascending order (Figure 9.21). The predicate in Figure 9.21 states that for all integers i and j in the sequence ddict, it is true that if i is less than j then the associated names are related in the same way. We assume here the existence of an ordering over entities which are members of NAME but we do not discuss this here.

The next step in the redefinition of ddict is to redefine the operations on the data dictionary and (presumably) define some operations which make use of the fact that the dictionary is ordered. These will not be covered here.

```
┌─ DataDictionaryEntry ─────────────────────────────────┐
│                                                        │
│  ident: NAME                                           │
│  type: {process, data_flow, data_store, user_input, user_output} │
│  description: seq CHAR                                  │
│                                                        │
├────────────────────────────────────────────────────────┤
│  #description ≤ 2000                                   │
└────────────────────────────────────────────────────────┘
```

Figure 9.20
Revised format for a data dictionary entry.

```
┌─NewDataDictionary ────────────────────────────────────────┐
│                                                             │
│ DataDictionaryEntry                                         │
│ ddict: seq {DataDictionaryEntry}                            │
├─────────────────────────────────────────────────────────── │
│                                                             │
│ ∀ i, j : dom ddict · (i < j) ⇒ s(i).ident < ...NAME s (j).ident │
└─────────────────────────────────────────────────────────── ┘
```

Figure 9.21
Ordered data dictionary.

This brief introduction to model-based specification has done no more than scratch the surface of the technique and there are many other defined language operations which provide tremendous power to the specifier. It is true that neither Z nor model-based specification in general is yet completely mature and widely usable as a software engineering tool. In particular, the research workers in this area have not yet tackled the problem of structuring specifications at an architectural level. Although Z's schemas are helpful, they are concerned with low-level rather than architectural structuring.

Support tools for formal specification are only just becoming available and further development of these is required.

Space does not allow the description of more complex systems here but recent work on the specification of a software engineering environment (Earl *et al.*, 1986) and on the specification of IBM's CICS system (Johnson, 1987) has demonstrated that the technique can be scaled up to large-scale industrial software systems. Formal specification is valuable because it forces the software developers to analyse the system requirements in detail before design and implementation and it is clear that it can play an important role in the software process.

KEY POINTS

- Model-based specification relies on building a model of the system using mathematical entities such as sets which have a formal semantics. The principal model-based specification languages are VDM and Z.

- A Z specification is presented as a number of schemas where a schema introduces some typed names and defines predicates over these names. Schemas in Z may be presented using graphical highlighting.

- Schemas are building blocks which may be combined and used in other schemas. The effect of including a schema A in schema B is that schema B inherits the names and predicates of schema A.

- A commonly used technique in Z is to use functions as a means of specifying certain types of data structure. Functions are sets of pairs where the domain of the function is the set of valid inputs and the range the set of associated outputs.

- Z includes a number of operators such as domain subtraction which allow the domain of functions to be manipulated.

- If ordering is important (sets are unordered), sequences can be used as a specification mechanism. Sequences may be modelled as functions where the domain is the natural numbers greater than zero and the range is the set of entities which may be held in the sequence.

Further reading

Specification Case Studies. This is the only book available which is explicitly concerned with Z. It consists of a number of Z specification examples and although it is not a language tutorial (all of the language is not illustrated in the example), the examples are well presented and (relatively) easy to follow. (I. Hayes (ed.), 1987, Prentice-Hall.)

References

Abrial, J.R. (1980), *The specification language Z: basic library*, Oxford Univ. Programming Res. Group.

Earl, A.N., Whittington, R.P., Hitchcock, P. and Hall, A. (1986), 'Specifying a semantic model for use in an integrated project support environment', in *Software Engineering Environments*, Sommerville, I. (ed.), London: Peter Peregrinus.

Hayes, I. (ed.), (1987), *Specification Case Studies*, London: Prentice-Hall.

Johnson, P. (1987), 'Using Z to specify CICS', *Proc. SEAS Anniversary Meeting*, Edinburgh, 303–33.

Jones, C.B. (1980), *Software Development – A Rigorous Approach*, London: Prentice-Hall.

Jones, C.B. (1986), *Systematic Software Development Using VDM*, London: Prentice-Hall.

EXERCISES

9.1 Explain how the schema combination mechanism which is available in Z is used in constructing complex specifications.

9.2 Modify the specification of a hopper set out in Figure 9.3 by adding a fill warning light which indicates when the hopper is close to capacity. This should be switched on when the contents is some high percentage of the capacity.

9.3 Write a specification for an operation called Dispense which dispenses a given number of units from a hopper.

9.4 Modify the specification of OverFillHopper (Figure 9.9) so that the effect of the operation is to fill the hopper to capacity and to dump the over-capacity in another container called Overflow.

9.5 What do you understand by the terms domain and range of a function? Explain how functions may be used in defining keyed data structures such as tables.

9.6 Modify the specification of DataDictionaryEntry (Figure 9.12) so that the description of data flows is restricted to 500 characters in length, the description of outputs and inputs to 1000 characters in length, and the description of processes and data stores to 1500 characters in length.

9.7   Write a specification for an operation on data dictionaries called ExamineProcesses which discovers the description for all entities in a data dictionary of type process. (Hint: use the quantifier ∀ in the predicate.)

9.8   Modify the specification of the DeleteEntry operation on data dictionaries so that it produces an error report if the entry is not in the data dictionary.

9.9   Using a model-based specification technique, write a specification for the symbol table which was set out in the exercises in Chapter 8 (Exercise 8.7).

9.10 Using sequences, write a model-based specification of an array abstract data type. For simplicity, assume that the lower bound of the array is 1.

Part 2

Software Design

Contents

Chapter 10

Software Design

This introductory chapter to Part 2 is concerned with a general discussion of software design. The introduction considers the importance of design and its role in the software process. A discussion of top-down design follows and then systems design where the relationship between hardware and software design is discussed. Function-oriented and object-oriented design decomposition are described using examples and Section 10.4 is concerned with the elusive notion of design quality. Here, maintainability is seen as the most important design quality attribute and several factors governing the maintainability of a design are noted. Finally, an Ada-based design description language is introduced by means of some small examples.

Contents

Design is a creative process. It requires experience and a certain amount of flair on the part of the designer, and a final design is an iteration from a number of preliminary designs. Design cannot be learned from a book – it must be practised and learnt by experience and study of existing systems. Good design is the key to effective engineering yet, paradoxically perhaps, it is not possible to formalize the design process in any engineering discipline. Software systems are no different in this respect from any other systems.

A general model of a software design is a directed graph where the nodes represent entities in the design such as processes, functions or types and the links represent relations between these design entities. The target of the design process is the creation of such a graph where there are no inconsistencies and where all the relationships between design entities are legal ones.

Of course, it is unusual for software designers to arrive at a finished design graph immediately. The design process appears to be a process of adding formality as a design progresses with constant backtracking to correct earlier, less formal, designs. Thus, the designer starts with a very informal picture of the design and refines that by adding information and making the design more formal (Figure 10.1).

The general form of the design which usually emerges from such a design process is approximately hierarchical (Figure 10.2) inasmuch as the cross-links in the graph emerge at lower levels of the design tree. The reason for this is that designers seem to start the design process using a top-down approach to construct a tree but naturally identify possibilities for reuse at lower levels in the tree. Thus, design components created in one branch of the tree are reused in other branches. Fine-grain components naturally appear at lower levels in the tree and are more reusable, so cross-links appear at the bottom of the hierarchy.

It is still the case that, in many organizations, software design is largely an *ad hoc* process. Given a set of requirements, usually in natural language, an informal design is prepared. Coding then commences and the design is modified as the system is implemented. When the implementation stage is complete, the design has usually changed so much from its initial specification that the original design document is a totally inadequate description of the system.

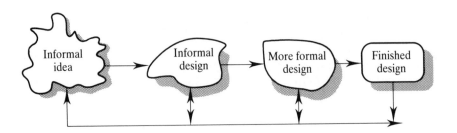

Figure 10.1
The design process.

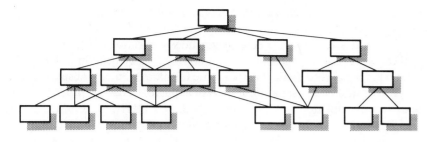

Figure 10.2
Software design structure.

A more methodical approach to software design is offered by so-called 'structured methods', which are basically sets of notations and guidelines about how to create a software design. Examples of structured methods are Structured Design (Constantine and Yourdon, 1979), Structured Systems Analysis (Gane and Sarson, 1979), RAPID/USE (Wasserman, 1981), Jackson System Development (Jackson, 1983) and Mascot (Simpson, 1986), which is a method used in real-time systems design. There have been a vast number of similar design methods suggested and used in different applications. A survey of these is given by Peters (1980) and by Blank and Krijger (1983).

The term 'structured methods' is a little misleading in that it suggests some kind of repeatable method whereby two designers given the same specification would generate the same design. In fact, these 'methods' are really standard notations and embodiments of good practice. By following these methods and applying the guidelines, a reasonable design should emerge, but designer creativity is still required to decide on the system decomposition and to ensure that the design adequately captures the system specification.

Structured methods are sometimes criticized because they are informal, sometimes incomplete and have no formal semantics. This criticism is usually made by members of the formal methods community who suggest that a very formal, transformation-based approach to design is superior. This approach was discussed in Chapter 7 and relies on taking a formal specification and transforming this systematically into a correct program. Recall that the conclusion drawn in Chapter 7 was that this approach has potential but its cost-effective application is still a research problem.

The criticism of structured methods on the grounds that they are informal and, by implication, of dubious value, is unfair. Structured methods have been applied successfully in many large projects and have resulted in significant cost reductions because they use standard notations and ensure that designs follow a standard form. They are usable, with some training, by engineers from a variety of backgrounds and are a significant improvement over no method at all. Indeed, the formal approach to design would benefit by adopting graphical notations as are common in most structured methods.

The relationship between design and specification is a very close one. Although the process of setting out a requirements specification as the basis of a contract is clearly a distinct activity, the formalization of that specification may be considered as a separate activity or as part of the design process. In this text, the specification process is described separately but, in practice, the designer iterates between the activities of specification and design.

It is sometimes said that the distinction between specification and design is that the specification represents 'what' is to be implemented and the design is a representation of 'how' it is to be implemented. This is quite arbitrary as at abstract design levels the difference between the design description and the actual implementation is so great that notions of 'what' and 'how' are meaningless.

The design process involves describing the system at a number of different levels of abstraction. It is an iterative process. As a design is decomposed, errors and omissions in earlier stages are discovered and these feed back to allow earlier design stages to be refined (Figure 10.3). Notice the overlap between the design stages. It is common to begin the next stage before a stage is finished simply to get feedback from the refinement process.

Figure 10.3 suggests that specification is an activity that follows the establishment of the component architecture rather than precedes that activity. At the very highest level, this implies that the designer sets out the architecture then defines precisely what each part of the architecture should do. As the design is decomposed, the design validation process should ensure that the specification of a component at one level matches the sum of the specifications of its sub-components. In Chapter 7, the architectural design stage was described as the establishment of a system model.

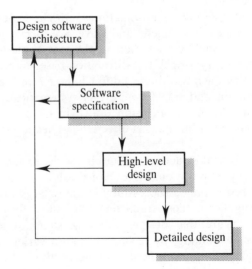

Figure 10.3
Design phases.

The process of setting out the system architecture then specifying the components continues until 'atomic' components can be identified. By atomic components, we mean components which have a single purpose such as a functional component 'sort' or an abstract data type 'list' or an object 'symbol table'. At this stage, the design of the component can be expressed directly in some design description language without the necessity for an architectural description. Using such a language is discussed later in this chapter.

10.1   Top-down design

A systematic approach to design simplifies the process and results in software which is understandable, verifiable and reliable without stifling the creativity of the software engineer. The most reliable approach is called top-down design which is based on the notion that the structure of the problem should determine the structure of the software solution.

The system is considered as an abstract entity without details of how that entity is actually realized. The designer identifies a set of components (themselves abstract entities) which make up the system and expresses the system design using these components. As a design progresses, each component is refined into its own fundamental parts with the process continuing until a low-level design is formulated in terms of constructs which can be mapped into a programming language.

The formulation and description of a software design involves a number of different stages which are repeated at each level in the design:

(1)   Study and understand the problem. Without this understanding, effective software design is impossible. Although the design process should be top-down this does *not* mean that thinking should necessarily be top-down. An understanding of the problem may be gained from a number of different angles and none of these should be excluded.

(2)   Identify gross features of at least one possible solution. At this stage it is often useful to identify a number of solutions and to evaluate each of these. The choice of solution depends on the experience of the designer (who is likely to choose a familiar, well-understood solution if one exists), the availability of reusable components, and the simplicity of the derived solutions. A good rule of thumb is always to choose the simplest solution if all other factors are equal.

(3)   Describe each abstraction used in the solution in some design description language which may be diagrammatic, textual or both.

Before creating formal documentation, however, the designer may find it necessary to construct an informal design description and debug this by developing it in more detail. Errors and omissions in the high-level design which are discovered during lower-level design may be corrected before formal design documentation.

After an initial solution has been formulated, the problem-solving process is repeated for each abstraction identified in the initial solution. This process of refinement continues until a low-level specification of each abstraction has been prepared. It is important that the representation of each stage of the design is clear and concise. A useful guideline is to express the design so that each design component is described on a single, standard-sized sheet of paper.

To be realistic, it is rare for large systems to be designed in a manner which is strictly top-down. The reason for this is that designers of such systems use their previous design knowledge in the design process. They do not need to decompose all abstractions as they may be aware exactly how one part of the design can be built. They might therefore concentrate on other problematical parts of the design before returning to that part. Indeed, project planning may require problematical parts of the design to be tackled first so that management can make more informed estimates of the system development time.

Furthermore, experienced designers may be aware of particular specific difficulties which may arise in a design. These may affect components which are critical to the whole project so the designer may concentrate on these components before designing other system parts. In essence then, although good designers usually adopt a strategy which is basically top-down, this is usually modified so that bottom-up and middle-outward strategies are also used.

10.2 Systems design

In large-scale embedded systems, the design process (Figure 10.4) includes an element of systems design in which functions are partitioned into software and hardware functions. Until recently, these decisions were not particularly difficult to make because only standard hardware with known functionality could be used. Thus, the hardware structure of a system often resolved itself leaving the software to coordinate and control the hardware units.

As the cost of special-purpose integrated circuits decreases and the speed of fabrication increases (for simple circuits, it is now possible to go from an idea to a delivered microchip in a few weeks), the borderline

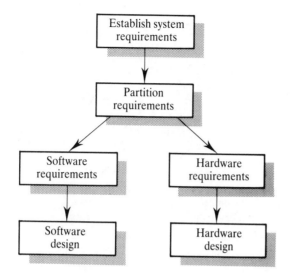

Figure 10.4
The system design process.

between hardware and software components is blurring. It is becoming increasingly cost-effective to delay decisions about which functions should be implemented in hardware and which functions should be software components.

The advantage of implementing functionality in hardware is that a hardware component delivers much better performance than the equivalent software unit. System bottlenecks can be identified and replaced by hardware components, thus freeing the software engineer from expensive software optimization. Providing performance in hardware means that the software design can be structured for adaptability and that performance considerations can take second place.

It is outside the scope of this book to discuss hardware and VLSI design. What is important in the design process is to delay hardware/software partitioning as late as possible in the design process, and this implies that the system architecture must be made up of stand-alone components which can be implemented in either hardware or software. Fortunately, building a design in this way is exactly the aim of the designer who is trying to design a maintainable system. Thus, following the quality guidelines set out in Section 10.4 should result in a system which can be implemented in either hardware or software.

10.2.1 Parallelism in the design process

A great many software systems, particularly embedded real-time systems, are structured as a set of parallel communicating processes as shown in Figure 10.5 which is an outline design of a simple control system. Indeed, it

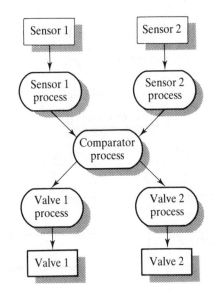

Figure 10.5
Parallel design of a
control system.

is sometimes suggested that this structure of parallel processes is a natural
and necessary approach for real-time systems construction. Historically,
this decomposition into parallel processes was probably correct.
Embedded systems must often perform to very strict time constraints and,
in situations where hardware is relatively slow, only a multiple process/
multiple processor approach could provide the necessary performance.
However, with fast processors, it may not be necessary to implement
embedded systems as parallel processes. A sequential system which uses
polling to interrogate and control hardware components may provide
adequate performance.

The advantage of avoiding a parallel systems design is that sequential programs are easier to design, implement, verify and test than parallel
systems. Time dependencies between processes are hard to formalize,
control and verify.

The design process should be considered as a two-stage activity:

(1)   Identify the logical design structure, namely the components of a
system and their inter-relationships.

(2)   Realize this structure in a form which can be executed. This latter
stage is sometimes considered detailed design and sometimes programming. It is this author's contention that decisions on parallelism
should be made at this stage rather than at earlier stages in the
design process.

On the other hand, there are some applications, such as vector processing,
where a parallel approach is a completely natural one. If n-element vectors

have to be processed with the same operation carried out on each element, the natural implementation is for a set of n-processes carrying out the same operation at the same time. Lower-cost hardware reduces the cost of building multiple processor machines and hence in supporting such parallelism. Such parallel machines offer challenges to the algorithm designer as existing algorithms, which may be very efficient on sequential machines, often do not map well onto parallel hardware. A discussion of parallelism, with particular attention paid to Ada's model of tasking, is provided by Sommerville and Morrison (1987).

10.3 Design decomposition

Effective software design is best accomplished by using a consistent approach to design decomposition. Until relatively recently, the usual mode of design decomposition involved considering the design as a number of functional components with the state information held in some shared data area. Although Parnas (1972) suggested an alternative view in the early 1970s and versions of Smalltalk (Goldberg and Robson, 1983) were in existence in the 1970s, it is only within the past few years that an alternative mode of decomposition, object-oriented design, has been recognized as of value.

These two modes of design decomposition may be summarized as follows:

(1) *Functional design* The system is designed from a functional viewpoint, starting with a high-level view and progressively refining this into a more detailed design. This methodology is exemplified by Structured Design (Constantine and Yourdon, 1979) and step-wise refinement (Wirth, 1971, 1976). Methods such as Jackson Structured Programming (Jackson, 1975) and the Warnier–Orr method (Warnier, 1977) are actually techniques of functional decomposition where the structure of the data is used to determine the functional structure used to process that data.

(2) *Object-oriented design* The system is viewed as a collection of objects rather than as functions, with messages passed from object to object. Each object has its own set of associated operations. Object-oriented design is based on the idea of information hiding which was first put forward by Parnas (1972) and which has been described more recently by Robson (1981), Abbott (1983) and Booch (1986, 1987). JSD (Jackson, 1983) is a design method which falls somewhere between function-oriented and object-oriented design.

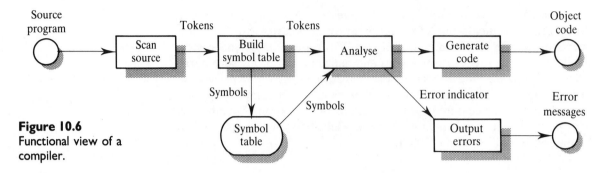

Figure 10.6
Functional view of a
compiler.

Top-down functional decomposition has been widely used for both small-scale and large-scale projects in diverse application areas. Object-oriented design is a relatively recent development which has not been widely tried but it is a technique which encourages the production of loosely coupled and highly cohesive systems.

To illustrate the difference between functional and object-oriented approaches to software design, consider the structure of a compiler. It may be viewed as a set of functional transformations with information being passed from one function to another (Figure 10.6). An alternative, object-oriented view of the same system is shown in Figure 10.7. Here, the objects manipulated by the compiler are central with transformation functions associated with object communications.

Proponents of particular design techniques naturally become very enthusiastic about their particular technique and sometimes suggest that a

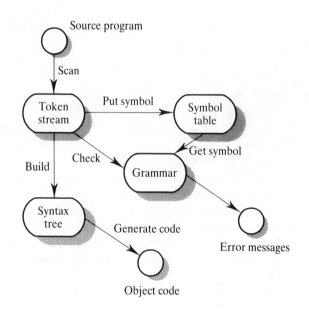

Figure 10.7
Object-oriented view of a
compiler.

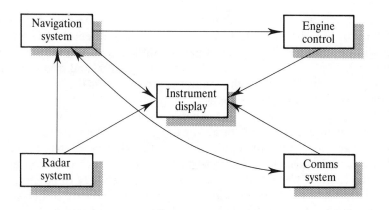

Figure 10.8
Interacting aircraft
subsystems.

technique is generally applicable and that other techniques need not be used. This is hyperbole. Large software systems are such complex entities that all of these approaches to design might be used at some stage in the design of different parts of the system. there is no 'best' design methodology for large projects and the pragmatic software engineer selects the msot appropriate approach for each stage in the design process.

In particular, functional and object-oriented approaches are complementary rather than opposing techniques and each may be applicable at different stages in the design process.

To illustrate this, consider the software systems (Figure 10.8) which might be part of a modern civil airliner. Some of these might be:

- The navigation system.
- The radar system.
- The external communications system.
- The instrument display system.
- The engine control system.

Our natural high-level view of the overall software system is as a set of objects (subsystems) rather than as a set of functions. Thus, at very abstract design levels, an object-oriented viewpoint seems to be appropriate. However, once the system is examined in more detail, its natural description is as a set of interacting functions rather than objects. For example, some of these functions might be:

(1)   Display_Track (radar subsystem)

(2)   Compensate_for_Wind_Speed (navigation subsystem)

(3)   Reduce_Power (engine control subsystem)

(4)   Indicate_Emergency (instrument subsystem)

(5)   Lock_onto_Frequency (communications sub-system)

This functional view may be that taken by the requirements definition. Although it may be possible to convert this to an object-oriented view, validation against the requirements may be difficult because there is not a simple correspondence between design components and requirements definitions. A single logical function in the requirements definition may be implemented as a complex sequence of object interactions.

As the system design is further decomposed, an object-oriented view may again become the natural way to view the system. At the detailed design stage, the objects manipulated might be The_engine_status, The_aircraft_position, The_altimeter, The_radio_beacon, etc. Thus an object-oriented approach to the lower levels of the system design is likely to be effective.

In summary, an object-oriented approach to software design seems to be the most natural at the highest and lowest levels of system design. At these levels, it may lead to higher component cohesion and lower component coupling and it is these characteristics that lead to a maintainable design. In between these levels, however, a functional view may be more apt. This confirms the notion that large software systems are such complex objects that it is unwise to adopt any single, dogmatic approach to the building of these systems.

10.4   Software design quality

There is no definitive way of establishing what is meant by a 'good' design. Depending on the application and project requirements, a good design might be a design that allows very efficient code to be produced; it might be a minimal design where the implementation is as compact as possible; or it might be the most maintainable design.

This latter criterion is the criterion of 'goodness' adopted here. A maintainable design implies that the cost of system changes is minimized and this means that the design should be understandable and that changes should be local in effect. Both of these are achieved if the software design is highly cohesive, loosely coupled and readily adapted.

Some work has been carried out to establish design quality metrics to establish whether or not a design is a 'good' design. These have mostly been developed in conjunction with Structured Design (see Chapter 12) and a description of possible metrics and their potential value is postponed until a later chapter on design validation.

10.4.1   Cohesion

A software component is said to exhibit a high degree of cohesion if the elements in that unit exhibit a high degree of functional relatedness. This means that each element in the program unit should be essential for that unit to achieve its purpose; for example, sort a file, look up a dictionary, etc. Elements which are grouped together in a program unit for some other reason such as to perform actions which take place at the same time or which implement a number of distinct functions have a low degree of cohesion.

Constantine and Yourdon (1979) identify seven levels of cohesion in order of increasing strength of cohesion from lowest to highest:

- *Coincidental cohesion*   The parts of a unit are not related but simply bundled together into a single unit.
- *Logical association*   Components which perform similar functions, such as input, error handling, etc. are put together in a single unit.
- *Temporal cohesion*   All of the components which are activated at a single time, such as start up or shut down, are brought together.
- *Procedural cohesion*   The elements in a unit make up a single control sequence.
- *Communicational cohesion*   All of the elements of a unit operate on the same input data or produce the same output data.
- *Sequential cohesion*   The output from one element in the unit serves as input for some other element.
- *Functional cohesion*   Each part of the unit is necessary for the execution of a single function.

These cohesion classes are not strictly defined and Constantine and Yourdon illustrate each by example. It is not always easy to decide under what cohesion category a unit should be classed.

Yourdon and Constantine's method is functional in nature and it is obvious that the most cohesive form of unit is the function. However, a high degree of cohesion is also a feature of object-oriented systems. Indeed, one of the principal advantages of this approach to design is that the objects making up the system are naturally cohesive.

A cohesive object is one where a single entity is represented and all of the operations on that entity are included with the object. For example, an object representing a compiler symbol table is cohesive if all of the functions such as 'Add a symbol', 'Search table', etc., are included with the symbol table object.

Cohesion is a desirable characteristic because it means that a unit represents one aspect of the problem solution only. If it becomes necessary to change the system, that aspect can be discovered in a single place and everything to do with it is encapsulated in a single unit. There is no need to modify many components if a change has to be made.

10.4.2   Coupling

Coupling is related to cohesion – it is an indication of the strength of interconnections between program units. Highly coupled systems have strong interconnections, with program units dependent on each other, whereas loosely coupled systems are made up of units which are independent or almost independent.

As a general rule, modules are tightly coupled if they make use of shared, global variables or if they interchange control information. Constantine and Yourdon call this common coupling and control coupling. Loose coupling is achieved by ensuring that, wherever possible, representation information is held within a component and that its data interface with other units is via its parameter list. If shared information is necessary, the sharing should be controlled as in an Ada package. Constantine and Yourdon call this data coupling and stamp coupling.

Figures 10.9 and 10.10 illustrate tightly and loosely coupled modules.

Other coupling problems arise when names are bound to values at an early stage in the development of the design. For example, if a program is concerned with tax computations and a tax rate of 30% is encoded as a number in the program, that program is coupled with the tax rate. Changes to the tax rate require changes to the program. On the other hand, if the program reads in the tax rate at run-time, it is very easy to accommodate rate changes.

Perhaps the principal advantage of object-oriented design is that the very nature of objects is such that loosely coupled systems are produced. It

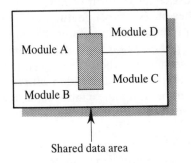

Figure 10.9
Tight coupling.

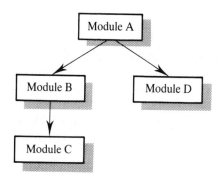

Figure 10.10
Loose coupling.

is fundamental to object-oriented design that the representation of an object is concealed within that object and is not visible to external components. Conceptually, objects communicate by passing messages to each other, and any one object can be replaced with another object that responds to the same set of messages.

10.4.3 Understandability

Changing a design component implies that the person responsible for making the change understands the operation of the component. This understandability is related to a number of component characteristics such as the use of meaningful names for design entities and the design documentation. However, perhaps the most crucial characteristic affecting the understandability of a component is its complexity.

We use the term complexity here in an informal way. High complexity implies many relationships between different parts of the design component and a complex logical structure which may involve deeply nested if–then–else statements. Complex components are hard to understand so the designer should strive for as simple as possible a component design.

Most of the work carried out in the general area of design quality metrics (Chapter 14) has concentrated on trying to measure the complexity of a component and obtain some measure of the component's understandability. However, while complexity is one determinant of understandability, there are a number of others such as the component documentation and the style in which the design is described. Thus, as discussed later, complexity measures provide an indicator rather than a quantitative assessment of the understandability of a component.

10.4.4 Adaptability

If a design is to be maintained, it must be readily adaptable. Of course, this implies that its components should be highly cohesive and loosely coupled. As well as this, however, adaptability means that the design should be well documented, the component documentation should be readily understandable and consistent with the implementation, and the implementation should be expressed in a readable way.

It is particularly important that the design exhibits a high level of visibility. This means that there should be a clear relationship between the different levels in the design (Figure 10.11) and it should be straightforward to incorporate changes made to the design in all design documents. This is important because changes made to a design description but not included in all descriptions mean that design documentation becomes inconsistent. Later changes are more difficult to make (the component is less adaptable) because the modifier cannot rely on the consistency of design documentation.

As well as the relationship between levels in the design being visible, it is equally important that the relationship between the specification and the design be clear. It is in this respect that there is an advantage in using the same design decomposition technique as is used to express the specification. That is, if the specification is expressed in an object-oriented way, the design should also be object-oriented; if the specification is described as a set of functions, it may be best to design the software in the same way. Although it is not impossible to maintain the relationship between a function-oriented specification and an object-oriented design, the differences in view can make this a difficult task as entities in the specification may be distributed over a number of design entities (Figure 10.12).

For optimum adaptability, a component should be as self-contained as possible. This is related to but distinct from coupling. A component may be loosely coupled in that it only cooperates with other components via message passing, say. This is not the same as being self-contained as the component may rely on other components, such as system functions or

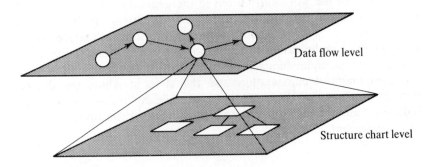

Figure 10.11
Design level visibility.

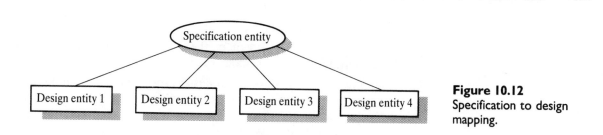

Figure 10.12
Specification to design mapping.

error handling functions. Adaptations to the component may involve changes to those parts of the component that rely on external functions, so these functions must also be considered by the modifier.

To be completely self-contained, a component should not use other components which are externally defined. However, this is contrary to good practice which suggests that existing components should be reused. Thus, some balance must be struck between the advantages of reusing components and the loss of component adaptability that this entails.

10.5   Design description languages

The lowest level of a software design is best described using a design description language. A design description language is a language with control constructs which allow the designer to write down the structure of a software solution to the design problem.

It has been argued that the most appropriate notation for this is a high-level programming language such as Ada or Pascal. This has the obvious advantage that the design is executable if a suitable language compiler is available, but there are disadvantages to this approach:

(1)   Programming languages must be compilable and so cannot be readily extended to encompass new concepts. For example, if a Pascal-based language is used and the designer wishes to describe an abstract data type, this is not possible.

(2)   The data types, structures and operations available as primitives in programming languages are often relatively low level. This means that the representation of some intuitively simple high-level constructs such as an unbounded sequence of data items sometimes becomes detailed and confused.

(3)   As thinking is constrained by language, the lower the level of constructs available to designers, the more their thinking is liable to be influenced by language constructs.

(4)   If an initial implementation of a design, specified in a programming language, must subsequently be reimplemented, it is difficult to carry out this reimplementation in a higher level language than the design specification language.

Rather than using an existing programming language as a vehicle for design expression, a better alternative is to use a design description language intended for documenting and communicating software designs. A number of such languages have been invented such as those described by Van Leer (1976) and Linger *et al.* (1979).

Design description languages make use of the familiar control constructs of high-level programming languages to specify flow of control but allow the designer considerable flexibility in the description of operations. In this chapter, a variant of Ada (Ada/PDL) is used as a design description language. This notation has been chosen because Ada is likely to become the most common language for large system construction and because Ada has a rich set of constructs encompassing control constructs, data abstraction, exception handling and tasking. It is only rarely necessary to go outside the language for descriptive purposes.

Ada is perhaps the best base language for a PDL but it still suffers from the disadvantages discussed above. For example, in the unlikely event of a design described in Ada being coded in LISP, the Ada design description would hardly be a reasonable definition of the LISP program. Furthermore, compiling requirements of Ada require representation information to be provided in packages and require all component dependencies to be stated using **with** clauses and this represents an unnecessary level of detail in a design. Names must be defined before use. This is unnatural if top-down design is practised.

Thus, the Ada design description language used here (described in Appendix A) is not proper Ada but a notation where natural language text may be substituted for statements or expressions and where it is unnecessary to declare all items before their use. This is particularly important in a PDL as top-down design relies on identifying abstractions then designing their realizations. If a name cannot be used without being defined, a top-down approach is inhibited as the designer is forced to concentrate on the details of the named entity rather than the component being designed.

A description of some of the facilities of Ada and the modifications introduced to cover design description is given in Appendix A. In the following examples, PDL control constructs have been used to describe the decisions made in the program but many operations have been described in natural language. Readers familiar with a high-level programming language like Pascal will have no difficulty understanding the examples.

```
procedure Spellcheck is
begin
    Unique_words := Get_all_unique_words_in_document ;
    Unknown_words := Lookup_the(
                            Dictionary => English_dictionary,
                            Wordlist=> Unique_words) ;
    Display (Unknown_words) ;
    Create_new_dictionary (Based_on => Unknown_words) ;
end Spellcheck ;
```

Example 10.1
The high-level design of a spelling checker.

Generally, a design in Ada/PDL is refined through a number of levels of abstraction from a high-level statement of the operation to a detailed design whose representation is close to the programming language. For example, consider the design of a program intended to detect misspelled words in a document (Example 10.1). Notice how named parameter association is used, where the formal parameter name is specified along with the actual parameter name, to help with readability. Thus, in the call of Lookup_the, the formal parameter is called Dictionary and the actual parameter is English_dictionary. The conjunction of the function name and the formal parameter name gives the readable name Lookup_the (Dictionary => English_dictionary...

This very high-level design description may be refined in more detail as shown in Example 10.2. It is sometimes useful to import a high-level design description into a refinement in the form of comments. Thus the comment symbol − −* means that the associated comment represents a higher level operational description. A refinement of Spellcheck is shown as Example 10.2.

One of the advantages of using a design description language is that new abstract data types may be introduced and used without previous definition. Naturally they must eventually be defined. This is illustrated in

```
procedure Spellcheck is
begin
− −* split document into words
    Word := The first word in the document ;
    loop
        Unique_words := Add Word to unique word list in
                                order, eliminating duplicates ;
        exit when the entire document has been processed ;
        Word := Get_next_word_from_document ;
    end loop ;
```

Example 10.2
Detailed design of a spelling checker.

Example 10.2
Detailed design of a
speller checker (cont.).

```
--* look up words in dictionary
        Word := The first word in Unique_words ;
        loop
            if Word is not in the dictionary then
                    Unknown_words := Add_the_word (Unknown_words,
                                                    Word) ;
            end if ;
            Word := Get_next_word_in (Unique_words) ;
            exit when all words in Unique_words have been checked ;
            end loop ;
--* display unknown words
        for_all words in Unknown_words loop
                Display ( Word = An unknown word ) ;
                if user marks word as correctly spelled then
                        Good_words := Add_the_Word (Good_words, Word) ;
                end if ;
--* create a new dictionary
            Dictionary := Merge (Dictionary, Good_words) ;
end Spellcheck ;
```

the next example, where an abstract data type called a sequence is used. A sequence is an unbounded list which may only be accessed in order, from the front. A package defining sequences is discussed in Appendix A.

Sequences are used in Example 10.3, which describes the final part of the spelling checker, namely the merging of the dictionary and the properly spelled words from the document which do not appear in the dictionary. Notice that this example starts with a statement of the type of entity which is arranged in the sequence. Ada supports the notion of generic sequences instantiated for particular types directly. This means that a generalized template for a sequence can be defined with a formal type for sequence members. The new statement in the package definition above defines a particular instance of the sequence for the type WORD.

Example 10.3
Dictionary merging.

```
package Word_sequence is new Sequence (Seqtype => WORD) ;

Dictionary, Good_words: Word_sequence.T ;

with Word_sequence ;
procedure Merge( In_seq1, In_seq2 : Word_sequence.T;
                    Out_seq: out WORDSEQ) is
        X, Y : WORD ;
```

Example 10.3
Dictionary merging
(cont.).

```
begin
    -- If one of the sequences is empty, the output is
    -- simply the other sequence
    if Word_sequence.Length (In_seq1) = 0 then
        Out_seq := In_seq1 ;
    elsif Word_sequence.Length (In_seq2) = 0 then
        Out_seq := In_seq2 ;
    else
        X := Word_sequence.Next (In_seq1) ;
        Y := Word_sequence.Next (In_seq2) ;
    end if ;
    -- execute till one sequence exhausted
    while Word_sequence.Length (In_seq1) > 0 and
            Word_sequence.Length (In_seq2) > 0 loop
        if X < Y then
            --select from 1st sequence
            Out_seq := Word_sequence.Add (Out_seq, X) ;
            X := Word_sequence.Next (In_seq1) ;
        else -- select from 2nd sequence
            Out_seq := Word_sequence.Add (Out_seq, X) ;
            Y := Word_sequence.Next (In_seq2) ;
            end if ;
    end loop ;
    -- assign remainder of non exhausted sequence
    if Word_sequence.Length (In_seq1) = 0 then
        Out_seq := Word_sequence. Catenate (Out_seq, In_seq1) ;
    else
        Out_seq := Word_sequence.Catenate (Out_seq, In_seq2) ;
    end if ;
end Merge ;
```

KEY POINTS

- Design is a creative process. Although methods and guidelines are helpful, judgement and flair on the part of the software engineer are still required to design a software system.

- Top-down design is an approach to design where the structure of the design matches the structure of the problem to be solved.

- Systems design includes hardware and software design. It is good design practice to delay partitioning of a design to hardware and software elements until as late as possible in the design process.

- A decision on whether a system should be implemented as a single sequential process or as a number of parallel processes is an implementation and not a design decision. The design process should partition the system into logical, interacting units which may be realized as either sequential or parallel components.

- Functional design decomposition involves considering a system as a set of interacting functional units. Object-oriented decomposition considers the system as a set of objects where an object is an entity with state and functions to inspect and modify that state.

- The most important design quality attribute is maintainability. Maximizing cohesion in a component and minimizing the coupling between components is likely to lead to a maintainable design.

- Design description languages are notations to describe detailed software design. A language based on Ada is used here because Ada is perhaps the most expressive of existing imperative programming languages.

Further reading

IEEE Transactions on Software Engineering, **SE-12** (2), 1986. This is a special issue of the journal devoted to design methods. It includes papers on various methods including object-oriented development, and papers on design documentation and design evaluation.

Programming in Ada. For readers who are unfamiliar with Ada, this is a readable introduction to the language. However, for complete information it must be supplemented by the language reference manual. (J.G.P. Barnes, 1984, Addison-Wesley.)

Software Development with Ada.   This book is concerned with software engineering and the use of Ada in building well engineered systems. A significant part of the book is devoted to a discussion of software design. (I. Sommerville and R. Morrison, 1987, Addison-Wesley.)

References

Abbott, R. (1983), 'Program design by informal English descriptions'. *Comm. ACM*, **26** (11), 882–94.

Blank, J. and Krijger, M.J., (eds) (1983), *Software Engineering: Methods and Techniques*, New York: Wiley Interscience.

Booch, G. (1986), 'Object-oriented development', *IEEE Trans. Software Eng.*, **SE-12** (2), 211–21.

Booch, G. (1987), *Software Engineering with Ada*, 2nd edn, Menlo Park, Calif.: Benjamin/Cummings.

Constantine, L.L. and Yourdon, E. (1979), *Structured Design*, Englewood Cliffs, NJ: Prentice-Hall.

Gane, C. and Sarson, T. (1979), *Structured Systems Analysis*, Englewood Cliffs, NJ.: Prentice-Hall.

Goldberg, A. and Robson, D. (1983). *Smalltalk-80: The Language and its Implementation*, Reading, Mass.: Addison-Wesley.

Jackson, M.A. (1975), *Principles of Program Design*, London: Academic Press.

Jackson, M.A. (1983), *System Development*, London: Prentice-Hall.

Linger, R.C., Mills, H.D. and Witt, B.I. (1979), *Structured Programming – Theory and Practice*, Reading, Mass.: Addison-Wesley.

Parnas, D. (1972). 'On the criteria to be used in decomposing systems into modules', *Comm. ACM*, **15** (2), 1053–8.

Peters, L.J. (1980), 'Software representation and composition techniques', *Proc. IEEE*, **68** (9), 1085–93.

Robson, D. (1981), 'Object-oriented software systems', *BYTE*, **6** (8), 74–9.

Simpson, H. (1986), 'The MASCOT method', *BCS/IEE Software Eng. J.*, **1** (3), 103–120.

Sommerville, I. and Morrison, R. (1987). *Software Development with Ada*. Wokingham: Addison-Wesley.

Van Leer, P. (1976), 'Top down development using a program design language', *IBM Systems J.*, **15** (2), 155–70.

Warnier, J.D. (1977), *Logical Construction of Programs*, New York: Van Nostrand Reinhold.

Wasserman, A.I. (1981), 'User software engineering and the design of interactive information systems', *Proc. 5th Int. Conf. on Software Engineering*, IEEE Press, 387–93.

Wirth, N. (1971), 'Program development by stepwise refinement', *Comm. ACM*, **14** (4), 221–7.

Wirth, N. (1976), *Systematic Programming, An Introduction*, Englewood Cliffs, NJ: Prentice-Hall.

EXERCISES

10.1 Describe how you would approach the top-down design of a software system.

10.2 Explain why sequential software designs are easier to validate than designs that involve parallel processes.

10.3 Discuss the differences between object-oriented and function-oriented design.

10.4 Present outline object-oriented and function-oriented views of the following systems:

- A cruise control system for a car which maintains a constant speed as set by the driver. The system should adjust the car controls depending on measured road speed.
- An automated library catalogue which is queried by users to find which books are available and which books are on loan.
- A self-service petrol (gas) pump where the driver sets the pump as required and fills his or her own tank. The amount used is recorded in a booth and the driver may pay by direct credit card debit.

10.5 What do you understand by the terms cohesion, coupling, and adaptability? Explain why maximizing cohesion and minimizing coupling leads to more maintainable systems.

10.6 Using an Ada-based design description language, describe designs for the following systems:

- A program to find the maximum, minimum and mean values in an array of integers.

- A quicksort algorithm which sorts an array of integers.

- A linear search algorithm which searches an array for some key value.

- A program which reads a document, identifies each sentence (delimited by a full stop) and prints it on a separate line.

- A program which multiplies two matrices.

- A program which, given a stream of input with one input item per line, prints this in four columns on a page. The page has a finite width and the size of the input items is not restricted. Take sensible action if the input items are too long for the columns.

- A keyword retrieval program which searches a set of records and retrieves those containing a given keyword.

- A computerized combination lock which requires the user to input a sequence of five numbers in order to unlock a door.

Chapter 11

Object-Oriented Design

Objective

The objective of this chapter is to describe an approach to software design which is based on objects rather than functions. This method maximizes information hiding and, in many cases, leads to systems with lower coupling and higher cohesion than the functional approach. The relationship between object-oriented design and object-oriented programming is discussed and the process of object-oriented design is illustrated using an example of a weather station data collection system. Finally, it is shown that, for some applications, object-oriented design is not necessarily the most appropriate approach.

Contents

Information hiding is a design strategy in which as much information as possible is hidden within design components. The basic premise which underlies it is the notion that the binding of logical control and data structures to their realizations should be made as late as possible in the design process. This means that communication between design entities is minimized (thus increasing the understandability of the design) and that the design is relatively easy to change as modification affects only a minimal number of entities.

Object-oriented design is a design method which is based on information hiding. It differs from the more familiar functional approach to design in that it views a software system as a set of interacting objects, with their own private state, rather than as a set of functions. An object can be defined as follows:

> An entity which has a state and a defined set of operations to access and modify that state. Using the terminology of Chapter 8, the operations that modify the state are *constructor operations* and the operations to access the state are *access operations*.

The state of the object may not be accessed except via these operations. Conceptually, objects communicate by passing messages to each other and these messages initiate object operations. Thus, communication may be asynchronous and an object-oriented design may be realized as a parallel or a sequential program. In practice, object operation instantiation is often implemented as function or procedure calls but this is an implementation rather than a design decision.

Object-oriented design is often confused with object-oriented programming. Object-oriented programming languages, such as Smalltalk (Goldberg and Robson, 1983) support the notion of objects and allow an object-oriented design to be implemented directly. They also incorporate notions of inheritance and run-time binding of operations to objects (discussed in Section 11.1) with the result that they inevitably have a high run-time overhead. For this reason, they are unsuitable for some kinds of system building and have not been widely used for large-scale software engineering.

Object-oriented design is a way of considering a software design and is not dependent on any specific implementation language. Features such as data encapsulation (Ada packages or Modula-2 modules) make an object-oriented design simpler to realize, but the design can also be implemented in languages such as Pascal which do not incorporate such features.

The advantages of object-oriented design may be summarized as follows:

- All shared data areas are eliminated as communication between objects is via message passing. This reduces overall system coupling as there is no possibility of unexpected modifications to shared information.

- Objects are independent entities, which may readily be changed because all state and representation information is held within the object itself. No access and hence no deliberate or accidental use of this information by other objects is possible. Thus changes may be made without reference to other system objects.

- Objects may be distributed and may execute either sequentially or in parallel. Decisions on parallelism need not be taken at an early stage of the design process.

To illustrate how an object-oriented approach to design can simplify system maintenance, consider the following simple example:

> A temperature control system is required for individual rooms in a building. Each room has a heater unit, a temperature sensor and a thermostat which is used to set the required temperature. Users of the system set their desired temperature and the control system maintains that temperature by monitoring sensor values and switching the heater accordingly.

An obvious design for this system is to maintain an array of temperature values which is indexed by room number. Thus array element Temperature_ required (15) holds the desired temperature for Room 15 and so on. This system design might be expressed as shown in Example 11.1. Assume that the number of rooms in the building is held in a constant called Number_of_ rooms and that the functions Switch_heater and Temperature_sensor interface with the system hardware to carry out switching and sensing functions.

This is a simple and straightforward design as might be discovered in a number of control systems. Of course, this loop would normally be embedded in another control loop which repeats the cycle indefinitely.

An alternative system design which takes an object-oriented view of this control system is shown as Example 11.2. In this approach, the system is viewed as being made up of room objects each of which has a state which includes the actual room temperature and the temperature to be attained, and a heater object which can respond to messages to switch on and off and to evaluate its state. Most languages do not incorporate explicit message passing so message passing is simulated by calling functions or procedures which implement the access and constructor operations of the object. Thus, to send a message to switch on a heater, a procedure called Switch within object Heater is called.

The control loop that maintains temperatures is shown as Example 11.2.

Example 11.1
A heating control system.

```
type Heater_settings is (ON, OFF) ;
type TEMP is range 10..30 ;
Temperature_required: array (1..Number_of_rooms) of TEMP ;
Heater_status: array (1..Number_of_rooms) of Heater_settings ;

for i in 1..Number_of_rooms loop
    if Temperature_sensor (i) >= Temperature_required (i) then
        if Heater_status(i) = ON then
            Switch_heater (i, OFF) ;
            Heater_status(i) := OFF ;
        end if ;
    else
      if Heater_status (i) = OFF then
            Switch_heater (i, ON) ;
            Heater_status (i) := ON ;
        end if ;
    end if ;
end loop ;
```

Example 11.3 shows an Ada/PDL package specification for the Room object type. In general the dot notation, for example, Room.Temperature (Rooms (i)), is used to reference components of an object. Thus, Room.Temperature means the entity Temperature defined within the object Room. To create objects of type Room, Ada variables are declared to be of Room.T meaning the type declaration T within object Room.

Example 11.2
A heating control system using information hiding.

```
Rooms: array (1..Number_of_rooms) of Room.T ;

for i in 1..Number_of_rooms loop
  if Room.Temperature (Rooms (i)) >
            Room.Required_temperature (Rooms (i)) then
    if Room.Heater.Setting( In_room => Rooms (i)) = ON then
        Room.Heater.Switch (In_room => Rooms (i),
                                    Status => OFF) ;
    end if ;
  else
    if Room.Heater.Setting (In_room =>Rooms (i)) = OFF then
        Room.Heater.Switch (In_room =>Rooms (i),
                                    Status=> ON) ;
    end if ;
  end if ;
end loop ;
```

```
package Room is
    type T is private ; – – the type representation is not accessible
    type TEMP is range 10..30 ;
    function Temperature (R: T) return TEMP ;
    function Required_temperature (R: T) return TEMP ;
    procedure Set_temperature (R: T ; Temperature: TEMP) ;
    package Heater is
        type STATUS is (ON, OFF) ;
        function Setting (In_room: T) return STATUS ;
        procedure Switch (In_room: T; V:STATUS ) ;
    end Heater ;
private
    – – The representation of Room.T is not relevant to this design
end Room ;
```

Example 11.3
The specification of a
Room object type.

The package in Example 11.3 is not an object in its own right but defines the structure of a class of objects. In order to create objects, they must be instantiated to be of this type by declaring them to be of Room.T. We call this type T because the type declaration includes the package name and a meaningful name is thus composed. For example:

An_office: Room.T ;

The distinction between objects and object classes is discussed later in this chapter.

The designs shown in Examples 11.1 and 11.2 appear similar but the advantages of the information hiding approach become clear when the following (reasonable) changes to the system are proposed.

> The heating control system is to be modified so that there is no longer a one-to-one relationship between rooms, sensors and heaters. There may be more than one heater in a room and the system switches all heaters on or off depending on the sensor value. In addition, the system must also be able to handle shared heating situations where a number of rooms have a shared heater and temperature setting but individual sensors. The heating is switched on and off depending on the average value of all of the sensors associated with the area.

We leave it to the reader to try to modify Example 11.1 to accommodate this situation. It must, in fact, be completely rewritten because it is dependent on the assumption that the one-to-one relationship between rooms, heaters and sensors exists. This relationship has been used to optimize the design of the shared data structures used in the system with the result that, when the relationship is changed, almost everything else in the system must be changed.

Example 11.3, on the other hand, need not be changed. In order to effect the required changes, the procedure Switch in object Heater must be modified so that it can switch more than one heater and the function Temperature in object Room must be changed to accommodate the situation where the temperature is the mean of a number of individual sensor values. Note that a room is considered to be an individually controlled area as far as the heating system is concerned. It may actually encompass a number of different rooms in the building.

The key difference between these approaches to software design is that the object-oriented view localizes the required changes. If an error is discovered in the heater control software (say) and it has to be changed, the maintenance programmer need not think about any parts of the program except the Heater object. Unexpected interactions with other parts of the program as a result of the system change are unlikely.

11.1 Objects, object classes and inheritance

At the beginning of this chapter, an object was defined as an entity that had a state and a set of operations which could modify or interrogate that state. The representation of the state is inaccessible from outside the object so it may be changed by the object implementor without normally requiring changes to any other objects that use the object which has been changed.

An object-oriented approach to software design was derived from work on information hiding (Parnas, 1972), abstract data types (Liskov and Zilles, 1974) and, most significantly, from work on object-oriented programming languages like Smalltalk (Goldberg and Robson, 1983). Object-oriented languages obviously simplify the implementation of an object-oriented design but the principle of designing a system as a set of interacting objects is distinct from implementing that system.

This means that an object-oriented design need not be implemented in an object-oriented language. For example, in this book Ada is used as a standard description language as it is (or will be) the most important language for large-scale software engineering. Ada is not a true object-oriented programming language although it has some features which allow object implementation. As this book is not really concerned with implementation techniques, object-oriented languages are not discussed further here.

When deriving an object-oriented design, there are two ways of defining design objects. These are:

(1) By direct specification where the object and its operations are set out.
(2) By defining an object class (an object template) and defining objects to be members of this class. Another name for an object class which is perhaps better known to software engineers is an abstract data type.

The differences between these approaches is most evident at the implementation level and which technique is most appropriate depends on the implementation language which is being used. At the design level, a good rule of thumb which can be adopted is as follows:

If a single instance of an object is required it should be defined directly. If a number of instantiations of an object are required, an object class should be defined and the appropriate number of objects instantiated. If there is a need for the whole state to be made available outside the object, the object should be defined as an instantiation of an object class.

When using Ada as a design description language, both objects and object classes may be defined using packages. For example, Example 11.4 is an Ada package defining the interface to an object which is a collection of names and addresses. Assume that both the name and the address are considered as character strings and that the type STRING_ARRAY represents an array of strings.

In this example, procedures are provided to access the state of the object (Get_names, Get_addresses), to make the object state representation visible (Print) and to change the state of the object (Add_entry,

Example 11.4
An address list object.

```
package Address_list is
    procedure Add_entry (Name, Address: STRING) ;
    procedure Delete_entry (Name, Address: STRING) ;
    procedure Change_address (Name, Old_address,
                          New_address: STRING) ;
    procedure Change_name (Old_name, New_name,
                          Address: STRING) ;
    function Get_names (Address: STRING)
            return STRING_ARRAY ;
    function Get_addresses (Name: STRING)
            return STRING_ARRAY ;
    procedure Print ;
end Address_list ;
```

Example 11.5
Address list class
definition.

```
package Address is
    type LIST is private ;
    procedure Add_entry (Name, Address: STRING ;To: LIST ) ;
    procedure Delete_entry (Name, Address: STRING; From:LIST);
    procedure Change_address (Name, Old_address,
                        New_address: STRING ;Inn: LIST) ;
    procedure Change_name (Old_name, New_name,
                        Address: STRING; Inn: LIST) ;
    function Get_names (From: LIST ; Address: STRING)
                return STRING_ARRAY ;
    function Get_addresses (From: LIST ; Name: STRING)
                return STRING_ARRAY ;
    procedure Print (The_list: LIST) ;
private
    type ADDRESS_REC ;
    type LIST is access ADDRESS_REC ;
end Address ;
```

Delete_entry, Change_name, Change_address). Thus, to print the address list, the following procedure call is made:

Address_list.Print

Given this object description was implemented in Ada, the package body for the package specification given in Example 11.4 would include a specification of the representation of Address_list (probably as an array of records) and the code implementing the access and constructor functions of that object. Package bodies are discussed in Chapter 16.

The definition of objects may be contrasted with the definition of an object class Address.LIST which sets out a template for address lists of the same type (Example 11.5). Note that the names of the operations on that type are identical but that their signature has changed to include the object instance which is being accessed or modified.

The distinction between object and object class declarations is that an object class declaration includes a type name which is the name of that class. In Example 11.5, this type name is LIST. Declaring an object class does not create any objects in itself. Once an object class has been declared, instances of that class are brought into existence using the language declaration mechanism.

Subscriptions: Address_list.T ;

Each operation takes a parameter specifying the object instance. The naming of these formal parameters may appear rather eccentric but the names have been chosen so that, when the procedure is called, a meaningful description is created by using named parameter association. For example, to delete an entry from a list named Subscriptions, the following call might be made:

```
Address.Delete_entry (   Name => "Andrew Tough",
                         Address => "17 Mount Vale Rd, Aberdeen",
                         From => Subscriptions ) ;
```

One way of looking at object instantiation is to say that objects inherit the attributes and operations of their class. This is taken further in object-oriented languages where object classes are themselves considered as objects. Thus object classes can be defined to be of a particular super-class and inheritance networks established. Thus, from a super-class EMPLOYEE say, sub-classes MANAGER and PROGRAMMER may be defined. The attributes of EMPLOYEE which are inherited by the sub-classes include those which are shared by all employees (such as a name, address, etc.) whereas the attributes of MANAGER and PROGRAMMER are those which are unique to these jobs.

Inheritance and the dynamic (run-time) association of operations with objects is one of the distinguishing characteristics of object-oriented languages like Smalltalk and it assists with the rapid development of programs. Ada supports a limited form of inheritance through derived types and does not support run-time operation instantiation.

From the point of view of object-oriented design, my view is that inheritance, except from a class to an instance, is not essential and may sometimes confuse a design. Without inheritance, the operations of an object-class must be explicitly stated, thus reducing the possibility of misunderstandings when reading that design. Even Ada's simple inheritance mechanism can be confusing and inheritance is not used in any of the design examples here.

11.1.1   Object implementation as Ada tasks

The notion of an autonomous object communicating by passing messages to other objects lends itself to an implementation model based on objects implemented as concurrent processes. The process of design can be carried out as if the system is a simple sequential system and this can easily be mapped to a concurrent implementation. This further confirms the view that concurrency is a detailed design decision and that there are few designs which can be considered as naturally concurrent or naturally sequential. Objects which are implemented in Ada may be realized as either packages, tasks or a mixture of both.

In general, it is usually easier to understand object descriptions which are presented as Ada packages rather than Ada tasks. However, to illustrate the equivalence of these descriptions, consider the following Ada package specification which describes an object representing a simple counter. The allowed operations on this are:

- Add a positive integer value to the counter
- Subtract a positive integer value from the counter
- Set the counter to some integer value and return the current value of the counter.

The Ada package description of this object is as follows:

```
package Counter is
    procedure Add (N: NATURAL) ;
    procedure Subtract (N: NATURAL) ;
    procedure Set (N: NATURAL) ;
    function Evaluate return NATURAL ;
end Counter ;
```

The equivalent Ada task specification of the counter is as follows:

```
task Counter is
    entry Add (N: NATURAL) ;
    entry Subtract (N: NATURAL) ;
    entry Set (N: NATURAL) ;
    entry Evaluate (N: out NATURAL) ;
end Counter ;
```

These different specifications are obviously similar and task entries are like procedure calls. The only significant difference in this case is that the Evaluate operation cannot be implemented as a function but must return its result through an **out** parameter.

The task body (Example 11.6) which actually implements the task is, however, quite different from the package implementation. Each **accept** statement handles an entry and has an associated queue of 'calls'. Thus, when an entry is 'called', that call joins the queue associated with the accept statement and is processed (ultimately) by the task according to the code specified between **accept** and **end**. While an **accept** clause (between **accept** and **end**) is in execution, mutual exclusion is guaranteed. An object wishing to evaluate a counter enters into what is called a *rendezvous* with the counter task. This simply involves calling the appropriate entry in Counter. For example:

```
Counter.Evaluate (The_value)
```

This joins the queue of Evaluate entries and is eventually processed by the counter task.

```
task body Counter is
    Value: NATURAL := 0 ;
begin
    loop
      select
        accept Add (N: NATURAL) do
          Value := Value + N ;
        end Add ;
      or
        accept Subtract (N: NATURAL) do
          Value := Value - N ;
        end Subtract ;
      or
        accept Set (N: NATURAL) do
          Value := N ;
        end Set ;
      or
        accept Evaluate (N: out NATURAL) do
          N := Value ;
        end Evaluate ;
      end select ;
    end loop ;
end Counter ;
```

Example 11.6
Task implementation of a
Counter object.

A full discussion of Ada's tasking facilities is lengthy and outside the scope of this text. Interested readers are referred to Sommerville and Morrison (1987) for such a description.

The specification of this object as a task or as a package is similar and, indeed, its usage in a program is similar. However, it is important that the object user knows whether a parallel or sequential object implementation is provided because the run-time behaviour of the implementations may be different. In the sequential implementation, calls on the object operations are executed in sequence; in the task-based implementation this cannot be guaranteed. When there are a number of entries waiting to be accepted, the task may choose any one of them for execution.

Bearing in mind that readers of this text may not be familiar with Ada's fairly complex tasking mechanism, it has been decided to consider the realization of an object as a task or package as an implementation decision. Tasks are not used for object description. Objects are specified as packages and operations as functions and procedures. This allows the designer to concentrate on the logical design and ignore implementation considerations.

As is clear in the following example, this involves a further relaxation of Ada's rules in the design description language to allow delay statements to be used within a procedure. In Ada, delay statements are only meaningful within tasks. However, standardizing on packages for object description simplifies the discussion here so we believe this decision is justifiable.

11.2   A design example

The process of software design is a creative one which is reliant on the skill and experience of the designer. Good design can only be illustrated by example. Readers can learn from examples and improve their own design skills. Object-oriented design is therefore illustrated by considering an example of a weather data collection system.

It is impractical to reproduce a full requirements document for such a system so this section simply presents a high-level overview of the system functions. Because object-oriented design allows detailed decisions to be postponed, design can begin without a complete requirements specification and can be modified as requirements are added or changed.

This means that an object-oriented approach can be used to develop system prototypes which may actually evolve into the production system. Normally, evolutionary prototyping is not a recommended practice if reliability is of paramount importance as the structure of prototypes tends to degrade very quickly as they are modified to meet changing requirements.

If an object-oriented language (such as Smalltalk) is suitable for implementation, evolutionary prototypes may be developed. However, the reader should note that there are few practical object-oriented languages which are suitable for large-scale software engineering and it is unlikely that any of these languages would be used for real-time systems construction. As discussed in Chapter 6, it is recommended that prototypes should be discarded after the requirements have been established and the system restructured and reimplemented.

The example shown here is a data collection system described as follows:

> A weather data collection system is made up of a large number of automatic weather stations which collect environmental data, perform some local data processing and periodically send the collected, processed information to an area computer for further processing.

The data which is to be collected is the air temperature, the ground temperature, the wind speed and direction, the barometric pressure and the amount of rainfall.

This description says nothing about the frequency of collection or the data processing required. Nevertheless, it provides sufficient information to begin the object-oriented design process.

The first stage in object-oriented design is to identify the entities which are part of the system. In general, this initial identification of objects must be refined as the design progresses and we shall see this refinement process as this example is developed. In a system which includes a mix of hardware and software, it is perhaps useful to identify fixed 'hardware' objects first. The reason for this is that the hardware usually constrains the design of embedded systems and there is little point in developing an elegant design which cannot be mapped onto the available hardware. Although it is best to delay the assignment of functions to hardware or software until as late as possible in the design process, sometimes fixed hardware structures such as sensors, switches, etc., constrain the design.

The term 'hardware' object is not a precise one but in this context means an object which interacts directly with some hardware unit. It will normally also include embedded software to drive the associated hardware. By contrast, a 'software' object is an object which only interacts with other system objects. The 'hardware' objects which can be identified from an analysis of the data collection system description are:

- Weather_station
- Air_thermometer
- Ground_thermometer
- Anemometer (measures wind speed)
- Wind_vane (measures wind direction)
- Barometer (measures pressure)
- Rain gauge
- Clock (required for timing collections and transmissions)
- Modem (for communication with remote computer)

Each of these object has associated operations although, in most cases, the only defined operation is an operation to return the current reading. The operations and brief descriptions are set out in Table 11.1.

To achieve visibility in a design, it is often useful to document it as a diagram. Diagrammatic descriptions are valuable because of their immediacy but, unfortunately, there has been relatively little work done in deriving diagrammatic representations of object-oriented designs. Booch

Table 11.1
Hardware object
descriptions.

Object	Operation	Description
Weather_station	Operate	Initiated by manual switch. Starts weather station operation, collecting and reporting weather information.
	Self_test	Initiated by remote signal or manual switch. Starts a self-test procedure reporting results on plug-in display or over communications line.
	Shutdown	Initiated by manual switch. Shuts down operation.
Clock	Time_now	Returns the current time.
	Reset	Sets the clock to the time specified as an operation parameter.
Modem	Transmit	Sends data to a remote computer.
	Receive	Receives data from a remote computer.
Rain_gauge	Evaluate	Returns rainfall in mm since last Reset operation.
	Reset	Initializes rainfall reading.
Anemometer	Evaluate	Returns current wind speed in km/h.
Wind_vane	Evaluate	Returns wind direction in degrees.
Ground_thermometer	Evaluate	Returns ground temperature.
Air_thermometer	Evaluate	Returns air temperature.
Barometer	Evaluate	Returns pressure in millibars.

(1987) suggests a notation but I find this notation unsatisfactory as it is awkward to use with automated graphical editing systems.

The notation used here to represent software and hardware objects is shown in Figure 11.1. Each object is denoted by a rectangular box containing the name of the object where boxes representing software objects have rounded corners (round = soft). Operations on the object are defined in the lower part of the box. In situations where many operations are defined, these may be shown by ellipses (...). In this case, the reader must refer to a more detailed object description for operation information.

Figure 11.1
Hardware and software
object representations.

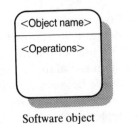

Software object

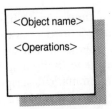

Hardware object

Two different kinds of diagram are needed to document an object-oriented design:

(1)   A network diagram showing which objects exchange messages. In many cases this will be broadly hierarchical as much inter-object communication is between a parent object and its sub-objects.

(2)   A hierarchical structure chart showing how objects are decomposed into sub-objects.

Figure 11.2 shows the hardware objects in the weather station system. This illustrates that the Thermometer, Rain_gauge, Clock, etc., are used by the weather station object. This is a hierarchy diagram showing that the weather station object consists of a number of sub-objects. As we shall see, the weather station object does not communicate with these objects directly but with intermediate level software objects. Hierarchy diagrams are distinguished from communication diagrams by the fact that, in communication diagrams, the lines joining objects are arrowed.

It is most appropriate to define Weather_station to be a single object rather than an instantiation of an object class. A possible package specification of this object is:

```
package Weather_station is
    procedure Operate ;
    procedure Self_test ;
    procedure Shut_down ;
end Weather_station ;
```

The weather station is a hardware unit which has a switch with three positions, namely on, off and self-test. It is connected via a telephone line and modem to some remote computer and information is transmitted along this line. It contains control software in a read-only memory and software functions are instantiated depending on the switch position.

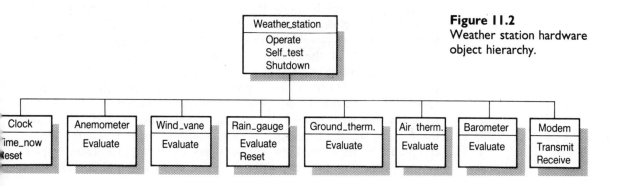

Figure 11.2
Weather station hardware object hierarchy.

Example 11.7
The weather station
Operate procedure.

```
with Weather_data, Clock, CALENDAR ;
procedure Operate is

-- This must be implemented as a task in Ada to allow it to be delayed

    Weather_info: Weather_data.REC ;
    Next_time: CALENDAR.TIME ;
    -- There is a gap of an hour (3600 seconds) between
    -- transmissions
    Transmission_gap: DURATION := 3600.0 ;
begin
    loop
        -- assume the loop terminates when selecting Shutdown
        -- generates an interrupt. Not shown here.
        -- Transmission_gap is the time between transmissions
        Next_time := Clock.Time_now + Transmission_gap ;
        Weather_data.Create (Weather_info) ;
        Weather_data.Check (Weather_info) ;
        Weather_data.Transmit (Weather_info) ;
        delay Next_time - Clock.Time_now ;
    end loop ;
end Operate ;
```

Not all of the operations on Weather_station will be defined here; only the Operate operation will be considered. As discussed above, the Ada/PDL is extended here to allow delay statements within a procedure. A procedure (Operate) will be shown using the delay statement within a loop. In Ada, only tasks can be delayed but this is really an implementation restriction. In practice, an implementation of this system would probably use parallel processes as the data collection operations must run continuously.

Example 11.7 shows the weather station Operate procedure. It makes use of the clock object and it is assumed that this has an operation called Time_now which returns the current time. The type TIME is exported by the standard package CALENDAR and DURATION is a built-in fixed-point type. It would be possible to use the Clock operation in CALENDAR for timing but, instead, the clock is made an explicit object here.

Notice in this example how the timing is carried out. Because data transmission tends to be error-prone and to require retries, the time required to carry out the creation, checking and transmitting of a weather record cannot be predicted. Rather than delaying for a fixed time before the next cycle, the time for the next transmission is computed before computations are carried out and the delay computed after these computations. This therefore takes into account the computation and trans-

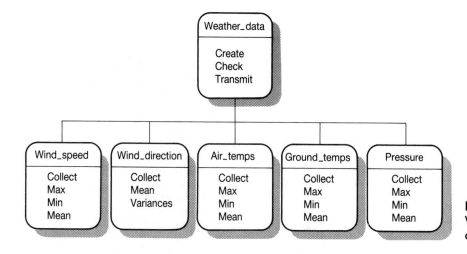

Figure 11.3
Weather station software
objects.

mission time. Timing considerations are discussed in more detail in
Sommerville and Morrison (1987).

The Operate procedure uses a 'software' object called Weather_data.
To identify other software objects and their relationships with Weather_
data, we need more system information.

> All of the weather parameters except the rainfall are collected
> every minute. Every hour (once 60 data collections have been
> made), the temperatures, the wind speed and the pressure are
> processed to determine mean, maximum and minimum values.
> The amount of rainfall is collected hourly immediately before this
> processing.
>
> The mean wind direction is computed and all wind directions
> which vary from this by more than 15° are returned for transmission
> to the remote computer.

This outline description allows us to identify the software objects shown in
Figure 11.3. This is a hierarchy diagram showing an object and sub-objects.
At this stage, it is not appropriate to look at the structure of the sub-objects
in more detail although they may themselves be implemented as a
hierarchy of sub-objects.

Table 11.2 is a description of some of these software objects. The
table is not complete as the operation description for the other objects is
similar to that shown.

Now that both the major hardware and software objects have been
identified, we can document the communication structure of the system as
shown in Figure 11.4. Notice the use of arrowed lines to indicate
communication.

Table 11.2
Some software object
descriptions.

Object	Operation	Description
Weather_data	Create	Creates a weather data record consisting of all information to be transmitted to remote computer.
	Check	Checks each field of the weather data record for validity. If apparently invalid, the field is tagged with a 'doubtful' indicator.
	Transmit	Sends the weather data record to the remote computer.
Rain_gauge	Evaluate	Returns the rainfall during the current time period.
	Reset	Zeros the rain-gauge
Wind_speed	Max	Returns the maximum wind speed during the current time period.
	Min	Returns the minimum wind speed
	Mean	Returns the mean wind speed during the current time period.
Wind_direction	Mean	Returns the mean wind direction during the current time period.
	Variances	Returns a list of wind directions which vary more than 15° from mean in current time period.

A specification of the interface to Weather_data is shown in Example 11.8. The Weather_data.Create procedure calls on the objects representing the collected temperatures, wind speeds, etc., to compute their means, maxima, minima, etc., and composes these into a transmission record. Note that this procedure need have no knowledge of how

Example 11.8
The Weather_data
object.

```
package Weather_data is
    type REC is private ;
    -- Create puts together a weather data record from raw collected
    -- data
    procedure Create ( Data: out REC ) ;
    -- Check examines the weather data record for inconsistencies
    -- and corrects these if they exist
    procedure Check (Data: in out REC) ;
    -- Transmit takes a weather data record and sends it to the
    -- remote collection computer
    procedure Transmit (Data: REC) ;
end Weather_data ;
```

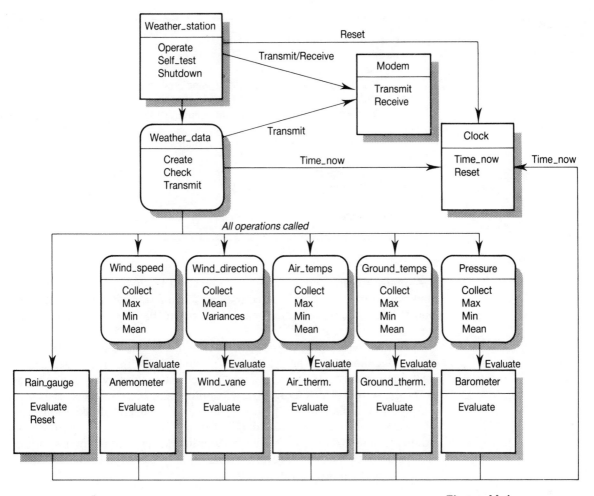

Figure 11.4
Weather station object communications.

the collected information is represented within the sub-objects. A fragment of this procedure is shown as Example 11.9. Assume that the weather information is held as a record with named fields.

An example of the interface specification of the wind speed sub-object is shown in Example 11.10. The implementation of Wind_speed is concealed completely within the body of the package. It may be changed without changing any of the objects which call on the operations defined on Wind_speed. There is no need for any other objects to have access to the collected wind speed information.

The object-oriented approach to design makes this system robust and tolerant to change. For example, say a new weather parameter, such as relative humidity, is to be collected. The only changes required to the

Example 11.9
The Weather_data.Create
procedure.

```
procedure Create (Data: out REC) is
begin
    Rain_gauge.Evaluate (Data.Rainfall) ;
    Wind_speed.Mean (Data.Mean_wind_speed) ;
    Wind_speed.Max ( Data.Max_wind_speed) ;
    Wind_speed.Min (Data.Min_wind_speed) ;
    ...
    -- Start collecting the next lot of data
    Rain_gauge.Collect ;
    Wind_speed.Collect ;
    Wind_direction.Collect ;
    ...
end Create;
```

system are to introduce a humidity object and to change Weather_data so that humidity is collected. Of course, we have not considered processing and the processing operation may also have to be changed when a new parameter is introduced.

Space does not permit us to continue this system decomposition but the reader should now have a general picture of how this is a feasible and useful approach to software design. To reiterate, the key to designing a software system which exhibits low coupling and high visibility is to use information hiding to its fullest extent and to delay all decisions on representation until the most detailed design stages. If this approach is adopted, shared data areas may be eliminated and data representation details do not affect the software structure. Subsequent data changes may be made without structural modifications.

Example 11.10
The Wind_speed object
interface.

```
package Wind_speed is
    type T is private ;
    -- Compute mean wind speed from raw data
    procedure Mean ( Average_speed: out T ) ;
    -- Find maximum wind speed
    procedure Max (Max_speed: out T ) ;
    -- find minimum wind speed
    procedure Min (Min_speed: out T ) ;
    -- Collect raw wind speed data into some internal data area
    procedure Collect ;
end Wind_speed ;
```

11.3   Deriving an object-oriented design

The advantages of adopting an object-oriented approach to system design are that it minimizes the coupling of the design and makes the design more resilient to change. Given that an object-oriented approach is to be adopted, the designer is faced with the problem of how to derive such a design from a specification which may not be expressed in an object-oriented way. In particular, how can relevant objects and associated operations be determined from a specification?

There is no simple formula or recipe that can be presented which allows a design to be derived. As discussed in Chapter 10, the process of design is a creative one relying on the skill, education, intuition and experience of the designer and, like other creative processes, it cannot be expressed in some kind of formula. The designer must postulate a number of possible designs, test these and iterate between them until an acceptable solution is found.

Of course, this process must start somewhere and an approach suggested by Abbott (1983) and Booch (1987) is useful as a starting point in the design process. This approach relies on producing a brief descriptive overview of the system, expressed in natural language, and then identifying relevant nouns (the objects) and verbs (the operations) from this overview. To illustrate this process, consider the following short description of a system which acts as an office information retrieval system (such a system is used as a design example in the following chapter).

> The Office Information Retrieval System (OIRS) is an automatic **file clerk** which can *file* **documents** under some **name** in one or more **indexes**, *retrieve* documents, *display* and *maintain* document indexes, *archive* documents and *destroy* documents. The system is activated by a **request** from the **user's terminal** and always *returns* a **message** to the **user** indicating the **success** or **failure** of the request.

The language analysis approach starts by identifying the nouns (shown emboldened above) and the verbs (shown italicized) in the system description.

- Documents
- Indexes
- User_requests

It is also possible to identify some operations:

- File documents
- Retrieve documents
- Archive documents
- Destroy documents
- Display indexes
- Maintain indexes
- Get user_request

We have thus identified some objects and operations but it is clear that the essential looseness of natural language can cause problems. For example, what exactly does 'maintain' an index mean? What does 'filing' mean and so on. It is not enough to rely on normal usage of these terms; a more complete explanation is required to derive the design. We can again turn to the system description for more information.

When a document is filed, the location of the document, a document name and the indexes under which it should be filed must be specified. Retrieval requests involve the specification of one or more indexes along with the document name. Index examination involves specifying an index name and a qualifier. This qualifier is a condition determining which parts of the index are required for examination.

From this paragraph, we see that the file operation involves specifying indexes. There is the implicit assumption that when a document is filed, its name is entered in an index. We get the information that index examination requires the specification of the index name and qualifier. There is also the implicit statement that all of this is specified as part of the user command. Thus the following object classes and operations can be derived:

Object class: Document
   Operations: File
               Retrieve
               Destroy
               Archive
Object class: Index
   Operations: Display
               Delete_entry
               Add_entry

Object class: User_request
       Operations: Get_request
                        Get_action
                        Get_index
                        Get_index_list
                        Get_qualifier
                        Get_location
                        Get_name

In fact, the description of the system stated above was not intended as a starting point for object-oriented design so was not written with this end in view. Nevertheless, it illustrates the general problem with this approach. The production of a complete description of a system is neither straightforward nor concise. We actually need much more detailed information about operations, system parameters, restrictions, etc., than can normally be provided in a one or two paragraph description. However, given the initial object and operation identification as a starting point, the derivation of the design can continue in a manner akin to that used in the above design example.

11.3.1   JSD and object-oriented design

It is sometimes suggested that Jackson's method (JSD) (Jackson, 1983) is an object-oriented method and can be used in the derivation of an object-oriented design. This author disagrees with such a suggestion. As Cameron (1986) states:

> JSD models are defined in terms of events (or synonymously actions), their attributes, and a set of processes which describe their time orderings and, by implication, possible parallelism.

The JSD approach relies on the user defining a model of the 'real world' which is expressed in terms of events but also includes the notion of objects (hence the confusion). Jackson suggests a method based on description analysis as described earlier to derive this model and it is certainly the case that the derived model has much in common with an object-oriented design.

The next stage in JSD is to transform this model into a specification expressed in terms of communicating sequential processes which can inspect each other's state vectors (definitely not objects whose state is concealed). The specification is finally transformed into an implementation where an indefinite number of processes are reduced to a manageable, implementable number of processes.

The method has much to commend it in that it represents one of the few methods which lead from initial system modelling through to implementation. Furthermore, the method is recommended if it is intended to implement an object-oriented design in a language like COBOL which is lacking in support for objects.

However, Jackson's method is not a way of deriving an object-oriented design although it does represent a systematic way of transforming such a design into an implementation. It suffers from the problems identified above, namely how can the entities and actions in a system be identified. This is, of course, the key problem in all approaches to design and it is unlikely that any method can actually formalize this task.

11.4   Inappropriate object-oriented design

Finally, a word of warning. It is unwise to be dogmatic about the design process and always to adopt an object-oriented approach irrespective of the system being developed. An object-oriented view of system design is not always the most natural. At some levels of abstraction, a functional view is easier to derive from system requirements than an object-oriented view. In particular, where systems retain only minimal state information, a functional rather than an object-oriented design may be used.

For example, consider an automated teller machine in a bank where the customer selects a particular function by pressing the appropriate function key. A natural view of this system is a functional one rather than an object-oriented one and this interaction might be coded as shown in the description of a simplified control algorithm for such a system in Example 11.11.

The important characteristic of this code is that again it is made up of independent sub-systems (Dispense_cash, Print_customer_balance, etc.) and that any one of these may be changed without reference to the others. Because the cash dispenser machine responds to customer function requests, a functional approach to system decomposition is appropriate. At this level in the design, information hiding is being practised using functions as representation details are not visible at this level.

None of the functional subsystems need retain state information (their action is independent of previous actions) and the overall system state is very simple. All that must be maintained are the customer's account number, personal identification number (PIN), account balance, cash available, cash dispensed and whether or not a statement or a cheque book has been ordered. Of this state, only the cash dispensed and the

```
loop
    loop
        Print_input_message ; – –" Welcome - Please enter your card"
        exit when Card_input ;
    end loop ;
    Account_number := Read_card ;
    Get_account_details (PIN, Account_balance, Cash_available) ;
    if Validate_card (PIN) then
        loop
            Print_operation_select_message ;
            case Get_button is
                when Cash_only =>
                Dispense_cash (Cash_available, Amount_dispensed) ;
                when Print_balance =>
                Print_customer_balance (Account_balance) ;
                when Statement=>
                Order_statement (Account_number) ;
                when Cheque_book=>
                Order_cheque_book (Account_number) ;
            end case ;
            Eject_card ;
            Print ("Please take your card or press CONTINUE") ;
            exit when Card_removed ;
        end loop ;
        Update_account_information (Account_number,
                                Amount_dispensed) ;
    else
        Retain_card ;
    end if ;
end loop ;
```

Example 11.11
A cash dispenser system.

cheque book or statement order is not read-only with updates to the other
variables made by the central computing system. Thus, an object-oriented
approach would be of little benefit in this case.

The key objective is to achieve a system design where the subsystems are mutually independent and communicate via abstract interfaces. The distinction between a functional and an object-oriented
approach is that data representation decisions have to be made earlier
when a functional view is adopted and state information is shared. This
tends to increase the coupling of the system and to make it more difficult to
change. A functional view may be more natural at some levels in the
design, but as soon as representation decisions have to be made, it is
recommended that the designer's approach should become object-
oriented.

KEY POINTS

- An object is an entity which has a private state and which has constructor and inspection functions allowing that state to be modified and examined. No other access to the state is allowed.
- Object-oriented design is a means of designing with information hiding. Information hiding allows the information representation to be changed without other extensive system modifications.
- Object-oriented design is not the same as object-oriented programming. Object-oriented programming languages support run-time operation binding and inheritance. An object-oriented design can be implemented in any programming language.
- Ada is not an object-oriented programming language.
- Objects may be realized as either Ada tasks (parallel processes) or as Ada packages. This realization is an implementation rather than a design decision.
- An approach to deriving an object-oriented design is to consider nouns and verbs in a natural language system description. Nouns represent objects and verbs operations. However, the inherent ambiguity of natural language descriptions means that this should be considered only as a guide to the designer. It is not a design method.
- It may be inappropriate to use object-oriented design to design systems that maintain minimal state information.

Further reading

Software Engineering with Ada, 2nd ed.   Booch is perhaps the foremost proponent of object-oriented design with Ada and this book is an excellent tutorial on the use of Ada and object-oriented design. He can be criticized a little because he makes it look so easy but that is a criticism which can be made of many textbooks, including, perhaps, this one. (G. Booch, 1987, Benjamin/Cummings.)

Languages and object-oriented programming. This is a paper about object-oriented programming rather than object-oriented design but it is a good introduction to the object-oriented approach. (S. Cook, IEE/BCS, *Software Eng. J.*, **1** (2) 1986.)

References

Abbott, R. (1983), 'Program design by informal English descriptions', *Comm. ACM*, **26** (11), 882–94.

Booch, G. (1987), *Software Engineering with Ada*, 2nd edn, Menlo Park, Calif.: Benjamin/Cummings.

Cameron, J.R. (1986), 'An overview of JSD', *IEEE Trans. Software Eng.*, **SE-12** (2), 222–40.

Goldberg, A. and Robson, D. (1983), *Smalltalk-80. The Language and its Implementation*, Reading, Mass.: Addison-Wesley.

Jackson, M.A. (1983), *System Development*, London: Prentice-Hall.

Liskov, B. and Zilles, S. (1974), 'Programming with abstract data types', *ACM Sigplan Notices*, **9** (4), 50–9.

Parnas, D. (1972), 'On the criteria to be used in decomposing systems into modules', *Comm. ACM*, **15** (2), 1053–8.

Sommerville, I. and Morrison, R. (1987), *Software Development with Ada*, Wokingham: Addison-Wesley.

EXERCISES

11.1 Explain why adopting a design approach based on information hiding is likely to lead to a design which may be readily modified.

11.2 Modify the heating system example presented in Examples 11.2 and 11.3 to implement the changes proposed in the paragraph following Example 11.3.

11.3 Write Ada packages describing the specifications for the following objects:

- A binary tree
- A compiler symbol table
- A personal computer printer
- A library catalogue
- A telephone

11.4 Using examples, explain the difference between an object and an object class.

11.5 If you are familiar with Ada, show how the object which you have specified in Example 11.3 might be implemented as Ada packages or as Ada tasks. If you are not familiar with Ada, suggest how the objects might be realized in another programming language.

11.6 Using an object-oriented approach, derive a design for the systems which are outlined below. Make any reasonable assumptions about the systems when deriving the design.

- A software components catalogue is intended to hold details of software components which are potentially reusable. A cataloguer may enter components in the catalogue, may delete components from the catalogue and may associate reuse information with a catalogue component. A user of the catalogue may query the catalogue to find a component using keywords associated with the component description. The catalogue user interface should be based on a structured form where the user enters some details of a component and the catalogue fills in the remainder of the form.

- A group diary and time management system is intended to support the timetabling of meetings and appointments across a group of co-workers. When an appointment is to be made which involves a number of people, the system finds a common slot in each of their diaries and arranges the appointment for that time. If no common slots are available, it interacts with the user to rearrange their personal diary to make room for the appointment.

- An overhead projector slide preparation system is to be built which allows users to prepare slides on a workstation. It should support multiple font text, variable sized text and simple graphical shapes (boxes, lines, circles, ellipses, etc.), and should allow shapes to be shaded. It should also support the preparation of overlay slides where a complete slide is created by using a number of different overlays.

- An automated vending machine can vend coffee, tea and soup depending on a user selection. Coins of the appropriate value are input and the user selects the drink required. A cup with soluble powder is dispensed and the user puts this under a tap. A button is pressed and hot water dispensed to make the drink. After inputting coins the user may terminate the transaction by pressing a coin return button. (Note: as an alternative, use any other vending machine model with which you are familiar.)

• A petrol (gas) station is to be set up for fully automated operation. A driver inputs his or her credit card into the pump, the card is verified by communication with a credit company computer and a fuel limit established. The driver may then take the fuel required and, on completion of delivery (when the pump hose is returned to its holster), the driver's credit account is debited with the cost of the fuel taken. The credit card is returned after debiting. If the card is invalid, it is returned by the pump with no fuel dispensed.

Chapter 12

Function-Oriented Design

Objective

The objective of this chapter is to present a complementary approach to software design where the basic design component is a function rather than an object. The method used to derive the functional design makes use of data-flow diagrams and structure charts which are described by example. The design process is illustrated using the example of an office information retrieval system introduced in Chapter 11 and shown in more detail here. A sequential design is derived but the final section in the chapter illustrates that a concurrent designs can also be derived from data-flow diagrams. A concurrent design for the office system is presented to complement the sequential design.

Contents

Function-oriented design is an approach to software design where the design is decomposed into a set of interacting units which each have a clearly defined function. By comparison with object-oriented design, the design components in this approach are cohesive around a function whereas object-oriented cohesion is around an abstract data entity.

Function-oriented design has probably been practised informally since programming began but it was only in the late 1960s and early 1970s that it was brought to prominence. A number of papers and books were published on this notion, the best known of which are probably those by Wirth (1971, 1976). Myers' work on so-called 'Structured Design' (1975) adopted a functional view of design and this was refined and described in a definitive book by Constantine and Yourdon (1979).

Function-oriented design techniques have been used in the building of large software systems and, in this respect, this design technique has stood the test of practice. In the last few years, the value of an object-oriented approach has also been recognized and it is clear that these design techniques complement each other.

Recently, suggestions have been made that function-oriented design is obsolete and should be superseded by an object-oriented approach. However, many software development organizations have developed standards and methods based on functional decomposition and are understandably reluctant to discard these in favour of object-oriented design. Therefore, functional design is, and will continue to be, widely and successfully practised.

In this chapter, an approach to function-oriented design which is based on the work of Constantine and Yourdon (Structured Design) is described. This is based on the notion of deriving a design from data-flow diagrams which describe the logical data processing, through structure charts which show the software structure, to PDL which describes the design in more detail. However, their data-flow notation has been modified to make it more suitable for use with an automated diagramming system, and a slightly different form of structure chart which excludes control information is used.

12.1 Data-flow diagrams

Data-flow diagrams are descriptions of how data flows from one logical processing unit to another. These diagrams document how data input is transformed to output, with each stage in the diagram representing a distinct transformation. They represent one way of describing a system and have the advantage that they are intuitive and readily understood without special training. They should not include control information and data should never flow in a loop.

Data-flow diagrams are an integral part of a number of design methods and each method uses a slightly different notation. These notations are similar and transforming from one notation to another is straightforward. The notation chosen here is used because it is easy to draw diagrams using a personal computer diagram editing system. Such systems are now widely available and it is important that notations are designed so that diagrams may be easily drawn with an automatic system.

The symbols which are used in this notation are as follows:

(1) *Round-edged rectangles* These represent transformation centres where an input data flow is transformed to an output. The transformation centre is normally annotated with a mnemonic name describing the transformation taking place.

(2) *Rectangles* These represent a data store. Again, they are annotated with a mnemonic name.

(3) *Circles* These represent user interactions with the system. These interactions may provide input or receive output.

(4) *Arrows* These show the direction of data flow. They are annotated with a name describing the data flowing along that path.

(5) *The keywords* **and** *and* **or** These have their usual meanings as in boolean expressions. They are used to link data flows when more than one data flow may be input or output from a transformation centre.

(6) *An arc symbol linking data flows* This is only used in conjunction with **and** and **or** and is used to indicate bracketing. In general, **and** takes precedence over **or** but this may be changed by linking the appropriate data flows.

This notation is illustrated in Figure 12.1, which describes the logical design of a report generator system which might be used in conjunction with the design editor discussed earlier. This system takes a design produced by the editor and produces a report about each of the entities used in the design. The user inputs a design name and the report generator finds all of the names used in that design. The data dictionary is then consulted for information about the design entities and a report is produced. The information in the report is presented according to whether an entity is a node type or a link type.

One of the principal advantages of data-flow diagrams is that they show transformations without making assumptions about how these transformations are implemented. For example, a system described in this way might be implemented as a single program using program units to implement each transformation. Alternatively, it might be implemented as a number of communicating tasks or, perhaps, the implementation might be an amalgam of these methods. Again, we see that parallelism is a detailed design consideration.

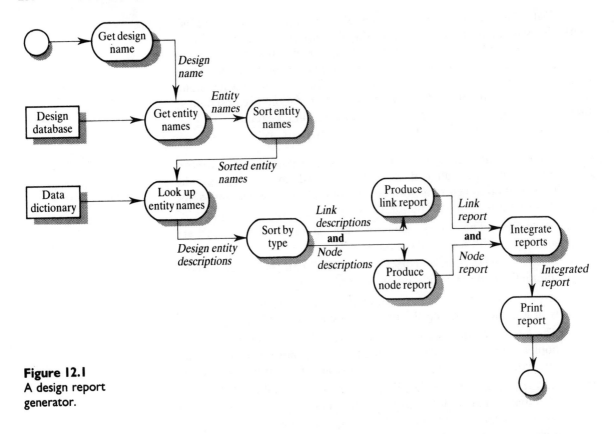

Figure 12.1
A design report generator.

12.2 Structure charts

When a system, described using data-flow diagrams, is to be implemented as a set of parallel processes, this logical organization may map directly onto a physical organization. Often, however, the software must be further structured into a hierarchy of components where data transformations are grouped together under a single parent.

Structure charts describe the programming system as a hierarchy of parts and display this graphically, as a tree. They document how elements of a data-flow diagram are realized as a hierarchy of program units. The purpose of a structure chart is to describe the organization of the software showing how components are formed from sub-components.

Although it is possible to use structure charts as a visual program
description with control information defining selection and loops
(Constantine and Yourdon's version of these charts do so), they are used
here to display the static organization of a design. Control information is not
included as I believe this is better displayed in a design description language.

The notation used here follows the usual convention of representing
a component on a structure chart as a rectangle. The hierarchy is displayed
by linking rectangles with lines and inputs and outputs to a component are
indicated by using annotated arrows. An arrow entering a box implies
input, leaving a box implies output. Data stores are shown as round-edged
rectangles and user inputs as circles. To save diagram space, some inputs
and outputs are unlabelled. This implies that the label associated with
these flows is that of the adjacent data flow.

Given a data-flow diagram showing logical transforms, it is usually
possibly to derive a number of possible structure charts from it. For
example, Figures 12.2 and 12.3 show alternative software structures for the
design report generator (Figure 12.1).

Figure 12.2
A structure chart for the
report generator.

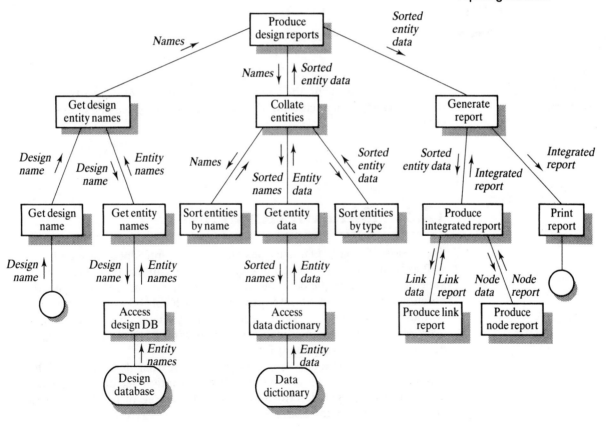

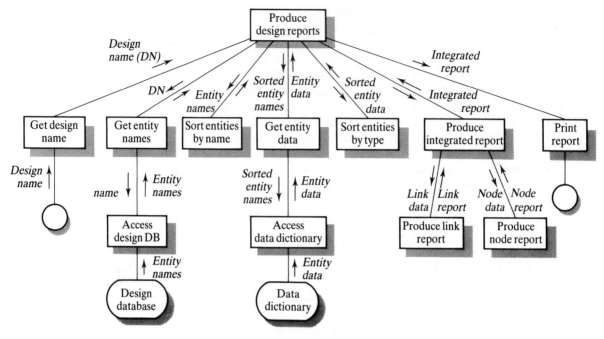

Figure 12.3
An alternative structure
chart for the report
generator.

A problem facing the software engineer is how to derive the 'best' structure chart from a data-flow diagram. This will be discussed later in the chapter.

12.3   Data dictionaries

The notion of a data dictionary has already been introduced in Part 1. As well as being useful in maintaining system specifications, data dictionaries are equally useful in the design process. Given the nature of diagrammatic notations, the amount of descriptive text which can be associated with a symbol is limited so it is important to supplement this with a fuller description. This is sometimes called a *minispec* standing for a short description of the component function.

The data dictionary entry might be a textual description of the component or might be a more detailed description set out in a design description language (described below). An example of part of the data dictionary entry for the above system is shown in Figure 12.4.

Entity name	Type	Description
Design name	Data	The name of the design to be processed.
Get design name	Transform	The design on which the report is to be generated is held in the system database as a named entity. This transform communicates with the user to get this name.
Get entity names	Transform	Using the design name, this transform finds the database entity holding the design and abstracts the names of design entities from it.
Sorted entity names	Data	The names of design entities in sort order.

Figure 12.4
Part of the design report generator data dictionary.

Data dictionaries are an appropriate way to link descriptive and diagrammatic design descriptions (Figure 12.5). This diagram shows a pop-up window describing the selected transform in the data-flow diagram. Some CASE toolsets such as Yourdon's Software Engineering Workbench provide automatic linkage between the data-flow diagram and the data dictionary and this reduces the cost of developing design diagrams. CASE workbenches are discussed in Chapter 18.

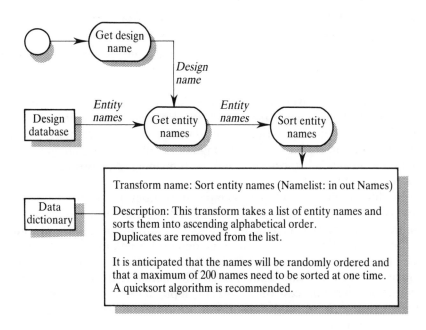

Figure 12.5
Transform information from a data dictionary.

12.4   Deriving structure charts

An important stage in the design process is the transformation of a data-flow diagram to a structure chart. This stage converts abstract transformations into a hierarchy of program units thus representing an important step in the transition from an abstract problem solution to a concrete realization of that solution.

Recall that, in the previous example of a design report generator, two different structure diagrams were derived from the system data-flow diagram. No comment was made at that stage as to which of these represented the best solution. Although this notion of a best solution is subjective, the designer's aim should be to derive a design where program units exhibit a high degree of cohesion and a low degree of coupling.

The identification of loosely coupled, highly cohesive units is simplified if units are considered to be principally responsible for dealing with one of four types of data flow.

(1)   *Input*   The program unit is responsible for accepting data from a unit at a lower level in the structure chart and passing that data on to a higher level unit in some modified form. Yourdon and Constantine use the term 'afferent' to describe such units.

(2)   *Output*   The program unit is responsible for accepting data from a higher level unit and passing it to a lower level unit. This is termed 'efferent' by Yourdon and Constantine.

(3)   *Transform*   A program unit accepts data from a higher level unit, transforms that data and passes it back to that unit.

(4)   *Coordinate*   A unit is responsible for controlling and managing other units.

The first step in converting a data-flow diagram to a structure chart is to identify the highest level input and output units. These units are those which are still concerned with passing data up and down the hierarchy but are furthest removed from physical input and output. This step, generally, does not include all transforms, and the remaining transforms are termed central transforms.

Identifying the highest level input and output transforms depends on the skill and experience of the system designer. One possible way to approach this task is to trace the inputs until a transform is found whose output is such that its input cannot be deduced from output examination. The previous bubble then represents the highest level input unit. Thus, processes which validate inputs or add information to them are not central transforms, but a process which sorts the input or filters data from it can be regarded as such. A similar criterion is used to establish the highest level output transform.

The first level of the structure chart is produced by representing the input and output units as single boxes and each central transform as a single box. The box at the root of the structure chart is designated as a coordinate unit. This factoring process may then be repeated for the first-level units in the structure chart until all bubbles in the data-flow diagram are represented.

In the design report generator data-flow diagram (Figure 12.1) it is clear that the output part of the system are those transforms which are concerned with producing reports for link and node type, report integration and printing. These are all concerned with the formatting and organization of design entity descriptions.

Deciding on which transforms in Figure 12.1 should be considered as input transforms is more difficult. Recall that the rule of thumb is to examine the transformation and, when it is not possible to determine the input from the output, a central transform has been discovered. From Figure 12.1, we decide that the sorting of entity names is a central transform. This results in the first-level structure chart (Figure 12.6).

Applying the same process to the sort unit to derive the second-level structure gives Figure 12.7.

The derivation process is applied a third time to derive the final structure chart as shown previously in Figure 12.2.

It is generally (although not necessarily) true that each node in the structure chart of a well structured design will have between two and seven subordinates. If a node has only a single subordinate, this implies that the unit represented by that node may have a low degree of cohesion. It suggests that the unit encompasses more than a single function and the existence of a single subordinate means that one of the functions may have been factored out. If a node has many subordinates, this implies that the design has been developed to too low a level at that stage. Determining design quality by analysing structure charts is covered in Chapter 14.

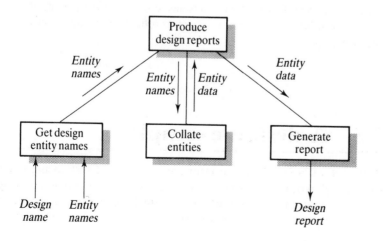

Figure 12.6
Initial design report generator structure.

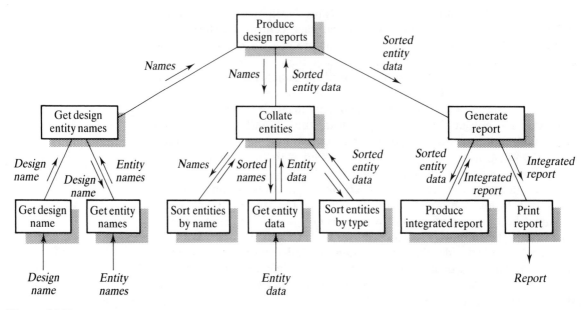

Figure 12.7
Expanded design report
generator structure chart.

The information available in data-flow diagrams is useful in deriving structure charts but, if these charts are seen as a description of the software component structure, other components may be included in a structure chart which are not directly concerned with data processing. For example, components which are concerned with logging-in and logging-out a user, system initialization and any other components which are concerned with system control rather than data processing may be necessary.

Thus, structure chart derivation is a two-stage process. From the data-flow design, an initial structure may be derived and this may be used in the construction of a design description expressed in a PDL. Following this design description, which includes control information, it may be necessary to modify the structure chart to reflect extra control components which are required.

12.5   A design example

In this section, a simple office information retrieval system is used as an example to illustrate function-oriented design. As a full system description is lengthy, only an overview of the system is presented. Aspects of the system will be expounded in more detail as required. This system is similar to the system described in the previous chapter and the function-oriented design may be compared with the object-oriented design shown there.

The Office Information Retrieval System (OIRS) is an automatic file clerk which can file documents under some name in one or more indexes, retrieve documents, display and maintain document indexes, archive documents and destroy documents. The system is activated by a request from the user's terminal and always returns a message to the user indicating the success or failure of the request.

The interface to this system is a form which has a number of fields (Figure 12.8). Some of these fields are menu fields where the user can choose a particular option. Other fields allow user textual input. Menu items may be selected by pointing with a mouse or by moving a cursor using keyboard commands.

The fields displayed in the form are as follows:

(1) *The operation field*   Selecting this field causes a menu of allowed operations to be displayed as shown in Figure 12.8.

(2) *The known indexes field*   Selecting this field causes a menu of index names to be displayed. These are the indexes known to the OIRS system. Selecting an item from this list causes it to be added to the current index list.

(3) *The current indexes field*   Selecting this field causes a list of the current indexes to be displayed. The current indexes are those indexes which are used in a particular retrieval operation. Thus, if the user issues a save command, the document name is entered in all of the current indexes.

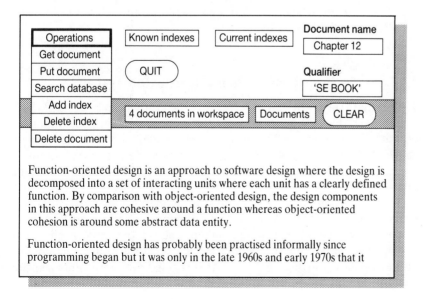

Figure 12.8
The OIRS system interface.

(4) *The document name field* This specifies the name under which the document is to be filed or the name of the document which is to be retrieved. If this name is not filled in, the user is prompted for a value.

(5) *The qualifier field* This is a pattern which is used in searching. For example, the pattern 'A-K' may be specified with a command to lookup the names of documents in the current index lists. The qualifier causes only those names which begin with a letter from A to K to be listed. Alternatively, the qualifier field might contain a keyword such as 'Software Engineering'. An index search retrieves all documents which contain this keyword.

(6) *The current workspace* Documents are retrieved to the current workspace which may contain several documents. The user may choose a document in the workspace by selecting its name from the workspace menu. Selecting Clear from the workspace menu bar causes the workspace selection to be removed from the workspace. Moving the cursor into the workspace causes the system to enter edit mode where documents may be edited using a simple word processor.

There are, of course, a number of alternative ways of realizing this design. The most appropriate depends on particular parameters such as the I/O devices connected to the system and the programming language to be used. For example, if a mouse is used for selection, a design must be adopted which enables the mouse position to be tracked.

In some situations, it may be appropriate to implement the system as a set of parallel process rather than as a single process. As already suggested, the early stages of a design should avoid such decisions as they limit the modifiability of the system.

12.5.1 Designing the office information system

The initial stage of the design of the OIRS can be tackled by considering the system as a black box and examining the inputs and outputs of the system. This can be represented as a data-flow diagram shown as Figure 12.9. Recall that the arc annotated with 'or' joining the output data flows means that one or the other but not both of these data flows occurs.

This initial step serves only to define the external inputs and outputs of the system. A possible development of this is to assume that a data-flow bubble exists to handle each input and each output. Connecting these bubbles might be a transform converting input to output as shown in Figure 12.10. At this stage, let us call this transform Execute Command.

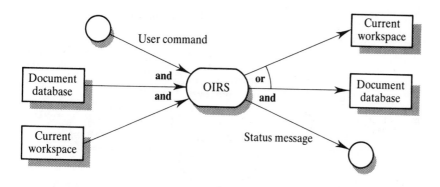

Figure 12.9
Inputs and outputs of
OIRS.

The Execute command transform can now be considered in isolation. The designer must now decide whether this central transform is, logically, a single transform or whether it is best implemented as a number of transforms. Clearly, there are several possible configurations but questions that the designer might use to help make the decision are:

- Are the input or output data flows processed independently or are they interdependent? If they are processed independently, this suggests that a transform should exist for each independent processing unit.

- Can the central transform be considered as a series of transforms where all of the data processed are passed through the series? If so, each logical processing element in the series might be represented as a single transform.

In fact, neither of these conditions hold in this case so it is reasonable, at the highest level, to represent the central transform as a single transformation unit. It is a complex transformation which can be broken down into simpler transformations (Figure 12.11).

Figure 12.10
Initial refinement of the
OIRS design.

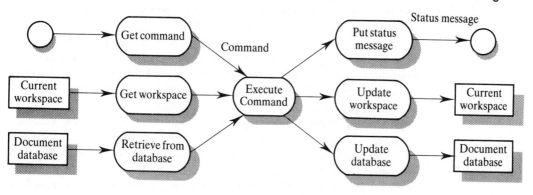

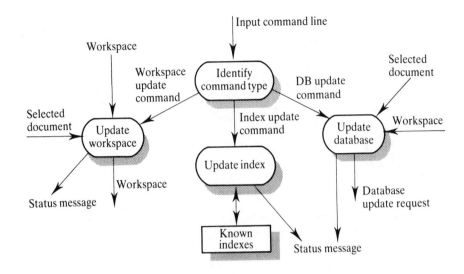

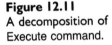

Figure 12.11
A decomposition of
Execute command.

Figure 12.11 shows how command execution can be partitioned: commands to update the workspace (Get document, Search database, Clear workspace and the implicit Edit command), commands to update the database (Put document, Delete document) and commands which operate on indexes (Add index, Delete index, Display index lists).

However, the data-flow diagram is not concerned with these individual commands unless they involve different data flows (in this case, they do not) so it is not appropriate to decompose the data-flow diagram further.

Decomposing Execute command in this way reveals a possible flaw in the initial design. It shows that the workspace and the database are exclusively accessed from within Execute command so there is no need for top-level transforms concerned with accessing these entities. These access procedures are subordinate to Execute command so the top-level description of the design should be modified (Figure 12.12).

The process of design refinement where a design is decomposed, flaws discovered and the higher levels redesigned is a natural part of the design process. I have deliberately tried to illustrate here that good designs do not come about all at once but are the outcome of an iterative refinement process.

Structure charts and data-flow diagrams are useful graphical notations which provide an overall description of the design but which do not, in the form used here, include control flow information. A structure chart shows how a system or components is made up of sub-components but does not describe when or how these sub-components are activated.

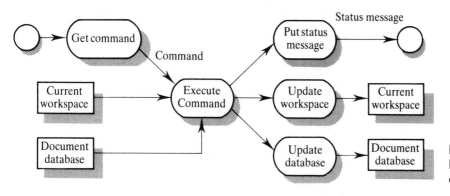

Figure 12.12
Modified OIRS data-flow design.

The form of structure charts described by Constantine and Yourdon does include some of this information but, in my view, control information is best provided using a design description language. Diagrammatic design descriptions are best for showing the relationships of design components. Textual descriptions are best for setting out detail. If too much detail is included in a diagram, it becomes untidy and cluttered and correspondingly difficult to read.

For each functional entity in the structure chart, an associated design description should be prepared. The level of detail at which this is expressed varies depending on the application and on the final implementation language. Indeed, individual organizations may develop their own standards for this. The control description should be provided after the structure chart has been completed as a supplement to it. Example 12.1 is an overall design description for the top-level of the OIRS. At this stage in the design, a simple description of the software has been set out without concern for details of the types of the design components. Thus, the design description does not include declarations of the entities which are used. However, the names used should be entered in a data dictionary along with a description of the entities which these names represent. Not only will this make it less likely that names are reused in error, but it also provides insight into the designer's thinking.

The design process continues by decomposing each of the design components. As an illustration of the decomposition process, consider the design of the Get_command component. For brevity, this is shown only as a PDL description in Example 12.2. Notice the use of natural language in this description.

The interface to the OIRS involves a number of menus to the user and the position of the screen cursor is used to choose which command to execute. This design suggests that the application system is responsible for finding out the cursor position, identifying the appropriate command and then calling another component to execute that command. The advantage of this approach is that command execution is localized and independent of

Example 12.1
High-level design of the
OIRS system.

```
procedure Office_system is
begin
      User := Login_user ;
      Workspace := Create_user_workspace (User) ;
      -- Get the users own document database using the user id
      DB_id := Open_document_database (User) ;
      -- get the user's personal index list;
      Known_indexes := Get_document_indexes (User) ;
      Current_indexes := NULL ;
      -- get/execute command loop
    loop
       Command := Get_command ;
       exit when Command = Quit ;
       Execute_command ( DB_id, Workspace, Command, Status) ;
       if Status = Successful then
          Write_success_message ;
       else
          Write_error_message (Command, Status) ;
       end if ;
    end loop ;
      Close_database (DB_id) ;
      Logout (User) ;
end Office_system ;
```

the interface. Should the interface be changed so that commands are typed (say), only the Get_command procedure need be changed.

The disadvantage of this approach is that additional overhead is involved in separating command identification and command execution. If a mouse is used for command selection, real-time tracking of the mouse and cursor display is necessary and the computer may include some hardware assistance to speed up this process. It may be necessary to adopt an alternative design strategy where a system procedure is used for mouse tracking. This is supplied with a list of 'action areas' and the names of functions to be called when these areas are entered.

12.6   Concurrent systems design

As with object-oriented design, a function-oriented approach to design does not preclude the realization of that design as a set of parallel communicating processes. Indeed, data-flow diagrams explicitly exclude control information so a standard implementation technique for real-time

Example 12.2
Command selection.

```
procedure Get_command is
begin
-- track the cursor until it is over a menu selection or in the workspace
   loop
      Cursor_position := Get_cursor_position ;
      exit when positioned in workspace or
            (positioned over menu and button clicked) ;
      Display_cursor_position ;
   end loop ;
   if In_workspace (Cursor_position) then
      Command := Edit_workspace ;
   elsif In_command_menu (Cursor_position) then
      Display_command_menu ;
      Command := Get_command_from_menu ;
   elsif In_Known_indexes (Cursor_position) then
      Command := Display_indexes ;
   elsif In_Current_indexes (Cursor_position) then
      Command := Display_current_indexes ;
   elsif In_clear_button then
      Command := Clear_workspace ;
   elsif In_Document_name (Cursor_position) then
      Command := Edit_document_name ;
   elsif In_Qualifier (Cursor_position) then
      Command := Edit_qualifier ;
   elsif In_documents (Cursor_position) then
      Command := Display_documents ;
   elsif In_quit_button (Cursor_position) then
      Command := Quit ;
   else
      System_error ;
   end if ;
end Get_command ;
```

systems is to take a data-flow diagram and to implement its transformations as separate processes.

To illustrate this approach, consider the data-flow diagram shown in Figure 12.13. This represents a system which collects data from six sensors monitoring the neutron flux in a nuclear reactor. The sensor data is placed in a buffer from which it is extracted and processed and the average flux level is displayed on an operator's display. Should the processed flux level exceed some maximum permitted value, an alarm process is activated and the reactor is shut down.

Each sensor has an associated process which converts the analogue input flux level into a digital signal and passes this, with the sensor identifier to the buffer (Sensor_data). The buffer must also be implemented as a

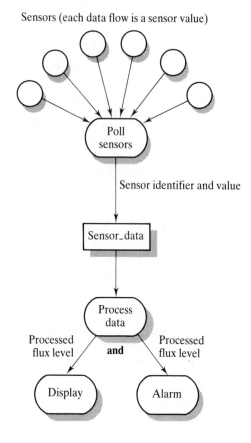

Figure 12.13
Reactor flux monitoring.

parallel process as this allows synchronization of the sensor processes producing the data and the processing functions which consume the data. The Process_data, Display and Alarm functions are also implemented as separate processes.

Space does not permit a complete description of this system design, but the buffer process is shown in Example 12.3 as an Ada task. Assume that the information passed to the buffer is of type SENSOR_RECORD. Descriptive comments have been included, but for a full description of Ada tasking a text such as that by Barnes (1984) should be consulted. Further examples of parallel design implementations and Ada tasking are given in Sommerville and Morrison (1987).

```
task Buffer is
    -- Get and Put are like procedures within Buffer which may
    -- execute in parallel. They are the sole interface to the buffer.
    entry Put ( Val: SENSOR_RECORD ) ;
    entry Get ( Val: in out SENSOR_RECORD) ;
end Buffer ;
```

This task specification describes the buffer interface and shows that Get and Put are the only operations defined on the buffer. The detailed design description (Example 12.3) shows that the buffer is implemented as a ring buffer with a maximum of 50 000 entries. If the number of entries exceeds 50 000, the processes calling Buffer must wait until there is buffer space available before making a buffer entry.

The OIRS system described above may also be realized using concurrent processes as shown in Example 12.4. Command input, command execution, and status reporting as shown in the data-flow diagrams for the system (Figure 12.12) are all implemented as separate tasks.

The Get_command task continually tracks the mouse and, when a command area is selected, initiates the command execution process. Similarly, the command execution process produces status messages which

```
        task body Buffer is
        Size: constant NATURAL := 50000 ;
        type BUFSIZE is range 1..Size ;
        Store: array (BUFSIZE) of SENSOR_RECORD ;
        Entries: NATURAL := 0 ;
        Front, Back:BUFSIZE := 1 ;
      begin
        loop
        -- The select construct is called a conditional entry.
        -- This means that a call to the Get and Put processes will
        -- only be accepted when one of the conditional expressions
        -- following is true.
        -- Thus, Put can only execute when there is space in the buffer,
        -- Get can only take items from the buffer when it is not empty.
          select
            when Entries < Size =>
            accept Put (Val: SENSOR_RECORD) do
              Store (Back) := Val ;
            end Put ;
            Back := Back mod BUFSIZE'LAST + 1 ;
            Entries := Entries + 1 ;
          or
            when Entries > 0 =>
            accept Get (Val: in out SENSOR_RECORD) do
              Val := Store (Front) ;
            end Get ;
            Front := Front mod BUFSIZE'LAST + 1 ;
            Entries := Entries - 1 ;
          end select ;
        end loop ;
      end Buffer ;
```

Example 12.3
A task implementation of a buffer.

Example 12.4
Concurrent design of
OIRS system.

```
procedure Office_system is
    task Get_command ;
    task Process_command is
      entry Command_menu ;
      entry Display_indexes ;
      entry Edit_qualifier ;
      -- Additional entries here. One for each command
    end Process_command ;
    task Output_message is
      entry Message_available ;
    end Output_message ;

    task body Get_command is
    begin
      loop
        Cursor_position := Get_cursor_position ;
        exit when cursor positioned in workspace or
              (cursor positioned over menu and button pressed)
        Display_cursor_position ;
      end loop ;
      if In_workspace (Cursor_position) then
        Workspace_editor.Enter ;
      elsif In_command_menu (Cursor_position) then
        Execute_command.Command_menu ;
      elsif In_Known_indexes (Cursor_position) then
        Execute_command.Display_indexes ;
      elsif In_Current_indexes (Cursor_position) then
        ...
        Other commands here
        ...
    end Get_command ;

    task body Execute_command is
      Command: COMMAND.T ;
      Index: INDEX.T ;
    begin
        loop
          accept Command_menu do
            Display_command_menu ;
            Get_menu_selection (Command) ;
            Execute_menu_command (Command) ;
          end ;
          accept Display_indexes do
            Display_current_indexes ;
            Get_index_selection (Index) ;
          end ;
          ...
          Other commands here
          ...
end Office_system ;
```

are processed by the output task. In this example, workspace editing is also implemented as a parallel task and the editor is initiated and suspended as the cursor is moved in and out of the workspace window.

This example illustrates the point made in Chapter 10 that design parallelism is often an option available to the designer. Some types of system (typically real-time embedded systems) are often implemented as collections of parallel processes with a process associated with each system hardware unit. However, problems often have both parallel and sequential design solutions and preconceived notions about the naturalness or otherwise of parallelism should be avoided.

KEY POINTS

- Function-oriented design is a complementary and not an opposing technique to object-oriented design.

- Data-flow diagrams are a means of documenting data flow through a system. They do not include control information and data-flow diagrams should never have loops in them.

- Structure charts are a way of representing the hierarchical organization of a system. In general, nodes in a structure chart should have more than one and less than seven subordinate nodes.

- Control information in a design is best presented using a design description language which includes powerful selection and looping constructs.

- Data-flow diagrams can be implemented directly as a set of cooperating sequential processes. Each transform in the data-flow diagram is implemented as a separate process. Alternatively, they can be realized as a number of procedures in a sequential program. Decisions on concurrency should be implementation rather than design decisions.

Further reading

Structured Design.   An exposition of the Structured Design method. This has been widely and successfully used, particularly in the United States. The book covers all aspects of the method including data-flow diagrams, structure charts and data dictionaries. (L.L. Constantine and E. Yourdon, 1979, Prentice-Hall.)

Software Development with Ada.   This is a book about the effective use of Ada and has a number of chapters on software design and on Ada's parallel processing constructs. (I. Sommerville and R. Morrison, 1987, Addison-Wesley.)

References

Barnes, J.G.P. (1984), *Programming in Ada*, 2nd edn, Wokingham: Addison-Wesley.

Constantine, L.L. and Yourdon, E. (1979), *Structured Design*, Englewood Cliffs, NJ: Prentice-Hall.

Myers, G.J. (1975), *Reliable Software through Composite Design*, New York: Petrocelli/Charter.

Sommerville, I. and Morrison, R. (1987), *Software Development with Ada*, Wokingham: Addison-Wesley.

Wirth, N. (1971), 'Program development by stepwise refinement', *Comm. ACM*, **14** (4), 221–7.

Wirth, N. (1976), *Systematic Programming, An Introduction*, Englewood Cliffs, NJ: Prentice-Hall.

EXERCISES

12.1 Using examples, describe how data-flow diagrams may be used to document a system design. Explain how these data-flow diagrams may be transformed to system structure charts.

12.2 Using a design description language, describe a possible design for the design report generator whose data-flow diagram is given in Figure 12.1 and structure chart in Figure 12.7.

12.3 Modify the design of the report generator so that it becomes an interactive system. The user may give a design entity name and the report generator provides information about that entity. Alternatively, the user may provide a type name and the report generator produce a report about each entity of that type in a design. Document your modified design using data-flow diagrams and structure charts.

12.4 The design of a spelling checker was discussed in Chapter 10 to illustrate design description languages. Document this design using data-flow diagrams and structure charts.

12.5   Explain how data dictionaries are used to supplement design information in data-flow diagrams and structure charts.

12.6   Develop the data-flow diagrams shown in Figure 12.10 so that all transforms are documented with more detailed data-flow diagrams.

12.7   Describe the design of Execute command in the office information retrieval system using a design description language.

12.8   Develop function-oriented designs for the following systems:
- A software components catalogue
- A group diary and time management system
- An overhead projector slide preparation system
- A drinks vending machine
- An automated fuel pump

Descriptions of these were given in Chapter 11. Compare your function-oriented design with the object-oriented design for the same systems.

Chapter 13

User Interface Design

The objective of this chapter is to cover an aspect of design which is often neglected in software engineering texts. User interface design has now been recognized as a critically important part of system design and this chapter presents a topic overview and some guidelines to the user interface designer. It is particularly concerned with the design of interfaces making use of windows, icons, menus and pointing, and with user guidance systems. However, command language interfaces are also discussed. The final section in the chapter gives some guidelines on the effective use of colour in user interfaces.

Contents

As computer systems become more pervasive because of reduced hardware costs, more and more individuals use computers as everyday tools. Interface design should reflect this and should ensure that the computer is seen as a useful and powerful tool. The interface should not have human characteristics, otherwise the user may ascribe human abilities to the machine. Human abilities and computer power are complementary and it is the task of the interface designer to ensure that they work well together.

It is now generally recognized that the user interface of a system is the yardstick by which that system is judged. An interface which is difficult to use will at best result in a high level of user errors. At worst, it will cause the software system to be discarded, irrespective of the functionality that it offers.

A badly designed interface can cause the user to make potentially catastrophic errors. If information is presented in a confusing or misleading way, the user may accidentally misunderstand the meaning of an item of information and, on that basis, initiate a sequence of dangerous actions. Although this chapter cannot cover user interface design in any depth, it is the intention to provide enough information for software engineers that dangerous design errors can be avoided. For a fuller discussion of user interface design, the reader is referred to texts such as that by Shneiderman (1986) or Monk (1984).

Since the first edition of this book was published in 1982, the possibilities open to the user interface designer have opened up enormously. It is now possible to assume that the user's terminal will include a significant amount of processing power and it is increasingly likely to have a bit-mapped high-resolution display supporting multiple text fonts and mixed text and graphics display.

Many systems are now equipped with a 'mouse' which allows the user to point at items on the screen and this has opened up computer use to many people who are reluctant to type. Thus, the emphasis in this chapter is on designing for this class of system. I believe that it will almost completely supplant text-only interfaces in the near future.

13.1   User interface design objectives

The design of a user interface should not be undertaken by the software engineer alone. It is essential to consult with system users and discuss their background and their needs. In some situations, it may be impossible to develop a single interface which is suitable for all system users. In such cases, multiple interfaces might be provided, each tailored for a particular class of user.

The most fundamental principle in user interface design is that the interface must be designed to suit the needs and abilities of the individual user. Users should not be forced to adapt to an interface because it is convenient to implement or because it is suited to the systems designer. Tailoring the interface to the user means that the interface must be couched in terms familiar to the user and that the objects manipulated by the system should have direct analogues in the environment with which the user is familiar.

For example, if a system is designed for use by secretarial staff, the objects manipulated should be letters, documents, diaries, folders, etc., at least as far as the secretary is concerned. In practice, these objects may be implemented using different files or database entities but the secretary should not be forced to cope with such computing concepts as workfiles, directories, file identifiers and so on. The allowed operations might be 'file', 'retrieve', 'index', 'discard', etc.

Examples of systems based on an office metaphor are now commercially available. In these systems, the user is presented with pictures (called icons) of familiar office objects such as calculators, trashcans, pencils, erasers, etc. To select an operation, the user points at the appropriate picture and that operation is initiated. For example, to perform calculations the user points at the calculator icon, to draw diagrams he or she points at the pencil icon, to discard items the trashcan icon is indicated and so on.

This type of interface is suitable for users with no previous experience of computers as they are not intimidated by the terminology associated with the machine. However, it has the disadvantage that completely new operations, which have no non-automated analogue, cannot be represented with a familiar icon. Indeed, it may be very difficult to devise any kind of icon for automated operations. For example, how might multi-file comparisons be pictorialized?

The second principle of interface design is that the user interface must be consistent. Consistency should be maintained within a system and across subsystems running on the same machine. Interface consistency means that system commands and menus should have the same format, parameters should be passed to all commands in the same way, and command punctuation should be similar. Subsystems which offer the same facilities as a menu should display these menus in the same way.

A consistent interface means that when a user takes time to learn about one command of the interface that knowledge is applicable to all other commands in the system. For example, say system commands accept parameters which may be filenames or which may be flags controlling command operation. If it is necessary to distinguish flags from filenames by some means (such as preceding flags with a '–' character), this should be the convention for every system command.

If a particular flag name is used to signify a particular operation in one system command, exactly the same name should be used in all compatible commands. For example, if a command to print a file takes a flag '–d' specifying that the file is to be deleted after printing, the same flag name should be used in every other command which can delete a file, such as archive commands, copy commands, etc.

Interface consistency across subsystems is equally important. Many large systems are made up of subsystems which can be independently activated. These subsystems should be designed so that commands with similar meanings in different subsystems are expressed in the same way. It is dangerous for a command, say 'k', to mean 'keep this file' in a system editor and the same command 'k' to mean 'kill this transaction' in an information retrieval system. Users of both systems will inevitably confuse the commands at some stage, with possibly dire consequences.

The third principle of interface design is that the interface should have built-in 'help' facilities. These should be accessible from the user's terminal and should provide different levels of help and advice. These should range from very basic information on how to get started with the system up to a full description of system facilities and how to use them. These help facilities should be structured so that the user is not overwhelmed with information when he or she asks for help. Help systems are discussed in more detail in Section 13.4.

These principles set out the notion that the system design should be user-centred (Norman and Draper, 1986). Computer users are trying to solve some problem using the computer and many existing systems concentrate on the fact that the computer is used rather than on the problem to be solved. The designer should always bear in mind that system users have a task to accomplish and the interface should be oriented towards that task.

13.2   Interface metaphors

The need for consistency in a user interface was identified as a basic principle of user interface design in the first part of this chapter. One way of helping achieve such consistency is to establish a consistent metaphor for user interaction with the computer system. A metaphor is a scheme of representing system entities in such a way that they can be equated with other entities familiar to the system user.

The best known metaphor is, of course, the desktop metaphor. This was put forward in the OfficeTalk system (Ellis and Nutt, 1980) where it was suggested that the user's screen represented a desktop and the system entities were represented by forms on that desktop. Activities such as deleting an entity were accomplished by dragging it to a trashcan, reading electronic mail was accomplished by 'opening' a mailbox, and storing documents involved dragging them into a filing cabinet. The Apple Macintosh interface (shown in Figure 13.2) adopted a modified and simplified form of this metaphor.

This particular metaphor is reasonably intuitive and suitable for some system interactions. It suffers from the problem that the system screen size is restricted. Rather than a desktop, which is usually a wide expanse, the user has the equivalent of the pull-down tables attached to the back of aircraft seats! There has to be a continual shuffling and rearrangement of windows on the screen to make sure the required information is visible when required.

Although the desktop metaphor is appropriate for some general interactions, it is not suitable for supporting complex system interactions. An alternative metaphor, which was developed specifically for interacting with a range of software tools, is the Control Panel metaphor (Reid and Welland, 1986), used in a software engineering environment. This metaphor is based on the notion that controlling a complex software tool is comparable to controlling a complex piece of machinery, which humans often do using built-in control panels.

An example of this style of interface is shown in Figure 13.1 which illustrates the Control Panel used in the design editing system described in the first part of the book.

The entities which may be represented on a control panel are as follows:

(1)   *Buttons*   Picking a button causes a single action to be initiated. In Figure 13.1, buttons are represented as shaded, named round-edged boxes. Two buttons are shown, Print and Quit.

(2)   *Switches*   Switches may be set at a number of positions to configure a system or to move a system from one state to another. In Figure

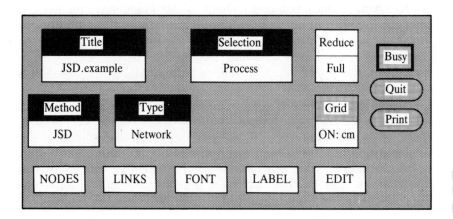

Figure 13.1
Design editor control panel.

13.1, the boxes marked Grid (which turns a screen grid on and off) and Reduce (which scales the display) are shown.

(3) *Menus* Menus are in essence collections of buttons or switches which may be made visible and selected. Menus are represented as named, unshaded rectangles in Figure 13.1. Picking one of these rectangles causes a menu to appear.

(4) *Lights* Lights are activated to show that some action is taking place. The shaded rectangle marked Busy in Figure 13.1 is a light.

(5) *Signs* Signs are visible representations of the system state showing, for example, the name of the file being processed. Signs are represented by two rectangles containing text. The filled rectangle is the title of the sign and the unfilled rectangle contains the sign value. Thus, in Figure 13.1, the sign Title always holds the name of the design being edited and, in this case, the actual design is JSD.example.

This metaphor has been used to provide a consistent interface to a range of software tools from information retrieval systems to the design editing system discussed above. Although there are overheads in using this approach which slow down some interactions, the interface consistency across tools more than compensates for this.

These general-purpose interface metaphors (Desktop and Control Panels) have been successfully applied but are general rather than system-specific metaphors. There seems to be an opportunity to develop specific application interfaces based on an application-oriented metaphor but, to my knowledge, there has been little work done on this approach.

13.3 WIMP interfaces

Since the first edition of this book was published in 1982, perhaps the most radical change which has come about is the availability, on low-cost computers, of a style of user interface which relies on multiple screen windows, iconic (pictorial) representations of entities manipulated by the system, pull-down or pop-up menus, and pointing devices such as cursor mice. The term 'WIMP interface' is derived from Windows, Icons, Menus and Pointing.

This style of interface was invented at Xerox PARC Laboratories in the mid-1970s but it was not until the 1980s that it became economically feasible to provide it on low-cost personal computers. Its first instantiation on personal computers was in the Apple Lisa and subsequently in the Apple Macintosh. Other examples of this interface style are in GEM, in MS-Windows and in the interface provided on many single-user workstations such as those marketed by Sun, Symbolics, etc.

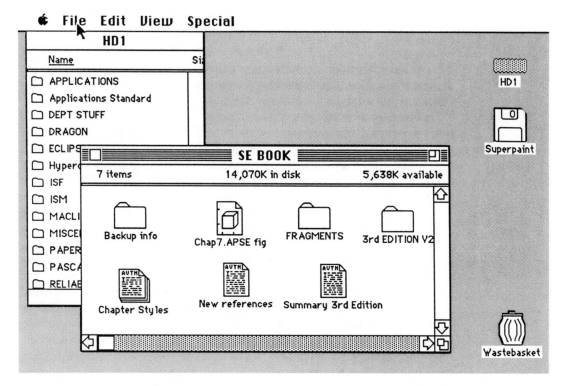

Figure 13.2
A WIMP interface.

An example of this interface style is shown in Figure 13.2. Two windows are displayed on the screen with each window showing a collection of documents. In one window these are represented iconically as are system disks (on the right edge of the screen) and a trashcan. In the other window, only mini-icons are shown and the documents are listed by name. To delete documents, they are selected by moving the cursor over them and clicking the mouse. They are then dragged, using the mouse, to the trashcan.

The advantages of this style of interface are:

* It is easy to learn and use. Even users with no computing experience whatsoever can adapt to this style of interface after a brief training session.

* Instead of a single screen, the user has multiple screens (windows) for system interaction. Switching from one task to another does not necessarily mean the complete loss of information generated during the first task. Although some WIMP interfaces do not support multi-tasking (several tasks executing in parallel), multiple views are very useful.

- It offers fast, full-screen interaction rather than the line-oriented interaction required by command interfaces. This makes some types of interaction much faster than is possible with command interfaces.

- It requires a high-resolution display for effective presentation and this means that graphical presentation of information is straight-forward.

This style of interface represents a radical step forward in computer systems design. If properly designed and if used in conjunction with command interfaces where necessary, a WIMP interface can reduce the time taken both to learn about and to interact with a computer system. It can also reduce the number of user errors made during that interaction.

The relative newness of this style of interface means that we have not yet established standards or guidelines about how best to make use of its facilities. A multi-window interface offers the opportunity of presenting different views of the user's information space but, if badly presented, can confuse rather than help the user. The most common mistake in this type of interface is to use too many windows. Each window is small and the user has to spend time scrolling the display in each window to view the data or moving and resizing windows.

Icon design can also be difficult. Icons are pictorial entities of system entities such as files or processes such as a mail process, a console process, an editor, etc. An example of some icons is shown in Figure 13.3. The icons displayed are a shell icon representing the system console process and a clock icon showing the current time. A terminal icon is used to represent a C-shell interaction and the mailbox icon represents the mail process. In this system, icons represent processes rather than entities such as documents.

For users familiar with the UNIX system, these icons are probably straightforward to understand. Other users, however, may be baffled by

Figure 13.3
Icon display.

the shell icon (the shell is the name given to the UNIX command language). This illustrates the difficulty facing the icon designer. Many entities which are manipulated by a computer are abstract and there is no obvious pictorial representation for them. Inevitably, the icons used are arbitrary and may not be readily understood by system users.

The complexities of window system and icon design are beyond the scope of this book. However, the following section does discuss menu system design because menus can be used without windows and icons. It represents the most effective technique available for designing interfaces for casual and inexperienced computer users.

13.3.1 Menu systems

In a menu-type interface, users must select one of a number of possibilities and indicate their choice to the machine. There are several ways in which the choice may be indicated. Users may type the name or the identifier of the selection; they may point at it with a mouse or some other pointing device; they may use cursor-moving keys to position the cursor over it or, on some types of touch-sensitive terminals, they may even be able to point at the selection with a finger.

The advantages of using a menu-based interface are as follows:

(1) *Users need not know the names of individual commands* They are always presented with a valid command list and they select one of these.

(2) *Typing effort is usually minimal* This is particularly important for occasional system users who cannot type quickly.

(3) *It is impossible for users to put the system into an erroneous state* If an incorrect menu selection is made, the system indicates that the selection is invalid and that another choice should be made.

(4) *Context-dependent help can be provided* With a menu system, it is straightforward to keep track of the user's context and to link the system with a help system.

Figure 13.4 shows an example of a menu which might be presented by a word processor system. This style of menu is similar to that used on the Apple Macintosh computer. This menu gives the user of the word processor several options. It is not worth going into details of these here but this menu display reveals two important features of menu-based interfaces. Firstly, options which are inappropriate should, somehow, be switched off and, secondly, options which require further input should be indicated.

In Figure 13.4 inappropriate options are displayed in grey rather than in black. Choosing these options is disallowed. Options which require

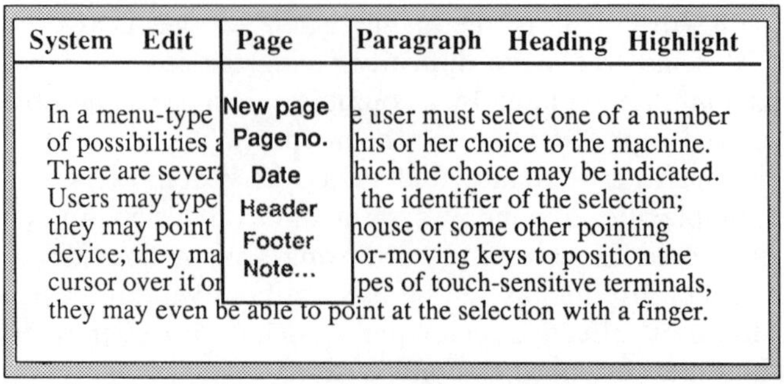

System Edit	Page	Paragraph Heading Highlight
In a menu-type of possibilities a There are severa Users may type they may point device; they ma cursor over it or	**New page** **Page no.** **Date** **Header** **Footer** **Note...**	e user must select one of a number his or her choice to the machine. hich the choice may be indicated. the identifier of the selection; ouse or some other pointing or-moving keys to position the pes of touch-sensitive terminals,

they may even be able to point at the selection with a finger.

Figure 13.4
A word processor menu.

further user input are indicated by following them by ellipses (...). Choosing one of these results in a window popping up and the user may have to make a further menu choice or carry out some other operation.

The type of menu shown in Figure 13.4 is called a 'pull-down' menu. In a pull-down menu system, the menu title is on continuous display and picking that menu title (usually using a mouse or other pointing device) causes the menu to appear. An alternative approach, used in some WIMP systems, is to use pop-up menus. These are menus which appear at the cursor position when a mouse button is pressed. In systems without a pointing device, menus usually pop-up but at a fixed screen position.

Menu systems, however, do suffer from a number of disadvantages.

(1)   Certain classes of action, particularly those queries which involve logical connectives (and/or/not) are awkward or even impossible to express using a menu system.

(2)   If there are a large number of possible choices, the menu system must be structured in some way so that the user is not presented with a ridiculously large menu. The most common structuring technique is hierarchical. The disadvantages of this approach are discussed in more detail below.

(3)   For experienced users, menu systems are sometimes slower to use than a command language.

The major problem with menu interfaces is the need to structure large menus. There must be sufficiently few choices so that all possibilities can be displayed on the terminal screen at the same time. In some cases, this is no problem but, in others, there may be tens, hundreds or thousands of possibilities. Techniques must be devised to classify these possibilities and to allow the user to identify his or her requirements with the minimum number of interactions.

An example of a menu-driven system with thousands of possibilities is the UK's Prestel teletext system. This is an on-line information retrieval

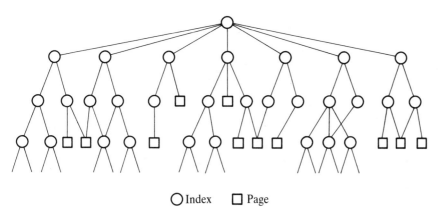

○ Index   □ Page

Figure 13.5
Hierarchical index
organization.

system containing pages of information. It is publicly accessible via the telephone network and the pages may be displayed on a domestic television set. Prestel offers about 250 000 separate pages and, to allow a menu-type interface to be used, classifies these pages as information pages and index pages.

A tree structure of indexes exists and, by starting at the root of this tree, users work their way through the indexes, keying in an abbreviated version of the page number of the next page required (Figure 13.5). All pages in the system have a unique number rather than a number relative to some index so the system does not suffer from the most common drawback of hierarchically indexed systems. On many such systems, the user must progress through every level in the hierarchy from 1 to $(n - 1)$, in order to reach level n. This is necessary because items at some level m, are only identified to the higher level $(m - 1)$. Using Prestel, the user may access any page by keying in the number of that page.

In some hierarchical menu systems, it is not possible for users to work their way up the index hierarchy from level n to level 1. There is no physically recorded relationship between an index and its contents. Users must always start at the top and work their way down the indexes.

An alternative to providing an index hierarchy is to present the user with a screenful of information with the added choice of 'go on to next page'. If this option is selected the following page is displayed and the process continues until the required item is finally displayed. This method is suitable for situations where there are tens rather than hundreds or thousands of possibilities. With such a system, it is important to include a skip forwards and backwards capability so that the user can flip through the pages looking for the one required. Otherwise, if a user accidentally misses the required page, he or she must start all over again at page 1.

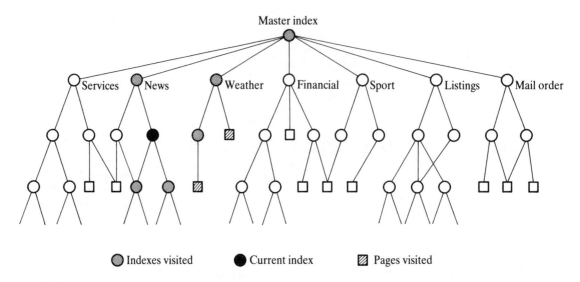

Figure 13.6
Index hierarchy map.

Fortunately, the availability of multiple window systems offers a way round some of the problems of navigating through menu structures. As well as a menu window, another display window can also be maintained which is, in effect, a map of the menu hierarchy. This shows the user's current position in the hierarchy, perhaps the path that he or she has followed to reach that position, and other reachable parts of the hierarchy. Figure 13.6 shows a possible map of the hierarchy displayed in Figure 13.5. The black node indicates the user's position and the shaded nodes show which parts of the hierarchy have been visited.

As well as being able to deduce position in a hierarchy, users should also be able to move around the menu hierarchy by pointing at the place they wish to go to. Thus, rather than using the limited movement commands provided with the system menus, large jumps from one part of the hierarchy to another may be made with ease. All users need to do is to point to the node they wish to visit and a transfer is made directly to that node.

13.3.2 Graphical information display

Although interactive computer graphics systems have been available for several years their use, until recently, has been limited. Because of the cost of terminal hardware and the processor power needed to drive the graphics display, user interfaces based on interactive graphics have only been used in systems such as CAD systems where there is no possible alternative. Now, cheap personal computers support bit-mapped graphics and the user interface designer can assume that simple graphical facilities, at least, will be available.

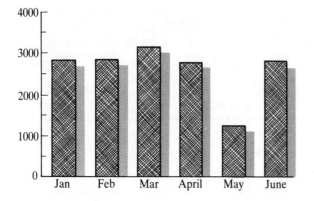

Figure 13.7
Histogram display.

Graphics are usually used for information presentation rather than for providing input to a system. The advantages of using graphics derive from human information processing capabilities which allow users to assimilate some types of information from pictures more readily than from an equivalent textual display.

Graphical systems have the advantage that the information stored and processed by the computer can be displayed in such a way that users can gain an overall impression of the entities described by that information. For example, consider a system which records and summarizes the sales figures for a company on a monthly basis. These figures may be presented exactly, using alphanumeric text:

Jan   Feb   Mar   April May   June
2842   2851   3164   2789   1273   2835

By reading those figures, it can be seen that higher sales were recorded in March and much lower sales in May. To abstract this information requires each monthly figure to be studied. Graphical presentation of this information, as a histogram (Figure 13.7), makes the anomalous figures in March and May immediately obvious. Once an overall impression is gained, further, more precise details can be obtained about these figures.

This type of overall impression is what many computer users require. Managers, using an information system, are often more interested in trends and patterns in their data than in exact figures. These trends can be difficult to discern if the data is presented alphanumerically, particularly when correlations are sought. Graphical display of the data, on the other hand, makes trends immediately obvious.

The ability of graphics systems to present approximate information in an easily assimilated way can also be used in designing the user interface

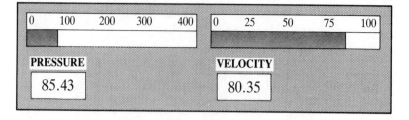

Figure 13.8
Graphical and digital
information display.

to built-in computer control systems. Consider, for example, the sensor information available to the pilot of an aircraft. Traditionally, this information was displayed on electromechanical dials. Glancing at a dial provides enough information to tell the pilot whether action is needed or not. He or she does not necessarily need to see the exact value registered on the dial. The needle position is enough to indicate that all is well or that some corrective action is required.

The introduction of computer-controlled sensor and display systems has meant that it is easier, cheaper and more reliable to display information electronically than using an electromechanical dial. The most common electronic display is a digital display based on liquid crystal technology which shows exact values. The operator must examine and mentally check the information rather than acquire this information from a needle position.

Where a large number of sensor displays are provided, digital displays are confusing and time consuming to check. Rather than use digital displays in such situations, it is better to convert the display output to an analogue form and display this graphically. A dial can be simulated on a display screen by blocking in segments of a circle or, alternatively, an expanding/contracting line can be displayed whose length is proportional to the value displayed.

A further advantage of continuous rather than digital displays is that they give the viewer some sense of relative value. In Figure 13.8, the values of velocity and pressure are approximately the same but the graphical display shows that velocity is close to its maximum value whereas pressure has not reached 25% of its maximum. With only a digital value, the viewer has to be aware of the maximum values and mentally deduce the relative state of the reading.

When such at-a-glance displays are provided, they may be supplemented by more exact digital displays activated at the request of the user or displayed alongside the graphical output (Figure 13.8).

When used wisely, graphics can improve a user interface. However, when graphical facilities are available, the user interface designer is sometimes tempted to over-use these facilities and to use graphics when it is inappropriate. The rule of thumb is that graphical information display should

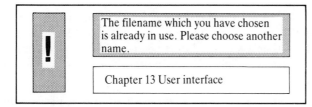

Figure 13.9
Graphical highlighting of textual information.

be used when it is intended to present trends and approximate information. If exact information is necessary, it should be presented alphanumerically.

When alphanumeric information is presented, graphics can be used as a means of highlighting. Rather than simply presenting a line of information, it might be presented in a box or indicated using some icon (Figure 13.9). In Figure 13.9, the box displaying the message overlays the screen display of the application and the user's attention is immediately drawn to it.

13.3.3   Direct manipulation

Direct manipulation is a form of interface style which becomes possible when users have a pointing device, such as a mouse, to pick areas on the display. A direct manipulation interface presents users with a model of their information space and they modify their information by direct action. It is not necessary to type any form of command to cause information modification.

A familiar example of a direct manipulation interface is that presented by many word processors or screen editors. To insert text the cursor is positioned at the appropriate place in the display and text is typed. It appears immediately showing the user the effects of his or her action. Another example is in manipulating a filestore where the user is presented with a list of filenames. In a system like UNIX, a command must be issued to change a filename. In a direct manipulation interface, the user points at the filename to be changed then types the new name.

The advantages of this form of interaction are:

- Users feel in control of the computer and are not intimidated by it.
- Typical user learning time is short.
- Users get immediate feedback on their actions so mistakes can be detected and corrected very quickly.

To build a direct manipulation interface, it is necessary to display some model of the user's information space and then allow the user to act directly on that model. User actions result in immediate change to the information space. The difficulties are twofold:

(1)   How can an appropriate model be derived? In some cases, this is
        straightforward. For example, in the Apple Macintosh, deletion of
        an entity is accomplished by dragging an icon representing the entity
        into a trashcan (Figure 13.2). In other applications, it can be difficult
        to derive an appropriate model.

(2)   Given that users have a large information space (normally the case
        in large systems), how can they navigate around that space and
        always be aware of their current position? This is comparable to the
        problem of dealing with multi-level menus and it is necessary to
        adopt a similar strategy, namely providing a map, to deal with it. Of
        course, it should be possible for the user to move from place to place
        by direct manipulation of the map.

As computer systems are used more and more by casual and untrained
users, direct manipulation interfaces will become more common. This style
of interface along with the derivation of appropriate information space
models is currently the subject of a great deal of research.

13.4   Command interfaces

Command interfaces involve the user inputting a command to the
computer system which takes some action depending on the command.
The command may be a query or the initiation of some subsystem, or it
may call up a sequence of other commands.

At the time of writing, this class of user interface is the most
common, principally because of the preponderance of IBM PC computers
and simple terminals which are in use. The user interacts with the system
via a terminal made up of a typewriter keyboard and a display screen which
can display discrete alphanumeric characters or very limited graphics
characters. The size of the screen is such that normally 24 lines of 80
characters can be displayed.

This class of interface is a direct derivation from off-line interfaces
where data was punched onto cards and input to the system. Such
interfaces were the norm before the advent of timesharing computer
systems and personal computers. Some application interfaces are simply a
conversion from an off-line interface supported in previous batch versions
of the software.

The advantages of a command interface are:

(1)   The interface may be implemented using simple, cheap alpha-
        numeric displays.

(2)   Language processing techniques are well developed because of the work done on compiler techniques. Thus, creating a command language processor is a relatively cheap task.

(3)   Commands of almost arbitrary complexity can be created by combining individual commands. Indeed, it is sometimes argued (Bourne, 1978) that one of the principal advantages of using the UNIX system is its facility to write powerful command language programs.

(4)   The interface can be made concise with little typing effort on the part of the user.

Its disadvantages are:

(1)   Users have to learn a command language which is sometimes very complex. In some cases (such as the UNIX shell language) few users ever learn the complete language.

(2)   Users inevitably make errors in expressing commands which requires additional error handling and message generation software. In a menu system, for example, it is impossible for users to input an incorrect action so the system can always assume its input is correct.

(3)   System interaction is through a keyboard. The interface cannot make use of pointing devices, like a mouse.

For casual and inexperienced users, this class of system interface is not suitable. It is simply asking too much of them to learn a command language. The time taken to learn the language is disproportionate to the time spent interacting with the computer so for such users a menu-based interface (or, sometimes, a natural language interface) is the only acceptable interface style.

Experienced, regular computer users sometimes prefer a command-based interface. The reason for this is that it allows for faster interaction with the computer and simplifies the input of complex requests. Indeed, there are some forms of query where logical connectives (and/or/not) link expressions that are very difficult indeed to formulate using a menu-based interface system. Furthermore, experienced users often wish to combine commands into procedures and programs. Such a facility is also difficult to provide using a menu-based interface.

In designing a command-language interface, there are a number of design decisions which must be made:

(1)   Should it be possible to combine interface commands to create new command procedures? This is a powerful facility in the hands of experienced users but is probably unnecessary for the majority of system users.

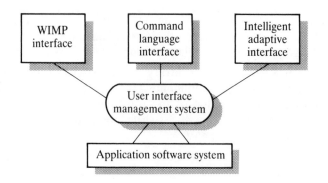

Figure 13.10
Multiple user interfaces.

(2)   What mnemonics should be chosen for system commands? The designer must try and develop as meaningful mnemonics as possible yet retain terseness to minimize the amount of typing required. Again, there is a trade-off between more and less experienced users. The more experience a user has, the more he or she prefers a terse interface.

(3)   Should users be allowed to redefine command names to suit their own preferences? The advantage of redefinition is that the command name can be terse for experienced users or expanded for those who are new to the system. Thus 'pc' and 'Compile_with_Pascal' can represent the same operation, namely the initiation of the Pascal compiler. The disadvantage is that wide-scale redefinition means that users no longer share a common language for communicating with the system.

Of course, command language interfaces and menu-based interfaces are not mutually exclusive. Many large software systems must accommodate a wide variety of users, from experienced computer professionals to casual users with no computing background. Given the resources, it is possible, in principle, to attach a number of different user interface processors to a system so that different interface styles may be provided for different classes of user (Figure 13.10).

13.4.1   Natural language interfaces

One class of command interface is a natural language interface. It is argued that computer systems will not become truly accessible to casual users until natural or quasi-natural language exchanges with the computer system become possible. A number of such interfaces to large database systems such as LADDER (Hendrix *et al.*, 1978) and PLANES (Waltz, 1978) have been implemented and are reportedly successful. The particular systems

> What is the next port of call of the Santa Inez

> How many ships carrying oil are within 300 miles of the Enterprise

> Where are they

>Where are they headed

Figure 13.11
Natural language queries.

are information retrieval systems geared to queries concerning a particular type of subject. This is ships in the case of LADDER, aircraft in the case of PLANES.

Both of these systems are interfaces to database systems and it is intended that they should be usable by people with no computing experience. Examples of the type of query, taken from the paper by Hendrix *et al.*, which may be posed in the LADDER system are shown in Figure 13.11. The system is sophisticated enough to recognize context so that queries such as 'Where are they?' are processed in the context established by the previous query.

The software problems involved in implementing quasi-natural language interfaces are immense – natural languages are inherently ambiguous and resolving ambiguities is generally difficult and sometimes impossible. Systems such as PLANES and LADDER operate successfully because knowledge about the entities in the database is built into the user interface. Using this knowledge, many ambiguities can be resolved. All natural language systems presently implemented confine themselves to specialized applications, and techniques for developing a general-purpose natural language understanding system have not been discovered.

Even if the implementation of a quasi-natural language system such as LADDER is feasible, it is not necessarily the case that a natural language interface is the most acceptable to users. The fundamental problems with such an interface are:

(1)   It is verbose. Users have to type long commands.
(2)   The resolution of ambiguities may involve much time-wasting system/user dialogue. Thus even more typing is involved.

Natural language command systems require users to type too much. If general-purpose speech recognition and understanding systems can be developed, this situation may change. The verbosity of the language will no longer be a problem as users will be able to talk directly with the computer.

However, there is no evidence from current research that general-purpose speech understanding systems are likely to be available in the near future.

A further problem which may result from the use of a natural language interface is that inexperienced users might overestimate the capabilities of the computer system. If the computer appears to communicate like a human, it is natural for those unfamiliar with computers to ascribe other human abilities to the machine, such as the ability to make deductions on the basis of incomplete information. The consequent disappointment may discourage users from investigating the real potential of the system and may even cause them to abandon usage of the system altogether.

Natural language interfaces may be superficially attractive but they are only likely to be useful in a few cases. They were first developed at a time when the difficulties of command languages were recognized but the technology supporting graphical interfaces was not available at low cost. As the population in general becomes more computer literate and familiar with devices such as mice and joysticks, they will be less intimidated by computers and there will be less need to make the machines appear to be human.

13.5   User guidance

In an earlier section in this chapter, it was suggested that all good user interfaces should provide an on-line help system. In fact, help systems are one facet of a general part of user interface design, namely the provision of user guidance. User guidance covers three areas:

- The documentation provided with the system
- The on-line help system
- The messages produced by the system in response to user actions

In this chapter, we are concerned with two of these areas, namely the help system and the system-generated messages. Documentation is covered later in the book (Chapter 29) as it is of general importance in the software engineering process and not just the user interface design.

Although a distinction is usually made between the provision of help (asked for by the user) and the output of messages (asynchronously produced by the system), this distinction is somewhat arbitrary. Many of the principles that apply to the help system apply equally to the messaging system; indeed some recent systems (Sommerville *et al.*, 1989) have integrated these functions into a single system (Figure 13.12). Both types of system are simply information presenters and the content of the information is critical to their success.

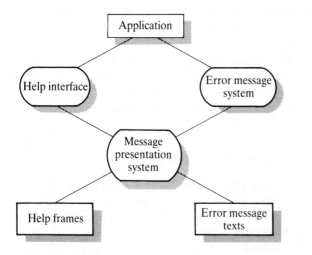

Figure 13.12
Help and message system.

When designing messages of any type, the following principles should be taken into account:

(1) *Messages should be tailored to the user's current context*   This means that the user guidance system should be aware of what actions the user is performing and should alter the output message if it is context dependent.

(2) *Messages should be tailored to the user's experience level*   As users become more familiar with a system and its messages, they become increasingly irritated with long, 'meaningful' messages. On the other hand, beginners find it difficult to understand short, terse statements of the problem. Thus, the user guidance system should allow user setting of the 'verbosity level' in any system and messages should be produced according to this setting.

(3) *Messages should be tailored to the user's skills*   This is quite distinct from the user's experience level. For example, secretarial staff and programming staff may both use an integrated environment. The secretaries may be very experienced in computer usage but their skills are quite different from those of programmers. Different terminology may be appropriate when generating messages.

(4) *Messages should be positive rather than negative*   They should use the active rather than the passive mode of address and should never be insulting or attempt humour.

The design of user guidance information should not be undertaken as an afterthought and should be part of a project plan and budget. Shneiderman (1983) suggests that professional editors and copy writers should be used to assist with message design, and stringent quality control and checking of messages should be imposed. Clearly, this is not a cheap process.

Even when the messages are constructed by technical staff, work on the ZOG system (Robertson *et al.*, 1981) which is a network of message frames, showed that each frame (a few sentences) took 10–12 minutes to write. A large system may have hundreds if not thousands of help message frames, so the total effort and cost of producing these is very significant.

13.5.1 Error message design

It is often the case that the first impressions a user gains of a computer system are those produced by the system error messages. An inexperienced user may start work with a terminal, make an initial error and immediately have to understand the error message which is generated. This can be difficult enough for skilled software engineers. It is often impossible for inexperienced or casual system users. As Brown (1983) points out, error message design is a neglected area of the user interface. Although more effort is now being devoted to this topic, the majority of current systems are sadly lacking in their provision of error information.

The error messages provided by the system should be polite, concise, consistent and constructive. Under no circumstances should they be abusive and, if the user's terminal might be in a public place, the error handling system should not cause audible tones to be emitted which might embarrass the user. Wherever possible, the message should try to suggest how the error might be corrected. If appropriate, the user should be given the option of accessing the on-line help system to find out more about the error situation.

The background and experience of the user should be anticipated when designing error messages. Lengthy, detailed messages are irritating if the user is experienced but essential if the user is a novice. For example, assume a system user is a nurse in an intensive-care ward in a hospital. Patient monitoring is carried out by a computer system. One command in such a system might be a command to display a patient's current state (heart rate, temperature, etc.). This command might be initiated by typing the word 'display' followed by the patient's name:

> *display* Jones, J.

This would cause the monitor readings for patient J. Jones to be displayed. However, say the nurse was new to the system and, rather than type *display*, he or she typed *print*. A badly designed system might respond with an error message as follows:

> *** ERROR *** Unrecognizable command

> **Your instruction (Print) is not a command which the system knows**
>
> For a list of commands which can be processed and help with how to use these commands, press the key marked **HELP**

Figure 13.13
User-oriented error message.

This message is negative (it accuses the user of making an error), it is not tailored to the user's skill and experience level, it does not take context information into account, and it makes no suggestion how the situation might be rectified. A much better error message for this situation is shown in Figure 13.13. This message is more positive, implying that the problem lies in the system rather than in the human use of that system. It explains what was not understood (the *print* command) and it suggests how the user might recover the situation.

Another common class of error is data input error where an invalid data value is entered. For example, in the above system, the nurse might make an error in typing the patient's name. The nurse might type:

display Jines, J.

A badly designed error message would be:

*** ERROR *** Invalid patient-id

As well as the negative connotation of user error, this message uses system specific terms (patient-id) rather than terms which are drawn from the user's domain. A better formulated message is shown in Figure 13.14. This message identifies the problem in the nurse's terms, gives him or her an easy way to correct the mistake by typing a single character, and suggests recourse to the help system if required.

When users are experienced and interact regularly with the computer system wordy human-like responses from the computer tend to

> **Patient (J.Jines) is not known to the system**
>
> Patients whose surnames begin with J are
>   1. Jones, J.
>   2. Jamieson, G.M.
> Type 1 to display readings for Jones
> Type 2 to display readings for Jamieson
>
> For a list of commands which can be processed and help with how to use these commands, press the key marked **HELP**

Figure 13.14
User-oriented error message 2.

become annoying after a few repetitions. Such users prefer more concise messages although these messages should still be expressed in plain language rather than jargon.

Much work remains to be done in this area, particularly in the tailoring of error messages to different classes of user. Many systems have both experienced and inexperienced users and, if they make regular use of the system, inexperienced users soon become experienced. Thus, it may be necessary to duplicate each message at a number of different levels of verbosity and to output the appropriate message for the background and experience of the user.

There are two ways of determining that background and experience:

(1)   The system maintains a user model which is built by observing the way in which the system is used. As the user gains experience, this is determined by the model and the level of the messages is automatically altered.

(2)   The user sets a parameter which determines the level of verbosity required. As he or she gains experience, that parameter is manually modified.

The first of these approaches is perhaps the ideal situation if the model can be correctly formulated. Unfortunately, this is beyond the current state of the art so that user models are imperfect with the result that the message level may be inappropriate. The second approach is simplistic, easy to implement and allows the human to judge when the message level should change. With current technology, this is the approach which should be adopted.

13.5.2 Help system design

As discussed above, the on-line help system and the error message generation system are closely allied. Perhaps the most frequent use of help systems arises when users are presented with an error message which they do not understand and they turn to the help system for information on what they should have done. This is an example of what Walker (1985) calls help! meaning 'help, I'm in trouble'. She also identifies another call of interaction with the help system, namely help? which means 'help, I want information'. She suggests that these are distinct requirements and that different system facilities and message structures are needed if both are to be properly supported.

Of course, the help systems required to provide both of these classes of help must be linked. Although the user may enter the help system because of a problem, solving that problem may require more than a detailed explanation of an error message. Fundamental concepts may have to be explained to the user involving different levels of information. Thus,

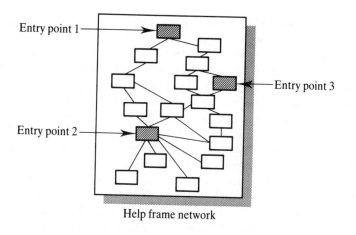

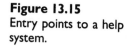

Figure 13.15
Entry points to a help
system.

a key criterion in help system design is to provide a system where there are
a number of different user entry points (Figure 13.15). In Figure 13.15, the
user may enter the help system network via the error message system, via
the application system (it should not be necessary to make an error in order
to get help) and independently when trying to discover what system
facilities are available.

A characteristic of all comprehensive help systems is that they have
a complex network structure where each frame of help information may
refer to several other information frames. The structure of this network is
usually hierarchical with cross-links. General information is held at the top
of the hierarchy, detailed information at the bottom (Figure 13.16). The
difficulties with this arrangement arise when a user enters a network at a
particular point which is not the top (as might happen via an error handling
system) and then navigates around the network. Within a short time, he or
she is likely to be hopelessly lost with no idea of the context in which help

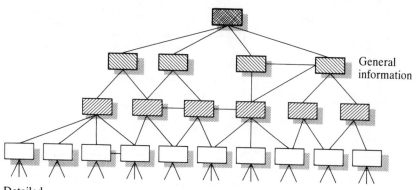

Figure 13.16
Help frame network.

information is provided. The user's only recourse is to abandon the session and start again at some known point in the network.

The author is not aware of any system in which this problem has been resolved although it is clear that the use of multiple windows can help alleviate the situation. Figure 13.17 shows a screen display where there are three distinct help windows. Window 1 is the help frame which is being viewed. Notice that it is relatively short. It is best not to overwhelm the user with information in any one frame. Three buttons are provided in the help frame allowing a user to request more information, to move onto the next logical help frame and to call up a list of topics on which help is available.

Window 2 is a 'history' window which shows the frames that have already been visited. It should be possible to return to these frames simply by picking an item from this list. Window 3 is a graphical 'map' of the help system network. The user's current position in this map should be highlighted by using colour, shading or, in this case, by annotation.

Navigation around the system can make use of any of these displays. The user may move to another frame by selecting it from the frame being read, may select a frame in the 'history window' to reread or to retrace his or her steps, or may select a node in the network 'map' to move to that node.

In the above example, movement from one help frame to another is dependent on an explicit user instruction. Recent developments in hypertext systems (Conklin, 1987) and the relatively low cost of such systems suggest that they will be used more and more for the provision of help information. Hypertext systems are systems where text is structured hierarchically rather than linearly. The hierarchy may be easily traversed by selecting parts of a message or display. Such systems are powerful and attractive and may sometimes be used as the basis of a complete user interface. However, they suffer, even more than help systems, perhaps, from problems of user navigation.

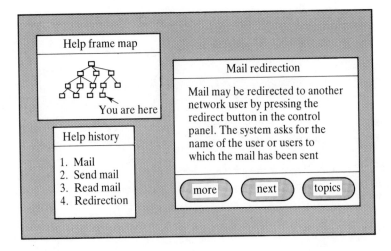

Figure 13.17
Help system windows.

The construction of the actual help information is a difficult, expensive and specialized task. It is best carried out in conjunction with the preparation of system documentation on paper, yet it is not usually appropriate simply to provide a screen listing of a paper manual. The reasons for this are as follows:

- A screen or a single window on a screen is usually smaller and can contain less information than a sheet of paper. Help information should be organized so that users do not have to scroll through pages of information to read a single help frame.
- A screen has dynamic characteristics which can be used to improve information presentation. For example, dynamic colour changes can be used to present different types of information.
- People are not as good at reading screens as they are at reading paper-based text.

The actual help text which is created is application dependent and is best prepared with the help of application specialists. This topic is beyond the scope of this book.

13.6   Using colour displays

In common with other display systems, the cost of colour displays has fallen dramatically over the last few years and it is now economically practical to consider using colour display systems to support the user interface. Indeed, the increasing audiovisual sophistication of the population in general, which has come about because of universal television, means that some types of system, particularly those used for entertainment, are only acceptable if they make use of colour displays.

Colour gives the user interface designer a new dimension which can be exploited to assist in the display of complex information structures. In some systems, such as VLSI layout systems, the display complexity is so high that, without colour, the display would be incomprehensible. In other cases, such as some safety-critical systems, colour may not be entirely essential but its use can draw the operator's attention to important events taking place in the underlying software system.

However, although colour is a powerful tool, it is easy to misuse it in user interface design and to produce displays which are error prone and disturbing to the user. There are two common mistakes which are made when designing colour interfaces:

- The interface designer uses colour to communicate meaning.
- Too many colours are used in the display and/or the colours are used in inconsistent ways.

The dangers of using colour to communicate meaning are threefold. Firstly, a significant percentage of the male population suffers from some form of colour blindness. Such people may not be able to perceive that a particular colour has been displayed. Secondly, individual colour perceptions differ dramatically so that users may misinterpret a display colour. Thirdly, there are no standard national or international conventions about the meaning of colours. In some situations (driving, for example) red means danger. In other cases (chemistry, for example) red means hot. Thus, different users may unconsciously ascribe different interpretations to the same colour display.

Colour then should not be used to set out meaning but should be used simply for highlighting to draw the user's attention to a particular part of the display. The designer must be careful to avoid over-use of colour or the use of colours which are very bright and saturated. These can disturb the user (in the same way that some abstract paintings cannot be viewed comfortably for a long time) and cause visual fatigue. Shneiderman (1986) sets out a number of guidelines for the effective use of colour. These are paraphrased below.

(1) *Don't use many colours*   No more than four or five separate colours should be used in any one display and no more than seven in a complete system interface.

(2) *Use colour coding to support the task which the user is attempting to perform*   If his or her role is to identify anomalous instances in a display, highlight these instances; if similarities are also to be discovered, highlight these using some different colour.

(3) *Give the user control of the colour coding*   He or she should have the option of turning it off. The exception to this might be in safety-critical systems where operator interference with the fault reporting system might not be acceptable. Even here, however, there are circumstances in which the operator might wish to turn off colour coding in order to remove a source of potential confusion.

(4) *Design for monochrome displays then add colour later to improve the display*   If a display is ineffective in monochrome, colour will only occasionally make it acceptable.

(5) *Use colour coding in a consistent way*   If one part of a system displays error messages in red (say), all other parts should do likewise and red should not be used for anything else. If it is, the user may interpret the display as an error message!

(6)   *Be careful about colour pairings*   Because of the physiology of the eye, humans cannot focus on red and blue simultaneously and operator eyestrain is a likely consequence of a red on blue display. Other colour combinations may also be visually disturbing or difficult to read.

(7)   *Use colour change effectively to show a change in system status*   If a display changes colour, it should indicate that some significant event has occurred in the underlying software system. Thus, in a fuel gauge, a change of colour may indicate that fuel is running low. Such changes are particularly important in complex displays where there may be hundreds of distinct entities displayed.

(8)   *Be aware of the fact that colour displays often have lower resolution than monochrome displays*   Sometimes using better graphics is better than using colour.

Colour offers us the opportunity of improving the user interface to complex systems by assisting the user to comprehend and manage the system complexity. However, there is still a great deal to be learned about how to use colour most effectively and, given our current knowledge, user interface designers should always err on the side of conservatism when designing colour displays.

KEY POINTS

- The quality of the user interface is the key system attribute as far as most users are concerned. Without a well designed interface, a system will not be used to its full potential or will be discarded by users.

- Interface design should be user-centred. This means that an interface should interact with users in their terms, should be logical and consistent, and should include facilities to help users with the system and to recover from their mistakes.

- Designing an interface metaphor is a good way to help users with a system.

- WIMP interfaces where the user has multiple windows, menus, iconic object representations and a pointing device are likely to be the most important class of interfaces for future systems.

- Menu systems are good for casual users because they have a low learning overhead. They can be difficult to use when the number of options is very large.

- Graphical information display should be used when it is intended to present trends and approximate values. Digital display should only be used when precision is required.

- Command language interfaces may be popular with regular experienced system users because complex commands can be created and because they can be faster to use than menu systems.

- User help systems should provide two kinds of help. Help! which is 'help, I'm in trouble' and Help? which is 'help, I need information'.

- Error messages should never be accusatory and suggest that the user is to blame. They should offer suggestions how to repair the error and provide a link to a help system.

- Colour must be used very carefully if it is not to confuse an interface.

Further reading

Designing the User Interface. This is a wide-ranging book discussing many different topics of user interface design by one of the foremost workers in this field. Unfortunately, the author has attempted to make the book both a

research monograph and a tutorial text and he has not been completely
successful in this respect. He would have been better to concentrate on
either one or the other. Nevertheless, it is still probably the best available
book on this subject. (B. Shneiderman, 1986, Addison-Wesley.)

Fundamentals of Human Computer Interaction.   This is a slightly older selection of
papers on user interface design. It complements Shneiderman's book well
because it is biased more towards cognitive science. (A. Monk (ed.), 1984,
Academic Press.)

References

Bourne, S.R. (1978), 'The UNIX shell', *Bell Systems Tech.J.*, **57** (6), 1971–90.

Brown, P.J. (1983), 'Error messages: the neglected area of the man/machine
interface', *Comm. ACM*, **26** (4), 246–50.

Conklin, J. (1987), 'Hypertext: an introduction and survey', *IEEE Software*, **20** (9),
17–42.

Ellis, C.A. and Nutt, G.J. (1980), 'Office information systems and computer
science', *ACM Computing Surveys*, **12** (1), 27–60.

Hendrix, G.G., Sacerdoti, E.D., Sagalowicz, D. and Slocum, J. (1978), 'Developing a natural language interface to complex data', *ACM Trans. Database
Systems*, **3** (2), 105–47.

Monk, A. (ed.) (1984), *Fundamentals of Human–Computer Interaction*, London:
Academic Press.

Norman, D.A. and Draper, S.W. (eds) (1986), *User-Centred System Design*,
Hillsdale, NJ: Lawrence Erlbaum.

Reid, P. and Welland, R.C. (1986), 'Software development in view', in *Software
Engineering Environments*, Sommerville, I. (ed.), Stevenage: Peter Peregrinus.

Robertson, G., McCracken. D. and Newell, A. (1981), 'The ZOG approach to
man-machine communication', *Int. J. Man Machine Studies*, **14**, 461–88.

Shneiderman, B. (1983), 'Designing computer system messages', *Comm. ACM* **25**
(9), 610–11.

Shneiderman, B. (1986), *Designing the User Interface*, Reading, Mass.: Addison-
Wesley.

Sommerville, I., Welland, R.C., Potter, S. and Smart, J.D. (1989), 'The ECLIPSE
user interface', to be published in *Software – Practice and Experience*.

Walker, J. (1985), 'Documentation and help online', Tutorial 9, *SIGCHI 1985*. San
Francisco.

Waltz, D. (1978), 'An English language question answering system for a large
relational database', *Comm. ACM*, **21** (7), 526–39.

EXERCISES

13.1 It was suggested in Section 13.1 that the objects manipulated by users should be drawn from their domain rather than a computer domain. Suggests appropriate objects for the following types of user and system.

- A warehouse assistant using an automated parts catalogue
- An airline pilot using an aircraft safety monitoring system
- A manager manipulating a financial database
- A policeman using a patrol car control system

13.2 Think of other interface metaphors apart from the desktop and control panel metaphors discussed here. (This is not an easy question!)

13.3 Describe why WIMP interfaces are well suited to inexperienced or casual computer users.

13.4 If you are familiar with MS-DOS, UNIX or some other command-based system, design an alternative menu-based interface for that system which would be better suited to occasional system users.

13.5 Discuss the advantages of graphical information display and suggest four applications where it would be more appropriate to use graphical than digital display of numeric information.

13.6 Explain what 'direct manipulation' means. Design a direct manipulation interface for UNIX, MS-DOS or some other operating system.

13.7 Study the command interface for MS-DOS or UNIX and discover the inconsistencies in that interface. Redesign the command interface so that these inconsistencies are removed.

13.8 Design a user guidance system for an application with which you are familiar. Pay particular attention to providing different levels of guidance for different levels of user experience.

13.9 Consider the error messages produced by MS-DOS, UNIX or some other operating system. Suggest how these might be improved.

13.10 What guidelines should be followed when using colour in a user interface? Suggest how colour might be used to improve the interface of an application system with which you are familiar.

Chapter 14

Design Quality Assurance

Objective

The objective of this chapter is to describe some aspects of design quality assurance. Design quality assurance is the assessment of whether or not a design meets its specification and should be considered a 'good' design. The principal means of making this assessment is via design reviews. The conduct of a design review is discussed and various design quality metrics are introduced. Unfortunately, these metrics are not yet well developed and are of limited value in assessing a design. Finally, the chapter considers the important topic of evaluating the design of the user interface to the software system and suggests some relatively low-cost ways in which this can be carried out.

Contents

Design quality assurance is an activity which can be carried out in a number of ways. It can simply be viewed as checking whether or not the design implements the system requirements. Alternatively it can be interpreted more generally, as an activity which involves checking the correspondence of the design and the requirements, checking whether or not the design has those attributes which are deemed to be desirable, and checking whether or not the user interface of the system is an appropriate one.

This more general definition is the one used here. Realistically, it is not possible to separate the notions of design–specification correspondence (does the design do what the specification defines) and requirements–specification correspondence (does the specification set out what the user really wants). Although as much validation as possible should be part of the requirements definition phase, it is only during design that a clear picture of the actual system to be delivered emerges and subtle requirements errors are detected.

In this chapter, we concentrate on three questions which must be resolved during design quality assurance:

(1)   What is the best practical way of checking the correspondence between a design and its specification?

(2)   What metrics can be associated with a design which will allow some estimate of its 'quality' to be determined?

(3)   How can the design of user interfaces be validated?

This chapter concentrates on the validation of the products of the design process. A complementary approach is concerned with the validation of the process itself. That is, a software procurer may require that a particular set of procedures is followed during the design process. The assumption is that those procedures lead to better designs so it is necessary to carry out some validation of the design process itself. Process validation is a more general quality assurance concern. It is discussed in Chapter 30.

Validation techniques which are appropriate for checking a software design have a great deal in common with static validation techniques discussed in Chapter 22. The program inspection process can equally well be applied to a detailed software design as can formal verification techniques. Sometimes, it may be more appropriate to apply these formal techniques to the software design rather than the program code.

If a design description rather than a program is verified, errors which are introduced between design and implementation are not discovered. However, there are advantages in applying formal verification techniques to the design:

(1)   The program may be written in such a way that verification is very difficult. Implementation-dependent constructs, whose semantics are not clear, may have been used in order to satisfy efficiency requirements.

(2)   The programming language used may be so low level that verification is impossible. There is no reasonable way to prove a FORTRAN or machine code program correct.

(3)   If verification follows implementation and design errors are discovered, this may involve considerable work in redesign and re-implementation of the program. It is far better to detect these errors at the design stage and accept the possibility of implementation errors which are usually relatively cheap to correct.

(4)   As an implementation may be larger than a design, program verification is longer, more complex and more expensive than design verification.

(5)   It may be possible to transform the design automatically into several different programs depending on the system required. Thus, by verifying the design, only a single verification is necessary for all of these generated programs.

Much depends, of course, on the implementation language. If this is close to or the same as the language used for specifying the detailed design it is obviously sensible to verify the program. If it is a lower-level language, it makes more sense to verify the detailed design. Verification techniques are covered in Chapter 22 and the interested reader should refer to that chapter for further details.

14.1   Design reviews

Design reviews are a quality assurance mechanism which involves a group of people examining part or all of of a software design with the aim of finding anomalies in that design. The conclusions of the review are formally recorded and passed to the author or whoever is responsible for correcting design faults.

Reviews are conducted in many different ways and go under different names such as 'program inspections' (Fagan, 1976), 'Structured Walkthroughs' (Yourdon, 1977) and simply reviews. It is impossible to be definitive about what a design review actually means or how it should be conducted. Any type of review is better than no review. They should be considered as an essential part of the design validation process.

It is possible to identify a number of distinct types of design review:

(1) *Design or program inspections* These are intended to detect detailed errors in the design and check whether or not standards have been adhered to. It is common practice for reviewers to make use of a checklist of possible errors and to use this checklist to drive the review process. This technique is discussed in Chapter 22 and can be equally well applied to detailed designs as to programs.

(2) *Management product reviews* This type of review is intended to provide information for management about the progress of the software design project. It is not intended for detailed design validation. Although the design is discussed, the main concerns of this type of review are design costs, plans and schedules. This type of review is an important project checkpoint where major decisions about the readiness of the project for implementation or even product viability are made. It is a management activity and is not part of the design validation process. Thus, the way in which this type of review might be conducted is not discussed further here.

(3) *Formal technical reviews* The design work of an individual or of a team is reviewed by a panel made up of project members and technical management. This type of review is distinct from a design inspection in that the design may not be described (or even developed) in detail. The review process is intended to detect serious design faults and mismatches between the design and the specification.

The discussion here concentrates on one approach to the reviewing process, namely technical reviews, and sets out one way in which these may be conducted. Further relevant material on design inspections is covered in Chapter 22.

As well as formal reviews, Weinberg (1971) suggests that informal reviews undertaken by project team members for each other are an effective means of discovering faults in a design or program. He refers to this process as egoless programming whereby a program or design is seen as a team rather than an individual responsibility. Individuals do not feel threatened by criticism from other team members and are thus willing to submit their work to scrutiny.

A formal technical review, as defined here, does not involve a detailed study of individual design components. It is more concerned with the validation of component interactions and with determining whether the design meets the user's requirements. The intention is that the review team will detect errors and inconsistencies in the design and point them out to the designer. If errors are detected, they should be noted for subsequent correction.

The stages involved in a design review are illustrated in Figure 14.1. The first step is the selection of a review team. It is important that this team includes all those project members who can make an effective contribution but, at the same time, it should not be too large. If the design is a subsystem design, it is particularly important that those team members who are responsible for designing related subsystems are included in the review. These people may bring important insights into subsystem interfaces which do not affect the design functionality. These insights may be missed if the design is only considered as a single unit.

There are two ways to approach review team selection. A small team of 3–4 people may be selected as principal reviewers. They are responsible for checking and reviewing the whole design. The remainder of the team may be made up of anyone else who is directly involved with the project and who feels that he or she has a contribution to make. These other team members may not be involved in reviewing the whole design but may simply concentrate on those parts of the design which affect their own work. During the review, any team member may comment at any time.

An alternative strategy is to restrict the formal review team to principal reviewers. However, the review documentation should be more widely circulated and written comments invited from other project members. During the review, the review chairman is responsible for ensuring that all written comments are considered by the review team.

The next stage in the process is to distribute the design specifications and, if necessary, the associated requirements specification. It is important that this is done well in advance of the formal review to allow reviewers time to read and understand the design documentation. This inevitable delay can disrupt the design process but premature reviewing causes problems if the review team is not given time to understand the subtleties of the design.

The technical review itself should be relatively short (two hours at most) and involves the designer 'walking through' the design with the review team. One member of the review team should be appointed chairman and he or she is responsible for organizing the review. Another should be responsible for recording all decisions made during the review. At least one review team member (often the chairman) should be a senior designer who can take the responsibility for making significant design decisions.

Depending on the organization, the design and the individuals concerned, this may mean presenting a design overview on a blackboard or may involve a more formal presentation by the designer using prepared slides. During this process, the team may identify problems and inconsistencies. These should simply be noted. No attempt should be made at this stage to resolve any of these problems.

On completion of the walkthrough, all of the comments made should be reconsidered along with any other written submissions to the review team. It may be the case that some of the comments are themselves

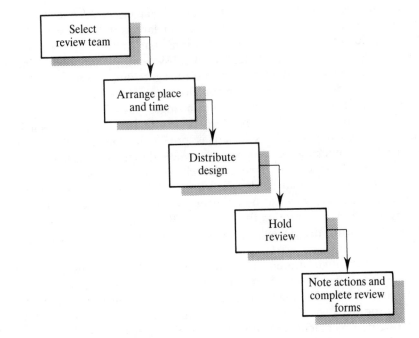

Figure 14.1
Stages in a design review.

incorrect and can be disregarded. The others should be classed under one of three categories:

(1) *No action*   The review discovered some kind of anomaly but it was decided that this was not critical and the cost of rectifying the problem was unjustified.

(2) *Refer to designer for repair*   The review detected a fault and it is the responsibility of the designer to modify the design to correct the fault.

(3) *Reconsider overall design*   The design impacts other parts of the system in such a way that changes must be made. However, the most cost-effective way to make these changes may not be to change the design being reviewed but to change other system components. The review chairman will normally set up a meeting between the designers involved to reconsider the problem.

On completion of the review, the actions are noted and the forms recording the comments and actions are signed by the designer and the review chairman. These are then filed as part of the formal project documentation. If only minor problems are discovered, it may be decided that a further review is unnecessary and the chairman will simply take responsibility for ensuring that the required changes are made. If major changes are necessary, it is normal practice to schedule a further design review.

An important task of the formal technical review is to decide how to handle errors in the software specifications and requirements definition which have been detected by design teams. Requirements errors must be reported to the software contractor and the impact of changing the requirements or the specification must be evaluated. The requirements may be changed. However, if the change involves large-scale modification of the design, it may be most cost-effective to live with the fault and instruct the design team to design around rather than correct that error.

As well as design validation, formal technical reviews may be used as part of the project management process and for training. Project management usually requires that designs be 'signed off' which means that approval must be given to the design before further work can go ahead. Normally, this approval is given after the review. Note that this approval is not the same as certifying the design to be valid. The review chairman may approve a design for further development before all problems have been repaired if the problems detected are such that they do not seriously affect further design development.

Finally, reviews are valuable for training purposes. They offer an opportunity for designers to explain their design to other project engineers. Newcomers to the project or designers who must interface with the system being designed may attend the review as observers as it offers an excellent opportunity to learn about the system design.

14.2   Design quality metrics

Chapter 10 identified attributes such as low coupling and high cohesion which it was suggested are characteristic of 'good' designs. As described in that chapter, these attributes are somewhat intangible. We require some way of quantifying these attributes, preferably automatically, so that we can decide whether or not a particular design is a good one. There are general problems in establishing software metrics which apply particularly to design metrics. These general problems are covered in Chapter 30.

The first problems we face are deciding what we mean by a 'good design' and discovering how this relates to the suggested attributes. In this book, maintainability is emphasized, so a good design is one which is readily adaptable and can be changed to meet new requirements. Adaptability is a difficult attribute to measure and empirical evidence relating coupling and coherence to adaptability is difficult to collect.

However, it is likely that these characteristics are a factor in the adaptability of a design. If a design component does not interact with other components, there is no need to be concerned with the affect of changes to the original component. If a component has a single function or role, the component need only be adapted if that role changes.

Thus, it would seem reasonable to measure the cohesion and coupling of a component. Low coupling and high cohesion should suggest adaptability. Here we are faced with a further set of problems. It is not possible to measure either cohesion or coupling directly. We can only measure other design attributes and hope that these relate to the cohesion and coupling of a component.

It is equally difficult to measure the understandability of a component although humans can often make rough assessments of this attribute. Automatically determining the meaningfulness or otherwise of entity names, for example, is currently impossible, although it is possible to measure certain types of design complexity. In particular, the cyclomatic complexity (McCabe, 1976) of a program can be measured and it has been suggested that low values of this metric imply more understandable programs or designs.

The computation of cyclomatic complexity is discussed in Chapter 21 as this metric may be used as a means of estimating the number of test cases required to provide full test coverage for a component. As a measure of the complexity as perceived by a human, however, it is not really adequate as it suffers from two fundamental drawbacks:

(1) It simply measures the decision complexity of a program as determined by the predicates in loops and conditional statements.
    If a program is data driven, it can have a very low value for the cyclomatic complexity yet still be complex and hard to understand.

(2) Exactly the same weight is placed on nested and non-nested loops. We know from experience that deeply nested conditional structures are much harder to understand than non-nested conditionals.

Oviedo (1980) has developed a metric which takes data references into account. He suggests that the complexity of a component can be estimated using the following formula:

$$C = aE + bN$$

where E is the number of edges in the flow graph and N is the number of references to data entities which are not declared in the component. Although this appears to get over some of the problems of measuring complexity, this metric has not really been properly validated.

Constantine and Yourdon (1979) suggest that the coupling of a design can be quantified by measuring the fan-in and fan-out of design components in a structure chart. The fan-in value for a component is the number of lines entering the component's box on the structure chart. It is equivalent to the number of other components which call that component. The fan-out value is the number of lines leaving a box on the structure chart. These can easily be computed automatically if the design is captured using some graphical editing tool.

A high fan-in value suggests that coupling is high because it is a measure of module dependencies. A high fan-out value suggests that the complexity of the calling component may be high because of the complexity of control logic required to coordinate the subordinate components.

Henry and Kafura (1981) identified another form of fan-in/fan-out which is informational fan-in/fan-out. This is a count of the number of local data flows from a component plus the number of data structures the component updates. The data-flow count includes procedure calls so informational fan-in/fan-out subsumes structural fan-in/fan-out discussed above.

Using the computed fan-in and fan-out, Henry and Kafura suggest that the complexity of a component can be computed according to the following formula:

$$\text{Complexity} = \text{Length} * (\text{Fan-in} * \text{Fan-out})^2$$

Length is any measure of length such as lines of code or McCabe's cyclomatic complexity. Henry and Kafura validated their metric using the UNIX system but I am not aware of any other independent validations. The advantage of this metric compared to structural fan-in/fan-out is that it takes into account data-driven programs. Its principal disadvantage is that it can give complexity values of zero if there is no fan-in or fan-out. Components at the lowest level may not call other components but may interact with hardware and be very complex. Similarly, components which interact with users have no fan-in but may also involve complex manipulations.

Given the current state of the art of software metrics, it is very difficult to provide any general guidelines concerning the usefulness or otherwise of design metrics. We simply do not have adequate evaluation data about the existing metrics, and organizations requiring some means of design quantification must use their own historical design data to establish local quality metrics.

14.3 User interface evaluation

We have already discussed the importance of effective user interface design, yet once a design has been outlined the designer is faced with the task of estimating the effectiveness or otherwise of that user interface. It is easy to be seduced by the attractiveness of the facilities provided on modern bit-mapped workstations and to assume that any interface which uses such facilities must be better than a simple command interface. However, this is not necessarily so and part of the overall design validation process should be concerned with validating the user interface design.

Unfortunately, proper evaluation of a user interface design is a very expensive process. It almost certainly requires the support of cognitive scientists such as psychologists and, perhaps, people trained in graphic design. It involves designing and carrying out a statistically significant number of experiments with typical users. This complete evaluation may be economically possible and sensible for very large and expensive systems development projects. However, it is simply economically unrealistic to carry out such an evaluation for most systems, particularly where these are developed by small organizations.

Of course, this does not mean that user interface evaluation should be ignored. It simply means that some simpler evaluation technique should be adopted and the results of the evaluation may be less reliable. However, in many cases the aims of the evaluation are to qualify rather than quantify user preferences and to detect particularly error-prone operations. Simple evaluation techniques may be used for this purpose.

Examples of simple techniques for user interface evaluation are:

- Questionnaires which collect information about what users thought of the interface.
- Video recording and analysis of typical system use.
- The inclusion in the software of code which collects information about what facilities are most used and what are the most common errors.
- The provision of a 'gripe' button which allows the user to feed back comments about the system to its designers.

Surveying users using a questionnaire is a relatively cheap way of evaluating an interface. However, it is important that the questions asked are precise rather than general. It is no use asking questions like 'Please comment on the usability of the interface' as the responses are likely to vary so much that no common trend can be discerned. Rather, specific questions such as 'Please rate the understandability of the error messages on a scale from 1 to 5 where one means very clear and 5 means incomprehensible' are more likely to provide useful information to improve the interface.

There is little point in providing a general set of questions here as the key to successful surveys is very specific system tailoring. The questions asked should be designed around the specific interface. Users should be asked to rate their own experience and background when filling in the questionnaire. This allows the designer to find out if users from any particular background have problems with the interface.

Relatively low-cost video equipment means that it is economically practical to record user sessions as they happen and to analyse the session systematically. Ideally, several cameras should be used with user's hand movements, screen display and head and eye movement recorded separately. Unfortunately, because of different scanning rates between the screen and the camera, it is difficult to photograph a screen directly. Some kind of direct video output from the display is necessary if stable images are to be produced.

Analysis of recordings allows the designer to find out if the interface requires too much hand movement (a problem with some systems is that the user must regularly move his or her hand from keyboard to mouse) and to see if unnatural eye movements are necessary. An interface which requires many shifts of focus may mean that the user makes more errors and misses parts of the display.

However, analysing video recordings is a time-consuming process. A detailed analysis of a one-hour recording is likely to take several hours so that an adequate budget must be assigned for an evaluation over many recording sessions and users.

The instrumenting of code to collect usage statistics allows interfaces to be improved in a number of ways. The most common operations can be detected and the interface can be organized so that these are the fastest to select. For example, if pop-up or pull-down menus are used, the most frequent operations should be towards the top of the menu and destructive operations towards the bottom. Code instrumentation also allows error-prone commands to be detected and subsequently modified.

Finally, a means of easy user response is very valuable. This can be provided easily by equipping each program with a 'gripe' command which the user can use to pass messages to the tool maintainer. Such a facility makes users feel that their views are being considered and provides a means whereby the interface designer (indeed, system designers in general) can gain very rapid feedback about individual problems.

KEY POINTS

- Design quality assurance as discussed here is concerned with checking product rather than process quality. Product quality concerns not just the relationship of the design to its specification but also an assessment of the 'goodness' of the design.

- Design reviews are the principal means of carrying out design quality assurance. They should involve all of those designers concerned with a design and its related systems.

- Design reviews are a way of discovering problems. They are not intended for fault repair.

- Making a quantitative assessment of a design is an attractive notion but existing metrics have serious disadvantages. The state of the art is such that reliable quantitative assessments cannot yet be made.

- User interface designs should be evaluated. To do this thoroughly is very expensive but lower-cost approaches can provide useful evaluation information.

Further reading

Designing the User Interface.   There is relatively little material which is concerned with design quality assurance. Shneiderman's book includes a chapter on interface evaluation. (B. Shneiderman, 1986, Addison-Wesley.)

Software Engineering: Design, Reliability and Management. This book is a software engineering text which has a quantitative bias and it includes a chapter on design assessment. It is much wider ranging than the material here and considers not just complexity but also other quality considerations such as storage and processing. (M.L. Shooman, 1983, McGraw-Hill.)

References

Constantine, L.L. and Yourdon, E. (1979), *Structured Design*, Englewood Cliffs, NJ: Prentice-Hall.

Henry, S. and Kafura, D. (1981), 'Software structure metrics based on information flow', *IEEE Trans. Software Eng.*, **SE-7** (5).

Fagan, M.E. (1976), 'Design and code inspections to reduce errors in program development', *IBM Systems J.*, **15** (3), 182–211.

McCabe, T.J. (1976), 'A complexity measure', *IEEE Trans. Software Eng.*, **SE-2** (4), 308–20.

Oviedo, E.I. (1980), 'Control flow, data flow and program complexity', *Proc. 4th COMPSAC*, Los Alaminitos, Calif.: IEEE Press.

Weinberg, G. (1971), *The Psychology of Computer Programming*, New York: Van Nostrand Reinhold.

Yourdon, E. (1977), *Structured Walkthroughs*, New York: Yourdon Press.

EXERCISES

14.1   What are the stages involved in a design review?

14.2   Design an electronic form which may be used to record design review comments and which could be used to electronically mail comments to reviewers.

14.3   Explain why design quality metrics do not allow a reliable estimate of design quality to be made.

14.4   Consult the literature and find other design quality metrics which have been suggested apart from those discussed here. Consider these metrics in detail and assess whether they are likely to be of real value.

14.5   Design a questionnaire which could be used to gather user feedback about the quality of the user interface to MS-DOS or UNIX. Carry out a similar exercise for a WIMP interface such as MS-Windows or the Apple Macintosh.

14.6   Discuss the advantages and disadvantages of using video recording as a means of user interface assessment.

Part 3

Programming Practice, Techniques and Environments

Contents

Chapter 15

Programming Practice

Objective

The objective of this chapter is to describe how particular approaches to program development affect the maintainability and reliability of a program. It starts with a comparison of top-down versus bottom-up development and concludes that, in practice, development is a mixture of these two approaches. Programming style is then covered, including the use of program names and program layout. Some layout guidelines are suggested. Finally, the chapter describes some aspects of error handling which is particularly important in high-reliability systems. The notion of defensive programming is introduced and exception handling is illustrated using Ada's exception mechanism.

Contents

Programming is a craft. It is dependent on individual skill, attention to detail, and knowledge of how to use available tools in the best way. Craftsmen must know their materials, understand the principles of their craft and learn by experience. Thus, programmers must understand both host and target computer systems, must know some theory of programming, and must practise programming. Although programming is a practical activity, learned by experience, the experience of others can be distilled to provide guidelines for the programmer in developing programming skills.

Good programming, the production of reliable and maintainable programs, is largely language independent. High-level languages, such as Ada or Pascal, simplify the process of converting a design into an implementation, but there is no reason why good programs may not be constructed in any language whatsoever. Even assembly code can be written in an understandable and reliable way, given that the programmer adopts a professional attitude to its development.

Readers may come across the term *structured programming* in discussions on programming methods and style. Structured programming is a term which was coined in the late 1960s to mean programming without using goto statements, adopting a top-down approach to design, and confining programming control constructs to while loops and if statements. The adoption of structured programming was important because it represented the first step away from an undisciplined approach to software development. Its notions should now be embodied in most programming teaching.

15.1 Program development

The process of developing a program from a software design may be tackled in two ways, namely top-down development and bottom-up development. If the program is viewed as a hierarchy of components, top-down development involves starting at the top of the hierarchy and working downwards whereas bottom-up development implies starting at the bottom and working upwards (Figure 15.1).

Top-down development parallels the top-down process used in system design, with the program structure being hierarchical. The programmer implements the higher levels of the design and represents the lower levels by stubs which simulate their function in a simplified way. As the implementation of a level is completed, the programmer moves on to the next lower level and implements that in terms of its sub-levels. Ultimately, the lowest level of the system is implemented using basic programming language facilities.

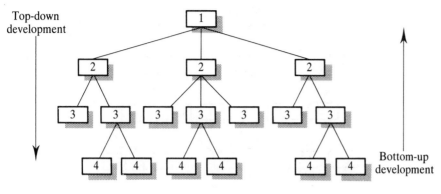

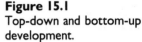

Figure 15.1
Top-down and bottom-up development.

Bottom-up development is the converse of this process. Implementation starts with the lower levels of the system and the system is built up until, finally, the highest design level is implemented. Effectively, the programmer creates basic building blocks and uses these to build more complex blocks which are themselves used as building blocks for higher levels of the system.

Authors such as Wirth (1971), Dijkstra (1968) and Naur (1972) argue that top-down development is a superior approach because it results in the creation of programs which are more readable and more reliable than those implemented using bottom-up techniques. Bottom-up development, it is argued, tends to result in local optimizations at the expense of system quality because the programmer is never given the opportunity to view the system as an entity. Rather, it always appears as a collection of parts.

For small programs which are hierarchical, a top-down approach to development results in the most elegant, modifiable and reliable programs. However, large software systems are usually built of interconnected subsystems so that it is impractical to build them as a strict component hierarchy. Their structure is that of a graph rather than a tree (Figure 15.2). Given this structure, the distinction between top-down and bottom-up development is less clear. The situation is further complicated by the fact that there may already exist some components which may be reused and that it may be virtually impossible to implement other components in stub form. An object-oriented approach to design further blurs the distinction between top-down and bottom-up software development as objects don't fit neatly into either model.

In practice, then, neither a strict top-down nor a bottom-up approach to development is appropriate for large system construction. A strict top-down approach is likely to lead to an unacceptable amount of component duplication and testing difficulties whereas a bottom-up approach has the disadvantages discussed above.

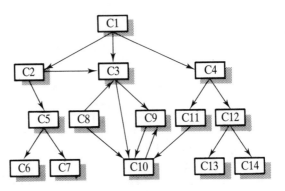

Figure 15.2
Large system structure.

What actually happens during large program development is that the programmer continually, perhaps unconsciously, switches between development modes. Top-down development identifies useful abstractions to be refined. Given existing components, these are taken into account by the programmer when constructing these abstractions so that they may be reused in the implementation of the abstractions.

Errors in the original model may become apparent but many of the abstractions remain useful so a new top-down model which is constrained by existing abstractions is developed. This iterative process continues until an adequate system model emerges. There is little point in being purist and rigidly adopting either development scheme . The human brain is such that a mixed scheme will be adopted as it is not possible to forget useful work which has already been carried out.

In this discussion of software development, it has been assumed that the majority of software components do not exist and have to be built by the programmer. If we compare this situation with hardware development, a quite different situation pertains. In hardware development, much more use is made of existing components with the minority of system components being specially built. In future, it seems likely that software development will involve much more component reuse than is currently practiced. This topic is discussed in Chapter 17.

Building systems in a component-rich environment implies that the main emphasis in programming will be on component interconnections rather than on program development. We need to develop new notations and methodologies to support this process, perhaps along the lines of that suggested by DeRemer and Kron (1976), by Lampson and Schmidt (1983) in the Cedar System Modeller, and by Sommerville and Thomson (1986). These notations concentrate on describing system structure in terms of its basic components and ignore details of how components operate. It seems likely that the development of such notations in combination with other automated support for software reuse will lead to new methods of program development.

15.2 Programming style

Programs are read more often than they are written as they are maintained during their useful lifetime. They should thus be readable and comprehensible and should not include arcane programming tricks which confuse the reader. The style in which a program is written contributes greatly to its readability and this includes the sensible use of naming, typing (discussed in Chapter 16) and error handling.

15.2.1 Program names

The named entities in a program, such as constants, variables, modules, procedures, functions and types, model real-world entities. The role or function of an entity in the real world is mirrored by the function of the corresponding program entity. Accordingly, the names of objects in a program should be closely related to or, if practical, identical to the names of the real-world entities which are modelled. The program names thus provide program readers with semantic clues which help them understand what the program is doing.

For example, say a program is computing satellite orbits. It is concerned with the mass of the satellite, the mass of the earth, the velocity of the satellite, the acceleration of the satellite and so on. These should be represented in the program by objects which might be named *Satellite_mass*, *Earth_mass*, *Satellite_velocity*, *Satellite_acceleration*, etc. Simpler names such as *mass*, *velocity*, and *acceleration* or abbreviations such as *SATVEL* should be avoided as they require the reader to do more work finding out what the program is doing.

Even worse, is to choose names which are unrelated to the entities being modelled such as the names of tennis players, cryptic abbreviations or single letter identifiers. Poor programmers frequently choose names which are short and therefore easy to type. This can result in programs which are almost incomprehensible.

Names should usually be more than a single word and use should be made of whatever language features are available to distinguish the parts of a name. Thus, the Ada programmer should make use of the underscore character and the Pascal programmer should use upper and lower case letters to distinguish name components. Some Pascal implementations allow underscores to be used but this is a non-standard feature. If program portability is required, this construct should be avoided.

Consider Example 15.1, where the same program has been programmed using short names and meaningful names. As well as illustrating the use of names, the example also illustrates that the use of a reasonable programming language such as Pascal does not guarantee that programs in that language are necessarily comprehensible. In the first

Example 15.1
A comparison of cryptic and meaningful program names.

```
program CT(input,output);
    var t,f:real;
begin
    read(t);
    f := t*9/5+32;
    write(f)
end.

program ConvertCentigradeToFahrenheit(input,output);
    var Fahrenheit, Centigrade : real;
begin
    read(Centigrade);
    Fahrenheit := Centigrade * 9/5 + 32;
    write(Fahrenheit)
end.
```

instance, if the reader did not know the formula for converting centigrade temperature to Fahrenheit temperature, it is unlikely that he or she would ever deduce what the program was doing. In the second example, not only does the program name explain the function of the program, but the conversion formula is also made explicit. The use of meaningful identifiers makes it immediately obvious that the program reads in an input value representing a temperature in degrees centigrade and outputs a number representing that value in degrees Fahrenheit.

Unfortunately, a commonly used programming language for scientific applications, FORTRAN, places an arbitrary restriction on the length of program names. Early versions of FORTRAN introduced this restriction to simplify the task of the compiler writer and revisions of the language have not removed the restriction. It is not clear why this is so. Compiler technology is now such that names of any length can easily be handled and longer names do not invalidate any existing programs. The FORTRAN programmer has no alternative but to choose abbreviations for program names and a consistent convention should be adopted in name abbreviation.

As a general rule, all program entities (constants, types, variables, procedures, etc.) should be given a name which reflects their use in the system being modelled by the program. Constant values within a program should only be used for program entities such as loop counters. Unfortunately, few programming languages provide for universal naming and they allow anonymous (unnamed) entities to exist and to be modified. For example, it is relatively common for programmers to make use of anonymous constants but this can cause problems when the program has to be changed.

Say a program is being used to compute sales tax which is normally taken as a percentage of the price of items. Assume that this is set at 5% so the sales tax computation is:

$$TotalPrice := BasePrice + BasePrice * 0.05;$$

This will work perfectly well until the rate of sales tax is changed to 6%. To modify the program, all statements which make use of the sales tax rate must be found and modified. It is not possible simply to change all instances of 0.05 to 0.06 as the constant 0.05 may be used to represent other entities apart from the sales tax. A better approach is to name the sales tax rate and to use this name in the program.

$$TotalPrice := BasePrice + BasePrice * SalesTaxRate;$$

To incorporate tax rate changes, only the constant SalesTaxRate need be modified and the programmer can be sure that the modification takes effect everywhere that it is required.

15.2.2 Program layout

The majority of programming languages are free format languages where the meaning of a program is not affected by how it is laid out on a page. Exceptions to this are FORTRAN and some assembly languages where the position of a field in an input record can affect its meaning. This is a hangover from the days when punched cards were almost universally used for preparing programs.

Layout affects the readability of a program. The liberal use of blank lines, reserved word highlighting and consistent paragraphing makes the program appear more elegant and easier to read. They act as separators which distinguish one part of the program from another. Examples 15.2a and 15.2b show how the readability of identical procedures is affected by the way the text is arranged. The same procedure laid out using consistent indentation, line spacing and reserved word highlighting (Example 15.2b) is much more readable. Distinct parts of the program such as the header comment, variable declarations and the procedure body should be distinguished by separating them with blank lines. Statements executed in the same loop and in each arm of a conditional statement are picked out by consistent indentation. Program reserved words are highlighted showing where each statement begins.

It is impossible to establish hard and fast rules for program layout which can optimize the layout of each and every program. There are, inevitably, circumstances such as very long or very short statements where layout rules break down and elegant layout relies on the judgement of the

Example 15.2a
Poor program layout.

```
procedure CountElementOccurrences(var inarray : intarray;
arraysize : integer);
{Given a sorted array of integers, this procedure prints each
distinct integer and the number of occurrences of that integer}
var i,count:integer; begin
count:=1;for i:=1 to arraysize–1 do
if inarray[i] = inarray[i+1] then count:=count+1 else
begin write(inarray[i],count); count:=1;
end; write(inarray[arraysize],count);
end;
```

programmer. For this reason, prettyprinters, programs which automatically lay out listings (covered in Chapter 18), are sometimes unsuccessful.

However, general guidelines can be established which are adequate for laying out the majority of Pascal programs. There is no single set of guidelines which are accepted as the 'best' and it is not particularly important which layout conventions are used. Any reasonable set of conventions, such as those set out below, will improve program readability.

Example 15.2b
Good program layout.

```
procedure CountElementOccurrences(var inarray : intarray;
                     arraysize : integer);

{ Given a sorted array of integers, this procedure prints each distinct
integer and the number of occurrences of that integer }

   var i,count : integer;
begin
  count := 1;
  for i := 1 to arraysize-1 do
    if inarray[i] = inarray[i+1] then
        count := count + 1
    else
      begin
        write(inarray[i],count);
        count := 1
      end;
    write (inarray[arraysize],count)
end;
```

In these guidelines, T stands for a standard tab indent and n is the block level of a procedure. In experiments to measure the effectiveness of indentation as an aid to program understanding, Miara *et al.* (1983) discovered that the value of T should be between 2 and 4 to be most effective. Smaller and larger values were found to be detrimental to the understandability of the program.

(1)   Label, constant, type, and variable declarations made at the outermost block level (level 0) should start in column 1 of a line. Declarations made at subsequent block levels should start at column T^*n.

(2)   In procedure declarations, the procedure header should start at column T^*n and the procedure body, that is, those statements between **begin** and **end** should start at column $T^*(n+1)$. The **begin** and **end** bracketing the procedure body should, however, be indented at column T^*n.

(3)   Local declarations should be separated from the procedure header by at least one blank line.

(4)   If the procedure has a header comment, it should appear before the local declarations and be separated from both the procedure header and the local declarations by at least one blank line.

(5)   The statement within a loop whose initial statement (**for**, **while**, **repeat**) is indented by N blanks should be indented by $N+T$ blanks. If this statement is a compound statement, however, the **begin** and **end** brackets of that statement should be on a line by themselves and should be indented by N spaces. Statements within these brackets should be indented by $N+T$ spaces.

(6)   Where a conditional statement is indented by N spaces, the statement in each arm of the conditional should be indented by $N+T$ spaces. If the statement is a compound statement, the rule for compound statements given above should be applied. If the conditional statement is a two-armed conditional, the reserved word **else** should be indented by N spaces and should be on a line by itself.

(7)   When records are declared, the reserved words **record** and **end** should occur on lines by themselves as should the declaration of each field of the record. The indentation of the field name declarations should be consistent and such that the field declaration with the greatest number of characters can fit on a single line.

(8)   Wherever possible, each assignment or input/output statement should appear on a line by itself.

These rules do not describe how every Pascal construct is to be laid out. Constructs which are not covered are those for which it is difficult to establish strict rules and the layout of these depends on the actual program text. The important principle which must be adhered to in program layout is consistency. Once a set of conventions has been established, the same conventions should be used throughout the same program.

15.3   Error handling

When an error of some kind or an unexpected event occurs during the execution of a program, this event is termed an exception. Exceptions are caused by hardware or software errors which may or may not have been anticipated by the programmer. In general, where an exception has not been anticipated explicitly by the programmer, control is transferred to a system exception handling mechanism which handles the exception. If the exception is serious the executing program is terminated. If an exception has been anticipated by the programmer, code must be included to detect that exception and to take appropriate action when it occurs.

Proper exception handling is important from the point of view of system reliability. A system which is reliable should always 'fail-soft'. That is, if an exception is generated during program execution, it should not cause immediate termination of the program. Rather, the exception should be detected by the program and the execution should be terminated in a controlled way. If the error causing the exception is recoverable, the program should correct the anomalous situation and continue execution. Coding in such a way that errors are detected and recovered from is sometimes called defensive programming.

If defensive programming is practised, it is a good general rule to associate an error state indicator with every procedure and to set this in the procedure to indicate whether the procedure call has been successful. If an error has been discovered, it should be set to indicate the type of error which has occurred. Even if this is not used in the initial system implementation, including such a feature makes subsequent modifications simpler. The Ada package to implement generalized lists, shown in Chapter 17, illustrates this feature.

Most programming languages offer the programmer little help in detecting and handling exceptions. The programmer must use the normal decision constructs of the language to detect the exception and the control constructs to transfer control to a section of code to handle the exception.

Although this is possible in a monolithic program, in programs where a sequence of procedure calls is nested, there is no convenient and safe mechanism for transmitting the exception from one procedure to another.

Example 15.3
Nested procedure calls.

procedure A;

...

    B;

...

end; {A}
procedure B;

...

    C;

...

end; {B}
procedure C;

...

end; {C}

Consider a number of nested procedure calls where procedure *A* calls procedure *B* which calls procedure *C* (Example 15.3). If an exception occurs during the execution of *C* this may be so serious that execution of *B* cannot continue. It may be necessary to transmit the fact that an exception has occurred from *B* to *A* so that it can take appropriate action.

The only mechanism the programmer has for this in Pascal is a global boolean variable which is set to indicate that an exception has occurred. This must either be passed as a parameter to every procedure or be set globally. The programmer must test the value of this variable after each procedure call so that, in a sequence of nested procedure calls, the same test is carried out a number of times. The existing mechanism forces the programmer to test for the exception each and every time that exception might occur. Unanticipated exceptions cause transfer to a system exception handler and, normally, program termination.

It may be acceptable for the operating system to handle unanticipated program exceptions in situations such as a student learning environment. It is not acceptable when reliability considerations are paramount. When the software is acting as a controller or providing an essential time-critical service, the system must not halt. Furthermore, program size is often critical in such situations. It is therefore also unacceptable to include a number of redundant statements to test for exceptions which lead to an increase in program size.

Ideally, an exception handling facility should not require programmers to increase the length of their programs and should support the transmission of exceptions from one program unit to another. Ada includes explicit exception handling facilities and the language provides powerful and adaptable constructs for indicating and handling exceptions.

In Ada, exception names are declared like any other names, that is, as a name associated with some type. Exception names are always declared to be of the special built-in type exception. Drawing attention to an exception is termed raising an exception in Ada. Executing a sequence of actions in response to an exception being raised is called handling the exception.

Any program unit in Ada may have an associated exception handler which must appear at the end of the unit. An exception handler resembles an Ada case statement in that it states exception names and appropriate actions for each exception. However, not every exception raised in a program unit need necessarily be handled by that unit. The exception may be propagated automatically to some other unit at a higher level.

Example 15.4 illustrates Ada exceptions and exception handling. This is a program fragment which implements a temperature controller on a food freezer. The required temperature may be set between −18 and −40°C and the control system maintains this temperature by switching a refrigerant pump on and off depending on the value of a temperature sensor. However, food may start to defrost and bacteria become active at temperatures over −18°C so the controller incorporates an alarm if, for some reason, it cannot maintain the required temperature. The current temperature is discovered by interrogating an object called Sensor and the required temperature by inspecting an object called Temperature_dial. A pump object responds to signals to switch its state.

Example 15.4
A temperature controller.

```
Ambient_temperature: FLOAT ;
Too_hot: exception ;
loop
    Ambient_temperature := Sensor.Get_Temperature ;
    if Ambient_temperature > Temperature_dial.Setting then
        if Pump.Status = OFF then
            Pump.Switch (State => ON) ;
        end if ;
        if Ambient_temperature > −18.0 then
            raise Too_hot ;
        end if ;
    elsif Pump.Status = ON then
-- Switch pump off because temperature is low
        Pump.Switch (State => OFF) ;
    end if ;
end loop ;
exception
    when Too_hot => Alarm.Activate ;
                    raise ;
end ;
```

In Example 15.4 the controller tests the temperature and switches the pump on and off accordingly. If the temperature is too hot, it transfers control to the exception handler which activates an alarm and re-raises the exception. Normally, when an exception is handled, the effect of the handling is to clear the exception condition, but in some circumstances it may be necessary to handle the exception then indicate to other parts of the system that an exception has occurred. This is accomplished by re-raising the exception within the exception handler.

Raising the exception within the exception handler has the effect of communicating the exception to some higher-level program unit and transferring control to its exception handler for this exception. In the above example, this higher-level unit might be responsible for re-starting the temperature controller after some response has been made to the alarm.

In some cases, it may not make sense to handle the exception within the program unit where that exception is raised. If an exception handler is not included, the exception is automatically propagated to the calling program unit and this process continues until an exception handler is found. If the application program does not include an exception handler, the exception is propagated to the system exception handler for processing.

The definition of Ada includes five built-in exceptions.

- CONSTRAINT_ERROR corresponds to something going out of range
- NUMERIC_ERROR occurs when some arithmetic operation goes wrong (division by zero, for example)
- PROGRAM_ERROR occurs when a control structure is violated
- STORAGE_ERROR occurs when storage space is exhausted
- TASKING_ERROR occurs when there is some failure of inter-task communication.

The Ada run-time system includes a handler for these exceptions and, of course, they may be handled by the application program. It is beyond the scope of this book to discuss them in more detail here.

As well as using exceptions to handle rare events which should not occur during normal program execution, the availability of an exception handling mechanism opens up the possibility of a style of programming where exceptions are used to handle particular, anticipated situations. For instance, Example 15.5 shows a short Ada program which copies characters from one file to another. The exception handling mechanism is used to handle the terminating condition of the file copy.

The exception handling mechanism of Ada is not a retry mechanism. It is not possible to handle an exception and restart the program at the point just before the exception occurred. Instead, an exception occurring within a program unit always results in the execution of that unit being

Example 15.5
File copying with
exceptions.

```
with TEXT_IO ; use TEXT_IO ;
procedure Main is

    -- This program copies characters from an input
    -- file to an output file. Termination occurs
    -- either when all characters are copied or
    -- when a NULL character is input

    Nullchar,Eof : exception ;
    Char : CHARACTER ;
    Input_file, Output_file, Console: FILE_TYPE ;
begin
   loop
      Open ( FILE => Input_file, MODE => IN_FILE,
                      NAME => "CharsIn") ;
      Open ( FILE => Output_file, MODE => OUT_FILE,
                      NAME => "CharsOut") ;
      Get (Input_file, Char);
      if END_OF_FILE (Input_file) then
         raise Eof;
      elsif Char = ASCII.NUL then
          raise Nullchar;
      else
          Put (Output_file,Char);
      end if ;
   end loop ;
exception
    when Eof => Put (Console, "no null characters" );
    when Nullchar => Put (Console, "null terminator" );
end Main;
```

terminated. However, the exception propagation mechanism can be used to effect recovery if an exception occurs in a program unit called X, say. That exception may be propagated to a higher level unit Y, the condition causing the exception corrected or modified and the program unit X may be explicitly reactivated after error recovery.

KEY POINTS

- In practice program development involves a mix of bottom-up and top-down techniques.

- Programs are read more often than they are written. Thus, it is important to pay attention to programming style.

- Program names should be meaningful and should reflect the real-world entities modelled in the program.

- Program layout conventions should be adopted and used in a large software project. The existence of a layout standard is more important than the details of that standard.

- In real-time systems with high reliability requirements it is important to pre-plan the handling of exceptions and not simply to leave exception handling to a system routine.

- Programming with exceptions is a programming technique which assumes exceptions to be normal although unusual events. The response to these events is set out in the exception handler.

Further reading

Software Tools in Pascal. Although ostensibly about software tools, this is really a more general text on programming practice and programming style. It contains many examples of how to program well. (B.W. Kernighan and P.J. Plauger, 1981, Addison-Wesley.)

A Discipline of Programming. Dijkstra was the first publicizer of 'structured programming' and good programming style and this book is an interesting compendium of his thoughts. However, it can be difficult going at times and it can be quite difficult to see how to scale up his small examples to large-scale problems. (E.W. Dijkstra, 1976, Prentice-Hall.)

References

DeRemer, F. and Kron, H.H. (1976), 'Programming in the large versus programming in the small', *IEEE Trans. Software Eng.*, **SE-2** (2), 80–6.

Dijkstra, E.W. (1968), ' A constructive approach to the problem of program correctness', *BIT*, **8**, 174–86.

Lampson, B.W. and Schmidt, E.E. (1983) 'Organizing software in a distributed environment', *ACM Sigplan Notices*, **18** (6), 1–13.

Miara, R.J., Mussleman, J.A., Navarro, J.A. and Shneiderman, B. (1983), 'Program indentation and comprehensibility', *Comm. ACM*, **26** (11), 861–7.

Naur, P. (1972), 'An experiment on program development', *BIT*, **12**, 347–65.

Sommerville, I. and Thomson, R. (1986), 'The ECLIPSE system structure language', *Proc. 19th Int. Conf. on Systems Science*, Honolulu, Hawaii.

Wirth, N. (1971), 'Program development by stepwise refinement', *Comm. ACM*, **14** (4), 221–7.

EXERCISES

15.1   Explain what you understand by top-down and bottom-up program development.

15.2   Using examples, explain under what circumstances the constants in a program should not be given names.

15.3   Produce a set of layout guidelines for Ada, C, Modula-2 or any other programming language with which you are familiar.

15.4   If you have access to a prettyprinter, document its layout conventions and discover situations where it might produce untidy layout.

15.5   Describe the exception handling mechanism which is provided in Ada. Consult the literature to discover other approaches to exception handling (start with PL/1) and compare these other approaches to that taken in Ada.

15.6   Using exceptions, write a routine which reads items from a user console and enters them in a table, in alphabetic order, according to their name. The routine should terminate when the user enters an item called STOP. Implement the table as a binary tree object.

15.7   Explain, using small examples, how the exception handling facility of Ada can be used in the writing of non-stop systems. (Hint: You must consider the handling of all built in exceptions.)

Chapter 16

Data Abstraction

Objectives

This chapter is concerned with data typing and, in particular, abstract data types. The notion and importance of a data type as used in Pascal is discussed and some deficiencies of Pascal's type facilities are described. Abstract data types are equivalent to object classes so are valuable when implementing an object-oriented design. Abstract data typing, the association of operations with a type, is discussed and illustrated with examples in Ada.

Contents

A security principle which is adopted by military organizations is the 'need to know' principle. Only those individuals who need to know a particular piece of information to carry out their duties are given that information. Information which is not directly relevant to their work is withheld.

When programming, an analogous principle should be adopted to control access to system data by program units. In principle, each program unit should be allowed access only to program data which is required to implement that unit's function. Access to other data, not needed by the unit, should be denied by using the scope rules of the programming language to conceal the existence of these objects. This is called 'information hiding'.

The advantage of hiding unnecessary information is that there is no way in which the hidden information may be corrupted by a program unit which is not supposed to use that information. This means that programs are more secure and, in some circumstances, may provide data independence. The data representation may be changed without changing the program units that make use of that data. Furthermore, if objects are declared close to where they are used, this improves the readability of the program. The reader need not search through pages of listing to find the definition of an object.

Effective information hiding is critically dependent on the data typing facilities provided in the system implementation languages. Although it is possible to implement information hiding in languages like C or Pascal, which have only limited data typing facilities, it is easier and more secure to use a language such as Ada which offers inbuilt support for information hiding.

16.1 Data typing

Most large software systems are now written using high-level programming languages (Ada, Pascal, C, Modula-2) which provide some facilities for programmers to define their own data types. The type name serves to classify the object and operations on the object are restricted to operations defined on that class of objects. If the programmer uses an object of a particular type in an invalid manner, this error can be detected and signalled by the compiler.

Type declarations in a programming language are not just a safety feature. As well as providing information which allows the compiler to carry out some program checking, they are also an important abstraction mechanism. The definition of type names allows reference to be made to entities such as personnel records, traffic light colours, etc, without considering the representation of these entities.

In general, for every type of entity which exists in the real-world system being modelled or controlled by the program, there should be a corresponding program type. Thus, if a system is concerned with entities such as names, counters and switches, there might be corresponding program types NAME, COUNTER and SWITCH which model these entities.

The notion of type checking was introduced in ALGOL60 and the concept has been considerably refined since then. The most important development was the language Pascal, which was the first widely used language to include type definition facilities. For example, if a traffic light system is being modelled in Pascal, the following declarations might be made:

> **type** *trafficlightcolour = (red, redamber, amber, green);*
> **var** *ColourShowing : TrafficLightColour;*

The object *ColourShowing*, which is modelling the colour displayed by the traffic light, may only be assigned the values *red*, *redamber*, *amber*, and *green*.

Contrast this with the modelling of such a situation in FORTRAN. Here, integers must be used to represent the entities associated with the traffic light:

```
INTEGER RED,REDAMB,AMBER,GREEN,COLSHW
DATA RED/1/,REDAMB/2/,AMBER/3/,GREEN/4/
```

Integers are associated with each possible colour, and assignments such as

```
COLSHW = RED
```

can be made. Disciplined programming in FORTRAN, which means associating a relevant name with each constant used to represent an entity, improves program readability. However, there is no mechanism to restrict statements which directly assign integers or real numbers to COLSHW. If names are not associated with constants, assignments such as:

```
COLSHW = 3
```

must be made, forcing the program to consult documentation or program comments to find out which colour is actually represented by 3.

The above example, defining type *TrafficLightColour*, is a Pascal type declaration which enumerates the values of a type. This declares a scalar type which is the name given to a type where the set of all possible values is known. By contrast, a real type is not a scalar type as it has a potentially infinite number of values. An alternative means of declaring a scalar type is the range declaration:

type POSITIVE = 1..MAXINT ;

This declares that the type *POSITIVE* consists of the set of integers between 1 and the maximum integer which may be represented on a particular computer. Although it would be possible (and very tedious) to enumerate all of these values, declaring the type as a range is a shorthand way of setting out the set of values associated with the type.

Declaring a set of values is one type facility provided in Pascal. The representation of these values is not under the control of the programmer and is decided by the implementors of the Pascal compilation system.

Another type of type declaration in Pascal which, confusingly, uses similar syntax allows structure templates to be named and associated with program variables. Using these templates, the representation of the type is defined. For example, a Pascal type representing a stack might be defined:

type STACK = array (1..100) of integer ;

This declares a stack to be an array of integers but doesn't enumerate the values that the stack may take. Access to the stack elements is according to their position in the array. It is also possible to declare records where the parts of the record are accessed by name rather than position:

type PERSON = record
Name: array (1..32) of char ;
Age: POSITIVE ;
Sex: (male, female) ;
end ;

These two classes of type declaration in Pascal are inconsistent. It would have been logical to distinguish the representation definitions by calling them something like structure declarations rather than type declarations. The inconsistency means that the reader of a program cannot always consider the type as an abstraction but must be aware of its details before the program can be properly understood.

This inconsistency (which is also present in Ada) is but one of the problems of the Pascal type system. Other problems are:

(1)   It is only possible for constants to be declared of predefined language types. It is not possible to declare a type then define constants to be of that type. Pascal imposes an ordering on declarations so that constants are declared before types.

(2)   The ordering rules of Pascal, which specify that declarations should be made in the order constants, types, variables then procedures,

don't allow type declarations and their associated operations (defined as procedures and functions) to be grouped together as a logical entity. Pascal was defined in the late 1960s and it is understandable that it does not include module facilities (like the Ada package) which allow control over the scope of type names. However, it is both irritating and contrary to modern thinking on good programming practice to make declarations in a pre-defined order. There is really no good reason for this restriction as it does not simplify the compiler writer's task.

(3) The bounds of arrays are deemed to be part of a Pascal type which means that it is impossible to create generalized functions and procedures which operate on arrays of any length. Thus, for every array which has a different number of elements, separate functions must be defined.

(4) It is permitted to declare anonymous types (types without a name).

Anonymous types are those types which are declared as part of variable declarations rather than using an explicit type declaration. For example, in Pascal, the following declarations of the composite type array is permitted:

> *var AnArray:* **array** *[1..10]* **of integer** *;*
> *AnotherArray:* **array** *[1..10]* **of integer** *;*

This declaration names variables called *AnArray* and *AnotherArray* and declares each of them to be an array of 10 integers. However, they are not of the same type. The type declared in these definitions is anonymous and each anonymous type declaration declares a different type, even although the type structures are identical. This is contra-intuitive unless you understand the Pascal type-checker, and learners of Pascal commonly make mistakes by assuming that types that look the same are the same.

Pascal uses what is called name equivalence for determining if types match. This means that two variables, *A* and *B* say, are only deemed to be the same type if they have been declared using the same type name. An alternative (but little used) form of type equivalence is structural equivalence where types are the same if they have the same structure. In a system with structural equivalence, the above declarations of *AnArray* and *AnotherArray* would have been of the same type.

The use of anonymous types is contrary to the notion that types should model classes of real-world system entities. If an anonymous type is used, the program reader is given no clues as to what the type is modelling and it is not possible to adopt an abstract view of that type. However, the programmer is not forced to use anonymous types and it is bad programming practice to do so. All types used in a program should be declared explicitly using a type declaration.

16.1.1 Derived types

Part of the role of types in a programming language is to act as a safety feature ensuring that some accidental mistakes are detected by the compiler. Equally important is their role as a structuring and abstraction mechanism where classes of entity in the system which the program is modelling are represented as system types.

Commonly, the values of system entities are comparatively simple. For example, if the program is controlling a car dashboard display, there might be a number of entities representing warning conditions such as low oil pressure, doors not closed properly, fuel level dangerously low and so on. These conditions are either true or false so it makes sense to represent them as boolean values. In Pascal:

var Low_oil_pressure, Door_open, Fuel_low: **boolean** ;

In itself, this is a meaningful declaration and the use of descriptive names perhaps makes accidental errors unlikely. However, there is nothing to stop the programmer assigning true to *Door_open* when the oil pressure is low or making any other similar accidental type error.

The problem is that, although these values may be represented as boolean values (and it makes sense to have boolean operations available), they are distinct types. This has been recognized in Ada where it is possible to derive a new type from an existing type. The new type inherits the operations of the existing type but each type derived from a common parent is distinct. Thus, in Ada types representing different lights might be declared as follows:

```
type OIL_STATUS is new BOOLEAN ;
type DOOR_STATUS is new INTEGER ;
type FUEL_STATUS is new BOOLEAN ;
```

Derived types are an example of type inheritance where the operations on a type are inherited from some parent type. Ada supports a limited form of inheritance via its derived type mechanism but other languages, particularly object-oriented languages, support a much more general inheritance mechanism. It is not appropriate to discuss inheritance in detail in a text of this nature but the reader should be aware that there are disadvantages as well as advantages to most of the inheritance schemes supported in current programming languages.

16.2 Abstract data types

The provision of user-defined types in Pascal was an important step forward in programming language design but, as we have seen, this early attempt at typing suffered from a number of flaws. The most important of these are the impossibility of concealing type representations and the impossibility of restricting the operations that are allowed on a type. The notion of an abstract data type, which was probably first publicized by Liskov and Zilles (1974), avoids these difficulties.

An abstract data type specification is made up of the following parts:

(1)	a type name
(2)	an optional specification of the domain of values for the type
(3)	a specification of allowed operations on that type

The implementation of the abstract type is distinct from its specification. The implementation includes details of the type representation and the implementation of operations on the type. If the specification part remains unchanged, the implementation part may be modified, by changing the representation perhaps, without requiring changes to other parts of the program which use the abstract data type.

As discussed in Chapter 11, abstract data types correspond to object classes and declaring a variable to be of a particular abstract type creates an object with its own operations. Programming with abstract data types and object-oriented programming have much in common although object-oriented programming languages also include type inheritance facilities (like a more general version of derived types discussed earlier) and, sometimes, dynamic binding of operations.

In Ada, abstract data types are implemented using packages. Ada allows the physical separation of the type specification (the package specification) and the type implementation (the package body) and gives the type specifier control over the visibility of the type representation. This means that the representation may be wholly or partially hidden from other parts of the program using that type. As a general rule, the representation is usually completely concealed.

As an example of an abstract data type, Example 16.1 is the specification of a simplified integer queue which can have a maximum of 100 elements. This package declares an abstract data type Queue.T and associated operations Queue.Add, Queue.Remove and Queue.Is_empty. The type T (the name is meaningful when prefixed by the package name to give Queue.T) is specified as a private type. This means that the only operations allowed on that type are assignment, test for equality and the operations defined in the Queue package.

Example 16.1
A package specification
for an integer queue.

```
package Queue is
    type T is private ;
    procedure Put (IQ : in out T; X: INTEGER);
    procedure Remove (IQ : in out T; X : out INTEGER);
    function Is_empty (IQ : T ) return BOOLEAN;
private
    type Q_RANGE is range 0..100 ;
    type Q_VEC is array (1..100) of INTEGER ;
    type T is record
        The_queue: Q_VEC ;
        front, back : Q_RANGE ;
    end record;
end Queue;
```

The private part of the package declares the representation for the queue. It may appear paradoxical that the intention of abstract data types is to conceal representation yet the representation of the queue is specified in the above example. The representation information is required by the Ada compiler so that it may make space allocation decisions. Without this information, the compiler cannot know the size of data elements and a very general allocation scheme with high run-time overhead would be required. As Ada was designed for writing efficient programs, this was not an acceptable approach, so the principle of information hiding was compromised to improve run-time efficiency.

The above package defines a type which is a queue but, as it stands, it is very specific. The queue size is fixed and the only allowed element type is integer. Queue is a general data structure and queue operations are usually independent of the type of queue element and the size of the queue. Thus, it is useful to declare this abstract type in a more general way which is independent of element type and size. This is possible in Ada using the generic facility. Ada generics are a way of creating parameterized, general-purpose templates for packages and subroutines. They are then instantiated, by associating values with the generic parameters, to form specific instances which operate on a particular type.

In Example 16.2, the type of queue element and the size of the queue are generic parameters which are assigned values when the package is instantiated. The queue type is specified as a private type which means that it is assumed that assignment and equality operations are defined over any actual type instantiated to ELEM. It is also possible to provide generic operations but a discussion of these is too specialized for this book.

Example 16.2
An Ada generic
specification of a queue.

```
generic
    type ELEM is private ;
    type Q_SIZE is range <> ;
package Queue is
    type T is private ;
    procedure Put (IQ : in out T; X: ELEM);
    procedure Remove (IQ : in out T; X : out ELEM);
    function Is_empty (IQ : in T ) return BOOLEAN;
private
    type Q_VEC is array (Q_SIZE) of ELEM ;
    type T is record
        The_queue: Q_VEC ;
        Front : Q_SIZE := Q_SIZE'FIRST ;
        Back: Q_SIZE := Q_SIZE'FIRST ;
    end record;
end Queue;
```

For example, the following instantiations define an integer queue with a maximum of 50 elements and a queue whose elements are lists (defined in another package, we assume) with 200 elements.

```
type IQ_SIZE is range 0..49 ; type LQ_SIZE is range 0..199 ;
package Integer_queue is new Queue (ELEM => INTEGER,
                                    Q_SIZE => IQ_SIZE ) ;
package List_queue is new Queue (ELEM => List.T,
                                 Q_SIZE => LQ_SIZE ) ;
```

Ada generics are static entities which means that creating a new version of a generic package is a compile-time operation. In essence, a generic declares a template for a package and the compile-time instantiation of this generic adds detail to the template. The effect is as if a completely new package had been declared.

This means that each instantiation of a generic package must have a different name. Dynamic, run-time instantiated generics would avoid this problem, but this facility would require the inclusion of run-time type checking. This contradicts the requirement that Ada programs should be as efficient as is practicable so it was not included as a language feature.

The package definition for Queue defines a type Queue.T and associated operations Queue.Add, Queue.Remove, and Queue.Is_empty but gives no information on queue implementation. Several implementations are possible. One example is shown in Example 16.3. Notice that the queue is circular. When the pointer to the front or back of the queue reaches the end of the array, it circles back to the front. For brevity, the procedures which operate on the queue have been simplified. In practice,

Example 16.3
The package body for the
Queue abstract type.

```
package body Queue is
    procedure Put (IQ : in out T; X : ELEM) is
    -- Adds an element to the back of the queue
    begin
        IQ.The_queue (IQ.back) := X;
        IQ.back := ( IQ.back + 1) rem Q_SIZE'LAST ;
    end Put ;

    procedure Remove (IQ: in out T; X: out ELEM) is
    -- Removes an element from the front of the queue
    begin
        X := IQ.The_queue IQ.front);
        IQ.front := (IQ.front +1) rem Q_SIZE'LAST ;
    end Remove;

    function Is_empty (IQ: in T) return BOOLEAN is
    begin
        if IQ.back = IQ.front then
            return TRUE ;
        else
            return FALSE ;
        end if ;
    end Is_empty;
end Queue;
```

code to check for queue overflow and underflow must be included in the queue operations. It is also assumed that the lower bound of the queue array is zero.

Let us assume that this implementation of a queue was put into use and, subsequently, it became necessary to cater for a situation where queues occasionally became very large but, normally, had only a few members. An array-based implementation in these circumstances is inefficient as the largest expected queue must be allowed for but, normally, most array elements will be unused. A more space efficient implementation makes use of a list of elements. A queue implementation making use of lists rather than arrays is shown in Examples 16.4 and 16.5.

Ada access types are equivalent to Pascal pointer types and reference entities of some other type. Linked lists are built in the usual way by creating a record which includes a field of type Queue.T. Representation specifications are only required in the private part so that the compiler can make space allocation decisions. As all access types occupy the same space (normally one machine word), there is no need to specify the type which is referenced by the access type. Its representation can be hidden in the

Example 16.4
Queue specification using
list implementation.

```
generic
    type ELEM is private ;
package Queue is
    type T is private ;
    procedure Put (IQ : in out T; X: ELEM);
    procedure Remove (IQ : in out T; X : out ELEM);
    function Is_empty (IQ : in T ) return BOOLEAN;
private
    type A_QUEUE ;
    type T is access A_QUEUE ;
end Queue;
```

package body (Example 16.5). Again queue underflow and overflow have been ignored in this example. In almost all cases, program components which used the Queue package need not be changed because the queue implementation is completely hidden. This is, of course, the major advantage of concealing type representations.

The representation of the queue in Example 16.5 is illustrated in Figure 16.1. A pointer to the front and back elements in the queue is maintained and each queue element includes a pointer to the next element. There is, however, one situation where it is not the case that the components using an abstract data type are completely insulated from representation changes. This is usually ignored by most commentators but can sometimes be critical.

Abstract type implementations cannot be changed arbitrarily in real-time systems where the change might modify the timing behaviour of a component. In most computers, an array based implementation of queues will result in a package where the queue operations operate more quickly than corresponding list based operations. If a real-time system is operating close to its performance requirements, changing the timing behaviour of a package might mean that the system no longer performs to specification. Such situations are unpredictable in advance but this problem must be borne in mind when modifying abstract data type implementations in real-time systems.

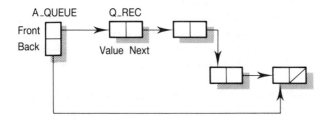

Figure 16.1
Queue implementation as
a linked list.

Example 16.5
Queue implementation
using lists.

```
package body Queue is
    type Q_REC ;
    type Q_POINTER is access Q_REC ;
    type Q_REC is record
        Value: ELEM ;
        Next: Q_POINTER ;
    end record ;
    type A_QUEUE is record
        Front, Back: Q_POINTER ;
    end record ;
    procedure Put (IQ : in out T; X : ELEM) is
    begin
        - - Deal with empty queue
        if IQ.front = null then
            IQ.Front := new Q_REC'(X, null) ;
            IQ.Back := IQ.front ;
        else
            IQ.Back := new Q_REC'( X, null) ;
        end if ;
    end Put ;

    procedure Remove (IQ: in out T; X: out ELEM) is
    begin
        IQ.Front := IQ.Front.Next ;
    end Remove;

    function Is_empty (IQ: in T) return BOOLEAN is
    begin
        if IQ.front = null then
            return TRUE ;
        else
            return FALSE ;
        end if ;
    end Is_empty;
end Queue;
```

Ada's support for abstract data types means that program components can be loosely coupled and independent so that changes to one component do not result in a cascade of other change requirements. However, Ada's provision of abstract data types is not problem free and it is important to understand its limitations if the most effective use is to be made of its facilities. Three problems can be identified:

(1)   Ada's compilation structure is such that a change to an abstract data type implementation means that all other programs which use that

must be recompiled and the system reconfigured. For large systems this can be a costly exercise and these costs must also be borne in mind when changes to abstract types are being considered.

(2)   It is not possible to have multiple implementations of the same specification included in the same program library. Each different implementation of the same logical specification must have a different name.

(3)   It is not possible to structure abstract data types so that abstract types declared within an enclosed package declaration can make their operations accessible. This is illustrated in Example 16.6 which is invalid Ada and shows what we would like to do.

Example 16.6
Nested abstract data types.

```
package T1 is
    type T is private ;
    function F1 (X:T) return BOOLEAN ;
    function F2 (X: T) return INTEGER ;
    package T2 ;
end T1 ;
```

Assume that some other type and type operations are declared in package T2 which is defined within the body of T1. A natural use of this is to export the package name T2 and thus make the enclosed type and its operations accessible through the interface to T1. We would thus refer to operations as T1.T2.op. Ada does not support this. To make the operations defined in T2 accessible, they have to be included explicitly in the specification of T1 along with functions F1 and F2. The benefits of structuring type definitions is lost.

Programming languages such as FORTRAN and Pascal do not have constructs that allow abstract data types to be created. FORTRAN's single level locality of declarations in subroutines and Pascal's simple block structure mean that, in most programs, unnecessary information is available to some or all program units. In languages without abstract type definition constructs, a disciplined approach to programming is necessary if information hiding is to be practised. The approach which must be adopted is to define special-purpose procedures to access particular types. Access to objects of these types in any other way should be avoided.

For example, an integer queue type may be defined in Pascal as follows:

```
type IntQueue = record
    Qvec : array [1..100] of INTEGER;
    front : 1..100;
    back : 1..100;
end;
```

Associated procedures *AddToQueue*, *RemoveFromQueue*, and *IsQueueEmpty* may be defined which operate on the array representing the queue. Although direct access to *IntQueue* is not forbidden by the language, disciplined use of these access procedures simulates the Ada information hiding mechanism. These procedures are not given here as they are similar to the Ada procedures above.

KEY POINTS

- The types in a program are an abstraction mechanism which can be used to model real-world entities.

- Pascal's type mechanism has a number of problems and inconsistencies. These include a lack of typed constants, the binding of array size with the type, the ability to create anonymous types and the inability to group type declarations and their associated operations.

- An abstract data type specification is made up of a type name, a specification of the domain of values for the type and a specification of operations defined over that type.

- Ada packages may be used to implement abstract data types.

- Ada generics are a means of creating abstract types with type parameters. These can be instantiated with a particular type to create a family of abstract data types.

- In general, the advantage of abstract data types is that the type representation can be changed without affecting other parts of the program which use that type. However, care must be taken in real-time systems if a representation change radically alters the dynamic behaviour of the type.

Further reading

Data Abstraction in Programming Languages. This is a reasonable book on data abstraction which tackles the topic from a programming language rather than an abstract viewpoint. One of its virtues is its conciseness although an extra chapter discussing the broader role of data abstraction in systems development would have certainly improved the book. (J. Bishop, 1986, Addison-Wesley.)

Programming in Ada, 2nd ed. This is an introductory Ada textbook which includes a very clear description of Ada packages. Other introductory texts might also be consulted. (J.G.P. Barnes, 1984, Addison-Wesley.)

Reference

Liskov, B and Zilles, S. (1974), 'Programming with abstract data types', *ACM Sigplan Notices*, **9** (4), 50–9.

EXERCISES

16.1 Write Pascal or Ada type declarations which might be used to model the following entities:

  - The entities which can appear on a data-flow diagram (discussed in Chapter 12)
  - The set of Pascal or Ada reserved words
  - A keyboard

16.2 Using examples, illustrate the problems with Pascal's type mechanism. Consult an Ada text and reference manual and describe how these deficiencies have been overcome in Ada (if they have been overcome!).

16.3 Using an example of a stack abstract data type, show how the representation may be changed without affecting other parts of a program using that type.

16.4 Write abstract data type specifications (in Ada) and implementations in Ada or another programming language for the following abstract types:

  - An ordered linked list (see Chapter 8)
  - A binary tree
  - A hash table with linear rehashing
  - A Cartesian coordinate including an equality operation
  - A compiler symbol table

16.5 Modify the representation of the hash table in Exercise 16.4 to support an alternative method of rehashing such as quadratic rehashing or chaining.

Chapter 17

Portability and Reuse

Objective

The objective of this chapter is to describe the problems which can arise in writing portable high-level language programs and suggest how non-portable parts of a program may be isolated. Particular attention is paid to operating system and machine architecture dependencies in high-level languages. The chapter is also concerned with software reuse. The advantages and disadvantages of reuse are discussed and guidelines given as to how reusable abstract data types can be designed.

Contents

The rate of change of computer hardware technology is so fast that computers become obsolete long before the programs that execute on these machines. It is therefore important that programs should be written so that they may be implemented under more than one computer/operating system configuration. This is doubly important if a programming system is widely marketed as a product. The more machines on which a system is implemented, the greater the potential market for it.

The initial proponents of high-level programming languages suggested that use of these languages would ensure program portability. It is certainly the case that the use of a high-level language is a necessary condition for portability but it is not sufficient. There are a number of hidden dependencies which can be introduced into high-level language programs, and part of this chapter is concerned with identifying and discussing how these dependencies may be avoided.

The other part of the chapter is concerned with the related subject of software reuse. Clearly, porting a program to another computer is an example of software reuse but it is possible to reuse software which is not portable and can only operate on a single computer. Software reuse is concerned with building software systems by using parts of other systems which have already been developed. It is now recognized that this approach offers one of the best opportunities of reducing overall software costs but systematic software reuse is still not widely practised.

17.1 Software portability

Techniques for achieving software portability have been widely documented (Brown, 1977; Tanenbaum *et al.*, 1978; Wallis, 1982; Nissen and Wallis, 1985). They include emulating one machine on another using microcode, compiling a program into some abstract machine language then implementing that abstract machine on a variety of computers, and using preprocessors to translate from one dialect of a programming language to another.

A characteristic of a portable program is that it is self-contained. The program should not rely on the existence of external agents to supply required functions. In practice, complete self-containment is almost impossible to achieve and the programmer intending to produce a portable program must compromise by isolating necessary references to the external environment. When that external environment is changed, those dependent parts of the program can be identified and modified.

Throughout this chapter, it will be assumed that a high-level language is used for programming and that a compiler for that language is available for each machine on which the program is to be implemented.

It is also assumed that some standard version of the high-level language is used rather than a dialect unique to a particular installation. The work involved in implementing a program on more than a single system is significantly increased if non-standard language 'extensions' are used in the initial coding of the program. Inevitably, compiler writers have different ideas concerning which 'extensions' should be made to a language and different compilers rarely include exactly the same additions.

This problem has bedevilled Pascal because the basic language lacks facilities and each implementation of Pascal has added its own features. Although there is now a standard for Pascal, this has come far too late and most Pascal implementations incorporate a significant number of non-standard features. To avoid this proliferation of dialects, the US Department of Defense has ensured that a standard for Ada was defined at an early stage of the language development. To check compliance with this standard, a set of validation programs have been produced and only language implementations which can successfully run this validation suite are considered as suitable for government-sponsored Ada development.

Even when a standard, widely implemented, high-level language is used for programming, it is difficult to construct a program of any size without some machine dependencies. These dependencies arise because features of the machine and its operating system are reflected directly in the language implementation. For example, the precision of numbers is dependent on the machine word size, and the access to backing store files is dependent on the primitives provided by the operating system. Even the character set available on different machines may not be identical, with the result that programs written using one character set must be edited to reflect the alternative character set.

Portability problems that arise when a standard high-level language is used can be classified under two headings. There are problems caused by language features influenced by the machine architecture and there are problems caused by operating system dependencies. Problems can be minimized, however, by making use of abstract data types and by ensuring that real-world entities are always modelled using such types rather than inbuilt program types.

The general approach which should be adopted in building a portable system is to isolate those parts of the system which depend on the machine architecture and the operating system in a portability interface (Figure 17.1). All operations which make use of non-portable characteristics should go through this interface.

The portability interface should be a set of abstract data types or objects which encapsulate the non-portable features and which hide any representation characteristics from the client software. When the system is moved to some other hardware or operating system, only the portability interface need be rewritten to reimplement the software.

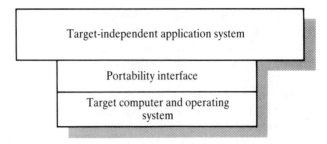

Figure 17.1
A portability interface.

This approach was adopted in the implementation of the design editing system which has been discussed in earlier chapters. The intention in building this system was to make it possible to store the design representation in either a UNIX file system or in one or more database systems. Thus, the objective was to avoid building representation dependencies into the system.

A logical design representation was specified and implemented in what was known as the abstract data interface (ADI). All operations on the design representation took place through this ADI (Figure 17.2) and porting the program to a different underlying database or filestore can be accomplished by rewriting the ADI code.

As an illustration of the relative amount of work involved, the ADI is implemented in about 1000 lines of C code whereas the entire system is about 14 000 lines of C. Given that some of the ADI code can be reused, it is estimated that porting the program to another data storage system would take about 1/20th of the effort required to rewrite the editing system.

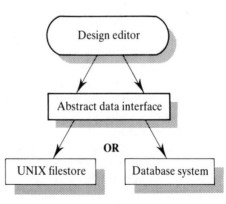

Figure 17.2
The portability interface of the design editor.

17.2 Machine architecture dependencies

The principal machine architecture dependencies arise in programs because the programming language must rely on the conventions of information representation adopted by the host machine. Different machines have different word lengths, different character sets and different techniques for representing integer and real numbers.

The length of a computer word directly affects the range of integers available on that machine, the precision of real numbers and the number of characters which may be packed into a single word. It is extremely difficult to program in such a way that implicit dependencies on machine word lengths are avoided.

For example, say a program is intended to count instances of some occurrence where the maximum number of instances that might arise is 500 000. Assume instance counts are to be compared. If this program is implemented on a machine with a 32-bit word size, instance counts can be represented as integers and comparisons made directly. However, if the program is subsequently moved to a 16-bit machine, it will fail because the maximum possible positive integer which can be held in a 16-bit word is 32 767.

Such a situation poses a difficult problem for the programmer. If instance counts are not represented as integers but as real numbers or as character strings this introduces an unnecessary overhead in counting and comparisons on the 32-bit machine. The cost of this overhead must be traded off against the cost of the reprogramming required if the system is subsequently implemented on a 16-bit machine.

If portability considerations are paramount in such a situation and if a programming language which permits the use of user defined types is available, an alternative solution to this problem is possible. An abstract data type, say *CountType*, whose range encompasses the possible values of the instance counter should be defined. In Pascal on a 32-bit machine this might be represented as follows:

type CountType = 0..500000;

If the system is subsequently ported to a 16-bit machine, then *CountType* may be redefined:

type CountType = array [1..6] of char;

Instead of using an integer to hold the counter value, it may be held as an array of digits. Associated with this type must be the operations permitted on instance counters. These can be programmed in Pascal as functions. On

Example 17.1
Large integer comparison
– 16-bit computer.

```
function Cequals(c1,c2 : CountType) : boolean;
      var i : integer;
      comp : boolean;
  begin
     comp:=true; i := 1;
     while comp and (i <= 6) do
     begin
        comp : = c1[i] = c2[i];
        i := i + 1
     end;
     Cequals := comp
  end {Cequals};
```

32-bit machines, these functions simply consist of the appropriate integer
operations. On 16-bit machines, on the other hand, the functions would
be more complex, and must simulate integer operations on digit strings.
For example, consider a Pascal function to compare counters for
equality. On a 32-bit machine, this function can be implemented as a
single statement:

```
function Cequals(c1,c2 : CountType) : boolean;
  begin
      Cequals := c1=c2
  end;
```

On a 16-bit machine, where large integers are represented as strings of
digits, the function could be written as shown in Example 17.1.

Irrespective of how the type *CountType* is represented, the user
always has exactly the same operations available and transporting the
program simply involves changing the type definition and rewriting the
functions which operate on that type.

Ideally, the type definition and its related operations should be
grouped together into a self-contained unit like an Ada package (Example
17.2). Only the type name and related operations need be visible outside
the package, with all representation details confined to the package. If the
program is ported to another system which uses a different counter
representation only the counter package need be changed. None of the
uses of counter are affected. In languages such as Pascal, where no module
facility is available, the operations on each type should be grouped and
delimited by comments.

```
package Counter is
    type T is limited private;
    procedure Inc (Cnt : in out T ) ;
    procedure Dec (Cnt : in out T ) ;
    procedure Copy (Cnt1: T ; Cnt2: out T ) ;
    function Cequals (Cnt1, Cnt2: T ) return BOOLEAN ;
private
    type T is range 0..500_000 ;
end;
```

Example 17.2
A counter package
specification.

Different machine word lengths also mean that the precision of real numbers varies from machine to machine. For example, if a real number is represented using 32-bits, 8-digit precision may be possible whereas 64-bit representation allows 17- or 18-digit precision. On a 32-bit machine, no distinction could be made between the numbers 10001.3214 and 10001.3210, whereas they would be considered different numbers on a higher precision machine.

The problem of differing precision has been recognized in Ada and, in defining a numeric type, the user may explicitly state the precision to which values of that type are held. For example, 6-digit precision is specified:

```
type short is digits 6 range 0..SOMEMAX ;
```

This specifies that numbers of type short lie in the range 0 to SOMEMAX and should be held to 6-digit precision.

This facility eliminates some of the problems involved in porting software which uses real numbers and, theoretically, implementations of Ada should support the specification of any precision whatsoever. In practice, the specification of precisions which cannot be accommodated in one or two machine words is difficult to implement and involves heavy run-time overhead.

A portability problem which is related to, but distinct from, the problems caused by machines having different word lengths is caused by the fact that different machines may represent exactly the same information in different ways. For example, a 16-bit machine which uses two's complement notation to represent negative numbers would represent -1 as 1111111111111111, whereas a machine which uses one's complement notation would represent the same number as 1111111111111110.

In some machines, the most significant bit of a number is the leftmost bit and on others it is the rightmost bit. On 16-bit machines where it is the leftmost bit, the number 2 would be represented as

0000000000000010, whereas if the rightmost bit is significant, 2 is represented 0100000000000000, assuming two's complement representation is used.

These representation considerations do not normally cause problems for high-level language programmers because the objects they use have values which are consistent from one representation to another. If, however, it is necessary to generate specific bit patterns and the programming language does not allow direct operations on bit strings, it may be necessary to simulate bit strings using integers. The representation of integers on a particular machine must be known if bit patterns are to be generated.

If the program is moved to another machine which uses a different representation for integers, the bit strings generated from integers will be incorrect. As a general rule, when bit strings are generated by using integers, absolute integer values should never be used in the program. Rather, the integers representing the bit strings should be given names appropriate to their function, with these names defined as constants. For example, if it is required to define a mask which will select the rightmost bit of a number, this might be declared:

const *RIGHTMOST* = *1;*

If the program containing this declaration is subsequently moved to a machine where the most significant bit is the rightmost bit, this constant might be redefined:

const *RIGHTMOST* = *−MAXINT − 1;*

Again, if packages are available, these declarations can be grouped in a package and their representation concealed from the remainder of the program. Otherwise, declarations of such machine dependent constants must be grouped together and clearly identified by comments in the program text.

Unfortunately there is no single worldwide standardization of the character sets used in computers. The majority of systems use a character set named ASCII (American Standard Characters for Information Interchange) but other representations are also used, principally EBCDIC (Extended Binary Coded Decimal) which is used on IBM and IBM compatible systems.

Not only do different character sets use different values to represent each character, they also differ in the punctuation characters provided. As a result, programs written using character set A, say, cannot be directly translated to another character set B. The programs in character set A must first be edited to replace characters available in A but not in B by some equivalent. For example, in the original definition of Pascal, it was specified that text enclosed in braces {} is treated as a comment. Many implementations of Pascal execute on machines which do not provide braces so, in these implementations, comments are enclosed within the compound symbols (* and *).

The editing procedure required to resolve character set differences is tedious but does not cause serious portability problems. The transformation is clearly defined and easy to implement if a reasonable context editor is available. Portability problems are caused by character representations when the system depends on a character having a particular value. For example, in ASCII, the digits 0–9 have values 60–69 and, to obtain the integer value of a digit, 60 is subtracted from the character value. In Pascal:

digitvalue := ord (digit) −60;

If this code were transported to machine using the EBCDIC character set, it would be legal but would deliver an incorrect result. In EBCDIC, digits are represented by the values 240–249, so the above statement would consider the character '2' to have an integer value of 182.

Assumptions about the values used to represent characters should never be built into a program. If the above statement were written:

digitvalue := ord (digit) − ord ('0');

no portability problems would arise. Not only is the statement character set independent, it is also a clearer description of the operation being implemented.

A further difficulty which arises because of different character sets results from the fact that different machines use different collating sequences for the letters of the alphabet. In ASCII, the letters A to Z are assigned ascending values in consecutive sequence whereas in EBCDIC, A to Z do not have consecutive values. A program statement may test a value to see if it represents a letter of the alphabet by checking that it lies between the value representing A and the value representing Z. For example:

if *(someval >= ord ('A'))* **and** *(someval <= ord ('Z'))* **then** ...

On EBCDIC machines, this is not guaranteed to work because the sequence of values between A and Z includes other characters. If the programmer is faced with such a situation and knows that the program may be implemented on machines with differing character sets, the only solution is to isolate such machine dependencies in clearly identified procedures. The above statement might be written:

if *letter (someval)* **then** ...

The procedure letter must be rewritten when the program is transferred to a machine with an incompatible character set.

17.3   Operating system dependencies

As well as machine architecture dependencies, the other major portability problem which arises in high-level language is dependencies on operating system facilities. Different machines support different operating systems. Although common facilities are provided, this is rarely in a compatible way.

Some *de facto* operating system standards have emerged (MS-DOS for personal computers, UNIX for workstations, for example) but these are not supported by some major manufacturers. At the time of writing, their future as general standards is uncertain. Until standards are agreed, the problem of dependencies on operating system facilities will remain.

Most operating systems provide some kind of library mechanism and, often, a set of routines which can be incorporated into user programs. These libraries fall into two classes:

(1)   Standardized libraries of routines associated with a particular application or operating system. An example of such routines are the NAG library routines for numerical applications. These routines have a standard interface and exactly the same routines are available to all installations which subscribe to the library.

(2)   Installation libraries which consist of routines submitted by users at a particular site. These routines rarely have a standard interface and they are not written in such a way that they may easily be ported from one installation to another.

The re-use of existing software should be encouraged whenever possible as it reduces the amount of code which must be written, tested and documented. However, the use of subroutine libraries reduces the self-containedness of a program and hence may increase the difficulty of transferring that program from one installation to another.

If use is made of standard subroutine libraries such as the NAG library, this will not cause any portability problems if the program is moved to another installation where the library is available. On the other hand, if the library is not available, transportation of the program is likely to be almost impossible.

If use is made of local installation libraries, transporting the program either involves transporting the library with the program or supplementing the target system library to make it compatible with the host library. The user must trade off the productivity advantages of using libraries against the dependence on the external environment which this entails.

One of the principal functions of an operating system is to provide a file system. Program access to this is via primitive operations which allow the user to name, create, access, delete, protect and share files. There are no standards governing how these operations should be provided. Each operating system supports them in different ways.

As high-level language systems must provide file facilities, they interface with the file system. Normally, the file system operations provided in the high-level language are synonymous with the operating system primitives. Therefore, the least portable parts of a program are often those operations which involve access to files.

There are a number of different problems which can arise because of file system incompatibilities:

(1)   The convention for naming files may differ from system to system. Some systems restrict the number of characters in a file name, other systems impose restrictions on exactly which characters can make up a file name, and yet others impose no restrictions whatsoever.

(2)   The file system structure may differ from system to system. Some file systems are hierarchically structured. Users may create their own directories and sub-directories. Other systems are restricted to a two level structure where all files belonging to a particular user must reside in the same directory.

(3)   Different systems utilize different schemes for protecting files. Some systems involve passwords, other systems use explicit lists of who may access what, and yet others grant permissions according to the attributes of the user.

(4)   Some systems attempt to classify files as data files, program files, binary files or as files associated with the application that created them. Other systems consider all files to be untyped files of characters.

(5)   Most systems restrict the user to a maximum number of files which may be in use at any one time. If this number is different on the host machine from that on the target machine, there may be problems in porting programs which have many files open at the same time.

(6)   There are a number of different file structuring mechanisms enforced by different systems. Systems such as UNIX support only character files whereas other systems consider files to be made up of logical records with many logical records packed into each physical block.

(7)   The random access primitives supported by different systems vary from one system to another. Some systems may not support random access, others allow random access to individual characters, and yet others only permit random access at the block level.

There is little that programmers can do to make file access over different systems compatible. They are stuck with a set of file system primitives and those parts of the system must be modified if the program is moved to another installation. To reduce the amount of work required, file access primitives should be isolated, whenever possible, in user defined procedures. For example, in UNIX, the mechanism to create a file involves calling a system function called create passing the file name and access permissions as parameters:

```
create ("myfile",0755)
```

This creates a file called myfile with universal read and execute access and owner write access. In order to isolate this call, a synonymous user function which calls create can be included:

```
access_permissions := "rwxr_xr_x"
create_file ("myfile", access_permissions)
```

In UNIX, create_file would simply consist of a single call to the system routine create. On other systems, create_file could be rewritten to reflect the conventions of the system. The parameters to create_file could be translated into the appropriate form for that system.

It might be imagined that the input/output facilities in a programming language would conceal the details of the operating system input/output routines. Input/output should therefore cause few problems when porting a system from one installation to another.

This is true to some extent. In some programming languages (FORTRAN and COBOL) input/output facilities are defined and each implementation of the language provides these facilities. In other languages, such as Pascal, the input/output facilities are poorly defined or inadequate. As a result, the implementors of a compiler 'extend' the I/O facilities to reflect the facilities provided by the operating system and this leads to portability problems because of incompatible extensions. In particular, the provision of interactive terminal support sometimes causes problems with Pascal as it was developed before interactive terminals were widely used.

Different systems consider interactive terminals in different ways. In UNIX, a terminal is considered as a special file and file access primitives are used to access it. In other systems, terminals are considered to be devices distinct from files and special terminal access primitives are provided.

There are advantages and disadvantages in considering a terminal as a file. The advantage is that input and output to and from a program can come from either a terminal or a file on backing store. The disadvantage is that the characteristics of a terminal are not exactly those of a file. In fact, a terminal is really like two distinct files, an input file and an output file. If this is not taken into account, portability problems are likely to arise.

Further problems with terminal I/O arise because terminal characteristics differ. Different terminals have different screen sizes; some terminals offer cursor addressability, others do not; some terminals support tab characters; and so on. Terminals make use of control characters which differ from machine to machine. Again, the only advice which can be given to the programmer wishing to write portable interactive programs is to isolate hardware specific code in clearly defined procedures. These procedures must be rewritten when the system is moved to another installation.

Alternatively, the user may choose to construct a special table-driven terminal driver which can handle all kinds of terminal likely to be used with the system. The terminal table contains details of terminal characteristics and the user must explicitly inform the driver what type of terminal is being used. All terminal access is via a set of routines which consult the terminal table to produce the appropriate responses for each type of terminal (Figure 17.3). This approach to isolating terminal dependencies is quite an expensive one but is probably worthwhile where a system (like UNIX) is to be used with a wide variety of terminal types.

The problem with non-portable terminal support is exacerbated when it comes to windowing facilities on bit-mapped workstations. There are a variety of window systems available which are sometimes radically different. Porting a program from one of these systems to another is at best awkward and, at worst, can involve a complete rewrite of the entire program.

Thankfully, however, a standard called X-windows (Scheifler and Gettys, 1986) in this area appears to be emerging and this has received the support of many workstation manufacturers. Again, unfortunately, very large manufacturers such as Apple and IBM have not yet given it their support and this will inevitably slow down its acceptance in the community in general.

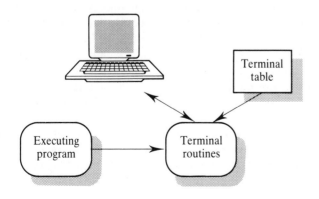

Figure 17.3
Table-driven terminal access.

Many systems are made up of a number of separate programs with job control language statements (in UNIX, these are called shell commands) used to coordinate the activities of these programs. Although it might be imagined that these would be relatively small programs, systems like UNIX encourage the use of job control languages as a programming language. Moderately large systems are sometimes written using this notation.

There is no standardization of job control languages across different systems with the consequence that all job control must be rewritten when transferring a system from one installation to another. The difficulties involved in this are exacerbated by the vastly different facilities provided in different languages and may be further compounded by WIMP interfaces such as that used in the Apple Macintosh. Only a move towards a standard operating system will help resolve these problems.

17.4 Software reuse

The notion of reusing software is one that developed at a very early stage in the history of computing, and the main motivation of the development of subroutine libraries was software reuse. Indeed, it was only about 20 years ago that the role of subroutines and procedures as program structuring concepts was articulated. Before that, they were seen simply as ways of reusing code.

An obvious advantage of software reuse is that costs should be reduced as the number of components that must be specified, designed and implemented in a software system is reduced. Reuse, of course, does not just encompass the reuse of code. It is possible to reuse specifications and designs and it has been suggested that code reuse is never likely to be cost effective. This is an arguable point, but what is clear is that reuse of logical software components, in any form, has obvious benefits.

It is difficult to quantify what the cost reductions might be. Indeed, there is no real guarantee that costs will always be reduced. Reusing the component might require modification to that component and this, conceivably, could cost as much as component development. However, cost reduction is not the only advantage of reuse and even if costs are not reduced, systematic software reuse offers a number of advantages:

(1) *System reliability is increased* It can be argued that only actual operational use adequately tests components and reused components, which have been exercised in working systems, should be more reliable than components developed anew.

(2)   *Overall risk is reduced* If a component exists, there is less uncertainty in the costs of using that component than in the costs of developing it. This is an important factor for project management as it reduces the overall uncertainty in the project cost estimation.

(3)   *Effective use can be made of specialists* Instead of application specialists joining a project for a short time and often doing the same work with different projects, as proposed by Brooks (1975), these specialists can develop reusable components which encapsulate their knowledge.

(4)   *Organizational standards can be embodied in reusable components* For example, say a number of applications present users with menus. Reusable components providing these menus mean that all applications present the same menu formats to users.

(5)   *Software development time can be reduced* It is often the case that bringing a system to market as early as possible is more important than overall development costs. Reusing components speeds up system production because both development and validation time should be reduced.

While standard subroutine libraries have been very successful in a number of application domains in promoting reuse, systematic software reuse as a general software development technique is not commonly practised. There are a number of technical and managerial reasons for this:

(1)   We do not really know what the critical component attributes which make a component reusable are. We can guess that attributes such as environmental independence are essential but assessing the reusability of a component in different application domains is difficult.

(2)   Developing generalized components is more expensive than developing a component for a specific purpose. Thus, developing reusable components increases project costs and manager's main preoccupation is keeping project costs down. To develop reusable components requires an organizational policy decision to increase short-term costs for possible, unquantifiable, long-term gain, and senior management is often reluctant to make such decisions.

(3)   Some software engineers are reluctant to accept the advantages of software reuse and prefer to write components afresh as they believe that they can improve on the reusable component. In most cases, this is probably true, but only at the expense of greater risk and higher costs.

(4)   We do not have a means of classifying, cataloguing and retrieving software components. The critical attribute of a retrieval system is that component retrieval costs should be less than component development costs.

The importance of systematic software reuse is now widely recognized and there is a great deal of research effort being expended on solving some of the problems of reuse. An overall view of some of this research is given by Horowitz and Munson (1984) and by Prieto-Diaz and Freeman (1987).

In one application domain, however, reuse is now commonplace. This is in data processing systems where fourth-generation languages (Martin, 1985) are widely used. Broadly, many data processing applications involve abstracting information from a database, performing some relatively simply information processing and then producing reports using that information. This stereotypical structure was recognized and components to carry out these operations devised.

On top of these was produced some control language (there is a close analogy here with the UNIX shell) which allowed programs to be specified and a complete application to be generated.

This form of reuse is very effective but it has not spread beyond the data processing systems domain. The reason for this seems to be that similar stereotypical situations are less obvious in other domains and there seems to be less scope for an approach to reuse based on applications generators.

The initial notion of reuse centred around the reuse of subroutines. The problem with reusing subroutine components is that it is not practicable to embed environmental information in the component so that only functions, whose values are not dependent on environmental factors, may be reused.

Subroutines are not an adequate abstraction for many useful components such as a set of routines to manipulate queues and it is likely that software reuse will only become widespread when languages such as Ada with improved abstraction facilities become widely used. Indeed, it is probable that the most effectively reusable component is the abstract data type which provides operations on a particular class of object.

Given this assumption, what are useful guidelines to adopt when developing abstract data types for reuse? It can be assumed that abstract data types are independent entities which behave in the same way irrespective of the environment in which they are used (except for timing considerations, perhaps). Thus, we have to be concerned about providing a complete and consistent set of operations for each abstract type. Unfortunately, there is a large number of possible operations on each abstract type and there is no way in which the component developer can anticipate every possible use. Some broad guidelines as to what facilities should be provided are:

(1)   An operation should be included to create and initialize instances of the abstract type. Creation is sometimes accomplished simply by language declarations but the programmer should not rely on default initializations provided by the implementation language.

(2) For each attribute of the abstract type, access and constructor functions should be provided. Access functions return attribute values; constructor functions allow attribute values to be changed.

(3) Operations to print instances of the type and to read and write type instances to and from filestore should be provided.

(4) Assignment and equality operations should be provided. This may involve defining equality in some arbitrary way which should be specified in the abstract type documentation.

(5) For every possible exception condition which might occur in type operations, a test function should be provided which allows that condition to be checked for before initiating the operation. For example, if an operation on lists might fail if the list is empty, a function should be provided which allows the user to check if the list has any members.

(6) If the abstract type is a composite type (that is, is made up of a collection of other objects), operations to add objects to and to delete objects from the collection should be provided. If the collection is ordered, multiple add and delete functions should be provided. For example, for a list type, operations should be available to add and delete an element to and from the front and the end of the list.

(7) If the abstract type is a composite type, functions to provide information about attributes of the composition (such as size) should be provided.

(8) If the abstract type is a composite type, an iterator should be provided which allows each element of the type to be visited. Iterators allow each component of a composite to be visited and evaluated without destroying the structure of the entity.

(9) Wherever possible, abstract types should be parameterized using generic types. However, this is only possible when parameterization is supported by the implementation language.

As an example of the abstract type structures which result when these guidelines are observed, consider the specification of two abstract types which have been designed for reuse. These are a type Coord (Example 17.3) which represents Cartesian coordinates on a diagram and a type List (Example 17.4) which represents lists of objects of any type. The specifications are given as Ada package headers and the semantics of the operations are not defined.

Even for this very simple type, following the reusability guidelines results in 10 functions being defined for the Cartesian.COORD abstract type. In this case, no parameterization is necessary and no exception conditions can occur. Notice that the type has been declared as a limited private type.

Example 17.3

The abstract type Coord.

```
with TEXT_IO ;
package Cartesian is
    type COORD is limited private ;
    function Create ( X, Y: INTEGER) return COORD ;
    function Equals (C1, C2: COORD) return COORD ;
    function X (C: COORD) return INTEGER ;
    function Y (C: COORD) return INTEGER ;
    procedure Put_x (C: in out COORD ; X: INTEGER ) ;
    procedure Put_y (C: in out COORD ; Y: INTEGER ) ;
    procedure Assign (C1: in out COORD ; C2: COORD ) ;
    procedure Print ( C: COORD ) ;
    procedure ToDisk (F: TEXT_IO.FILE_TYPE ; C: COORD) ;
    procedure FromDisk (F: TEXT_IO.FILE_TYPE ;
                                    C: out COORD) ;
private
    type COORD is record
        X_part: INTEGER ;
        Y_part: INTEGER ;
    end record ;
end Cartesian ;
```

Example 17.4

The abstract type List.

```
with TEXT_IO ;
generic
    type ELEMENT is private ;
package Linked is
    type LIST is limited private ;
    type STATUS is range 1..10 ;
    -- Creation procedure
    procedure Create (Error_level: out STATUS) ;
    -- Assignment
    procedure Assign (L1: in out LIST ; L2: LIST ;
                            Error_level: out Status) ;
    -- Procedures to find out things about the list
    procedure Is_empty (L: LIST; Result: out BOOLEAN ;
                            Error_level: out STATUS ) ;
    procedure Size_of (L: LIST ; Size: out NATURAL ;
                            Error_level: out STATUS ) ;
    procedure Contains (E: ELEMENT; Result: out BOOLEAN ;
                            Error_level: out STATUS ) ;
    procedure Head (L: LIST; E: in out ELEMENT ;
                            Error_level: out STATUS ) ;
    procedure Tail ( Outlist: in out LIST ;
                            Error_level: out STATUS ) ;
    -- State change procedures
    -- Append adds an element to the end of the list
    procedure Append ( E: ELEMENT; Outlist: in out LIST ;
                            Error_level: out STATUS ) ;
```

Example 17.4
The abstract type List
(cont).

```
-- Add adds an element to the front of the list
procedure Add ( E: ELEMENT; Outlist: in out LIST ;
                  Error_level: out STATUS ) ;
-- Add_before adds an element before element value E
procedure Add_before ( E: ELEMENT ; Outlist: in out LIST ;
                  Error_level: out STATUS ) ;
-- Add_after adds an element after element E
procedure Add_after ( E: ELEMENT; Outlist: in out LIST ;
                  Error_level: out STATUS ) ;
-- Replace replaces the element matching E1 with E2
procedure Replace (E1, E2: ELEMENT; Outlist: in out LIST ;
                  Error_level: out STATUS ) ;
-- Clear deletes all members of a list
procedure Clear ( Outlist: in out LIST ;
                  Error_level: out STATUS ) ;
-- Prune removes the last element from the list
procedure Prune ( Outlist: in out LIST ;
                  Error_level: out STATUS ) ;
-- Prune_to deletes the list up to and including
-- the element matching E
procedure Prune_to ( E: ELEMENT; Outlist: in out LIST ;
                  Error_level: out STATUS ) ;
-- Prune_from deletes list after element matching E
procedure Prune_from( E: ELEMENT; Outlist: in out LIST ;
                  Error_level: out STATUS ) ;
-- Remove deletes the element which matches E
procedure Remove ( E: ELEMENT; Outlist: in out LIST ;
                  Error_level: out STATUS ) ;
-- Remove_before and Remove_after delete the element before
-- and after E respectively
procedure Remove_before ( E: ELEMENT; Outlist: in out LIST;
                  Error_level: out STATUS ) ;
procedure Remove_after ( E: ELEMENT; Outlist: in out LIST ;
                  Error_level: out STATUS ) ;
-- I/O procedures
procedure Print_list (L: LIST; Error_level: out STATUS ) ;
procedure Save_list (F: TEXT_IO.FILE_TYPE ; L: LIST;
                  Error_level: out STATUS ) ;
procedure Restore_list (F: TEXT_IO.FILE_TYPE ;
         Outlist: out LIST ;Error_level: out STATUS ) ;
procedure Explain_error (Level: STATUS ;
                  Message: out STRING) ;
private
type LIST_ELEM;
type LIST is access LIST_ELEM ;
end Linked ;
```

This means that only the operations defined in the package may be applied to entities of that type so it is necessary to define an assignment operation (Assign) and an equality operation (Equals).

For a generalized list type, which is a composite type, even more functions must be included. In Example 17.4, an Ada generic package has been used to parameterize the component with the type of list element. Notice how defensive programming is practised and that each list operation returns an error status indicator. This status indicator is set depending on the success or otherwise of the operation. The particular values which are assigned for each operation in the package should be part of the component documentation.

It is clear from the size of these examples that the cost of producing a generalized component is inevitably greater than the cost of producing a component for a single application where all of the functions are not required. Unless a management decision is made to incur such expenditure, it is unlikely that effectively reusable components will be produced in the normal course of a software development project.

KEY POINTS

- To make a program portable it must be as self-contained as possible. Wherever practical, the use of external agents should be avoided.

- When using a high-level language, the major portability problems arise because of machine architecture and operating system dependencies.

- Dependencies on machine architecture or operating system features should be localized in a portability interface. This should be represented as a set of abstract data types which can be rewritten when the system is moved to another computer.

- Software reuse is an effective way of reducing the costs and risk associated with software development.

- The problems associated with software reuse are both technical and non-technical. Perhaps the most difficult to solve are the non-technical factors which require people to be convinced that reuse is worthwhile.

- Abstract data types can be considered as reusable components. To make them reusable, care has to be taken in the design of the operations provided with these types.

Further reading

Portable Programming.   This book is now a few years old but it covers many of the general problems of portability, which have not changed. There seems to be relatively little more recent material available on this topic. However, it does not discuss the use of information hiding to achieve portability. (P.J.L. Wallis, 1982, Macmillan Press.)

IEEE Trans. Software Eng., **SE-10** (5), 1984. A special issue of this journal which is devoted to reusability. It is perhaps a measure of the state of the art that many of the papers are speculative rather than descriptive of practical experience.

IEEE Software, **4** (4), 1987. Again, a journal special issue which is devoted to reusability. The papers have been deliberately selected to reflect practical experience which was generally positive. However, these illustrate that we have only taken the first steps in software reuse and have a great deal further to go.

References

Brooks, F.P. (1975), *The Mythical Man Month*, Reading, Mass.: Addison-Wesley.

Brown, P.J. (ed.), (1977), *Software Portability*, Cambridge: Cambridge University Press.

Horowitz, E. and Munsen, J.B. (1984), 'An expansive view of reusable software', *IEEE Trans. Software Eng.*, **SE-10** (5), 477–87.

Martin, J. (1985), *Fourth Generation Languages*, Englewood Cliffs, NJ: Prentice-Hall.

Nissen, J. and Wallis, P.J.L. (eds) (1985), *Portability and Style in Ada*, Cambridge: Cambridge University Press.

Prieto-Diaz, R. and Freeman, P. (1987), 'Classifying software for reusability', *IEEE Software*, **4** (1), 6–16.

Scheifler, R.W. and Gettys, J. (1986), 'The X window system', *ACM Trans. on Graphics*, **5** (2).

Tanenbaum, A.S., Klint, P. and Bohm, W. (1978), 'Guidelines for software portability', *Software – Practice and Experience*, **8**, 681–98.

Wallis, P.J.L. (1982), *Portable Programming*, London: Macmillan.

EXERCISES

17.1 Explain why the use of a standard high-level language does not guarantee that software will be portable across a range of machines.

17.2 You have been given the task of implementing a calendar and clock which gives time and data information. This has to operate on a range of computers from 8-bit micros to 64-bit special processors. Design an abstract data type which can be ported from machine to machine.

17.3 Suggest suitable implementations on 8-bit and 32-bit computers for the clock and calendar abstract data type designed in Exercise 17.2.

17.4 Design the architecture of a Pascal (or some other programming language) compiler so that it may be implemented on a range of computers. Identify the key features of the portability interface in your design.

17.5 Discuss the problems which can arise when an interactive terminal is considered as a file. Define an abstract data type TERMINAL which avoids these difficulties and which represents a portability interface for terminals.

17.6 What are the major technical and non-technical factors which militate against widespread software reuse? From your own experience, do you reuse much software? If not, why not?

17.7 Write a set of guidelines for the Pascal or C programmer when writing functions or procedures that set out how to make these functions or procedures more reusable.

17.8 Using the suggestions set out in the chapter, construct reusable packages for the following abstract data types:
- A stack
- A table with keyed access to table elements
- A binary tree
- A priority queue
- An array
- A character string

Chapter 18

Computer-Aided Software Engineering

Objectives

This chapter introduces the notion of computer-aided software engineering and discusses how the use of support tools can improve the productivity of the software engineer. Three classes of tool are discussed here, namely CASE workbenches, text editing systems and language processing systems. The advantages and disadvantages of current CASE workbench products are described, different types of text editing system including structured editors are discussed, and particular attention is paid to the important topic of separate compilation which is essential in large systems development. The chapter is not intended to cover all CASE tools. Other tools, such as testing and debugging tools, are discussed in later chapters.

Contents

Historically, the most significant productivity increases in manufacturing or building processes have come about when human skills have been augmented by powerful tools. For example, one man and a bulldozer can probably shift more earth in a day than 50 men working with hand tools. Similarly, the productivity of engineering designers is enhanced when they are supported by CAD systems which take over tedious drawing chores and which check the design to ensure its validity.

The practice of software development has some similarities with manufacturing, so supporting software engineers with automated tools can lead to improvements in productivity. Recently, the term computer-aided software engineering (CASE) has come into use when discussing support tools for software engineers. However, this is a new term for an old concept. Software tools to support programming have been available for some time, but new cheap personal computers means that automated tools can now be made available to many more software developers than was previously possible.

Before the widespread introduction of timesharing computer systems, the majority of program development was carried out off-line. Programs were prepared and debugged without the aid of the computer system. Preparing a program involved punching it onto cardboard cards, submitting the cards to a batch processing system and then retrieving the cards along with a listing of the results of executing or compiling the program. Program modifications were made by repunching those cards in the deck that contained the program statements to be modified.

Even in this situation, some programming tools were available. Apart from compilers, assemblers and other language processors, most systems provided a link editor which allowed parts of the program to be independently compiled then linked together to form an executable program. If a generally useful subroutine is prepared by one individual, that routine can be entered in a public library of subroutines and any other user may refer to that subroutine in his or her program. The link editor searches the appropriate subroutine libraries, abstracts the code of the called routine, and links the referenced routine with the calling program.

As well as these tools, a variety of other CASE tools to assist the process of software development are now available. The use of timesharing systems allows interactive editors and debugging tools to be used and large amounts of backing store means that library programs to keep track of code and documentation can be developed. However, timesharing systems offer a restricted amount of computational power to each user and it is only now, with the introduction of powerful, networked single-user workstations to support software development, that the full productivity benefits from tool use can be realized.

Individual software tools, used in conjunction, are very valuable but the true power of a CASE toolset can only be realized when these tools are integrated into a common framework or environment. In an integrated environment, any one tool can access the data produced by other tools. This allows both serendipitous tool combinations and incremental toolsets where operations common to a number of tools are implemented once and provided as a single tool. The structure and components of software engineering environments are described in the following chapter.

18.1   CASE workbenches

Perhaps the most publicized CASE tools are so-called CASE workbench systems which are designed to support the analysis and design stages of the software process. These systems are oriented towards the support of graphical notations such as used in the various design methods. They are either intended for the support of a specific method, such as Structured Design, or support a range of diagram types which encompasses those used in the most common methods.

Typical components of a CASE workbench (Figure 18.1) are:

(1)   A diagram editing system that is used to create data-flow diagrams, structure charts, entity-relationship diagrams, etc. The editor is not just a simple drafting tool but is aware of the types of entities in the diagram. It captures information about these entities and saves this information in a central repository (sometimes called an encyclopaedia). The design editing system discussed in previous chapters is an example of such a tool.

(2)   Design analysis and checking facilities that process the design and report on errors and anomalies. As far as possible these are integrated with the editing system so that the user may be informed of errors during diagram creation.

(3)   Query language facilities that allow the user to browse the stored information and examine completed designs.

(4)   Data dictionary facilities that maintain information about named entities used in a system design.

(5)   Report generation facilities that take information from the central store and automatically generate system documentation.

(6)   Forms generation tools that allow screen and document formats to be specified.

(7)   Import/export facilities that allow the interchange of information from the central repository with other development tools.

(8)   Some systems support skeleton code generators which generate code or code segments automatically from the design captured in the central store.

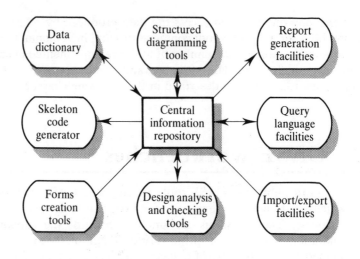

Figure 18.1
CASE workbench
facilities.

CASE workbench systems, like structured methods, have been mostly used in the development of data processing systems, but there is no reason why they cannot be used in the development of other classes of system. Chikofsky and Rubenstein (1988) suggest that productivity improvements of up to 40% may be achieved with the use of such systems. They also suggest that, as well as these improvements, the quality of the developed systems is higher, with fewer errors and inconsistencies, and the developed systems are more appropriate to the user's needs.

Current CASE workbench products are first-generation systems and Martin (1988) identifies a number of deficiencies in these tools. For example:

(1)   The workbenches are not integrated with other document preparation tools such as word processors and desktop-publishing systems. Import/export facilities are usually confined to ASCII text.

(2)   There is a lack of standardization which makes information interchange across different workbenches difficult or impossible.

(3)   They lack facilities which allow a method to be tailored to a particular application or class of application. For example, it is not usually possible for users to override a built-in rule and replace it with their own. In this respect, most CASE workbenches are different from the design editing system previously discussed. It provides explicit tailoring facilities.

(4)   The quality of the hard-copy documentation which is produced is often low. Martin observes that simply producing copies of screens is not good enough and that the requirements for paper documentation are distinct from those for screen documentation.

(5)   The diagramming facilities are slow to use so that even a moderately complex diagram can take several hours to input and arrange. He suggests that there is a need for automated diagramming and diagram arrangement given a textual input.

A more serious omission, from the point of view of large-scale software engineering, is the lack of support for configuration management provided by these systems. Large software systems are in use for many years and, in that time, are subject to many changes and exist in many versions.

Configuration management is discussed in Chapter 28 and is probably the most critical management activity in the software engineering process. Configuration management tools allow individuals versions of a system to be retrieved, support system building from components, and maintain relationships between components, and their documentation.

The user of a CASE workbench is provided with support for aspects of the design process, but these are not automatically linked to other products such as source code, test data suites and user documentation. It is not usually possible to create multiple versions of a design and to track these, nor is there a straightforward way to interface the workbench systems with other configuration management tools.

The lack of data standards makes it difficult or impossible to transfer information in the central repository to other workbench systems. This means that users may be faced with the prospect of maintaining obsolete CASE workbenches and their supporting computers for many years in order to maintain systems developed using these workbenches. This problem has not yet manifested itself because of the relative newness of these systems but is likely to arise as new, second-generation CASE products come onto the market.

18.2   Text editing systems

Program and document preparation is probably the activity which most software engineers carry out most of the time. This involves making use of one or more text editing systems. The function of a text editor is to enable the user to create and modify files kept on-line in the system, and most environments used for software development offer a number of different editors. Because this is such a common activity, the power of the editor contributes significantly to the productivity of the software engineer.

Although some editors, such as UNIX's *vi* editor, have facilities which are designed to support program preparation, most editors are general-purpose text preparation systems. This naturally means that it is possible for the user to prepare syntactically incorrect programs with these editors but it has the advantage that the same editing system may be used to produce any type of document. There is no need for the user to learn more than one editing system.

To support program preparation and editing, some work has been done in developing language-oriented editors (sometimes called structure editors) designed to prepare and modify programs in a specific programming language. An example of such a system is the Cornell Program Synthesizer, described by Teitelbaum and Reps (1981), which is intended to help beginners prepare programs written in a subset of PL/1 called PL/C. Such a system must include a PL/C syntax analyser as well as editing features. Rather than manipulate unstructured text, the system actually manipulates a tree structure representing the program. In fact, the Cornell system is more than just a syntax-directed editor. It is a complete language-oriented environment with integrated editing, translation and program execution facilities.

Such systems are valuable for beginners wrestling with the idiosyncrasies of our current programming languages. However, they do have limitations. Passing information about context-sensitive language constructs is difficult, particularly in large programs where the whole program is not visible on the screen. More fundamentally, perhaps, these systems do not recognize the fact that many experienced programmers work by laying out an (incorrect) program skeleton then filling in that skeleton correcting inaccuracies and inconsistencies. Structure editors force a mode of working on the user which does not always conform to professional practice.

Some of the limitations of existing editing systems (particularly for program editing) are a result of display inadequacies where simple 80 by 24 character terminals are used. Such hardware forces documents or programs to be viewed sequentially. A sequential representation is hardly ever the most appropriate for programs where the reader wishes to look at and modify program parts which are logically rather than textually related. Furthermore, it may be appropriate to view and edit programs as diagrams rather than text. As bit-mapped workstations become the normal tool of the software engineer, new editing systems such as that described by Shneiderman *et al.* (1986) will become commonly used.

Such systems use multiple windows to present different parts of the program and allow interaction in terms of program concepts. For example, one window might show the code of a Pascal procedure, with the program declarations displayed beside this in another window. Changing one part of the program (for example, modifying a procedure parameter list) results in related parts being immediately identified and presented for modification.

Multi-window program preparation systems offer such productivity advantages that they are likely to supplant the use of general-purpose text editors for the preparation of programs, specifications and software

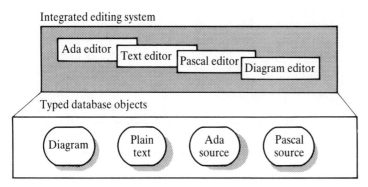

Figure 18.2
Integrated editing.

designs. However, the software engineer will still have to produce many documents which are not programs and there is a need for integrated, standardized editing systems which allow any type of object (programs, text, forms and diagrams) to be prepared and edited using a consistent and context-sensitive set of commands.

Such systems are impractical in development environments such as UNIX where the files are untyped. However, in an integrated development environment, stored entities are normally typed so that the editing system can examine what is being edited and present appropriate facilities to the user. Thus, as a user moves through a document containing text, programs, tables and diagrams, the editor identifies the working context and gives the user editing facilities geared to the type of object being edited. There is no need to prepare diagrams separately and paste them into documents or to move explicitly between program and text editors (Figure 18.2).

18.3   Language processing systems

The most important tool available to programmers is the language processing system used to convert their programs to machine code. The provision of a helpful compilation system reduces the costs of program development by making program errors easier to find and by producing program listings which include information about program structure as seen by the compiler.

Obviously, the error diagnostic facilities of a compiler are partially dependent on the language being compiled. A Pascal compiler, for example, can detect many more errors than a FORTRAN compiler. Not only are the rules that govern the validity of a program more strict for Pascal than for FORTRAN, but the Pascal programmer must also supply more information to the compiler about the entities to be manipulated by the program. This information allows the compiler to detect forbidden operations on these entities.

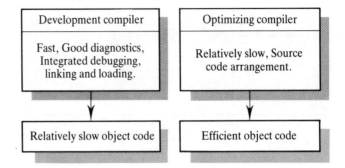

Figure 18.3
Development and
optimizing compilers.

As well as providing information to the programmer, a compilation system must also generate efficient machine code. This latter task involves a good deal of program analysis and can be very time consuming. This has the consequence that it is generally uneconomic to carry out this operation for anything apart from completely developed programs. A software engineering environment, therefore, might contain two compatible compilers for each language – a development compiler and an optimizing compiler (Figure 18.3).

Development compilers should be written to compile code as quickly as possible and to provide the maximum amount of diagnostic information to the programmer. Optimizing compilers, on the other hand, should be tailored to generate efficient machine code without considering compilation speed and diagnostic facilities. Programs are developed using the development system and, when complete, the optimizing system is used to produce the final version of the program for production use.

Within the confines of the language being processed, development compilers should provide as much information as possible about the program being compiled. For instance:

(1)	The compiler listing of the program should associate a line number with each program line.

(2)	When a program syntax or semantic error is discovered, the compiler should indicate where it found the error and what the error appears to be. It may also be appropriate to indicate the possible cause of the error. Error message design has already been discussed in Chapter 13.

(3)	The compiler should include directives which allow the programmer some control over the program listing generated by the compiler. These directives should allow the suppression of parts of the listing, control over the pagination of the listing, and the enhancement of program keywords by bold printing or underlining.

(4)   When a program in a block-structured language is compiled, the compiler should indicate the lexical level at the beginning and the end of each block. This allows misplaced 'begin'/'end' brackets to be easily identified.

(5)   The compiler should separate source text provided by the user from information provided by the compiler. This can be accomplished by delimiting the input source using special characters such as '|' and prefacing compiler messages by some string of punctuation characters such as '****'.

(6)   The compiler should identify where each procedure in a program starts and finishes. When a program listing is searched for a particular procedure, the location of that procedure is often not immediately obvious because the name of the procedure is not distinguished from the remainder of the source text. When compiling a procedure heading, the procedure name should be abstracted and, as well as listing the procedure heading normally, the procedure name should be reprinted so that it stands out from the rest of the program text.

These facilities were supported in the XPL compiler (McKeeman *et al.*, 1970), which was part of a compiler construction system. It is unfortunate that many of the display facilities provided by XPL have not been taken up by later compilers.

If an environment supports both development and optimizing compilers, there is no need for the optimizing compiler to provide comprehensive diagnostic facilities. Rather, given that code optimization is a time-consuming business, the compiler may allow the user to specify the degree of optimization to be carried out by the compiler or whether time or space considerations are most important. Ada has a specific construct called a pragma which, amongst other things, provides some facilities for the user to control compiler optimization.

18.3.1   Separate compilation

Separate compilation of program units means that units may be compiled separately and subsequently integrated to form a complete program. The integration process is carried out by another software tool known as a linker or link editor. Without the facility of separate compilation, a programming language should not be considered as a viable language for software engineering.

A large program may consist of several thousand lines of source code and it may take hours or even days to compile the complete program. If every program unit needed to be recompiled each time any one of the

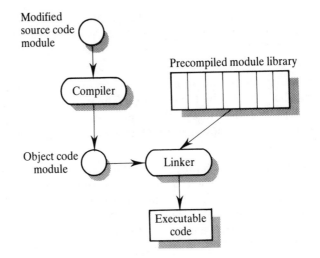

Figure 18.4
Separate compilation.

units was changed, this would impose significant overhead and increase the costs of program development, debugging and maintenance. If separate compilation is available, compiling the whole system is unnecessary. Only modified units need be recompiled and the system relinked (Figure 18.4).

A separate compilation facility is vital for the development of large systems and this is one of the principal reasons why FORTRAN, in spite of its shortcomings, has been so widely used in software engineering projects. The design of FORTRAN subroutines is such that independent compilation is straightforward and large libraries of precompiled FORTRAN routines can be developed. As well as this, routines specific to some application such as the mathematical routines are available at almost all large FORTRAN installations and this increases the real power of the language enormously.

In FORTRAN, the basic program unit which is separately compiled is the subroutine. Because FORTRAN is not a block-structured language, there is no concept of global names. All names used in a subroutine are either parameters, locally declared or explicitly stated in a COMMON block. A COMMON statement specifies those program variables which are defined outside the subroutine. If reference is made to other subroutines, the FORTRAN compiler assumes them to be externally declared and creates a list of external references to be resolved by the link editor. Because the user need not specify external references made in a subroutine, the compiler assumes that all external references whether to subroutines or COMMON variables are correct. It cannot check, for example, if a subroutine call has the correct number of parameters. Consequently programmer errors across compilation units cannot be detected.

The design of true block-structured languages like Pascal means that separate compilation must be implemented as a special feature. Restrictions must be imposed on language usage if separate compilation is provided. The scope rules of block-structured languages mean that all names accessed in a block need not be declared in that block – access to names declared in outer blocks are permitted. Consequently, according to the rules of the language, a procedure may refer to global variables and the compiler must obtain the specifications of these variables by compiling their declarations. Clearly, procedures that refer to global variables cannot be separately compiled.

Non-standard implementations of block-structured languages which offer a separate compilation facility generally forbid the use of global names in separately compiled procedures. In order that separately compiled procedures may make reference to other procedures, the language is usually extended by the provision of an external procedure specification facility.

An external procedure specification allows the programmer to introduce the name of an external procedure and to specify the types of its parameters. There may be a restriction on the parameter types permitted in an external procedure, or alternatively, the system may not guarantee compiler checking of external procedure references. Each external procedure which is referenced must be specified and after compilation a special-purpose linker is used to create the final program.

In Ada, the need for separate compilation of programs has been explicitly recognized by the language designers. An Ada program may be submitted to the compiler as a single unit or as a number of separate compilation units. A compilation unit may take several forms but, simplistically, it is either a subprogram or a package.

An integral part of the Ada compilation system is one or more libraries containing those compilation units which have already been processed. When a compilation unit requires the services of a library unit, this is indicated by a **with** statement. For example:

    with Queues, Stacks, Lists ;

This statement tells the Ada compiler that library units called Queues, Stacks and Lists are required. The specifications for these program units are held in the program library and are accessible to the compiler. Therefore, when a reference to one of these units is made, that reference may be checked against the specification. Compiler checking is not compromised by the separate compilation.

An additional separate compilation facility is also provided in Ada. This is the ability to define the body of a compilation unit as separate and to compile the unit specification (package header, etc.) before the unit body. This allows the parallel development of dependent units to take place. Once the specification of a unit is available in a library it may be used by any other unit. Obviously, execution is impossible until the unit body is available.

Separate compilation of the bodies of compilation units is indicated by means of the keyword **separate**:

```
package body Lists is separate;
procedure Count (X : in SOMEARRAY) is separate;
```

The separate compilation facilities of Ada make the separate development of Ada components a reasonably straightforward task. However, a disadvantage with Ada's approach to separate compilation is that the order of compilation of units is critical. A unit must be compiled before it is referenced. This causes problems when units in the library are being changed at the same time as some other units are relying on their services. For example, consider the Ada package structure in Example 18.1. If package A and package C are changed, all of the packages must be compiled in the order A then B then C irrespective of the order in which the changes were made. This is because of the checking which the compiler has to do using the package specifications in the program library. If the recompilations are not carried out in the correct order, this checking cannot be reliable.

Example 18.1
Ada package
dependencies.

```
package A
end A ;

with A ;
package B
...
end B ;

with A, B ;
package C
...
end C ;
```

To assist with this compilation ordering problem and to reduce clashes between unit versions, the management of Ada libraries is best automated using a configuration management system although, at the time of writing, few Ada compilers are properly integrated with configuration management tools.

18.3.2 Compiler support tools

The compilation process involves an analysis of the support text and, given this analysis, it is possible to provide additional information for the programmer and to lay out the program code, automatically, in a standard way. Commonly, these facilities are embedded in a compilation system (Figure 18.5). Other analysis tools, called static program analysers, are intended to detect anomalies in the source code. These tools are discussed in Chapter 22.

A simple example of a compiler support tool is a program cross-referencer. Such a tool provides a collated listing of the names used in the program, the types of the named objects, the line in the program where each name is declared, and the line numbers where a reference is made to that object. More sophisticated cross-referencers can also provide, for each procedure in the program, a list of the procedure parameters and their types, the procedure local variables and the global variables referenced in the procedure.

This latter facility is particularly useful to the programmer who must modify the value of some global variable. By examining the cross-reference listing, either manually or with an automatic tool, those procedures which reference that variable can be identified. They can be checked to ensure that global variable modification will not adversely affect their actions.

In addition to cross-reference systems, other source code analysis tools include layout programs (prettyprinters) which set out programs in some standard way. Prettyprinters are tools which incorporate standard layout conventions such as those discussed in Chapter 15, and it is sometimes suggested that the availability of such tools makes disciplined layout on the part of the programmer redundant. Furthermore, if all listings are produced using a prettyprinter, the maintenance programmer will not be presented with the problem of getting used to different layout conventions.

As an example of prettyprinter output, the Pascal program which was deliberately laid out badly in Chapter 15 is shown in Example 18.2. This may

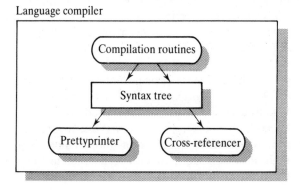

Figure 18.5
Embedded compiler tools.

Example 18.2
Prettyprinter output.

```
procedure CountElementOccurrences (var inarray : intarray;
                                   arraysize : integer);
{Given a sorted array of integers, this procedure prints each}
{distinct integer and the number of occurrences of that integer}
var
  i, count : integer;
begin
  count := 1;
  for i := 1 to arraysize do
    if inarray[i] = inarray[i + 1] then
      count := count + 1
    else
    begin
      write(inarray[i], count);
      count := 1;
    end;
  write(inarray[arraysize], count);
end;
```

be compared with the manually laid out version of the same procedure. In fact, the system used here is combined with an editor so that programs are neatly laid out as they are typed in. Notice that this system avoids the common Pascal error of leaving out a closing comment bracket by inserting comment symbols at the beginning and end of each comment line.

The problem with most prettyprinting systems is that they incorporate a set of conventions which have been invented by the tool designer and which are rarely explicitly specified. This means that, if an organization has existing standards, it is not possible to tailor prettyprinters to these standards. This may preclude the use of a prettyprinter and the programmers may revert to manual code layout.

All tools for static program analysis are language-oriented and must include a language syntax analyser. This has led to suggestions that the process of analysis normally carried out by the compiler should be factored out. Program analysis would be distinct from compiling and the analyser output would be processable by translation tools, editors, analysis tools, etc. (Figure 18.6).

Figure 18.6 shows how a lexical analysis and parsing package can create a symbol table and syntax tree which encapsulate the information in the program source code. These can be used by a code generator to produce object code, by a prettyprinter to list the program neatly, and by a cross-referencer to generate information about name usage. Of course, other tools might also be integrated with such a system, such as a language directed editor.

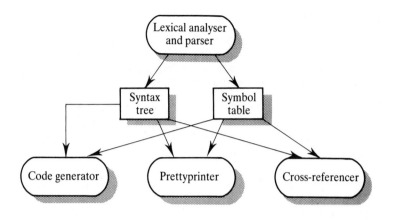

Figure 18.6
Language processing
toolkit.

KEY POINTS

- Computer-aided software engineering is the term used to refer to the support of the software engineer using software tools.

- CASE workbenches tend to be oriented towards the support of the earlier stages of the life-cycle and incorporate powerful diagramming and report generation facilities.

- The principal disadvantage of CASE workbenches is that they are not integrated with other software tools such as programming tools and configuration management systems.

- Multi-window editing systems offer an opportunity to improve the process of document editing.

- It is useful to provide both development and optimizing compilers. Development compilers should be designed for fast compilation and to provide extensive user information. Optimizing compilers should be developed to generate efficient code.

- Separate compilation is the process of compiling parts of a large system without all other parts being present. It is essential for large systems development because of the time required for the compilation process.

- Various tools can be integrated with a compilation system such as a prettyprinter and a cross-reference generator. These can either be tightly or loosely integrated with the system.

Further reading

Software Tools in Pascal.   This book covers the development of a set of tools, mostly oriented towards text processing. It illustrates tool facilities and shows how tools can be built by modifying other tools. (B.W. Kernighan and P.J. Plauger, 1981, Addison-Wesley.)

IEEE Software, **5** (2), March 1988. This is a special issue of this journal which is concerned with CASE tools. It does not simply discuss current systems but also includes articles on research projects which are investigating the facilities which will be available in the next generation of CASE products.

References

Chikofsky, E.J. and Rubenstein, B.L. (1988), 'CASE: reliability engineering for information systems', *IEEE Software*, **5** (2), 11–17.

Martin, C.F. (1988), 'Second-generation CASE tools: a challenge to vendors', *IEEE Software*, **5** (2), 46–9.

McKeeman, W.M., Horning, J.J. and Wortman, D. (1970), *A Compiler Generator*. Englewood Cliffs, NJ: Prentice-Hall.

Shneiderman, B., Shafer, P., Simon, R. and Weldon, L. (1986), 'Display strategies for program browsing: concepts and experiment', *IEEE Software*, **3** (3), 7–15.

Teitelbaum, T. and Reps, T. (1981), 'The Cornell Program Synthesizer: a syntax-directed programming environment', *Comm. ACM*, **24** (9), 563–73.

EXERCISES

18.1   Outline the key features that CASE workbenches should include. Discuss the disadvantages of the present generation of such systems.

18.2   If you have access to a CASE workbench or similar system, rate your system against the features and disadvantages you have identified in Exercise 18.1. Does your system have any other advantages or disadvantages not covered here?

18.3   If you have access to a UNIX system, suggest how the *vi* editor could take advantage of a multi-window editing capability. If you use some other editor, suggest how it could be used with multiple windows.

18.4 Consider the error diagnostic facilities provided with a compiler that you use. Suggest how these might be improved.

18.5 Discuss the advantages and disadvantages of separate compilation. If you are familiar with C, describe how independent compilation is handled in that language. Why is it impossible to provide separate compilation with some programming languages?

18.6 Apart from the compiler support tools identified here, suggest other tools that require knowledge of language syntax to be effective.

Chapter 19

Software Engineering Environments

Objectives

The objective of this chapter is to introduce the concept of a software engineering environment and to describe a typical structure for an environment. It can be represented as a layered model, and layers such as the database layer, the object management system, the tools and the user interface layer are described. Ada support environments are briefly discussed and the difficulties and problems of introducing a software engineering environment are covered. Finally, the limitations of existing environments and facilities which may be available in the next generation of software engineering environments are described.

Contents

The term *environment* is used to encompass all of the automated facilities that the software engineer has available to assist with the task of software development. Thus it may include tools as described in Chapter 18, documentation support, electronic mail and so on. There are a number of different classes of environment such as language-oriented environments intended to support programming in one particular programming language, educational environments which are intended to help beginners learn to program, and software engineering environments to support the development of large software systems. Surveys by Howden (1982) and, more recently, by Dart *et al.* (1987) describe these in broad terms.

Software development and maintenance are specialized activities and the most effective way to support these activities is to devote a separate system to them. In some cases, the application software under development may be for a machine with no software development facilities; in other cases, the machine may be application-oriented (a vector processor, say) and not well suited to supporting software development environments.

Thus, software development environments usually run on a host computer system (or network) and the software is developed for a separate target computer (Figure 19.1).

The environments which are of most interest to us here are software engineering environments such as ENCOMPASS (Terwilliger and Campbell, 1986) and ISTAR (Dowson, 1987). We will not consider programming environments such as the UNIX Programmers' Workbench (Ivie, 1977; Dolotta *et al.*, 1978). Nor will we discuss single language, integrated development environments such as those environments developed for the support of LISP (Teitleman and Masinter, 1984) or Smalltalk (Goldberg, 1984) programming. A simple classification of environments is shown in Figure 19.2.

Although programming environments often include very powerful tools and, for single-language environments (LISP and Smalltalk) may be tightly integrated with an excellent user interface, they are designed to support programming rather than software engineering. They do not include support facilities for all software process activities nor, crucially, do

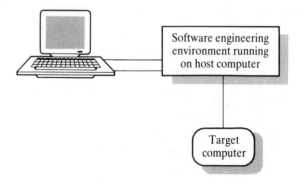

Figure 19.1
Host–target working.

Environment type	Example	Applicability
Programming, language independent	UNIX/PWB	Small to medium size systems development. Can be used for larger systems but poor integration facilities.
Programming, language-specific	Smalltalk	Exploratory programming and prototyping. Excellent user interface and tight integration.
Software engineering	ISTAR	Large, long-lifetime systems development and maintenance.

Figure 19.2
Environment classification.

they include an integrated configuration management system. Similarly, CASE workbenches, in spite of the claims of some vendors, are not software engineering environments.

Software engineering environments are designed to support all stages of the software process from initial feasibility studies to operation and maintenance. Because of this wide-ranging support such environments are sometimes called *integrated project support environments* (IPSEs). Of course, programming environments and IPSEs will usually offer some of the same software tools as it is increasingly common for IPSEs to be built on top of the UNIX operating system. The terms 'software engineering environment' and 'integrated project support environment' are used synonymously here.

UNIX is a file-oriented programming environment where the user may interconnect different tools either explicitly via shared files or by using UNIX pipes. This file-oriented approach has the disadvantage that the user must be aware of the specific I/O conventions of cooperating tools and, if these do not happen to match, it is not easy to use these tools in combination.

To allow tool inter-operability, current thinking now suggests that environments should be built around a database management system. All tools should output information to and collect information from this database which thus provides a standard tool interface. Furthermore, the use of a database system also opens up the possibility of building powerful information retrieval tools which can collate and present component information generated at different stages in the life-cycle. Integrated tools to support all stages of the software process may be provided.

An integrated project support environment is intended to support all of the activities in the software process from initial feasibility studies through to software maintenance and evolution. At the time of writing, there are few IPSEs in use and many IPSEs under construction in North America, Europe and Japan. It is clear that, by 1990, a great many of these current development projects will be in operation. To be realistic, however, current tool technology is such that some activities will not be supported in the first generation of IPSEs. We are not yet able to understand all of the underlying process fragments and hence cannot provide tool support for some activities.

The advantages of using a software engineering environment are:

(1) All available software tools are interfaced to a database management system so that the output of any one tool can potentially be an input to any other tool. It is normally the case that tool interactions are predictable but there are many cases of serendipitous tool combinations and the IPSE database allows these combinations to occur when required. Recall that one of the problems with CASE workbenches is the problem of exchanging information with other tools.

(2) Project management has direct access to project information and management tools can use actual data collected during the course of a project.

(3) All of the documents produced in the course of a project from feasibility studies to fault reports can, if necessary, be put under configuration control and managed by the configuration management tools which are an integral part of the environment. Furthermore, the database facilities are rich enough to allow relationships between documents to be recorded so that designs (say) can be linked to their associated code and changes to each automatically tracked. This is probably the single most important reason for adopting a software engineering environment.

(4) If the environment is properly integrated, all of the support tools will present the user with a consistent interface so that the task of learning to use new tools is reduced.

(5) The use of a database allows fine-grain (small) objects to be recorded, named and subjected to configuration control. This means that the structure of the storage system can reflect the structure of the software system rather than an artificial file organization being imposed on the program.

(6) It becomes possible to build more powerful software tools because these tools can make use of the relationships recorded in the database. Standard database management systems will be ported to new hardware as it becomes available so that the IPSE can also migrate as new machines are developed.

A typical structure for software engineering environments is shown in Figure 19.3. The structure is like an onion where there are a number of layers of functionality provided by different levels in the system. Although it can be argued (Blair *et al.*, 1986) that IPSEs should be built in conjunction with a special-purpose operating system tailored to support the environment, the need for portability has meant that the innermost

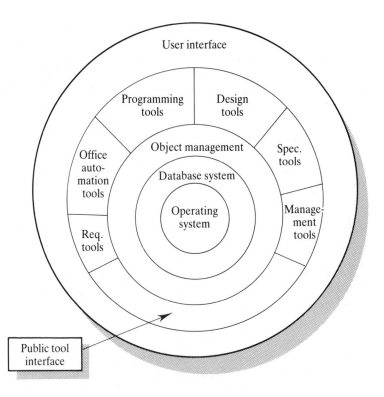

Figure 19.3
The structure of an IPSE.

kernel in the 'IPSE onion' is a standard operating system. The majority of IPSE projects have chosen to build the IPSE on top of the UNIX operating system. The reasons for this are partly to make use of the software tools provided by UNIX. More importantly, it is used because UNIX is implemented on a wide range of computers. It is an emerging operating system standard. This means that, in principle at least, the costs of rehosting an IPSE on another UNIX machine should be significantly less than initial implementation costs.

Some IPSEs (Higgs and Stevens, 1986) are built directly on top of the UNIX system and make use of the UNIX file system for data storage. However, as discussed earlier, the majority of IPSE projects make use of a database management system to store project data so the next 'onion layer' is generally a database layer which allows a much richer set of object relationships to be recorded. A variety of different database management systems, both proprietary and special-purpose, have been used for IPSE support.

The third 'onion layer' is the layer which distinguishes an IPSE from a software toolkit or CASE workbench. This is the object management layer which is responsible for controlling and managing all of the entities (conventionally termed objects although these are different from the objects of object-oriented programming) produced during software development. Broadly, the object management layer allows objects to be named, to exist in a number of different versions and it provides facilities for relationships, such as *part-of*, to be recorded between objects.

The next layer out is the tool layer and the tools supported by an IPSE normally fall into three categories:

(1)   *Integrated tools*   Tools which have been built or modified by the IPSE developers so that they can make intimate use of the facilities provided by the object management system.

(2)   *Imported tools*   These are tools which are less tightly integrated with the object management system and which communicate with the IPSE via the PTI or public tools interface. Such tools may communicate using system objects but will generally not be able to make use of inbuilt information about objects in the same way as integrated tools.

(3)   *Foreign tools*   These are tools which do not integrate with the object-management system but which interface directly to the underlying operating system. In order for IPSEs to be viable, they must support an upgrade path from existing toolkit machines so that users can continue to use familiar file-based tools when an IPSE is introduced. Thus most IPSEs support file-based tools and, in particular, support the tools provided with UNIX.

The final layer is the user interface layer. If an IPSE is to be an integrated system, it is not acceptable for that integration to be simply concerned with tool inter-operability. It is equally important that the tools provided by the IPSE should be integrated at the user interface level so that users are not faced with the daunting cognitive task of learning lots of different tool interfaces. Although it is clearly impossible for foreign tools to be integrated at this level, integrated and imported tools should offer some common interface to their users.

19.1   The operating system layer

The operating system layer is the most fundamental IPSE layer and, as discussed above, UNIX or one of its variants has become the most common base for IPSE development. It is likely that this situation will persist well into the 1990s so, in spite of the disadvantages of basing a system on UNIX, there is little point in wishing otherwise. The undoubted advantages of UNIX are its availability on a wide range of machines, its standardization and the vast amount of existing software available which runs under UNIX.

From a cost-effectiveness point of view these make UNIX the obvious choice as an IPSE host but the system suffers from a number of technical disadvantages:

(1)   The process structure of UNIX is hierarchical (processes spawn children) so that it is difficult to implement a system as a collection of loosely interacting processes.

(2)   UNIX is essentially a single processor system and its architecture is not well suited to multiple-processor hosts. Such machines are becoming increasingly viable as hardware costs fall.

(3)   The security and access controls on the UNIX filestore (on which any database must ultimately be implemented) are less than adequate. This is a particular problem for IPSE developers as much of the market for IPSEs is in defence software development which requires stringent security controls.

(4)   UNIX is essentially a character-oriented system which has been built on the assumption that user interaction is via a character terminal. The result of this is that it is awkward to make use of many of the graphics facilities offered by modern bit-mapped workstations.

None of these problems are insuperable. Different variants of UNIX have been built which incorporate solutions to one or two of them although, as far as I am aware, there is no single system which has solved them all. These variants are non-standard and, if one of them is chosen for an IPSE host, some of the portability advantages of using UNIX are lost. Although a definitive UNIX standard has not yet been established, the indications are that the standard which is emerging will suffer from the deficiencies set out above.

The fundamental problem caused by these operating system deficiencies is that it imposes a centralized IPSE architecture where a single database system runs on top of the operating system. Indeed, the above model is largely the result of choosing a system like UNIX as a base for the IPSE. Distribution of processing and data is always awkward and sometimes impossible and this limits the functionality and performance of IPSEs which may be built.

19.2 The database layer

The database built into an IPSE provides all of the data storage facilities for project information and allows relationships between project entities to be specified and maintained. Although many types of database have been used in research projects, environment products usually seem to be based on either a proprietary relational database (Earl *et al.*, 1986) or use a database, such as PCTE (Campbell, 1986) or CAIS (1985) which is specifically intended to support a software engineering environment.

It is not clear whether it is best to use a proprietary relational database product or a specially designed environment support system. Theoretically, the database model used in most environment databases is subsumed by the relational model. The argument for using environment-specific databases is that they are tuned to support likely operations and thus provide superior performance. Furthermore, they may also provide direct support for some object management facilities as discussed in the following section.

PCTE and CAIS are systems which have been developed to support software engineering environments. CAIS is a US development which stemmed directly from work on Ada support environments. It is explicitly intended to be the Kernel-APSE as discussed later in this chapter. However, it is broader in concept than this and could act as a general support facility. PCTE is a corresponding European development which is emerging as a European standard. It is UNIX-oriented rather than Ada-oriented.

Both PCTE and CAIS have particular advantages and disadvantages which are not covered here. Both are in need of further development and it appears that in future these systems are likely to converge so that a single standard environment support database and support facility will be defined.

From the point of view of the object management system, the most important characteristic of the project database is its granularity (Figure 19.4). The granularity is the minimum size of entity which may be efficiently stored and manipulated in the database. Coarse-grain databases tend to have higher performance but the minimum entity size which may be stored could be something like an entire Ada package or a complete design document. Fine-grain databases allow much smaller entities (such as a single declaration) to be stored but overall performance is generally poorer.

The current generation of software engineering environments do not make use of object-oriented databases (Andrews and Harris, 1987). However, there are obvious advantages in using such systems and it is likely that next-generation environment products will be based on an object-base rather than a database. It is not clear, at this stage, how this will influence the development of standards such as CAIS and PCTE.

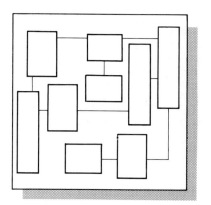

Coarse-grain database

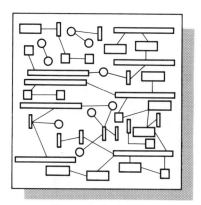

Fine-grain database

Figure 19.4
Fine-grain and coarse-grain databases.

19.3   The object management system

The object management system (OMS) is that part of the environment which provides control over the name space and which implements configuration control on environment objects. The term 'object' here does not refer to objects as entities with state and defined operations. Rather, the entities managed by an OMS are static entities which have a number of attributes such as a type, a creator, a representation language, etc.

Given the existence of an object management system, the user may simply refer to environment objects using some local name and the OMS handles all of the problems of mapping that name to a database identifier. The user should not need to have any knowledge of how the underlying database is structured and, in general, the name space model provided by the OMS is simpler than the underlying database schema.

A more important function of the OMS, perhaps, is to provide configuration management facilities on all environment entities. In the context of an IPSE, configuration management is not an option. It is imposed on all entities by the OMS.

It is the object management system's responsibility to maintain and name the different versions of system entities as they are created. It is good practice to support the notion of immutable (unchangeable and undeletable) entities so that, when an object is changed, it is never overwritten but a new version of that object is created. Clearly this may lead to many thousands of entities being created and the underlying database must be able to support entities which are held on some kind of archival medium such as optical disk or magnetic tape.

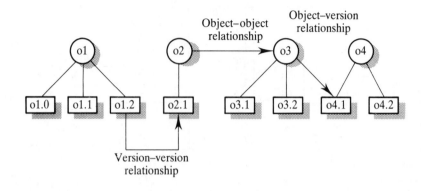

Figure 19.5
OMS relationships.

Given that objects can exist in a number of different versions, the OMS must be able to maintain three different classes of relationship (Figure 19.5). These are:

(1)   *Object–object relationships* All versions of one object have the same relationship with all versions of another object. An example of such a relationship is the relationship between design descriptions and associated program components. Given that they are updated in step, it is sufficient to maintain the relationship between the objects and to compute which versions of each object correspond.

(2)   *Object–version relationships* All versions of an object have a relationship with a single version of another object. An example of such a relationship is where an object represents a component intended for use on a specific operating system. The relationship may be between that object and a version of a library component for that operating system. Another example of such a relationship is where a component makes use of another component but always wishes to use the most up-to-date version of that component. By utilizing sensible defaults, the user of the component need not be informed when new versions of the 'used' component are produced.

(3)   *Version–version relationships* A version of an object has a relationship with a version of another object. An example of such a relationship is where a component uses another specific component. Given that the combined component works in a predictable way, it is important to ensure that changes to either component do not affect the particular workings of an instantiation.

In some cases, the user interacts directly with the OMS, particularly when browsing through the system information space. However, it is more common to interact via some specific tools such as an editor. Tools which are integrated with an IPSE must make use of recognizable OMS entities rather than files.

This requirement poses problems for IPSE designers as it is clearly desirable to be able to interface tools to the IPSE which were not developed at the same time as the IPSE. As discussed above, it is essential for the OMS to provide a public-tool interface (PTI) which defines the way in which other tools interface to the system. In general, the PTI is concerned with defining primitive configuration management facilities and access to the underlying database. Indeed, it is possible to consider both PCTE and CAIS as defining public tool interfaces.

As IPSEs are introduced, there will be a need to use these in conjunction with existing file-based tools and an OMS must provide a way of transferring environment objects to files so that they may be manipulated by such tools. Such a facility is usually called 'check-in/check-out' as objects are checked out from the control of the OMS, operated upon and then checked back in. It is comparable with import/export facilities in CASE workbenches.

This is less than ideal as the IPSE loses effective control of that object. However, until IPSEs are in widespread use and PTI standards are established, it is likely that file-based tools will be produced and used within an IPSE.

19.4   The environment toolset

The toolset provided with an environment should be tailored to the application domain which it is intended to support and the development paradigm used in that domain. Some facilities, such as object management, are required by all classes of system, but other tools are specific to particular application domains. It is impossible or at least impractical for all tools to be supported in an IPSE.

As an illustration of the tools which might populate an environment for developing real-time software on a target microprocessor system, the following tools might be made available:

(1)   *Host target communications software*   This linking the development computer to the computer on which the software is to execute (the target machine).

(2)   *Target machine simulators*   These are used when target-machine software is being developed so that it may be executed and tested on the host machine.

(3)   *Cross-compilers*   These are language processing systems which execute on the host machine and generate code for the target machine.

(4)   *Testing and debugging tools*   These might include test drivers, dynamic and static program analysers and test output analysis programs. Debugging on the host of programs executing on the target should be supported if possible.

(5)   *Graphical design editors*   These are comparable to those incorporated in CASE workbenches but are tailored to support a real-time method such as MASCOT (Simpson, 1986) or DARTS (Gomaa, 1984).

(6)   *Text processors*   These support documentation development on the same machine as program development. This simplifies the task of producing and updating documentation as the system is developed. Documentation tools are discussed in Chapter 29.

(7)   *Project management tools*   These software tools allow estimates of the time required for a project and the cost of that project to be made. Furthermore, they may provide facilities for generating management reports on the status of a project at any time.

As well as these tools, which are supportive of a particular application domain, the environment should provide a number of tools which would be standard in all instantiations. These include tools for configuration management, supporting change control, and version and variant management (see Chapter 28). Text editing tools and an electronic mail system to support communications between local and remote users should also be part of the standard toolset.

The term project support environment implies that a range of tools is available to support all of the activities which are involved in the software process. In practice, given our current understanding of that process, it is unlikely that such a range of tools will be available. Although programming tools such as compilers, debuggers and program analysers are well developed, tools to support activities such as requirements analysis, design transformation and program maintenance are in an early stage of development and may not be included in an IPSE.

19.5   The user interface

The user interface is the means by which users actually carry out productive work and it is now recognized that effective user interfaces have a significant effect on productivity. User interface design is discussed in general in Chapter 13 but the designer of an environment interface is faced with some particular problems:

(1)   The activities involved in software development are diverse. How can a user interface be produced which integrates the different facilities provided by these tools? For example, can a word processor and a program debugger share interface concepts? This concept sharing is essential if an integrated interface is to be produced and, as discussed in Chapter 13, it does appear to be possible to some extent.

(2)   IPSE users vary tremendously from project secretaries with no training in software engineering through project managers with little recent technical experience to software engineers who use the system for several hours every day. These users have different requirements. Secretaries may prefer non-technical terminology, managers may only use the IPSE occasionally and so prefer a helpful interface, and software engineers may prefer an interface which maximizes their speed of interaction. It is not clear if a single interface suitable for all of these classes of user can be built.

(3)   The entities represented in an environment may be very abstract and it may be difficult to represent these entities in such a way that they may be readily understood. For example, say one entity is composed of 20 others – how might this be displayed on a user's screen?

As well as these particular problems, software engineering environments are like all large information processing systems in that it is difficult to navigate around the system information space. It is the responsibility of the user interface to provide facilities to support such navigation.

One approach to assisting with the problems of user interface construction is to adopt a metaphor for interaction (the desktop metaphor is now well known) and to ensure that all tools in the IPSE conform to this metaphor. Such an approach as been adopted in the ECLIPSE IPSE (Sommerville *et al.*, 1989) where the metaphor is a control panel as is used in other complex hardware systems such as aircraft, power stations, etc.

The presumption is that interacting with a complex entity such as an IPSE is analogous to interacting with other complex systems and that if the user is provided with buttons, switches, signs, etc., this provides a consistent means of interacting with the system in general and with specific tools. An illustration of the control panel interface is shown in Figure 19.6. The details of this interface are discussed in Chapter 13.

19.6   Ada support environments

When the Ada programming language was under development, the need for an associated support environment was recognized and a number of requirements documents for such an environment were developed. These

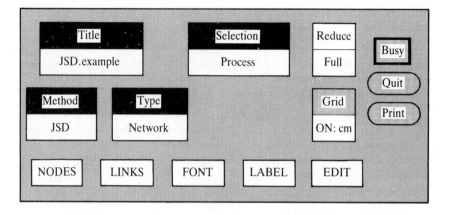

Figure 19.6
The control panel metaphor used in ECLIPSE.

culminated in the Stoneman proposals as discussed in Chapter 5. However, the requirements for an integrated generic support environment and an Ada support environment overlap to such an extent that it is likely that Ada environments will be built by configuring general-purpose environments with Ada-specific tools.

The Stoneman proposals for an Ada programming environment (APSE) envisage that the APSE should be portable and available on a variety of different machines. To achieve this degree of portability, three levels of program support are required – a kernel environment, KAPSE, a minimal environment, MAPSE and the full Ada support environment, APSE (Figure 19.7).

The innermost level of the APSE is the Kernel-APSE which provides the interface between Ada programs and the underlying operating system. Thus the KAPSE must include an Ada run-time support system, database primitives and the interface to peripheral devices such as terminals. In principle, the KAPSE should insulate the remainder of the APSE from the underlying machine. Therefore, to transfer the APSE from machine to machine should simply require a reimplementation of the KAPSE system.

The next level in the APSE is the so-called Minimal-APSE. This is built on top of the KAPSE and should provide facilities for the development of Ada programs. Obviously the MAPSE must include an Ada compiler, an editor and a loader, but other tools such as static and dynamic program analysers, command interpreters and configuration management systems are also to be provided at this level.

The top-level APSE was defined in a very general way and, even now, no examples of a complete APSE have been developed and put into use. As described in the requirements document, the APSE might provide tools to support all phases of the software life-cycle and tools to support particular development methodologies. As well as providing a

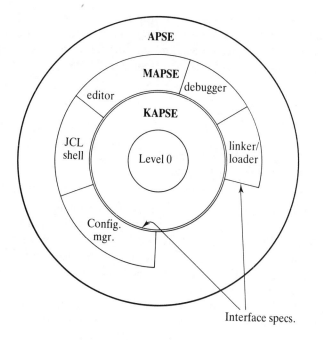

Figure 19.7
The organization of an APSE.

comprehensive toolkit to support the development of Ada programs, an APSE must also provide database facilities for tools to communicate and to allow relationships between objects to be recorded and maintained. The information in the database may be used to produce management reports detailing the current state of a project, project development cost, etc. A more detailed description of an APSE is provided in McDermid and Ripkin (1984).

It was never envisaged that there would be a single definitive APSE for all Ada support. Rather, it was intended that a number of different APSEs would evolve to support different classes of application domain. The Stoneman document was a very general document which unfortunately included some quite specific requirements. It has not been updated to reflect changes in technology, such as the widespread use of personal workstations, and the general feeling now is that an APSE is simply an IPSE which is configured to support Ada. In fact, careful reading of the Stoneman report reveals that the majority of the Ada support tools are generic rather than specific, so viewing an APSE as a specific IPSE does not conflict with the majority of the requirements in that document.

A valid criticism which may be made, however, is that the Stoneman report was not quickly followed up by a more detailed interface specification for the KAPSE. It has taken almost ten years for proposals in this area to emerge and this delay has undoubtedly hindered the production of

Ada support environments. A set of proposals called CAIS-1 (1985) have now been agreed but these are lacking in important facilities such as transactions, a schema mechanism and support for bit-mapped graphics. A development of these (CAIS-2) is presently underway.

19.7 Introducing a support environment

At the time of writing, software engineering environments have only been available for a short time. There is little reported experience on the organizational difficulties posed by such systems or of costs and cost savings. However, it is reasonable to postulate that moving software development to an IPSE will involve considerable disruption and costs and it is useful to try to anticipate what these might be. Some of these difficulties are clearly comparable with those experienced when changing operating or database systems so we can learn from these experiences when introducing a software engineering environment.

The first obvious difficulty which is likely to arise is user resistance. With few exceptions, humans are innately conservative and tend to resist new developments unless they have very obvious advantages. The present generation of IPSEs have obvious advantages for software management as they provide more control over the software process. The advantages for the individual software developer are less clear. Indeed, it can be argued that IPSEs are prescriptive and constrain the creativity of the individual engineer. Thus, they do not enhance his or her working environment but deskill the process of software engineering and hence reduce the overall satisfaction to be gained from software development.

A properly designed software engineering environment should provide tools which take over or assist with some of the tedious chores inherent in software development (such as redrawing design diagrams, finding associated code and documentation, etc.) thus leaving individual engineers more time for the creative and fulfilling parts of their job. They do not deskill the activities involved in the software process.

A further reason for user resistance is that some engineers may feel that new developments are inherently difficult and that they might be unable to understand some of the facilities provided by an IPSE. This is most likely to be a problem with staff who have learned by experience and have little formal training in software engineering. Furthermore, the pace of change in software development has been such that they may just have adapted to working with some new operating system and they may be reluctant to spend time learning another new system.

Some managers too may be resistant to introducing an environment into a known development process. The reason for this is that much of the activity of software management is fundamentally concerned with cost control. The cost advantages of introducing a software engineering environment are unquantifiable. Thus, they may argue that using an unknown support environment increases the risk associated with a project. Indeed, because of initial training costs, there are unlikely to be cost advantages for IPSE pioneers.

The other major problem of adopting an environment are the costs of converting existing development projects to work in that context. It may not be possible to justify the costs of the IPSE unless it is generally used, yet the costs and upheaval associated with converting to this development may be very great indeed. The reason for this is that the environment records and stores a great deal of project information which may be collected automatically but which, outside of the IPSE, may exist only on paper or in people's heads. This must be collected, encoded and input which is a very expensive process.

These difficulties mean that management must adopt a sensitive approach when introducing an IPSE. They must make realistic estimates of the start-up costs of moving to an automated environment. Attempting to introduce an environment without an understanding of the concerns of the software developer are liable to lead to an exodus of the workforce. The cost advantages of an IPSE ensue in the long-term rather than the short-term and this must be understood by all levels of company engineers and management.

It is important that an adequate budget is available for training and that the move to IPSE-based development is incremental. Rather than move all projects at one time, the environment should be introduced in conjunction with existing support systems. As new projects are started, they should make use of environmental support. As the cost advantages of environment usage become quantifiable, the costs of converting existing project work to an IPSE-based development may be assessed. A decision is necessary on whether this conversion should be made or whether parallel development support should continue until project completion.

A related problem to that of initially adopting a software engineering environment is the problem of moving development from one environment to another. It is clear that this will be necessary in many organizations for the following reasons:

(1)   The first available environments have limited functionality and will be superseded by improved systems relatively quickly.

(2)   Mistakes will be made in choosing an environment product and these may not become apparent until that product is put into use.

(3)   External software purchasers may make it a condition of contract that a particular environment is used for software development. This is most likely if an IPSE standard emerges and government agencies insist on the use of this standard as part of their terms of contract.

Clearly, the problems of moving from one environment to another are akin to those of moving to IPSE-based development, but the conversion costs may be even greater. Different object relationships may be supported and these may have to be derived from existing relationships. Users may have learned a rich set of facilities and may have to repeat this process for a new environment. From cost studies of moving from one database management system to another, it is reasonable to postulate that moving from one environment to another is a slow and expensive process which may last three or four years.

The inevitability of multiple-IPSE support implies that the use of agreed or *de facto* standards should be a major factor in choosing an environment as these may allow later conversion without major disruption. On the other hand, we know from experience that computing standards are rarely technically innovative and far superior functionality may be offered by non-standard systems.

19.8   Future developments

The approach adopted in this book is to discuss practical software engineering and to describe tools and techniques which are either in use or which will be introduced in the near future. This is not a book about research developments. We make an exception in this case because an overview of the state of the art in environment research may help the reader to understand the role of IPSEs in software support and the limitations of the environments which are now available.

Although there is little experience with IPSE-based development, it is already clear that the present generation of software engineering environments suffer from a number of deficiencies. This does not imply that the designers of these systems have been negligent. It simply means that we know some of the problems which we would like environments to solve but that the solution technology is not yet in such a state that it may be applied in IPSE products.

The major identifiable deficiencies in most present environments are the following:

(1)   *The object store is a passive rather than an active store*   This means
      that it is impossible to encode rules and actions in that store and to
      specify that actions are triggered when particular rules are checked.
      It is the responsibility of users to decide on how most exception
      conditions are handled and how to schedule the activities involved in
      the software process.

(2)   *Most environments are single-paradigm systems*   This means that
      they make use of an implicit view of software development such as a
      conventional life-cycle approach, exploratory programming, formal
      transformations or whatever and this imposes a structure on the
      environment and its tools. As discussed in Chapter 1, there is no
      'correct' paradigm and, increasingly, systems must be built which
      require different paradigms to be used for different parts of the
      system. To support this style of development requires an
      environment which supports multiple paradigms. This need has
      been explicitly recognized in the REFINE environment (Smith
      et al., 1985) which goes some way to providing a multi-paradigm
      approach.

(3)   *Only simple management tools which help with computations are
      supported*   Although an IPSE might include a PERT scheduler and
      a cost modelling system, we do not yet know how to build tools
      which assist with management activities such as allocating
      programmers to projects, deciding when and how to re-plan
      projects, etc.

There are a number of research projects currently underway (Kaiser *et al.*,
1988; Ambras and O'Day, 1988) which are investigating how the next
generation of environments might be built. In general, these projects are
making use of AI techniques and, as well as or instead of a database, the
environment is equipped with a less structured knowledge base in which
facts, rules and (sometimes) a process model are embedded.

KEY POINTS

- A software engineering environment or integrated project support environment (IPSE) is intended to support all software process activities. Programming environments like UNIX or Smalltalk are not software engineering environments.

- Current software engineering environments are based around a database of all project information. This allows tool inter-operability, configuration control of all project documents, and management access to project information.

- One view of an environment is a set of layers; an operating system layer, a database layer, an object management system layer, a tool layer and a common user interface.

- Object and configuration management is the principal distinguishing feature of a software engineering environment. All project documents may be placed under configuration control.

- The tool population of an environment depends on the type of development that the environment is intended to support. Given current technology, it is not possible to support all process activities.

- An Ada support environment can be created by populating a more general software engineering environment with the appropriate tools.

- Introducing a support environment is expensive. Its benefits are long-term rather than short-term. Some users are wary of environments because they believe that the support offered de-skills the activity of software engineering.

- The next generation of environments will be based around an active object base rather than a passive database.

Further reading

Software Engineering Environments. The proceedings of a conference on environments, which provides a picture of work in this area going on in the UK and in Europe. (I. Sommerville, 1986, Peter Peregrinus.)

'Software development environments'. This is a recent survey article which discusses the different kinds of software engineering environments. In fact, the journal in which it appears is a special issue on environments and other papers there are also valuable as background to this chapter. (S.A. Dart, R.J. Ellison, P.H. Feiler and A.N. Habermann, *IEEE Computer*, **20** (11), 1987.)

References

Ambras, J. and O'Day, V. (1988) 'MicroScope: a knowledge-based programming environment', *IEEE Software*, **5** (3), 50–8.

Andrews, T. and Harris, C. (1987), 'Combining language and database advances in an object-oriented development environment', *Proc. OOPSLA'87*, Orlando, Fla.: 430–40.

Blair, G.S., Lea, R., Mariani, J.A., Nicol, J.R. and Wylie, C. (1986), 'Total system design in IPSEs', in *Software Engineering Environments*, Sommerville, I. (ed.), Stevenage: Peter Peregrinus, 85–104.

CAIS (1985), *Common Apse Interface Set*, MIL_STD-CAIS, Washington: US Dept. of Defense.

Campbell, I. (1986), 'PCTE proposal for a public common tool interface', in *Software Engineering Environments*, Sommerville, I. (ed.), Stevenage: Peter Peregrinus, 57–72.

Dart, S.A., Ellison, R.J., Feiler, P.H. and Habermann, A.N. (1987), 'Software development environments', *IEEE Computer*, **20** (11), 18–28.

Dolotta, T.A., Haight, R.C. and Mashey, J.R. (1978), 'The Programmers Workbench', *Bell Systems Tech. J.*, **57** (6), 2177–200.

Dowson, M. (1987), 'Integrated project support with ISTAR', *IEEE Software*, **4** (6), 6–15.

Earl, A.N., Whittington, R.P., Hitchcock, P. and Hall, J.A. (1986), 'Specifying a semantic model for use in an integrated project support environment', in *Software Engineering Environments*, Sommerville, I. (ed.), Stevenage: Peter Peregrinus.

Goldberg, A. (1984), *Smalltalk-80 – The Interactive Programming Environment*, Reading, Mass.: Addison-Wesley.

Gomaa, H. (1984), 'A software design method for real-time systems', *Comm. ACM*, **29** (7), 938–49.

Higgs, M. and Stevens, P. (1986), 'Developing an environment manager for an IPSE', in *Software Engineering Environments*, Sommerville, I. (ed.), Stevenage: Peter Peregrinus, 39–56.

Howden, W.E. (1982), 'Contemporary software development environments', *Comm. ACM*, **25** (5), 318–29.

Ivie, E.L. (1977), 'The Programmers Workbench – a machine for software development', *Comm. ACM*, **20** (10), 746–53.

Kaiser, G.E., Feiler, P.H. and Popovich, S.S. (1988), 'Intelligent assistance for software development and maintenance', *IEEE Software*, **5** (3), 40–9.

McDermid, J. and Ripkin, K. (1984), *Life Cycle Support in the Ada Environment*, Cambridge: Cambridge University Press.

Simpson, H. (1986), 'The MASCOT method', *BCS/IEE Software Eng J.*, **1** (3), 103–20.

Smith, D.R., Kotik, G.B. and Westfold, S.J. (1985), 'Research on knowledge-based software environments at Kestrel Institute', *IEEE Trans. Software Eng.*, **SE-11** (11), 1278–95.

Sommerville, I., Welland, R.C., Potter, S.J. and Smart, J.D. (1989) 'The ECLIPSE user interface', *Software – Practice and Experience* (in press).

Teitleman, W. and Masinter, L. (1984), 'The Interlisp Programming Environment', *in Interactive Programming Environments*, Barstow, D.R., Shrobe, H.E. and Sandewall, E. (eds), New York: McGraw-Hill.

Terwilliger, R.B. and Campbell, R.H. (1986), 'ENCOMPASS: a SAGA-based Environment for the composition of programs and specifications', *Proc. 19th Hawaii Int. Conf. on System Sciences*.

EXERCISES

19.1 Describe why UNIX should not be considered as a software engineering environment.

19.2 Outline the structure of a software engineering environment and describe the role of the components in that structure.

19.3 Suggest tools which should be included in a software engineering environment to support the development of (a) software engineering environments and (b) transaction processing systems.

19.4 Explain why it is important that tools in an environment offer a consistent user interface.

19.5 What support tools might be included in an Ada support environment?

19.6 If you have access to the CAIS and PCTE documentation, compare and contrast these two approaches to providing environment support.

19.7 Explain why the initial costs of introducing an IPSE are high.

19.8 Study the literature and draw up an outline of the facilities which might be included in the next generation of project support environments.

Part 4

Software Validation

Contents

Chapter 20

Program Verification
and Validation

Objectives

The objective of this chapter is to introduce program
verification and validation and, in particular, to discuss the
processes of testing and debugging a program. Testing and
debugging are not the same thing. Testing is the process of
establishing the presence of faults. Debugging is concerned
with finding and removing faults. The testing process and
the stages of testing and the advantages and disadvantages
of top-down testing are discussed. Test planning and
scheduling is covered and hints on how to debug a
program are given.

Contents

The validation of a software system is a continuing process through each stage of the software process. Previous chapters have discussed validation of software requirements and design but it is only after implementation is complete that true product validation can begin. There is sometimes confusion over the distinction between verification and validation but the important difference is succinctly summarized by Boehm (1979):

- Validation: Are we building the right product?
- Verification: Are we building the product right?

Verification involves checking that the program conforms to its specification. Validation involves checking that the program as implemented meets the expectations of the user. Although requirements validation activities such as prototyping help in this respect, sometimes flaws and deficiencies in the requirements can only be discovered when the final system implementation is complete.

Until recently, the only post-implementation validation and verification technique employed was program testing. Even now, many organizations still rely completely on testing for system validation. Testing is a dynamic technique. It involves running the program, observing its inputs and outputs, and looking for unexpected behaviour. However, it is now clear that static techniques can also be used which complement testing and reduce the overall costs of the verification and validation process. The possible use of static and dynamic techniques is illustrated in Figure 20.1.

Static techniques include program inspections, analysis and formal verification, and it is sometimes suggested that they can completely replace dynamic techniques in the verification and validation process. This notion is flawed partly because static techniques can only check the correspondence between a program and its specification (verification) and because they cannot reveal non-functional program characteristics. A separate chapter (Chapter 22) is devoted to static verification techniques.

At the time of writing, static verification techniques require a good deal of development, and program testing is the predominant verification and validation technique. Program testing is that part of the software process which is normally carried out during implementation and also, in a different form, when implementation is complete. Testing involves exercising the program using data which is similar to the real data on which the program is designed to execute. The program outputs are observed, and the existence of program errors or inadequacies inferred from anomalies in these outputs.

It is important to understand that testing can never show that a program is correct. It is always possible that undetected errors exist even

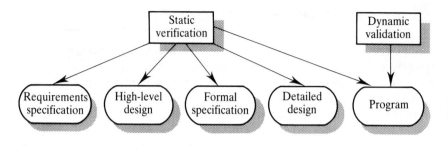

Figure 20.1
Static and dynamic
verification and validation.

after the most comprehensive testing. Program testing can only demonstrate the presence of errors in a program, it cannot demonstrate their absence. Following Myers (1979), therefore, a successful test can be considered to be one which establishes the presence of one or more errors in the software being tested.

This differs from the frequently used definition of a successful test which is a test displaying no output anomalies. This alternative definition is appealing in some ways (statements such as 'the system has passed all its tests' are seductive) but it can lead to complacency. Simply because the test suite for a program does not detect errors does not mean that the program does not contain errors. It means that the tests chosen have not exercised the system in such a way that errors are revealed. Large programs are rarely, if ever, bug-free.

Program testing is a destructive process. It is intended to cause a program to behave in a manner that was not intended by its designer or implementor. As it is a natural human trait for an individual to feel some affinity with objects that he or she has constructed, the programmer responsible for system implementation is not the best person to test a program. Psychologically, programmers do not want to 'destroy' their creations with the result that, consciously or subconsciously, program tests will be selected which fail. These tests will not demonstrate the presence of system errors.

On the other hand, detailed knowledge of the structure of a program or programming system can be extremely useful in identifying appropriate test cases and the system implementor plays an important part in this. The key to successful program testing is to establish a working environment where system implementors and outsiders involved in program testing can play a complementary role. These outside testers should not be part of the project team but should be part of the overall quality assurance function in an organization. Quality assurance is a management function and is discussed in Chapter 30.

20.1 The testing process

Except for small computer programs, it is unrealistic to attempt to test systems as a single unit. Large systems are built out of subsystems which are built out of modules which may themselves be built out of procedures. If an attempt is made to test the system as a single entity, it is unlikely that more than a small percentage of the system 'errors' will be identified. The testing process, like the programming process, must proceed in stages where each stage is a logical continuation of the previous stage. It is possible to identify five distinct stages in the testing process (Figure 20.2).

Unit testing is the basic level of testing where individual components (which may be functions or objects) are tested to ensure that they operate correctly. In a properly designed system, each component should have a precise specification, and test cases must be defined to check that the component meets its specification. Unit testing considers each component to be a stand-alone entity which does not require other system components to be present during the testing process.

A module is a collection of components which are interdependent. After each program unit has been tested, the interaction of these components when they are put together must be tested. A module encapsulates related components and it should be possible to test a module as a stand-alone entity, without the presence of other system modules.

Subsystem testing is the next step up in the testing process where modules are put together to form subsystems. Subsystems may be designed and implemented by different software engineers and experience has shown that the most common problems which arise in large software systems are interface mismatches. Thus, the subsystem test process should concentrate on the detection of interfacing errors by rigorously exercising these interfaces.

Integration is carried out when the subsystems are integrated to make up the entire system. At this stage, the testing process is concerned with finding errors which normally result from unanticipated interactions between subsystems and components. It is also concerned with validating that the overall system provides the functions specified in the requirements and that the dynamic characteristics of the system match those required by the system procurer.

As well as tests which exercise system functions and which demonstrate its performance, it may be appropriate to devise tests which place an unnatural load on a system. This is sometimes called stress testing. For example, say a system was designed to handle 100 transactions per second. Stress testing involves devising tests which increase the number of transactions until this limit is reached and beyond, until the system breaks down.

The rationale for stress testing is that it exercises the system to its limit and that it tests the systems facilities when it is overloaded. When

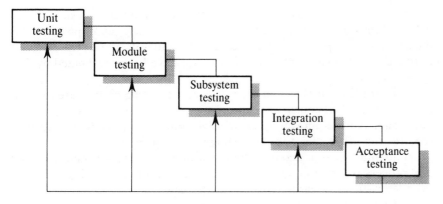

Figure 20.2
Stages of testing.

systems fail, it may be desirable for them to 'fail-soft' which means that they do not simply stop but degrade gracefully and preserve system information. Stress testing is a means of causing failure and checking that the system fails in an acceptable way.

Until this stage, all testing is carried out using data generated by the organization responsible for constructing the system. The testing process is principally concerned with detecting program faults and checking that the program conforms to its specification.

Acceptance testing is the process of testing the system with real data – the information which the system is intended to manipulate. As well as a verification process, it is also a validation process. Acceptance testing often demonstrates errors in the system requirements definition. The requirements may not reflect the actual facilities and performance required by the user, and testing may demonstrate that the system does not exhibit the anticipated performance and functionality.

This type of testing is sometimes called *alpha testing* where the system developer tests in the system in the presence of the system procurer, using real test data. For bespoke systems (systems developed specially for a single client), the alpha testing process continues until the system developer and the system procurer reach agreement that the delivered system is an acceptable representation of the system requirements.

Of course, this does not mean that the system is error-free or, even, necessarily meets all its requirements. It simply means that the delivered product is of reasonable and acceptable quality and that the procurer is willing to complete payment for the system. In some cases, the system will not be adequate but, rather than reject the system completely, the procurer may negotiate a reduced price with the system contractor.

Where it is intended that a system is to be distributed as a software product, a process of testing called *beta testing* is commonplace. The beta testing process involves delivering a system to a number of customers or potential customers who agree to use that system and to report problems to the system developers. This has the advantage that it exposes the product to real use and detects errors which may not have been anticipated by the system builders.

Figure 20.2 implies that the stages of the testing process are carried out in sequence. Of course this is simplistic. As errors are discovered at any one stage, they require program modifications to correct them and this requires the other stages in the testing process to be repeated. Errors in program units, say, may come to light at a later stage of the testing process. The process is therefore an iterative one with information being fed back from later stages to earlier parts of the process.

Correcting some program errors (or making any modifications) may result in new errors being introduced. It is not sufficient simply to re-test those components which have been modified. All components which interact with the modified component must also be tested. This is sometimes called *regression testing*.

20.2   Top-down and bottom-up testing

There are two different testing philosophies which have been used in testing a software system, namely top-down testing and bottom-up testing (Figure 20.3).

Top-down testing involves starting at the subsystem level with modules represented by stubs – objects which have the same interface as the module but which are very much simpler. After subsystem testing is complete, each module is tested in the same way – the functions are represented by stubs. Finally, the program components are replaced by the actual code and this is tested.

Bottom-up testing reverses this process. The components making up a module are tested individually. Then they are integrated to form a module and this is tested. After each module has been tested, the modules are integrated and, finally, the subsystem is tested.

Top-down testing is not an activity which should be carried out in isolation. Rather it is used in conjunction with top-down program development so that a module is tested as soon as it is coded. In principle, therefore, coding and testing are a single function with no clearly defined component or module testing phase.

If top-down testing is used, it is likely that unnoticed design errors will be detected at an early stage in the testing process. These errors are

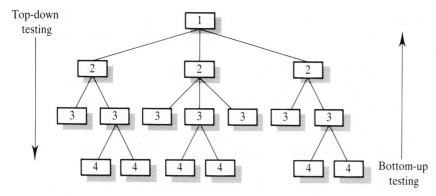

Top-down testing

Bottom-up testing

Figure 20.3
Top-down and bottom-up testing.

usually built into the top levels of the system. If they are detected early, a good deal of time can be saved. Early error detection before much of the system has been implemented means that extensive redesign and re-implementation may be avoided.

As well as this, top-down testing has the advantage that a working, albeit limited, system is available at an early stage in the development process. Not only does this provide an important psychological boost to those involved in the system development, it also demonstrates the feasibility of the system to management. It means that validation, as distinct from verification, can begin early in the testing process rather than after much testing has been completed.

Unfortunately, strict top-down testing can be difficult because of the requirement that program stubs, simulating lower levels of the system, must be produced. The mechanism for implementing these program stubs involves either producing a very simplified version of the component, returning some random value of the correct type, or interacting with the tester who inputs an appropriate value or simulates the action of the component.

If the component is a complex one, it may be impractical to produce a program stub which simulates it accurately. For example, consider a function which relies on the conversion of an array of objects into a linked list. The result of that function involves internal program objects, the pointers linking elements in the list.

It is unrealistic to generate some random list and return that object. The list components must correspond to the array elements. It is equally unrealistic for the programmer to input the created list as he or she probably has no knowledge of the internal representation of pointers. Therefore, the routine to perform the conversion from array to list must exist before top-down testing is possible.

A further disadvantage of top-down testing is that test output may be difficult to observe. In many systems, the higher levels of that system do not generate output but, in order to test these levels, they must be forced to do so. The tester must create an artificial situation, in order to generate test results.

Bottom-up testing, on the other hand, involves testing the modules at the lower levels in the hierarchy, and then working up the hierarchy of modules until the final module is tested. The advantages of top-down testing are the disadvantages of bottom-up testing and vice versa.

If bottom-up testing is used, drivers must be constructed for the lower level modules which present these modules with appropriate inputs. Using a bottom-up approach to testing usually means that it is easier to create test cases and observe test input. Bottom-up testing has the disadvantage that no demonstrable program is available until the very last module has been tested. Furthermore, if design errors exist in high-level modules these are not detected until a late stage in the system test. Correction of these errors might involve the rewriting and consequent re-testing of lower-level modules in the system.

In view of the advantages and disadvantages of each method of testing, there is no 'best' method of testing a program. The techniques adopted must depend on the programming organization, the application being programmed and the individual programmers working on a project. In practice, some combination of top-down and bottom-up testing is usually used to test a system. It is normal to test at least some of the lower-level components illustrated in Figure 20.3 in parallel with the components nearer the top of the tree.

One approach to testing is to test each system module individually. Once satisfied that modules are fully tested, all modules are put together to make up the final system. That system is then tested as an integrated whole. This approach usually leads to a non-working system with no clear indicators of exactly which aspects of the system are causing the problems. A much better approach, which should be adopted irrespective of whether a top-down or bottom-up strategy is being used, is to introduce modules incrementally, one at a time (Figure 20.4).

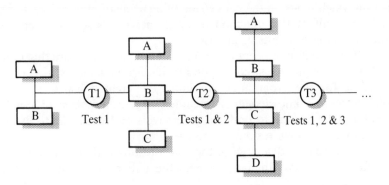

Figure 20.4
Incremental testing.

The system should start off as a single module and this should be tested using appropriate test cases. Once satisfied with the testing of this module a second module can be introduced and further testing carried out. The process continues until all modules have eventually been integrated into a complete system. If a module is introduced at some stage in this process and tests, which previously did not detect faults, now detect errors it is likely that these faults are due to the introduction of the new module. The source of the error is thus localized, simplifying the task of locating and correcting the error.

20.3   Test planning and scheduling

System testing is an expensive process. For large systems, particularly real-time systems with complex timing constraints, system testing may consume about half of the overall development costs. Thus, to get the most out of testing and to minimize testing costs, careful planning is essential.

Test planning is concerned with setting out standards for the testing process rather than describing product tests. The major components of a test plan are:

- A description of the major phases of the testing process. These might be as described earlier in this chapter.

- A description of how traceability of testing to requirements is to be demonstrated. Users are most interested in the system meeting its requirements and testing should be planned so that all requirements are individually tested.

- An overall testing schedule and resource allocation for this schedule. This, obviously, is linked to the more general project development schedule.

- A description of the relationship between the test plan and other project plans.

- A description of the way in which tests are to be recorded. It is not enough simply to run tests. It must be possible to audit the testing process to check that it been carried out correctly.

The test plan should include significant amounts of contingency so that slippages in design and implementation can be accommodated and staff allocated to testing can be usefully deployed in other activities.

Ideally, all parts of a system should be formally specified and this specification should be used to derive a complete set of test cases for the component being tested. Hayes (1986) illustrates this process using a specification for a symbol table package.

These tests should be developed at the same time as the design and implementation by an engineer who is not involved in the design. The tests are thus available for immediate application when the implementation is complete.

In practice, such an ideal situation rarely occurs. The costs of adopting this approach are high, particularly as specifications usually change as a design is developed. Thus, the test data must also be changed. Furthermore, the specification process is only rarely developed to a detailed level and program units are sometimes only identified during the system design. Thus, project management must arrive at some compromise approach which makes best use of existing resources yet still provides adequate test coverage.

It is normal practice for unit testing and module testing to be carried out by the programmer or the programming team without a formal test specification. The programmer makes up his or her own test data and incrementally tests the code as it is developed. This is an economically sensible approach as the programmer knows the component best and is most able to generate test data.

However, it should be subject to some monitoring procedure to ensure that the components have been properly tested. This means that some of the components tested by the developer should be selected by an independent tester and tested using a different set of test cases. Given that the independent testing and the programmer testing come to the same conclusions, it may be assumed that the programmer has adequately tested his or her components.

Later stages of testing involve integrating work from a number of programmers and must be planned in advance. They are usually undertaken by an independent team of testers. The testing process should be precisely specified and set out in the project plan. It is desirable to start test planning at a relatively early stage in the software development process. Module and subsystem testing should be planned as the design of the subsystem is formulated. System test and acceptance test specifications should be prepared either at the system design stage or while system implementation is in progress.

As part of an overall project plan, a test plan should be created which sets out the resources required for testing, the costs of testing and the scheduling of the tests. Such a plan will undergo very regular revision as testing is an activity which is dependent on implementation being complete. If only a single part of a system is incomplete, the system testing process cannot begin.

20.4   Program debugging

It is sometimes thought that program testing and debugging are one and the same thing. Although closely related, they are distinct processes. Testing is the process of establishing the existence of program errors. Debugging is the process of locating where these errors occurred in the program and correcting the code which is incorrect. Debugging is dependent on testing; it relies on test output to show the presence of errors in a program.

There are various debugging stages (Figure 20.5). Those parts of the program code which are incorrect must be located and the program must be modified so that it meets its requirements. After modification, program testing must be repeated to ensure that the change has been carried out correctly. The first stage, error location, is the most difficult stage and debugging tools are intended to assist this activity.

Debugging can simply be viewed as a problem-solving process. The debugger must generate hypotheses about the observable behaviour of the program then test these hypotheses in the hope of finding the error in the system. Testing the hypotheses may involve manually tracing the program code or may require new test cases to be generated which help to localize the problem.

It is impossible to present a set of instructions about how to go about debugging a program. Although the cognitive processes involved are by no means clear, it seems that the skilled debugger looks for patterns in the test output where the error is exhibited and uses knowledge of the error, the pattern and the programming process to locate the error. Process knowledge is important. The debugger knows of common errors (such as failing to increment a counter) and matches these common errors against the observed patterns.

After the error in the program has been discovered, it must be corrected. If the error is a simple coding error, it is usually fairly easy to correct that error without affecting other parts of the program. On the other hand, if the error is a design error or involves a misunderstanding of the program requirements, correcting this may involve much work.

It may be necessary to redesign parts of the program and consequently re-test the whole system. Error correction is expensive so design reviews and static validation before coding commences are cost-effective error avoidance techniques. Apart from avoiding such errors, all the programmer can do to minimize their effect is to program in such a way

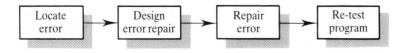

Figure 20.5
Debugging stages.

that the program is made up of independent functional units. If a design error is discovered, it may affect only a single unit and only that unit need be redesigned and recoded.

If, on the other hand, program components are logically dependent and make use of many shared variables, this is a recipe for disaster if a major redesign is required. In such programs, it is difficult to determine the effects on the overall system caused by redesigning one module. An apparently straightforward modification can result in errors in functionally unrelated modules. This process may snowball as these errors are corrected, causing other errors whose correction then causes more errors and so on.

The most important aid for the debugger is the listing of the test results which display the error to be corrected. If the programmer is familiar with the code, the nature and location of the error can often be determined by examination of these results. Code inspection can then determine which statement or statements are incorrect.

Many programmers approach code inspection thinking that they know what the program does and, subconsciously, they read the code as if its operation is what the programmer thinks it is. The most useful debugging aid is the ability to approach code in an open-minded, sceptical manner and to perform a 'thought execution' of that code.

20.4.1 Error location

In some circumstances, code inspection alone is inadequate. Those circumstances arise where programming errors do not cause immediate failure or obvious corruption to test output. Rather, these errors may cause incorrect, although not necessarily invalid, output to be generated at some later stage of the program's execution. A symptom of the problem rather than the problem itself may be all that is apparent from the test output. The execution of the program must be traced to determine where the corruption causing the error is taking place.

A useful technique is to include program statements which print important data values at appropriate places in the program. Examination of the output involves comparing subsequent values of the same object and, when an anomaly is detected, the coding error must lie between the output statement that printed the correct values and the output statement that printed the incorrect values.

The process of adding output statements can be continued, if necessary, until individual statements are bracketed. At this stage, the statement where the error manifests itself can be determined. This need not necessarily mean that this statement is incorrect. The error may be a design error or may involve the failure of some program component, previously thought to be correct.

This technique is certain to detect the program statement where the error is manifested, although this need not be the statement in error, irrespective of how 'correct' the program appears to be. It is, however, a laborious and time-consuming process to include output statements and recompile the program after it has been written. It is much better to anticipate that there will be program errors and include some of these output statements when the program is first constructed.

Clearly, when the program is finally delivered, it should not produce debugging output so it is necessary somehow to switch off the statements used to produce diagnostic information. This can be accomplished in three ways:

(1) Each statement can be identified by some string such as ***DEBUG*** and, using this string as an identifier, can be edited or commented out of the final program.

(2) The output statements can be conditionally compiled into the program. When the program is being tested, a compiler directive can cause the output statements to be included; when the production version of the program is delivered the compiler directive is switched off so that no debugging code is included.

(3) The output statements can be conditionally executed depending on some global debugging switch which may be set by the program user. The switch is set while the program is being debugged and unset in the production version of the program.

Each of these approaches has disadvantages. Editing out diagnostic statements is a final process – it requires time and effort to put them back. Conditional compilation although potentially the best technique is not offered by all compilers and the permanent inclusion of diagnostic information increases the size of the program.

The inclusion of anticipatory diagnostic statements shares a disadvantage with a number of other error location techniques provided by software tools. Unless carefully controlled, voluminous amounts of information can be generated. Examining all this information is a time-consuming process.

If output statements are included in a program, excessive output is most easily controlled by controlling diagnostic output via a multi-way, rather than a two-way, switch. Levels of output detail can be controlled by switch settings – setting 1, say, may cause global information to be printed only at important checkpoints whereas setting 5 might cause diagnostics to be output more frequently and in greater detail.

Over the last few years, tools to assist the testing and debugging processes have improved markedly and, depending on the language being used, debuggers which act at the source code level may be available to assist the programmer. Such systems and other testing and debugging tools are the subject of Chapter 23.

KEY POINTS

- Testing is a process which is concerned with both the verification and the validation of programs. Verification is intended to show that a program meets its specification. Validation is intended to show that the program does what the user wants it to do.

- Testing can only demonstrate the presence of errors. It cannot prove their absence.

- The testing process involves unit testing, module testing, subsystem testing, integration testing and acceptance testing.

- The most effective testing strategy is a mixture of top-down and bottom-up testing.

- It is important that testing should be scheduled as part of the project planning process and that adequate resources should be made available for testing.

- Testing and debugging are distinct. The aim of testing is to discover the presence of faults in a program. Debugging is the process of locating erroneous code and repairing it.

- An experienced debugger works by generating hypotheses about the problem then confirming or denying these hypotheses by a process of elimination.

Further reading

The Art of Software Testing.   This is now a relatively old book on the subject but it has not, in my opinion, been improved upon by later texts. As well as an excellent general discussion of testing, it is also appropriate reading for the other chapters in this section. (G.J. Myers, 1979, Wiley.)

References

Boehm, B.W. (1979). 'Software engineering: R & D trends and defense needs', in *Research Directions in Software Technology*, Wegner, P. (ed.), Cambridge, Mass.: MIT Press.

Hayes, I. (1986), 'Specification directed module testing', *IEEE Trans. Software Eng.*, **SE-12** (1), 124–33.

Myers, G.J. (1979), *The Art of Software Testing*, New York: Wiley.

EXERCISES

20.1 Discuss the differences between verification and validation and explain why validation is a particularly difficult process.

20.2 Suggest alternative models of the testing process which might be used when a system is (a) to be built from reusable components and (b) to be built as a support tool and not part of a software product.

20.3 What is the distinction between alpha and beta testing? Explain why this form of testing is particularly valuable.

20.4 Using a program you have written, devise top-down and bottom-up testing strategies for it.

20.5 Draw up a testing schedule and estimate the resources required to implement that schedule for the suggested programming projects in Appendix B.

20.6 Based on your programming experience, draw up debugging guidelines for locating errors in programs which have been written in Pascal, C or some other programming language.

20.7 Design an interactive software tool which allows debugging statements to be readily included or deleted from a program. Suggest how such a tool might be integrated with a language processing system as discussed in Chapter 18.

Chapter 21

Testing Techniques

Objective

The objective of this chapter is to describe a number of techniques which can be used in systematically testing a program. These include black-box testing with equivalence partitioning and structural or 'white-box' testing. The limitations of this latter technique are described and the particular problem of testing real-time systems is discussed.

Contents

Planning the testing of a programming system involves formulating a set of test cases which are akin to the real data that the system is intended to manipulate. Test cases consist of an input specification, a description of the system functions exercised by that input and a statement of the expected output. Thorough testing involves producing cases to ensure that the program responds as expected to both valid and invalid inputs, that the program performs to specification and that it does not corrupt other programs or data in the system.

In principle, testing of a program should be exhaustive. Every statement in the program should be exercised and every possible path combination through the program should be executed at least once. In practice, this is impossible in a program which contains loops as the number of possible path combinations is astronomical. The best that can be done in reality is to derive test cases which cause each path through the program to be executed. This also ensures that each statement in the program is executed at least once.

Thus, it is necessary to select a subset of the possible set of test cases and conjecture that this subset will adequately test the program. The subset might be selected using the guidelines discussed here and should be supplemented by other tests generated using knowledge of the program, its application domain and its users. Petschenik (1985) suggests that test cases should be selected using the following heuristics:

(1)   'Testing a system's capabilities is more important than testing its components.' This means that users are interested in getting a job done and test cases should be chosen to identify aspects of the system which will stop them doing their job. Although errors, such as screen corruption, are irritating, they are less disruptive than errors which cause loss of data or program termination.

(2)   'Testing old capabilities is more important than testing new capabilities.' If a program is a revision of an existing system, users expect existing features to keep working. They are less concerned by failure of additional capabilities which they may not even use.

(3)   'Testing typical situations is more important than testing boundary value cases.' It is more important that a system works under normal usage conditions than under occasional conditions which only arise with extreme data values. This does not mean that boundary value testing (discussed below) is unimportant. It simply means that, if it is necessary to restrict the number of test cases, it may be advisable to concentrate on typical input values.

Test cases and test data are not the same thing. Test data are the inputs which have been devised to test the system; test cases are input and output specifications plus a statement of the function under test. It is sometimes possible to generate test data automatically but impossible to generate test cases as the generator would have to have the same functions as the program being tested.

It is impossible to present an example of the test cases for even a moderate system as their listing would occupy a volume much thicker than this book. Rather, to illustrate the number of test cases which might be required, consider the testing of a simple routine to search a table of integers to determine if some given integer is present in that table.

Assume that this routine is called as follows:

```
S := Search (AnArray, InValue);
```

If AnArray has an element equal to InValue, the index of that element in AnArray is returned by Search, otherwise -1 is returned. If Search is written in a programming language which permits type checking, such as Ada, the compiler detects parameters of incorrect type. There is no need to test Search with parameters of the wrong type or with incorrect numbers of parameters. The size of the array can be determined using the predefined Ada attributes FIRST and LAST which return the lower and upper bounds of the array.

If the program is written in a language like C or FORTRAN which has less strict type checking, additional testing may be required to ensure that the types of the parameters to the function are correct. This demonstrates that the use of a language with compile-time type checking can reduce the costs of later stages of the software process.

Search should be tested for its reaction to valid and invalid input, system corruption and performance. As input of the wrong type is trapped by the compiler and performance is not specified there is no need to design specific test cases for them. The requirement that a call of Search should not modify any program variables apart from that assigned the value returned by Search cannot be tested using specific test cases.

To detect if Search actually corrupts global values, a dump of the program global variables must be taken. This is taken each time Search is called and repeated immediately after the call of the procedure. These dumps may then be compared automatically, to ensure that only the variable assigned a value by Search has been changed. It is not realistic to require this process to be explicitly programmed into the system and a software tool designed to assist with program testing should be used. Of course, if the source code of the function is available, it is possible to inspect that code to check if any global variable modifications are made.

Now let us consider the minimum set of test cases which are required to establish a reasonable level of confidence in the function Search. We require to test the possibilities shown below.

(1) Array size of l, element in array.

(2) Array size of 1, element not in array.

(3) Empty array.

(4) Even array size, element first element in array.

(5) Even array size, element last element in array.

(6) Even array size, element not in array.

(7) Odd array size, element first element in array.

(8) Odd array size, element last element in array.

(9) Odd array size, element not in array.

(10) Even array size, element in array, not first or last.

(11) Odd array size, element in array, not first or last.

To test these situations, the following set of test cases might be derived:

(1) Array is a single value equal to required value.
Input : AnArray = 17; InValue = 17
Output : function returns 1

(2) Array is a single value not equal to required value.
Input : AnArray = 17; InValue = 0
Output : function returns −1

(3) Array is empty, no values assigned.
Input : AnArray = —; InValue = 1
Output : function returns −1

(4) The array size is even and the first value is the required value.
Input : AnArray = 17, 23, 28, 33; InValue = 17
Output : function returns 1

(5) The array size is even and the last value is the required value.
Input : AnArray = 17, 18, 21, 23; InValue = 23
Output : function returns 4

(6) The array size is even and no value matches the required value.
Input : AnArray = 17, 23, 28, 33; InValue = 3
Output : function returns −1

(7) The array size is odd and the first value is the required value.
Input : AnArray = 17, 23, 29, 32, 36; InValue = 17
Output : function returns 1

(8) The array size is odd and the last value is the required value.
Input : AnArray = 17, 23, 29, 32, 36; InValue = 36
Output : function returns 5

(9) The array size is odd and no value matches the required value.
Input : AnArray = 17, 23, 29, 32, 36; InValue = 4
Output : function returns −1

(10)   The array size is even and the element is neither first nor last.
        Input : AnArray = 17, 23, 29, 35, 41, 45; InValue = 23
        Output : function returns 2

(11)   The array size is odd and the element is neither first nor last.
        Input : AnArray = 17, 23, 29, 35, 41; InValue = 23
        Output : function returns 2

In this situation, the tester is simply provided with a description of the routine and does not have access to the code of that routine. This is called 'black-box testing' where the routine is considered to be a black-box – we have no idea how the search routine works. By contrast, white-box or structural testing makes use of knowledge of the program code to derive test cases. This is the topic of a later section in this chapter.

The apparently arbitrary set of test cases set out for the search routine has been derived using the following heuristics:

- Search programs are most likely to go wrong when the key element is either the first or last element in the array.

- Programmers often don't consider situations where there are an unusual number of elements (such as zero or one) in the collection.

- From experience, we know that search routines sometimes behave differently depending on whether the number of values in the array is even or odd so both possibilities are tested.

The set of input values used to test Search is in no way exhaustive. The routine may fail if the input array happens to be 1, 2, 3, 4 but there are no grounds for supposing this. Test cases have been designed to check Search for a number of classes of input and it is reasonable to surmise that, if it works successfully for one member of a class, it will do so for all members of that class. For example, a test case has been designed to check that Search works with arrays which have an odd (3) number of values. It may be that Search would fail if an array whose size is a different odd number is used but there is no reason to suspect that this will be the case.

21.1   Equivalence partitioning

The form of input classification for determining the test inputs for the search routine above is called equivalence partitioning. Equivalence partitioning is a technique for determining which classes of input data have common properties. If a program does not display an erroneous output for one member of a class, it should not do so for any member of that class.

The equivalence classes must be identified by using the program specification or user documentation and by the tester using experience to predict which classes of input value are likely to detect errors. For example, if an input specification states that the range of some input value must be a 5-digit integer, that is, between 10 000 and 99 999, equivalence classes might be those values less than 10 000, values between 10 000 and 99 999 and values greater than 99 999. Similarly, if four to eight values are to be input, equivalence classes are less than four, between four and eight and more than eight.

Sometimes, program specifications may not be precisely detailed so testers must use their experience to determine equivalence classes. For example, if a program accepts an integer as input, it should be tested using integers less than zero. If a program manipulates tables, it should be tested using tables with no entries, a single entry and many entries.

When equivalence classes have been determined, the next step is to choose values from each class which are most likely to lead to a successful test. The values chosen should cause the program to display an erroneous output. Testing experience has shown that the most useful values to select for test input are those at the boundaries of each equivalence class.

Not only input equivalence classes should be considered. Output equivalence classes should also be taken into account and the input values which generate outputs at the boundary of each output class should be chosen as test input. For example, say a program is designed to produce between three and six outputs, with each output lying in the range 1000–2500. Test input should be selected which produces three values at 1000, three values at 2500, six values at 1000 and 6 values at 2500. Furthermore, input should be selected so that erroneous output values would result if that input was processed as correct input. This input should attempt to force the program to produce less than three values, more than six values, values less than 1000 and values greater than 2500.

To illustrate this technique of choosing test input, consider a procedure designed to convert a string of digits to an integer. Assume that the procedure is implemented in Ada and is intended to operate in an environment where 16-bit two's complement notation is used to represent integers.

This conversion procedure header and associated type declaration are as follows:

```
type SHORTSTRING is array [1..6] of CHAR;
function String_to_integer (Digits : SHORTSTRING) return
                 INTEGER;
```

The string of digits to be converted to an integer is right justified in Digits and may be positive or negative. If less than six characters long, Digits is

Table 21.1
Equivalence classes for
testing String_to_integer.

Identifier	Type	Class
C1	Input	1 – 5 non-blank characters
C2	Input	6 non-blank characters
C3	Input	Empty
C4	Input	Single minus sign, no characters
C5	Input	Minus sign as most significant character
C6	Input	Digit as most significant character
C7	Input	Left padded with non-blank and not 0
C8	Input	Left padded with 0
C9	Input	Digit as significant character but with invalid characters in number
C10	Input	Gap between minus sign and number
C11	Output	Negative integers ≥ MinInt and < 0
C12	Output	Zero
C13	Output	Positive integers > 0 and ≤ MaxInt

padded with blanks on the left and, if the input is negative, a minus sign occupies the character position immediately to the left of the most significant digit. Because of built-in compiler checking, there is no need to test this function using arrays of more or less than six characters or to test it with any other invalid type of parameter.

By inspecting the function description, we can identify the input and output equivalence classes shown in Table 21.1. Using two's complement 16-bit representation for integers means that the minimum integer which may be represented is −32 768 and the maximum positive integer is 32 767.

Once the equivalence classes have been identified, the next step is to select values in these classes to test the program. Myers (1979) suggests that the values which are most likely to cause anomalous results to be generated are those at the boundaries of the equivalence classes as, from experience, we know that programmers often overlook the exceptional states which sometimes occur at class boundaries.

Thus, an appropriate set of test data where the values are at the boundaries of the equivalence classes might be as shown in Table 21.2. The letter 'b' represents a blank character in this table. The letter 'x' represents any character except '−' or a digit. Thirteen input and output equivalence classes can be identified and from these nineteen test cases identified. Note that tests derived from input and output equivalent classes can overlap. For example, testing the function with the input −32 768 tests the function's reaction to an input containing six significant characters and also if it converts strings representing the maximum negative integer correctly.

The technique of equivalence partitioning is a useful one for selecting instances of each possible input for test. However, even when a program operates successfully for individual test inputs, combinations of

Table 21.2
Test cases for String_to_
integer routine.

Number	Input	Expected output	Classes tested
1	"bbbbb1"	1	C1, C6, C13
2	"000001"	1	C8, C6, C2
3	"bbbb−1"	−1	C5, C11
4	"−00001"	−1	C8, C5, C2
5	"000000"	0	C2, C12
6	"bbbbb0"	0	C6, C12:
7	"b32767"	32767	C1, C6, C13
8	"032767"	32767	C2, C13
9	"−32768"	−32768	C2, C5, C11
10	"b32768"	Error – invalid input	C1, C13
11	"−32769"	Error – invalid input	C2, C5, C11
12	"123456"	Error – invalid input	C2
13	"xxxxx1"	Error – invalid input	C7
14	"xxxx−1"	Error – invalid input	C7
15	"bbbbbb"	Error – invalid input	C3
16	"bbb2x1"	Error – invalid input	C9
17	"bbb2−1"	Error – invalid input	C9
18	"bbb−b1"	Error – invalid input	C10
19	"bbbbb−"	Error – invalid input	C4

these inputs may detect program error. Equivalence partitioning provides no help in selecting these combinations. The experience and intuition of the tester must be used to select combinations likely to cause program failure.

21.2   Structural testing

Black-box testing is the name given to testing where the tester is presented with the specification of a component to be tested and uses this to derive the test cases. This approach has the advantage that testers need not have access to the source code of the routine and need not understand the program which is being tested. The disadvantage, of course, is that the tester cannot get clues from the program about which test inputs best exercise the program.

An alternative approach to testing is sometimes called 'white-box', 'glass-box' or structural testing in that it relies on the tester using knowledge about the code and the structure of a component to derive the test data. The advantage of structural testing is that test cases can be derived systematically and test coverage measured. Thus, the quality assurance mechanisms which are set up to control testing can quantify what level of testing is required and what has been carried out.

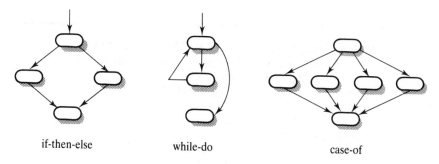

Figure 21.1
Flow graph
representations.

if-then-else   while-do   case-of

The starting point for structural testing is to derive a program flow graph which is simply a representation of the program where all paths through the program are explicit. A program flow graph consists of nodes representing decisions and edges showing flow of control. The flow graph representations for if-then-else, while-do and case statements are shown in Figure 21.1.

Given that goto statements are not used in a program, it is a straightforward manual or automatic process to derive the flow graph for any program by substituting these representations for program statements. Sequential statements (assignments, procedure calls and I/O statements) can be ignored in the flow graph construction.

For example, the flow graph for the binary search procedure in Example 21.1 is shown in Figure 21.2, where the compound condition in the **while** statement has been simplified into a simple **while** and an **if** statement.

```
while Bott <= Top loop
    if Found then
        exit
    else
    ...
```

The reason for this simplification is that flow graphs are intended to show all program decisions and a compound logical expression is simply shorthand for two conditions.

An exhaustive structural test involves testing all possible combinations of all paths through the program. For any components apart from very trivial ones without loops, this is an impossible objective. Thus, the aim of structural testing is not to test all possible path combinations but to ensure that test data are selected so that all possible paths are traversed at least once.

The number of independent paths in a program can be discovered by computing the cyclomatic complexity (McCabe, 1976) from the program flow graph. An independent program path is one which traverses at least one new edge in the flow graph. In program terms, this means exercising

Example 21.1
Binary search procedure.

```
procedure Binary_search (Key: ELEM ; T: ELEM_ARRAY ;
            Found: in out BOOLEAN ; L: in out ELEM_INDEX ) is
    -- Assume that T'FIRST and T'LAST are both
    -- greater than or equal to zero and T'LAST >= T'FIRST
    Bott : ELEM_INDEX := T'FIRST ;
    Top : ELEM_INDEX := T'LAST ;
    Mid : ELEM_INDEX;
begin
    L := (T'FIRST + T'LAST ) mod 2;
    Found := T( L ) = Key;
    while Bott <= Top and not Found loop
        Mid := (Top + Bott) mod 2;
        if T( Mid ) = Key then
                Found := true;
                L := Mid;
        elsif T( Mid ) < Key then
            Bott := Mid + 1;
        else
                Top := Mid − 1;
        end if;
    end loop;
end Binary_search;
```

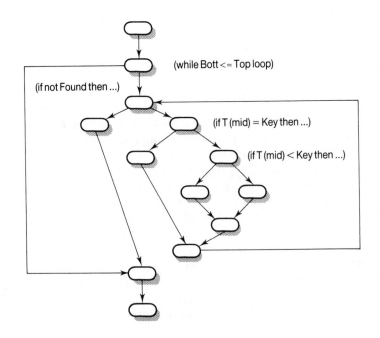

Figure 21.2
Flow graph for a binary
search procedure.

one or more new conditions. Thus, the maximum possible number of tests required to test all conditions is equal to the cyclomatic complexity.

The cyclomatic complexity of a graph, G (any graph, not just a program flow graph) may be computed according to the following formula:

$$\text{Cyclomatic\_complexity } (G) = \text{Number\_of\_edges} - \text{Number\_of\_nodes} + 1$$

For programs, it is not necessary to construct a flow graph in order to compute the cyclomatic complexity. Its value is equal to the number of conditions in the program where compound conditions with N simple predicates are counted as N rather than 1. Thus, if there are six if-statements and a while loop, with all conditional expressions simple, the cyclomatic complexity is 7. If one of the conditional expressions is a compound expression with one **and** and one **or**, the cyclomatic complexity is 9.

Of course, knowing the number of tests required does not necessarily make it any easier for the tester to derive test cases. Generally heuristic techniques are used, based on the tester's experience. An initial set of test data is proposed and then refined using the experience and judgement of the tester. A testing tool such as a dynamic program analyser (see Chapter 23) can indicate which parts of the program have been executed and its output used to guide the tester in selecting further test cases.

Unfortunately, cyclomatic complexity is limited in its usefulness and is only loosely related to the adequacy of the program testing. Indeed, using metrics such as this one can be dangerous as it may give an impression that the program has been thoroughly tested whereas all that can be said is that some percentage (perhaps 100%) of the independent paths in a program have been executed.

Its fundamental difficulty is that it does not take into account programs which are data-driven. For example, the program fragments in Example 21.2 are equivalent in function but have quite different cyclo-

---

Example 21.2
Control and data-driven programs.

```
case A is                          Strings: array (1..4) of STRING :=
    when "One" => i := 1 ;             ("One", "Two", "Three", "Four", "Five");
    when "Two" => i := 2 ;             i := 1 ;
    when "Three" => i := 3 ;       loop
    when "Four" => i := 4 ;            exit when Strings (i) = A ;
    when "Five" => i := 5 ;            i := i + 1 ;
end case ;                         end loop ;

        (a)                                (b)
```

matic complexities. They are equivalent and simply use different ways of representing a table. Complete testing requires that A should take all of the values "One", "Two", "Three", "Four", "Five". However, code fragment (a) has a cyclomatic complexity of 5 and fragment (b) a cyclomatic complexity of 1. This implies that the exhaustive testing of fragment (b) requires only a single test case. Of course, this is nonsense. Both fragments should be tested in exactly the same way.

For non-trivial programs, it is impossible to judge whether or not exhaustive testing using the cyclomatic complexity is adequate or not. Although this metric can be useful in testing, it must be used with care.

21.3   Testing real–time systems

Real-time systems are those systems, such as control systems, where the processes making up the system must respond to events under time constraints. These are, typically, less than a second and may be as little as a few milliseconds. If the system response is not timely, information may be lost. The effective testing of such systems poses particular problems for the tester.

The testing of real-time systems is particularly critical because the reliability requirements of these systems are usually greater than the requirements for systems which are not time critical. The reason for this lies in the applications for which real-time systems are used, such as controlling complex machinery, air traffic control, military communications, etc. The consequences of system failure are potentially disastrous. Thus, the testing process must be very comprehensive. It is normal in real-time systems development for the costs of system testing to be more than half of the total system development costs.

Real-time systems are usually made up of a number of distinct cooperating processes and are often interrupt driven. This means that an external event such as an input from a sensor causes control to be transferred from the currently executing process to the process which handles that event.

The peculiar problems of testing real-time systems are caused by the subtle interactions which may arise between the various processes in the system. System errors may be time dependent, only arising when the system processes are in a particular state. The exact state of the system processes when the error occurred may be impossible to reproduce. Testing is obviously simplified if parallel processes are avoided and a design method adopted which allows decisions on parallelism to be postponed. However, there are some systems where performance dictates that the software must be made up of parallel processes.

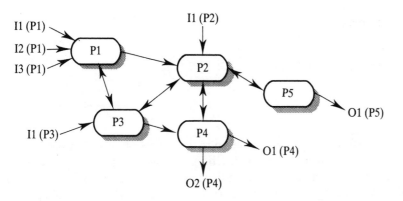

Figure 21.3
A real-time system.

Consider the real-time system made up of five processes shown in Figure 21.3. These processes interact with each other and some of them collect inputs from their environment and generate outputs to that environment. These inputs may be from sensors, keyboards or from some other computer system. Similarly, outputs may be to control lines, other computers or user terminals.

Because real-time systems are composed of a number of processes, the first step in testing such systems is to test each process individually. In the above system model, therefore, P1, P2, P3, P4 and P5 would first be tested in isolation and debugged until each process appeared to meet its specification.

Following this, it may be appropriate to test threads, that is, test the system's reaction to a single event. This will normally involve control passing from process to process as actions 'thread' their way through the system. Two possible threads are shown in Figures 21.4 and 21.5 where an input is transformed by a number of processes in turn to produce an output. Of course, complete thread testing may be impossible because of the number of possible input and output combinations. In such cases, the most commonly exercised threads should be selected for testing.

After a single thread has been tested, that thread can then be exercised by introducing multiple events of the same class but without introducing events of any other class. For example, a multi-user system might first be tested using a single terminal then multiple terminal testing gradually introduced. In the above model, this type of testing might involve processing all inputs in multiple-input processes. Figure 21.5 illustrates an example of this process where three inputs to the same process are used as test data.

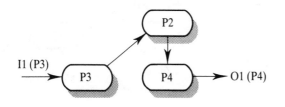

Figure 21.4
Thread testing.

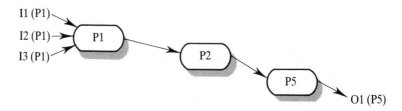

Figure 21.5
Multiple inputs to thread testing.

After the system's reaction to each class of event has been tested, it can then be tested for its reactions to more than one class of event occurring simultaneously. At this stage, new event tests should be introduced gradually so that system errors can be localized. In the above model, this might be tested as shown in Figure 21.6.

One of the difficulties of testing real-time systems is that they are designed to interface and control hardware systems. These may not be available when the software is being tested, or interfacing the hardware to potentially faulty software may be dangerous. The incorrect software could cause invalid control signals to be generated and the hardware or its testers might be damaged.

Furthermore, safety-critical software is intended to handle rare unexpected, dangerous events and it is unthinkable to introduce these events because of their potential danger. To cope with these situations, the normal practice is to use a simulator which produces the same responses as the hardware interfaced to the system. Simulators as testing tools are discussed in Chapter 23.

The testing of safety-critical systems presents even more problems than testing real-time systems. The reason for this is that many events which can cause system failure are, by their very nature, rare and difficult to anticipate. Formal verification (see Chapter 22) can be of use in verifying safety-critical systems but the fundamental difficulty is that the requirements of the system cannot set out all possible events which might happen. Thus, the system may be verified but code to handle a dangerous event may simply not be included in the program. This is a very specialized topic and is not discussed further here.

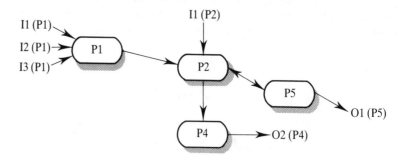

Figure 21.6
Multiple thread testing.

KEY POINTS

- When testing a program it is more important to test those parts of the system that are commonly used rather than those parts that are only rarely exercised.

- Even simple programs require many test cases if they are to be thoroughly tested.

- Equivalence partitioning is a way of deriving test cases. It depends on finding partitions in the input and output data sets and exercising the program with at least one value from these partitions. Often, the value which is most likely to lead to a successful test is a value at the boundary of a partition.

- Black-box testing does not need access to source code. White-box testing uses source code information to derive test cases.

- Structural testing is a way of analysing a program to determine paths through it and using this analysis to derive test cases. It has the advantage that a test coverage metric can be produced but this is unreliable because it is simply based on program control flow.

- Real-time systems are difficult to test because of timing dependencies between processes in the system. Incremental testing is used in testing such systems. Safety-critical systems are even more difficult to test because the testing team must anticipate very rare events.

Further reading

The Art of Software Testing. Contains excellent material on black-box testing, equivalence partitioning and boundary value analysis as well as much wisdom on testing. It has little on structural testing but this is hardly a fault as the value of this technique is a dubious one. (G.J. Myers, 1979, Wiley.)

References

McCabe, T.J. (1976), 'A complexity measure', *IEEE Trans. Software Eng.*, **SE-2**, 308–20.

Myers, G.J. (1979), *The Art of Software Testing*, New York: Wiley.

Petschenik, N.H. (1985), 'Practical priorities in system testing', *IEEE Computer*, **2** (5), 18–23.

EXERCISES

21.1   Discuss the differences between black-box and white-box testing and suggest how they can be used together in a testing program.

21.2   Derive a set of test cases for the following routines:
- A keyed table where entries are made and retrieved using some alphabetic key.
- A sort routine which sorts arrays of integers.
- A routine which takes a line of text as input and counts the number of non-blank characters in that line.
- A routine which takes a line of text as inputs where lines may have leading blank characters. The output from the routine is the text with leading blank characters stripped from the line.
- An abstract data type called STACK which supports stack push, pop and test for empty operations (see specification chapters).
- A routine which examines a line of text and replaces sequences of blank characters with a single blank character.
- An abstract data type called STRING which provides operations on character strings. These include concatenation, length (to give the length of a string) and substring selection.

21.3   Program the above routines using a language of your choice and, for each routine, derive its cyclomatic complexity.

21.4   By examining the code of the routines which you have written, derive further test cases in addition to those you have already considered. Has the code analysis revealed omissions in your initial set of test cases?

21.5   Describe the difficulties encountered when verifying and validating real-time systems. Explain how these can be tackled by program testers.

21.6   For the following safety-critical systems, list some rare events which might cause system failure and which the tester should consider.
- A car brake control system
- A system to control the bow doors on a car ferry
- An aircraft auto-pilot system
- A nuclear reactor control system
- A system controlling gas flow to a heating boiler

Chapter 22

Static Program Verification

Objectives

The objective of this chapter is to describe a number of static verification techniques where static techniques are ways of verifying a program by examination and analysis of its source code. Execution is not required. The first technique covered is an informal one called program inspections. This is a form of code review intended to detect program errors. Formal program verification, where a mathematical argument demonstrates the correspondence between a program and its specification, is illustrated by example. Finally, static analysis tools which analyse source code to detect certain kinds of program error are covered.

Contents

The testing of a program is a dynamic verification and validation technique. It involves executing the program with appropriate input data and examining the program output to detect anomalies. The problem with testing, particularly in its early stages, is that each test run tends to discover one or only a few faults. A fault can cause system data corruption so it is sometimes difficult to tell if output anomalies are a result of a new fault or simply a consequence of a fault which has already been discovered. Systematic program testing requires a large number of test runs to be made, thus contributing to the high cost of system testing.

Static verification techniques do not require the program to be executed. Rather, they are concerned with examining the source code of a program (or, perhaps, a detailed PDL design specification) and detecting faults in that code before execution. The advantage of this approach is that each error can usually be considered in isolation. Error interactions are not significant and an entire component can be validated in a single session.

Static verification is effective in finding errors in programs. Fagan (1986) reports that, typically, 60% of the errors in a program can be detected using informal static verification techniques before the program is executed. Mills *et al.* (1987) suggest that more formal static validation techniques using mathematical verification can result in more than 90% of the errors in a program being detected before execution.

As an indication of the costs of informal verification, Fagan suggests that about 100 lines of code can be inspected per hour and that this requires about another hour's preparation. Given that four people may be involved in a program inspection, the cost of inspecting 100 lines of code is equivalent to roughly the cost of one person working for one day.

It is impossible to know, in general, whether or not this represents a saving over testing. Testing costs are dependent on the ability of the testers, the equipment available (fast turnround can reduce testing costs), the tools available and the application domain. In some cases, discovering faults by testing will be cheaper; in others static verification will result in a lower cost per fault detected. Fagan suggests, however, that in most cases systematic inspection results in a lower cost per defect discovered than testing.

However, static and dynamic techniques are not in opposition. As well as detecting errors, static verification is part of the overall quality assurance process (see Chapter 30) and is the principal means of ensuring that programming standards have been followed. The effective combination of static validation and testing can result in higher product quality and lower overall life-cycle costs.

22.1   Program inspections

The notion of formalized inspection has already been introduced in Chapter 14 where design reviews were discussed. However, design reviews are multi-functional and are intended for defect detection, education and overall strategy decisions. A complementary process, which is exclusively aimed at defect detection, is formalized program inspections. This validation technique was developed by Fagan (1976, 1986) at IBM.

Although the term 'program inspection' is used here, the techniques used in this process may be applied to any of the outputs of the software process. Requirements specifications, detailed design definitions, data structure designs, test plans and user documentation can all be inspected in the same way. The benefits gained from the inspection process apply to all of these but, for convenience, only program inspection is discussed here.

The key difference between inspections and reviews is that inspections are solely intended to detect defects in a component. They do not have an explicit educational function nor are they part of the design process where strategy decisions are made. This means that to conduct an inspection effectively there are a number of conditions which must hold:

(1)   A precise specification of the code to be inspected must be available. It is impossible to inspect a component at the level of detail required to detect errors unless such a specification has been produced.

(2)   The members of the inspection team must be familiar with any organizational standards which are to be checked.

(3)   A version of the code which is completely up-to-date and which is free from syntax errors must be available. There is no point in inspecting code which is 'almost complete' even if delaying causes schedule disruption.

(4)   A checklist of likely errors should be available to assist with the inspection process. This should be established initially from the distilled experience of experienced staff and should be refined as inspections are carried out.

(5)   Project management must be supportive of the notion of static verification and must be prepared to accept that this will tend to 'front-load' the project cost but with a significant reduction in testing costs. It is particularly important that project management sees inspections as part of the verification process and not as personnel appraisals. Inspection results should never be used in individual career reviews as it is important that those involved in inspections are not defensive about the process.

The process of inspection is a formal one carried out by a small team of about four people. The roles adopted by these individuals are:

- *Author* The programmer or designer is responsible for producing the component or components to be inspected.
- *Reader* The reader presents the code to the team during the inspection process.
- *Tester* The tester views the code from a testing point of view.
- *Chairman or moderator* the chairman is responsible for conducting the inspection and motivating the other participants. Ideally, he or she should not be directly involved in the development of the product being inspected although it is sometimes impractical, in small organizations, to bring in people from outside the project.

Fagan suggests that there are six stages in the inspection process (Figure 22.1) and that it is unwise to leave any of them out. The planning stage involves arranging an inspection team, organizing a meeting room and ensuring that the material to be inspected and its specifications are complete. The overview stage is concerned with presenting a general description of the material to be inspected to the inspection team. This is followed by a period of individual preparation where each member of the inspection team examines the code and its specification.

The inspection process itself takes place. This should be relatively short (no more than two hours) and should be exclusively concerned with identifying product defects. It is not the function of the inspection team to suggest how these defects should be corrected or to recommend that other components might be modified.

Following inspection, a rework stage is entered and the program modified by its author to correct the identified defects. Re-inspection is then necessary as new defects may be introduced during the rework. However, it may not be necessary to repeat the entire inspection process. The inspection chairman may simply check that the changes have been made correctly.

The amount of code which can be inspected in a given time varies depending on the experience of the inspection team, the programming

Figure 22.1
Stages in the inspection process.

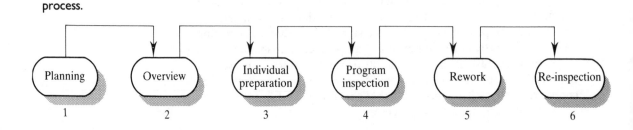

| Planning | Overview | Individual preparation | Program inspection | Rework | Re-inspection |
| 1 | 2 | 3 | 4 | 5 | 6 |

language and the application domain. Fagan provides approximate figures as follows:

(1) About 500 source code statements per hour can be considered during the overview stage.

(2) During individual preparation, about 125 source code statements per hour can be examined.

(3) From 90 to 125 statements per hour can be inspected.

Fagan suggests that the maximum time spent on inspection should be about two hours as the efficiency of the defect detection process falls off after that time. This suggests that inspection should be a frequent process, carried out on relatively small software components, during program development. Inspection should not be considered as a process which is initiated once an entire software development is complete.

It is useful to drive the inspection process using a checklist of likely errors which commonly arise. This checklist will vary, depending on the checking provided by the language compiler. For example, an Ada compiler checks that functions have the correct number of parameters, a C compiler does not. Examples of checks which might be made during the inspection process are:

(1) Are all program variables initialized before their values are used?

(2) Have all constants been named?

(3) For each conditional statement, is the condition correct?

(4) Is each loop certain to terminate?

(5) When arrays are processed, should the lower bound be 0, 1, or something else? Should the upper bound be equal to the size of the array or Size −1?

(6) If character strings are used, is a delimiter explicitly assigned?

(7) If dynamic storage is used, has space been allocated correctly?

(8) Do all function and procedure calls have the correct number of parameters?

(9) Do formal and actual parameter types match? This is not a problem if a strongly typed language is used.

(10) If a linked structure is being modified, have all links been correctly reassigned?

(11) Are compound statements correctly bracketed?

(12) Have all possible error conditions been taken into account?

(13) If the component is concerned with checking keyword input, have all keywords been checked?

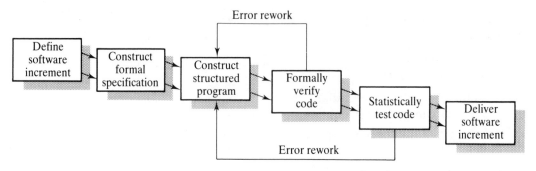

Figure 22.2
'Cleanroom' software
engineering.

The inspection process can be particularly effective when combined with mathematical program verification (Mills *et al.*, 1987; Selby *et al.*, 1987). This has been discovered in experiments in IBM's so-called 'Cleanroom' approach to software development (Figure 22.2). This is named by analogy with semiconductor fabrication units where defects are avoided by manufacturing in an ultra-clean atmosphere. The Cleanroom approach to software development is based on the notion that defects in software should be avoided rather than detected and repaired. It relies on static verification techniques during development to ensure that fault-free software is developed. Instead of unit and module testing, software components are formally specified and mathematically verified as they are developed. The process forces specification development and stability and then verifies the developed software against that specification without executing the software.

Incremental development of software is also important. The software is produced and delivered in parts which are made available for user assessment. Users can then feed back reports of the system and propose changes that are required. Rather than continuous requirements change during software development, which is common in some development, this approach controls the changes made to a system (Figure 22.3). Users can still request changes but with a less disruptive effect on the development process.

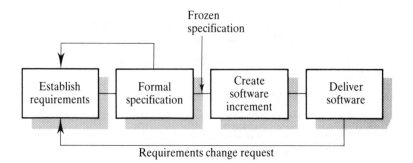

Figure 22.3
Controlling requirements
change requests.

The first stage of testing is an integration test of the complete system (or a major increment of it) and statistical techniques are used during testing to assess reliability. A model of expected usage patterns of the product is created and used to drive the testing process. Reliability growth models, as discussed in Chapter 30, are used to determine when the system has been tested adequately.

The cleanroom approach is reportedly no more expensive than conventional development and testing but it results in software with very few errors. Mills *et al.* (1987) report that, in a 20 000 line language processor, only 53 errors were discovered during the testing of the system. By comparison, the estimated industry average error count is of the order of 50 errors per thousand lines of code.

The cleanroom approach is a very interesting experiment in software development and it suggests that formal verification may be currently applicable. Like most experiments in software engineering, there are many dependent variables such as specification development, formal verification and the skill and experience of the staff involved. It is not possible to tell which of these is most significant. Of course, it does not matter if the software development process is improved but this has not been demonstrated in an environment where staff are less skilled and less committed to the concept.

22.2 Mathematical program verification

Given that programming language semantics are formally defined, it is possible to consider a program as a mathematical object. Using mathematical techniques, it is possible to demonstrate the correspondence between a program and a formal specification of that program. Essentially, the program is proved to be correct with respect to its specification. If such a proof can be established, the program has been verified and no testing to check verification is required.

It has been suggested by some formal verification zealots that the development of effective methods of program verification will make the need for a system testing phase redundant. This is a false premise. Part of the testing activity involves checking that a program meets its specifications but testing also checks that these specifications are correct and appropriate for the user's needs and that non-functional constraints are satisfied by the system. Furthermore, we know from the history of mathematics that proofs may themselves be incorrect. Although formal verification may reduce testing costs, it cannot replace testing as a means of system validation.

The verification of programs by providing a mathematical proof of their correctness was built on the work of McCarthy (1962), and a number of other authors such as Floyd (1967), Hoare (1969), Dijkstra (1976) and Manna (1969). There are a number of different techniques for proving program correctness and an axiomatic approach is illustrated here. Linger *et al.* (1979) describe an alternative function-based approach which has been used with some success within IBM.

The basis of the axiomatic approach is as follows. Assume that there are a number of points in a program where the software engineer can provide assertions concerning program variables and their relationships. At each of these points, the assertions should be invariably true. Say the points in the program are P(1), P(2),...P(n). The associated assertions are $a(1)$, $a(2)$,...,$a(n)$. Assertion $a(1)$ must be an assertion about the input of the program and $a(n)$ an assertion about the program output.

To prove that the program statements between points P(i) and P($i+1$) are correct, it must be demonstrated that the application of the program statements separating these points causes assertion a(i) to be transformed to assertion $a(i+1)$. Given that the initial assertion is true before program execution and the final assertion is true after execution, verification is carried out for adjacent program statements. This demonstrates that the input assertion plus the program leads directly to the output assertion. Partial correctness has been demonstrated. Complete correctness can be demonstrated if it can be shown that the program terminates; that is, does not contain an endless loop.

The demonstration of correctness of a program with respect to its specification can be developed with varying degrees of rigour. Correctness may be demonstrated using completely formal mathematical techniques. Alternatively, less rigorous correctness arguments may be presented which are based on mathematical verification but which are elaborated in an informal way. This latter approach is successfully used in the Cleanroom experiment.

It might be thought that the more rigorous the mathematical demonstration of correctness, the lower the probability of error in the program would be. This is not necessarily the case. A reasonable assumption is that the number of errors in a symbolic text is proportional to the number of symbols in that text. Thus, the larger a program (or a proof), the more errors it will contain. Informal arguments are much shorter than formal proofs so are less likely themselves to contain errors.

A rigorous, formal discussion of program verification requires a book, such as that by McGettrick (1983), to itself and cannot be effectively summarized here. Rather, less rigorous correctness arguments are exemplified using two small examples. The first of these is an Ada function which determines the maximum value in an array, and the second example is the well-known binary search algorithm.

Example 22.1
Specification for function
Max_value.

```
generic
      type ELEM is private ; type ELEM_INDEX is range <> ;
      type ELEM_ARRAY is array (ELEM_INDEX) of ELEM ;
      with function ">" (A, B: ELEM) return BOOLEAN is <> ;
function Max_value (X: ELEM_ARRAY) return ELEM ;
-- FIRST and LAST are predefined attributes giving the lower and
-- the upper bounds of the array respectively
--| Pre: X'LAST - X'FIRST >= 0 and
--|          for_all i in {X'FIRST..X'LAST}, Initialized (X(i))
--| Post: for_all i in {X'FIRST..X'LAST}, Max_value (X) >= X (i) and
--|          exists j in {X'FIRST..X'LAST}, Max_value (X) = X (j)
```

The convention used in these examples is to set out the function specification where the function signature (its parameters and their types) and pre- and post-conditions are defined. The pre-condition is a predicate which must be true for the function to execute correctly and the post-condition is a predicate which holds after function execution. The combination of pre- and post-conditions specifies the operation of the function. The value returned by the function is referenced in the post-condition by using the function name.

A mnemonic notation is used in the examples. The existential quantifier ($\exists$) is replaced by a mnemonic **exists**. The universal quantifier ($\forall$) is replaced by the mnemonic **for_all**. The membership operator ($\in$) is replaced by the keyword **in** and this may be applied to arrays as well as to sets.

Slices of an array may be specified, as in Ada, by writing their upper and lower bounds. For example, A (3..6) specifies the part of the array which includes elements indexed from 3 to 6 inclusive. Pre-conditions and post-conditions are distinguished by appropriate keywords and names may be given to predicates using a define declaration.

The specification of a function to find the maximum value in an array is shown in Example 22.1. This sets our pre- and post-conditions for the function Max_value. The body of function Max_value is shown as Example 22.2. Assertions are written as special comments introduced by the symbol --|.

The pre-condition states that the function will only work properly when the array has one or more elements and these elements have been assigned values. The predicate Initialized is true if an entity has been assigned a value.

The post-condition states that the value returned by Max_value is greater than or equal to the values of all members of the array X. It also states that this value is equal to a value of an array element. This is

Example 22.2
Maximum function
annotated with assertions.

```
function Max_value (X: ELEM_ARRAY) return ELEM is
--|    Pre: X'LAST − X'FIRST >= 0 and
--|            for_all i in {X'FIRST..X'LAST}, Initialized (X(i))
        Max : ELEM := X (X'FIRST) ;
        Index: ELEM_INDEX := X'FIRST ;
begin
-- loop invariant
--|1.  Is_largest (X ( X'FIRST..Index), Max) and
--|            Has_member (X ( X'FIRST..Index), Max)
while Index < X'LAST loop
        Index := Index + 1 ;
        --|2.  Is_largest (X ( X'FIRST..Index), Max) and
        --|            Has_member (X ( X'FIRST..Index), Max)
        --|or
        --|   X (Index) > Max and
        --|            Has_member (X(X'FIRST..Index), Max)
        if X (Index) > Max then
        --|3.  X (Index) > Max and
        --|            Has_member (X(X'FIRST..Index), Max)
            Max := X (Index) ;
        --|4.  Is_largest (X ( X'FIRST..Index), Max) and
        --|        Has_member (X ( X'FIRST..Index), Max)
        end if ;
end loop;
--|5.        Is_largest (X ( X'FIRST..Index), Max) and
--|            Has_member (X ( X'FIRST..Index), Max)
        return (Max) ;
--| Post:   for_all i in {X'FIRST..X'LAST}, Max_value (X) >= X (i) and
--|            exists j in {X'FIRST..X'LAST}, Max_value (X) = X (j)
end Max_value ;
```

necessary as some large value which is not in the array might satisfy the first part of the post-condition.

To make the assertions used in the function more readable, predicates may be named and parameterized. The first of these, Has_member, specifies that an entity must have the same value as an element of an array. The second predicate, Is_largest, specifies that the value of an entity must be greater than or equal to all of the values in an array.

```
--| define Has_member (X: ELEM_ARRAY, V: ELEM) is
--|    exists j in {X'FIRST..X'LAST}, V = X (j)
--| define Is_largest (X:ELEM_ARRAY ; V: ELEM) is
--|    for_all i in {X'FIRST..X'LAST}, V >= X (i) and
--|                    Has_member (X, V)
```

The advantage of defining names for predicates is that the assertions in a program become much easier to read. The code of the function Max_value and associated assertions is given as Example 22.2.

To demonstrate the correctness of this function, we must show that the function terminates and that the initial assertion plus the program inevitably leads to the final assertion. Termination can be established by showing, for each program loop, how the loop termination condition will inevitably be achieved.

Termination argument

The program contains a single while loop and will terminate if that loop terminates. The loop terminates when the value of Index equals or exceeds the value of X'LAST. Index is initially equal to X'FIRST which from the pre-condition we know is less than X'LAST. Index is increased by 1 during each loop execution. Given that X'LAST cannot be infinite, Index must eventually attain the value X'LAST and the loop must terminate.

Correctness argument

To prove that this design is correct, it must be shown that the output assertion follows from the input assertion and the program.

(1)   Assertion 1 is called a loop invariant and is an assertion which should hold for every loop execution. It must hold for every loop execution because a static analysis cannot reveal how many times the loop will be executed. The invariant here states that *for the portion of the array X which has been examined*, the value of Max exceeds or is equal to the value of all array elements and the value of Max equals the value of at least one of these elements. Initially, it is tri-
vially true as the portion of the array under consideration has only one element (X'FIRST) and the variable Max has been assigned this value.

(2)   The value of the counter Index is increased by 1, thus referencing the next array element. If the array element referenced is less than Max, the previous condition holds. If it is greater than Max, the second part of the assertion holds.

(3)   The **if** statement selects the case where the array element is greater than Max. This is reflected in Assertion 3.

(4)   The assignment of the array element value to Max means that Max is now greater than or equal to all array values examined and is equal to an array element. The loop invariant therefore always holds at the end of the loop and thus for all loop executions and loop termination.

(5) When the loop terminates, the loop invariant which states that Max is greater than or equal to a value in the portion of the array which has been examined holds and all elements of the array have been examined. Thus, Max must be equal to the largest value in the array. The function returns the value of Max so the function post-condition which refers to the value of the function holds.

This correctness argument demonstrates that even informal verification of a simple program is lengthy. The detail required in a proof is one of the factors which militate against the widespread use of program proving as a verification technique. As proofs may be longer than programs, it is at least feasible that the proof will contain as many errors as the program being verified.

As a further illustration of verification, consider a binary search routine. Its specification is given in Example 22.3 and its code in Example 22.4. Assertions have been included as commentary in the program. The pre-condition states that the upper bound of the array is greater than the lower bound, that the array T is ordered and that the lower and the upper bound of the array are both non-negative. The predicate Ordered may be defined as follows:

```
--| define Ordered (T: ELEM_ARRAY) is
--|    for_all i, T'FIRST >= i <= T'LAST-1, T (i) <= T (i + 1)
```

The post-condition states that either the boolean variable Found is set true and the value of L indexes an element of the array T equal to Key or that Found is false and there is no value in the array T which is equal to Key. This latter condition is stated by writing down that there does not exist a value i which is a valid array index such that T(i) is equal to Key. It is important to return both a boolean and an integer result as the value of L is undefined if Found is false.

Example 22.3
Specification of a binary search procedure.

```
generic
    type ELEM is private ; type ELEM_INDEX is range <> ;
    type ELEM_ARRAY is array (ELEM_INDEX) of ELEM ;
    with function "<" (A, B: ELEM) return BOOLEAN is <> ;
procedure Binary_search (Key : ELEM ;T: ELEM_ARRAY;
        Found : in out BOOLEAN; L: in out ELEM_INDEX) ;
--| Pre: T'LAST - T'FIRST > 0 and Ordered (T) and T'FIRST >= 0
--| Post: ( Found and T (L) = Key) or ( not Found
--| and not (exists i, T'FIRST >= i <= T'LAST, T (i) = Key ))
```

Example 22.4
An annotated binary
search procedure.

```
procedure Binary_search (Key: ELEM ; T: ELEM_ARRAY ;
        Found: in out BOOLEAN ; L: in out ELEM_INDEX ) is
--| Pre: T'LAST − T'FIRST > 0 and Ordered (T) and T'FIRST >= 0
    Bott : ELEM_INDEX := T'FIRST;
    Top : ELEM_INDEX := T'LAST ;
    Mid : ELEM_INDEX;
begin
    L := ( T'FIRST + T'LAST ) mod 2;
    Found := T( L ) = Key;
    -- loop invariant
    --|1. Found and T(L) = Key or
    --|     not Found and not Key in
    --|            T(T'FIRST..Bott−1, Top+1..T'LAST)
    while Bott <= Top and not Found loop
        Mid := (Top + Bott) mod 2;
        if T( Mid ) = Key then
            Found := true;
            L := Mid;
            --| 2. Key = T(Mid) and Found
        elsif T( Mid ) < Key then
            --| 3. not Key in T(T'FIRST..Mid)
            Bott := Mid + 1;
            --| 4. not Key in T(T'FIRST..Bott-1)
        else
            --| 5. not Key in T( Mid..T'LAST )
            Top := Mid - 1;
            --| 6. not Key in T(Top+1..T'LAST)
        end if;
    end loop;
--| Post: Found and T (L) = Key or ( not Found
--|    and not (exists i, T'FIRST >= i <= T'LAST, T (i) = Key ))
end Binary_search;
```

Recall that the earlier discussion of specification required changes to
input parameters to be specified. As this routine is written in Ada and the
language rules state that parameters passed by value cannot be modified,
this is unnecessary. We also ignore the circumstances where the procedure
is presented with input which does not match the precondition. The
keyword **in** used in the assertions in Example 22.4 means array membership. Thus, A **in** B where B is an array means that at least one of the
elements of B has a value matching that of A.

Termination argument

The program contains a single while loop which terminates when Found becomes true or when Bott becomes greater than Top. If the search succeeds, that is, if an element equal to the key exists, Found is explicitly set true; thus the loop will terminate.

The condition Bott <= Top implies that (Top − Bott) >= 0. Thus, if it can be demonstrated that (Top−Bott) < 0, loop termination is guaranteed. If an element matching Key is not found during an execution of the loop, either the statement Bott := Mid + 1 or the statement Top := Mid −1 must be executed. We know from the meaning of the mod operation that the value of Mid is less than Top and greater than or equal to Bott. The effect of assignments to Top or Bott is to reduce (Top − Bott). Eventually (Top − Bott) must become negative. The loop and thus the program terminates.

Correctness argument

Proving this design correct involves demonstrating that the final assertion follows from the initial assertion.

(1)　Assertion 1 is the loop invariant which specifies either that a value matching Key does not lie in the portion of the array already examined or that the value at the mid-point of the array matches Key. This is true on the first entry to the loop because none of the array has been examined so a value matching Key does not lie in the portion of the array examined.

(2)　Assertion 2 follows because of successful test, Key = Mid.

(3)　Assertion 3 follows from the fact that T is ordered and T(Mid) < Key. All values between T'FIRST and Mid must therefore be less than Key.

(4)　Assertion 4 follows by substituting Bott−1 for Mid.

(5)　Assertion 5 follows using a similar argument to 4 for values greater than Key. All values between Mid and T'LAST must be greater than Key.

(6)　Assertion 6 follows from 5 by substituting Top−1 for Mid.

(7)　At the end of a loop execution, it follows from the loop invariant that T(L) = Key and Found is true or, alternatively, Found is false and there is no value in the part of the table searched so far that equals key. On termination Bott is greater than Top so the expression T(T'FIRST..Bott−1, Top+1..T'LAST) includes the entire array. There is no value in T = Key. Therefore, the binary search program is correct.

Authors such as Macro and Buxton (1986) do not consider program proving to be a cost-effective software engineering technique. On the other hand, reports of work at IBM's Federal Systems division (Mills *et al.*, 1987) suggest that they make successful use of verification techniques in the development of large programming systems. They suggest that the effort to develop informal demonstrations of correctness is less than the effort required to verify a program by testing.

22.2.1 Automated verification tools

The notion of a mathematically formal verification of correctness of a program is an attractive one but the amount of work involved in this task means that it is probably not a cost-effective validation technique for large software systems. However, some efforts have been made to develop software tools to reduce this effort. An excellent summary of available systems is given by Lindsay (1988). The state of the art now is that completely automated program verifiers have not been developed but that current theorem provers can provide assistance in developing a proof and can help check proofs which have been developed.

Other tool developments in this area, include notations such as Anna (Luckham and Von Henke, 1985), have introduced the interesting idea of self-checking code where verification tool activation and program execution are integrated. The programmer includes verification information with his or her program and, during execution, this is automatically checked (Figure 22.4). If the verification tool signals a potential inconsistency, program execution may be suspended or some other exception handling mechanism activated.

Tools to support formal verification are not yet mature enough to be available as products and much research is still required in this area. Formal verification will not become common until tool support is available although informal correctness arguments will be used increasingly as formal specifications are developed. This suggests, perhaps, that investment should be made in tool support for this technique.

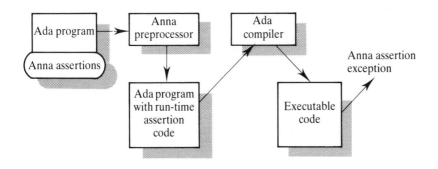

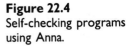

Figure 22.4
Self-checking programs using Anna.

22.3 Static program analysers

Static program analysers are software tools which scan the source text of a program and detect possible faults and anomalies. They do not require the program to be executed. They may be used as part of the verification process to complement the error detection facilities provided by the language compiler.

Static analysers are perhaps most useful when programming languages such as FORTRAN, which do not allow much compile time checking, are used. The analyser takes over much of the checking which would be carried out by the compiler in a stricter language like Pascal or Ada. For example, an installation may have a rule that all variable names used in a FORTRAN program must be declared and that the default conventions of the language are not to be used. A static analyser can scan a program and mark undeclared variables in the same way as a Pascal compiler can detect undeclared names.

As well as syntax checking, a static analyser can also check that no parts of the program are unreachable because goto statements always branch around a section of code. This situation arises when a program with goto statements is modified and a previously used code section is no longer executed (Figure 22.5). The programmer may think it safest to leave the code section in the program as some other (unknown) code may branch to it but, if there are no branches to that code, this can be detected by the analyser program. This indicates either that a program branch is incorrect or that the redundant code can be removed.

Static analysis can check for variable initializations by flagging instances where a variable name is used on the left side of an assignment before it has been given a value on the right side of an assignment. The analyser can highlight subprogram calls where the number of actual

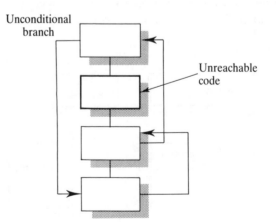

Unconditional branch

Unreachable code

Figure 22.5
Unreachable code.

> Unreachable code
> Unconditional branches into loops
> Undeclared variables
> Parameter type mismatches
> Parameter number mismatches
> Uncalled functions and procedures
> Variables used before initialization
> Non-usage of function results
> Possible array bound violations
> Misuse of pointers

Figure 22.6
Static analysis checks.

parameters differs from the number of formal parameters. A summary of the checks which static analysers can make is given in Figure 22.6.

A number of static analysers such as DAVE (Osterweil and Fosdick, 1976), AUDIT (Culpepper, 1975) and FACES (Ramamoorthy and Ho, 1975) have been developed for use with FORTRAN programs. These analysers all detect anomalies and inconsistencies which normally cause errors. These tools check subroutine interfaces to ensure that the number and types of subroutine parameters are consistent with the routine declaration, and locate COMMON block errors and flag error-prone practices such as branching into a DO-loop. FORTRAN-based static analysers are particularly useful because FORTRAN compilers do not do much program checking.

Static analysers are not just useful with FORTRAN. A program called LINT (Ritchie *et al.*, 1978) has been developed for use with C programs and its authors claim that use of LINT provides static checking equivalent to that provided by the compiler in a language such as ALGOL 68. Thus the reliability advantages of a strictly typed language are combined with the ability to generate efficient code using a systems implementation language. Unfortunately, many C programmers don't always use LINT to check their programs before execution and hence spend time in unnecessary debugging.

An example of the output produced by LINT is shown in Example 22.5. This is a transcript of a UNIX terminal session where commands are shown in italics. The first command lists the program which is complete nonsense. It defines a function with one parameter called printarray then causes this function to be called with three parameters. Variables i and c are declared but never assigned values. The value returned by the function is never used.

The line numbered 139 shows the C compilation of this program with no errors reported by the C compiler. This is followed by a call of the

Example 22.5
LINT static analysis.

```
138% more lint_ex.c
#include <stdio.h>
printarray (Anarray)
    int Anarray;
{
    printf("%d",Anarray);
}
main ()
{
    int Anarray[5]; int i; char c;
    printarray (Anarray, i, c);
    printarray (Anarray) ;
}
139% cc lint_ex.c
140% lint lint_ex.c
lint_ex.c(10): warning: c may be used before set
lint_ex.c(10): warning: i may be used before set
printarray: variable # of args. lint_ex.c(4) :: lint_ex.c(10)
printarray, arg. 1 used inconsistently lint_ex.c(4) :: lint_ex.c(10)
printarray, arg. 1 used inconsistently lint_ex.c(4) :: lint_ex.c(11)
printf returns value which is always ignored
```

LINT static analyser which detects and reports program errors. The static analyser points out that the scalar variables c and i have been used but not initialized and that printarray has been called with a different number of arguments than are declared. It also points out the inconsistent use of the first argument in printarray and the fact that the function value is never used.

Static analysers are useful tools which can take over some of the error checking functions of the program inspection process. However, they should not be considered as a substitute for inspections as there are a significant number of error types which they cannot detect. For example, they can detect uninitialized variables but they cannot detect initializations which are incorrect. They can detect (in a language like C) functions which have the wrong numbers and types of arguments but they cannot detect situations where an incorrect argument of the correct type has been correctly passed to a function.

KEY POINTS

- Static verification techniques involve examination and analysis of the program source code to detect errors. They complement program testing.

- Program inspections are effective in finding program errors. They involve a team of four people manually checking the program code. The aim of an inspection is to locate faults and the inspection process is often driven by a fault checklist.

- Cleanroom software development is an experimental approach which relies on static techniques for program verification. It has reportedly been successful in producing systems with a low percentage of errors.

- Mathematical program verification involves producing a mathematically rigorous argument that a program conforms to its specification. The misleading term 'proof of correctness' is sometimes used for this process.

- Verification is accomplished by setting out a program pre- and post-condition and demonstrating that the application of the program statements leads invariably from the pre- to the post-condition. It also involves showing that the program terminates.

- Program proofs are usually long and expensive to produce. Mathematical verification will only come into widespread use when support tools are available which reduce error-prone human effort.

- Static analysers are software tools which process a program source code looking for anomalies such as unused code sections and uninitialized variables.

Further reading

There are no single texts known to the author which are exclusively concerned with different approaches to static analysis. However, the following articles and book are readable introductions to their topics.

'Cleanroom software engineering'. This article describes the development technique used in IBM's Federal Systems Division which is based on program correctness arguments and statistical quality checks. (H.D. Mills, M. Dyer and R.Linger, *IEEE Software*, **4** (5), 1987.)

'A survey of mechanical support for formal reasoning'. This is an excellent survey of the state of the art in theorem proving systems as applied to the formal verification of programs. (P.A. Lindsay, *IEE/BCS Software Eng. J.*, **3** (1), 1988.)

Program Verification using Ada. This is a gentle introduction to formal program verification which is particularly suited to software engineers as it discusses verification in terms of a real, widely used, rather than in an invented programming language. (A.D. McGettrick, 1981, Cambridge University Press.)

'Advances in software inspections'. An article by the inventor of the notion of program inspections which sets out the excellent results which the inspection process has achieved. (M.E. Fagan, *IEEE Trans. Software Eng.*, **SE-12**, 7, 1986.)

References

Culpepper, L.M. (1975), 'A system for reliable engineering software', *IEEE Trans. Software Eng.*, **SE-1** (2), 174–8.

Dijkstra, E.W. (1976), *A Discipline of Programming*, Englewood Cliffs, NJ: Prentice-Hall.

Fagan, M.E. (1976), 'Design and code inspections to reduce errors in program development', *IBM Systems J.*, **15** (3), 182–211.

Fagan, M.E. (1986), 'Advances in software inspections', *IEEE Trans. Software Eng.*, **SE-12** (7), 744–51.

Floyd, R.W. (1967), 'Assigning meanings to programs', *Proc. Symposium in Applied Maths.*, 19–32.

Hoare, C.A.R. (1969), 'An axiomatic basis for computer programming', *Comm. ACM*, **12** (10), 576–83.

Lindsay, P.A. (1988), 'A survey of mechanical support for formal reasoning', *IEE/BCS Software Eng. J.*, **3** (1), 3–27.

Linger, R.C., Mills, H.D. and Witt, B.I. (1979), *Structured Programming – Theory and Practice*, Reading, Mass.: Addison-Wesley.

Luckham, D. and Von Henke, F.W. (1985), 'An overview of Anna, a specification language for Ada', *IEEE Software*, **2** (2), 9–23.

Macro, A. and Buxton, J. (1986), *The Craft of Software Engineering*, Wokingham: Addison-Wesley.

Manna, Z. (1969), 'The correctness of programs', *J. Computer System Sci.*, **3**, 119–27.

McCarthy, J. (1962), 'Towards a mathematical science of computation', *IFIP 62*, 21–8. Amsterdam: North-Holland.

McGettrick, A.D. (1982), *Program Verification Using Ada*, Cambridge: Cambridge University Press.

Mills, H.D., Dyer, M. and Linger, R. (1987), 'Cleanroom software engineering', *IEEE Software*, **4** (5), 19–25.

Osterweil, L.J. and Fosdick, L.D. (1976), 'DAVE – a validation, error detection and documentation system for FORTRAN programs', *Software – Practice and Experience*, **6**, 473–86.

Ramamoorthy, C.V. and Ho, S.F. (1975), 'Testing large software with automated software evaluation systems', *IEEE Trans. Software Eng.*, **SE-1** (1), 46–58.

Ritchie, D.M., Johnson, S.C., Lesk, M.E. and Kernighan, B.W. (1978), 'The C programming language', *Bell Systems Tech. J.*, **57** (6), 1991–2020.

Selby, R.W., Basili, V.R. and Baker, F.T. (1987), 'Cleanroom software development: an empirical evaluation', *IEEE Trans. Software Eng.*, **SE-13** (9), 1027–37.

EXERCISES

22.1 The technique of program inspections was derived in a large organization which had a plentiful supply of potential inspectors. Suggest how the method might be revised for use in a small programming group with no outside assistance.

22.2 Using your knowledge of Pascal, C or some other programming language, derive a checklist of common errors (not syntax errors) which could not be detected by a compiler but which might be detected in a program inspection.

22.3 Write a set of routines to implement an abstract data type called SYMBOL_TABLE which could be used as part of a compilation system. Organize a program inspection of your routines and keep a careful account of the errors discovered. Test the routines using a black-box approach and compare errors which are revealed by testing with those discovered by inspection.

22.4 Modify the routine in Example 22.1 (Max_value) so that it sums the elements of the array and returns the value of that sum. Modify the correctness arguments accordingly.

22.5 Write and produce correctness arguments for the following routines:

- A linear search routine
- A routine that sorts an array of integers using bubblesort
- A routine that finds the greatest common divisor of two integers
- A routine that inserts an element into an ordered list

22.6 Examine the literature and write a management report outlining the state of the art in automated verification tools.

22.7 If you have access to a UNIX system, process some C source code using the LINT static analyser. Modify the code so that the anomalies revealed by LINT are removed.

22.8 Produce a list of conditions which could be detected by a static analyser for Pascal or Ada.

Chapter 23

Testing and Debugging Tools

Objectives

This chapter describes the capabilities of a number of types of tool which are of use during the testing and debugging process. Testing and debugging tools are now widely available and play an important role in testing high-level language programs. Their effective use reduces the cost of testing and debugging activities. The particular classes of tool discussed here include test data generators, dynamic analysers, file comparators, simulators, symbolic dump programs, tracing tools and debugging environments.

Contents

It has always been recognized that testing is an expensive and laborious phase of the software process. This has had the result that testing and debugging tools were among the first software tools to be developed. They now, perhaps, offer the most sophisticated range of facilities of any software tools and their use reduces the cost of the testing and debugging process.

It is inherent in the nature of many testing and debugging tools that they are programming language dependent. For example, a dynamic analyser depends on a compiler instrumenting a program and, the more mature a language system, the better are the available testing and debugging tools. Unfortunately, this means that when a new language is introduced it takes some years before good support tools become available. Thus, we now have good testing and debugging tools for Pascal and C but only a few of the Ada compilers available at the time of writing have adequate testing and debugging support.

23.1   Test data generators

Test data generators are programs which automatically generate a large number of test inputs for some system. Unfortunately, it is not possible for test data generators to produce the corresponding outputs. If they could, they would be equivalent to the program under test.

Test data generators are most useful in situations where the performance of a system in a practical environment must be tested. For example, the testing of a database management system may start by using very small databases. That testing is initially designed to detect program errors resulting in incorrect output being produced. This small-scale testing does not actually reflect the actual environment where the program is to be used. It would normally operate using very large databases. Given the specification of a database, a test case generator can generate large amounts of data so that the performance of the system may be tested in a realistic environment.

Another instance where test data generators can be useful is that situation where the syntax of the input to and output from an application program can be specified in a formal way. Given an input specification, the test data generator can produce a large volume of input data which is presented to the system under test. The output of the generator is input to a syntax checker. If errors are found, this may be due to errors in the program being tested.

An example of such a situation might be the testing of the syntax analysis phase of a compiler. The output from such a phase for a correct program may be simply whatever program was input. If an incorrect

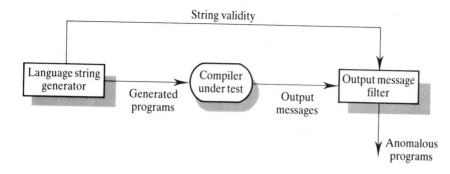

String validity

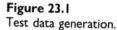

Anomalous
programs

Figure 23.1
Test data generation.

program is presented, the output also includes error indicators. A test data generator might accept a specification of the syntax of the language being compiled and from that generate correct and incorrect programs. The output from the compiler can be checked automatically (Figure 23.1) to ensure that error messages are not generated for correct programs and, conversely, error messages are generated for incorrect programs. Of course, it is still necessary to check the error messages manually to make sure that they are correct.

In Figure 23.1, the language generator generates both correct and incorrect programs and informs the message filter whether a program is correct or incorrect. The message filter analyses the compiler output and highlights those correct programs which cause error messages to be generated and vice versa.

23.2 Execution flow summarizers

Execution flow summarizers, such as that described by Satterthwaite (1972), are programs used to analyse how many times each statement in some other program has been executed. They are sometimes called dynamic analysers and have two fundamental parts:

(1) *An instrumentation part* This adds instrumentation statements to a program either while it is being compiled or before compilation. When the program is executed, these statements gather and collate information on how many times each program statement is executed.

(2) *A display part* This collects the information provided by the instrumentation statements and prints it in a form which can be understood by the reader. Typically, this produces a program listing where each line is annotated with the number of times that line has been executed.

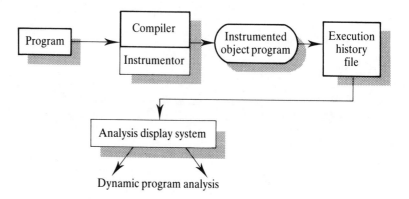

Figure 23.2
Dynamic analysis.

Dynamic program analysis

In order to instrument a program, all decision statements and loops must be identified and instrumentation code placed at the beginning of each loop and decision. A sequence of statements without loops or decisions need only have a single instrumentation section at the beginning of the sequence. Because the instrumentation phase needs knowledge of the language syntax, the easiest way to provide this facility is to build it into the compiler. The user may switch it on with a compiler directive. Alternatively this phase of the system may be implemented as a preprocessor which adds high-level language statements to collect information about the program execution. These are compiled by the standard compiler and flow information is output to a 'history' file (Figure 23.2). This history file is then input to the flow display program which associates the history information with the statements in the original program. Example 23.1 is an example of a typical flow summary. It was generated using the Pascal execution flow summarizer available under the Berkeley UNIX system.

Dynamic analysers reformat the program and number the reformatted statements. Each statement or statement sequence has an associated number indicating how many times that sequence has been executed. In Example 23.1, statement 15 has been executed 700 times and each branch of the if-then-else statement has been executed 350 times.

There are two principal uses of execution flow summarizers:

(1)   *To assist in program optimization*   Normally, programs spend most of their time in a few tight loops and the best way to optimize the program is to optimize these loops. The flow summarizer helps the engineer discover the loops in the program which are executed most often.

(2)   *To detect unexecuted program segments*   During testing, it is desirable to ensure that all program statements are executed at least once. Using a dynamic analyser, those parts of the program which are not executed can be discovered and test cases devised to ensure that the statements in these segments are tested.

Example 23.1
An execution flow
summary of a Pascal
program.

```
Berkeley Pascal PXP – – Version 2.12 (5/11/83)
Mon Oct 19 15:30 1987 pascflow.p
Profiled Mon Oct 19 15:38 1987
    1 1.– – –| program primes(input, output);
    {Prints all prime numbers between 3 and MAXPRIME.
    Uses Sieve of Eratosthenes method }
    6        | const
    6        |   MAXPRIME = 700;
    8        | type
    8        |   boolvec = array [1..MAXPRIME] of boolean;
   10        |var
   10        |   primes: boolvec;
   11        |   i, j, k: 1..MAXPRIME;
   13        |begin
   14        |   for i := 1 to MAXPRIME do
   15      700.– – –|   if odd(i) then
   16        350.– – –|   primes[i] := false
   16      350.– – –|   else
   18        350.– – –|   primes[i] := true;
   19        |   i := 3;
   20        |   k := trunc(sqrt(MAXPRIME));
   21        |   while i <= k do begin
   23        8.– – –|   j := i + i;
   23             |   while j <= MAXPRIME do begin
   26      688.– – –|   primes[j] := true;
   27             |   j := j + i
   27         |   end;
   29         |   j := i + 2;
   30         |   while primes[i] and (i <= k) do
   31        4.– – –|   i := i + 2
   31         |   end;
   33         |   i := 3;
   34         |   while i <= MAXPRIME do begin
   36      349.– – –|   if not primes[i] then
   37        123.– – –|   writeln(i, ' is prime');
   38         |   i := i + 2
   38         |   end
   38         |end.
```

Execution flow summarizers are useful tools but rely on all of the program source code being instrumented. This is not always possible if precompiled program components are used as it is normal to compile a component without such instrumentation once it has been completely validated. If a program includes library components, the dynamic flow analyser may not work properly and it may not be possible to abstract information about the program flow.

Another difficulty which sometimes inhibits the use of dynamic analysers is that the inclusion of code to collect program information affects the timing of that program. In real-time systems, timing is often critical and the timing overhead incurred by dynamic data collection is unacceptable. Real-time systems are among the most difficult to test and it is unfortunate that one of the most useful testing tools often cannot be used.

23.3   File comparators

A file comparator is a general-purpose software tool which reports differences between files. As testing involves the examination of large volumes of test output, it is not unusual for the reader to miss erroneous output. To avoid this, as much of the checking and comparison process as possible should be automated.

Automation involves preparing a file containing the output expected from a program if no errors are detected. The tests are then executed and the actual output directed to some other file. Both files may then be compared using a file comparator and differences in the files highlighted. If the expected output from the program and the actual output are the same, the tests failed to detect any errors.

Another situation where file comparators may be used is in checking that procedures and functions do not have unwanted side-effects which affect global program variables. A global dump may be taken before and after exercising a function. These dumps are then automatically compared. Notice that global dumping cannot be automated using an external tool but must be implemented using a specially written procedure.

Those globals which have been changed are then highlighted by the file comparison program. This is illustrated in Examples 23.2(a) and (b) which show the output produced by the UNIX file comparator **diff** after comparing dumps of globals used in a Pascal program. Example 23.2(a) shows the input files which are the same except for the change in value of Y from 17 to 18 and the change in name from 'J Smith' to 'F Jones'. Example 23.2(b) shows the output produced by the **diff** program.

Example 23.2(a)
Files to be compared.

X : integer = 20	X : integer = 20
Y : integer = 17	Y : integer = 18
Z : integer = 34	Z : integer = 34
name : chararray = 'J Smith'	name : chararray = 'F Jones'
(a)	(b)

Example 23.2(b)
diff output.

```
diff Ex23.2aa Ex23.2ab
2c2
< Y : integer = 17
– – –
> Y : integer = 18
4c4
< name : chararray = 'J Smith'
– – –
> name : chararray = 'F Jones'
```

The use of file comparators is particularly helpful when many tests are submitted to a program at once. Generally, only some of these tests will succeed and a file comparison program can detect these successful tests and bring them to the attention of the tester.

File comparators may be completely general purpose, comparing any two files character by character for equality. Alternatively, such programs can be constructed for a specific application and information about the structure of the test output built into the program.

General-purpose comparators are most useful when the expected output from a program can be compared with other program-generated data. A typical situation where this arises is in regression testing (Figure 23.3) where a modified program is tested to ensure that the changes have

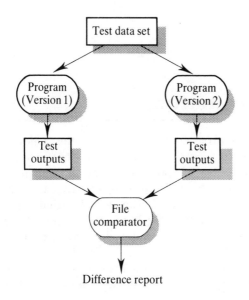

Figure 23.3
Regression testing.

not affected existing program functions. The steps involved in regression testing are:

(1)   Prepare a general-purpose set of test cases.

(2)   Exercise the existing program version with these test cases and save the results in one or more files.

(3)   Make program modifications.

(4)   Exercise the modified program with the existing set of test cases and save the results in one or more files.

(5)   Automatically compare the files produced by the modified and unmodified program versions.

If the modifications have been made correctly, the file comparison will show the output files to be identical. Of course, it may be that the modifications were intended to affect existing functions in which case some of the output will clearly be different. However, it should be possible to predict which files have changed and use the file comparator to check that the changes are as predicted.

General-purpose comparison programs are less useful when the expected output file is manually input. A trivial input error such as the input of an extra blank which does not affect the meaning will cause a character-by-character file comparison to fail. In such cases, it is necessary to build special-purpose file comparison programs which have some embedded knowledge of the syntax of the outputs which they are comparing. Thus, spurious separators can be ignored by the program and the comparison made correctly.

23.4   Simulators

A simulator is a program which imitates the actions of some other program, hardware device, or class of devices. They are particularly important in the testing of real-time programs. They provide a way for a sequence of events to be repeated exactly, thus allowing timing-dependent errors to be detected. They are also used to simulate hardware facilities in situations where the hardware is unavailable or where it is possible that faulty software could damage the interfaced hardware system (Figure 23.4).

There are advantages and disadvantages in using a simulator in place of real hardware. Apart from the obvious advantage that software faults

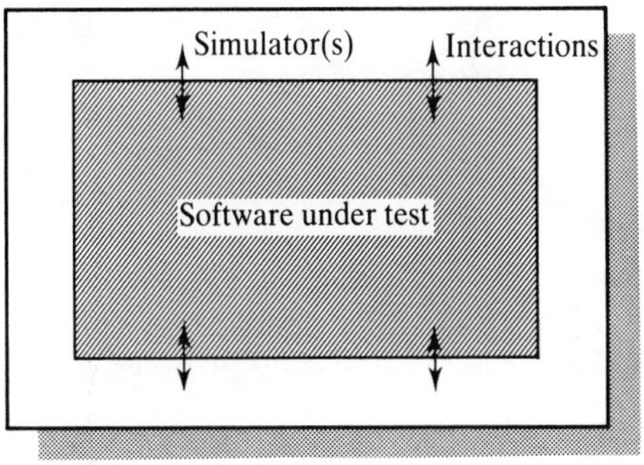

Figure 23.4
Simulators in system
testing.

cannot cause hardware damage, the other advantage is that it is usually easy to instrument the simulator and thus gather information about the combined hardware/software system. The main disadvantage is that the simulator is very much slower than the hardware it is imitating. Thus, it is not possible to test functions properly which are dependent on the hardware timing although some mapping of simulator to real-time may be possible.

In some cases, simulation is by far the only way to mimic the events that a real-time system must process. For example, if a program is used for controlling a nuclear reactor that program must obviously be able to deal with failure of the reactor cooling system. This failure will normally be signalled by sensor inputs indicating a rise in temperature, drop in pressure, etc. Obviously, this cannot be tested operationally so it is necessary to simulate these sensor inputs using some other program. The reactions of the reactor control program to these inputs may then be observed.

The ability of simulators to reproduce sequences of events exactly is particularly important. Consider a situation where a system is accepting input from many sensors and a system failure occurs (Figure 23.5). Each sensor presents different information and the failure may be due to a particular information combination being processed simultaneously or may be due to some historical event sequence which has caused corruption of information. If the system is tested using real sensors interfaced to a changing environment it is impossible to reproduce the exact information and timing from each sensor. However, if a simulator is used, this can be driven by a prepared script. The exact sequence of inputs and their timings can be repeated (Figure 23.6).

As well as providing repeatable inputs, simulators also allow the system to be tested under load. If a system is required to support a number of terminals with some average response time, a terminal simulator can be set up to imitate these terminals. The simulator can then measure the system response using different combinations of input to ensure that the average response is that required.

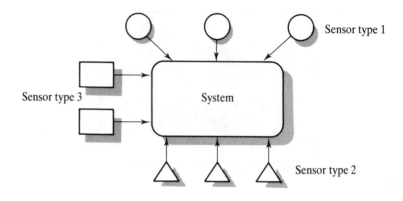

Figure 23.5
A real-time system with
multiple inputs.

When imitating terminal inputs, the relatively slow simulator speed is not usually a problem as humans inputting information will typically work much more slowly than any simulator. Thus, in this case, the actual timings of the system can be observed.

The UNIX/PWB system, a UNIX-based programming environment, provides a general purpose terminal simulator called LEAP (Dolotta *et al.*, 1978). This simulator is designed to run on the host machine and to test programs running on some target connected to that machine. High-level languages have been developed for use with LEAP which allow the actions of terminal-operator pairs to be simulated.

Running the terminal simulator and the program under test on different computers ensures that timings are not affected by interactions between the simulator and the program under test. If the machines are connected by a high-speed LAN, the communication time between the systems is not significant and will not perturb the simulator timings.

23.5   Symbolic dump programs

Debugging tools that rely on the user manipulating store addresses are of little use to the high-level language programmer. When using a high-level language the programmer needs a debugging tool which relates the names of the objects used in a program to their values. A symbolic dump program is such a tool.

Symbolic dumps can be either interactive or batch, although the almost universal use of interactive systems for software development means that batch systems are used less and less. In the batch form the system lists the names of all program variables along with their values

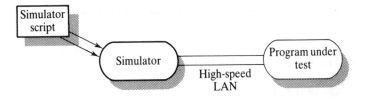

Figure 23.6
Script-driven simulation in
program testing.

either when the program terminates or at the specific inclusion of a
program directive. Such a system saves the programmer including explicit
output statements to trace the values of his variables.

A properly designed symbolic dump will not only generate
information about global variables but will also present information about
local variable values in all activated procedures. It should associate the
name of the appropriate procedure with the variable name in order to
avoid confusion where variables of the same name are used in different
procedures.

Modern dump programs usually provide an interactive program for
analysing the symbolic information. This allows the user to request the
value of individual variables by name so that only relevant values can be
examined. Again, local variables should be accessible by specifying the
procedure name followed by the variable name.

An example of an interactive symbolic dump system is included in
the Pascal debugging package **pdx**, available under Berkeley UNIX. In
combination with a Pascal interpreter, this system allows the user to
request the values of variables, to set breakpoints in his or her code, to find
out the types of variables, to find out where variables are used, etc.

Interactive tools of this kind are most useful if they allow users to
scan the dump information in a number of ways. They should be allowed to
specify conditions relating to object values and all name/value pairs
satisfying these conditions should be printed. It should also be possible to
display structures involving pointers in some readable way, perhaps by
drawing these structures and their links. Many program errors are the
result of misdirected pointers and a facility to detect these is invaluable.
This graphical display facility is difficult to implement and very few systems
which include pointer display have been built. One such experimental
system for Pascal is described by Getz *et al.* (1983).

23.6 Trace packages

Symbolic dump systems allow the user to examine values once the program
has terminated but they do not provide information about the dynamic
execution of the program. Program trace packages provide such

Example 23.3
Trace package output.

```
> initially (at line 14): i = 0
initially (at line 14): j = 0
trace: 14 for i := 1 to MAXPRIME do
after line 14: i = 36
trace: 19 i := 3;
after line 19: i = 3
trace: 20 k := 6;
trace: 21 while i <= k do
after line 21: i = 7
after line 21: j = 40
trace: 33 i := 3;
after line 33: i = 3
trace: 34 while i <= MAXPRIME do
after line 34: i = 37
execution completed
```

information, printing information about procedure entry and exit, transfers of control, branch selection in if statements, etc.

Early trace packages produced all of this information and generated a huge amount of data, which had to be manually examined. More sophisticated systems are now equipped with a number of options and switches, which provide the user with much finer control over what program information is traced. It is possible to set up the trace package simply to print the values of particular variables when they are changed, to print procedure parameter values when a procedure is called, and to print values on entry to and on exit from a loop.

Some of the output produced by the trace package built into the Pascal programming debugging system available under Berkeley UNIX is shown in Example 23.3. The program traced is a modified version of the prime numbers program (Example 23.1). The modification made is to print only the prime numbers to 36. Otherwise, more output than is necessary would be produced for this illustration.

The Pascal debugging system allows high-precision tracing to be specified so that the volume of output can be controlled. Trace options in this system include tracing the value of variables, line number tracing, expression value tracing, procedure call tracing, etc. In Example 23.3, the trace system has been set up to print the values of i and j each time they are changed in the program.

Trace packages involve instrumenting the program automatically so that the relevant information can be collected. This instrumentation obviously involves overhead both in terms of space and speed. Thus, tracing affects that timing of systems. In testing real-time systems, where tracing might be particularly useful, tracing may be impossible because of the degradation to system timing.

23.7   Interactive debugging environments

The most sophisticated debugging tools are systems which give the programmer the impression that he or she can interact with a program while it is executing and can display variable values, reverse execution sequences and so on. In essence, they are an integrated, interactive version of all of the debugging tools which have been discussed in this chapter.

Such systems may operate by executing the program and constructing a 'history' file recording all program state changes. They provide facilities for interrogating this history file in program terms. The user can watch control flow and/or data flow in the program as each statement executes and the statement causing the error can then be detected.

The Cornell Program Synthesizer (Teitelbaum and Reps, 1981) which integrates the preparation, translation and execution of programs written in a subset of PL/1 has provided an interactive execution/debugging environment for programs. In the Cornell Program Synthesizer, the execution of the user's program is controlled by an interpreter and, as particular statements in the program are executed, they are picked out by the cursor on the user's terminal.

Because of the interpretive nature of the system, the user can 'single-step' the program executing statements one by one until a previously observed error manifests itself. Should the user overshoot, the Cornell Program Synthesizer also provides a 'reverse gear' facility which allows backwards execution of the program. The user can thus quickly converge on the statement in error.

Debugging systems which allow the programmer to reverse execution sequences consume a great deal of resources and are not widely available. However, somewhat less sophisticated yet still very powerful debugging environments such as dbxtool for debugging C programs on a Sun workstation are now widely used. The screen window used by dbxtool is shown in Figure 23.7. The display is split into a number of subwindows. The top window, under the title bar, provides information about the file in which the displayed program is stored (text1.c), the function where execution has stopped (init), the line where execution has stopped (25) and the numbers of the lines which are on display (19–38).

The largest window in the display is the program display window. Several lines of the program are shown, with the arrow indicating the current execution point.

The menu window below the program display provides a number of buttons. Picking one of these buttons causes a debugger command to be executed. The user may single-step through the program, set breakpoints, move through the program, execute it and so on.

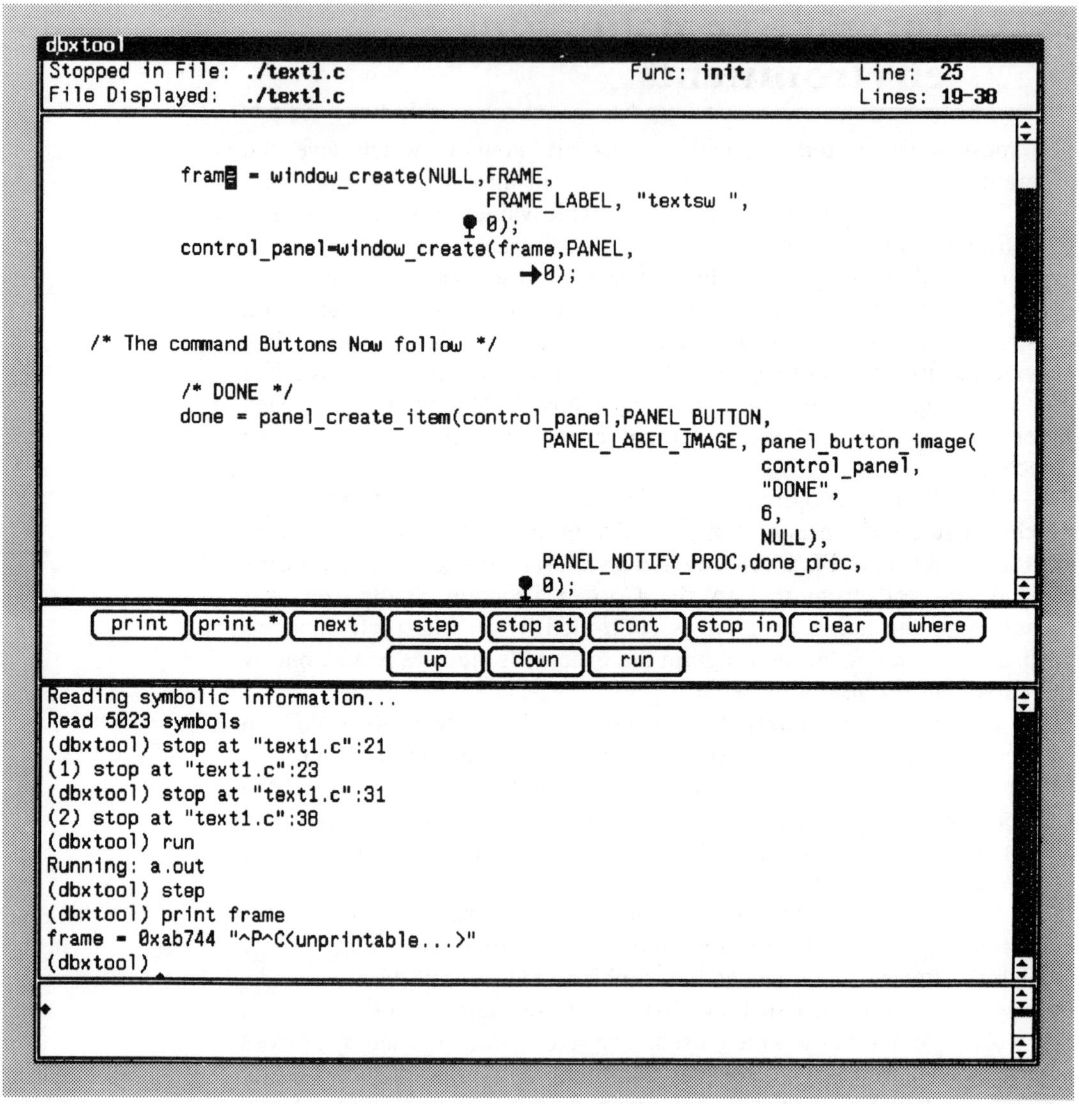

```
dbxtool
Stopped in File:   ./text1.c                              Func: init        Line:   25
File Displayed:    ./text1.c                                                 Lines: 19-38


            frame = window_create(NULL,FRAME,
                                        FRAME_LABEL, "textsw ",
                                  ♥ 0);
            control_panel=window_create(frame,PANEL,
                                  →0);


    /* The command Buttons Now follow */

            /* DONE */
            done = panel_create_item(control_panel,PANEL_BUTTON,
                                     PANEL_LABEL_IMAGE, panel_button_image(
                                                        control_panel,
                                                        "DONE",
                                                        6,
                                                        NULL),
                                     PANEL_NOTIFY_PROC,done_proc,
                                  ♥ 0);
```

```
( print )( print * )( next )( step )( stop at )( cont )( stop in )( clear )( where )
                      ( up )( down )( run )
```

```
Reading symbolic information...
Read 5023 symbols
(dbxtool) stop at "text1.c":21
(1) stop at "text1.c":23
(dbxtool) stop at "text1.c":31
(2) stop at "text1.c":38
(dbxtool) run
Running: a.out
(dbxtool) step
(dbxtool) print frame
frame = 0xab744 "^P^C<unprintable...>"
(dbxtool)
```

Figure 23.7
dbxtool display.

The bottom window is the dbxtool interaction window where messages from the program and some user inputs are displayed. The range of possible commands far exceeds those set out in the menu display and users must type less commonly used commands in the interaction window.

Interactive debuggers such as dbxtool, used in a multi-window environment where the program and the debugging tool displays can both be seen at the same time, have changed the activity of debugging. Before the advent of such systems, programmers may have used a debugger to find out about the dynamic execution sequence but had to view the program text via a listing. Edits had to be marked on this and entered later, the program executed and the debugger again used to view the output.

Now, the whole debug–edit–compile–execute cycle has been speeded up significantly and overall programmer productivity is markedly improved when interactive debugging systems are available.

KEY POINTS

- The use of testing and debugging tools reduces the costs of program verification and validation.
- Execution flow summarizers or dynamic analysers instrument the program then output a listing of the program statements along with a count of how often these have been executed. This can be used to identify parts of the program for optimization (those loops which are executed most) and for identifying unexecuted program sections. Test cases can then be derived to exercise these sections.
- Simulators are essential in the testing of real-time systems. They may simulate unavailable hardware or they may be used in conjunction with a prepared script to simulate terminal or device inputs to a system. Their advantage is that their timing behaviour is always predictable.
- Various tools such as symbolic dump programs and trace packages are available which provide information about the execution history of a program. These can be combined in an interactive debugging system which allows the programmer to interact with the program as it is executing and examine program information.

Further reading

In spite of, or perhaps because of, their ubiquity, surprising little material has been published which is dedicated to the topic of testing and debugging tools. There are no modern papers which can be recommended for further reading. Rather, it is suggested that the reader actually uses such tools; they are available with many microcomputer implementations of languages like Pascal and C.

References

Dolotta, T.A., Haight, R.C. and Mashey, J.R. (1978), 'The Programmers Workbench', *Bell Systems Tech. J.*, **57** (6), 2177–200.

Getz, S.L., Kalliyiannis, G and Schach, S.R. (1983), 'A very high level interactive graphical trace for the Pascal heap', *IEEE Trans. Software Eng.*, **SE-9** (2).

Satterthwaite, E. (1972), 'Debugging tools for high level languages', *Software – Practice and Experience*, **2**, 197–217.

Teitelbaum, T. and Reps, T. (1981), 'The Cornell Program Synthesizer: a syntax-directed programming environment', *Comm. ACM*, **24** (9), 563–73.

EXERCISES

23.1 Describe how a dynamic analyser can be used in the structural testing of a program.

23.2 Apart from a compiler, describe situations where a test data generator which generated sentences in a formal language might be used in system testing.

23.3 What are the difficulties of using a dynamic analyser when developing large software systems which are made up of independently compiled routines?

23.4 Give examples of hardware simulators that might be required when testing real-time systems. Explain why system tests which are based on simulators are not always reliable.

23.5 Suggest other software tools which might be useful in assisting program testing. Consider specific application domains when making your suggestions.

Part 5

Software Management

Contents

Chapter 24

Software Management

Objective

The objective of this chapter is to introduce the activity of software management and to set the scene for the remainder of the chapters in this section. The introduction emphasizes the importance of management and the first section sets out typical management activities. This is followed by a discussion of management structures and programming team organizations. Programming productivity and the difficulties of defining what productivity means are covered in the final section in this chapter.

Contents

The failure of several large software projects in the 1960s and early 1970s brought the problems involved in software management to light. These projects did not fail because the project managers or programmers working on the project were incompetent. Indeed, the nature of these large projects was such that they attracted people of above average ability. The fault lay in the management techniques used. As these were the first really large programming projects, management techniques derived from small-scale development projects were used and this approach to project management proved to be inadequate. The delivered software was late, unreliable, cost several times the original estimates and often exhibited poor performance characteristics (Brooks, 1975).

The software manager is responsible for planning project development and overseeing the work, ensuring that it is carried out to the required standards, on time and within budget. Good management cannot guarantee project success but bad management or inadequate management support will probably result in software which is delivered late, exceeds cost estimates and which may be expensive to maintain.

There are a number of reasons why software project management is distinct from other types of engineering project management.

(1) *The product is intangible* The manager of a shipbuilding project or of a civil engineering project can see the product which is being developed. If a schedule slips it has an obvious effect on the product in that parts of the structure are obviously unfinished. Software is intangible. It cannot be seen or touched and the project manager is dependent on documentation to review the progress of the project.

(2) *We do not have a clear understanding of the software process* In engineering disciplines with a long history, the stages of development are well understood and predictable. In software engineering, this is not the case and models such as the life-cycle model, discussed in Chapter 25, are artificial process representations which are used to make software management possible.

(3) *Large software systems tend to be 'one-off' projects.* They are distinct from previous projects. Historical experience is of limited value in predicting how these projects should be managed.

Because of these problems, it is not surprising that software projects are often late, over-budget and behind schedule. Each large software system development is a new and technically innovative project and many engineering projects (such as new transport systems, bridges, etc.) which are innovative often also have schedule problems. Given the difficulties involved, it is perhaps remarkable that so many software projects are delivered on time and to budget!

24.1 Management activities

It is impossible to write a standard 'job description' for a software manager. The job varies tremendously depending on the organization involved in development and on the particular software product being developed. However, there are a number of activities which most managers are involved with at some stage in a project. These are:

- Proposal writing
- Project costing
- Project planning and scheduling
- Project monitoring and reviews
- Personnel selection and evaluation
- Report writing and presentations

In many organizations, the first stage in a software project involves writing a proposal to carry out that project. This applies whether or not the project is to be commissioned by some client, is specified by some other part of an organization or is an internal development. In each case, the proposal sets out an outline of the project work, cost and schedule estimates and a justification of why the project contract should be awarded to a particular organization or team.

It is often the case that it is the project manager who is responsible for writing this proposal, perhaps in conjunction with some senior technical staff. Proposal writing is a critical task as the prosperity or otherwise of many software organizations depends on them having a sufficient number of proposals accepted and contracts awarded. There can be no set guidelines for this task, and proposal writing is a skill which is acquired by experience. It is really part of an overall marketing activity and is outside the scope of this book. Aron (1983) includes a discussion of proposal writing which is recommended to interested readers.

Project planning and scheduling and project costing are probably the major management activities and are the subject of Chapters 25 and 26. They are not discussed further in this chapter.

Project monitoring is a continuing task throughout a project. The manager must keep track of the progress of the project and compare actual and planned progress and costs. Although most organizations have formal mechanisms for monitoring, it is often the case that a skilled manager can form a clear picture of what is going on by informal discussion with project staff. Indeed, such informal monitoring activities can often be used to predict potential project problems as they may reveal difficulties as they occur.

For example, daily discussions with project staff might reveal a particular problem in finding some software fault. Rather than waiting for a schedule slippage to be reported, the software manager might assign some expert to the problem or might decide that it should be programmed around.

In the course of a project, it is normal to have a number of formal project management reviews. These are not technical reviews in that they are not intended for fault finding or for making detailed technical decisions. Rather, they involve looking at the overall progress and technical development of the project and considering the project's status against the overall aims of the organization commissioning the project.

The development time for a large software project may be many years and during that time organizational objectives are likely to change. These changes may mean that the software is no longer required or that the original project requirements are inappropriate. Thus, the management review may decide to stop software development or to change the structure of the project in some radical way to accommodate the changes to the objectives of the organization.

The manager of a project usually has the responsibility of selecting personnel to work on that project. Clearly, the ideal is to have available staff who are talented and who have the appropriate experience to carry out the project but, in the majority of cases, this will be impossible. The reasons for this are:

(1)   The overall project budget may be such that it precludes the use of many highly paid staff and requires that less experienced, less well paid staff be utilized.

(2)   Staff with the appropriate experience may simply not be available either within an organization or externally. At the time of writing, there is an international shortage of software engineers and this is likely to continue until at least the end of the 20th century. It may be impossible to recruit new staff to the project given the existing project budget. Within an organization, the most appropriate staff may be required for work on other projects.

(3)   Long-term organizational goals for staff development and training may require staff without experience to gain that experience on the project.

Thus, the software manager must work within these constraints when selecting project staff. Again, it is not appropriate to discuss staff selection techniques in this book but a clear requirement is that at least one project member should have experience of developing comparable systems to that proposed. Without this experience, many simple mistakes are likely to be made. It is also important that appropriate provision is made for training other staff during the course of the project.

Although all members of a project team are likely to have some responsibility for producing documentation, the project manager is principally responsible for reporting on the project to both the client and contractor organizations. This means that he or she must be able to write concise, coherent documents which abstract the salient features from more detailed project reports. Furthermore, he or she must be able to present this information during progress reviews. Again, detailed discussion of this reporting is outside the scope of this book.

24.2   Software management structures

Traditional management structure is hierarchical with individuals at each level in the hierarchy reporting to the level above. Typically, a manager might be responsible for 12–25 subordinates. This hierarchical structure is retained to some extent in software management except that each software manager should handle only about six direct subordinates because of the complexity of the software projects under his or her control.

In a large organization undertaking a number of simultaneous software development projects, the software management structure might be as shown in Figure 24.1. This structure suggests that there should be an overall director or vice-president in charge of software development and that a number of programme managers should report to that director. Each

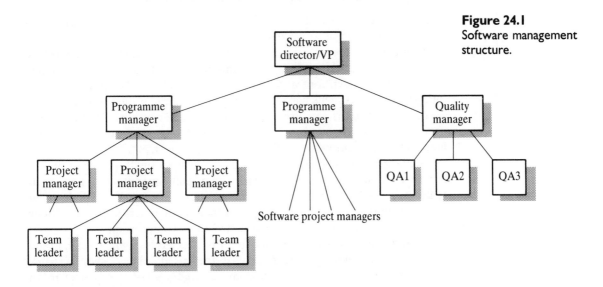

Figure 24.1
Software management structure.

programme manager is responsible for a particular area of development such as business systems development, avionics systems development, tools development, etc. Each individual development project has its own project manager reporting to the programme manager and within each project there may be a number of team leaders responsible for managing individual sub-projects.

Figure 24.1 shows the quality assurance function as distinct from individual project management. Quality assurance may have its own quality manager and a number of quality teams will report to that manager. These teams work in conjunction with individual projects but, to maintain their independence, do not report to the individual project manager. Quality assurance is discussed in Chapter 30.

It is an unfortunate characteristic of some software development organizations that technically skilled staff reach a career plateau fairly rapidly. To progress further, they must take on managerial responsibilities which are quite different from the technical skills which they have already exhibited. It certainly does not follow that skilled software engineers necessarily make the best software managers. Promotion of these people to managerial status means that useful technical skills are lost.

In order to avoid this loss of technical skills to a project, some organizations have developed parallel technical and managerial career structures which are of equal worth. As an individual's career develops, he or she may either specialize in technical or in managerial activities or may move between them without loss of status.

24.2.1 Programming team organizations

It is now generally accepted that software projects should not be tackled by a single large team of software engineers. As discussed in Chapter 2, large teams mean that the time spent in communication among team members is greater than the time spent programming. Furthermore, it is usually impossible to partition a software system into a large number of independent units. This has the result that, if a large programming team is used, program units are often arbitrary and have complex interfaces with each other. Consequently, the probability of interface error is high and additional verification and validation costs are incurred.

Programming team sizes should be relatively small. A rule of thumb is that a team should have not more than eight members. When small teams are used, communication problems are reduced. The whole team can get round a table for a meeting, can meet in members' offices and does not require complex communication structures to be set up.

If a project is so big that it cannot be tackled by a single team in the time allowed, multiple teams must be used. They should work independently with each team tackling a large part of the project in an autonomous way. The overall system design should be such that the interface between the parts of the project produced by the independent teams is well defined and as simple as possible.

As well as minimizing communication problems, small programming teams have a number of other benefits:

(1) *A team quality standard can be developed*   Because this is arrived at by consensus, it is more likely to be observed than arbitrary standards imposed on the team by software management.

(2) *Team members work closely together*   The team can learn from each other. Inhibitions caused by ignorance are minimized as mutual learning is encouraged.

(3) *Egoless programming can be practised*   Programs are regarded as team property rather than personal property.

(4) *Team members can get to know each other's work*   Continuity can be maintained should a team member leave.

Small programming teams are usually organized in an informal way. Although a titular team leader exists, he or she carries out the same tasks as other team members. Indeed, a technical team leader may emerge who effectively controls software production without having the title of team leader.

In an informal team, the work to be carried out is discussed by the team as a whole and the tasks are allocated to each member according to ability and experience. High-level system design is carried out by senior team members but low-level design is the responsibility of the member allocated a particular task.

Informal teams can be very successful, particularly where the majority of team members are experienced and competent. The team functions as a democratic team, making decisions by consensus. Psychologically, this improves team spirit with a resultant increase in cohesiveness and performance. On the other hand, if a team is composed mostly of inexperienced or incompetent members, the informality can be a hindrance. No definite authority exists to direct the work, causing a lack of coordination between team members and, possibly, eventual project failure.

A serious problem which sometimes arises is a lack of experienced team members. Often, teams tend to be composed of relatively inexperienced members because the career and reward structure of the organization is such that able and experienced team members are promoted to management positions. They are not directly involved in software development. This situation is exacerbated by distinctions made between so-called systems analysts and programmers where design and programming work are separated. Programmers are reduced to simple coders with the result that talented people strive to get out of programming as soon as possible.

In order to utilize the skills of experienced and competent programmers, these individuals should be given responsibility and rewards commensurate with what they would receive in a management position. A parallel technical career path should be established to achieve this without any implication that it is inferior to a management-oriented career path. The team organization discussed below is one way of achieving this.

24.2.2 Chief programmer teams

An alternative programming team organization to the informal democratic team was suggested by Baker (1972) and also described, in a slightly different form, by Brooks (1975) and Aron (1974). The development of this approach was motivated by a number of considerations:

(1) Projects tended to be staffed by relatively inexperienced people as discussed above.

(2) Much programming work is clerical in nature involving the management of a large amount of information.

(3) Multi-way communications are time consuming and hence reduce programmer productivity.

The chief programmer team is based on utilizing experienced and talented staff as chief programmers, providing clerical support for these programmers using both human and computer based procedures, and funnelling all communications through one or two individuals (Figure 24.2). The chief programmer team has been compared to a surgical team undertaking an operation. The ultimate responsibility in such a team rests with the surgeon but he or she is helped by skilled, specialized staff members such as an anesthetist, chief nurse, etc. who carry out particular roles.

The nucleus of a chief programmer team consists of the following members:

(1) A chief programmer who is experienced and highly qualified. He or she takes full responsibility for designing, programming, testing and installing the system under development.

(2) A backup programmer who is also skilled and experienced. He or she works with the chief programmer and should be able to adopt that role if necessary. The backup programmer's main function is to provide support by developing test cases and analyses to verify the work of the chief programmer.

(3) A librarian whose role is to assume all the clerical functions associated with a project. The librarian is assisted by an automated library system.

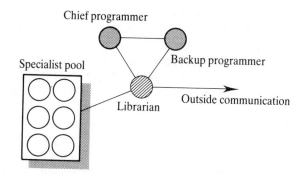

Figure 24.2
A chief programmer team.

Depending on the size and type of the application, other experts might be added temporarily or permanently to a team. These might include:

(1)   A project administrator who relieves the chief programmer of administrative tasks.

(2)   A toolsmith who is responsible for producing software tools to support the project.

(3)   A documentation editor who takes the project documentation written by the chief programmer and backup programmer and prepares it for publication.

(4)   A language/system expert who is familiar with the idiosyncrasies of the programming language and system which is being used and whose role is to advise the chief programmer on how to make use of these facilities.

(5)   A tester whose task is to develop objective test cases to validate the work of the chief programmer.

(6)   One or more support programmers who undertake coding from a design specified by the chief programmer. These support programmers are necessary when the scale of the project is such that detailed programming work cannot be carried out by the chief programmer and backup programmer alone.

The principal objective of using a chief programmer team is to improve productivity, and measurements by Baker (1972) and Walston and Felix (1977) suggest that a chief programmer team is approximately twice as productive as teams which are not organized in this way. However, it is not clear whether this improvement is a result of the team organization or whether it results simply from using better programmers who would be more productive in any case.

Shneiderman (1980) points out that there may be psychological problems in introducing chief programmer teams. These derive from the position of the chief programmer who is the kingpin of the project and, if the project is successful, takes the credit for this success. Other team members may feel that they have no definite function and be resentful of the status of the chief programmer.

Another problem is that the success of the project is dependent on one or two individuals working closely together. If they should fall ill at the same time (very common in winter) or if both should choose to leave, the project may have to be abandoned. No-one else in the team or the organization may be able to take over their role and maintain the project schedule.

Other political problems in using chief programmer teams are described by Yourdon (1979). In large organizations it may be impossible to fit the chief programmer team into the existing organizational structure and adequately reward the chief programmer. The introduction of chief programmer teams may entail the complete reorganization of existing staff and this might be resisted. It may be impossible to attract suitably qualified chief programmers to work in certain application areas.

In spite of these disadvantages, the basic premise underlying chief programmer teams, namely the need to utilize the talent of experienced programmers, is sound. The practice of programming is too difficult and important to be left entirely in the hands of novices.

24.3   Programmer productivity

The estimation of programmer productivity is important for two reasons. Firstly, without some estimate of productivity, project scheduling is impossible. Productivity measurement provides data which allows estimates to be made and cost models to be tuned. Secondly, some of the advantages which result from the use of improved software engineering practices and management techniques can only be demonstrated by showing that their use results in improved productivity over the whole of the software life-cycle.

Unfortunately, because software is intangible, it is not possible to measure productivity directly. Productivity in a manufacturing system can be measured by counting the number of units output and dividing this by the number of hours input to the work. In software systems, what we really want to estimate is the cost of deriving a particular system with given functionality. This is only indirectly related to some tangible measure such as the system size.

It is not possible to derive a hard and fast formula which allows us to measure function production per hour. Thus, productivity measures can act only as a subjective and relative guide to overall productivity. They must be supplemented by human judgement and intuition to estimate the real process productivity.

A number of different units have been devised to measure programmer productivity. These include:

- Lines of code written per programmer-month
- Object instructions produced per programmer-month
- Pages of documentation written per programmer-month
- Test cases written and executed per programmer-month

The most commonly used measure is lines of source code per programmer-month. This is computed by taking the total number of lines of source code which are delivered and dividing that number by the total time in programmer-months required to complete the project. This time includes analysis and design time, coding time, testing time and documentation time. Coding takes up only a relatively small part of the total development time (Figure 24.3).

As Jones (1978) points out, this measure of productivity is subject to a number of problems. The most fundamental of these is determining exactly what is meant by a line of code. Programs are made up of declarations, executable statements and commentary, and may also include macro instructions which expand to several lines of code. Different counting techniques adopt different definitions of a line of code. Some consider executable statements only, some executable statements and data declarations, and some each distinct non-blank line in the program, irrespective of what is on that line. Because of these different conventions, published measures of programmer productivity cannot readily be compared.

Another problem which arises when languages such as Pascal are used is how source lines containing more than a single statement should be treated. If such lines are treated as a single line, this implies that higher productivity can apparently be achieved by the judicious use of new lines! There is no evidence that any one line-counting technique is superior and, as long as the same technique is used consistently, comparisons can be drawn.

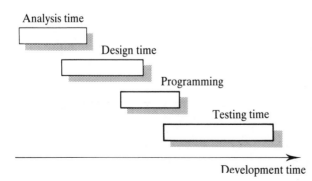

Figure 24.3
System development time.

However, a more serious problem which results from using lines of code/month as a measure of productivity is the apparent productivity advantages which it indicates when assembly code is used. The problem also occurs, to a lesser extent, when programs in different high-level languages are compared. If lines of code per month are used as a raw productivity measure, it appears that the low-level language programmer is more productive than the high-level language programmer for comparable systems.

This paradox results from the fact that all tasks associated with the programming process (design, documentation, testing, etc.) are subsumed under the coding task in spite of the fact that the coding time normally represents much less than half the time needed to complete a project (Figure 24.4). The measure places undue emphasis on coding and considers other stages of the life-cycle less important. Analysis, design and documentation time are language-independent and low level language programs have more lines of code than high level language programs. Dividing code produced by development time gives a very biased result.

For example, consider a system which might be coded in 5000 lines of assembly code or 1500 lines of high-level language code. The development time for the various phases is shown in Table 24.1. The assembler programmer has a productivity of 714 lines/month and the high-level language programmer less than half of this, 300 lines/month. Yet the development costs for the high-level language system are lower and it is produced in less time. Because of this paradox, individual productivity standards for each programming language are required and productivity comparisons between projects coded in different languages should not be made.

To avoid some of the problems associated with using lines of code per month as a productivity measure, an alternative method uses the number of object instructions generated per programmer-month. Although this unit is more objective than lines of code – there is no difficulty in defining what is meant by an object instruction – there are also disadvantages in using this measure of productivity.

Low-level language

Analysis	Design	Coding	Validation

Figure 24.4
Development times with high-level and low-level languages.

High-level language

Analysis	Design	Coding	Validation

	Assembly code	High-level language
Analysis	3 weeks	3 weeks
Design	5 weeks	5 weeks
Coding	8 weeks	4 weeks
Testing	10 weeks	6 weeks
Documentation	2 weeks	2 weeks
Size	5000 lines	1500 lines
Effort	28 weeks	20 weeks
Productivity	714	300

Table 24.1
System development time.

Firstly, it is difficult to estimate the source code/object code expansion ratio with most compilers. This means that object code/month is not useful for productivity estimation before code is actually produced. Secondly, the amount of object code generated by a compiler is very dependent on high-level language programming style. A programmer who takes more care over coding and produces tight code is apparently less productive than a programmer who codes in such a way that large object programs are generated.

Other measurements that have been used, such as pages of documentation per programmer-month, also suffer from disadvantages. If productivity is measured simply by volume of documentation produced, this militates against the documenter who takes time to express himself or herself clearly and concisely.

The problem with all productivity units expressed in volume/time is that they take no account of the quality of the finished system. They imply that more always means better and take no account of the fact that apparently higher raw code productivity may ultimately involve increased system maintenance costs.

Productivity cannot be measured over the whole of the system life-cycle so productivity over the software development stage is measured. If poor quality software is produced quickly, the developers of that software may appear to be more productive than those programmers who produce reliable and easy to maintain systems.

24.3.1 Factors affecting programmer productivity

Although the present units for measuring programmer productivity are imperfect, let us assume that productivity can be roughly measured and examine what factors influence it.

A study by Sackman *et al.* (1968) showed that individual productivity differences can be very large. The best programmers may be ten times more productive than the worst. This aptitude factor is likely to be dominant in individual productivity comparisons. Accordingly, the factors discussed below are only relevant to programming teams made up of programmers who have a range of abilities.

Walston and Felix (1977) carried out a productivity survey to identify productivity improvements that result from using methodologies such as top-down development, structured programming, etc. They collected data from over 60 projects ranging from small commercial DP programs to large complex process control systems. They selected 68 variables for analysis and identified 29 of these as correlating significantly with productivity. These variables included characteristics of the system being developed, the experience of the developers, hardware constraints, the use of new system development technology, program design constraints and the quantity of documentation required.

The most important single factor affecting productivity was the complexity of the user interface. Projects with a low interface complexity showed a productivity of 500 lines/programmer-month whereas high complexity interfaces were produced at 124 lines/programmer-month.

Other significant factors were found to be the extent of user participation in requirements definition and the overall experience of the programming team. Where the user did not participate in requirements definition, productivity was measured at 491 lines/programmer-month but where there was significant user participation this dropped to 205 lines/month. Teams with a good deal of experience produced at a rate of 410 lines/programmer-month whereas inexperienced teams produced 132 lines/month.

The effects on productivity of user interface complexity and team experience are what might be intuitively expected although the study by Walston and Felix is useful for quantifying the effects. It might also be expected that if the user had little to do with requirements definition, productivity would be higher although, in such cases, there must be some doubt that the finished product meets the user's needs.

Design and programming methodologies such as structured programming, design and code reviews, and top-down development had a positive influence on productivity although this was not as great as that of the factors previously discussed. However, productivity improvements resulting from the use of these techniques must be seen as a bonus as their principal function is to improve the reliability and maintainability of software.

Another factor which obviously affects productivity is the amount of time that a software engineer actually spends working on software development. Ignoring holidays and illness, each member of a software development team spends time training, attending meetings and dealing with administrative tasks. If a project involves new techniques, training will be required; if the project involves more than one geographical location, travel time between locations is involved; and the larger the programming group, the more time must be spent communicating. A study by McCue (1978) showed that 20–30% of an engineer's tasks might be spent on 'non-productive' activities.

Because of the difficulties in establishing a unit of productivity measurement and because of the variety of factors which influence productivity, it is very difficult to give a figure which can be taken as the average productivity of a programmer. For large, complex real-time systems, productivity may be as low as 30 lines/programmer-month whereas for straightforward business application systems which are well understood it may be as high as 600 lines/month. These figures are approximately independent of the programming language used. Thus, it always pays to use as high-level a language as possible for software projects.

Because of the differences between organizations and individuals, it is meaningless to suggest a standard productivity figure. Effective estimation can only be carried out using historical data derived from previous projects using the same programming language and carried out to the same quality standards. Without such data, productivity estimation is simply guesswork.

KEY POINTS

- Good software project management is essential if software engineering projects are to be developed on schedule and within budget.

- Software management is different from other engineering management because software is intangible, because we don't understand the software process and because many projects are novel and innovative.

- A software manager has diverse roles but the most significant activities are project planning, estimating and scheduling.

- There have been various development team organizations adopted. Democratic teams work well with experienced and competent staff. Chief programmer teams try to make best use of a scarce resource, namely, programming skills.

- The dominant factor in programmer productivity is the aptitude of the individual programmer.

- Inter-language comparisons using lines of code produced per month should not be made.

- Existing measures of programming productivity do not take the quality of the finished product into account.

Further reading

The Mythical Man Month. An interesting and readable account of management problems which arose during the development of one of the first very large software projects, the IBM OS/360 Operating System. The author was manager of this development and distilled much wisdom from the experience. (F.P. Brooks, 1975, Addison-Wesley.)

The Program Development Process: Part 2 – The Programming Team. Another text on software management from an author whose experience is at IBM. This is a very practical book. Although it is not, perhaps, as entertaining as Brooks's book, it is an equally valuable complement to this chapter. (J.D. Aron, 1983, Addison-Wesley).

IEE/BCS Software Eng. J., **1** (1), 1986. This is a special issue of a relatively new journal devoted to software engineering topics. The first issue of this journal contains a number of papers on the management of software projects.

References

Aron, J.D. (1974), *The Program Development Process*, Reading, Mass.: Addison-Wesley.

Aron, J.D. (1983), The Program Development Process: Part 2 – The Programming Team, Reading, Mass.: Addison-Wesley.

Baker, F.T. (1972), 'Chief programmer team management of production programming', *IBM Systems J.*, **11** (1).

Brooks, F.P. (1975), *The Mythical Man Month*, Reading, Mass.: Addison-Wesley.

Jones, T.C. (1978), 'Measuring programming quality and productivity', *IBM Systems J.*, **17** (1), 39–63.

McCue, G.M. (1978), 'IBMs Santa Teresa Laboratory – architectural design for program development', *IBM Systems J.*, **17** (1), 4–25.

Sackman, H., Erikson, W.J. and Grant, E.E. (1968), 'Exploratory experimentation studies comparing on-line and off-line programming performance', *Comm. ACM*, **11** (1), 3–11.

Shneiderman, B. (1980), *Software Psychology*, Cambridge, Mass.: Winthrop Publishers Inc.

Walston, C.E. and Felix, C.P. (1977), 'A method of programming measurement and estimation', *IBM Systems J.*, **16** (1), 54–73.

Yourdon, E. (1979), *Managing the Structured Techniques*, Englewood Cliffs, NJ: Prentice-Hall.

EXERCISES

24.1 Using reported instances of project problems in the literature, list management difficulties which occurred in these failed programming projects. (Start with Brooks's book as suggested in Further Reading.)

24.2 Given the list of management activities in Section 24.2, explain why it is not always the case that the best programmers do not make the best software managers.

24.3 Using the information on human factors given in Chapter 2, carry out an analysis of democratic and chief programmer team organizations. Suggest problems that might arise in each of these organizations.

24.4 List those metrics which have been used to measure programmer productivity. Suggest other metrics which might be used, taking into account that a software engineer is also involved in specification and design activities.

24.5 From your own experience, list those factors which have most effect on your own programming productivity. Suggest how your productivity might be improved.

Chapter 25

Project Planning and Scheduling

Objectives

This chapter is concerned with those management activities
which take up most managerial effort on a large software
project. After an introduction setting out planning
activities, the notion of a project milestone and the
importance of milestones are discussed. This is followed by
a description of option analysis where it is suggested that
the best managerial strategy is to reduce risk. Finally,
scheduling is discussed and graphical schedule
representations (activity graphs and bar charts) are
described. The use of automated tools for scheduling is
covered in this section.

Contents

Effective management of a software project depends on thoroughly planning the progress of the project, anticipating problems which might arise and preparing tentative solutions to those problems in advance. A project plan is drawn up at the outset of a project and should be used as the driver for the project. Of course, the initial plan is not static but must be modified as the project progresses and more information becomes available to the project manager.

It will be assumed here that the project manager is responsible for planning from requirements definition to the delivery of the completed system. The planning involved in assessing the need for a software system, the feasibility of producing that system, and the assignment of priority to the system production process will not be discussed. For a discussion of these topics, the reader is referred to Fried (1979) and also to Pressman (1987).

The planning process encompasses a number of related activities and is really inseparable from the process of cost estimation discussed in the following chapter. All software engineering projects are carried out in an environment where resources are subject to some budget and the planning process is constrained by that budget. However, the particular activities involved in the process are the same irrespective of the budget and it is possible to discuss these in isolation.

The following pseudo-code sets out planning activities and demonstrates that planning is an iterative process which is only complete when the project itself is complete.

```
Define constraints under which the project must be carried out
Make initial assessments of the project parameters
Define project milestones and deliverables
while project has not been completed or cancelled loop
      Draw up project schedule
      initiate activities according to schedule
      delay (for a while)
      review project progress
      revise estimates of project parameters
      apply revisions to project schedule
      re-negotiate project constraints and deliverables
      if (problems arise) then
            initiate technical review and possible revision
      end if
end loop
```

The planning process starts with an assessment of the constraints (required delivery date, staff available, overall budget, etc.) affecting the project. This is carried out in conjunction with an estimation of project parameters such as its structure, size and distribution of functions. The progress milestones and deliverables are then defined.

The process then enters a loop. A schedule for the project is drawn up and the activities defined in the schedule are initiated or given permission to continue. After some time (usually about 2–3 weeks), progress is reviewed against the plan and discrepancies noted. Because estimates of project parameters can only be tentative when they are initially drawn up, it is inevitable that the plan will need to be modified.

Given that more information becomes available during an iteration of the planning loop, the project manager can revise his or her assumptions about the project and assess how these revised assumptions affect the schedule. If their effect is to delay the project, it may be necessary to try and re-negotiate the original project constraints and deliverables with the project customer. If this re-negotiation is unsuccessful and does not allow the schedule to be met, it may then be necessary to initiate a project technical review. The objective of this review is to determine whether some alternative approach is viable which falls within the project constraints and which meets the project schedule.

Of course, the wise project manager does not assume that all will go well. From experience, we know that problems of some description nearly always arise in the course of a project and the initial assumptions and scheduling should be conservative. There should be sufficient contingency built into the plan that the project constraints and milestones need not be re-negotiated every time round the planning loop.

The above activities are those involved in the software development plan but this is only one of the plans which must be drawn up for the project. Other plans which may be required are:

- A validation plan
- A configuration management plan
- A staff training and development plan
- A maintenance plan

Validation plans, configuration management and maintenance are discussed in other chapters. Staff training is outside the scope of this work and a training plan is not discussed.

25.1   Project milestones

Effective management is reliant on information and, as software is intangible, this information can only be provided in the form of documents describing the work which has been carried out. Without this information, control of the project is lost and cost estimates and schedules cannot be updated.

When planning a project, a series of milestones should be established. At each milestone, a formal progress report should be presented to management. As Metzger (1973) points out, it is important that these milestones each represent the culmination of a distinct stage in the project. There is little point in planning indefinite milestones where it is impossible to decide unequivocally if a milestone has been reached.

A good milestone is characterized by finished documentation, for example, 'High-level design complete' or 'Test plan formulated'. On the other hand, a poor milestone is something like 'Coding 80% complete'. What exactly does this mean and how can it be determined whether coding is 80% complete or not?

A useful starting point for identifying milestones is a detailed view of the software life-cycle. The macro life-cycle view where the life-cycle is broken into five stages is too coarse for this purpose and each stage must be broken into sub-stages for reporting.

There is no single definitive detailed view of the software life-cycle. The particular organization of each phase must depend on a number of factors such as the application being developed, the programming team organization, the project documentation required by the contractor, etc. One possible micro-life-cycle view with reporting milestones associated with each sub-stage is shown in Figure 25.1. For brevity, only specification and design milestones are shown but comparable milestones should be established for the other phases of the software process.

Milestones should not necessarily be established for each and every project activity, otherwise the project team will spend more time on management reporting than on system development. An approximate rule

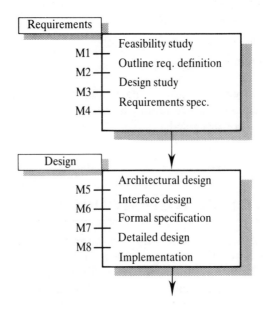

Figure 25.1
Life-cycle reporting milestones.

of thumb is that milestones should be scheduled at two to three week intervals although this can vary by up to 100% depending on particular project activities.

One of the reasons for the widespread adoption of the 'waterfall' model of the software process is that it allows for the straightforward definition of milestones throughout the course of a project. Alternative approaches, such as exploratory programming, are such that milestone definition is a more difficult and a less certain process. Consequently, it is my opinion that in spite of its known deficiencies the waterfall model or some variant of it will continue to be the most commonly adopted process model for the majority of software engineering projects.

25.2   Option analysis

In the course of formulating a software project plan, the project manager is usually presented with a set of goals which must be achieved and goals which are desirable but not essential. It is almost always the case that some of the goals are mutually opposing. For example, one goal might be to minimize project costs, another to maximize system reliability. In general, increased reliability can only be achieved by increasing costs so some balance point where acceptable cost and reliability levels are achieved must be discovered.

Usually, a set of options can be derived which, partially or completely, achieves the project goals. In carrying out an analysis of the different options available, the first stage is to define all of the organizational and project-specific goals which are of relevance. For example, project-specific goals might be high maintainability, low cost, high reliability, etc. Organizational goals might be the production of reusable components, the development and support of particular areas of expertise (because these may lead to future contracts), and the career development of particular members of staff.

Unfortunately, it is often the case that goals are left implicit rather than set out at the start of a project. This has the result that the project team do not really know what they are trying to achieve and why particular management decisions have been made.

Given a goal definition, the different options available to the project manager can be scored against these goals. Of course, this scoring is usually relative rather than absolute, and the actual values involved are often arbitrary. The scoring system should also take goal weighting into account. For example, high reliability might be paramount and must be achieved irrespective of the other goals. Thus it would be given a higher weighting than staff development, say. Weighting may be either positive or

Table 25.1
Project options.

	Option A	Option B	Option C
Cost (£million)	1.2	0.8	1.75
Schedule (months)	33	30	36
Reliability	5	9	13
Reuse (%)	40	40	30
Portability (%)	90	75	30
Efficiency	0.35	0.75	1

negative so that the benefit or cost from a particular option may be reduced or increased.

This is perhaps best illustrated by example. Say there are three optional approaches to product development open to a project manager. The goals and the scoring of each of the options is shown in Table 25.1. For simplicity, weighting has not been included. Some of the scores have been expressed as percentages. For example, reuse is the percentage of system components that might be reused and efficiency is expressed a percentage of the most efficient option. Other scores are absolute such as the cost and the reliability, which is expressed as rate of occurrence of failures (see Chapter 30).

Given this analysis, how can the project manager then decide which option should be chosen? One possible approach is to use what are sometimes called polar graphs which are derived from techniques used in computer performance evaluation (Ferrari, 1978). Boehm (1981) shows how they can also be used in making multivariate comparisons and in evaluating software project options.

A polar graph is a graph with a number of radial axes where, in this context, each axis corresponds to one of the goals which are to be achieved. The particular options are plotted on each axis and the option which offers the best overall payoff is the one which encloses the greatest area. The polar graph for the options shown in Table 25.1 is illustrated in Figure 25.2.

The most desirable attainments should be plotted at the extremes of the radii and the least desirable at the origins. For example, in Figure 25.2, reliability is measured as a rate of fault occurrence so the lower this value the better. Thus, the lowest value is at the extreme end of the radius and the highest in the centre. By contrast, efficiency (expressed as a percentage of the most efficient) is represented in the opposite manner.

Of course, these polar graphs are simply intended as a guide to project management and are not to be interpreted completely literally. For example, it may be the case that one of the options scores best on the polar graph but conflicts with a critical organizational or project objective. It must then be rejected in favour of some other option. For example, the organization may anticipate other projects in the same application area so

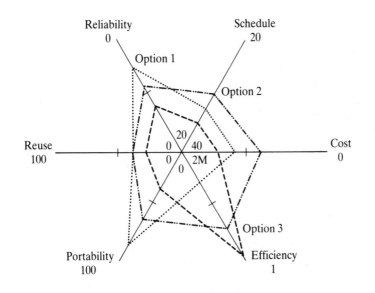

Reliability
0

Schedule
20

Option 1

Option 2

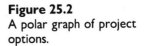

Reuse
100

20
0   40
0   2M
0

Cost
0

Option 3

Portability
100

Efficiency
1

Figure 25.2
A polar graph of project options.

may select the option that provides the highest number of reusable components so as to save development costs in later projects.

Boehm (1981) describes a technique for option analysis called the payoff matrix where the maximum benefit and penalty of each possible strategy is tabulated. For example, say two possible strategies of project implementation are proposed and the maximum and minimum costs of each strategy estimated. The possibilities are shown in Table 25.2.

Faced with these possibilities, which option should a project manager select? Clearly, if all goes well, Option A leads to the lowest cost project, but if things do not go well it is the most expensive option to choose. Boehm identifies three decision-making strategies which can be used in this situation.

The maximin strategy is a conservative strategy which aims at the minimization of losses. In the above example, the minimum loss is $15 000 ($70 000 − $55 000) so Option B would be selected. An alternative strategy is an optimistic strategy which selects the option which offers the greatest gains. In the above example, Option A would therefore be selected.

Neither of these strategies takes the relative magnitudes of the gains or losses into account. So if the potential gains in Option A were just

Table 25.2
Option costs.

	Cost ($)	
	Maximum	**Expected**
Option A	100 000	40 000
Option B	70 000	55 000

slightly larger than the gains from Option B but the losses were, say, 10 times larger, the maximax strategy would select Option A whereas the majority of project managers would select the safer alternative option.

The problem is that neither of these approaches takes into account the notion of risk, where risk can be expressed as a probability that the estimated value will not be exceeded. The sum of the probabilities of each possible outcome should equal 1. In situations of complete uncertainty, the probability of each outcome, in a binary situation, is 0.5.

If we consider the figures in Table 25.2 and estimate that each possible outcome is equally likely, we can compute the probable payoff from any one option:

$$\text{Option A: Probable cost} = (0.5 * \$100\ 000) + (0.5 * \$40\ 000)$$
$$= \$70\ 000$$
$$\text{Option B: Probable cost} = (0.5 * \$70\ 000) + (0.5 * \$55\ 000)$$
$$= \$62\ 500$$

On the basis of these figures, Option B should be selected as the most acceptable option. This option is more likely to lead to lower software costs than Option A.

Of course, in reality we rarely have to deal with situations of complete uncertainty. Indeed, if a manager is completely uncertain about an estimate it can be argued that he or she ought to be carrying out some kind of analysis (prototyping, simulation or whatever) to reduce that uncertainty. In general, it is possible to assign subjective probability estimates to each option and to use these estimates in option analysis.

For example, say the probability of Option A succeeding is 65% and the probability of it failing is 35%. Option B has a success probability of 70% and a failure probability of 30%. Redoing the computation shows that Option B should again be selected as the best option.

$$\text{Option A: Probable cost} = (0.65 * \$40\ 000) + (0.35 * \$100\ 000)$$
$$= \$61\ 000$$
$$\text{Option B: Probable cost} = (0.70 * \$55\ 000) + (0.30 * \$70\ 000)$$
$$= \$59\ 500$$

Of course, this analysis is simplistic and the project manager should use it as a guide to decision-making and not as an automated decision-making technique. However, it does illustrate the role of risk estimation which is a critical part of project management.

When project management decisions are made, each decision should have a risk estimate associated with it where, informally, the risk associated with a decision is the probability that the decision will not have adverse consequences. Note that it is not a measure of the probability of the correctness of a decision. A decision may be incorrect but may not have adverse effects (it could be an over-estimate, say) and the risk associated with such a decision is low. In general, the best project management strategy is to minimize risk even if this means that, on some occasions, costs are not minimized.

For example, say one way of tackling the project depends on hiring a specific expert whereas an alternative option allows the project to be tackled with existing staff. The first option may be cheaper but has much higher risk because, if a specialist cannot be found, the project may be cancelled. The second option may cost more but the risk of project failure is lower. A wise project manager would accept the higher costs and not face the uncertainties of staff recruitment. Success is always cheaper than project failure!

25.3   Project scheduling

Project scheduling is one of the most difficult tasks of software management. Unless the project being scheduled is similar to a previous project, previous experience is of limited relevance. More typically, projects break new ground with the consequence that previous estimates cannot be simply modified. Different projects use different programming languages and methodologies which further complicates the task of estimating the project schedule.

Because of these uncertainties, scheduling is an iterative process. An initial schedule must be estimated but this should not be considered inviolate. As the project progresses, information is fed back to the scheduler and the initial estimate modified.

The preparation of the initial schedule must be based on the experience and intuition of the manager. If the project is technically advanced, the initial estimate will almost certainly be optimistic in spite of endeavours to consider all eventualities. In this respect, software scheduling is no different from scheduling any other type of large advanced project. New aircraft, bridges and even motor cars are frequently late because of unanticipated problems and it is unrealistic to expect software projects to be different from other complex engineering projects.

Project scheduling involves separating the total work involved in a project into distinct tasks and assessing when these tasks will be completed. When a number of individuals or teams are working on a project, some of these tasks are carried out in parallel. The project scheduler must coordinate these parallel tasks and organize the work so that the workforce is used optimally. The scheduler must strive to avoid a situation arising in which the whole project is delayed because a critical task is unfinished.

In estimating schedules, it should not be assumed that every stage of the project will be problem free. Individuals working on a project may fall ill or may leave, hardware may break down and essential support software or hardware may be late in delivery. If the project is new and technically advanced, certain parts of it may turn out to be more difficult and hence take longer than originally anticipated. A rule of thumb in estimating is to estimate as if nothing will go wrong, increase that estimate to cover anticipated problems and then add a contingency factor to cover unanticipated problems. This extra factor must be determined by the manager's experience and knowledge of his staff.

As a rough guide for the scheduler, requirements analysis and design normally takes twice as long as coding. So too does validation. To estimate the total time required for the project, the system size must be estimated and divided by the expected programmer productivity to give the number of programmer-months required to complete the project. The resulting figure is very approximate because of the difficulties involved in estimating system size and the variations in programmer productivity. Estimation techniques are discussed in the following chapter.

Estimating the actual duration of a project cannot simply be carried out by dividing the number of programmer-months by the number of available programmers. There are two reasons for this. Firstly, as the number of programmers increases, communication problems arise and productivity falls. Indeed, Fried suggests that, once the number of programmers working on a project exceeds a certain maximum, productivity is actually negative. This is also suggested by Lehman's laws, discussed in Chapter 1 and in Chapter 27. Secondly, some tasks are indivisible and no matter how many programmers work on them, the time required cannot be reduced. Again, experience is required to identify these indivisible tasks and to estimate the duration of a project.

The output from the scheduling process is usually a set of charts which show the work breakdown, task dependencies and staff allocations. These charts are discussed in the following section. Manual preparation of these charts is a time-consuming chore but various tools are now available which automate the task of chart production. Using such tools allows the manager to experiment with different schedules until the most appropriate is discovered.

25.3.1 Bar charts and activity networks

Bar charts and activity networks are graphical notations which are used in project scheduling. Bar charts illustrate who is responsible for each part of the project and when that part is scheduled to start and finish. Activity networks show the different activities making up a project, their projected durations and interdependencies.

As an illustration of these notations, consider the set of activities shown in Table 25.3. This table shows various subtasks, their duration, and

Task	Duration (days)	Dependencies
T1	8	
T2	15	
T3	15	T1
T4	10	
T5	10	T2, T4
T6	5	T1, T2
T7	20	T1
T8	25	T4
T9	15	T3, T6
T10	15	T5, T7
T11	7	T9
T12	10	T11

Table 25.3
Task durations and
dependencies.

the task interdependencies. From Table 25.3, we can see that Task T3 is
dependent on Task T1. This means that T3 must be completed before T1
starts. For example, T1 might be the preparation of a software design and
T3 the implementation of that design. Before implementation begins, the
design should be complete.

Given dependency and estimated duration of tasks, it is possible to
generate a number of graphical representations of the project schedule.
One such chart is an activity network which shows task dependencies. This
is illustrated in Figure 25.3. Notice that dates in this diagram are written in
British style where the day precedes the month.

It is not generally useful to subdivide tasks into units that take less
than a week or two to execute. Finer subdivision means that a disproportionate amount of time must be spent on estimating and chart revision. It is

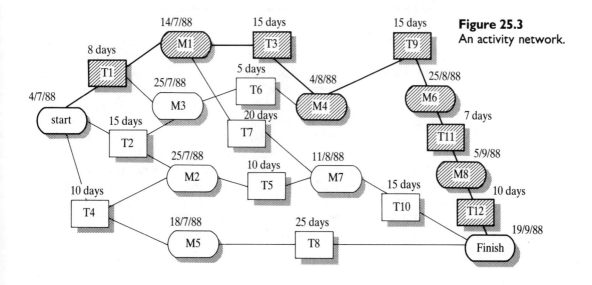

Figure 25.3
An activity network.

also useful to set a maximum amount of time for any task on the chart – about 10–12 weeks is reasonable.

Rectangular nodes in Figure 25.3 represent tasks and the task duration is shown alongside each node. Rounded nodes represent the culmination of activities or project milestones and these are annotated with the expected completion date of the dependent activities.

Before progress can be made from one milestone to another, all paths leading to that milestone must be complete. For example, task T9, shown in Figure 25.3, cannot be started until both T3 and T6 are complete and milestone M4 has been reached. The diagram shows the interdependence of activities, illustrating what activities can be carried out in parallel and what must be done in sequence.

The duration of the project can be estimated by considering the longest path in the activity graph. This is called the critical path and, in Figure 23.3, it is represented by shaded boxes. The critical path is the activity series on which the overall schedule of the project depends and any slippage in completion in any critical activity causes project delays. On the other hand, a delay in T8 in Figure 25.3, assuming it was not excessive, would have no effect on the project completion date.

PERT charts are a more sophisticated form of activity chart where, instead of making a single estimate for each task, pessimistic, likely, and optimistic estimates are made. Considering each of these and combinations of them makes critical path analysis very complex and it must be carried out automatically.

As well as using activity graphs for estimating, it is useful for management to construct these charts when allocating project work. They can provide insights into the interdependence of tasks which are not intuitively obvious. In some cases, it may be possible to modify the system design so that the critical path is shortened. The duration of the project may be reduced because the time spent waiting for activities to complete might be reduced.

Now that personal computers are widely used, it is normal practice for automated tools to be used in activity network generation and maintenance. Figure 25.3 was created with a project management tool and, given an initial starting date and the task durations, the dates for completion of all tasks were computed automatically. Furthermore, other representations of the schedule can be computed with little effort.

Figure 25.4 shows a bar chart (or Gantt chart) illustrating a project calendar and how tasks start and finish at various dates. Some of the tasks in Figure 25.4 are followed by a shaded bar. This indicates that there is a measure of flexibility in the completion date of these tasks and if a task does not complete on time the critical path will not be affected until the end of the period marked by the shaded bar. Of course, tasks which lie on the critical path have no margin of error allowed.

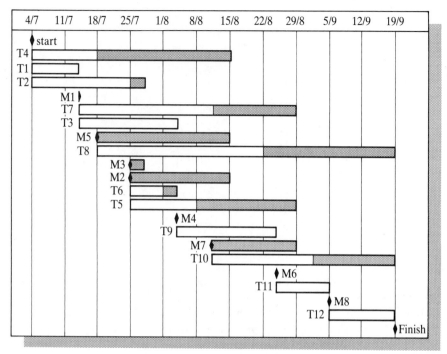

Figure 25.4
Activity bar chart.

In practice, of course, the situation illustrated in Figures 25.3 and 25.4 is an unlikely one as few managers would produce estimates without some contingency. Estimating errors and unexpected delays are a fact of life for project management and some slippage should always be allowed for in project estimates.

As well as considering schedules, project managers must also consider resource allocation and, in particular, the allocation of staff to project tasks. Table 25.4 suggests an allocation of programmers to the tasks illustrated in Table 25.3.

Staff allocations can also be processed by project management support tools and a bar chart generated which shows how the time periods where staff are employed on the project (Figure 25.5).

Not all staff need be occupied at all times on the project. During intervening periods they may be on holiday, working on other projects, attending training courses or occupied in some other activity.

A common practice in large organizations is to employ a number of specialists and for these specialists to work on a project as required. This is attractive in principle but can cause scheduling problems. If one project is delayed while a specialist is working on it, this may have a knock-on effect and other projects may also be delayed because that specialist is not available.

Table 25.4
Staff/task allocations.

Task	Programmer
T1	Jane
T2	Anne
T3	Jane
T4	Fred
T5	Mary
T6	Anne
T7	Jim
T8	Fred
T9	Jane
T10	Anne
T11	Fred
T12	Fred

Inevitably, initial project schedules will be incorrect and, as a project develops, it is important to compare estimates with actual elapsed time. This comparison can be used as a basis for revising the schedule for later parts of the project. When actual figures are known, it is also important to review the activity chart and perhaps repartition the later project tasks in order to reduce the critical path.

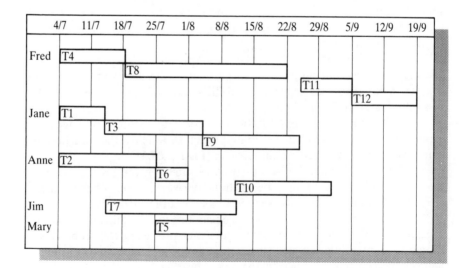

Figure 25.5
Staff allocation chart.

KEY POINTS

- Effective management of a software project depends on good planning and problem anticipation.

- Planning and estimating are iterative processes which continue throughout the course of a project. As more information becomes available, plans and schedules must be revised.

- A project milestone is a predictable state where some formal report of progress may be presented to management. They should occur regularly throughout the course of a software project.

- Managers should carry out some kind of option analysis when deciding on how best to organize a project. The risk of each option should be considered and a management strategy which minimizes risk should be adopted. Techniques such as polar graphs may be useful in this analysis.

- Project scheduling involves the creation of PERT charts showing the inter-relationships of project activities and bar charts. These are best prepared using software tools which are now widely available on personal computers.

Further reading

Software Engineering Economics. This is a first class general text on software management which has excellent chapters on risk analysis. (B.W. Boehm, 1981, Prentice-Hall.)

Software Engineering Concepts. This is a general software engineering text which has a particularly good chapter on project planning. (R.E. Fairley, 1985, McGraw-Hill.)

'A spiral model of software development and enhancement'. This paper discusses an alternative process model where the analysis of risk is an integral part of the software process. In general, the paper is an excellent discussion of the importance of risk estimation in project management. (B.W. Boehm, *IEEE Computer*, **21** (5), 1988.)

References

Boehm, B.W. (1981), *Software Engineering Economics*, Englewood Cliffs, NJ: Prentice-Hall.

Ferrari, D. (1978), *Computer Systems Performance Evaluation*, Englewood Cliffs, NJ: Prentice-Hall.

Fried, L. (1979), *Practical Data Processing Management*, Virginia: Reston.

Metzger, P.W. (1973), *Managing a Programming Project*, Englewood Cliffs, NJ: Prentice-Hall.

Pressman, R.S. (1987), *Software Engineering – A Practitioner's Approach*, 2nd edn, New York: McGraw-Hill.

EXERCISES

25.1 Explain why the process of project planning is an iterative one and why a plan must be continually reviewed during the course of a software project.

25.2 A number of development projects are suggested in Appendix 2. For some or all of these projects, draw up a project plan showing the major milestones and the development schedule.

25.3 Describe the contingencies you have allowed for in drawing up the project plans in Exercise 25.2. Suggest how you might recover from some complete disaster such as the project team being wiped out in an air crash.

25.4 Draw up alternative project plans which will allow the projects in Appendix 2 to be completed in 70% of your original development schedule. What assumptions have you had to make? Estimate the risk associated with the different options and present an option analysis as discussed in Section 25.2.

25.5 Table 25.3 gives task durations for software project tasks. Assume that a serious, unanticipated setback occurs and, instead of taking 10 days, task T5 takes 40 days. Revise the activity chart accordingly, highlighting the new critical path. Draw up new bar charts showing how the project might be organized. (Use a project management tool if you have access to one.)

25.6 Table 25.5 sets out a number of tasks, durations and dependencies. Draw up activity charts and bar charts for these tasks.

Task	Duration (days)	Dependencies
T1	10	
T2	15	T1
T3	10	T1, T2
T4	20	
T5	10	
T6	15	T3, T4
T7	20	T3
T8	35	T7
T9	15	T3, T6
T10	5	T5, T9
T11	10	T9
T12	20	T10
T13	35	T3, T4
T14	10	T8, T9
T15	20	T9, T14
T16	10	T15

Table 25.5
Task durations and dependencies.

25.7 If you have access to a project management package, draw up activity charts and bar charts for your project plans devised in Exercise 25.2. (You can try this without automated tools but it is long and tedious!)

Chapter 26

Software Cost Estimation

Objectives

This chapter is devoted to a discussion of software cost estimation. Different estimation techniques are summarized and it is suggested that more than one technique should be used in practical cost estimation. The general advantages and problems of algorithmic cost modelling are discussed and the algorithmic technique is illustrated using the COCOMO model. The final section of the chapter suggests that algorithmic modelling is an effective tool for the manager to use in deciding on particular project strategies.

Contents

One of the principal roles of a software project manager is to control the costs of a project. In order to do so, he or she must be able to make estimates of how much a software development or part of that development is going to cost. Clearly, this estimation activity is carried out in tandem with the scheduling process as the human effort expended in a project makes up the major part of the costs.

The components of project costs are:

- Hardware costs
- Travel and training costs
- Effort costs (the costs of paying software engineers)

Of these costs, the dominant cost is the effort cost although travel and training costs can make up a substantial and controllable budget cost. The discussion here will concentrate on the cost of effort in a project as this is the most difficult to estimate and has the most significant effect on project costs.

Software cost estimation is a continuing activity which starts at the proposal stage and continues throughout the lifetime of a project. It is the usual practice for projects to be allocated a budget and continual cost estimation is necessary to ensure that that budget will not be exceeded.

A survey of various techniques of software cost estimation is given by Boehm (1981). He identifies seven different techniques:

(1) *Algorithmic cost modelling*   A model is developed using historical cost information which relates some software metric (usually its size) to the project cost. An estimate is made of that metric and the model predicts the effort required.

(2) *Expert judgement*   One or more experts on the software development techniques to be used and on the application domain are consulted. They each estimate the project cost. The cost estimate is arrived at by consensus judgement.

(3) *Estimation by analogy*   This technique is applicable when other projects in the same application domain have been completed. The cost of a new project can be estimated by analogy with these completed projects.

(4) *Parkinson's law*   Parkinson's law states that work expands to fill the time available. In software cost terms, a project will cost whatever there is available to spend on it.

(5) *Pricing to win*   The software cost is estimated to be whatever the customer has available to spend on the project.

(6) *Top-down estimation*   A cost estimation is arrived at by considering the overall properties of the product. This cost is then split among its components.

(7) *Bottom-up estimation*   The cost of each component is estimated. All these costs are added to produce a final cost estimate.

Each technique has advantages and disadvantages. The most important point made by Boehm is that no single technique is adequate in isolation. He suggests that, for large projects, several cost estimation techniques should be used in parallel and their results compared. If these predict radically different costs, this implies that not enough costing information is available. More information should be sought and the costing process repeated.

It is usually impossible to separate project costing from broader organizational, economic, political and business considerations. Much of the discussion in the literature about project costing assumes that a firm set of requirements has been drawn up and costing is carried out using these requirements as a basis.

Although this is an appropriate model of some projects (particularly military projects which have funded a separate requirements phase), the costs of many projects must be estimated using only an outline of the work which is to be done. This can be justifiably criticized as a very unscientific approach but it may be cost effective from a business point of view. Drawing up requirements is an expensive activity and its cost may not be justified if the project does not gain approval from higher management.

Although the notion of pricing to win may seem amoral, the reality of product development is such that this is, perhaps, the most common approach to costing. In essence, a project cost is agreed on the basis of some broad, outline proposal and negotiations then begin between client and customer to establish the detailed project specification. This specification is constrained by the agreed contract and the buyer and seller must agree on what is acceptable system functionality. The fixed factor in many projects is not the project requirements but the cost. The requirements may be changed in order that the cost is not exceeded.

Software costing is often simply a matter of experience or political judgement and there are no ways to describe these skills in a book of this nature. Thus, the remainder of this chapter concentrates on one specific costing technique, namely algorithmic cost modelling. This does not mean that I consider it superior to other techniques – on the contrary, we shall see that it suffers from a fundamental flaw which means that its accuracy is hard to determine without a great deal of historical project information – but it is a technique which is often promoted as significant.

26.1   Algorithmic cost modelling

The most scientific approach to software costing and scheduling is to use an algorithmic costing model. Such a model can be built by analysing the costs and attributes of completed projects. A mathematical formula or formulae can be established linking costs with one or more metrics such as project size, number of programmers, etc.

There have been a number of such models built and used in software costing and these are compared by Mohanty (1981) and Boehm (1981). Mohanty exercized a number of these models with the same hypothetical project data. This was a system with about 36K executable instructions, mostly mathematical software but with elements of interactive working and real-time command and control and with an assumed labour cost of $50 000 per year. He received cost estimates from different models ranging from $362 000 to $2 766 667 for the same input data.

The vast discrepancy in these figures does not, in itself, discredit algorithmic cost modelling but it does illustrate that the parameters associated with each model are highly organization dependent. Because of different measurement techniques for quantities such as lines of code, the number of days in a person-month, etc., it is impossible to establish a single costing model which is applicable across a wide range of organizations and projects.

The fundamental flaw in the algorithmic cost modelling approach is that it relies on the estimate of some metric of the finished software product. Cost estimation is probably most critical early in the software process long before the product is completed so the manager must estimate the appropriate metric for input to the costing model.

The most commonly used metric is the number of lines of source code in the finished system. Although it may be possible in some projects to use application domain knowledge to provide a reasonable cost estimate, many projects break new ground and estimating their size is very difficult indeed. I am not ashamed to admit that I have no idea how to estimate the source code size of a large system accurately and I would argue that few people are able to do so.

Furthermore, code size estimates depend on hardware and software choices. The use of a commercial database management system might mean that database code need not be written. The use of a language such as Ada might mean that more lines of code are necessary then if FORTRAN (say) were used. However, these lines provide redundant information and checking, and Ada programmers are likely to be more productive than FORTRAN programmers. Hardware and software selection is often an integral part of a project and the selected choices may not be known to project managers when making initial size estimates.

Thus, users of such models for project costing must be wary of the figures they produce. It is only in situations where the product to be developed is well understood, where it is similar to previous products and where language and hardware choices are pre-defined that the margin of error in the model estimate is likely to be small. In other cases, the estimate produced must be treated with caution.

This warning is not really contradicted by reports of successful usage of such models. Project cost estimates are often self-fulfilling as the estimate is used to define the project budget and the product is adjusted so that the budget figure is realized. I know of no controlled experiments with cost modelling systems where the model outputs were not used to bias the experiment. A controlled experiment would not reveal the cost estimate to the project manager and then would compare actual with estimated costs.

Although the margin of error in initial cost estimates produced by these models is likely to be high, this does not mean that this approach to cost estimation is useless. It may provide more accurate results during the development of a project when a better estimate of product size may be made. Furthermore, as we shall see in the following section, they provide a decision-making aid to project managers, allowing alternative means of tackling a project to be compared.

26.2   The COCOMO model

The best documented software costing model, whose parameters can be tailored to particular modes of working, is the COCOMO model described by Boehm (1981). Other models such as the Putnam Estimation Model (Putnam, 1978) are different but embody comparable principles. This section concentrates on the COCOMO model to give the reader a general overview of algorithmic cost estimation. The suggested further reading with this chapter includes a book covering Putnam's approach.

The COCOMO model exists in basic (simple), intermediate and detailed forms but a full description of all of these is outside the scope of this book. Rather, an overview of the basic and intermediate COCOMO models is presented with the intention of introducing algorithmic cost modelling and to illustrate the advantages to management of using this technique.

The basic COCOMO model is intended to give an order of magnitude estimation of software costs. It uses only the estimated size of the software project and the type of software being developed. Versions of the estimation formula exist for three classes of software project:

(1)   *Organic mode projects*   These are projects where relatively small teams are working in a familiar environment developing applications with which they are familiar. In short, communications overhead is low, and team members know what they are doing and can quickly get on with the job.

(2)   *Semi-detached mode projects*   This mode of project represents an intermediate stage between organic mode projects and embedded mode projects described below. In semi-detached mode projects, the project team may be made up of experienced and inexperienced staff. Team members have limited experience of related systems and may be unfamiliar with some (but not all) aspects of the system being developed.

(3)   *Embedded mode projects*   The principal characteristic of embedded mode projects is that they must operate within tight constraints. The software system is part of a strongly coupled complex of hardware, software, regulations and operational procedures. Therefore, requirements modifications to get round software problems are usually impractical and software validation costs are high. Because of the diverse nature of embedded mode projects, it is unusual for project team members to have a great deal of experience in the particular application which is being developed.

The formulae to compute costs or, more precisely, the effort required for software development all have the same form, namely:

$$\text{Effort} = A \, (\text{KDSI})^b$$

A and b are constants which vary depending on the type of project. The equation suggests that cost is an exponential function of size although, in fact, the value of b is usually close to 1. KDSI is the number of thousands of delivered source instructions.

Boehm's interpretation of a delivered source instruction is any line of source text irrespective of the actual number of instructions on that line. Therefore, if there are two or more statements on a line this counts as a single delivered source instruction and if a statement is spread over five lines this counts as five DSIs. Comments are excluded. The definition of a delivered source instruction also excludes undelivered support software even although the effort involved in this may be significant.

This is a very arguable definition of a delivered source instruction and it is clearly based on FORTRAN programming where one statement per line is the norm. It is probably inappropriate for languages such as Ada where statements may span several lines. However, the detailed definition of a DSI is not critical for this model, given that all estimates are based on the same source instruction definition.

The values which should be assigned to these constants in any particular situation can only be determined by analysis of historical project data. Using data from other organizations is likely to increase the margin of model error because of different inherent assumptions and working practices. From an analysis of his organization's data, Boehm reports the

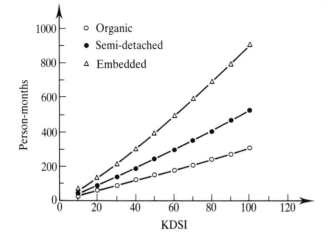

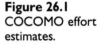

Figure 26.1
COCOMO effort
estimates.

following formulae for the different classes of project:

Organic mode	$PM = 2.4 \, (KDSI)^{1.05}$
Semi-detached mode	$PM = 3 \, (KDSI)^{1.12}$
Embedded mode	$PM = 3.6 \, (KDSI)^{1.20}$

These equations are illustrated in Figure 26.1, which shows the estimated effort for a range of project sizes.

The result of the estimate is PM, the number of person-months required to complete the project. In the version of the COCOMO model described by Boehm, a person-month is defined as consisting of 152 hours of working time. This figure takes into account the average monthly time off for holidays, training and sick leave. This clearly varies from organization to organization.

Note that these effort curves, particularly for the smaller systems, are very close to straight lines. It can actually be argued that the margin of error in the estimates is likely to be such that a linear estimating function may produce equally valid estimates, particularly as the basic COCOMO model is simply intended to provide an approximate 'ball-park' figure.

The basic COCOMO model assumes that the software requirements will not be significantly changed after software development. There is also an implicit assumption that the project will be well managed by both the customer and the software developer.

As well as providing effort equations, the basic COCOMO model provides equations to estimate the development schedule of a project. The development schedule is the time required to complete the project given that sufficient personnel resources are available. The development schedule equations for the different modes of the project are:

Organic mode	$\text{TDEV} = 2.5\,(\text{PM})^{0.38}$
Semi-detached mode	$\text{TDEV} = 2.5\,(\text{PM})^{0.35}$
Embedded mode	$\text{TDEV} = 2.5\,(\text{PM})^{0.32}$

The development schedule for different sizes of semi-detached mode projects is shown in Figure 26.2. In fact, the shapes of the curve for different project modes are very similar and it is not really clear if the differences between the exponents in the above development schedule equations are significant.

To illustrate the basic COCOMO model, assume that an organic mode software project has an estimated size of 32 000 delivered source instructions. From the effort equation, the number of person-months required for this project is:

$$\text{PM} = 2.4\,(32)^{1.05} = 91 \text{ person-months}$$

From the schedule equation, the time required to complete the project is:

$$\text{TDEV} = 2.5\,(91)^{0.38} = 14 \text{ months}$$

The number of personnel required to complete the project in the timescale is:

$$N = \text{PM} / \text{TDEV} = 91 / 14 = 6.5 \text{ people}$$

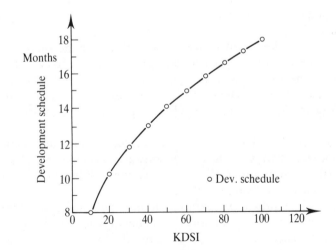

Figure 26.2
COCOMO development schedule curve.

Consider now a large embedded mode software project consisting of about 128 000 delivered source instructions. The basic COCOMO equations give results as follows:

$$PM = 3.6 \, (128)^{1.20} = 1216 \text{ person-months}$$
$$TDEV = 2.5 \, (1216)^{0.32} = 24 \text{ months}$$
$$N = 1216 \, / \, 24 = 51 \text{ people}$$

The basic COCOMO model is intended to give an order of magnitude estimate of the effort required to complete a software project. Before going on to look at the intermediate COCOMO model which takes factors apart from system size and type into account, let us look at some of the assumptions which are embedded in the basic COCOMO model.

First of all, the model has an implicit productivity estimate built into it which was presumably derived from existing project data. In the case of the organic mode system above, the productivity is 352 DSI/person-month which is about 16 instructions per person-day. The effort required for the embedded system implies a productivity of 105 DSI/person-month which is about four instructions per person-day. These figures roughly correspond to productivity estimates from other sources.

A more interesting implication of the COCOMO model is that the time required to complete the project is a function of the total effort required for the project and not a function of the number of software engineers working on the project. This confirms the notion that adding more people to a project which is behind schedule is unlikely to help that schedule to be regained.

The COCOMO model is not particularly helpful in estimating schedules when personnel resources are limited but delivery schedules are flexible. It is not clear whether a project schedule of 14 months for 6.5 people can be simply increased to 30 months if only three people are available. This is clearly a result of its ancestry in a large organization with many development staff.

The basic COCOMO model is a useful starting point for project estimation but it is clear that there are many factors apart from project size and type which affect the effort involved in a project. The intermediate COCOMO model takes some of these factors into account.

The intermediate COCOMO model for software estimation takes the basic COCOMO effort and schedule computations as its starting point. It then applies a series of multipliers to the basic COCOMO figures which take into account factors such as required product reliability, database size, execution and storage constraints, personnel attributes and the use of software tools. In all, in Boehm's organization, 15 factors are taken into consideration. These are divided into four classes – product attributes, computer attributes, personnel attributes and project attributes.

Product attributes are:

(1) *Required software reliability (RELY)*   This is rated on a scale from very low where a software failure would only result in slight inconvenience, through nominal where a failure would result in moderate recoverable losses, to very high where failure involves risk to human life.

(2) *Database size (DATA)*   This is rated from low where the size of the database (in bytes) is less than 10 times the number of DSIs, through nominal where the database size is between 10 and 100 times the system size, to very high where the database is more than 1000 times larger than the program.

(3) *Product complexity (CPLX)*   This is rated on a scale from very low to extra high. Low complexity code uses simple I/O operations, simple data structures and 'straight line' code. Nominal complexity implies some I/O processing, multi-file input/output, the use of library routines and some inter-module communication. Very high and extra-high complexity means possibly re-entrant or recursive code, complex file handling, parallel processing, complex data management, etc.

Computer attributes are those hardware constraints such as speed and space constraints which affect software productivity. There are four attributes which are classed as computer attributes. These are:

(1) *Execution time constraints (TIME)*   This is rated from nominal to extra high. A nominal rating means that less than 50% of available execution time is used and an extra-high rating means that 95% of available time must be used.

(2) *Storage constraint (STOR)*   This is rated in the same way as TIME with a nominal value meaning that less than half the available store is used and an extra-high rating meaning that 95% of available store is used.

(3) *Virtual machine volatility (VIRT)*   The virtual machine is the combination of hardware and software on which the software product is built. A low rating for this factor means that it is only changed occasionally (once a year), a nominal rating implies major changes every six months, and a very high rating suggests that the virtual machine will change once every two weeks.

(4) *Computer turnround time (TURN)*   This is rated from low which implies interactive systems development to very high which means that turnround time is more than 12 hours. This attribute is less relevant now than when the model was formulated. Most systems development now takes place using timesharing systems or workstation networks so that the turnround attribute is low.

There are five personnel attributes taken into consideration which reflect the experience and capabilities of development staff working on the project. These attributes are analyst capability (ACAP), application experience (AEXP), virtual machine experience (VEXP), programmer capability (PCAP) and programming language experience (LEXP). These are all rated from very low, which means little or no experience, through nominal, which means at least one year's experience, to very high, which means more than three years experience.

The project attributes are concerned with the use of software tools, the project development schedule and the use of modern programming practices. Boehm defines modern programming practices as practices such as top-down design, design and code reviews, structured programming, program support libraries, etc. It was decided to classify these under a single heading rather than attempt to assess the effect of each factor in isolation.

The project attributes are as follows:

(1)   *Modern programming practices (MODP)*   This attribute is rated on a scale from very low which implies no use of such practices through nominal which implies some use to very high which means that the use of modern practices is routine and that staff are experienced in their use.

(2)   *Software tools (TOOL)*   The availability of software tools can have a significant effect on the effort required to develop a software system. A very low value assessment of this attribute means that only basic tools such as an assembler are available. A nominal value means that a more complete set of implementation, testing and debugging tools are available and a high value suggests that tools to support all life-cycle phases are available.

(3)   *Required development schedule (SCED)*   This attribute is a measure of how well the required development schedule fits the nominal development schedule estimated using the basic COCOMO model. A very low value for this attribute means an accelerated schedule whereas a high value implies an extended schedule. Both low and high attribute values actually increase the effort required for product development.

The multipliers associated with each of these 15 attributes are shown in Table 26.1 reproduced from Boehm (1981). The particular values associated with these attributes are organization-specific and the model must be calibrated for each organization using it.

In the estimation of maintenance costs, discussed in the following chapter, these ratings are the same for all attributes except RELY (reliability), MODP (modern programming practice) and SCED (schedule). In maintenance cost estimation, the original development schedule is

Table 26.1
Project attribute
multipliers.

Cost driver	Ratings					
	Very low	**Low**	**Normal**	**High**	**Very high**	**Extra high**
RELY	0.75	0.88	1	1.15	1.4	—
DATA	—	0.94	1	1.08	1.16	—
CPLX	0.7	0.85	1	1.15	1.3	1.65
TIME	—	—	1	1.11	1.3	1.66
STOR	—	—	1	1.06	1.21	1.56
VIRT	—	0.87	1	1.15	1.3	—
TURN	—	0.87	1	1.07	1.15	—
ACAP	1.46	1.19	1	0.86	0.71	—
AEXP	1.29	1.13	1	0.91	0.82	—
PCAP	1.42	1.17	1	0.86	0.7	—
VEXP	1.21	1.1	1	0.9	—	—
LEXP	1.14	1.07	1	0.95	—	—
MODP	1.24	1.1	1	0.91	0.82	—
TOOL	1.24	1.1	1	0.91	0.83	—
SCED	1.23	1.08	1	1.04	1.1	—

irrelevant so this attribute always has a nominal value. The use of modern programming practices has a more significant effect on maintenance costs and this effect increases with product size. A low value for the reliability attribute reduces development effort but may mean increased maintenance effort will be required. Furthermore, a high development reliability means that achieving high reliability in the maintained product is easier than with a product which exhibits lower development reliability.

The modified values for RELY and MODP, also taken from Boehm (1981), are set out in Tables 26.2 and 26.3. The MODP attribute depends on the size of the delivered product in KDSI (Table 26.3).

These attributes have been determined by an analysis of historical data and the list of attributes is neither exhaustive or exclusive. Some other organization might use a different set of attributes as cost multipliers. For example, the availability of a library of software components, the use of an integrated software engineering environment or the availability of personal workstations might all be taken into account.

The basic and intermediate COCOMO models suffer from the disadvantage that they consider the software product as a single entity and apply multipliers to it as a whole. In fact, most large systems are made up

Table 26.2
Maintenance effort
multipliers.

	Very low	**Low**	**Normal**	**High**	**Very high**
RELY	1.35	1.15	1	0.98	1.1

Tables 26.1 to 26.4 are reprinted by permission of Prentice-Hall Inc., Englewood Cliffs, NJ.

Product size	Very low	Low	Normal	High	Very high
2	1.25	1.12	1	0.9	0.81
8	1.3	1.14	1	0.88	0.77
32	1.35	1.16	1	0.86	0.74
128	1.4	1.18	1	0.85	0.72
512	1.45	1.2	1	0.84	0.7

Table 26.3
MODP attribute values.

of subsystems which are not homogeneous. Some may be considered to be organic mode systems, some embedded mode, for some the reliability requirements may be high, for others low, and so on.

The complete COCOMO model takes this into account and estimates the total system costs as the sum of subsystem costs with each subsystem estimated separately. This approach reduces the margin of error in the final cost estimate but a full discussion is outside the scope of this text. Interested readers should turn to Boehm's book for a complete description of the model.

26.2.1   Model tuning

After some experience of using an estimation model such as COCOMO it may be discovered that the constants built into the model should be changed to reflect local circumstances. Boehm discusses how the model may be recalibrated by comparing actual costs to predicted costs and by using a least squares approximation to fit estimated to measured costs. This allows the constant factor and the scale factor in the basic COCOMO model to be recomputed.

For example, Table 26.4 shows the predicted project costs and a set of measured project costs. These figures are graphed in Figure 26.3. The least squares technique is a statistical technique which allows the best-fit line to the measured values to be discovered and the constant value in the COCOMO equation to be recalibrated. Many graphical packages include curve-fitting capabilities and these can be used in model recalibration.

Size	Predicted effort	Measured effort
14	57.65	65.72
17	71.65	82.40
26	115.32	131.46
40	186.82	249.10
55	266.89	304.25
60	294.21	323.63
64	316.26	302.55
97	503.86	571.04

Table 26.4
Predicted and measured software costs.

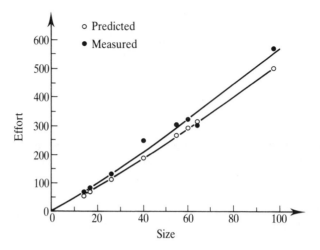

Figure 26.3
Predicted and measured
cost curves.

The exponent value can be calculated in a similar way but probably requires more data, particularly for large projects, for a valid calibration to be made. As we have seen, this value is normally close to 1. It is possible to compute new exponent values but the difference between the new value and the current published value is probably not significant.

Depending on particular modes of working within an organization, it may be possible to eliminate or combine intermediate COCOMO attributes or to add new attributes which are of particular importance. For example, the personnel attributes might be combined into a single attribute, interactive working may be the only development mode, and the use of a standard development system such as UNIX may mean that a standard toolset is always available. New attributes which might be added include the effect of working with classified data and its associated security and privacy considerations and an attribute reflecting the type of application being developed.

Values for multipliers may be computed by estimating the product costs without using a particular multiplier, measuring the actual costs then finding the best multiplier value which fits estimated to measured data.

The difficulty, of course, in adjusting the multipliers is that they are not independent variables. Few organizations have time for controlled experiments which allow the values to be calibrated. For example, say an organization decides to invest in a software engineering environment, thus affecting the tools attribute, the virtual machine volatility attribute and the turnround attribute. Calibrating the model accurately would require each attribute to be considered in isolation and the new system might have to be degraded to isolate the different attributes. It is unrealistic to expect any organization which has invested in support to reduce the effectiveness of that support in order to calibrate a costing model.

26.3 Algorithmic cost models in project planning

The problem with the COCOMO model and other algorithmic models for absolute project cost estimation is that the scope for error is high. It is very difficult to estimate product size, the amount of support software required for different products may vary dramatically, products don't just fall into three classes, the multiplier values are average rather than specific and so on. Furthermore, it is equally difficult to estimate the margin of error so we cannot readily ascribe a confidence factor to the project estimates.

However, given that errors are fairly constant, algorithmic cost models can be used for computing relative project costs where the model parameters are varied and the cost differences observed. Thus, the technique provides some quantitative basis for management on how to tackle a particular project. It allows a reasoned consideration of how resources are best used. This is valuable for reducing risk, even if the actual cost estimates produced by the model are inaccurate.

Consider a situation where the basic COCOMO model predicts an effort of 45 person-months to develop an embedded software system on microcomputer hardware. The hardware consists of a 16-bit processor with a speed of 0.2 MIPS and 64 Kbytes of store. The effort multipliers for the intermediate COCOMO model all have nominal values apart from the following:

RELY	1.15
STOR	1.21
TIME	1.10
TOOL	1.10

Thus, using the intermediate COCOMO model to estimate development effort gives the following figure:

$$PM = 45 * 1.15 * 1.21 * 1.10 * 1.10 = 76 \text{ person-months}$$

Given that the average costs per software engineer amount to $7000 per person per month the total costs of developing this project is:

$$C = 76 * 7000 = \$532\ 000$$

From the effort multipliers, it is clear that hardware constraints have a significant effect on the total software costs. Say a proposal was made to use a compatible processor which ran at twice the speed with 128K of store.

However, this requires special interfaces to be developed so the total additional hardware cost is $30 000. Furthermore, it would mean that the TOOL attribute would be very low rather than low but, because the hardware is compatible, personnel attributes are not affected.

With this new processor, both TIME and STOR attributes are reduced to nominal values so the predicted software cost is:

$$C = 45 * 1.24 * 1.15 * 7000 = \$449\ 190$$

Thus, the project cost is reduced by almost $83 000 for an additional hardware expenditure of $30 000. The overall saving is more than $50 000. Of course, the estimates are subject to error but they should be biased in the same way. Thus, the absolute saving may be less than $53 000 but the model indicates that a saving is likely if investment is made in new hardware.

Say a further proposal was made to invest in a software engineering environment at a cost of $120 000. Rather than off-line transfer of the software from the host to the target, this system might support a direct communications link between the systems. Users could write and debug target programs remotely on the host environment.

The effect of this on the cost attributes would be to reduce the turnround attribute because of interactive working, and increase the virtual machine experience attribute because the project team are not familiar with the environment. It would also probably decrease the TOOL attribute because the environment would be well populated with tools. The revised project cost if such a development system were used is:

$$C = 45 * 0.91 * 0.87 * 1.10 * 1.15 * 7000 = \$315\ 472$$

The saving from using the environment is $133 718. The cost of the development system might be recovered in the savings for this project alone. Given that a general-purpose development environment which would be available for future projects is purchased, investment in such a system is clearly cost effective. Even if the cost estimate is wildly inaccurate, it reveals that investment in the environment produces some savings which would accumulate over several projects to recover the costs of the support system.

KEY POINTS

- There are various techniques of software cost estimation. In preparing an estimate, several of these should be used. If the estimates diverge widely, this reveals that inadequate estimating information is available.

- The reality of estimation is that estimates are priced to gain a contract and the functionality of the system is adjusted to meet the estimate.

- Algorithmic cost modelling suffers from the fundamental difficulty that it relies on attributes of the finished product to make the cost estimate. At early stages of the project, these attributes are difficult to estimate accurately.

- The COCOMO costing model is a well developed model which takes project, product, hardware and personnel attributes into account when formulating a cost estimate. It also includes a means of estimating development schedules.

- To be useful, the COCOMO model has to be tuned to the needs of a user organization using historical project data. Unfortunately, such historical data is not always available.

- Algorithmic cost models are perhaps most valuable to management in helping with quantitative option analysis. They allow the cost of various options to be computed and, even with errors, the options can be compared on an objective basis.

Further reading

Software Engineering Economics. This is the definitive book on cost estimation and it covers a range of techniques. It has a complete and thorough discussion of the COCOMO model which was invented by Boehm and his collaborators. The one slight criticism which can be made is that it is a little dated in places and does not reflect trends such as workstation usage. (B.W. Boehm, 1981, Prentice-Hall.)

Cost Estimation for Software Development. This recent text is an excellent complement to Boehm's book. It provides a more concise summary of cost estimation problems and techniques and concentrates on Putman's cost estimation model rather than the COCOMO model. (B. Londeix, 1987, Addison-Wesley.)

References

Boehm, B.W. (1981), *Software Engineering Economics*, Englewood Cliffs, NJ: Prentice-Hall.

Mohanty, S.N. (1981), 'Software cost estimation: present and future', *Software – Practice and Experience*, **11** (2), 103–21.

Putnam, L. H. (1978), 'A general empirical solution to the macro software sizing and estimating problem', *IEEE Trans. Software Eng.*, **SE-4** (3), 345–61.

EXERCISES

26.1 Make an estimate of the costs of carrying out the projects described in Appendix B. Use more than one estimating method and compare the results. Given that different people make estimates, compare the different results and account for their discrepancies.

26.2 If you decide to implement any of the projects in Appendix B, use the COCOMO model *after implementation* to predict the cost and development schedule. Compare this with the original estimates and with the actual development schedule.

26.3 Write an interactive program in Pascal, C or some other programming language which implements the basic and intermediate COCOMO models and allows users to experiment with various parameter values.

26.4 Using the basic COCOMO model, estimate the costs of the following projects:

- A semi-detached mode project delivering 50 000 lines of code
- An embedded mode project delivering 25 000 lines of code
- An embedded mode project delivering 300 000 lines of code
- An organic mode project delivering 80 000 lines of code

26.5 It has been suggested that the US SDI initiative will require about 10 million lines of code to be written. Leaving aside the feasibility of this project, estimate the costs of constructing the software for such a system.

26.6 Using the examples set out in Exercise 26.4, illustrate how project multipliers such as support tool availability affect the costs of a project.

26.7 Explain how an algorithmic modelling approach can be used for option analysis and discuss why the inaccuracies of the model are less important in such situations.

26.8 A software project manager is responsible for the construction of a project with an estimated cost of $9 000 000. Given that the average monthly cost of a junior software engineer is $5000, an experienced software engineer is $7000 and a senior software engineer is $9000, that $500 000 are fixed costs (travel, etc.), and that hardware but no support software is available, derive a number of options setting out how the project budget might be allocated. You may assume that costs may be spent on either software support or people. Support software at different levels of functionality is available at an annual cost of $3000, $6000 and $10 000 per project engineer. You may assume that the associated cost multipliers for these levels of support are 0.9, 0.83 and 0.77.

Chapter 27

Software Maintenance

Objectives

This chapter is concerned with part of the software process which is often ignored but which consumes the majority of software costs. Maintenance is discussed in this part of the book because it is seen as a managerial issue. Types of maintenance, maintenance costs and cost estimation are described in this chapter. A relatively new approach to maintenance, namely program restructuring, is discussed and the notion of program evolution covered in more detail than was possible in Chapter 1.

Contents

Historically, the term 'maintenance' has been applied to the process of modifying a program after it has been delivered and is in use. These modifications may involve simple changes to correct coding errors, more extensive changes to correct design errors or drastic rewrites to correct specification errors or accommodate new requirements.

As Turski (1981) pointed out, this is a gross abuse of the term 'maintenance'. The addition of a new wing to a building would never be described as maintaining that building, yet adding new facilities to a program is considered as maintenance activity. However, as the term maintenance is widely and generally used, it will be used here to mean changing a program in order to correct errors and to provide new facilities.

This chapter has been deliberately included in the management section of the book as most of the material covered is managerial rather than technical. It is concerned with planning and predicting the process of change and is complemented by the following chapter which discusses configuration management which is the management of change.

It is impossible to produce systems of any size which do not need to be maintained. Over the lifetime of a system, its original requirements will be modified to reflect changing needs, the system's environment will change, and obscure errors, undiscovered during system validation, will emerge. Because maintenance is unavoidable, systems should be designed and implemented so that maintenance problems are minimized.

Software maintenance falls into three categories:

- Perfective maintenance
- Adaptive maintenance
- Corrective maintenance

Perfective maintenance means those changes demanded by the user or the system programmer which improve the system in some way without changing its functionality. Adaptive maintenance is maintenance due to changes in the environment of the program and corrective maintenance is the correction of undiscovered system errors. A survey by Lientz and Swanson (1980) discovered that about 65% of maintenance was perfective, 18% adaptive and 17% corrective (Figure 27.1). Furthermore, they found that large organizations devoted about 50% of their total programming effort to maintaining existing systems.

The techniques involved in maintaining a software system are essentially those used in building the system in the first place. New requirements must be formulated and validated, components of the system must be redesigned and implemented and part or all of the system must be tested. The techniques used in these activities are the same as those used during development. There are no special technical tricks which should be applied to software maintenance.

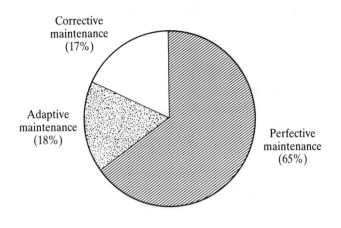

Figure 27.1
Maintenance effort
distribution.

It is particularly important that the program maintainer pays attention to the principles of information hiding discussed earlier as, for a long-lived system, it is quite possible that a set of changes to a system may themselves have to be maintained. It is a characteristic of any change that the original program structure is corrupted. The greater the corruption, the less understandable the program becomes and the more difficult it is to change. The program modifier should try, as far as possible, to minimize effects on the program structure.

One of the problems of managing maintenance is that maintenance has a poor image among software engineers. It is seen as a less skilled process than program development and, in many organizations, maintenance is allocated to inexperienced staff. The end result of this negative image is that maintenance costs are probably increased because staff allocated to the task are less skilled and experienced than those involved in system design.

Boehm (1983) suggests that the following steps should be taken to improve the motivation of maintenance staff:

(1) Couple software objectives to organizational goals.

(2) Couple software maintenance rewards to organizational performance.

(3) Integrate software maintenance personnel into operational teams.

(4) Create a discretionary perfective maintenance budget.

(5) Involve maintenance staff early in the software process during standards preparation reviews and test preparation.

In short, management must demonstrate that maintenance is of equal value and is as challenging as software development.

27.1 Maintenance costs

The costs of maintenance are difficult to estimate. Evidence from existing systems suggests that maintenance costs are, by far, the greatest cost incurred in developing and using a system. In general, these costs were dramatically underestimated when the system was designed and implemented. As an illustration of the relative cost of program maintenance, it was estimated that one US Air Force System cost $30 per instruction to develop and $4000 per instruction to maintain over its lifetime (Boehm, 1975).

These figures are perhaps exceptional as the system in question was a highly optimized, tightly coded control system. Almost certainly, performance was its principal requirement and this can sometimes be achieved by sacrificing the understandability, structuredness and, therefore, the maintainability of a program. Maintenance costs certainly vary widely from application to application but, on average, they seem to be between two and four times development costs for large embedded software systems.

As systems age, relatively more effort must be expended in maintaining those systems. One reason for this is that these systems may be written in obsolete programming languages which are no longer used for new systems development. Special provision may have to be made to train staff members to maintain these programs. This problem is likely to become particularly apparent as Ada supplements languages such as FORTRAN in large systems development.

It is obviously worthwhile to invest time and effort when designing and implementing a system to reduce maintenance and hence overall system costs. Extra development effort is a negative multiplier on maintenance costs (Figure 27.2). A percentage increase in development costs, if it leads to a comparable percentage decrease in maintenance costs, results in an overall saving. The guidelines and techniques discussed in previous chapters recognize this. They have been formulated with the explicit intention of explaining how an understandable and maintainable program can be designed, developed and tested. As the previous chapters are based on the assumption that the software engineer should produce easily maintained programs as a matter of course, further technical discussion is not presented here.

Table 27.1
Maintenance cost factors.

Non-technical factors	Technical factors
Application domain	Module independence
Staff stability	Programming language
Program age	Programming style
External environment	Program validation
Hardware stability	Documentation

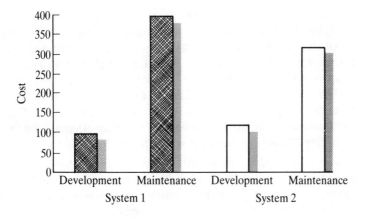

Figure 27.2
Development and
maintenance costs.

27.1.1 Maintenance cost factors

Estimating maintenance costs for any particular program is difficult. The difficulties arise because these costs are related to a number of technical and non-technical factors (Table 27.1). Some of the non-technical factors which must be taken into account are:

(1) *The application being supported*   If the application of the program is clearly defined and well understood, the system requirements may be definitive and maintenance due to changing requirements minimized. If, alternatively, the application is completely new, it is likely that the initial requirements will be modified frequently, as users gain experience with the system.

(2) *Staff stability*   It is easier for the original writer of a program to understand and change a program rather than some other individual who must understand the program by study of its documentation and code listing. Therefore, if the programmer of a system also maintains that system, maintenance costs will be reduced. In practice, the nature of the programming profession is such that individuals change jobs regularly. It is unusual for one person to develop and maintain a program throughout its useful life.

(3) *The lifetime of the program*   The useful life of a program depends on its application. Programs become obsolete when the application becomes obsolete or their original hardware is replaced and conversion costs exceed rewriting costs. Program lifetimes are much longer than originally anticipated and some of today's systems were coded in the 1960s. The older a program, the more it has been maintained and the more degraded its structure. Thus, maintenance costs tend to rise with program age.

(4)   *The dependence of the program on its external environment* If a program is dependent on its external environment it must be modified as that environment changes. For example, changes in a taxation system might require payroll, accounting, and stock control programs to be modified. Taxation changes are relatively common and maintenance costs for these programs are related to the frequency of these changes. By contrast, a program used in a mathematical application does not normally depend on humans changing the assumptions on which the program is based.

(5)   *Hardware stability* If a program is designed to operate on a particular hardware configuration and that configuration does not change during the program's lifetime, no maintenance costs due to hardware changes will be incurred. However, hardware developments are so rapid that this situation is rare. The program must be modified to use new hardware which replaces obsolete equipment.

Apart from these non-technical considerations, maintenance costs are also governed by less unpredictable, technical factors. Some technical factors affecting program maintenance are:

(1)   *Module independence* It should be possible to modify one program unit of a system without affecting any other unit.

(2)   *Programming language* Programs written in a high-level programming language are usually easier to understand (and hence maintain) than programs written in a low-level language.

(3)   *Programming style* The way in which a program is written contributes to its understandability and hence the ease with which it can be modified.

(4)   *Program validation and testing* Generally, the more time and effort spent on design validation and program testing, the fewer errors in the program and, consequently, maintenance costs resulting from error correction are lower. Maintenance costs due to error correction are governed by the type of error to be repaired. Coding errors are usually relatively cheap to correct; design errors are more expensive as they may involve the rewriting of one or more program units. Errors in the software requirements are usually the most expensive to correct because of the drastic redesign which is usually involved.

(5)   *The quality and quantity of program documentation* If a program is supported by clear, complete yet concise documentation, the task of understanding the program can be relatively straightforward. Consequently, program maintenance costs tend to be less for well documented systems than for systems supplied with poor or incomplete documentation.

Because of this multiplicity of factors affecting maintenance costs, it is impossible to present any technique of maintenance cost estimation which has general applicability. Such cost estimates can only be made using cost data from past projects and even then are only likely to be accurate when previous cost information was collected for the same type of system. However, if this information is available, the maintenance cost estimation technique described below may be useful.

27.2 Maintenance cost estimation

Using data gathered from 6.3 projects in a number of application areas, Boehm (1981) has established a formula for estimating maintenance costs. This is part of the COCOMO software cost estimation model, discussed in Chapter 26.

Boehm's maintenance cost estimation is calculated in terms of a quantity called the Annual Change Traffic (ACT) which he defines as follows:

> The fraction of a software product's source instructions which undergo change during a (typical) year either through addition or modification.

Boehm's estimation method for maintenance costs uses the ACT and the estimated or actual development effort in person-months to derive the annual effort required for software maintenance. This is computed as follows:

AME := 1.0 * ACT * SDT

AME and SDT are the annual maintenance effort and the software development time and the units of each are person-months. Note that this is a simple linear relationship. Figure 27.3 shows the maintenance costs for systems of various sizes assuming ACTs of 10, 20 and 30%.

For example, say a software project required 236 person-months of development effort and it was estimated that 15% of the code would be modified in a typical year. The basic maintenance effort estimate is:

AME := 1.0 * 0.15 * 236 = 35.4 person-months.

Boehm does not claim that this formula gives any more than a rough approximation to maintenance costs. However, it serves as a basis for computing a more accurate figure. This is based on the notion that software

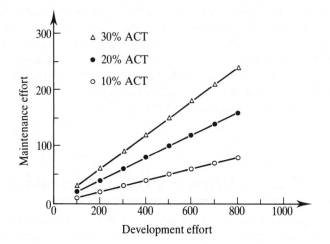

Figure 27.3
Maintenance costs.

costs and maintenance costs depend on the size of the software and a number of other factors including the reliability required, the type of software, hardware constraints and the skill of the software development personnel. Details of these factors and their effect on software costs are covered in Chapter 26.

The maintenance cost estimate may be refined by judging the importance of each factor which affects the cost and selecting the appropriate cost multiplier. The basic maintenance cost is then multiplied by each multiplier to give the revised cost estimate.

For example, say in the above system the factors having most effect on maintenance costs were reliability (RELY) which had to be very high, the availability of support staff with language and applications experience (AEXP and LEXP) which was also high, and the use of modern programming practices for system development (very high). From Boehm's table, reproduced in Chapter 26, these have multipliers as follows:

RELY   1.10
AEXP   0.91
LEXP   0.95
MODP   0.72

By applying these multipliers to the initial cost estimate, a revised figure may be computed as follows:

AME := 35.4 * 1.10 * 0.91 * 0.95 * 0.72 = 24.2 person-months.

The reduction in estimated costs has come about partly because experienced staff are available for maintenance work but mostly because modern programming practices had been used during software development. As an illustration of their importance, the maintenance cost estimate if modern programming practices are not used at all and other factors (including the development cost!) are unchanged is as follows:

$$AME := 35.4 * 1.10 * 0.91 * 0.95 * 1.40 = 47.1 \text{ person-months.}$$

This is a gross estimate of the annual cost of maintenance for the entire software system. In fact, different parts of the system will have different ACTs so a more accurate figure can be derived by estimating initial development effort and annual change traffic for each software component. The total maintenance effort is then the sum of these individual component efforts. It is outside the scope of this book to look at cost estimation at this level of detail and interested readers are referred to the original source by Boehm.

One of the problems encountered when using an algorithmic cost estimation model for maintenance cost estimation is that it takes no account of the fact that the software structure degrades as the software ages. Using the original development time as a key factor in maintenance cost estimation introduces inaccuracies as the software loses its resemblance to the original system. It is not clear whether this cost estimation model is valid for geriatric software systems.

The cost estimation model used by Boehm estimated maintenance costs which fitted reasonably well with measured actual costs. Boehm does not claim that his organization is necessarily typical and the estimation model may not work so well in other organizations or for other types of work. It may also be the case that the predicted maintenance cost affected the actual cost if it was used to set maintenance budgets.

The existence of a cost estimation model which takes into account factors such as programmer experience, hardware constraints, software complexity, etc., allows decisions about maintenance to be made on a quantitative rather than a qualitative basis. For example, say in the above example system that management decided that money might be saved by using less experienced staff for software maintenance. Assume that inexperienced staff cost $5000 per month compared to $6500 for more experienced software engineers.

Using experienced staff, the total annual maintenance costs are:

$$AMC := 24.23 * 6500 = \$157\ 495$$

Using inexperienced staff, the effort required for software maintenance is increased because the staff experience multipliers change:

$$AME := 35.24 * 1.10 * 1.07 * 1.13 * 0.72 = 33.89 \text{ person-months.}$$

Thus, total costs using inexperienced staff are:

AMC := 33.89 * 5000 = $169 450

Therefore, it appears to be more expensive in this example to use inexperienced staff rather than experienced engineers.

This emphasizes our conclusions in Chapter 26 which are that the most useful characteristic of algorithmic cost models are in assessing relative rather than absolute costs. It may be impossible to predict the annual change traffic of a system to any degree of accuracy but the inaccuracy is reflected in all computations. Although the absolute cost figure may be out of step with reality, the information allows management to make reasoned decisions about how best to allocate resources to the maintenance process.

27.3   Measuring program maintainability

The key to effective management is not to be taken by surprise. To predict what maintenance effort a system will require, some way of assessing the maintainability of system components is required. This is particularly useful when it is not clear whether a component should be changed or rewritten. If a maintainability metric can be derived, its value can help management make an informed decision on this matter.

Maintainability metrics do not measure the cost of making a particular change to a system nor do they predict whether or not a particular component will have to be maintained. Rather, they are based on the assumption that the maintainability of a program is related to its complexity. The metrics measure some aspects of the program complexity. It is suggested that high complexity values correlate with difficulties in maintaining a system component.

Halstead (1977) suggests that the complexity of a program can be measured by considering the number of unique operators, the number of unique operands, the total frequency of operators and the total frequency of operands in a program. Using these parameters, Halstead has devised metrics allowing program size, programming effort and program 'intelligence count' to be computed.

McCabe (1976) has devised a measure of program complexity using graph theoretic techniques. His theory maintains that program complexity is not dependent on size but on the decision structure of the program. Measurement of the complexity of a program depends on transforming the program so that it may be represented as a graph and counting the number of nodes, edges and connected components in that graph.

Both of these techniques may have some validity. Both suffer from the same disadvantage that they do not take into account the data structures used in the program, the program comments or the use of meaningful variable names. Shepherd *et al.* (1979) have conducted experiments using both techniques. Their results were inconclusive. Hamer and Frewin (1981) have evaluated Halstead's metrics and are dubious of their validity.

Rather than use a single metric, Kafura and Reddy (1987) use a spectrum of seven metrics to assess the complexity of a system. These included Halstead's effort metric, McCabe's complexity metric, the code size, and other metrics which take into account the way in which a component uses its data. Their experiments demonstrated that there was a high correlation between the values of the metrics produced and the perceived maintainability as assessed by human maintainers.

They suggest that it is not perhaps the absolute values of the metrics which are important but rather their relative values. If some components have a much higher value than most others, their experiments suggested that these would cause particular problems in maintenance and may well contain a higher proportion of system faults. For example, say the average complexity value for system components was X but three components had complexity rating which were much greater than X. This indicates that the design of these components should be assessed to see if it might be simplified to facilitate future component modifications.

The problem, of course, is that maintainability is related to many factors, as discussed earlier. Complexity is one of these and the metrics suggested above assume it is the dominant one. We do not know if this is actually the case so it is difficult to say whether or not these maintainability metrics are of value.

27.4   System restructuring

One of the reasons why maintenance costs are so high is that the structure of the systems which have to be modified may be non-existent or, perhaps, not obvious to the program reader. The reasons for this may be that the system is geriatric and developed without the use of information hiding or, perhaps, continuing maintenance has meant that the original structure has become so corrupt that it is no longer discernible.

There comes a stage in the life of a program where the cost of making incremental changes to a system is so high that it must either be scrapped and rewritten or completely or partially restructured. Restructuring involves examining the existing system and rewriting parts of it to improve its overall structure. Restructuring may be particularly useful when changes are confined to part of the system. Only this part need be restructured. Other parts need not be changed or revalidated.

If a program is written in a high-level language, it is possible to restructure that program automatically although the computer time required to do so may be great. Bohm and Jacopini (1966) demonstrated that any program may be rewritten in terms of simple if-then-else conditionals and while loops and that unconditional goto statements were not required. This theorem is the basis for program restructuring.

The process starts by constructing a program flow graph (discussed in Chapter 21). This is relatively simple for structured programs (those without gotos) but is more complex when goto statements are included. Once this graph has been constructed, simplification and transformation techniques are applied to the graph and, ultimately, a program which only uses while loops and simple conditional statements can be generated. This may contain some inefficiencies but these are often readily detectable and can be manually optimized.

This reduces the complexity of a program and hence should make the system easier to maintain. However, it only affects the program control structure and is of no help in improving the structure of abstractions used to represent the system. Nor can it improve systems which are difficult to maintain because of high coupling caused by the use of shared global tables.

An alternative approach which can be applied to both assembly language and high-level language programs is described by Britcher and Craig (1986). This work involved taking a large software system written in assembly language, discovering its structure and documenting that structure using functional and data abstractions. This was necessary because the system had been operating on obsolete hardware and had to be rehosted on modern computers. It was not, however, necessary to change all of the program and it was clear that the cost of restructuring was less than the cost of a complete system rewrite.

Many parts of the system were not well structured and the effort really involved the imposition of structure onto the program. For example, shared data areas were reconstructed as data abstractions and control structures were all rebuilt as simple conditionals or loops. The outcome of the work was a well documented system whose life was considerably extended by the restructuring process.

It may well be that a combination of automatic and manual system restructuring is the best approach. The control structure could be improved automatically and this makes the system easier to understand. The abstraction and data structures of the program may then be discovered, documented and improved using a manual approach.

Decisions on whether to restructure or rewrite a program can only be made on a case-by-case basis. Some of the factors which must be taken into account are:

(1) Is a significant proportion of the system stable and not subject to frequent change? If so, this suggests restructuring rather than rewriting as it is only really necessary to restructure that part of the program which is to be changed.

(2) Does the program rely on obsolete support software such as compilers, etc.? If so, this suggests it should be rewritten in a modern language as the future availability of the support software cannot be guaranteed.

(3) Are tools available to support the restructuring process? If not, manual restructuring is the only option.

System restructuring offers an opportunity to control maintenance costs and I believe that it will become increasingly important. The rate of change of hardware development means that many embedded software systems which are still in use must be changed as the hardware on which they execute cannot be supported. Systems developed in the early 1970s often fell into this category and structured development techniques were only occasionally used at that time. If the life of these systems is to be extended, it will be essential to carry out some restructuring.

27.5 Program evolution dynamics

Program evolution dynamics is the study of system change and the majority of work in this area has been carried out by Lehman and Belady (1985). We have already come across these ideas in Chapter 1 where Lehman's laws were introduced. Lehman and Belady's work has been concerned with the process of change and it is instructive to look at their work in a little more detail in this chapter and in the following chapter on configuration management.

Interestingly, Lehman's laws are one of the few examples in software engineering of theories which have been derived from observations. It is normal practice in other sciences to base theories on observations, but objective observations in software engineering are difficult and expensive to make. Consequently, most theories are based on subjective analysis, prejudice and, sometimes, commercial opportunism. It is important to consider many theories with a degree of scepticism.

Lehman and Belady examined the growth and evolution of a number of large software systems and the proposed laws were derived from these measurements. The 'laws' (hypotheses, really) may be paraphrased as follows:

(1)   A program that is used in a real-world environment necessarily must change or become less and less useful in that environment (the law of continuing change).

(2)   As an evolving program changes, its structure becomes more complex unless active efforts are made to avoid this phenomenon (the law of increasing complexity).

(3)   Program evolution is a self-regulating process and measurement of system attributes such as size, time between releases, number of reported errors, etc., reveals statistically significant trends and invariances (the law of large program evolution).

(4)   Over the lifetime of a program, the rate of development of that program is approximately constant and independent of the resources devoted to system development (the law of organizational stability).

(5)   Over the lifetime of a system, the incremental system change in each release is approximately constant (the law of conservation of familiarity).

The first law tells us that system maintenance is an inevitable process and much of this book is indeed based on this assumption. We have already seen that fault repair is only part of the maintenance activity and that changing system requirements will always mean that a system must be changed if it is to remain useful. Thus, the constant theme of this text is that software engineering should be concerned with producing systems whose structure is such that the costs of change are minimized.

The second law states that, as a system is changed, its structure is degraded and additional costs, over and above those of simply implementing the change, must be accepted if the structural degradation is to be reversed. The maintenance process should perhaps include explicit restructuring activities which are simply aimed at improving the adaptability of the system. It suggests that program restructuring, as discussed earlier in this chapter, is an appropriate process to apply.

The third law is, perhaps, the most interesting and the most contentious of Lehman's laws. It suggests that large systems have a dynamic all of their own and that is established at an early stage in the development process. This dynamic determines the gross trends of the system maintenance process and the particular decisions made by maintenance management are overwhelmed by it.

In essence, this law says that maintenance management cannot really do whatever it wants as far as changing the system is concerned. It does not have a free hand in setting targets for maintenance activity. Lehman and Belady suggest that this law is a result of fundamental structural and organizational effects. They use the terms inertia, momentum and feedback to describe these but it is my opinion that these terms confuse rather than illuminate their argument.

As changes are made to a system, these changes introduce new system faults which then require more changes to correct them. Once a system exceeds some minimal size it acts in the same way as an inertial mass. It inhibits major change because these changes are expensive to make and result in a system whose reliability is degraded. Thus, even if management would like to make a system change, it may not be possible to do so. In essence, the fact that change requires further change imposes a stabilizing factor on the system and means that it is necessary to limit the total changes made.

An organizational constraint to major system change is a result of the fact that large systems are so expensive that they must be produced by relatively large organizations. These organizations have their own internal bureaucracies which impose checks and balances to change and which determine the budget allocated to a particular system. Major system changes require organizational decision making and, almost certainly, changes to the project budget.

Such decisions usually take some time to make and, during that time, other system changes may be proposed which must be allocated higher priority. It may be necessary to shelve the changes to a later date with the consequent requirements for the approval process to be re-initiated. Thus, the rate of change of the system is governed by the overall decision-making processes of the organization.

Lehman's fourth law suggests that most large programming projects work in what he terms a 'saturated' state. That is, a change of resources or staffing has imperceptible effects on the long-term evolution of the system. Of course, this is also suggested by the third law which essentially says that program evolution is independent of management decision making. Again this may seem to be contra-intuitive but it backs up the notion that large software development teams are unproductive as the communication overheads are such that they dominate the work of the team.

Lehman's fifth law is concerned with the change increments in each system release and is discussed in the following chapter on configuration management.

It must be emphasized that Lehman's laws are really hypotheses and it is unfortunate that more work has not been carried out to validate them. Nevertheless, they do seem to be sensible and maintenance management should not attempt to circumvent them but should use them as a basis for planning the maintenance process. It may be that business considerations require them to be ignored at any one time (say it is necessary to make several major system changes). In itself, this is not impossible but management should realize the likely consequences for future system change.

KEY POINTS

- There are three identifiable types of software maintenance. These are perfective maintenance which is system improvement; adaptive maintenance which is system evolution; and corrective maintenance which is system repair.

- The cost of software maintenance usually exceeds the cost of software development. Typically maintenance costs are a factor of 2 to 4 higher than development costs for large systems.

- There are a variety of technical and non-technical factors affecting maintenance costs. These include application factors, environmental factors, personnel factors, programming language factors and documentation.

- An algorithmic approach can be used for maintenance cost estimation but its accuracy is dubious.

- We do not, at the moment, have effective metrics which allow the maintainability of a program or a component to be measured.

- System restructuring is a relatively new approach to maintenance. It involves restructuring those parts of a program which are subject to change. It is cost effective when changes are mostly confined to an identifiable segment of a system.

- There appear to be a number of invariant relationships (Lehman's laws) which affect the evolution of a software system.

Further reading

IEEE Software, **3** (3), 1986.   This is a special issue of this very readable journal devoted to software maintenance. It contains a number of papers on maintenance topics including program reading, program understanding and program restructuring.

Program Evolution. Processes of Software Change.   This is an edited collection of papers from these authors which charts their thoughts on software evolution from its inception in the early 1970s to the mid-1980s. It is a very interesting text in this respect although it would have been improved with a little more linking text from the editors. (M.M. Lehman and L. Belady, 1985, Academic Press.)

References

Boehm, B.W. (1975), 'The high cost of software', in *Practical Strategies for Developing Large Software Systems*, Horowitz, E. (ed.). Reading, Mass.: Addison-Wesley.

Boehm, B.W. (1981), *Software Engineering Economics*, Englewood Cliffs, NJ: Prentice-Hall.

Boehm, B.W. (1983), 'The economics of software maintenance', *Proc. Software Maintenance Workshop*, Washington DC, 9–37.

Bohm, C. and Jacopini, G. (1966), 'Flow diagrams, Turing machines and languages with only two formation rules', *Comm. ACM*, **9** (5), 366–71.

Britcher, R.N. and Craig, J.J. (1986), 'Using modern design practices to upgrade aging software systems', *IEEE Software*, **3** (3), 16–26.

Halstead, M.H. (1977), *Elements of Software Science*, Amsterdam: North-Holland.

Hamer, P.G. and Frewin, G.D. (1981), 'Halstead's software science – a critical examination', *Proc. 6th Int. Conf. on Software Engineering*, Tokyo.

Kafura, D. and Reddy, G.R. (1987) 'The use of software complexity metrics in software maintenance', *IEEE Trans. Software Eng.*, **SE-13** (3), 335–43.

Lehman, M.M. and Belady, L. (1985), *Program Evolution. Processes of Software Change*, London: Academic Press.

Lientz, B.P. and Swanson, E.B. (1980), *Software Maintenance Management*, Reading, Mass.: Addison-Wesley.

McCabe, T.J. (1976), 'A complexity measure', *IEEE Trans. Software Eng.*, **SE-2** (4), 308–20.

Shepherd, S.B., Curtis, B., Milliman, P., Borst, M. and Love, T. (1979), 'First year results from a research program in human factors in software engineering', *AFIPS*, 1021–7.

Turski, W. (1981), 'Software Stability', *Proc. 6th ACM European Conf. on Systems Architecture*, London.

EXERCISES

27.1 Describe the technical and non-technical factors which affect system maintenance costs. Explain how, as a software manager, you would attempt to minimize maintenance costs in projects you are managing.

27.2 Given that the annual change traffic in a system is 14% per year and the initial development cost was $245 000, compute an estimate for the annual system maintenance cost. Given that the lifetime of the system is 12 years, what is the total cost of that software system?

27.3 Explain the difficulties involved in measuring program maintainability. Describe why the notion of relating maintainability to complexity is oversimplistic.

27.4 Explain the rationale underlying Lehman's laws. Under what circumstances might the laws break down?

27.5 Go back to a program you wrote some time ago and write documentation describing the structure of that program. Keep a log of the difficulties encountered in understanding the program.

27.6 Seek out papers on program maintenance and compile a list of hints and tips for the maintainer of large Pascal or C programs.

Chapter 28

Configuration Management

Objective

The objective of this chapter is to discuss the process of configuration management which is critical to the maintenance of large software systems. The introduction defines configuration management as the management of system change. This is followed by a section discussing the planning of configuration management in a large project. Section 28.2 covers change control and Section 28.3 the activity of building a system from its components. This is followed by a description of version and release management strategies, and the final part of the chapter covers CASE tools to assist the configuration management process.

Contents

Configuration management is that part of the software management process which is concerned with the development of procedures and standards for managing an evolving software system. In essence, it is concerned with change: how to control change, how to manage systems which have been subject to change, and how to release these changed systems to customers.

Configuration management (CM) is closely allied with the quality assurance process and, in some organizations, the same manager may share quality assurance and configuration management responsibilities. The relationship between these activities is due to the fact that they are both post-development activities. Software is first released by the developers to quality assurance and, once certified, it is passed on to the configuration management team who take control of that software.

The need for configuration management arises because software systems, particularly large ones, have a long lifetime and, during that lifetime, are subjected to change. Furthermore, that change is a team activity and it is exceptional for it to be the responsibility of the original software developer. Configuration management is intended to ensure that the changes to the software are made in such a way that overall costs are minimized and, most importantly, that minimum disruption is caused to existing users of the software.

There are various activities which can be considered under the general heading of configuration management and different organizations adopt different roles for their configuration management teams. This chapter considers four configuration management activities, namely configuration management planning, change control, system building, and version and release management.

It is inevitable that a useful software system will exist in a number of versions for different computers, for different operating systems, incorporating client-specific functions and so on. The configuration manager is responsible for keeping track of the differences between versions of the software and for ensuring that new versions are derived in a controlled way. He or she may also be responsible for ensuring that these new versions of the software are released to the correct customers at the appropriate time.

Software versions are created by applying changes to existing software and perhaps the most critical role of the configuration management team is change control. Uncontrolled change quickly leads to chaos and configuration management is concerned with assessing the impact of changes, costing these changes and deciding if and when they should be applied. Once changes have been made, the configuration management team is also often responsible for rebuilding the software system from its components.

Military software procurers normally insist that their own standards and procedures are used and the IEEE has published a standard (828-1983) for configuration management plans. Software companies may develop their own in-house standards based on these external standards. The material in these standards documents is very detailed and it is not appropriate to discuss it in this context. As with all standards, the important thing is to have some standard which is consistently applied rather than simply to rely on informal management practices.

28.1   Configuration management planning

Configuration management is concerned with the management of software systems after they have been developed, yet the success of the configuration management process relies on planning which should take place before and during the software development. Configuration management planning is not an activity which is carried out in isolation. It is an integral part of the overall project planning process and relates to almost all other activities in that process.

In the course of developing a large software system there are, literally, thousands of documents produced. Many of these are technical working documents which present a snapshot of ideas used as a basis for further development and such documents are subject to frequent and regular change. Others are inter-office memos, minutes of group meetings, outline plans and proposals, etc. Although these documents may be of interest to a project historian, they are not critical for future maintenance of the system.

Thus, one of the key tasks of the configuration management planning process is to decide exactly which items (or classes of item) are to be subject to formal configuration control. The documents chosen would typically be project plans, specifications, designs, programs and test data suites. In short, all of the documents which may be necessary for future system maintenance must be placed under configuration control. We refer to these documents as formal documents.

Having established what documents are to be managed, the configuration management planning process must then define the following:

- A document naming scheme
- The relationships between formal documents
- Who is responsible for checking the quality of a formal document
- Who is responsible for delivering each formal document to CM

The document naming scheme must be such that a unique name is given to all documents under configuration control. Furthermore, the naming scheme chosen should be such that related documents such as specifications and designs have related names. This can be accomplished using a hierarchical naming scheme. Thus examples of names might be:

> ECLIPSE/UI/TOOLS/DE/ADI/FS
> ECLIPSE/UI/TOOLS/DE/ADI/CODE

These names have a number of components – the project (ECLIPSE), the sub-project (UI), the part of the sub-project (TOOLS), the particular tool being developed (DE, abbreviation of Design Editor), the part of the tool which is documented (ADI, Abstract Data Interface) and the type of document (FS or CODE, Functional Specification or program source).

Defining the relationships between formal documents means drawing up the document hierarchy which is embodied in the naming scheme. For example, the above names suggest a hierarchy as shown in Figure 28.1. The leaves of the documentation hierarchy are required formal documents. Figure 28.1 shows that four formal documents are required for each managed entity. These are a functional specification (FS), a design specification (DS), the code of the component and a test specification (TS).

The description of this hierarchy is a critical project document as it allows document names to be generated and documents to be located. Thus it should itself be placed under configuration control and should not be changed in an arbitrary way.

The configuration management plan should define the individuals responsible for document quality control and document delivery. Note that the individual responsible for document delivery need not be the person

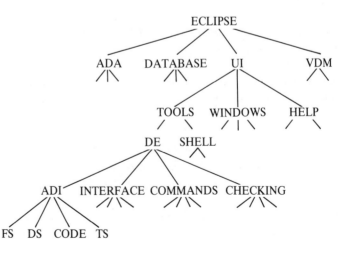

Figure 28.1
Documentation hierarchy.

responsible for producing the document. To simplify interfaces, it is usually convenient to make project managers or team leaders responsible for all of the documents produced by their team.

The CM planning process also involves drawing up procedures for change control, system building and version management. These are discussed later in this chapter.

Another aspect of configuration management planning is the definition of a database schema to record configuration information. The configuration database is used to record all relevant information relating to configurations and is used as a project management tool after the software has been delivered.

A configuration database must be able to provide answers to a variety of queries about system configurations. Typical queries might be:

(1) Which customers have taken delivery of a particular version of the system?

(2) What hardware and operating system configuration is required to run a given system version?

(3) How many versions of a system have been created and what were their creation dates?

(4) What versions of a system might be affected if a particular component is changed?

(5) How many change requests are outstanding on a particular version?

(6) How many reported faults exist in a particular version?

The database schema drawn up during the CM planning process should be such that information which will allow anticipated queries to be answered is recorded in the database. Furthermore, as well as defining the schema, procedures for recording and retrieving project information must also be defined.

Some CM databases, particularly for old systems, are still paper rather than computer databases. The range of queries which can be supported with such paper databases is more limited than is possible with computerized systems. Given the existence of low-cost hardware and database management systems, there is no justification for continuing with paper-based systems for new developments.

28.2 Change control

Change control is perhaps the most important responsibility of a project CM team. We have already discussed how the necessity for change is inherent in software systems and, irrespective of improvements in the

Example 28.1
Change request
procedure.

Request change by completing a change request form
Analyse change request
if change is valid **then**
        Assess how change might be implemented
        Assess change cost
        Submit request to change control board
        if change is accepted **then**
            repeat
                make changes to software
                submit changed software for quality approval
            until *software quality is adequate*
            create new system version
    else
        reject change request
else
    reject change request

---

software process, there will always be a need to apply changes to existing software systems.

Change control procedures ensure that the changes to a system are made in a controlled way so that their effect on the system can be predicted. Of course, during a system development it is counter-productive to impose rigid change control but the change control process should come into effect when the software (or associated documentation) is delivered to configuration management. Items accepted for change control are sometimes called a *baseline*.

The basic change control procedure can be defined as shown in Example 28.1. The first stage in the procedure is to complete a change request form. This is a formal document where the requester sets out the change required to the system. As well as recording the change required, this form records the recommendations regarding the change, the estimated costs of the change, the dates when the change was requested, approved, implemented and validated. It may also include a part where the maintenance engineer outlines how the change is to be implemented.

Defining the change request form (CRF) is part of the CM planning process although, for many contracts, forms conforming to some client standard must be used. The information provided in the change request form is the basis of much of the information which is recorded in the CM database.

Once a change request form has been submitted, it is analysed to ensure that the change is a valid one. It is sometimes the case that users of a system submit change requests setting out apparent system errors and the fault is not with the system but in the way in which it has been used. It is also common for different users to request the same or very similar changes. If the analysis process discovers that a change request is invalid, duplicated or has already been considered, the change is rejected.

For valid changes, the next stage of the process is change assessment and costing. The impact of the change on the overall system must be determined and a means of implementing that change discovered. The cost of making the change and possibly changing other system components to accommodate the change is then estimated and recorded on the change request form. This assessment process is much simplified if a configuration database is available where all component inter-relationships are recorded.

There are some classes of change which do not require any further assessment. For example, change requests which point out typographical errors in documents, which have no other impact on the system and which may be implemented very cheaply may be immediately accepted and put into effect. Again, part of the CM planning process is to set out which classes of change fall into this category.

The majority of changes, however, should be submitted to a change control board who decide whether or not the change is to be accepted. The change control board considers the impact of the change from a strategic and organizational rather than a technical point of view and decides whether or not the change is economically justified.

Formally structured change control boards, including senior client and contractor staff, are a requirement of military projects. For other projects, the make-up of the change control board depends on the project and the organization. It may simply consist of a single reviewer. What is important, however, is that the change control board should be independent of the project and should be able to consider the change from a broad organizational perspective.

If the change is approved by the change control board, it may then be applied to the software. The revised software then undergoes quality assurance to check that the change has been properly made and that it has not adversely affected other parts of the system. Once this has been done, the changed software is handed over to the CM team and, ultimately, it is incorporated in a new version of the system.

As software components are changed, it is important that a record of all of the changes which were made to each component is maintained. This is sometimes called the derivation history of a component and is very valuable to maintenance engineers. The most effective way to maintain such a record is in a standardized comment prologue kept at the beginning of the component. If a standard is adopted, tools may be written to process these prologues and produce reports about component changes.

An example of a standardized comment prologue incorporating change information (taken from the design editing system, described in Part 2) is shown in Figure 28.2.

```
/* ────────────────────────────────────────────────── */
/*                                                      */
/* ALVEY ECLIPSE PROGRAMME                              */
/*                                                      */
/* Identity: ECLIPSE/UI/DESIGN_EDITOR/ADI/CC10          */
/*                                                      */
/* Title: Node.c                                        */
/*                                                      */
/* Author: I.Sommerville                                */
/*                                                      */
/* Date: 20/1/86                                        */
/*                                                      */
/* (C) COPYRIGHT ALVEY ECLIPSE CONSORTIUM, 1986         */
/*                                                      */
/* Modification history                                 */
/*                                                      */
/* Version No.   Modifier    Date      Change           Reason            */
/* 1.1           J. Brown    20/1/86   CM info added     Submitted to CM   */
/* 1.2           S. Beer     16/5/86   Links altered     Bug rep. 063      */
/* ────────────────────────────────────────────────── */
```

Figure 28.2
A component header comment.

28.3 System building

System building is the process of taking the components of a system and combining them into a single unit which executes on a particular target configuration. This may not appear to be a particularly difficult task but, for large systems, the process may take several days. It is a very expensive part of the configuration management process.

System building requires particular care when the system is built using one computer yet must execute on some other machine. The first sign of build problems may be when the target system simply does not start up. In such situations it is difficult to diagnose the problem. The build team may have to redo much of the building process to correct the fault.

The factors which the system building team must take into account are:

(1) Have all the components which make up a system been included in the build instructions?

(2) Has the appropriate version of each required component been included in the build instructions?

(3) Are all required data files available?

(4) If data files are referenced within a component is the name used the same as the name under which the data file is installed on the target machine?

(5)   Is the appropriate version of the compiler and other required tools available? Sometimes particular configurations have to be built using a non-current compiler version because they are dependent on some peculiarities of that compiler.

A complete system build may require the compilation and relinking of all the components of a system. For large systems with many hundreds of components this can be a lengthy process and several days may be required simply to complete all of the compilations. Normally, however, the compilation process is carried out incrementally and the majority of the components which are assembled are in compiled form.

When component source code exists in multiple versions, it is sometimes unclear which version of the source has been used to derive an object-code component. This is a particular problem in environments where systems are typically built using the most recent component version which has the same name as previous versions (most UNIX environments fall into this category).

However, this problem can be tackled using a software tool which examines the modification and creation dates of source and object code and only recreates the object code from the source when the source has been modified after the creation of the available object code component. MAKE, discussed later, is an example of such a tool which is used in UNIX systems.

The fundamental problems in system building arise because the build process requires that build instructions are specified in terms of physical storage components (typically files but perhaps database entities). It is usually the case that these are fairly sizeable objects and each file may be made up of a number of logical software components. There is rarely a one-to-one mapping between physical storage organizations and logical software structure.

One way to tackle this problem is to use a module interconnection language (DeRemer and Kron, 1976; Sommerville and Thomson, 1986) to describe the software structure and to use this description to create the system build instructions (Figure 28.3).

The structural description is simply a specification of the static relationships of the software components and, as such, is a valuable document for software maintenance. The name mapping system relates logical components to their physical storage entity and the system build instruction generator takes component type information and transformation rules and generates a set of instructions to build the system.

This approach simplifies the process because the build team need not be involved with generating the low-level build instructions. Given that different system versions have the same logical structure, each version is specified by a different mapping from logical to physical components.

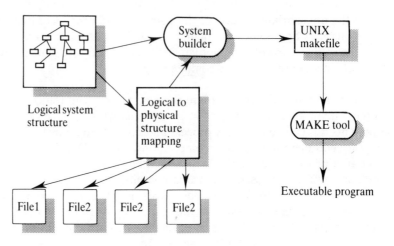

Figure 28.3
System building from a
logical structure
description.

Logical system
structure

Logical to
physical
structure
mapping

System
builder

UNIX
makefile

MAKE tool

Executable program

File1   File2   File2   File2

28.4   Version and release management

Version and release management involves drawing up an identification scheme for different versions of a system, ensuring that that scheme is applied when new system versions are created, and planning when new releases of a system should be distributed to customers.

At first sight, the naming of versions of a system appears to be a simple notion. The first version of a system is simply called 1.0, subsequent versions are 1.1, 1.2 and so on. At some stage, it is decided to create version 2.0 and the process starts again at version 2.1, 2.2, etc. For convenience, we refer to the base version (1.0, 2.0, etc.) as a system release and to intermediate versions simply as versions. In essence, the scheme is a linear one based on the assumption that system versions are created in sequence. Version management tools such as SCCS (Rochkind, 1975) support such a naming scheme.

This scheme has an attractive simplicity but begs several questions:

(1)   When should a new release rather than a new version be created?

(2)   If a number of versions are created from a single parent, how should they be numbered? For example, say a system is intended to run on a number of different computer architectures and these are all derived from a single base release numbered 1.0. Should the versions be numbered 1.1, 1.2, etc., implying sequential derivation?

(3)   If very many versions of a system are created and distributed to
       different customers, how can the version naming scheme include
       some customer identifier? It may well be the case that each customer
       or system user has a unique version of the system.

These identification problems arise because the naming scheme implies a
linear derivation of versions whereas the actual logical derivation structure
is a network structure such as that shown in Figure 28.4. In this example,
version 1.0 has spawned two versions 1.1 and 1.1a. Version 1.1 has also
spawned two versions, namely, 1.2 and 1.1b. Version 2.0 is not derived
from 1.2 but from 1.1a. Version 2.2 is not a direct descendent of version 2
as it is derived from version 1.2.

From any one version of the system, it is possible to derive some
new system version which is in some way observably distinct from it. This
derivation may add new functionality or performance, or may repair
system faults. As well as this, however, it is possible to derive system
versions which are functionally equivalent but which are tailored for
different hardware or software configurations. These are sometimes
termed system variants. Of course, each of these may also act as a base for
further development and so may have its own set of associated versions and
variants.

An alternative to a numeric naming structure is to use a hierarchical
naming scheme in conjunction with symbolic naming. For example, rather
than refer to version 1.1.2, a particular instantiations of a system might be
referred to as V1/VAX_VMS/11_750, implying that this was a version for a
DEC VAX computer running the VMS operating system and configured
for an 11-750 computer. This has some advantages over the linear scheme
but, again, it does not truly represent the derivation structure.

Given that a workable naming scheme can be devised, a decision has
to be made on the criteria for incorporating system changes to create a new
system version. Furthermore, the criteria for distributing a new system
release must also be established. These are not by any means the same

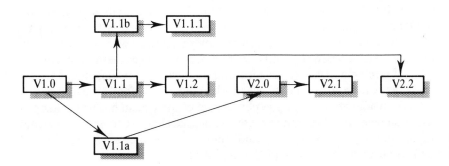

Figure 28.4
Version derivation
structure.

thing. Creating a system release involves expensive system validation and (probably) documentation, whereas a new version may simply be created for the purposes of internal development.

It is important that the creation of system versions should be the responsibility of a single team or individual within a project even when the version created is not intended for external release. It is only possible for the configuration management database to be assuredly consistent if version control is centralized within the project.

Over the lifetime of a system, changes are likely to be proposed on a fairly regular basis. These fall into the categories discussed in the previous chapter. Corrective changes are intended to fix faults, perfective changes are intended to improve the non-functional behaviour of the system, and adaptive changes are intended to change the system functionality. A decision which must be made by configuration management is how often the components affected by these changes should be reconfigured to create a new version or release of the system.

In some cases, this decision is forced on management. It may be that a particularly serious fault is discovered in a released system and it is imperative that a new system version is produced which incorporates a repair for that fault. More commonly, however, management can decide when to apply system changes.

The problem posed by change is that it is likely that changing a system will introduce new faults into that system or bring other existing faults to light. If a release incorporates a large number of changes, it is likely that there will be a correspondingly large number of new faults. System reliability may be impaired. The need for future fault repair changes will be intensified.

We have already looked at Lehman's laws (Lehman and Belady, 1985) in previous chapters and his fifth law, the law of conservation of familiarity suggests that, over the lifetime of a system, the incremental system change in each release is approximately constant. The measure of change was the number of system modules which were modified in any one release.

This law was proposed by observing changes to large systems which showed that if a large number of changes were made in one release of the system it had to be followed fairly quickly by a system with a smaller number of changes which were exclusively concerned with fault repair. Over the lifetime of a system, it was observed that this was a self-regulating process which tended to a constant number of changes per system release.

Lehman and Belady suggest that it is wise for management to take this observation into account when planning release and to avoid system releases where an unduly large percentage of the system has been changed. They suggest that an appropriate change strategy is to interleave fault repair releases of a system and releases which change the system's behaviour or its functionality (Figure 28.5).

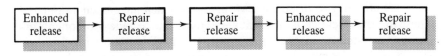

Figure 28.5
System release strategy.

A common sense analysis suggests that this approach is the correct one. If some of the changes to be made to a system are concerned with fault repair and others with changing the system behaviour, mixing these change types could cause problems. The faults reported apply to a given version of the system code and if that code is changed to amend its behaviour it is expensive to determine if the faults still apply.

Of course, it is unlikely that a state will be reached where a fault-free version of the system will be produced whose functionality may then be changed. However, it is certainly the case that all serious faults (faults which cause system corruption) should be repaired before functional or behavioural changes are contemplated.

A common difficulty of release management is the fact that customers may not actually want a new release of the system! A system user may be happy with an existing system version and may consider the cost of changing to a new version unwarranted. Eventually, however, as the system's functionality is enhanced, it is likely that the customer will decide to change.

This causes CM problems because it makes it unwise to make new releases of the system dependent on the existence of previous releases. For example, say Release 1 of a system is distributed and put into use. Release 2 follows which requires the installation of new data files but some customers do not need the facilities of Release 2 so remain with Release 1. Release 3 requires the data files installed in Release 2 and has no new data files of its own. However, it cannot be assumed that these files have already been installed in all sites where Release 3 is to be installed. Thus, these data files must also be distributed and installed with Release 3 of the system.

28.5 Configuration management tools

Major problems which exist with any large software system are keeping track of the development and maintenance of program modules, determining the interdependence of modules and ensuring that the common code in different versions of a system is consistent. This is an immense information management problem which is best tackled with tool support.

There are two principal CM functions which have been automated. These are the tracking of different versions of source code components and building a system from its component parts. This latter chore involves both specifying what components make up a system and deciding on how these are to be processed to make up an executable system.

MAKE (Feldman, 1979) and SCCS (Rochkind, 1975) are described here as examples of configuration management tools. SCCS keeps track of system modifications and different system versions, whereas MAKE ensures the consistency of source code and its corresponding object code. Both of these programs are part of the UNIX system. Other configuration management systems have been described by Tichy (1982), by Lampson and Schmidt (1983) who discuss the problems of system building in a distributed environment and by Leblang and Chase (1987). One of these environments (DSEE) is briefly discussed later in this section.

SCCS (Source Code Control System) was originally developed for IBM 370 hardware but is now distributed with UNIX. The aim of SCCS is to allow different versions of the system to be maintained without unnecessary code duplication. It controls system updates by ensuring that no part of the system can be updated by more than one programmer at any one time. It also records when updates were made, what source lines were changed and who was responsible for the change.

SCCS is principally a system for storing and recording changes to system modules. Each time a module is changed, that change is recorded and stored in what is termed a delta. Subsequent changes are also recorded as deltas. To produce the latest version of a system, SCCS applies the deltas in turn to the original module until all deltas have been processed (Figure 28.6). The user of SCCS can specify that the system should be generated up to any point in the delta chain, allowing systems at different stages of development to be produced.

An extension of this feature is the ability to freeze a system at any point in the chain. When a module is added to SCCS initially, it is deemed to be Release 1.0. Subsequent deltas create 1.1, 1.2, 1.3, etc. At some stage, the programmer may wish to freeze the system, for testing say, although further system development, including the addition of more deltas, may be continuing in parallel. Freezing a system involves specifying that a set of deltas constitutes a new release of the system (Figure 28.7). In order to obtain Release 1 of the system, the SCCS user requests that release, and only those deltas pertaining to Release 1 are applied.

Figure 28.6
Deltas in SCCS.

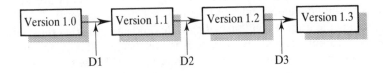

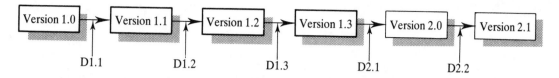

Figure 28.7
Freezing a system using SCCS.

Furthermore, Release 1 can be modified after development of Relase 2 is in progress by adding new level 1 deltas. In the above example, D1.4 could be inserted between D1.3 and D2.1.

As deltas are date stamped and owner stamped, and the user of SCCS can specify that a system version at any particular date should be created and can also generate management reports on system development.

MAKE is a complementary system which maintains the correspondence between source code and object code versions of a system. It is a file-based system and the user must describe the system structure in terms of the files where components are stored. In some cases, dependencies exist between those files, that is, changing one file also necessitates changing some other file or group of files. MAKE provides a mechanism for specifying those dependencies. Using built-in information and user specified commands, MAKE can cause the object code of a system to be recreated when a change is made to part of the system source code.

Using MAKE, the programmer must initially state file dependencies. For example, if the object code file x.o depends on the source code files x.c and d.c, this can be stated. If d.c is changed, this change can be detected by MAKE and x.o recreated by recompiling x.c and d.c. There is no need for the user to recompile files after an editing session – MAKE works out necessary recompilations and initiates them automatically.

As an example of how MAKE can be used, consider a situation where a program called comp is created out of object modules scan.o, syn.o, sem.o and cgen.o. For each object module, there exists a source code module called scan.c, syn.c, sem.c and cgen.c. A file of declarations called defs.h is shared by scan.c, syn.c and sem.c (Figure 28.8). Modifications can be made to any of scan.c, syn.c and sem.c without requiring any other files to be recompiled, but a modification to defs.h requires the recompilation of the associated source code. MAKE represents this dependency graph textually and includes commands which are invoked to build the system.

There are two major problems with MAKE as a system building utility. The first of these is that it is difficult to write and to understand makefiles for even moderately large systems as the dependency graph quickly becomes complicated. This is particularly true when the order of compilation is important, as it is in Ada. Some Ada systems provide makefile generators which process Ada component dependencies and automatically create a makefile. Of course, makefile generators don't help makefile readers.

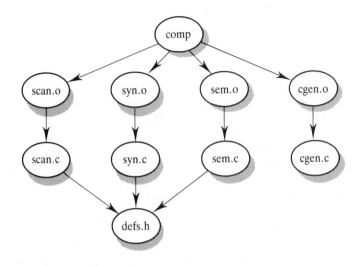

Figure 28.8
Component depedency
graph.

The second problem is inherent in the design of MAKE and cannot be resolved by tool improvement. MAKE assumes that a system is structured as a set of files and allows the dependencies of these files to be defined. In reality, a system is actually structured as a set of language abstractions (procedures, functions, packages, etc.). MAKE relies on the programmer to maintain the correspondence between files and the abstractions stored in these files. As discussed above, the resolution of this problem depends on building a system from a logical rather than a physical component description.

Both MAKE and SCCS are relatively old systems which were designed for use with timesharing machines. A more recent configuration management system is DSEE (Leblang and Chase, 1987) which is designed to operate on a network of workstations. Like MAKE and SCCS, DSEE supports version management and system building but includes a number of innovative features:

(1)   It allows different versions of a system to be built in parallel.

(2)   It supports the parallel building of system components by distributing build command sequences to idle nodes on the workstation network.

(3)   It uses a rule-based 'configuration thread' to describe system versions.

Conceptually, DSEE does little more than MAKE and SCCS but it represents a new generation of configuration management tools which offer richer functionality and much improved performance to their users.

KEY POINTS

- Configuration management is the management of system change. When a system is maintained, it is important that changes are incorporated in a controlled way and it is the role of the CM team to ensure this.

- In a large project, a formal document naming scheme should be established and used as a basis for managing the project documents.

- The CM team should be supported by a configuration database which records information about system changes and change requests which are outstanding. Projects should have some formal means of requesting system changes.

- System building is the process of assembling system components into an executable program to run on some target computer system. Problems can arise in this process because the physical storage organization of the components does not match the logical system structure.

- When setting up a configuration management scheme, some consistent means of version numbering should be established.

- System releases should be phased so that a release which provides new system functionality is followed by a release to repair errors.

- Some tools are available to assist with the process of configuration management. The best known of these is the version management tool SCCS and the system building tool MAKE.

Further reading

Software Configuration Management.   Configuration management is not a well documented area of software engineering, partially because it has not attracted a great deal of academic interest. This is one of the few available books and although it is sometimes annoyingly informal, it contains much wisdom. (W. A. Babich, 1986, Addison-Wesley.)

References

DeRemer, F. and Kron, H.H. (1976), 'Programming in the large versus programming in the small', *IEEE Trans. Software Eng.*, **SE-2** (2), 80–6.

Feldman, S.I. (1979), 'MAKE – a program for maintaining computer programs', *Software – Practice and Experience*, **9**, 255–65.

Lampson, B.W. and Schmidt, E.E. (1983), 'Organizing software in a distributed environment', *ACM Sigplan Notices*, **18** (6), 1–13.

Leblang, D.B. and Chase, R.P. (1987), 'Parallel software configuration management in a network environment', *IEEE Software*, **4** (6), 28–35.

Lehman, M.M. and Belady, L. (1985), *Program Evolution. Processes of Software Change*, London: Academic Press.

Rochkind, M.J. (1975), 'The Source Code Control System', *IEEE Trans. Software Eng.*, **SE-1** (4), 255–65.

Sommerville, I. and Thomson, R. (1986), 'The ECLIPSE system structure language', *Proc. 19th Int. Conf. on System Sciences*, Hawaii.

Tichy, W. (1982), 'Design, implementation and evaluation of a revision control system', *Proc. 6th Int. Conf. on Software Engineering*, Tokyo.

EXERCISES

28.1 Using the project examples in Appendix B, design an appropriate formal document naming scheme for these projects.

28.2 Using the relational approach to data modelling set out in Chapter 4, design a model of a configuration database recording information about system components, versions, releases and changes.

28.3 Design a change control form which might be used to request changes in a large system.

28.4 Describe the difficulties which can be encountered in system building. What are the particular problems that can arise when a system is built on a host computer for some target machine?

28.5 With reference to system building, explain why it may sometimes be necessary to maintain obsolete computer systems on which large software systems were developed.

28.6 A common problem with system building occurs when physical file names are incorporated in system code and the file structure implied in these names differs from that of the target machine. Write a set of programmer's guidelines which help avoid this and other system building problems you can think of.

28.7 What do you understand by Lehman's fifth law and how does it relate to configuration management?

28.8 Outline the working of SCCS and MAKE. If you have access to these tools, experiment with them and comment on their advantages and disadvantages.

Chapter 29

Documentation

Objectives

This chapter is concerned with the documentation which is an integral part of all large software systems. The structure of user and system documentation is described and the importance of producing high-quality documentation is emphasized. Tools to assist with the documentation process are discussed, including text formatters, proof checking tools and desktop publishing systems. In the same way as software systems should be designed to be maintainable and portable, so too should their associated documentation. The final parts of the chapter comment on document maintainability and document portability.

Contents

All large software systems, irrespective of application, have a prodigious amount of documentation associated with them. This documentation can be classed as either user documentation or system documentation. User documentation consists of the documents which describe the functions of the system, without reference to how these functions are implemented. System documentation, on the other hand, describes all aspects of the system design, implementation and testing.

The documentation provided along with a system can be useful at any stage in the lifetime of the system. It need not necessarily be produced in the same order as the system itself. Indeed, it is useful during system specification to have user documentation available so that the specifier is aware of the constraints within which he or she must operate.

All kinds of documentation need effective indexing. A good index, which allows the user to find the information he or she needs, is probably the most useful feature that can be provided but, sadly, is often the most neglected part of document production. A comprehensive index can make a badly written document usable but, without an index, even the best written prose is unlikely to convince the reader that the document is effective.

29.1 User documentation

The documentation provided for system users is usually the first contact they have with the system. It should provide an accurate initial impression of the system. It is not sales literature. It should not over-emphasize system features which are novel or very powerful nor should it be unrealistic about the system's capabilities. The user should not have to read most of the documentation to find out how to make simple use of the system. The documentation should be structured in such a way that the user may read it to the level of detail appropriate to his or her needs.

There are at least five documents (or perhaps chapters in a single document) which are an essential part of user documentation. These are:

(1)   *A functional description*, which explains what the system can do.

(2)   *An installation document*, which explains how to install the system and tailor it for particular hardware configurations.

(3)   *An introductory manual*, which explains, in simple terms, how to get started with the system.

(4)   *A reference manual*, which describes in detail all of the system facilities available to the user and how these facilities can be used.

(5)   *A system administrator's guide* (if necessary), explaining how to react to situations which arise while the system is in use and how to carry out system housekeeping tasks such as making a system backup.

The role of each of these documents is shown in Figure 29.1.

The functional description of the system outlines the system requirements and briefly describes the aims of the system implementors. It should outline what the system can and cannot do, introducing small, self-evident examples wherever possible. Diagrams should be plentiful. For example, the functional description of an operating system which has a hierarchical file system might illustrate the structure of the file system as a tree, and instructions on how to move up and down the tree may be shown as examples.

This document should not attempt to go into detail nor need it cover every system facility. Rather, it should provide an overview of the system and, when read in conjunction with an introductory manual, should enable users to decide if the system is appropriate for their needs.

The introductory manual should present an informal introduction to the system, describing its 'normal' usage. It should describe how to get started on the system and how the user might make use of the common system facilities. It should be liberally illustrated with examples. The introductory manual should also tell the system user how to get out of trouble when things go wrong. Inevitably beginners, whatever their background and experience, will make mistakes. Easily discovered information on how to recover from these mistakes and restart useful work should be provided.

The system reference manual is the definitive document on system usage. The most important characteristic of a reference manual is that it

Figure 29.1
System document roles.

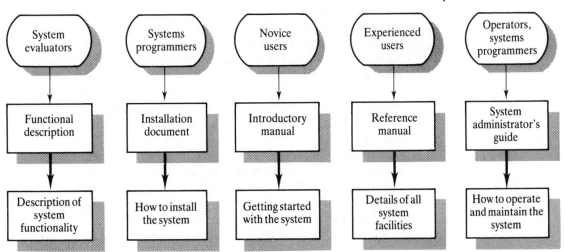

should be complete. Wherever possible, formal descriptive techniques should be used to ensure that completeness is achieved. Although the style of the reference manual should not be unnecessarily pedantic and turgid, it is acceptable to sacrifice readability for completeness.

The writer of this manual may assume that the reader is familiar with both the system description and introductory manual. He or she may also assume that the reader has made some use of the system and understands its concepts and terminology. As well as describing, in detail, the system facilities and their usage, the system reference manual should also describe the error reports generated by the system. It should describe the situations where these errors arise and, if appropriate, refer the user to a description of the facility which was in error. A comprehensive index is particularly important in this document.

The system installation document should provide full details of how to install the system in a particular environment. It must contain a description of the machine-readable media on which the system is supplied – its format, the character codes used, how the information was written, and the files making up the system. It should then describe the minimal hardware configuration required to run the system, the permanent files which must be established, how to start the system, and the configuration-dependent files which must be changed in order to tailor the system to a particular host system.

For systems which require operator intervention, a system administrator's manual must be provided. This should describe the messages generated at the system console and how to react to these messages. If system hardware is involved, it might also explain the operator's task in maintaining that hardware. For example, it might describe how to clear faults in the system console, how to change printer ribbons, etc.

Depending on the size of the system, these documents may be provided as separate manuals or bound together as one or more volumes. If the latter method of presentation is chosen, each part should be distinguished so that readers may easily find and use the information that they require. This distinction might be made by separating the sections and providing thumb indexes or by printing the different parts of the manual on different colours of paper.

As well as manuals, other easy-to-use documentation might be provided. For example, a quick reference card listing available system facilities and how to use them is particularly convenient for experienced system users. On-line help systems, which contain brief information about the system, are another facility which saves the user spending time in consultation of manuals. Help systems are discussed in Chapter 13.

Some organizations consider that the production of user documentation should not be the task of the software engineer. Rather, professional technical authors are employed to produce such finished documentation using information provided by the engineers responsible for constructing the system. There is some merit in this approach inasmuch as it frees software staff to do their principal job which is to write software. However, it does have the disadvantage that communications between authors and software engineers can be almost as time consuming as writing the documentation so, in practice, the use of technical authors may not be cost effective.

29.2   System documentation

System documentation encompasses all of the documents describing the implementation of the system from the requirements specification to the final acceptance test plan. Documents describing the design, implementation and testing of a system are essential if the program is to be understood and maintained. Like user documentation, it is important that system documentation is structured, with overviews leading the reader into more formal and detailed descriptions of each aspect of the system.

The documents making up the system documentation should include:

(1) The requirements definition and specification and an associated rationale.

(2) An overall system specification showing how the requirements are decomposed into a set of interacting programs. This document is not required when the system is implemented using only a single program.

(3) For each program in the system, a description of how that program is decomposed into components and a statement of the specification of each component.

(4) For each unit, a description of its operation. This need not extend to describing program actions as these should be documented using intra-program comments.

(5) A comprehensive test plan describing how each program unit is tested.

(6) A test plan showing how integration testing, that is, the testing of all units/programs together is carried out.

(7) An acceptance test plan, devised in conjunction with the system user. This should describe the tests which must be satisfied before the system is accepted.

Each of these documents is a different representation of the same software system and one of the most common problems which arises during system maintenance is ensuring that all of these representations are kept in step when changes to the system are made. To help with this, the relationships and dependencies between documents and parts of documents should be recorded along with the documents in a project database.

Configuration management tools should be used to maintain different versions of the documentation and to record when and by whom document changes were made.

29.3 Document quality

It is a sad reflection on the current state of software engineering that much computer system documentation is badly written, difficult to understand, out-of-date or incomplete. With some honourable exceptions, little attention has been paid to producing system documents which stand on their own as well written pieces of technical prose.

Document quality is as important as program quality. Without information on how to use a system or how to understand it, the utility of that system is degraded. Producing good documents is neither easy nor cheap and the process is at least as difficult as producing good programs.

A standard procedure for producing, checking and laying out documentation is an important aid to document quality control (Figure 29.2). The importance of quality control mechanisms in document production cannot be overemphasized. Poor quality documentation is likely to confuse rather than help the reader with the consequence that minimal use is likely to be made of that documentation.

Documentation standards should describe exactly what the documentation should include and should describe the notations to be used in the documentation. Within an organization, it is useful to establish a standard 'house style' for documents and require that all documents conform to that format. This standard might include a description of a front-cover format to be adopted by all documents, page numbering and page annotation conventions, methods of reference to other documents and the numbering of headings and sub-headings.

The numbering of headings and sub-headings may appear a trivial point. However, when a large number of separate documents are produced which reference each other, a consistent numbering scheme is vital. Documents should be subdivided using exactly the same system so that corresponding sections in each document each refer to the same entity. Cross-referencing should be avoided wherever possible and, when unavoidable, should reference by section heading and section number.

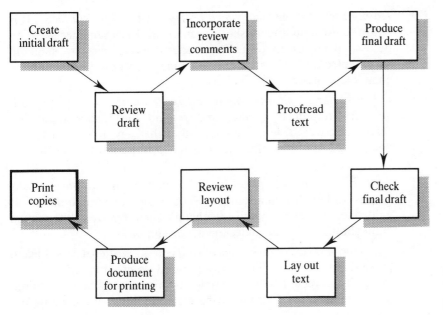

Figure 29.2
The document production process.

29.3.1 Writing style

Although standards and quality assessment are essential if good documentation is to be produced, the most fundamental factor affecting documentation quality is the ability of the writer to construct clear and concise technical prose. In short, good documentation requires good writing. In a book of this nature, devoted to a technical subject, it may appear presumptuous to include notes on writing style. However, it is unfortunately the case that some talented engineers responsible for software production have great difficulty constructing well written, clear and concise documentation.

Writing documents well is neither easy nor is it a single-stage process. Written work must be written, read, criticized and then rewritten, and this process should continue until a satisfactory document is produced. As in many other aspects of software engineering, it is impossible to present a set of rules which govern exactly how to set about this particular task. Technical writing is a craft rather than a science and only broad guidelines about how to write well may be given. These guidelines, set out in a style that might be used in software instruction manuals, are:

(1)   *Use active rather than passive tenses*   It is better to say 'You should see a flashing cursor at the top left of the screen' rather than 'A flashing cursor should appear at the top left of the screen'.

(2) *Do not use long sentences which present several different facts* It is better to use a number of shorter sentences. Each sentence can then be assimilated on its own. The reader does not need to maintain several pieces of information at one time in order to understand the complete sentence.

(3) *Do not refer to information by reference number alone* Instead, give the reference number and remind the reader what that reference covered. For example, rather than say 'In section 1.3....' you should say 'In section 1.3, which described software evolution, ...'

(4) *Itemize facts wherever possible* It is usually clearer to present facts in a list rather than in a sentence. You might have found this set of guidelines harder to read if they hadn't been itemized. Use textual highlighting (italics or underlining) for emphasis.

(5) *If a description is complex, repeat yourself* It is often a good idea to present two or more differently phrased descriptions of the same thing. If the reader fails to completely understand one description, he or she may benefit from having the same thing said in a different way.

(6) *Don't be verbose* If you can say something in five words do so, rather than use ten words so that the description might seem more profound. There is no merit in quantity of documentation. Quality is more important.

(7) *Be precise and define the terms you use* Computing terminology is very fluid and many terms have more than one meaning. Therefore, if specialized terms (such as module or process) are used, make sure that your definition is clear. If you need to define a number of words or if you are writing for readers with little or no knowledge of computing terminology, you should provide a glossary with your document. This should contain definitions of all terms that might not be completely understood by the reader.

(8) *Keep paragraphs short* As a general rule, no paragraph should be made up of more than seven sentences. This is because of short-term memory limitations (described in Chapter 2). Our capacity for holding immediate information is limited, so by keeping paragraphs short all of the concepts in the paragraph can be maintained in short-term memory.

(9) *Make use of headings and sub-headings* These break up a chapter into parts which may be read separately. Always ensure that a consistent numbering convention is used for these.

(10) *Use grammatically correct constructs and correct spelling* To boldly go on splitting infinitives (like this) and to misspell words (like mispell) irritates many readers and reduces the credibility of the

writer in their eyes. Unfortunately, English spelling is not standardized and both British and American readers are sometimes irrational in their dislike of alternative spellings.

A mechanism which should be used for checking and improving documents is to establish document inspections. These can be used in the way that code inspections can be used for the detection of program errors. During a document inspection, the text is criticized, omissions pointed out and suggestions made on how to improve the document. In this latter respect, it differs from a code inspection which is simply an error finding rather than an error correction mechanism.

As well as personal criticism, it is also possible to make use of software tools whose function is to read text and find ungrammatical or clumsy uses of words. These tools might also point out where sentences and paragraphs are too long and where passive rather than active tenses are used. A set of such tools has been packaged together under UNIX to form a so-called 'Writer's Workbench'. This is discussed in the following section.

29.4   Documentation tools

This section discusses software tools which can be used to develop and maintain project documentation on a computer system. Although not essential, this should preferably be the same system as is used to develop the software system so that programs and documentation can be developed and stored together. The advantages of developing documentation in this way rather than on a separate word processing system are:

(1) *The documentation is always on hand*   Software developers or users need not search for a manual if they have access to the computer. In the case of user documentation, copies of this should be maintained on the same system as the application so that, again, reference to manuals may be unnecessary. The need for effective indexing of documents is particularly important when the documentation is maintained on-line. There is no point in having the information available if the reader cannot easily and quickly find the information required.

(2) *Documents are easy to modify and maintain* This has the consequence that the project documentation is more likely to be kept up to date.

(3) *Documents may be automatically analysed* The text can be analysed in various ways to produce different types of index and to check for spelling and typing errors.

(4) *Document production may be shared*   Several individuals may work on the production of a document at the same time.

(5) *Documentation management is simplified*   All associated documents can be collected under a common heading. The state of development of these documents may be ascertained. Configuration management tools may be used to maintain different versions of documents and to control changes.

(6) *Automatic information retrieval is feasible*   Information retrieval systems may operate on documents retrieving all documents which contain particular keywords, for example.

The most important documentation tool is a powerful editing system which allows documents to be generated and modified. A general-purpose text editor, as described in Chapter 18, may be used for this task or a word processing system may be preferred. There are advantages and disadvantages to each approach.

Word processing systems are screen based and are organized so that the operations of text editing and formatting are combined. This means that the image of the document on the user's terminal is, more or less, the same as the final form of the printed document. Thus, finished layout is immediately obvious. Errors can be corrected and layout improved before printing the document. On the other hand, programmers who already use an editor for program preparation may be reluctant to learn how to use another type of editor and, for them, use of a separate editor and text formatting system may be more appropriate.

Using an editor, a computer terminal can be treated as a typewriter and the document formatted directly by the typist. Unfortunately, the screen size of most terminals is such that it does not conform to standard paper sizes. The typist must adapt to the smaller terminal screen and, when typing, mentally translate screen layout to layout on paper. Although each line is formatted as it will be printed, visualizing how changes affect lines which are not currently on the screen is a difficult task.

This problem can be avoided by processing input text using a text formatting program such as the NROFF/TROFF system (Kernighan *et al.*, 1978). Such systems are very powerful but are not particularly easy to use. A text formatter allows the typist to input text in free format. The formatter then automatically rearranges that text and lays it out neatly on standard paper. The final layout of the document is specified by the author by interspersing formatting commands with the text of the document.

Word processing systems and formatting systems are compared in Figure 29.3.

Although an editor/text formatter or word processor is the most important documentation tool, there are a number of other programs which are useful in document production. These include programs to assist with proofreading, programs to help lay out complicated tables and

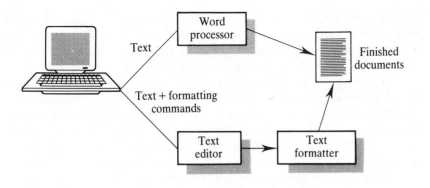

Figure 29.3
Word processing and text formatting systems.

mathematical expressions, graphics systems to assist diagram production, pattern matching systems for document retrieval and programs to identify and control changes in documents (Figure 29.4).

Proofreading is one of the most onerous chores associated with authorship. Although the process cannot be completely automated, some help can be given by documentation tools. For example, a spelling checker program might be used that points out words that appear in the document but not in the system dictionary. Similarly, a punctuation checker can detect common errors such as unbalanced parentheses, spaces before punctuation marks, etc.

A spelling checker should be designed so that the dictionary may be passed as a parameter to the program. This means that, after a document has been checked using the standard system dictionary, the spelling checker can be rerun, checking those words not found in the standard dictionary against the user's private dictionary. This dictionary might contain specialized terms or proper names which are particular to a user or an application.

In addition to these simple proofreading tools, which are widely available, a comprehensive set of proofreading and document checking tools has been developed to run under the UNIX system. This toolkit is called the 'Writer's Workbench' (Cherry and MacDonald, 1983). It

Table and equation formatters	Graphics editor
Proofreading tools	Information retrieval tools

Figure 29.4
Documentation tools.

contains programs to detect common typographical errors such as repeated words or badly used spacing, programs that detect clumsy phraseology and suggest alternatives, programs to measure the clarity (fog factor) of the text, and programs that comment on the user's style.

Programs which assist the user with complicated layout problems normally operate in conjunction with a formatting system. Rather than users devising a complex set of formatting commands, they provide a table specification, say, along with the data to be included in that table. A table formatter reads the specification and the data and generates the appropriate sequence of formatting commands for inclusion in the user's document.

Document retrieval software is, of course, generally useful but it has a specialized application in a document production environment. If the document retrieval system includes a sufficiently powerful pattern matching system, a database of existing documents can be scanned to find any text which is associated with that being produced. This text may then be reused. As in program production, reuse of existing work can increase productivity and reduce the amount of proofreading (testing) and modification (debugging) required.

Information retrieval systems are also useful in bibliography production. When a document is produced, its bibliography may be added to a bibliography database and this database made publicly accessible. Not only does this help the user find source material, it also ensures that making references to other documents is simplified. The appropriate reference can be copied directly from the bibliography database thus ensuring the correctness of the reference.

Finally, desktop publishing systems may be used to produce the finished versions of system documents. Desktop publishing systems are programs designed to automate the layout of text and graphics and they take over some of the functions of traditional printworkers.

The advantage of using a desktop publishing system is that the cost of producing high-quality documents is reduced because some of the steps in the production process are eliminated (Figure 29.5). Even documents which are produced in small numbers can be produced to a high standard. The disadvantage of using desktop publishing systems is that they do not automate the skills of the graphic designer; it is easy to produce documents which are unattractive and badly designed.

29.5 Document maintenance

As a software system is modified, the documentation associated with that system must also be modified to reflect the changes to the system. Unfortunately, documentation maintenance is often neglected, with the

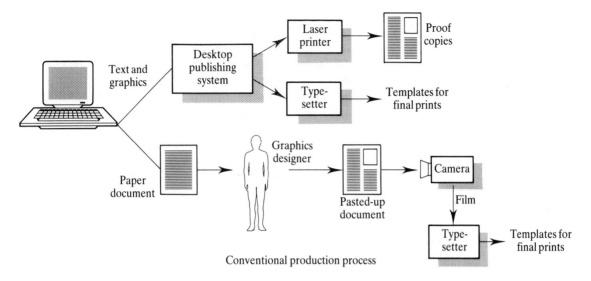

Figure 29.5
Desktop publishing and
conventional production.

result that the documentation becomes out of step with its associated
software. This introduces problems for both users and maintainers of the
system.

All associated documents should be modified when a change is made
to a program. Assuming that the change is transparent to the user, only
documents describing the system implementation need be changed. If the
system change is more than the correction of coding errors, this will mean
revision of design and test documents and, perhaps, the higher level
documents describing the system specification and requirements.

One of the major problems in maintaining documentation is keeping
different representations of the system in step with each other. The natural
tendency is to meet a deadline by modifying code with the intention of
modifying other documents later. Often, pressure of work means that this
modification is continually set aside until finding what is to be changed
becomes very difficult indeed. The best solution to this problem is to
support document maintenance with software tools which record document relationships, remind software engineers when changes to one
document affect another, and record possible inconsistencies in the
documentation.

If the system modification affects the user interface directly either by
adding new facilities or by extending existing facilities, this should be
intimated to the user immediately. In an on-line system, this might be
accomplished by providing a system noticeboard which each user may
access. When a new item is added to the noticeboard, users can be
informed of this when they log in to the system.

System changes can also be indicated on a real noticeboard and in a
regular newsletter distributed to all system users. At periodic intervals,

user documentation should be updated by supplying new pages which describe the changes made to the user interface.

This updating process is simplified if manual pages are not consecutively numbered but are numbered according to their chapter or section. For example, pages in Chapter 3 should be numbered 3-1, 3-2, 3-3.... If this numbering scheme is adopted, parts of the manual may be replaced without disrupting page numbering in the unchanged parts of the document.

Paragraphs which have been added or changed should be indicated to the reader. New versions of documents should be immediately identifiable. The fact that a document has been updated should not be concealed on an inner page. Rather, the version number and date should be clearly indicated on the cover of the document and, if possible, different versions of each document should be issued with a different colour or design of cover.

29.6   Document portability

When a computing system is moved from one machine to another, the documentation associated with that system must be modified to reflect the new system. In some circumstances, the work involved in this is comparable to the work involved in moving the programs themselves. If portability is a system design objective, the documentation must also be designed and written with the same aim.

Just as the property of self-containedness is the key to program portability, portable documentation should also be self-contained. This means that the information provided in the documentation should be as complete as possible. Reference should not be made to any other documents, such as an operating system manual, which are not directly associated with the system being documented.

For example, say a programming language allows the user access to mathematical functions such as sin, cos, tan, log, etc. In some installations, these functions may be provided in a library of similar functions shared by all of the programming languages implemented at that installation. When discussing available functions, the programming language documentation should not simply refer to the documentation describing the mathematical library. Should that language be implemented on another machine without a mathematical library the language documentation would be incomplete. The language manual itself should describe fully the functions available.

Those parts of the system which generally cause portability problems are obviously the sections describing non-portable parts of the programming system. These include file organization, file naming conventions, job control, input/output, and so on. When the system is moved from one computer to another, those parts of the documentation must be rewritten.

To make this rewriting easier, descriptions of system dependent functions should be confined to separate sections. These sections should be clearly headed with information about their system dependence and they are replaced when the system is moved to another installation. If possible, other references to system dependent features should be avoided. If this is impossible, an index of such references should be maintained so that they may be located and changed when the program is moved.

As transporting a program and its documentation is really a specialized form of system maintenance, the availability of machine readable documentation and appropriate software tools reduces the work involved in producing documentation for a new system. System dependent parts of the document may be located, rewritten and a new version of the document produced automatically.

KEY POINTS

- There are two classes of documentation associated with a computer system. These classes are user documentation which describes how to use the system and system documentation which describes the system design and implementation.

- User documentation should be structured so that it is not necessary to read almost all the documentation before starting to use the system. It should be integrated with on-line help but it is not sufficient simply to print help frame text as user documents.

- One of the major difficulties with documentation (particularly system documentation) is the maintenance of consistency across the different documents describing the system. To keep track of changes, it is recommended that documents should be placed under the control of a configuration management system.

- The most fundamental factor affecting documentation quality is the ability of the writer to construct clear and concise technical prose. The best way to produce comprehensible documents is to keep them as simple as possible.

- There is a variety of software tools available to help with the production of documents. In general, documentation should be produced and stored on the same computer as is used to develop the system software.

- In the same way as a software system must be maintained, so too must its documentation. The same guidelines apply. Information hiding and localization are the keys to easily maintained and portable documents.

Further reading

Software Validation, Verification, Testing and Documentation. There is little material which is devoted exclusively to the topic of computer system documentation. This book, which is a collection of US National Bureau of Standards reports contains two extensive sections discussing documentation. (S.J. Andriole (ed.), 1986, Petrocelli Books.)

References

Cherry, L. and MacDonald, N.H. (1983), 'The UNIX Writer's Workbench software', *BYTE*, **8** (10), 241–52.

Kernighan, B.W., Lesk, M.E. and Ossanna Jr, J.F. (1978), 'Document preparation', *Bell Systems Tech. J.*, **57** (6), 2115–35.

EXERCISES

29.1 Write a user manual for each of the software system projects suggested in Appendix 2.

29.2 Explain why simply providing hard copies of help frame text does not lead to good user documents.

29.3 Under what circumstances would you suggest using professional technical authors to prepare documentation?

29.4 Suggest five further style guidelines in addition to those set out in Section 29.3.1.

29.5 Using the style guidelines as a basis, write a critique of one or more chapters of this book. Identify the major style problems that you discover and write to the author about them.

29.6 You have been given the task of creating a toolset for supporting document production. Suggest what components would be included in such a toolset and investigate the literature to see what documentation tools are available. What checking tasks cannot be readily supported with current software tools?

29.7 Under what circumstances would you recommend the use of a desktop publishing system as a means of creating computer system documentation?

29.8 Describe the documentation difficulties that might be encountered when a program is ported from a mainframe with character terminals onto a workstation with a bit-mapped screen.

Chapter 30

Software Quality Assurance

Objective

The objective of this chapter is to describe the essentials of software quality assurance. Software quality assurance is a management activity which is concerned with ensuring that software products meet some acceptable standard. Reliability is seen here as the most important product attribute and it is discussed in more detail than in Chapter 1. The importance of standards is discussed and the final part of the chapter is concerned with a short discussion of software metrics. It concludes that metrics can be useful but their use must be tailored to individual circumstances.

Contents

Software quality assurance (QA) is closely related to the verification and validation activities carried out at each stage of the software life-cycle. Indeed, in some organizations there is no distinction made between these activities. However, quality assurance and other verification and validation are actually separate activities. Simplistically, quality assurance is a management function and verification and validation are a technical part of the software development process.

Within an organization, quality assurance should be carried out by an independent software quality assurance team who report directly to management above the project manager level. The quality assurance team should not be associated with any particular development group but should be responsible for quality assurance across all project groups in an organization (see Figure 24.1).

A further important distinction is that verification and validation are concerned with fault detection. Quality assurance has a broader remit. Rather than software faults, quality assurance is concerned with software reliability as well as other software attributes such as maintainability, portability, readability, etc. We have already seen in Chapter 14 that design quality assurance, for example, is concerned with the 'goodness' as well as the correctness of a design.

An appropriate definition of software quality assurance is given by Bersoff (1984):

> Quality assurance consists of those procedures, techniques and tools applied by professionals to ensure that a product meets or exceeds prespecified standards during a product's development cycle; and without specific prescribed standards, quality assurance entails ensuring that a product meets or exceeds a minimal industrial and/or commercially acceptable level of excellence.

The problem which arises in developing software standards for quality assurance and which makes the assessment of the level of excellence of a software product difficult is the elusive nature of software quality. Boehm *et al*. others (1978) suggest that quality criteria include, but are not limited to, those attributes shown in Table 30.1. Some of these attributes are subjective and difficult to assess. Assessment of software quality relies on the judgement of skilled individuals although this does not mean that it is necessarily inferior to quantitative assessment. After all, we cannot assess a painting or a play quantitatively yet this does not preclude a judgement of its quality. The general problem of quantification and metrics is discussed later in this chapter.

Buckley and Poston (1984) point out that some of these quality criteria may have no relevance for a particular product. It may be possible to transfer a system from a microcomputer to a large mainframe (portability) but this is often a nonsensical thing to do. The attributes in Table 30.1

Economy	Correctness	Resilience
Integrity	Reliability	Usability
Documentation	Modifiability	Clarity
Understandability	Validity	Maintainability
Flexibility	Generality	Portability
Interoperability	Testability	Efficiency
Modularity	Reusability	

Table 30.1
Software quality
attributes.

are not general attributes but must be modified for each specific software product.

A commonly held view of software quality assurance is that it is an activity which takes place after completion of a software system. It is true that much quality assurance work involves product analysis, but quality planning should begin at an early stage in the software process.

A quality plan should set out the attributes which the product being developed should exhibit and should define how these are to be assessed. Probably the most common error made in quality assurance is the assumption that there is a common understanding of what 'high quality' software actually means. No such common understanding exists. Situations arise where different software engineers strive, in a mutually antagonistic way, to ensure that particular, but different, product attributes are achieved.

Therefore, the quality plan should clearly set out which of the quality attributes listed in Table 30.1 are most important for a particular product. It may be that efficiency is paramount and other factors are to be sacrificed to achieve this. If this is set out in the plan, all of the engineers working on the development can cooperate to achieve this. The plan should also define how the quality is to be assessed or measured. There is little point in trying to attain some quality if there is no way of assessing whether that quality is present in the product.

The quality plan should set out which standards are appropriate to the product and to the process and (if necessary) define the plan for developing these standards. Although the plan may not actually include details of particular standards, it should reference these and quality management should ensure that the standards documents are generally available.

One of the underlying assumptions of quality assurance is that the quality of the software process affects the quality of delivered software products. Although quality assurance is ultimately about product quality, the difficulty of assessing product attributes has meant that a great deal of emphasis is placed on ensuring the quality of the software process. It is (reasonably) assumed that a well planned, managed process is more likely to lead to high-quality products.

This assumption is derived from manufacturing systems where product quality is intimately related to the production process. Indeed, in automated mass production systems, once an acceptable level of process quality has been attained, product quality follows. However, each software system is unique so the relationship between process and product quality is more tenuous.

It is reasonable to assume that such a relationship exists but it cannot be assumed that a high-quality process will necessarily produce a high-quality product. External factors, such as the novelty of an application or commercial pressure for an early product release might mean that product quality is impaired irrespective of the process used.

However, the notion of process quality affecting product quality is widely accepted and part of the QA function is ensuring the quality of the process. This involves:

(1)   Defining process standards such as how reviews should be conducted, when reviews should be held, etc.

(2)   Monitoring the development process to ensure that the standards are being followed.

(3)   Reporting the software process to project management and to the buyer of the software.

Unfortunately, process QA sometimes disrupts the development of the software and results in an artificial process being followed simply because some arbitrary process model has been defined by quality assurance.

For example, the QA standards may specify that specification must be complete and approved before implementation can begin. However, some systems may require prototyping which involves implementation. The QA team may suggest that this prototyping should not be carried out because its quality cannot be monitored. In such situations, senior management must intervene to ensure that the QA process supports rather than retards product development.

30.1   Software reliability

The subject of software reliability was discussed briefly in the opening chapter of this book. It was suggested that reliability was probably the most important product attribute as unreliable systems are discarded or never brought into use. The increasing use of software systems in life-critical applications means that the reliability of these systems must be so high that system behaviour does not pose a threat to life. Thus, I consider reliability to be the most important software quality attribute. The primary task of the QA process is to assure product reliability.

Software reliability theory is an important discipline in its own right and it cannot be discussed in any detail here. The intention of this section is simply to highlight some of the complexities of reliability assessment and to illustrate that simplistic assumptions about reliability are not enough when assessing software quality.

The difficulties of saying what exactly reliability means were discussed in Chapter 1. In short, what is most important to system users is perceived reliability rather than some arbitrary reliability metric related to fault counts, etc. However, it is difficult to predict the seriousness of fault which arise so most reliability assessments are concerned with the likely occurrence of any unexpected software behaviour, irrespective of its practical effects.

There is a distinction between unexpected software behaviour and software faults although, in most cases, unexpected behaviour is the result of a fault. However, it can also occur in circumstances where the software conforms to its requirements but the requirements themselves are incomplete. Omissions in software documentation can also lead to unexpected behaviour although the software system may not contain faults.

As far as reliability is concerned, the quality assurance process is concerned with assessing the operational reliability of a product and not with the estimation of the number of latent software faults. Mills *et al.* (1987) point out that not all software faults have an equal probability of manifestation. Removing software faults from parts of the system which are unlikely to be exercised makes little difference to the perceived reliability. Their work suggested that, for the products studied, removing 60% of product defects would only lead to a 3% improvement in reliability.

This is illustrated in Figure 30.1, derived from Littlewood (1989), which shows a software product as a mapping of an input to an output set. A subset of the input set causes erroneous behaviour (unexpected outputs) and the product reliability is related to the probability that a particular use of the product will involve the selection of one of the inputs which causes erroneous behaviour. The input set which causes erroneous behaviour, I_e, contains a number of members and it is not equally likely that any one of these will be selected. In fact, it is likely that there will be a small number of members of I_e which are much more likely to be selected than others and the reliability of the program is related to that probability rather than the mean probability of selecting an erroneous input. Indeed, in a study of errors in IBM software products, Adams (1984) noted that many errors in the products were only likely to occur after hundreds or thousands of months of usage.

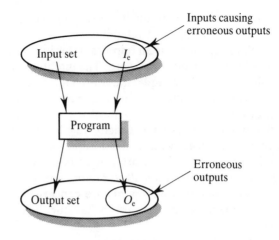

Figure 30.1
A program as an input/
output mapping.

The fact that reliability is related to the probability of an error occurring in operational use is the reason why a program may contain a significant number of known defects but still be perceived as reliable by its users. Their mode of operation may never involve selection of an erroneous input so they perceive the program as reliable. Furthermore, experienced users may 'work around' known software faults and deliberately avoid exercising the code which includes these faults. Repairing these faults may make no practical difference to the reliability as perceived by these users.

30.1.1   Reliability metrics

The role of quality assurance is to assess product reliability and to do so involves deciding upon the use of some reliability metric. As we shall see, there are a number of such metrics, each of which has its own advantages and disadvantages.

Unfortunately, there is no way of certifying the reliability of a program in any absolute way. Program reliability is not a constant but is dependent on the way in which the program is exercised. Different users and environments are likely to use the program in different ways, so faults that affect the reliability of the system for one user may never manifest themselves under a different mode of working (Figure 30.2).

For example, the word processor used to write this book has an automatic hyphenation capability which may or may not contain faults. This facility is used when text columns are short and any faults might manifest themselves when users produce multi-column documents. I rarely if ever use the hyphenation facility so, as far as I am concerned, faults in that facility have no effect on the perceived reliability of the word processing system.

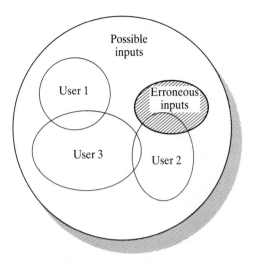

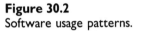
Figure 30.2
Software usage patterns.

In Figure 30.2, the set of inputs which exercise faulty code is shaded. From the diagram, it is clear that only User 2 will discover these faults. Users 1 and 3 will see the software as completely reliable.

One of the difficulties in quality assurance is assessing the most likely pattern of operational usage of a product. This problem is particularly acute for safety-critical systems, which must include features that cause them to fail-safe in the presence of unanticipated, occasional, life-threatening, exceptional situations. By their very nature, such situations are uncommon and unanticipated. It is thus difficult to assess whether or not the program will behave correctly when such situations occur.

The metrics which have been developed to assess reliability have, by and large, evolved from the much older discipline of hardware reliability assessment. The important distinction between hardware and software systems is that a hardware component failure tends to be permanent in that the component stops working until repair is effected. Thus, there is an obvious relationship between system availability and mean time to failure, say.

By contrast, software component failures are transient in that they are only exhibited for some inputs, so the system can continue in operation in the presence of these failures. This distinction has meant that commonly used hardware reliability metrics such as mean time to failure are much less relevant in software systems reliability. It is not simple to relate system availability to system fault occurrence because it depends on factors such as restart time, the degree (if any) of data corruption caused by the fault and so on.

Some of the metrics which have been used to assess software reliability are:

(1)   *Probability of failure on demand*   This is a measure of the likelihood that the system will behave in an unexpected way when some demand is made on it. It is most relevant for safety-critical systems and 'non-stop' systems whose continuous operation is critical. In these systems, a measure of fault occurrence is less important than the chance that the system will not perform as expected.

(2)   *Rate of fault occurrence (ROCOF)*   This is a measure of the frequency of occurrence with which unexpected behaviour is likely to be observed. For example, if the ROCOF is 2/100 this indicates that two faults are likely to occur in each 100 operational time units. Appropriate time units are discussed shortly. This is probably the most generally useful reliability metric.

(3)   *Mean time to failure (MTTF)*   This is a measure of the time between observed failures. As discussed above, it is of limited utility as a software reliability metric because software failures are transient. It is more useful when assessing hardware component reliability.

(4)   *Availability*   This is a measure of how likely the system is to be available for use. For example, an availability of 998/1000 means that, in every 1000 time units, the system is likely to be available for 998 of these. This measure is most appropriate for systems, like telecommunication systems, where the repair or restart time is significant and the loss of service during that time is important.

Time is a factor in all of these metrics and it is important that appropriate time units are chosen when using the metrics. Time units may be calendar time, processor time or some discrete unit such as number of transactions. This depends on the application and on the time as perceived by system users. For systems which have a regular usage pattern, it may be appropriate to use calendar time. For systems which are used periodically but which are idle for much of the time (for example, a bank auto-teller system), the number of transactions would be a more appropriate time unit.

No single one of these metrics is universally appropriate, and the particular reliability metric used most be chosen with care depending on the application domain and the expected usage of the system. Indeed, for large systems it may be appropriate to use different reliability metrics for different parts of the system.

In order for reliability metrics to be used in the quality assurance process, the software requirements must state the reliability required. Unfortunately, it is often the case that requirements analysts have little knowledge of reliability theory and state reliability requirements in subjective, irrelevant or unmeasurable ways.

For example, statements such as 'The software shall be as reliable as possible' means very little. Quasi-quantitative statements such as 'The software shall exhibit no more than N faults/1000 lines' are equally irrelevant. Not only is it impossible to measure the number of faults per 1000 lines of code (how can you tell when all have been discovered?), but the statement means nothing in terms of the dynamic behaviour of the system. As we have already discussed, reliable operation in the presence of faults is quite possible.

The reliability requirements should state reliability in terms of the dynamic behaviour of the system. For example, the requirement for a management information system might state that the probability that the system should be available on demand should be 99.99%. This means that, on average, 9999 requests for service out of 10 000 should be satisfied.

30.1.2 Reliability growth models

A reliability growth model is a mathematical model of software reliability which can be used to predict when (or if) a particular level of reliability is likely to be attained. These are important to the quality assurance process as they provide a means of assessing whether or not the software quality is improving with time and allow the QA team to decide when the software is likely to be of adequate quality for release.

Reliability growth models are used by the QA team when a software product has been delivered for quality assessment but does not exhibit acceptable reliability. During quality assurance, faults are discovered and repair requests submitted. As these repairs are made, the reliability of the software should (but need not) increase. The reason why reliability will not necessarily increase after a fault has been repaired is that the repair may introduce new faults whose probability of occurrence might be higher than the occurrence probability of the fault which has been repaired.

The earliest developed and most simplistic reliability growth model is a step function model where the reliability increases by a constant increment each time a fault repair is effected. Such a model was first discussed by Jelinski and Moranda (1972) and its form is illustrated in Figure 30.3.

There are two main problems with this model. It assumes that software repairs are always perfect and never increase the number of faults present in the software. Secondly, it assumes that all faults contribute equally to reliability and that each fault repair contributes the same amount of reliability growth. However not all faults are equally probable. Repairing faults which are more likely to occur contributes more to reliability growth than repairing faults which only manifest themselves very occasionally.

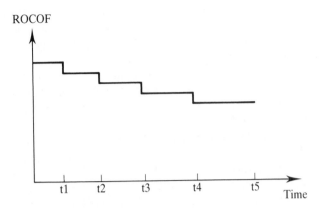

Other models, such as that described by Littlewood and Verrall (1973), take these problems into account by introducing a random element into the reliability growth improvement effected by a software repair. Thus, each repair does not result in an equal amount of reliability improvement but varies depending on the random perturbation (Figure 30.4).

Not only does Littlewood and Verrall's model take into account that reliability growth can be negative when a software repair introduces further errors, it also models the fact that, as faults are repaired, the average improvement in reliability per repair decreases. This is a result of the fact that the most probable faults are likely to be discovered early in the investigation process and repairing these contributes most to reliability growth.

This has been a simplified discussion of reliability growth. A proper discussion on reliability growth models requires an understanding of statistical theory and is outside the scope of this book. A paper by Abdel-Ghaly *et al.* (1986) compares the various reliability growth models which have been developed.

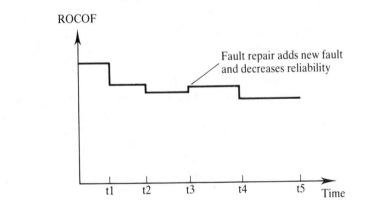

Littlewood (1989) points out that no one model is universally applicable and that all of the models can be useful in different circumstances. He recommends that reliability growth predictions should be based on fitting observed data to one of the growth models and that whichever model exhibits the best fit should be used for that system.

30.2 Software standards

One of the most important roles of the quality assurance team in a large software project is the development of appropriate product and process standards. Product standards set out attributes which all product components should exhibit; process standards set out how the software process should be conducted. An example of a product standard is a programming language standard which sets out how a language should be used. An example of a process standard is a standard setting out how design reviews should be conducted and documented.

Standards are important for a number of reasons:

(1)   They provide an encapsulation of best, or at least most appropriate, practice. This knowledge is often only acquired after a great deal of trial and error and building it into a standard avoids the repetition of past mistakes. In essence, the standard captures some wisdom which is of value to an organization.

(2)   They provide a framework around which the quality assurance process may be implemented. Given that standards encapsulate best practice, quality assurance becomes the activity of ensuring that standards have been properly followed. Of course, the current state of the art is such that much wisdom concerning the software process and software products cannot be written down as standards.

(3)   They assist in continuity where work carried out by one person is taken up and continued by another. Standards ensure that all engineers within an organization adopt the same practices so that the learning effort when starting new work is reduced.

It is a truism that the need to adhere to standards is often resented by software engineers. They see standards as being bureaucratic and irrelevant to the technical activity of software development. Although they usually agree about the value of standards in general, engineers often find good reasons why standards are not appropriate to their particular project.

Product standards such as standards setting out program formats, design documentation and document structures are often tedious to follow and to check. It is unfortunately the case that these standards are often written by staff who are remote from the software development process and who are not aware of modern practices. Thus, to the software engineer, the standards appear to be out of date and unworkable.

To avoid these problems, the quality assurance organization must be adequately resourced and must take the following steps:

(1) Involve software engineers in the development of product standards. They should understand the motivation behind the standard development and be committed to these standards. The standards document should not simply state a standard to be followed but should include a rationale of why particular standardization decisions have been made.

(2) Review and modify standards on a regular or even on a per project basis to reflect changing technologies. One of the principal problems with standards is that once developed they tend to be enshrined in a company standards handbook. Once included in such a handbook, they become difficult to change. A standards handbook is essential but it should be a dynamic rather than a static document.

(3) Where standards set out clerical procedures such as document formatting, software tools should be provided to support these standards. Such clerical standards are the cause of many complaints not because of their substance but because of the tedious work involved in implementing them. If tool support is available, the effort involved in development to the standards and in standards checking is minimal.

Process standards also cause difficulties because of the fact that they are predicated on the notion that there is a single software process and that we understand and can articulate this process. There are many different approaches to software production and it is probably the case that each large project is developed according to a unique process. Furthermore, much of this process is implicit and badly understood and we have not discovered how to express it in a formal way.

This is not to say that process standards are of no value. Some, such as those relating to quality assurance activities, are essential to ensure that the necessary checks have been carried out. For example, a process standard might define the procedure for accepting a component for configuration control and the quality assurance process requires that this standard is followed for all components.

Other process standards, however, can be no more than guidelines which must be sympathetically interpreted by individual project managers. There is no point in prescribing a particular way of working if that mode of working is appropriate for a project or the project team. Each project manager must have the authority to modify process standards according to individual circumstances.

The development of software engineering project standards is a difficult and time-consuming process. National and international bodies such as the US DoD, ANSI, BSI, NATO and the IEEE have been active in the production of standards but these are usually of a general rather than a specific nature. Bodies such as NATO and other defence organizations may require that their own standards are followed in software contracts but it is probably more appropriate to use national and international standards as a starting point for more specific standard development.

National and international standards have been developed covering software engineering terminology, notations such as charting symbols, procedures for deriving software requirements, quality assurance procedures, programming languages such as Pascal and Ada, ways of using languages such as Ada, and software verification and validation.

30.3   Software metrics

It has been suggested that the distinction between a craft and an engineering discipline is that craftsmen use qualitative methods whereas engineering is based on quantitative techniques. Engineering is concerned with measurement and the application of these measurements to improving the engineering process. This is a rather restricted notion of engineering and, if it is accepted, software engineering cannot be considered as a true engineering discipline.

The ability to quantify aspects of software products and processes would be of immense value to software quality assurers. Although there has been a great deal of research in software metrics and many claims made about the efficacy of particular metrics, the current state of software measurement is such that few software metrics have been demonstrated to be usefully predictive or related to product attributes which we are interested in discovering.

A software metric is any measurement which relates to a software system, process or related documentation. Examples are measures of the size of a product in lines of code, the Fog index (Gunning, 1962) of a product manual, the number of reported faults in a delivered software product and the number of person-days required to develop a system component.

Metrics fall into two classes (Figure 30.5). Control metrics are those used by management to control of the software process. Examples of these metrics are effort expended, elapsed time and disk usage. Estimates and measurements of these metrics can be used in the refinement of the project planning process.

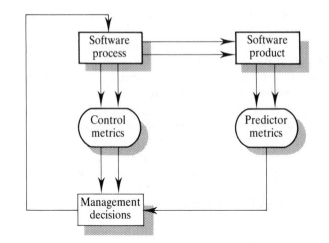

Figure 30.5
Predictor and control metrics.

Predictor metrics are measurements of a product attribute which can be used to predict an associated product quality. For example, the readability of a product manual may be predicted by estimating its Fog index, or the ease of maintenance of a software component may be predicted by measuring the cyclomatic complexity (McCabe, 1976) of the component. Whether or not valid quality predictions can be made from such measurements is open to question. Fundamentally, we can't measure directly what we really want to measure and we have to assume that a relationship exists between what we can measure and what we want to know.

Kitchenham (1989) articulates the three assumptions on which predictor metrics are based:

(1)   We can accurately measure some property of the software.

(2)   A relationship exists between what we can measure and what we would like to know about the product's behavioural attributes.

(3)   This relationship is understood, has been validated and can be expressed in terms of a formula or model.

She points out that this critical third assumption is often ignored. For example, McCabe's complexity measure is said to be related to the ease of maintenance of a component. The higher the cyclomatic complexity, the more difficult the component is to maintain. However, as discussed in Chapter 14, this relationship is not well understood and thus the value of this metric as a quality predictor is in doubt.

It is not the intention in this section to discuss individual quality metrics. The reason for this is that there are no software metrics which have been unequivocally demonstrated to be generally useful as quality

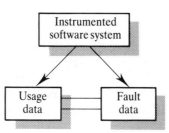

Figure 30.6
Automated data
collection.

predictors. It is clear that individual organizations must assess the validity of particular metrics to their own products and software process. The reading list associated with this chapter includes references to fuller discussions of software metrics.

To find out if any particular metric is a useful predictor of product quality, quality management must evaluate that metric in a systematic way. Firstly, management must convince itself of the existence of a relationship between the measurement and the product quality of interest. Secondly, a model must be formulated which allows the quality prediction to be made.

An essential prerequisite for metric evaluation in the context of a particular product or product class is the collection of data from previously developed products of the same type. Unfortunately, this data may not have been collected during product development and the costs of collecting it by a post-release analysis of products is often very high.

In order for metrics to be evaluated statistically, it is necessary to have a reasonable quantity of data. In circumstances where product data has not been collected during development, and management is unwilling to accept high data collection costs, there is little point in attempting to evaluate any software metric with small and perhaps untypical data sets.

Kitchenham (1989) suggests that data collection is unlikely to be successful unless it is automated and integrated into the development process (Figure 30.6). Furthermore, data which cannot be automatically collected should be collected during development and should not be based on recollections of past events. Little time should elapse between data collection and data analysis. Finally, product data should be maintained as an organizational resource and historical records of all projects should be maintained even when data has not been used during a particular project.

Once an appropriate data set is available, model evaluation involves identifying the functional form of the model (linear, exponential, etc.), identifying the parameters which are to be included in the model and calibrating these using existing data. Such model development, if it is to be trusted, requires significant experience in statistical techniques and it is recommended that a professional statistician should be involved in the process.

Metrics clearly have a role to play in the quality assurance process but unfortunately we do not know enough about software metrics to arrive at any general conclusions of what that role should be. Measurements are seductive and it is easy to fall into the trap of accepting figures which appear to confirm prejudices and beliefs. Individual experimentation is essential if metrics are to be useful. Quality assurance must be applied to suggested metrics as well as the software process and products!

KEY POINTS

- Software quality is more than verification and validation. It encompasses software attributes such as maintainability, reliability, portability,etc. Some quality attributes are subjective and difficult to assess.

- A software quality plan should explicitly identify those quality attributes which are most significant for a particular project and should set out how these attributes can be judged.

- The reliability of a software system is not a simple measure which can be associated with the system. It depends on the pattern of usage of that system. It is quite possible for a system to contain faults yet be completely reliable.

- There are a number of ways of measuring reliability. The particular metric chosen depends on the individual system and application domain. The reliability required should be set out in the system requirements specification.

- Reliability growth models are a means of assessing the change in reliability as a product is developed. They should not assume that reliability always increases with changes to the system.

- Software standards are important to quality assurance as they represent an identification of 'best practice'. If standards can be developed, quality assurance is the activity of checking that the process and the product conforms to these standards.

- The notion of quantifying software products and processes is an attractive one. However, current development in software metrics means that it is very difficult to make general statements concerning how this quantification can be carried out.

Further reading

Software Reliability Handbook.   In spite of its title this book has a much broader scope than simply reliability issues. It also has excellent sections on metrics and quality assurance. (P. Rook (ed.), London: Elsevier, 1989.)

Software Engineering, Design Reliability and Management.   This is a general text on software engineering which pays particular attention to reliability issues. For readers who wish to explore the topic of reliability in more detail, it contains a good introduction to the underlying theory. (M.L. Schooman, 1983, McGraw-Hill.)

IEEE Software, **4** (5), 1987. This is a special issue of the journal, containing a number of papers on quality assurance. It is also relevant reading for the previous chapter on software maintenance.

ANSI/IEEE 730-1981 IEEE Standard for Software Quality Assurance Plans, IEEE, Piscataway, NJ, 1981. This is included simply as an example software engineering standard. It is not light reading and is only really for those very interested in quality assurance.

References

Abdel-Ghaly, A.A., Chan, P.Y. and Littlewood, B. (1986), 'Evaluation of competing software reliability predictions', *IEEE Trans. Software Eng.*, **SE-12** (9), 950–67.

Adams, E.N. (1984). 'Optimizing preventative service of software products', *IBM J. R & D*, **28** (1), 2–14.

Bersoff, E.H. (1984), 'Elements of software configuration management', *IEEE Trans. Software Eng.*, **SE-10** (1), 79–87.

Boehm, B.W., Brown, J.R., Kaspar, H., Lipow, M., Macleod, G. and Merrit, M. (1978), *Characteristics of Software Quality*, TRW Series of Software Technology, Amsterdam: North-Holland.

Buckley, F.J. and Poston, R. (1984), 'Software quality assurance', *IEEE Trans. Software Eng.*, **SE-10** (1), 36–41.

Gunning, R. (1962), *Techniques of Clear Writing*, New York: McGraw-Hill.

Jelinski, Z. and Moranda, P.B. (1972), 'Software reliability research', in *Statistical Computer Performance Evaluation*, Frieberger, W. (ed.), New York: Academic Press.

Kitchenham, B. (1989), 'Software metrics', in *Software Reliability Handbook*, Rook, P. (ed.), London: Elsevier.

Littlewood, B. (1989), 'Software reliability growth models', in *Software Reliability Handbook*, Rook, P. (ed.), London: Elsevier.

Littlewood, B. and Verrall, J.L. (1973), 'A Bayesian reliability growth model for computer software', *Applied Statistics*, **22**, 332–46.

McCabe, T.J. (1976), 'A complexity measure', *IEEE Trans. Software Eng.*, **SE-2**, 308–20

Mills, H.D., Dyer, M. and Linger, R. (1987), 'Cleanroom software engineering', *IEEE Software*, **4** (5), 19–25.

EXERCISES

30.1 Given that you have been assigned the role of a quality manager, write a quality plan which would be appropriate for a QA team assessing the quality of real-time systems products embedded in software used by the general public.

30.2 Explain why assuring the quality of the software process should lead to high quality software products. Discuss also the difficulties with this system of QA.

30.3 Assess the reliability of some software system which you use regularly by keeping a log of system failures and observed faults. Write a user's handbook which describes how to make effective use of the system in the presence of these faults.

30.4 Suggest appropriate reliability metrics for the following classes of software system. Give reasons for your choice of metric. Suggest, also, approximate acceptable values for the system reliability.

- A system which monitors patients in a hospital intensive care unit
- A word processor
- An automated vending machine control system
- A system to control braking in a car
- A system to control a refrigeration unit
- A management report generator

30.5 Using the literature as background information, write a report for management (who may be technically illiterate) on the use of reliability growth models.

30.6 Suggest standards for the following documents and activities:

- A software requirements specification
- A software design expressed using data-flow diagrams
- A program inspection
- The quality assurance process

30.7 Assume you work for an organization which develops database products for microcomputer systems. This organization is interested in quantifying its software development. Write a report suggesting appropriate metrics and suggest how these can be collected.

Appendix A

Ada/PDL Description

Objectives

This appendix sets out an outline description of Ada and of the PDL used to describe designs in this book. It includes brief descriptions of Ada control structures, types and packages and of the relaxations of Ada's rules which have been introduced to make the notation more suitable as a language for describing designs. It is clearly impossible to describe all of Ada in a short appendix and no attempt to do so is made here. The differences between Pascal and Ada are described and the reader is given pointers to other parts of the text where specific Ada constructs are described.

Contents

Ada is a programming language which was sponsored by the US Department of Defense for the building of real-time embedded computer systems. The need for such a language arose because of the vast number of languages used for implementing such systems with the associated cost and expense of language support.

Ada embodies much programming language research which was carried out in the 1970s and it is now a mandatory standard in the US and in the UK for implementing military systems. The language is a large and comprehensive one and its introduction has not been as rapid as was once anticipated. Part of the reason for this was the difficulty of writing efficient compilers but there are now a number of good compilers available. It is reasonable to predict that Ada will become the standard language for large-scale software engineering.

One of the aims of the designers of Ada was to include as much compile-time checking as possible so that program errors could be detected by the language compiler rather than at run-time. This is a laudable aim but it requires the programmer to provide a lot of information which the compiler can use for checking. Sometimes, it forces decisions to be made and this is not desirable when the language is used for describing abstract designs. Thus, when used as a PDL, it makes sense to relax some of Ada's rules. These relaxations are discussed later in this appendix.

A.1   Ada and Pascal

Pascal was a 'base-language' for Ada and many of the ideas embodied in Ada were first introduced in Pascal. However, Ada includes many more constructs to support information hiding, exception handling and parallelism.

The similarities between Ada and Pascal are:

- Types are defined in a similar way although Ada uses a slightly different syntax which should be obvious to readers who know Pascal (Example A.1). However, Ada does not require declarations to be made in any particular order so typed constants are allowed. It includes a sub-typing mechanism which means that array sizes need not be bound into the type declaration (thus permitting more general array operations) and a derived type mechanism which is a means of supporting a limited form of inheritance. Variables are declared as in Pascal but there is no need to precede the variable name with the reserved word **var**. Pointers in Ada are called access types.

Example A.I
Ada declarations.

```
-- Scalar type declarations
type COLOUR is (red, orange, yellow, green, blue, indigo, violet) ;
type SMALL_INT is range 0..255 ;
-- Array declaration
type INT_ARRAY is array (1..10) of INTEGER ;
-- Array declaration without fixed bounds
type TEXT is array (NATURAL range <>) of CHARACTER ;
-- Record declaration with pointer component
-- Use a forward declaration of the pointer reference type to allow it to
-- be used in the pointer declaration
type ELEM ;
type LISTP is access ELEM ;
type ELEM is record
    Val: INTEGER ;
    Next: LISTP ;
end record ;
-- Some variable declarations
Rainbow: COLOUR ;
Char_value: SMALL_INT ;
First_10: INT_ARRAY ;
```

Example A.2
Ada control statements.

```
-- An Ada if statement
if A = B and X = Y then
    Some_action ;
else
    Some_other_action ;
end if ;
-- An Ada for loop
for J in (1..10) loop
    Do_something (J) ;
end loop ;
-- An Ada while loop
while J < 20 loop
    Do_something (J) ;
    J := J + Some_function (J) ;
end loop ;
-- An Ada case statement
case Sensor is
    when Red => Do_danger ;
    when Amber => Do_warning ;
    when Green => Do_safe ;
end case ;
```

- Control structures (selection and loops) are similar although, again, a slightly different syntax is used in Ada (Example A.2). Perhaps the most obvious difference is the explicit **end** statement which must be associated with an Ada control structure. These are actually very valuable for the reader looking for the end of loops and selection statements. A further difference is the introduction of an **exit** statement which allows exit from a loop at any point. Pascal only supports exit from the beginning (*while* loop) and at the end (*repeat* loop) of loops. Again, readers familiar with Pascal will have no difficulty in understanding Ada's control constructs.

- A program may be structured into functions and procedures. Instead of referring to parameter passing by reference as *var* parameters, Ada calls parameters which are passed by reference **out** parameters. Again a slightly different syntax is used for function and procedure declaration but this should be obvious to Pascal programmers. Examples of procedure and function declarations are given in the discussion of Ada packages (Section A.2).

A.1.1   Additional features in Ada

Ada has much in common with Pascal, and many Ada programs are easily understood by those who have Pascal knowledge. However, Ada includes a number of additional features which Pascal programmers may not be familiar with. Some of these are:

- *Packages*   These are information hiding constructs which allow a group of declarations to be encapsulated and given a name. As far as the use of Ada in this book is concerned, packages are the most important Ada construct. They are described in Section A.2.

- *Tasks*   These are sections of code which can operate in parallel rather than sequentially. Ada's model of tasking is very complex and we have tried to avoid using tasks here for program or design description. There are some illustrative examples in the design chapters (11 and 12).

- *Exceptions*   Exceptions are a means of handling error situations or unusual events in an Ada program. This is particularly valuable for a real-time system which must continue in operation in the presence of system faults. Exceptions are discussed in Chapter 15.

- *Representation clauses*   Representation clauses are a way of providing machine-specific information while still staying within the Ada language. They are discussed in Chapter 5.

- *Independent compilation*   Components of an Ada program may be compiled separately. Independent compilation is discussed in Chapter 18.

- *Generics*   Generics are a means of parameterizing entities such as packages and procedures so that they can operate on any type. However, to ensure strict type checking, the generic must be instantiated at compile-time where instantiation means specifying which actual type the generic component operates on. Generics are discussed below where a generic package is illustrated.

A.2   Ada packages

Ada packages are a means of implementing information hiding. They allow a set of declarations (of constants, variables, procedures, functions, other packages, etc.) to be grouped together and named. They provide facilities which give the programmer control over which of these names can be used outside the package and which are purely internal. They provide the important facility of separation of specification and implementation. A package specification must be produced but its implementation can be delayed.

An Ada package is made up of two parts:

- A package specification which sets out the declarations made in the package which may be accessed from outside the package.
- A package body which can include additional declarations which are completely inaccessible from outside the package. The package body also includes the code of any procedures or functions declared in the package specification.

There is no requirements for these parts to be together in source program. It is common practice to provide a package specification and a package body quite separately.

Within a package, a type may be declared to be a private or a limited private type. This means that the type name may be used outside the package but its representation is private to the package within which it is declared. When a type is declared to be a **private** type, this means that only the procedures and functions declared within the same package may operate on the representation of that type. It is also assumed that equality and assignment operations are valid. When a type is a **limited private** type, only package operations are allowed. If equality and assignment operations are required, they must be declared within the package specification.

Ada packages are not, in themselves, executable objects. To access an executable object such as a function within a package, the package name and the function name must both be specified, separated by a dot (see later). Packages are introduced below by illustrating how a generic package describing a sequence may be defined. Comments are used within this package for additional explanation.

This package sets out the specification for a sequence and, during a system design, it is often only necessary to construct a package specification. The specification defines the package interface and this can be used by other components without knowledge of the package body. The body is not included here. Examples of package bodies are given in Chapter 16.

The sequence package shown in Example A.3 is a generic package. Generics are a useful feature of Ada which are based on the fact that the

Example A.3
An Ada package defining a sequence.

```
generic
    - - Declaring a generic type means that ANY_TYPE is the formal
    - - type name. The package is instantiated with an actual type
    - - before the package is used. By using generics, the implementor
    - - need not write a separate package for each type of element
    type ANY_TYPE is private ;
    - - A generic size parameter is used to set up a default length for
    - - sequences. This may be instantiated before use but, if not, its
    - - default value is 100.
    Max: NATURAL := 100 ;
package Sequence is
    - - Declaring a type as private means that its representation is
    - - completely concealed within the package. It may not be
    - - accessed by any external agent.
    type T is private ;
    - - Create brings a sequence into existence
    function Create (Seq: T) return T ;
    - - Add adds an item to the end of the sequence
    function Add (Val: ANY_TYPE; Seq: T) return T ;
    - - Next returns the current front item of the sequence which is
    - - referenced by some notional sequence pointer. The operation
    - - updates this notional pointer so that it refers to the sequence
    - - item following that returned. However, the returned item is not
    - - removed from the sequence but may be accessed again by
    - - resetting the sequence pointer and traversing the sequence
    - - again.
    function Next (Seq: T) return ANY_TYPE;
    - - Reset sets the notional sequence pointer to refer to the
    - - beginning of the sequence
    function Reset (Seq: T) return T ;
    - - AtEnd determines if the notional pointer refers to the last
    - - sequence member
    function AtEnd (Seq: T) return BOOLEAN ;
```

```
        -- IsEmpty determines if the sequence has any members
        function IsEmpty (Seq: T) return BOOLEAN ;
        -- Length returns the number of sequence members
        function Length (Seq: T) return NATURAL ;
        -- Catenate puts two sequences together
        function Catenate (Seq1, Seq2: T) return T ;
private
        -- Ada requires that the sequence representation is specified in
        -- the package specification although this is not necessary for
        -- design specification.
        -- Ada requires this so that the compiler knows how much space to
        -- allocate for objects declared of this type. It is included here for
        -- completeness although it need not be used in our design
        -- description language.
        type SEQ_ARRAY is array (1..Max ) of ANY_TYPE ;
        type T is record
             Pointer: NATURAL ;
             Values: SEQ_ARRAY ;
        end record ;
end Sequence ;
```

operation of many algorithms is independent of the type manipulated by
the algorithm. Given that an ordering exists, sort is type independent as
are most collections of elements. Using generics, it is possible to specify a
general algorithm then instantiate that with a particular type before use.

Generic instantiation is a compile-time and not a run-time operation. A generic is simply a template and the programmer must create the
actual package or routine from the generic. Example A.4 shows the
package Sequence being instantiated with types INTEGER, COORD and
TAG.

```
        -- Create a sequence of integers with a maximum length of
        -- 100 elements
        package Integer_seq is new Sequence (ANY_TYPE => INTEGER) ;
        -- Create a sequence of COORD with a maximum size of 500 elements
        package Coord_seq is new Sequence (ANY_TYPE => COORD ;
                                           Max =>500) ;
        -- Create a sequence of TAGS with a maximum length of 300
        package Tag_sequence is new Sequence (ANY_TYPE => TAG,
                                              Max => 300) ;
```

Example A.5
Abstract type
declarations.

```
with Integer_seq, Coord_seq, Tag_sequence ;
First_100_primes: Integer_seq.T ;
Zig_zag_line: Coord_seq.T ;
Labels, New_labels: Tag_sequence.T ;
```

Once a generic has been instantiated, it is, of course, possible to declare variables to represent abstract sequences.

Example A.5 illustrates the declaration of abstract types and also the use of Ada's **with** clause. Ada's information hiding strategy means that information is concealed unless it is explicitly made visible. A package is made visible by using a **with** clause. Thus, in Example A.5, the **with** clause makes the packages Integer_seq, Coord_seq and Tag_sequence visible. Therefore, the names declared in these sequences may be used in those parts of the program where the package is visible. Example A.6 shows how names within a package are accessed. A dot notation (similar to record access) is used with the package name preceding the name of the entity within the package.

Example A.6
Accessing package
elements.

```
First_100_primes := Integer_seq.Create ;
Zig_zag_line := Coord_seq.Add (Next_point, Zig_zag_line) ;
Labels := Tag_sequence.Catenate (Labels, New_labels) ;
```

It is possible to combine the **with** clause with a **use** clause which allows names declared within a package to be used without preceding them with the package name. This is not particularly good style and is not recommended.

A.3 Ada/PDL extensions

As suggested in the introduction, Ada is a programming language and requires the programmer to provide redundant information to enable compiler type checking. It sometimes forces the programmer to make early decisions which are logically unnecessary at a particular stage of development.

A good design principle is to delay detailed decision making as long as possible in the design process. The later a decision is made, the less effect subsequent change to that decision is likely to have. For this reason, when the language is used to express a design, it is allowable to relax some of the rules of the language. In particular, the following are allowed in a PDL but not in standard Ada.

(1)   Names do not have to be declared before use. In general, the purpose of a name may be obvious because the name is meaningful, or the precise type may be unimportant at an early stage in the design.

(2)   It is unnecessary to make a package name visible using a **with** clause before referencing the names declared in that package.

(3)   The private part of a package specification where the representation of types is set out may be excluded. This part included purely for implementation reasons as it provides space allocation information to the compiler.

(4)   A statement or expression may be replaced by descriptive English text describing the effects of that statement or expression. Where this is used here, the English text is italicized. For example:

   Word := *The first word in the sequence* ;

(5)   A delay statement may be used in a procedure or function to specify a time delay. This is used to describe the design. In an implementation, delay statements are only meaningful in tasks, otherwise the whole system stops.

(6)   It is sometimes useful to specify an operation on all elements of a collection without defining how that collection is represented. The **for_all** statement is used here to indicate that the same action is carried out on each element. This may be used with sets, sequences, lists, arrays, etc. For example:

   -- Execute an action for all elements in a set Nodes
   for_all i **in** Nodes **loop**

Further reading

There are a multiplicity of introductory Ada texts which, in general, cover more or less the same ground. My recommendations are as follows but I have not actually looked at all available texts.

Software Engineering with Ada, 2nd ed., G. Booch, 1987, Benjamin/Cummings.

Programming in Ada, 2nd ed., J.G.P. Barnes, 1984, Addison-Wesley.

Ada: Language and Methodology, D. Watt, B. Wichmann and W. Finlay, 1987, Prentice-Hall.

The following texts are not Ada primers but are intended for readers who have some language experience.

Software Development with Ada, I. Sommerville and R.Morrison, 1987, Addison-Wesley.

Software Components with Ada, 2nd ed., G. Booch, 1987, Benjamin/Cummings.

Appendix B

Instructor's Notes

Objectives

This appendix is a collection of notes for instructors using the book to support a course in software engineering. It includes a discussion of course structures into which the book might fit, some suggestions for other courses that might supplement a software engineering course, a description of the my approach to the difficult problem of setting practical software engineering work and some suggestions for design and implementation projects.

Contents

Users of earlier editions of this book will have noticed a marked increase in the amount of material covered in this text and a significant reorganization in the way that it has been presented. The reason for this is the increasing emphasis given to courses in software engineering in universities, colleges and industry. These courses have different emphases and not all courses might include all of the subjects covered in this book.

As before the material in the book is based on my own teaching of software engineering. The additional material reflects the fact that software engineering courses are now a more important part of a university computer science course. More of the subject is covered than was the case a few years ago. Software engineering courses now discuss software process models, software design, formal specification, requirements derivation, program validation, software management, environments and software reliability.

It is not really possible to give any detailed guidelines about how the book fits into existing course structures. The second edition of this book was used by students in the UK, in several European countries, in North America, in Asia and in Australia. It is intended that the modular structure of the book will make it possible to use it effectively in the different course structures adopted in different countries.

Figure B.1 illustrates how the book is used at Lancaster. The undergraduate course is a three-year course in computer science and the software engineering part of the course is also taken by students taking a joint major in computer science and electronics. After courses in introductory programming, computer science and data structures, students are required to take three software engineering modules in their second year. In their third and final year, a core software engineering course must be taken covering more advanced topics (Figure B.2).

It is clear from Figures B.1 and B.2 that the book is not really designed to be used sequentially. Unless a very intensive approach is taken, there is probably too much material to be covered in a single unit. However, a possible course structure based on two software engineering units might use the book as shown in Figure B.3.

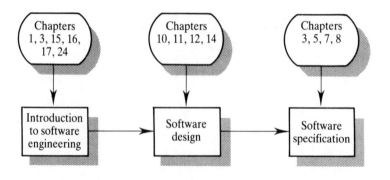

Figure B.1
Introductory software engineering.

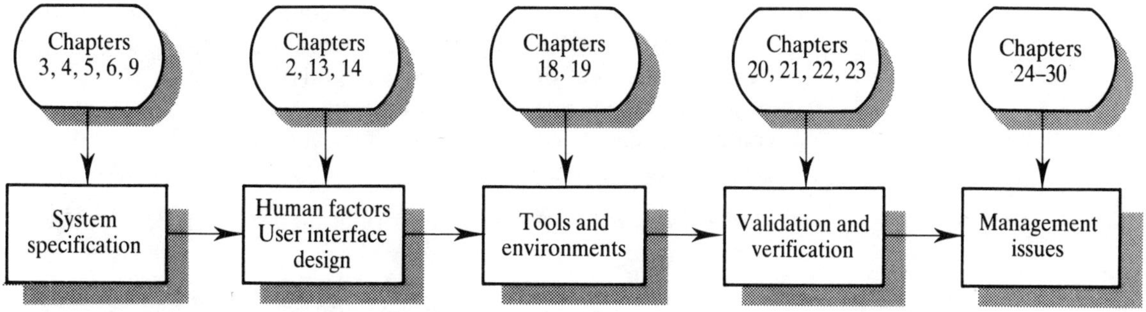

Figure B.2
Advanced software engineering.

B.1 Complementary courses

As well as being a course text in its own right, the book may also be used as background material in a number of other courses. For example, a course on a particular design method such as JSD might use Chapters 10–12 to present an alternative approach; a course on algebraic specification might not use Chapter 8 but might recommend Chapter 9 as a comparison. Figure B.4 shows some courses which the book might support.

This text is intended to stand alone and, apart from an elementary programming course, there are no prerequisites for using the book. However, it may be the case that individual students may wish to choose a set of courses which are oriented towards software engineering. If available, the following courses are recommended as complementary to the material in this book.

Unit 1

Introduction (Chapter 1)
Human factors (Chapter 2)
Software design (Chapters 10–14)
Programming issues (Chapters 15–16)
Portability and reuse (Chapter 17)
Verification and validation (Chapters 20–23)

Unit 2

Software specification (Chapters 3–9)
Tools and environments (Chapters 18–19)
Software management (Chapters 24–30)

Figure B.3
A two unit software engineering course.

- *Embedded real-time systems* Such a course might cover real-time executives, parallel programming, real-time languages (Ada and Modula-2), real-time design methods, hardware interfacing, interrupt management, software safety, etc. In Lancaster, students may take such a course in their final year after the core software engineering course.

- *Formal methods* A course in formal methods can be an effective complement to a software engineering course if it is oriented towards formal specification and, to a lesser extent, the study of algorithms. Some courses with this title are more concerned with theoretical computer science (computability, Turing machines, etc.) or language semantics and, although these have a value in their own right, they are only vaguely related to software engineering.

- *User interface design* In this book, it has been possible only to touch on the topic of user interface design. Chapter 13 is really intended to present an overview of the topic to those students who do not have an opportunity for a more detailed study of this topic. Topics which might be covered in such a course include user psychology, adaptive user interfaces, icon and window design, command language design, user guidance systems, collaborative working, etc.

- *Advanced programming or software design* This title can cover a multitude of different topics from design methods to a study of algorithms. In general, most of these complement the material here and, as suggested, it may be possible to use this book to broaden the student's experience.

- *Management* The chapters here on software management concentrate on the problems of software management but software managers also have to cope with general management problems which should be covered in a management course.

Figure B.4
Complementary courses.

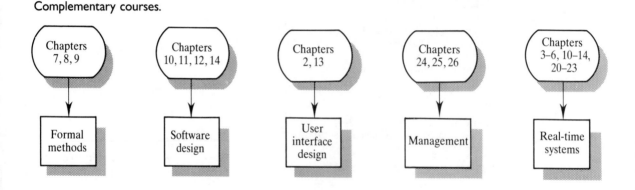

B.2   Exercises and other coursework

Each of the chapters in the book is accompanied by a set of exercises. These range from simple descriptive exercises, whose answers can be discovered in the text, through exercises which require some thought about the descriptive material to problems which rely on the application of the ideas discussed in the chapter.

In a software engineering text, it is inevitable that much of the material is descriptive in nature and is simply intended to illustrate the state of the art to students. Where this is the case, it is unrealistic to devise exercises requiring the application of problem-solving skills. I have an intense dislike of some of the very artificial exercises included in other texts and, in some of the descriptive chapters, only a few exercises have been included. Many of the exercises have several possible solutions.

It is unlikely that students will do all of the exercises associated with a chapter and instructors should select those which are most appropriate to their style of presentation. Wherever possible, it is recommended that exercises are supplemented with practical work. Because of the range of backgrounds of readers and equipment available to them, this can only be devised by a particular course instructor.

As well as short practical exercises, it is recommended that students also undertake more substantial project work. The difficulty which arises in setting such work is that courses normally run for a relatively short time (10–12 weeks) and it is simply impossible to complete realistic projects in the time available. The approach taken by the author to this problem is twofold:

(1)   Group projects are set which simply involve a single aspect (not programming) of building a system. This might be the writing of a requirements specification, the construction of a non-trivial formal specification, the writing of a user manual, etc. As well as this document, students are also requested to schedule and cost their work, thus illustrating some of the management problems discussed in Chapters 25 and 26.

(2)   Students involved in other courses where practical work is set are expected to employ the techniques discussed in the software engineering course when doing that work. Thus, a course in compiling techniques, say, may suggest that an object-oriented approach is taken to compiler design; a course in embedded systems construction may involve the production of a comprehensive test specification for the system being built.

I consider it particularly important that projects should be group projects rather than individual projects. Furthermore, students should be assigned to groups rather than left to choose their own group. Each group may do a different project and, again, these should be assigned rather than chosen. As discussed in Chapter 2, we try to form mixed-sex groups but this is not always possible.

The intention is to illustrate the problems of group working and, sometimes personality clashes arise. Depending on the individuals involved, instructors may step in and resolve outstanding issues or may simply leave the group to sort out its own problems.

An aspect of software engineering which students find unsettling is the fact that system users and procurers usually have a vague and potentially contradictory set of requirements. The approach I have adopted is to act as a user and deliberately be vague and contradictory and present impossible requirements. This approach leads to entertaining classes!

The argument against group projects is, of course, that it makes individual assessment more difficult. This is correct. However, in my opinion education is more important than assessment and the loss of precision in assessment is compensated for by the improved education provided by group working. In general, students working in groups find the experience very instructive and enjoyable, especially when they are working on non-programming aspects of the subject.

Individuals within groups may be assessed by interviewing the group members after some grade for the group as a whole has been assigned. During that interview, the individual contribution of group members can be assessed and the mark re-allocated. In my experience students are content with this system (especially after the inherent imprecision of any grading system is explained to them) and few raise complaints about it.

B.3   Project work

The fundamental difficulty in proposing projects is that the majority of realistic examples all require some application domain knowledge and there are few general applications which can be understood. Hence, patient monitoring systems and electronic mail systems are often used as a source of examples in textbooks simply because the concepts are easily understood by most students.

The projects suggested here fall into two classes. Design projects are very general projects which are not implementable in most university or college laboratories. They may be large applications, require access to special hardware or require detailed domain knowledge to complete an implementation. It is intended that students construct high-level specifications and designs of such systems. The aim of the work is to illustrate the problems of writing specifications and designs rather than to design a valid system. In some cases, it may be possible to prototype parts of the system if appropriate languages and equipment are available.

The documents which might be produced are:

- A requirements definition and (partial) specification
- An outline architectural design
- A project plan and schedule
- A prototype of part of the system user interface

In all cases, it is recommended that a requirements definition be produced to expand on the suggested project outlines. Of course, this may bear little resemblance to the true requirements for the system but, given that the requirements are reasonable, this does not really matter.

The second class of project is smaller scale projects that a student or group might take through from initial specification to implementation. Depending on the time available, these may also be considered simply as design projects. In these projects, students might be expected to produce some or all of the following documents:

- A requirements specification which expands the outline below in more detail
- A formal specification for part of the project
- An outline architectural design
- A detailed design specification
- A test specification
- A user manual and associated help frames
- A project plan and schedule setting out milestones, resource usage and estimated costs
- A quality plan setting out quality assurance procedures

B.3.1 Design project suggestions

1. A police vehicle command and control system

It is a requirement of a police service that it respond as quickly as possible to reported incidents, and the objective of a command and control system is to ensure that incidents are logged and routed to the most appropriate police vehicle. Factors which must be taken into account in deciding which vehicle to send to which incident include:

(1) *The type of incident* Some incidents are more serious than others and require a more urgent response. It is recommended that classes of response be identified and incidents allocated to these classes.

(2)   *The position of available vehicles*   In general, the best strategy is to send the closest vehicle to respond to an incident. Take into account that the position of vehicles may not be known exactly and that it may be necessary to send a message to vehicles to determine their current position.

(3)   *The type of vehicles available*   Some incidents require a number of vehicles; others, such as traffic accidents, may require specialized vehicles and so on.

(4)   *The location of the incident*   In some areas, it may be unwise simply to respond to an incident by sending a single vehicle. In other areas, a single vehicle or policeman may be all that is needed to respond to the same type of incident.

(5)   *The need to alert other emergency services*   The system should automatically alert services such as fire and ambulance services if necessary.

(6)   The system should allow details of the reporter of incidents to be logged.

A system such as this one is open to almost indefinite expansion. For example, police vehicles may include fax terminals so that written information may be faxed when a vehicle is routed to an incident. A user interface for a system control room might be prototyped and so on.

2. A fire and security alarm monitoring system

A large building may require an automated alarm system which monitors and controls all fire and security alarms in the building. Normally, the building is divided into zones and a number of alarms are associated with each zone. Alarms alert personnel at a central manned control area who may pass these on to the emergency services or may respond personally.

Factors which have to be taken into account in building such a system are:

(1)   If the control area is unmanned and an alarm is activated this alarm should not be ignored if it is potentially serious. Emergency services should be automatically called.

(2)   Some but not all parts of the building may be equipped with sprinkler systems or systems to shut down electrical equipment. These should be activated if a fire alarm is confirmed. They should not be activated if there are people in the same room.

(3)   The building may be equipped with direction indicators which illuminate the route to the nearest exit. These should be activated when a fire alarm is confirmed. At the same time, an audible signal should sound alerting occupiers to leave the building.

(4)   A security alarm may cause some internal doors to be locked automatically. It should be possible to isolate complete zones by automatic door locking.

(5)   False alarms are common and it might be normal practice to have an alarm confirmed before alerting emergency services. There are different ways of confirming an alarm. In the case of a fire alarm, it may be confirmed by multiple sensors detecting a problem.

3.   An integrated university department information system

University computer science and engineering departments often have budgets which are comparable with those of small companies and an integrated system to support all aspects of departmental administration is required. This should support student records, laboratory administration, the ordering of goods and services, input and output payments, payments made for teaching assistants, research contract reporting, etc. It should be linked to a wider university system responsible for staff salaries, etc.

Factors which should be taken into account include the following:

● Departmental chairmen who use such a system are usually very busy. Even if they are computer literate, they require a system with a straightforward user interface.

● Users of the system range from secretaries through technicians to teaching and administrative staff. The range of users to be supported is very wide.

● In some countries, the trend is for universities to devolve administration from a central organization to the individual departments. The system must be able to be expanded to handle future, unforeseen tasks.

● Subsystems should be automatically linked so that, for example, the costs of a particular class or laboratory can be computed by considering payments made and received.

4.   A management conferencing system

Simple conferencing or bulletin board systems are now widely used but these usually have a character-based user interface (because they can be accessed via dial-up lines), a command language which is cryptic and text-only presentation. This project involves the building of a management conferencing system to be used by managers via their personal workstations. Multiple conferences should be supported.

This system is different from more general conferencing systems in a number of ways:

● The workstations all have bit-mapped graphic screens and are connected by a fast local area network. There is no need to support slow dial-up lines.

- The managers using the system require a very easy-to-use user interface. A text-based, command language interface is not acceptable.
- Mixed text and graphics should be supported.
- It should incorporate an electronic mail facility.
- The user community is a closed one. It is possible to incorporate knowledge of particular roles and individuals in the system. This may lead to some individuals only being concerned with particular conferences.

5. A library automation system

A library requires a completely integrated automated system which handles book ordering, cataloging, book issue and recall. It is intended that the catalogue be accessible by library users and that users should be able to access this remotely via dial-up lines. Users should also be able to request books which are currently on loan by marking that book in the library catalogue.

The following factors should be taken into account:

- Users of the library may have no specific computer experience. However, the requirement for remote catalogue browsing means that a text-based interface is required.
- Book ordering depends on a buying budget. If this is exhausted, no books may be ordered. There may be multiple book purchase budgets to be administered.
- The system should be able to generate reports about books on order, loan frequency, etc., for library staff.
- Books are marked with a bar code when purchased and this is read to issue the book. Library users also have identification cards incorporating a bar code.

B.3.2 Term projects

(1) *Software components catalogue*   The aim of this project is to build a software components catalogue which users may browse through to discover reusable software components. It may be accessed using keywords associated with each component. It must be possible to enter and classify components. An extension to such a system is to provide a graphical browsing capability.

(2) *Group diary and appointments system*   This project is concerned with providing a shared diary where appointments for a group are recorded. When a meeting involving more than one group member

is required, their diaries are consulted and a mutually suitable time discovered. Appointments may be moved to make a suitable time. Note that some appointments are not movable.

(3) *OHP transparency system*   The object of this project is to design and implement a system which runs on a personal computer and which assists with the preparation of overhead projector transparencies. It should support multiple font text, simple graphics, the importing of material from other editors, and the use of standard template slides incorporating a company name, say. Individual elements on the slide should be movable so this is not a word processing problem. It should also support the preparation of overlays where several slides are overlaid to form a whole picture.

(4) *Ideas processor*   This project is concerned with providing a means of organizing ideas. It should support the input of headings, the moving of headings, the association of text with headings, etc. Do not assume that a simple hierarchical structure is appropriate. It should be possible to form a network of ideas. Make use of graphical capabilities if these are available.

(5) *A Pascal toolset*   The aim of this project is to build a set of Pascal tools such as static and dynamic analysers, structure editors, viewing systems, compilers for a range of machines and so on. Of course, it is probably not possible to do all of these in a single project but different parts can be created during one project and used as new tools are added. The system should be built around a syntax tree representation of a Pascal program. The use of data abstraction and object-oriented techniques is recommended.

(6) *Diagram editor*   The aim of this project is to write a simple object-oriented graphical editor (like MacDraw for those who know the Macintosh). This should support a range of shapes, shape combination, the addition of texts in different fonts, shape scaling, etc. The possibilities are limitless.

(7) *Visual interface to UNIX*   UNIX is a widely used system but its shell command language has been widely condemned as difficult to use. The aim of this project is to write a direct manipulation interface which allows the filestore (for example) to be displayed graphically and modified by direct manipulation. Other possibilities include iconic displays, the use of file suffixes to restrict operations on these files and so on.

(8) *Personal data management system*   The aim of this project is to build a small database management system used to record personal information such as details of records and books, information about recipes and so on. There may be a diversity of different kinds of information recorded and the system should be usable by those

without a computing background. One possible approach would be to build a Macintosh-like HyperCard system.

(9) *Photograph library sales system*   This system should record and retrieve information about photographs in a library and the worldwide sales of these photographs. It should support keyword classification and retrieval requests for different types of photograph. It should also maintain details of fees received and due for each photograph which is published. Again, the system should be designed for use by people who are not familiar with computing concepts.

(10) *A student record system*   The aim of this project is to maintain a student record system within a single university or college department. The system should allow personal details to be recorded as well as classes taken, grades, etc. It should provide summary facilities allowing information about groups of students to be retrieved. Assume that the system is intended for use by departmental administrative staff with no computing background.

(11) *A laboratory management system*   This sytem is intended to support the administration of an undergraduate laboratory where different equipment is available to students for different experiments at different times. The system should assist with experiment scheduling and keep records of equipment purchases, reliability and maintenance.

(12) *System change control and reporting system*   This system is intended to support a change reporting and control system as discussed in Chapter 28. It should allow changes to be logged, submitted for approval and subsequently tracked. It might be integrated with an electronic mail system so that the change reports can be passed automatically to the change control board.

(13) *A writer's workbench*   The objective of this project is to build a set of tools which analyse text and make suggestions to the writer as to how this text might be improved. To get an idea of what to include with such a system, study the reports on the UNIX Writer's Workbench (Chapter 29).

(14) *A program visualizer*   The objective of this system is to generate structure charts automatically by analysing Pascal source programs. As well as structure charts displaying the procedure and function hierarchies, you might also consider the graphical display of other program characteristics such as the static nested structure, etc.

(15) *A Pascal or C program viewing system*   The objective of this project is to build a multi-window viewing system for Pascal or C programs. The system should be aware of language elements such as functions and procedures and allow these to be viewed at the same time as the

main text. You should also consider how to highlight user-specified program features in the display.

(16) *A testing system for Pascal compilers*   The objective of this project is to build a compiler input generator as discussed in Chapter 23. The system should generate Pascal strings and strings which are similar but illegal, submit these to the compile and collect anomalous results in some file for processing. You may also consider integrating such a system with a file comparator to support regression testing.

(17) *An integrated help and message system*   This system should be designed as a set of abstract data types so that it may be incorporated as a component in other systems. Your design should take into account that the system may have to present help and messages at different levels of detail and in different languages.

(18) *A screen and forms generator*   The objective of this project is to build a system which allows the user to create form and screen designs interactively by specifying fields on the form, their contents and their constraints. The system may be interfaced with some database management system. Pay attention to the fact that the text displayed in fields may exceed the field size so scrolling of each individual field should be supported.

(19) *An animated presentation system*   The objective of this system is to use a personal computer as a means of making presentations. Rather than prepare transparencies, the presenter sets out a series of frames on a screen and displays these to the audience. The project should make use of the machine's ability to provide animation, zoom and dissolve effects. Graphical and textual presentations using a range of fonts should be supported.

Collected References

Abbott, R. (1983), 'Program design by informal English descriptions', *Comm. ACM*, **26** (11), 882–94.

Abdel-Ghaly, A.A., Chan, P.Y. and Littlewood, B. (1986), 'Evaluation of competing software reliability predictions', *IEEE Trans. Software Eng.*, **SE–12** (9), 950–67.

Abrial, J.R. (1980), *The specification language Z: basic library*, Oxford Univ. Programming Res. Group.

Adams, E.N. (1984), 'Optimizing preventative service of software products', *IBM J. R & D*, **28** (1), 2–14.

Alderson, A., Falla, M. and Bott, M.F. (1985), 'An overview of the ECLIPSE project', in *Integrated Project Support Environments*, McDermid, J. (ed.), Stevenage: Peter Peregrinus.

Alford, M.W. (1977), 'A requirements engineering methodology for real time processing requirements', *IEEE Trans. Software Eng.*, **SE–3** (1), 60–9.

Alford, M.W. (1985), 'SREM at the age of eight: the distributed computing design system', *IEEE Computer*, **18** (4), 36–46.

Ambras, J. and O'Day, V. (1988) 'MicroScope: a knowledge-based programming environment', *IEEE Software*, **5** (3), 50–8.

Andrews, T. and Harris, C. (1987), 'Combining language and database advances in an object-oriented development environment', *Proc. OOPSLA'87*, Orlando, Fla.: 430–40.

Aron, J.D. (1974), *The Program Development Process*, Reading, Mass.: Addison-Wesley.

Aron, J.D. (1983), *The Program Development Process: Part 2 – The Programming Team*, Reading, Mass.: Addison-Wesley.

Baker, F.T. (1972), 'Chief programmer team management of production programming', *IBM Systems J.*, **11** (1).

Balzer, R. (1985), 'A 15 year perspective on automatic programming', *IEEE Trans. Software Eng.*, **SE–11** (11), 1257–67.

Balzer, R.M., Goldman, N.M. and Wile, D.S. (1982), 'Operational specification as the basis for rapid prototyping', *ACM Software Eng. Notes*, **7** (5), 3–16.

Barnes, J.G.P. (1984). *Programming in Ada*, 2nd ed., Wokingham: Addison-Wesley.

Bass, B.M. and Dunteman, G. (1963), 'Behaviour in groups as a function of self, interaction and task orientation', *J. Abnorm. Soc. Psychol.*, **66** *(4)*, 19–28.

Bell, T.E., Bixler, D.C. and Dyer, M.E. (1977), 'An extendable approach to computer aided software requirements engineering', *IEEE Trans. Software Eng.*, **SE–3** (1), 49–60.

Bersoff, E.H. (1984), 'Elements of software configuration management', *IEEE Trans. Software Eng.*, **SE–10** (1), 79–87.

Blair, G.S., Lea, R., Mariani, J.A., Nicol, J.R. and Wylie, C. (1986), 'Total system design in IPSEs', in *Software Engineering Environments*, Sommerville, I. (ed.), Stevenage: Peter Peregrinus Ltd., 85–104.

Blank, J. and Krijger, M.J., (eds) (1983), *Software Engineering: Methods and Techniques*, New York: Wiley Interscience.

Boehm, B.W. (1974), 'Some steps towards formal and automated aids to software requirements analysis and design', *IFIP 74*, Amsterdam: North-Holland.

Boehm, B.W. (1975), 'The high cost of software', in *Practical Strategies for Developing Large Software Systems*, Horowitz, E. (ed.), Reading, Mass.: Addison-Wesley.

Boehm, B.W. (1979). 'Software engineering: R & D trends and defense needs', in *Research Directions in Software Technology*, Wegner, P. (ed.), Cambridge, Mass.: MIT Press.

Boehm, B.W. (1981), *Software Engineering Economics*, Englewood Cliffs, NJ : Prentice-Hall.

Boehm, B.W. (1983), 'The economics of software maintenance', *Proc. Software Maintenance Workshop*, Washington DC, 9–37.

Boehm, B.W. (1984), 'A software development environment for improving productivity', *IEEE Computer*, **17** (6), 30–44.

Boehm, B.W. (1987), 'Improving software productivity', *IEEE Computer*, **20** (9), 43–58.

Boehm, B.W., Brown, J.R., Kaspar, H., Lipow, M., Macleod, G. and Merrit, M. (1978), *Characteristics of Software Quality*, TRW Series of Software Technology, Amsterdam: North-Holland.

Bohm, C. and Jacopini, G. (1966), 'Flow diagrams, Turing machines and languages with only two formation rules', *Comm. ACM*, **9** (5), 366–71.

Booch, G. (1986), 'Object-oriented development', *IEEE Trans. Software Eng.*, **SE–12** (2), 211–21.

Booch, G. (1987), *Software Engineering with Ada*, 2nd ed., Menlo Park, Calif.: Benjamin/Cummings.

Borgida, A., Greenspan, S. and Mylopoulos, J. (1985), 'Knowledge representation as a basis for requirements specification', *IEEE Computer*, **18** (4), 82–101.

Bourne, S.R. (1978), 'The UNIX shell', *Bell Systems Tech. J.*, **57** (6), 1971–90.

Britcher, R.N. and Craig, J.J. (1986), 'Using modern design practices to upgrade aging software systems', *IEEE Software*, **3** (3), 16–26.

Brooks, F.P. (1975), *The Mythical Man Month*, Reading, Mass.: Addison-Wesley.

Brown, P.J. (ed.) (1977), *Software Portability*, Cambridge: Cambridge University Press.

Brown, P.J. (1983), 'Error messages: the neglected area of the man/machine interface', *Comm. ACM*, **26** (4), 246–50.

Buckley, F.J. and Poston, R. (1984), 'Software quality assurance', *IEEE Trans. Software Eng.*, **SE–10** (1), 36–41.

Buxton, J. (1980), *Requirements for Ada Programming Support Environments: Stoneman*, US Department of Defense, Washington DC.

CAIS (1985), *Common Apse Interface Set*, MIL_STD-CAIS, Washington DC: US Dept. of Defense.

Cameron, J.R. (1986), 'An overview of JSD', *IEEE Trans. Software Eng.*, **SE–12** (2), 222–40.

Campbell, I. (1986), 'PCTE proposal for a public common tool interface', in *Software Engineering Environments*, Sommerville, I. (ed.), Stevenage: Peter Peregrinus Ltd., 57–72.

Card, S., Moran, T.P. and Newell, A. (1983), *The Psychology of Human–Computer Interaction*, Hilldale, NJ: Lawrence Erlbaum Associates.

Chen, P. (1976), 'The entity relationship model – towards a unified view of data', *ACM Trans. Database Systems*, **1** (1), 9–36.

Cherry, L. and MacDonald, N.H. (1983), 'The UNIX Writer's Workbench software', *BYTE*, **8** (10), 241–52.

Chikofsky, E.J. and Rubenstein, B.L. (1988), 'CASE: reliability engineering for information systems', *IEEE Software*, **5** (2), 11–17.

Clocksin, W. and Mellish, C. (1982), *Programming in PROLOG*, Heidelberg: Springer-Verlag.

Codd, E.F. (1970), 'A relational model of data for large shared data banks', *Comm. ACM,* **13**, 377–87.

Cohen, B., Harwood, W.T. and Jackson, M.I. (1986), *The Specification of Complex Systems*, Wokingham: Addison-Wesley.

Conklin, J. (1987), 'Hypertext: an introduction and survey', *IEEE Software,* **20** (9), 17–42.

Constantine, L.L. and Yourdon, E. (1979), *Structured Design*, Englewood Cliffs, NJ: Prentice-Hall.

Cougar, J.D. and Zawacki, R.A. (1978), 'What motivates DP professionals', *Datamation*, **24** (9).

Culpepper, L.M. (1975), 'A system for reliable engineering software', *IEEE Trans. Software Eng.*, **SE–1** (2), 174–8.

Dart, S.A., Ellison, R.J., Feiler, P.H. and Habermann, A.N. (1987), 'Software development environments', *IEEE Computer*, **20** (11), 18–28.

Date, C.J. (1983), *An Introduction to Database Systems*, Reading, Mass.: Addison-Wesley.

Davis, C.G. and Vick, C.R. (1977), 'The software development system', *IEEE Trans. Software Eng.*, **SE–3** (1), 69–84.

Davis, W.S. (1983), *Systems Analysis and Design*, Reading, Mass.: Addison-Wesley.

DeMarco, T. (1978), *Structured Analysis and System Specification*, New York: Yourdon Press.

DeRemer, F. and Kron, H.H. (1976), 'Programming in the large versus programming in the small', *IEEE Trans. Software Eng.*, **SE–2** (2), 80–6.

Dijkstra, E.W. (1968), ' A constructive approach to the problem of program correctness' *BIT*, **8**, 174–86.

Dijkstra, E.W. (1976), *A Discipline of Programming*, Englewood Cliffs, NJ: Prentice-Hall.

Dolotta, T.A., Haight, R.C. and Mashey, J.R. (1978), 'The Programmers Workbench', *Bell Systems Tech. J.*, **57** (6), 2177–200.

Dowson, M. (1987), 'Integrated project support with ISTAR', *IEEE Software*, **4** (6), 6–15.

Earl, A.N., Whittington, R.P., Hitchcock, P. and Hall, A. (1986), 'Specifying a semantic model for use in an integrated project support environment', in *Software Engineering Environments*, Sommerville, I. (ed.), London: Peter Peregrinus.

Ellis, C.A. and Nutt, G.J. (1980), 'Office information systems and computer science', *ACM Computing Surveys*, **12** (1), 27–60.

Fagan, M.E. (1976), 'Design and code inspections to reduce errors in program development', *IBM Systems J.*, **15** (3), 182–211.

Fagan, M.E. (1986), 'Advances in software inspections', *IEEE Trans. Software Eng.*, **SE–12** (7), 744–51.

Feldman, S.I. (1979), 'MAKE – a program for maintaining computer programs', *Software – Practice and Experience*, **9**, 255–65.

Ferrari, D. (1978), *Computer Systems Performance Evaluation*, Englewood Cliffs, NJ: Prentice–Hall.

Festinger, L.A. (1957), *A Theory of Cognitive Dissonance*, Evanston, Ill.: Row Peterson.

Floyd, R.W. (1967), 'Assigning meanings to programs', *Proc. Symposium in Applied Maths*, 19–32.

Fried, L. (1979), *Practical Data Processing Management*, Virginia : Reston.

Futatsugi, K., Goguen, J.A., Jouannaud, J.P. and Meseguer, J. (1985), 'Principles of OBJ2', *Proc. 12th ACM Symp. on Principles of Programming Languages*, New Orleans, 52–66.

Gane, C. and Sarson, T. (1979), *Structured Systems Analysis*, Englewood Cliffs, NJ: Prentice-Hall.

Getz, S.L., Kalliyiannis, G. and Schach, S.R. (1983), 'A very high level interactive graphical trace for the Pascal heap', *IEEE Trans. Software Eng.*, **SE–9** (2).

Gladden, G.R. (1982), 'Stop the life cycle – I want to get off', *ACM Software Engineering Notes*, **7** (2), 35–9.

Goldberg, A. (1984), *Smalltalk–80: The Interactive Programming Environment*, Reading, Mass.: Addison-Wesley.

Goldberg, A. and Robson, D. (1983), *Smalltalk–80: The Language and its Implementation*, Reading, Mass.: Addison-Wesley.

Gomaa, H. (1983), 'The impact of rapid prototyping on specifying user requirements', *ACM Software Eng. Notes*, **8** (2), 17–28.

Gomaa, H. (1984), 'A software design method for real-time systems', *Comm. ACM*, **29** (7), 938–49.

Gunning, R. (1962), *Techniques of Clear Writing*, New York: McGraw-Hill.

Guttag, J. (1977), 'Abstract data types and the development of data structures', *Comm. ACM*, **20** (6), 396–405.

Guttag, J.V., Horning, J.J. and Wing, J.M. (1985), 'The Larch family of specification languages', *IEEE Software*, **2** (5), 24–36.

Halstead, M.H. (1977), *Elements of Software Science*, Amsterdam: North–Holland.

Hamer, P.G. and Frewin, G.D. (1981), 'Halstead's software science – a critical examination', *Proc. 6th Int. Conf. on Software Engineering*, Tokyo.

Hayes, I. (ed.) (1987), *Specification Case Studies*, London: Prentice-Hall.

Hayes, I.J. (1986), 'Specification directed module testing', *IEEE Trans. Software Eng.*, **SE–12** (1), 124–33.

Hendrix, G.G., Sacerdoti, E.D., Sagalowicz, D. and Slocum, J. (1978), 'Developing a natural language interface to complex data', *ACM Trans. Database Systems*, **3** (2), 105–47.

Heninger, K.L. (1980), 'Specifying software requirements for complex systems. New techniques and their applications', *IEEE Trans. Software Eng.*, **SE–6** (1), 2–13.

Henry, S. and Kafura, D. (1981), 'Software structure metrics based on information flow', *IEEE Trans. Software Eng.*, **SE–7** (5).

Higgs, M. and Stevens, P. (1986), 'Developing an environment manager for an IPSE', in *Software Engineering Environments*, Sommerville, I. (ed.), Stevenage: Peter Peregrinus, 39–56.

Hill, A. (1983), 'Towards an Ada-based specification and design language', *ADA UK News*, **4** (4), 16–34.

Hiltz, S.R. and Turoff, M. (1979), *The Network Nation*, Reading, Mass.: Addison-Wesley.

Hoare, C.A.R. (1969), 'An axiomatic basis for computer programming', *Comm. ACM,* **12** (10), 576–83.

Horowitz, E. and Munsen, J.B. (1984), 'An expansive view of reusable software', *IEEE Trans. Software Eng.*, **SE–10** (5), 477–487.

Howden, W.E. (1982), 'Contemporary software development environments', *Comm. ACM*, **25** (5), 318–29.

Ivie, E.L. (1977), 'The Programmers Workbench – a machine for software development', *Comm. ACM*, **20** (10), 746–53.

Jackson, M.A. (1975), *Principles of Program Design*, London: Academic Press.

Jackson, M.A. (1983), *System Development*, London: Prentice-Hall.

Janis, I.L. (1972), *Victims of Groupthink. A Psychological Study of Foreign Policy Decisions and Fiascos*, Boston: Houghton Mifflin.

Jelinski, Z. and Moranda, P.B. (1972), 'Software reliability research', in *Statistical Computer Performance Evaluation*, Frieberger, W. (ed.) New York: Academic Press.

Johnson, P. (1987). 'Using Z to specify CICS', *Proc. SEAS Anniversary Meeting*, Edinburgh, 303–33.

Jones, C.B. (1980), *Software Development – A Rigorous Approach*, London: Prentice Hall.

Jones, C.B. (1986), *Systematic Software Development Using VDM*, London: Prentice–Hall.

Jones, T.C. (1978), 'Measuring programming quality and productivity', *IBM Systems J.*, **17** (1), 39–63.

Kafura, D. and Reddy, G.R. (1987), 'The use of software complexity metrics in software maintenance', *IEEE Trans. Software Eng.*, **SE–13** (3), 335–43.

Kaiser, G.E., Feiler, P.H. and Popovich, S.S. (1988), 'Intelligent assistance for software development and maintenance', *IEEE Software*, **5** (3), 40–9.

Kernighan, B.W., Lesk, M.E. and Ossanna Jr, J.F. (1978), 'Document preparation', *Bell Systems Tech. J.*, **57** (6), 2115–35.

Kitchenham, B. (1989), 'Software metrics', in *Software Reliability Handbook*, Rook, P. (ed.), London: Elsevier.

Lampson, B.W. and Schmidt, E.E. (1983), 'Organising software in a distributed environment', *ACM Sigplan Notices*, **18** (6), 1–13.

Lampson, B.W., Horning, J.J., London, R.L., Mitchell, J.G. and Popek, G.L. (1977), 'Report on the programming language Euclid', *ACM Sigplan Notices*, **12** (2), 1–79.

Leavitt, H.J. (1951), 'Some effects of certain communication patterns on group performance', *J. Abnorm. Soc. Psychol.*, **54** (1), 38–50.

Leblang, D.B. and Chase, R.P. (1987), 'Parallel software configuration management in a network environment', *IEEE Software*, **4** (6), 28–35.

Lehman, M.M. (1980), 'Programs, life cycles and the laws of software evolution', *Proc. IEEE*, **15** (3), 225–52.

Lehman, M.M. and Belady, L. (1985), *Program Evolution. Processes of Software Change*, London: Academic Press.

Lewin, K., Lippit, R. and White, R.K. (1939), 'Patterns of aggressive behaviour in experimentally created social climates', *J. Soc. Psychol.*, **10**, 271–99.

Lientz, B.P. and Swanson, E.B. (1980), *Software Maintenance Management*, Reading, Mass.: Addison-Wesley.

Lindsay, P.A. (1988), 'A survey of mechanical support for formal reasoning', *IEE/BCS Software Eng. J.*, **3** (1), 3–27.

Linger, R.C., Mills, H.D. and Witt, B.I. (1979), *Structured Programming – Theory and Practice*, Reading, Mass.: Addison-Wesley.

Liskov, B. and Zilles, S. (1974), 'Programming with abstract data types', *ACM Sigplan Notices*, **9** (4), 50–9.

Littlewood, B. (1989), 'Software reliability growth models', in *Software Reliability Handbook*, Rook, P. (ed.), London: Elsevier.

Littlewood, B. and Verrall, J.L. (1973), 'A Bayesian reliability growth model for computer software', *Applied Statistics*, **22**, 332–46.

Looney, M. (1985), *CORE – A Debrief Report*, Manchester: NCC Publications.

Luckham, D. and Von Henke, F.W. (1985), 'An Overview of Anna, a specification language for Ada', *IEEE Software*, **2** (2), 9–23.

Macro, A. and Buxton, J. (1986), *The Craft of Software Engineering*, Wokingham: Addison-Wesley.

Mander, K.C. (1981), 'An Ada view of specification and design', *Tech. Rep. 44*, Department of Computer Science, University of York, York, UK.

Manna, Z. (1969), 'The correctness of programs', *J. Computer System Sci.*, **3**, 119–27.

Marshall, J.E. and Heslin, R. (1976), 'Boys and girls together. Sexual composition and the effect of density on group size and cohesiveness', *J. Personality Soc. Psychol.*, **36**.

Martin, C.F. (1988), 'Second-generation CASE tools: a challenge to vendors', *IEEE Software*, **5** (2), 46–49.

Martin, J. (1985), *Fourth-generation Languages*, Englewood Cliffs, NJ: Prentice-Hall.

McCabe, T.J. (1976), 'A complexity measure', *IEEE Trans. Software Eng.*, **SE–2**, 308–20.

McCarthy, J. (1962), 'Towards a mathematical science of computation', *IFIP 62*, 21–8. Amsterdam: North–Holland.

McCracken, D.D. and Jackson, M.A. (1982), 'Life cycle concept considered harmful', *ACM Software Engineering Notes*, **7** (2), 28–32.

McCue, G.M. (1978), 'IBMs Santa Teresa Laboratory – architectural design for program development', *IBM Systems J.*, **17** (1), 4–25.

McDermid, J. and Ripkin, K. (1984), *Life Cycle Support in the Ada Environment*, Cambridge: Cambridge University Press.

McGettrick, A.D. (1982), *Program Verification Using Ada*, Cambridge: Cambridge University Press.

McKeeman, W.M., Horning, J.J. and Wortman, D. (1970), *A Compiler Generator*, Englewood Cliffs, NJ: Prentice-Hall.

Metzger, P.W. (1973), *Managing a Programming Project*, Englewood Cliffs, NJ: Prentice-Hall.

Miara, R.J., Mussleman, J.A., Navarro, J.A. and Shneiderman, B. (1983), 'Program indentation and comprehensibility', *Comm. ACM*, **26** (11), 861–7.

Miller, G.A. (1957), 'The magical number 7 plus or minus two: some limits on our capacity for processing information', *Psychol. Rev.*, **63,** 81–97.

Millington, D. (1981), *Systems Analysis and Design for Computer Applications*, Chichester: Ellis Horwood.

Mills, H.D., O'Neill, D., Linger, R.C., Dyer, M. and Quinnan, R.E. (1980), 'The management of software engineering', *IBM Sys. J.*, **24** (2), 414–77.

Mills, H.D., Dyer, M. and Linger, R. (1987), 'Cleanroom software engineering'. *IEEE Software*, **4** (5), 19–25.

Mohanty, S.N. (1981), 'Software cost estimation: present and future', *Software – Practice and Experience*, **11** (2), 103–21.

Monk, A. (ed.) (1984), *Fundamentals of Human–Computer Interaction*, London: Academic Press.

Morgan, C. and Sufrin, B. (1984), 'Specification of the UNIX filing system', *IEEE Trans. Software Eng.*, **SE–10** (2), 128–42.

Mullery, G. (1979), 'CORE – a method for controlled requirements specification', *Proc. 4th Int. Conf. on Software Engineering*, Munich.

Myers, G.J. (1979), *The Art of Software Testing*, New York: Wiley.

Myers, G.J. (1975), *Reliable Software through Composite Design*, New York: Petrocelli/Charter.

Naur, P. (1972), 'An experiment on program development', *BIT*, **12**, 347–65.

Nissen, J. and Wallis, P.J.L. (eds) (1985), *Portability and Style in Ada*, Cambridge: Cambridge University Press.

Norman, D.A. and Draper, S.W. (eds) (1986), *User-Centered System Design*, Hillsdale, NJ: Lawrence Erlbaum.

Osterweil, L.J. and Fosdick, L.D. (1976), 'DAVE – a validation, error detection and documentation system for FORTRAN programs', *Software – Practice and Experience*, **6**, 473–86

Oviedo, E.I. (1980), 'Control flow, data flow and program complexity', *Proc. 4th COMPSAC*, Los Alaminitos, Calif.: IEEE Press.

Parnas, D. (1972), 'On the criteria to be used in decomposing systems into modules', *Comm. ACM*, **15** (2), 1053–58.

Perry, D.K. and Cannon, W.M. (1966), 'A vocational interest scale for programmers', *Proc. 4th Annual Computer Personnel Conf.*, ACM, New York.

Peters, L.J. (1980), 'Software representation and composition techniques', *Proc. IEEE*, **68** (9), 1085–93.

Petschenik, N.H. (1985). 'Practical priorities in system testing', *IEEE Computer*, **18** (5), 18–23.

Porter, L.W. and Lawler, E.E. (1965), 'Properties of organisation structure in relation to job attitudes and behaviour', *Psychol. Bull.*, **64**, 23–51.

Pressman, R.S. (1987), *Software Engineering – A Practitioner's Approach*, 2nd ed., New York: McGraw-Hill.

Prieto-Diaz, R. and Freeman, P. (1987), 'Classifying software for reusability', *IEEE Software*, **4** (1), 6–16.

Putnam, L. H. (1978), 'A general empirical solution to the macro software sizing and estimating problem', *IEEE Trans. Software Eng.*, **SE–4** (3), 345–61.

Ramamoorthy, C.V. and Ho, S.F. (1975), 'Testing large software with automated software evaluation systems', *IEEE Trans. Software Eng.*, **SE–1** (1), 46–58.

Randell, B. (1975), 'System structure for software fault tolerance', *IEEE Trans. Software Eng.*, **SE–1** (2), 46–58.

Reid, P. and Welland, R.C. (1986), 'Software development in view', in *Software Engineering Environments*, Sommerville, I. (ed.), Stevenage: Peter Peregrinus.

Ritchie, D.M., Johnson, S.C., Lesk, M.E. and Kernighan, B.W. (1978), 'The C programming language', *Bell Systems Tech. J.*, **57** (6), 1991–2020.

Rittel, H. and Webber, M. (1973), 'Dilemmas in a general theory of planning', *Policy Sciences*, **4**, 155–69.

Robertson, G., McCracken. D. and Newell, A. (1981), 'The ZOG approach to man–machine communication', *Int. J. Man–Machine Studies*, **14**, 461–88.

Robson, D. (1981), 'Object-oriented software systems', *BYTE*, **6** (8), 74–9.

Rochkind, M.J. (1975), 'The Source Code Control System', *IEEE Trans. Software Eng.*, **SE–1** (4), 255–65.

Ross, D.T. (1977), 'Structured Analysis (SA): a language for communicating ideas', *IEEE Trans. Software Eng.*, **SE–3** (1), 16–34.

Royce, W.W. (1970), 'Managing the development of large software systems', *Proc. WESTCON*, Calif., USA.

Sackman, H., Erikson, W.J. and Grant, E.E. (1968), 'Exploratory experimentation studies comparing on-line and off-line programming performance', *Comm. ACM*, **11** (1), 3–11.

Salter, K.G. (1976), 'A methodology for decomposing system requirements into data into data processing requirements', *Proc. 2nd Int. Conf. on Software Engineering*, San Francisco.

Satterthwaite, E. (1972), 'Debugging tools for high level languages', *Software – Practice and Experience*, **2**, 197–217.

Scheifler, R.W. and Gettys, J. (1986), 'The X window system', *ACM Trans. Graphics*, **5** (2).

Schoman, K. and Ross, D.T. (1977), 'Structured analysis for requirements definition', *IEEE Trans. Software Eng.*, **SE–3** (1), 6–15.

Selby, R.W., Basili, V.R. and Baker, F.T. (1987), 'Cleanroom software development: an empirical evaluation', *IEEE Trans. Software Eng.*, **SE–13** (9), 1027–37.

Shaw, M.E. (1964), 'Communication networks', in *Advances in Experimental Social Psychology*, New York: Academic Press.

Shaw, M.E. (1971), *Group Dynamics. The Psychology of Small Group Behaviour*, McGraw-Hill, New York.

Shepherd, S.B., Curtis, B., Milliman, P., Borst, M. and Love, T. (1979), 'First year results from a research program in human factors in software engineering', *AFIPS 79*, 1021–7.

Shneiderman, B. (1980), *Software Psychology*, Cambridge, Mass.: Winthrop Publishers.

Shneiderman, B. (1983), 'Designing computer system messages', *Comm. ACM*, **25** (9), 610–11.

Shneiderman, B., Shafer, P., Simon, R. and Weldon, L. (1986), 'Display strategies for program browsing; concepts and experiment', *IEEE Software*, **3** (3), 7–15.

Shneiderman, B. (1986), *Designing the User Interface*, Reading, Mass.: Addison-Wesley.

Simpson, H. (1986), 'The MASCOT method', *BCS/IEE Software Eng. J.*, **1** (3), 103–20.

Smith, D.R., Kotik, G.B. and Westfold, S.J. (1985), 'Research on knowledge-based software environments at Kestrel Institute', *IEEE Trans. Software Eng.*, **SE–11** (11), 1278–95.

Soloway, E., Ehrlich, K., Bonar, J. and Greenspan, J. (1982), 'What do novices know about programming', in *Directions in Human–Computer Interaction*, Badre, A. and Shneiderman, C. (eds), Norwood, NJ: Ablex Publishing Co.

Sommerville, I. and Morrison, R. (1986), *Software Development with Ada*, Wokingham: Addison-Wesley.

Sommerville, I. and Thomson, R. (1986), 'The ECLIPSE system structure language', *Proc. 19th Int. Conf. on System Sciences*, Honolulu, Hawaii.

Sommerville, I., Welland, R.C., Potter, S. and Smart, J, D. (1989), 'The ECLIPSE user interface', to be published in *Software – Practice and Experience*.

Tanenbaum, A.S., Klint, P. and Bohm, W. (1978), 'Guidelines for software portability', *Software – Practice and Experience*, **8**, 681–98.

Teichrow, D. and Hershey, E.A. (1977), 'PSL/PSA: a computer aided technique for structured documentation and analysis of information processing systems', *IEEE Trans. Software Eng.*, **SE–3** (1), 41–8.

Teitelbaum, T and Reps, T. (1981), 'The Cornell Program Synthesiser: a syntax-directed programming environment', *Comm. ACM*, **24** (9), 563–73.

Teitleman, W. and Masinter, L. (1984), 'The Interlisp Programming Environment', in *Interactive Programming Environments*, Barstow, D.R., Shrobe, H.E. and Sandewall, E, (eds). New York: Macgraw-Hill.

Terwilliger, R.B. and Campbell, R.H. (1986), 'ENCOMPASS: a SAGA–based environment for the composition of programs and specifications', *Proc. 19th Hawaii Int. Conf. on System Sciences*.

Tichy, W. (1982), 'Design, implementation and evaluation of a revision control system', *Proc. 6th Int. Conf.on Software Engineering*, Tokyo.

Turski, W. (1981), 'Software stability', *Proc. 6th ACM Conf. on Systems Architecture*, London.

Van Leer, P. (1976), 'Top down development using a program design language', *IBM Systems J.*, **15** (2), 155–70.

Walker, J. (1985), 'Documentation and help online', Tutorial 9, *SIGCHI 1985*. San Francisco.

Wallis, P.J.L. (1982), *Portable Programming*, London: Macmillan.

Walston, C.E. and Felix, C.P. (1977), 'A method of programming measurement and estimation', *IBM Systems J.*, **16** (1), 54–73.

Waltz, D. (1978), 'An English language question answering system for a large relational database', *Comm. ACM*, **21** (7), 526–39.

Warnier, J.D. (1977), *Logical Construction of Programs*, New York: Van Nostrand Reinhold.

Wasserman, A.I. (1981), 'User software engineering and the design of interactive information systems', *Proc. 5th Int. Conf. on Software Engineering*, IEEE Press, 387–93.

Wasserman, A.I., Pircher, P.A., Shewmake, D.T. and Kersten, M.L. (1986), 'Developing interactive information systems with the user software engineering methodology', *IEEE Trans. Software Eng.*, **SE–12** (2), 326–45.

Weinberg, G. (1971), *The Psychology of Computer Programming*, New York: Van Nostrand Reinhold.

Wirth, N. (1971), 'Program development by stepwise refinement', *Comm. ACM*, **14** (4), 221–7.

Wirth, N. (1976), *Systematic Programming, An Introduction*, Englewood Cliffs, NJ: Prentice-Hall.

Yeh, R.T. and Zave, P. (1980), 'Specifying software requirements', *Proc. IEEE*, **68** (9), 1077–85.

Yourdon, E. (1977), *Structured Walkthroughs*, New York: Yourdon Press.

Yourdon, E. (1979), *Managing the Structured Techniques*, Englewood Cliffs, NJ: Prentice-Hall.

Index